The Film Theory Reader

The Film Theory Reader brings together a range of key theoretical texts, organized thematically to emphasize the development of specific critical concepts and theoretical models in the field of film theory.

Each section presents well-known or significant texts, which have introduced a particularly influential concept, followed by texts that have developed or extended the concept, or that have offered explicit critiques or arguments against the original model. The collection thus represents and reproduces the debates and arguments that have shaped the theoretical landscape of film studies, guiding the reader through the complex terrain of theoretical debate, and offering suggestions for further reading and research.

An Introduction from the editor contextualizes the essays and provides a logical guide to the book, clarifying the links between articles and tracing the development of key arguments. The notes to the Introduction include extensive references, for readers to explore and further their own studies, as they are guided through the history of debate in film theory.

Contributors include:

Béla Balázs, André Bazin, John Belton, Noël Carroll, Gilles Deleuze, Anne Friedberg, Marc Furstenau, Tom Gunning, bell hooks, E. Ann Kaplan, Lev Manovich, Christian Metz, Daniel Morgan, Laura Mulvey, Hugo Münsterberg, D.N. Rodowick, Malcolm Turvey, Peter Wollen.

Marc Furstenau is Assistant Professor of Film Studies at Carleton University, Canada. He is co-editor, with Bruce Bennett and Adrian Mackenzie, of *Cinema and Technology: Cultures, Theories, Practices* (2008). He has also published on the topics of cinema and semiotics, film theory, the philosophical cinema of Terrence Malick and the photographic theory of Susan Sontag.

The Film Theory Reader

Debates and Arguments

Edited by

Marc Furstenau

 Routledge
Taylor & Francis Group

LONDON AND NEW YORK

First published 2010
by Routledge
2 Park Square, Milton Park, Abingdon, Oxon OX14 4RN

Simultaneously published in the USA and Canada
by Routledge
270 Madison Avenue, New York, NY 10016

Routledge is an imprint of the Taylor & Francis Group, an informa business

Typeset in Perpetua and Bell Gothic by
RefineCatch Limited, Bungay, Suffolk
Printed and bound in Great Britain by
CPI Antony Rowe, Chippenham, Wiltshire

British Library Cataloguing in Publication Data
A catalogue record for this book is available from the British Library

Library of Congress Cataloging-in-Publication Data
The film theory reader : debates & arguments / edited by Marc Furstenau.
    p. cm.
  Includes index.
  1. Motion pictures—Philosophy.   I. Furstenau, Marc, 1963–
PN1995.F4675 2010
791.4301—dc22   2009043527

ISBN 10: 0-415-49317-X (hbk)
ISBN 10: 0-415-49322-6 (pbk)

ISBN 13: 978-0-415-49317-8 (hbk)
ISBN 13: 978-0-415-49322-2 (pbk)

Contents

Acknowledgments

WE GRATEFULLY ACKNOWLEDGE PERMISSION to reproduce the essays below. Whilst every effort has been made to trace copyright holders and obtain permission, this has not been possible in all cases. Any omissions brought to our attention will be remedied in future editions.

D.N. Rodowick. "An Elegy for Theory." *October*, 122, Fall 2007: pp. 91–109. © 2007 by October Magazine Ltd. and the Massachusetts Institute of Technology.

Malcolm Turvey. "Theory, Philosophy, and Film Studies: A Response to D.N. Rodowick's 'An Elegy for Theory'." *October*, 122, Fall 2007: pp. 110–20. Reproduced with permission of the author.

Hugo Münsterberg. "The Psychology of the Photoplay." *The Photoplay: A Psychological Study*. New York: Arno Press, 1970 [1916].

Noël Carroll. "Film/Mind Analogies: The Case of Hugo Münsterberg." *Journal of Aesthetics and Art Criticism*, 1988 / Vol. 46 / No. 4 / pp. 489–99. Reproduced with permission of Blackwell Publishing Ltd.

Béla Balázs. *Visible Man, or The Culture of Film* (1924), with Introduction by Erica Carter, Rodney Livingston, trans., *Screen*, 48.1, 2007: pp. 91–108. By permission of Oxford University Press.

Malcolm Turvey. "Balázs: Realist or Modernist?" *October*, 115, Winter 2006: pp. 77–87. © 2006 by October Magazine, Ltd. and the Massachusetts Institute of Technology.

André Bazin. "The Ontology of the Photographic Image" and "The Evolution of the Language of Cinema." *What Is Cinema?* Trans. Hugh Gray. University of California Press, 1967, pp. 9–16, 23–40.

Daniel Morgan. "Rethinking Bazin: Ontology and Realist Aesthetics." *Critical Inquiry*, 32, Spring 2006: pp. 443–81. Reproduced with permission of Chicago University Press.

Christian Metz. "The Cinema: Language or Language System?" *Film Language: A Semiotics of the Cinema*. Trans. Michael Taylor. New York: Oxford University Press, 1974 [1964]. pp. 31–91. By permission of Oxford University Press, Inc.

Peter Wollen. "The Semiology of the Cinema." *Signs and Meaning in the Cinema*. Bloomington: Indiana University Press, 1972. pp. 116–54. Reproduced with permission of Indiana University Press and Palgrave Macmillan.

Gilles Deleuze. "Recapitulation of Images and Signs." *Cinema 2: The Time-Image*, trans. Hugh Tomlinson and R. Galeta, University of Minnesota Press and Continuum, 1991. pp. 25–43. With permission of Continuum International Publishing Group.

Laura Mulvey. "Visual Pleasure and Narrative Cinema." *Screen*, 16.3, Autumn 1975, pp. 6–18. By permission of Oxford Journals.

E. Ann Kaplan. "Is the Gaze Male?" from *Women and Film: Both Sides of the Camera*. New York: Methuen, 1983, pp. 23–35. Reproduced with permission of Routledge.

Laura Mulvey, "Afterthoughts on 'Visual Pleasure and Narrative Cinema' inspired by King Vidor's *Duel in the Sun* (1946)," in *Visual and Other Pleasures*, Indiana University Press, 1989: 29–38. Reproduced with permission of Indiana University Press and Palgrave Macmillan.

bell hooks. "The Oppositional Gaze: Black Female Spectators" from *Black Looks: Race and Representation*, 1992, pp. 115–31. Reproduced with permission of Between the Lines and South End Press.

Lev Manovich. "Digital Cinema and the History of a Moving Image." *The Language of New Media*, pp. 293–308, © 2001 Massachusetts Institute of Technology, by permission of The MIT Press.

Tom Gunning. "Moving Away from the Index: Cinema and the Impression of Reality," in *differences*, Volume 18, no. 1, pp. 29–52. Copyright, 2007, Brown University and *differences: A Journal of Feminist Cultural Studies*. All rights reserved. Used by permission of the publisher, Duke University Press.

Anne Friedberg. "The End of Cinema: Multimedia and Technological Change," *Reinventing Film Studies*. Eds. Christine Gledhill and Linda Williams. © 2000 Arnold. pp. 438–52. Reproduced by permission of Edward Arnold (Publishers) Ltd.

John Belton. "Digital Cinema: A False Revolution." *October*, 100, Spring 2002: pp. 98–114. © 2002 by October Magazine, Ltd. and the Massachusetts Institute of Technology.

Marc Furstenau

INTRODUCTION
FILM THEORY:
A HISTORY OF DEBATES

It is inevitable that in theorizing about film one at some point speculates about its origins,
because despite its recentness, its origin remains obscure.
(Stanley Cavell)[1]

I

THEORIES OF FILM began as expressions of wonder. As soon as moving, photographic images were projected on to screens, critics, writers, poets, philosophers, artists,
and even filmmakers themselves began describing the new medium, speculating about film's
nature, debating its various effects, and arguing for its value and significance. Almost all of the
early observers agreed that they were witnessing the advent of something new and
unprecedented, and they sought immediately to provide some sort of account of it.[2] Maxim
Gorky, the Russian writer, in an often cited review of one of the very first public film screenings,
in 1896, tried to describe the powerful experience of entering a "kingdom of shadows," which
seemed so realistic and familiar, yet so ghostly and strange. How, he asked, anticipating the
questions of later theorists, could he be so moved by such obvious artifice? How could mere
shadows affect him so powerfully? What effects might this powerful new art have?[3] Of all the
resources that film seemed to possess, Gorky suggested, the most potent was its ability to
confuse reality and illusion. This was revealed during a particularly dramatic moment in one of
the films in the Lumière program, which Gorky describes, seeking to communicate the full
force of the experience. "Suddenly," he wrote, "a train appears on the screen. It speeds
straight at you—watch out! It seems as though it will plunge into the darkness in which you sit
. . . crushing into dust and into broken fragments this hall and this building."[4]

Confronted by such an effect, Gorky wonders if it is even susceptible to explanation. It
may be, he suggests, that film's powers are incapable of being fully understood, but he is
determined nevertheless to try to account for them. "The extraordinary impression that it
creates," he wrote, "is so unique and complex that I doubt my ability to describe it with all its

nuances. However, I shall try to convey its fundamentals."[5] Gorky presents, in these two short lines, the basic contours of the theoretical discourse on film that would subsequently emerge. Many more would describe film as a unique, perhaps even unprecedented, new medium—a strange amalgam of art and technology, illusion and reality—capable of producing effects unlike any other mode of representation. It would present an acute critical challenge, stretching the explanatory abilities of scholars and theorists. The task of describing and explaining film and its effects emerged as one of the central critical undertakings of the twentieth century, and it has not yet exhausted the interest of those seeking to understand the source of its effects, and to explain its significance. Over the past hundred years or so, there has been no shortage of those who have endeavored to "convey its fundamentals."

The intense interest in film as a critical problem was driven by the rapid growth and development of the new medium. From its early years as a sensational novelty, complex and affecting as it may have been, film would emerge as the most significant and influential popular art of the last century, in a multitude of forms and styles, with an extensive repertoire of techniques and conventions. Film theorists have endeavored to catalogue and to explain these, but they have also speculated about film's proper function, arguing not only about film's aesthetic significance, but about its cultural, social, and psychological implications. The obviously enormous power of cinematic representation had to be accounted for, but also guided and directed, and film theory has often had a decidedly prescriptive tone. Gorky himself was dubious about the new art's value, and wary of its effects, but there was, he thought, very real promise in the future of film, if properly utilized. "I do not yet see the scientific importance of Lumière's invention," he wrote, "but, no doubt, it is there, and it could probably be applied to the general ends of science, that is, of bettering man's life and the developing of his mind."[6] While Gorky had specific hopes for the new medium's edifying capacities, others were to see in film far greater significance, extending beyond its specific visual effects. It would, many thought, transform social and cultural structures, alter our conceptions of art, representation and experience, and play a key role in the development of a new kind of visual culture. The enduring critical interest in film has been sustained by a sense that film has had an enormous influence, and that it has required critical consideration in order either to reveal and extend those influences, or to control and ameliorate them.

The social significance of film was immediately obvious, and accounts of its broader impact, and predictions of future effects, were a staple of the early discourse. Vachel Lindsay, the American poet, produced rather eccentric accounts of the new medium, but he can be seen as an early and representative enthusiast. He was an ardent movie fan, and his fervor matched the passions that the movies were already eliciting among dedicated audiences, anticipating the enduring popular fascination with cinematic culture. He wrote love letters in verse to new movie stars like Mary Pickford and Blanche Sweet. More than just a fan, though, Lindsay published one of the first critical accounts of cinema. In it he wondered how film would change the world.[7] He saw the dawning of a new utopian age of worldwide visual communication and understanding. Could it be, he asked, that a universal language of images had been created, heralding a new era of global unity? The advent of film, like so many other new media at the time, prompted often delirious predictions about its benefits and positive effects, and Lindsay was a significant figure among its early champions. The chance to describe a new art, at the moment of its emergence, was too important an opportunity to miss. "There can never be but one first of anything," he wrote, and film, if it was to realize its potential, had to be subjected to careful analysis as quickly as possible. While often dismissed as eccentric, Lindsay's book can be understood to have set the tone for many subsequent accounts of film's promise and potential, and to have provided an important foundation for the serious study of the medium.[8]

While Lindsay sang the praises of the new art of film, others at the time were less san-
guine, and saw the movie theater not as a site of moral improvement and political progress, or
even of significant aesthetic developments, but rather as a "recruiting station for vice."[9] Film
was often seen as a new social and political problem, a threat to traditional conceptions of
class, gender, and race. Men and women, from all walks of life and all backgrounds, were able
to mingle in the new public space of the cinema (significantly, a *darkened* space), to witness an
unprecedented and dynamic form of representation. According to many concerned observers
at the time, there was no telling what effect this would have on the minds of spectators, on the
behavior of the new mass audiences that were flocking to the moving pictures. Film seemed to
pose very real threats to the social order, confusing traditional cultural and aesthetic categories, and radically altering received conceptions of public decorum and conduct.

Film inspired both hopes and fears, then, but the early celebrations and critiques of the new
medium quickly formed the basis for subsequent critical considerations. From such early speculations, an extensive theoretical discourse emerged, and film has become, over the last century, a
key critical issue, the source of fervent debate and often very passionate argument. Film was
very quickly understood to be worthy of serious study. As Dana Polan has recently shown,
courses in film study were created in many colleges and universities in the United States in the
very early years of the twentieth century, establishing an enduring foundation for later film
teaching and research. "Many of the questions of this early pedagogy," writes Polan, "would
recur in the discipline, and film studies scholars still wrestle with them today."[10] The activities
of contemporary theorists are shaped by a relatively brief but very rich history of enthusiastic
claims for and concerned critiques about the power of the new medium, and are the legacy of a
long series of debates and arguments about what film is and what its effects are.

There is no singular "theory of film," of course, the final elaboration of which scholars
are diligently working towards. Rather, film theorists participate in an ongoing and wide-ranging
conversation, arguing and debating about a medium whose scope, complexity and importance
seems to belie its short history. While still relatively "new," film has undergone many significant changes in its brief life—in style, technique, effect, and value—and it seems thereby to
resist any easy definition. As Stanley Cavell has observed, film's origins have remained obscure,
despite its "recentness," but this has not been the result of any shortage of theoretical effort
to explain it.[11] The early and extensive critical analyses of film have provided a firm foundation
for subsequent study. Film has now become the focus of a distinct and clearly defined discipline, and has been fully incorporated within the institutions of higher education, supported by
an extensive academic apparatus—university departments, graduate programs, scholarly publishing, academic associations, and international conferences. Yet there is considerable concern
that the discipline is threatened by the advent of newer media, which are challenging film's
status as the key visual medium of the last century, eroding its identity as a unique medium,
and putting its significance as a distinct object of academic inquiry into question. There is a
strong sense, though, among many of those who study film, that it will remain an integral
object of scholarly analysis, and that the debates about film have not come to an end. As the
discipline advances, though, in a complex multimedia era, it is important to consider the history of those debates, in order to chart new directions for theory in the future.

II

If film studies *is* to advance, there will need to be a renewed effort to revitalize film theory,
which had long been understood to be at the core of the discipline. As Malcolm Turvey notes,

though, in an essay included here, the last decade or so has been characterized by a "retreat from theory" (p. 38).[12] This anthology seeks to counter that retreat, if only by modestly gesturing to various significant theoretical debates that have animated, and that continue to animate, the field of film studies. This book can be read as an introduction to several key theoretical debates, for those new to the discipline, or as a guide to those who are seeking to extend those debates, or turn them in new directions, or to initiate entirely new debates. At the core of this book, though, is a sustained confidence in the importance of theoretical reflection, in the value of debate and argument, and in the enduring place of film theory within the broader field.[13] Film theory has played a key role in the history of the discipline. It has sought to define and analyze the object of study, to reveal and to account for its unique qualities and characteristics. That object is "film"—the specific medium at the heart of the complex technical apparatus for the production and presentation of moving, photographic images, which provides the material foundation for the "cinema," the extensive industrial, economic and cultural structure for the distribution and exhibition of those images. One of the primary tasks of theories of "film" has been to explain how this medium has functioned as the basis for the broader cinematic enterprise, to describe the relations between the medium and the institution.[14] As a component within broader technological, industrial, and commercial structures, "film" has been subject to more, and more dramatic, changes than the other arts, and it has, arguably, been more significant, or at least more ubiquitous, than the other arts. Given all of this, "film" seems to have required its own particular field of study, capable of addressing all aspects of the multifaceted phenomenon, and "film studies" has emerged over the past century, through a quite complex process,[15] which has included the development of a specific branch of inquiry within the discipline, "film theory."[16]

Some find the focus of *film* theory too narrow, especially today in our multimedia environment, and advocate instead for a broader account of the whole range of moving images, not only the specific film images of the cinema. Noël Carroll has recently made such an argument. "Film," he writes, "was undoubtedly the most important early implementation of the moving image (a.k.a. *movies*), but the impression of movement . . . can be realized in many other media including kinetoscopes, video, broadcast TV, CGI, and technologies not yet even imagined."[17] Given these technical and historical facts, given the dispersed character of moving image technologies, Carroll argues for a broader domain for the analyses of motion pictures. Such an expansion is, in fact, well underway, and film theorists pay more attention now to the relations between cinema and the very many other sources of moving imagery, and to other media generally. But an acknowledgment of the fact that there are other such sources does not diminish the importance of "film" as an early and still very significant manifestation of moving image technology. "Film," as a concept, continues to structure our thinking about moving images generally. As Carroll himself is ready to admit, the term "film" is often used in everyday speech "to designate things that are really the product of other media."[18] Many "films" today are actually shot on digital video, or are computer animations, but we do not make a distinction between going to see a film and going to see a video. We perhaps blur this distinction by saying that we are going to the "movies," but this term itself is intimately tied, historically, to the specific medium of film. Carroll insists, though, that the persistence of the use of the term "film," when theorizing about moving images, is the source of some significant conceptual confusion—"it can and does," he says, "cause philosophical mischief"—and he calls for a shift from film theory to a more broadly conceived "philosophy of motion pictures."[19]

Carroll is not alone in his proposal for conceptual clarification, but few seem as eager as he is to dispense with film theory altogether in favor of a more expansive philosophical project. A quite animated debate is underway among film theorists about the present status and future prospects of the enterprise, and there are various *philosophical* prescriptions that are being offered as solutions, including the very different proposals of D.N. Rodowick and Malcolm Turvey, whose recent debate about the status and prospects of film theory is reprinted in this anthology. But while film theory is being asked to become more philosophical, the concept of "film" is still central, and it persists even in an era when film as a physical object may be disappearing. This is partly a result of the fact that in the realms of production and reception, in the everyday parlance of *film*making and *film*going, the word "film" still rolls easily off the tongue. As we move into the digital era, *films* continue to be made (and most, in fact, are still made *on* film), and they are still understood as the basic product of the larger enduring enterprise that is *cinema*. Whether we need to radically extend the theoretical focus at this point in history, to address certain technological changes that are taking place, is still an open question.

The project of film theory persists, and remains robust, and it will, I think, for as long as the word "film" remains a part of the ordinary language of cinematic culture, and for as long as "films" continue to be made, in whatever format. The word still serves a vital descriptive function, both in everyday use, and in the technical language of theory. The importance of the word "film" for film theory is the historical legacy of a longstanding debate about the nature and character of the cinema, about its material basis, a debate that has been reignited as the physical constitution of the medium is being altered. As D.N. Rodowick says, in the essay included here, "one powerful consequence of the rapid emergence of electronic and digital media is that we can no longer take for granted what 'film' is—its ontological anchors have come ungrounded—and thus we are compelled to revisit continually the question, What is cinema?" (p. 24). But the question of cinema is still posed here in terms of the putatively more basic question of film—even if, as Rodowick claims, we can no longer take film's identity for granted.

Given the technological changes that are underway, given that film's identity is once again in question, there is a growing consensus that film theory needs to be revived and reinvented, if it is to fruitfully contend with these changes. If the solution is not to comprehensively transform film theory into a more broadly conceived philosophy of motion pictures, though, there is a sense that a certain amount of philosophical clarification is needed, that film theory should look to philosophy for guidance and support. But the debate is about which philosophical tradition film theorists should turn to, and what, precisely, one means by philosophy. Rodowick argues for a broadening of film theory's purview, and asks us to imagine "what a film philosophy might look like" (p. 29). Whatever it is, it would certainly be very different from Carroll's philosophy of motion pictures. Rodowick explicitly rejects what he describes as Carroll's "scientific" approach. He argues that, "it is important . . . to find and retain in theory the distant echo of its connection to philosophy" (p. 29), but this, for him, means finding the links between philosophy and art, rather than those between philosophy and science. A philosophically inflected film theory would not emulate the methods or approaches of the natural sciences, he insists, or of the scientifically informed tradition of analytic philosophy, but would, instead, acknowledge philosophy's role in "liberating humanistic inquiry from the bonds of empirical and causal explanation" (p. 29). Film theory should, Rodowick argues, be less like science. It should be more speculative, more contemplative, more discursive—in a word, more artful.

In his response, also reprinted here, Malcolm Turvey agrees with Rodowick that theory has become a "'contested concept' in film studies," and that we need to reverse the "retreat from theory" that has characterized film studies since the 1980s. Theory is important, Turvey insists, and we need to "[take] seriously the recent debates among film theorists and analytical philosophers about what film theory is, or should be" (p. 38). While he agrees with Rodowick in principle about the value of theory, and while he also calls for a turn to philosophy, Turvey's prescriptions for the revitalization of film theory are in stark contrast to Rodowick's. He rejects Rodowick's characterization of analytical philosophy as strictly modeled on the scientific method—film theory, for Turvey, is not and should not be understood as a "science"—but he does insist that it is only the application of a rigorous logic, the analytical legacy, that will provide conceptual clarification for film theory. "Under the aegis of analytical philosophy," writes Turvey, film theory "has become much more dialectical, rigorous, and clear, ridding itself of much of the 'fashionable nonsense' and dogma of psychoanalytical-semiotic film theory" (p. 42). Film theory should, Turvey argues, be clearer, more rigorous, more precise. Film theory would benefit, Turvey seems to be saying, by being *less* artful.

While the current state of film theory is the subject of vigorous debate, and while very different solutions to theory's problems are being proposed, there is a general consensus that any conceptual clarification will benefit from a historicization of theory. Both Rodowick and Turvey are busy investigating the historical origins of theoretical concepts, and both understand film theory as a fundamentally historical phenomenon—as a process, as a history of conceptual development, a series of debates and arguments. One way of clarifying the concepts of film theory is to revisit earlier articulations of those concepts, and to put them into dialogue with contemporary theory. This can reveal significant differences between historical moments, but it can also reveal important continuities. The history of film theory is, fundamentally, a continuous history of debates and arguments about what "film" is, what its nature and effects might be, what its broader social and cultural value is. This history has provided us with a store of concepts and ideas that are proving surprisingly useful again in our own era, which is characterized by the proliferation of new visual media. As another dramatic technological transformation seems to be underway, as the cinema is "digitized," and as the medium of film is again put into question, there is a renewed interest in earlier debates, and contemporary film scholars are returning to the work of previous film theorists. Whether reconsidering Béla Balázs' account of a newly emerging "culture of film" in the 1920s, which can be compared to the emergence of a new digital visual culture, or returning again to "rethink" André Bazin's "ontological" analysis of film, in light of recent technological developments, old film theory is being revisited to answer the questions posed by new media. As we again confront new forms of representation, which are supposed to be altering our access to reality and transforming our knowledge and understanding of the world, accounts of previous moments of comparable change seem worth revisiting. Malcolm Turvey, in another essay reprinted in this volume, reconsiders Balázs' early film theory, and while he does not explicitly address our contemporary conditions, his account of an earlier argument for the dramatic effects of film as a "new medium" seems timely. Daniel Morgan, in his essay included here, *is* explicit, insisting that a re-evaluation of the ontological theories of André Bazin is especially important now, given that "[t]he advance in digital technologies of image production and manipulation has seriously challenged traditional views about photography and film" (p. 104). Bazin, he argues, offered compelling accounts of the photograph and film which cannot easily be dismissed, and which may in fact helpfully guide us in our thinking about the changes underway in those media. The present moment requires new thought, of course, but, Morgan argues, "[i]f we need to develop new theories to keep up with a rapidly changing media landscape, it is also important not to forget the ambitions of classical theories" (p. 104).

The history of film theory should be understood as a conceptual reserve, and its development can only proceed with an historical awareness of the continuing effects of these concepts. Noël Carroll had made this argument some years ago, in an essay reprinted here. Re-reading the early film theory of Hugo Münsterberg, Carroll finds in it one of the first articulations of an analogy between film and mind, which, he argues, persists as a concept. Carroll, rather audaciously, traces a link between Münsterberg's early psychological analysis and later developments in film theory. He insists on the "exemplary historical value" of Münsterberg's work, which, he argues, "presages recent psychoanalytic explorations in film theory" (p. 58). Münsterberg, he says, "can be seen as the pioneer of the mind/film analogy-approach to film theory, and his writings, therefore, can be discussed within the context of the contemporary debate about whether the mind/film paradigm is a useful one" (p. 58). Whether one agrees or not with Carroll's conclusion—his insistence that "this line of inquiry should be jettisoned" (p. 67), and that psychoanalytic film theory be rejected—his essay is a model of historically informed theoretical work, and an early instance of the historicization of theory that is increasingly understood as a necessary component of theoretical activity.[20]

As part of this broader historical effort, we need to trace the specific conceptual development of film theory, which is best conceived of as a process, a collective discursive endeavor, with various paths and trajectories. These are not leading to any particular conclusion, to any single solution. Rather, the historical movement of ideas in film theory can be understood as a manifestation of what Mieke Bal has described as a kind of conceptual itinerary, a traveling of concepts that characterizes humanities inquiry generally, as interests and concerns, goals and ambitions, are articulated and revised.[21] Film theory has roamed widely in its conceptual travels, and as its objectives have changed it has absorbed material from a broad range of other disciplines, from linguistics and semiotics, psychology and psychoanalysis, cognitive theory and media analysis, and it has established very close ties with, for instance, feminist and queer theory, cultural studies, and analyses of race and class. The history of these, and the very many other conceptual collaborations, should be carefully recounted, and film theory's and film studies' place within broad, interdisciplinary networks needs to be carefully considered.

But film theory has also maintained its specific focus on its named object of inquiry, and the challenge now is to address the role of film theory in a multimedia era, which seems to call for a more interdisciplinary approach, but which may also require a renewed focus on the persistence of film as a key component in a multifaceted visual culture. The fact that film theory has not simply been absorbed by a larger, interdisciplinary enterprise—whether a philosophy of motion pictures advocated by Carroll, or the related disciplines of media and cultural studies, or the emergent field of visual studies—is testament to the enduring significance of "film" as a term and as a concept. To ask whether we should still be studying film, whether we should still conceive of it as a discrete and distinct medium in a multimedia world, is to acknowledge the immense importance of the term in the history of thinking about cinema, and about moving images generally.

Even Carroll, in his provocative call for the end of film theory, seems historically aware of the force and significance of the term "film." He knows that his call will likely prompt strong reactions, that film theory still has many committed practitioners and passionate advocates, and he is well aware that any conceptual or terminological change will be the result only of argument, not the effect of a simple declaration on his part (even if he does seem to suggest that recent technical changes are enough, in themselves, to force a new theoretical alignment). Theory is, in this respect, fundamentally a *process*. Carroll himself had, before calling for a shift to philosophy, urged that we replace the word "theory" with "theorizing," in order, he says, "to lay emphasis on theorizing as an activity—an ongoing process rather than a product."[22] That process consists of a series of exchanges, dialogues, and disputes, which, if they seem not to be heading to an ultimate conclusion, do help us refine our thinking about an important and influential technical and cultural phenomenon, which we may or may not continue to call "film."

The most recent debate, then, about the very status of the term "film"—focused on the specific changes that are being wrought by the so-called "digitization" of film, a debate represented in the essays that conclude this anthology—should be understood as merely the latest instance in a long history of debates about "film," and be seen as a sign of the robust state of film theory, rather than of its imminent demise. It is also a sign of the inherent theoretical value of debate. Debate is constructive, even if it sometimes seems fierce. Carroll, for instance, has strongly disagreed with other theorists, but he acknowledges that it is the process of debate that allows us to proceed productively in our theoretical activity. He has, as he puts it, been a "dogged critic of contemporary film theorists," and he has loudly declared that "their theories have been consistently misguided," but he does admit that "many of the topics they have put on the table for discussion have been good ones."[23] Some find the argumentative nature of film theory, its emphasis on debate, somewhat objectionable. "Although film theory has often involved debates," writes Robert Stam, "argument is only one, rather narrow, dimension of film theorizing." He prefers what he calls "a real dialogue," which, he says, "depends on the ability of each side to articulate the adversary's project fairly before critiquing it."[24] While there have certainly been some rather heated quarrels between film theorists, and while it is the case that some have presented their arguments in rather strident terms, very real insights have emerged. Film theory has mainly been characterized by debate, by argument, and less by the sort of ideal dialogue hoped for by Stam. Indeed, Francesco Casetti, in his history of film theory, has emphasized this fact. "A theory," he writes, "in order to be such, must function as both a testing ground and a reason for discussion, and it must be acknowledged and appropriated by a . . . group of scholars." According to such a model, he says, the history of film theory should "privilege above all those contributions that 'initiated a debate'."[25]

III

Following Casetti, then, a number of key debates in the history of film theory are presented in this anthology, not as an exhaustive account of the field, but rather as an indication of the conceptual development that characterizes theorizing about film. And it is *film* that is at the heart of these debates—what it is, what its uses are, what its functions and effects are, what its future might be. Despite the specific focus, though, no single question is posed here, nor has film theory been guided by any particular or even a dominant method. Film's complexity has produced a surprising plurality of approaches. The field of "film theory" is a very broad domain of rhetorical and conceptual activity, where basic questions are posed about an enormous and multifaceted phenomenon—the extensive technological, industrial, artistic, and social apparatus for the production, exhibition, and consumption of moving, photographic images. The basic components of this apparatus appeared, rather suddenly, at the end of the nineteenth century, and observers and commentators, as we've seen, began almost immediately to try to describe it, speculating about its possible effects and assessing its likely artistic value. Given that it emerged fully formed, so to speak, recognized almost immediately as a distinct, new medium, whose aesthetic potential lay in the utilization of the specific mechanical, chemical, and optical technologies for the photographic reproduction of movement, it has been customary to identify the entire phenomenon by reference to its basic material component. Its complexity is perhaps obscured, though, by the singular noun, "film," that has come to designate it, and it is worth reflecting on how *film* has come to be the object of a distinct kind of *theory*, why a separate realm of "film theory" emerged for the analysis and evaluation of this new form. Despite the fact that there were techniques for the production of moving images before the cinema, and have been many others since, it is "film" that has been at the heart of the most long-standing and perhaps most significant moving image medium of the last century, and it is film theory that has emerged as the most coherent approach to the analysis of moving imagery.

The story of its emergence, though, is a complex one. "Retrospectively," observes Rodowick, in the essay reprinted here, "it is curious that early in the twentieth century film would become associated with theory, rather than with aesthetics or the philosophy of art" (p. 24). As early as 1924, Rodowick notes, Béla Balázs, writing in German, called for a *Theorie des Films*, and, "from this moment forward," as he says, "one would rarely speak of film aesthetics or a philosophy of film, but rather, always, of film *theory*" (p. 24). This, argues Rodowick, is "representative of a nineteenth-century tendency in German philosophies of art to portray aesthetics as a *Wissenschaft*, comparable in method and epistemology to the natural sciences" (p. 24). The study of film has never really been "scientific," though—despite the ambitions of some. As Rodowick notes, the "theory" in film theory is related more to "the Greek sense of *theoria* as viewing, speculation, or the contemplative life" (p. 24), than to the modern, scientific sense of theory.

But the new medium of film did seem to call for a separate and distinct kind of analysis, a modern approach, logical and precise, like the theory that Turvey advocates, capable of clearly revealing the novel and specifically technological character of film, which provided the material basis for the cinema. The "film" in film theory has been understood as both the actual physical surface upon which the photographic images are registered, and the finished products that are then distributed and exhibited by large commercial concerns, and consumed by mass audiences; and it is "film theory" that has emerged as the term for that broad field of inquiry dedicated to the description, analysis, and explanation of the material manifestations of the immense and complex cinematic apparatus. This is the case, at least, in the English-speaking world. In France there is *théorie du cinéma*; in Italy *teoria del cinema*. But the English term, like Balázs' German term, draws our attention to the fact that, in theoretical speculations about the *cinema*, it is the question of the specific medium of *film*—both the material process for the photographic reproduction of movement, and the actual finished product of the cinema—that has been central.

The cinema has long been distinguished from the other traditional arts, and from other media, primarily on the basis of its "filmic" character, and those who made the first comprehensive efforts to establish a rigorous theoretical model for the analysis of the medium have emphasized this distinction. When Hugo Münsterberg, professor of philosophy and psychology at Harvard University, wrote his book-length study in 1916 of what was still called the "photoplay," an excerpt of which is included in this volume, he began with the problem of *film* as a photographic medium, wondering whether it would limit the aesthetic potential of the new form. "Do the photoplays," he asked, "furnish us only a photographic reproduction of a stage performance?" (p. 49). If this is the case, he argued, then the "photoplay" could simply be understood and analyzed as an extension of the traditional art of the theater. But there was, he insisted, something that clearly distinguished the *photo*play from its stage-bound predecessor. A merely technical description of the new medium would not help us to see this distinction, however. Münsterberg's approach, instead, was to analyze those specific material qualities of the medium in terms of their capacity to produce new and powerful effects in the minds of the viewer.

It was important, Münsterberg argued, to provide not merely another technical description. He would avoid "all which books on moving pictures have so far put into the foreground, namely the physical technique of producing the pictures on the film or of projecting the pictures on the screen, or anything else which belongs to the technical or physical or economic aspect of the photoplay industry" (p. 49). What was required, instead, was a more careful consideration of the techniques as the source of film's *effects*. "Our esthetic interest," writes Münsterberg, "turns to the means by which the photoplay influences the mind of the spectator" (p. 49). Those "means," though, turn out to be the peculiar material qualities of the medium, understood as a technical system for the presentation of images—which produces images that *seem* to move, and that *appear* to have depth, despite their origin in the still, flat *film* surface. While we do not see the technological components directly, while, as Münsterberg says, "we do not see the passing by of the long strip of film," it is, nevertheless, its actual passing that produces the various effects in the minds of the spectators. "What objectively reaches our eye is one motionless picture after another," he observes. This, however, raises a difficult question, which can only be answered psychologically, which has to be approached theoretically: "Why do we, nevertheless, see a continuous movement?" (p. 53). It is this discrepancy between the limited technical origin of the photoplay's imagery and the rich perceptual and emotional effects that it can produce that is of concern to Münsterberg. Despite the apparent limitations of the medium, he insists, "we must recognize that the photoplaywright has . . . possibilities to which nothing corresponds in the world of the stage"—possibilities that are realized, he says, through the artistic use of a technological instrument, through what he calls, emphasizing the cinema's technical origins, "the subtle art of the camera".[26]

Many of the most significant debates in film theory have been about the "subtle art of the camera," about the rich perceptual, emotional, aesthetic, and ideological effects that are produced through the use of a quite basic technical device. Are we to understand those effects to be the result of a unique technical method, or are they no different than those produced by any artistic medium—by painting, poetry, or music? The answer has tended to be the former, which has in turn led to the elaboration of distinct concepts that have—for better or worse—guided the development of a distinct *film* theory. The effects of motion pictures have, since Münsterberg, as Carroll argues, typically been understood to be unique, and to derive, ultimately, from the particular technical processes for the production of moving, photographic images, from their filmic base. This has become a common claim in film theory. According to a familiar formula, the origins of the art of film are technological. "It was not," according to Erwin Panofsky, for example, in his analysis of style in motion pictures, "an artistic urge that gave rise to the discovery and gradual perfection of a new technique; it was a technical invention that gave rise to the discovery and gradual perfection of a new art."[27] Rudolf Arnheim argued along similar lines, claiming that "film art developed only gradually when the movie makers began consciously or unconsciously to cultivate the peculiar possibilities of cinematographic technique and to apply them toward the creation of artistic productions."[28] Béla Balázs, in the passage reproduced in this volume, from his 1924 book *Visible Man, or The Culture of Film*, establishes the material fact of film as the fundamental basis upon which to analyze its effects, which differ radically from the effects of other, more traditional aesthetic media, noting that "the purely visual nature of film enables us to see that *indeterminate something* that can only ever appear between the lines even in the best of novelists" (p. 76).

The tendency to find the origin of the particular effects of film in the unique material basis of the medium has continued to guide theorists, and has led to theoretical accounts that, while differing in many respects, share a fundamental assumption about the relation between form and effect, between the material basis of film and the cinematic experience. This is expressed in various terms, and with different emphases, but can be traced as a variation on a theme throughout the history of film theory. It is expressed in perhaps the most famous, certainly the most controversial, statement by André Bazin, in his essay "The Ontology of the Photographic Image," included here. Grounding film in its photographic material, Bazin argues that "[t]he photographic image is the object itself, the object freed from the conditions of time and space that govern it"[29] (p. 92). He goes on to say that "[t]he photograph as such and the object in itself share a common being, after the fashion of a fingerprint" (p. 93). The consequence of this, Bazin argues, is that photographs and films have a unique capacity to affect us, to force us to acknowledge the reality and significance of what they represent, in a manner that can only be compared to natural phenomena like flowers or snowflakes, to use two of his own examples. Daniel Morgan, in his reconsideration of Bazin, endeavors to explain the value of such a view, and argues for the enduring importance of Bazin's critical work. Morgan argues against later accounts of Bazin that, as he says, conceive of his argument in "semiotic" terms, as an anticipation of what would come to be called the "indexical" argument. If Bazin's argument has been accepted, it is as an anticipation of the later semiotic analysis of filmic expression. Morgan argues that this is a too limited reading of Bazin, and that we need to attend to "the complexities of the relation between ontology and style" (p. 106) in Bazin's theory. A retrospective account of Bazin's argument as proto-semiotic, he argues, does not do it justice.

The supposedly "indexical" argument in Bazin's critical writings finds its first explicit expression in Peter Wollen's "The Semiology of the Cinema," a chapter of his 1969 book *Signs and Meaning in the Cinema*, and is presented in rather different form in the later work of Gilles Deleuze, in his 1985 book *Cinema 2: The Time-Image*. Both Wollen and Deleuze offer their arguments as correctives to what they see as the limitations of the semiological analysis of Christian Metz, presented most fully in his groundbreaking 1964 essay "The Cinema: Language or Language System?" All three arguments are reprinted here. Wollen associates Metz with other "semiologists" such as Roland Barthes, Umberto Eco, and Pier Paolo Pasolini, all of whom had been influenced by the structural linguistics of Ferdinand de Saussure, and specifically by his proposal for a general science of signs, or semiology, which he thought would develop from linguistic analysis. But the extension of such an analysis to other, non-linguistic phenomena was, according to both Wollen and Deleuze, unsuccessful. Both argue that the limitations of a semiological analysis of the cinema are revealed most dramatically in Metz's most ambitious methodological statement, the "Language" essay. "Metz's position," argues Wollen, "involves him in a considerable number of problems which he never satisfactorily surmounts" (p. 173). What is needed, Wollen suggests, in order to overcome the obstacles that Metz had erected, is "a more precise discussion of what we mean by a 'natural sign'," which had been dismissed by Metz, in favor of the Saussurian notion of the conventional or "arbitrary" sign (p. 173).

The photographic images of the cinema, though, insists Wollen, are best understood not as arbitrary, but rather as motivated or continuous, as Bazin had argued two decades earlier—the effect of the specific qualities of the photographic process. But Wollen wants to provide firmer philosophical support to Bazin's argument, which had often been presented as too impressionistic, and he makes recourse to the semiotic theory of the nineteenth-century American philosopher Charles Peirce, in particular to his concept of the "indexical" sign, which he offers as the means out of the impasses of linguistic theories of cinema. Like Wollen, Deleuze also argues against Metz, and semiological theories of cinema generally, in favor of what he also presents as the richer conceptual resources of Peirce's semiotic. Deleuze rejects semiological analysis, and, in language that seems to directly echo Bazin, offers the alternative concept of the "movement-image," which, he says, "is not analogical in the sense of resemblance; it does not resemble an object that it would represent." Instead, he insists, "the movement-image is the object; the thing itself caught in movement as continuous function" (p. 187). Daniel Morgan explicitly cites Wollen and Deleuze as the two initial proponents of the so-called "indexical" argument, and as influential readers and interpreters of Bazinian theory. But Morgan resists their readings of Bazin, and rejects the "indexical" account that they offer. Instead, he insists, Bazin's arguments need to be understood in their own terms, and claims an ethical and moral dimension for Bazin, which transcends the strictly formal analyses of later semiologists like Metz, but also of the later indexical arguments of both Wollen and Deleuze.

The arguments of Wollen and Deleuze are only two instances in a wide-ranging debate about film language that followed from Metz's ambitious semiological analysis. Metz's essay, though, came late in the history of thinking about film as language. André Bazin himself had concluded his "Ontology" essay with the short and infamously enigmatic final sentence: "On the other hand, of course, cinema is also a language."[30] The concept of language seemed to naturally present itself as the most sensible way of thinking about cinematic expression, even to Bazin, who had just argued that the filmic image has a natural quality, that seems to distinguish it from the arbitrary and conventional quality of language. But film's "natural" images, as Bazin was willing to acknowledge, have been made to perform an *expressive* function, and, having described film's ontological character, he would then trace the evolution of the language of cinema.

Film too obviously "says" something. As Francesco Casetti has put it, "just like any natural language . . . cinema appears to be a place for an elaboration of meanings that makes them perceptible, formulates them, and allows for their exchange with other people. In a word, cinema appears as the sphere of a *signification* and of a *communication*."[31] "Grammars" and "rhetorics" of film, accounts of filmic language, of film's signifying and communicative capacities, have been produced throughout the history of film theory. It was Christian Metz, though, who first provided a distinct methodology for the rigorous analysis of filmic expression. In order to overcome the rather more impressionistic accounts of film language of earlier theorists, Metz applied the new method of semiology. As Metz writes, in his account of those earlier efforts, progress was limited by a "tempting" conceptual error: "Seen from a certain angle, the cinema has all the appearances of what it is not. It is apparently a *kind of language* (*une sorte de langage*), but it was seen as something less, a specific *language system* (*une langue*)" (p. 137). Metz then produces an elaborate argument for cinema to be understood as "*une sorte de langage*," or as a kind of language, rather than "*une langue*," or a language system. This basic semiological distinction, inherited from Ferdinand de Saussure, provides the means, Metz argues, to fully describe the communicative capacities of film.

The semiological project, despite its ambitions and its early promise, did not really proceed beyond Metz's efforts in the "Language" essay. Despite his declaration that "[g]oing from one image to two images, is to go from image to language" (p. 140), a semiology of cinema could not overcome the problems that Metz himself had identified. There is nothing comparable in film to the word in language, much less to the other linguistic components of the phoneme and morpheme. "One can of course conclude," wrote Metz, in the face of this fact, "that the cinema is not a language, or that it is so only in a sense that is altogether too figurative, and, consequently, it should not be dealt with through semiotics" (pp. 158–9).[32] Metz rejected this conclusion, though, and he saw in the semiological analysis of the cinema the possibility of realizing "the great Saussurian dream of studying the mechanisms by which human significations are transmitted in human society" (p. 160).

Within only a few years, though, Metz would revise that dream, as he turned more and more to the figure of Sigmund Freud, and to psychoanalysis, as the means by which he could overcome the limitations of a merely linguistic analysis of cinema. It would only be a combination of semiology and psychoanalysis, Metz argues, as proposed specifically by Jacques Lacan, that would allow for an accounting of what he calls "the *signification-fact* taken in itself."[33] The turn to psychoanalysis would allow Metz to account for those more ephemeral aspects of cinematic signification that a merely semiological, or linguistic, approach could not explain. Psychoanalysis seemed to offer the means with which to account for the specifically *visual* aspect of cinema, which would come to be understood as a system for the elaboration of a "scene," comparable to the "primal scene" of psychoanalysis. The cinema comes to be understood essentially as a site for the reproduction of an unsanctioned kind of looking. The cinematic spectator is understood as a kind of *voyeur*. The cinema's uniqueness lies in this effect, which other arts may also stimulate, but none as powerfully as film. "[C]inematic voyeurism," writes Metz, "*unauthorised* scopophilia, is from the outset more strongly established than that of the theatre in direct line from the primal scene."[34] The cinema, in its very material manifestations, creates a situation for the spectator that is strongly similar to that of the voyeur. "Certain precise features of the institution," writes Metz, "contribute to this affinity: the obscurity surrounding the onlooker, the aperture of the screen with its inevitable keyhole effect."[35]

The turn to a psychoanalytically inflected semiology was decisive for the emergence of a powerful new form of feminist film theory, which supplanted earlier emphases in feminist critiques of cinema on the content of film—specifically the negative representations of women. Psychoanalysis, as inflected by Jacques Lacan, would provide feminist theorists with the means to analyze the formal and structural effects of cinema, its power to shape how the spectator "sees." The question of the effect of film has been most acute for feminist film theorists, and one of the most significant debates in film theory has been about the cinematic "gaze." The debates prompted by Metz's "Language" essay, about film language and filmic representation, have been matched in significance and importance only by the debates that have followed the argument made by Laura Mulvey, in her decisive essay of 1975, "Visual Pleasure and Narrative Cinema." If Metz's essay prompted a keen debate about the value for film theory of semiology, Mulvey's has led to even keener debates about the value of psychoanalysis. Her essay was among the first comprehensive statements of a psychoanalytically informed feminist film theory, and has certainly been the most influential and the most controversial. It almost immediately generated a fierce debate, provoking direct interrogatory responses like that of E. Ann Kaplan, who, in an almost equally famous response, asked, "Is the Gaze Male?" While Mulvey had made a strong claim, arguing that the cinema's gaze is inherently gendered, and that the "language" of cinematic expression is male, Kaplan responded by pointing to the limits that Mulvey's argument set on actual female film-viewers. Is the gaze essentially male, she asks, "[o]r would it be possible to structure things so that women own the gaze?" (p. 211). Kaplan goes on in her essay to explore this possibility, and to carefully consider the various problems posed by psychoanalysis as a method for the analysis of cinema's role within a gendered and patriarchal society.

Mulvey herself would write a follow-up to her original essay, acknowledging the importance of the question that was persistently posed to her: "What about the women in the audience?" While she states that she stands by her original argument, she does endeavor to answer that question, and to offer a more subtle account of female spectatorship, specifically of the sort of spectatorial experience offered by the Hollywood melodrama (which had become a significant genre for feminist theorists seeking to ask the same sorts of questions about female audiences, and which would be the focus of many subsequent studies). Mulvey asks the question in relation to her viewing of King Vidor's 1946 film *Duel in the Sun*. This was, in many respects, a peculiar choice for Mulvey, since the film revolves as much (if not more) around issues of race (and in decidedly troubling ways) as around gender. Rather than settle some of the issues that had been raised by those who had argued with her original claims, it brought into focus for many the considerable limitations of psychoanalytic film theory, and its emphasis on the issue of gender, and its apparent inability to contend with the fact of race. As bell hooks writes, in the essay included here: "Mainstream feminist film criticism in no way acknowledges black female spectatorship. . . . Feminist film theory rooted in an ahistorical psychoanalytic frame-work that privileges sexual difference actively suppresses recognition of race" (p. 234). Out of these debates a rich and complex field of feminist film theory has emerged, which has carefully interrogated the value of psychoanalysis, and expanded its purview to include as many voices as possible.[36]

IV

The present state of film theory is the legacy of a century-long history of argument and debate, which has provided theorists with an extensive conceptual reserve, and grounded the discipline of film studies in a reflexive, analytic enterprise. Film has been a central critical issue over the past century, and film studies has emerged and become firmly established within the institutions of academia, as film has come to be understood as an object worthy of serious sustained study. The rise of the discipline coincided for many years with the continued rise in the popularity of cinema, and the increasing confidence of film scholars has certainly been sustained by the broad consensus that film was capable of producing works as significant as those produced by any of the other arts. The decades of film studies' incorporation within academia, the 1960s and 1970s, were also crucial decades in the history of film itself, and the increasingly serious ambitions of filmmakers sustained and encouraged those who pursued the serious study of film. The various crises that film studies has faced in the last two decades have, similarly, coincided with crises within the cinema. The 1980s saw the rapid corporatiza-tion of filmmaking, as studios were purchased and absorbed by enormous multinational entities, which have had as much, or as little, interest in their films as they did in any of the other products and commodities they produced. Internationally, filmmaking seemed to be less and less about the art of cinema and more about the art of deal making, as national cinemas struggled for existence, and as international co-productions, with all the inevitable meddling of the growing number of producers (complaining in many different languages), threatened the integrity of the film artist. (Jean-Luc Godard had already vividly warned about the threat of "international co-productions" in his 1963 film *Contempt.*)

Further threats seemed to loom, as new media challenged film's status as the preeminent popular form of the last century, and as new technologies transformed the nature and quality of film viewing. The advent of television and of the VCR had already challenged conceptions of film. Recent developments in computer-generated imagery and digitization seem to threaten film's very identity. The state of film, and the state of cinema, seem to be in question, and this anthology concludes with debates about the very future of the medium. There is a clear div-ision that has been established, between those theorists who see a radical transformation underway, and those who insist that, in most respects, the medium of film and the cinematic experience remain fundamentally the same. Lev Manovich has resurrected the "indexical" argument, re-establishing this as a key theoretical concept for contemporary film theory. Film, argues Manovich, as it has been transformed by digital media, has lost its indexical quality. It no longer refers directly to the objects it represents. The Bazinian era, he suggests, is over, and we must now reconceive film as wholly subordinated to the digital logic of new media. Tom Gunning, however, insists that the concept of the index, as reintroduced by Manovich, has lost its theoretical value—it has, he says, become "diminished"—and he argues that further pro-gress in our analyses of cinematic realism will come only with a change of emphasis, away from the indexical argument.

Debates about the nature of the medium of film in the digital age will no doubt continue.

So, too, will debates about the nature of the cinematic experience. In her very influential essay, Anne Friedberg announced the "end of cinema," describing the subordination of film to the larger and more extensive apparatus of the new media. The shift from the large, absorbing image of the movie theater has been largely replaced, she argues, by the smaller-scale experience of watching films on computer screens. More significantly, she insists, this has transformed film viewing from a contemplative experience—where we were allowed to be carried away by the image—to just another of the many "interactive" screen experiences available in the digital era. John Belton, though, argues against such claims, and wants to resist what he sees as premature announcements of the death of the cinema. In most respects, the cinematic experience remains intact, he insists. While there are many other means available for accessing films, the movie theater survives and remains distinct. It seems, in fact, to be thriving as a technology, with the number of movie-goers around the world only rising.

The intense focus of these debates on the question of film's very identity—the return to issues of indexicality, considerations of the varied aspects of an ever more extensive and heterogenous cinematic experience—seem to have breathed new life into the theoretical project. While I cannot hope with this anthology to have accounted for the whole breadth and scope of the history of film theory, I am confident that it reveals the dynamic and energizing force of "theorizing." This is especially evident now. The arguments about the present and future status of film have enlivened the discipline, and have generated significant debates about the present and future status of film theory.

Notes

1   Stanley Cavell, *The World Viewed: Reflections on the Ontology of Film*, enlarged edition (Cambridge: Harvard University Press, 1979): 37.

2   There is growing interest in the extensive and lively discourse on film in the first decades of its history. Laura Marcus has described the breadth and richness of early critical discourse on film, and considers the effect that cinema had, at the turn of the twentieth century, on the very concept of "newness." The new medium of film, she argues, provided an opportunity for a wide range of writers and critics to consider what "newness" might mean, just as the other older, traditional arts were in the process of being "modernised," or made new. See Laura Marcus, "How Newness Enters the World: The Birth of Cinema and the Origins of Man," *Forum for Modern Language Studies*, 37.2 (2001): 186–203. Marcus provides a broader consideration of modernist responses to the new art of film in her book *The Tenth Muse: Writing about Cinema in the Modernist Period* (New York: Oxford University Press, 2007). For an account of the specific effects of cinema on the work of key modernist writers of the early twentieth century, see David Trotter, *Cinema and Modernism* (Malden, MA: Blackwell, 2007).

3   "Last night I was in the Kingdom of Shadows," wrote Gorky. "If only you knew how strange it is to be there. . . . It is not life but its shadow, it is not motion but its soundless spectre." Gorky's text is a review of a program of films by the Lumière brothers, Auguste and Louis. Published in 1896 in a Russian newspaper under the pseudonym I.M. Pacatus, it is reprinted as an Appendix to Jay Leyda's *Kino: A History of the Russian and Soviet Film* (London: George Allen and Unwin, 1969): 407–409.

4   Quoted in Leyda, *Kino*, p. 408. Gorky's is one of the very first of many such accounts of this moment in the Lumières' *L'Arrivé d'un train en gare de la Ciotat* (*Arrival of a Train at the Ciotat Station*), which quickly became famous as a model for the very early cinema, which emphasized such effects. Countless similar scenes followed during the next decade or so. Trains, trams, buses, cars, bicycles, and all manner of conveyances and objects hurtled towards early movie audiences, prompting many stories of the effects that these scenes had on credulous spectators. The original scene from the Lumière film is supposed to have been met with gasps and shrieks, and there are stories of spectators even leaping out of the way of

the oncoming train, and rushing for the exits. The history of such claims has been carefully recounted, and the stories more or less debunked. Stephen Bottomore has shown that accounts of audiences panicking in the face of images of approaching trains were significantly exaggerated. Bottomore takes the *stories* seriously, though, and he traces their fascinating history, arguing that they were significant elements in the early advertising and marketing of film, but also in the emerging critical discourse about the possible effects of film. The stories may be understood as the first manifestation of the fear that certain people—the uneducated, children, rural people, and "primitives"—might be more susceptible to the illusory powers of film. Bottomore suggests that this was at least partly an expression of a more general anxiety about the effects of film. "One might argue," he writes, "that the myth of the train effect is part of the 'universal human response' to the early cinema; a way of resolving a certain discomfort about a new and uncomfortably realistic new [sic] medium" (p. 186). Bottomore, though, does not really pursue the ideological aspects of such displacement, and is more interested in the broader psychological issues that stories of actual early responses to film might shed light on. See Stephen Bottomore, "The Panicking Audience?: Early Cinema and the 'Train Effect'," *Historical Journal of Film, Radio and Television*, 19.2 (1999): 177–216. Bottomore builds on the work of film historian Martin Loiperdinger, in his essay "Lumière's *Arrival of the Train*: Cinema's Founding Myth," *The Moving Image* 4.1 (2004): 89–118. The essay was originally published in German as "Lumieres Ankunft des Zugs," *KINtop* 5 (1996): 36–70. Tom Gunning has pursued the broader issues of an "aesthetics of astonishment," elaborating the concept of an early "cinema of attractions" that was designed primarily to produce such effects. See Tom Gunning, "An Aesthetic of Astonishment," *Film Theory and Criticism*, eds. Leo Braudy and Marshall Cohen, seventh edition (New York: Oxford University Press, 2009): 736–50; and his seminal essay "The Cinema of Attraction: Early Film, Its Spectator and the Avant-Garde," *Wide Angle: A Film Quarterly of Theory, Criticism, and Practice*, 8.3–4 (1986): 63–70. For a detailed history of trains and early film, see Lynne Kirby, *Parallel Tracks: The Railroad and Silent Cinema* (Durham, NC: Duke University Press, 1997).

5   Quoted in Layda, *Kino*, p. 407.

6   Quoted in Layda, *Kino*, pp. 408–409.

7   Lindsay's main work is *The Art of the Moving Picture* (New York: Macmillan, 1915). A second, revised edition was published in 1922, and reprinted in 1970 with an Introduction by Stanley Kaufmann. See Vachel Lindsay, *The Art of the Moving Picture* (New York: Liveright, 1970). A later book of film criticism has been reprinted. See Vachel Lindsay, *The Progress and Poetry of the Movies*, ed. Myron Lounsbury (Lanham, MD: Scarecrow Press, 1995). While an early advocate of popular film, even Lindsay was ambivalent about the new medium, noting, in his 1914 poem to Blanche Sweet, the promise of film compared to the meager quality of its actual accomplishments, which were manifested in Sweet's performances in otherwise unremarkable films, shown in unsavory settings. "Though the tin piano/Snarls its tango rude,/Though the chairs are shaky/And the dramas crude,/Solemn are her motions,/Stately are her wiles,/Filling oafs with wisdom,/Saving souls with smiles." See Vachel Lindsay, *The Congo, and Other Poems* (New York: Macmillan, 1915): 25.

8   Dana Polan notes that Lindsay is often cited as a forerunner in historical accounts of film study, even though he produced what Polan describes as "poetic and often wacky ramblings" (p. 19). But Polan does acknowledge that "Lindsay did write a full-fledged aesthetics of film," and that, while "Lindsay never actually was a film professor, . . . his text became formative for the discipline" (p. 19). See Dana Polan, *Scenes of Instruction: The Beginnings of the U.S. Study of Film* (Berkeley: University of California Press, 2007). Lindsay's influence has been indirect, though, with very little written explicitly on his film criticism, but see Glenn Joseph Wolfe, *Vachel Lindsay: The Poet as Film Theorist* (New York: Arno Press, 1973). See also Miriam Hansen, *Babel and Babylon: Spectatorship in American Silent Film* (Cambridge: Harvard University Press, 1991), for an historical account of early film spectatorship in the United States, and a consideration of the kinds of claims that were being made about the social effects of film and its political value. Hansen provides a brief account of Lindsay, whom she describes as a "prophet of motion picture millennialism" (p. 77), a key figure in the broad discourse on film as a universal visual language, the basis for a utopian democratic future.

9   This is the phrase used by the early feminist and social reformer Dr. Anna Shaw, who said in 1910: "There should be a police woman at the entrance of every moving picture show and another inside. These places are the recruiting stations of vice." Quoted in Eileen Bowser, *The Transformation of Cinema: 1907–1915* (Berkeley: University of California Press, 1990): 38. While Shaw's comments were those of a social progressive, concerns about the moral effects of the cinema in its early years in the United States were expressed from every ideological perspective, as Bowser recounts in Chapter 3 of her book. The anxieties generated by the advent of the new medium are also described by Robert Sklar, in his *Movie-Made America: A Cultural History of American Movies*, revised edition (New York: Vintage, 1994). Sklar considers the "vast array of books and articles by educators, clergymen, academics, reformers, intellectuals, clubwomen, penal workers and politicians deploring the baneful influence of movies" (p. 122). The sense of concern was not only limited to the United States. The rise of new media and entertainments of mass popular culture was a global phenomenon, and these were widely understood to pose significant social and political threats. The new visual media were of particular concern. This was expressed in such late-nineteenth-century works as Gustav Le Bon's *The Crowd: A Study of the Popular Mind* (London: T. Fisher, 1897). "Crowds," wrote Le Bon, "being only capable of thinking in images are only to be impressed by images. It is only images that terrify or attract them and become motives of action. For this reason," he argues, "theatrical representations in which the image is shown in its most clearly visible shape, always have an enormous influence on crowds" (p. 35). Apprehension about the effects of the image were intensified with the advent of film and other more powerful visual media. The conservative Spanish philosopher José Ortega y Gasset, in his critique of mass society, bemoans the effects of new media. "The illustrated paper and the film," he wrote, "have brought . . . far-off portions of the universe before the immediate vision of the crowd." But, he argues, this is now within the grasp of the most common individual, when once "it was a question of honour for man to triumph over cosmic space and time" (p. 39) — an essentially aristocratic privilege. See José Ortega y Gasset, *The Revolt of the Masses* (New York: Norton, 1932). In contrast to the threat of film's dangerous excitement of the mass imagination seen by the political right, critiques from the left would tend to emphasize its restrictive and reductive powers. Theodor Adorno and Max Horkheimer would come to see film as a significant force *limiting* the progressive imagination of the masses. "The withering of imagination and spontaneity in the consumer culture of today," they wrote, "need not be traced back to psychological mechanisms. The products [of the culture industry] themselves, especially the most characteristic, the sound film, cripple those faculties through their objective makeup" (p. 100). See Max Horkheimer and Theodor W. Adorno, *Dialectic of Enlightenment: Philosophical Fragments*, trans. Edmund Jephcott (Stanford: Stanford University Press, 2002).

10   Dana Polan, *Scenes of Instruction*, p. 6. Some of the basic questions that Polan enumerates are: the connection between the critical study of film and the practice of filmmaking; the relation between the aesthetics of film and its psychosocial effects; film's uniqueness, its distinction from the other arts; and the influence of dominant, "Hollywood," film on the development of alternative modes of cinematic productions and filmic expression. "To a large degree," he says, "such questions still drive the field, and it is useful to look back on the ways the very first film pedagogues came to grips with them" (p. 6).

11   Writing in 1970, Cavell acknowledges that a great deal of work had been done recounting the history of the development of the cinema, and that this was an important part of the effort to produce a theoretical account of the medium. "The facts are well enough known," he writes, "about the invention and the inventors of the camera, and about improvements in fixing and then moving the image it captures. The problem is that the invention of the photographic picture is not the same thing as the creation of photography as a medium for making sense." A full theoretical account would have to explain how and why the cinema came to perform a primarily *realistic* function. Realism, he notes, was "the burning issue during the latter half of the nineteenth century," and the cinema immediately pursued what was being sought in the new realist forms of theater and painting. He insists that "unless film captured possibilities opened up by the arts themselves, it is hard to imagine that its possibilities as an artistic medium would have shown up as, and as suddenly as, they did." Stanley Cavell, *World Viewed*, pp. 37–39.

12   Page references in the text refer to this volume.

13   There is, of course, considerable debate about the position that film theory occupies within the broader field or discipline of film studies. For a recent account of those debates, and an argument for the enduring value of theory in the discipline, see Dudley Andrew, "The Core and the Flow of Film Studies," *Critical Inquiry* 35 (Summer 2009): 879–915. Andrew is a champion of "theory," but he does admit that its position has shifted, and that its function has changed. It is no less important, though, even after years of intense critique. As he says, "theory today no longer stands in the middle of the field like a tentpole, but rather spreads itself into every inquiry across the field that submits itself to sustained and coherent reflection" (pp. 905–906). Andrew is the author of two early and influential accounts of film theory, which have been instrumental in establishing the theoretical basis of the discipline. See Andrew, *The Major Film Theories* (New York: Oxford University Press, 1976); and Andrew, *Concepts in Film Theory* (New York: Oxford University Press, 1984). For another account of the state of film studies, see Gertrud Koch, "Carnivore or Chameleon: The Fate of Cinema Studies," *Critical Inquiry* 35.4 (2009): 918–928. This and the essay by Dudley Andrew are contributions to a special issue of *Critical Inquiry* on "Disciplines."

14   This theoretical distinction can be traced back to the "Filmology" movement, which emerged at the University of Paris after 1945. The main figure of the movement, Gilbert Cohen-Séat, established a distinction between what he called the "cinematic fact" and the "filmic fact." See Gilbert Cohen-Séat, *Essai sur les principes d'une philosophie du cinéma* (Paris: Presse Universitaires de France, 1946). Christian Metz developed this distinction, establishing the methodological grounds upon which the "cinematic fact" would be put aside, in favor of a rigorous formal analysis of the "filmic fact." As Metz argues, the distinction "allows us to restrict the meaning of the term 'film' to a more manageable, specifiable signifying discourse, in contrast with 'cinema,' which ... constitutes a larger complex." See Christian Metz, "Within the Cinema: The Filmic Fact," *Language and Cinema*, trans. Jean Umiker-Sebeok (The Hague: Mouton, 1974): 12. The history of filmology has been chronicled by Edward Lowry, in *The Filmology Movement and Film Study in France* (Ann Arbor, MI: UMI Research, 1985). More recently, the history and enduring influence of filmology have been traced in a special issue of *Cinémas: Revues d'études cinématographique*, edited by Martin Lefebvre. See *Cinémas* 19.2–3 (Autumn 2009).

15   The full complexity of the academic institutionalization of film studies is being revealed as the history of the discipline has begun to receive serious attention. The recently published anthology, edited by Lee Grieveson and Haidee Wasson, *Inventing Film Studies* (Durham, NC, and London: Duke University Press, 2008), provides a rich account of the historical complexities of film studies' emergence as a discipline. The story of film studies had long been presented according to what Grieveson and Wasson call "conventional narratives," and they write that "[w]hen one scratches at the surface of disciplinary certainties . . ., then one finds long and often complex histories that have been largely omitted from prevailing accounts of what the study of cinema has been and ought to be" (p. xii). A significant omission has been corrected by Dana Polan, in his recently published history of the very early years of film study in the United States, *Scenes of Instruction*. Polan describes the "seductive" but misleading history of the discipline of film studies that has so often been told, and which, he says, "allows film studies practitioners to imagine the beginnings of their discipline in heroic terms" (p. 4). Film scholarship had been understood to have emerged in the 1950s, in the resistance to the tendency then to denigrate popular culture and popular media like film. Such resistance is then understood to have been manifested in the 1960s in the formation of the discipline of film studies. Among other consequences, as Polan argues, the effect of this story is that "earlier efforts in the teaching of film have been downplayed" (p. 5), and he recounts the many and varied efforts, in the first half of the twentieth century, to incorporate the study of film within the university.

16   In *Scenes of Instruction*, Polan explicitly presents his account of the early history of the study of film as part of a broader tendency to consider and interrogate the conceptual and theoretical basis upon which the discipline of film studies has been built. That tendency is the positive result, he suggests, of the central position of theory in film studies. "[T]he emphasis on theory as a central activity of [the] field," he notes, "has encouraged reflexivity and self-interrogation. It becomes inevitable to ask such disciplinary questions as What does it mean

to do film theory? Which theory? Should one do something other than theory?" (p. 3). Theory is understood here as an animating and critical force within the discipline. Polan's history is partly intended to reveal the sources of the theoretical foundation in the context of what he calls the "concrete institutional operations" of the field's participants (p. 3).

17 Noël Carroll, *The Philosophy of Motion Pictures* (Malden, MA: Blackwell, 2008): 3.

18 Carroll, *Philosophy*, p. 3.

19 Carroll, *Philosophy*, p. 4.

20 Lee Grieveson has recently made an argument which is similar to Carroll's, if (slightly) less polemical in tone. Grieveson traces the origins of a certain conception of cinematic spectatorship, which, he argues, has affected the very structure of film studies as a discipline. Grieveson, like Carroll, describes the legacy of Münsterberg's argument about film's mental effects in subsequent theories of spectatorship and mass movie audiences, but he extends his purview to describe the broader context within which psychological and sociological models of influence were structuring the early analyses of cinema. Grieveson concludes by linking the early sociological and psychological accounts of cinema's effects with later film theory, informed by psychoanalysis and critical theory. While Grieveson accepts that "this later work included a much more nuanced approach to the analysis of the cinematic image, [when] viewed from a slightly different angle, it is perhaps the continuity of these traditions of thinking about cinema that may well be more striking" (p. 25). See Lee Grieveson, "Cinema Studies and the Conduct of Conduct," in Grieveson and Wasson, eds., *Inventing Film Studies*: 3–37. For broader historical accounts of the conceptual development of film theory, see Francesco Casetti, *Theories of Cinema: 1945–1995*, trans. Francesca Chiostri and Elizabeth Gard Bartolini-Salimbeni, with Thomas Kelso (Austin: University of Texas Press, 1999), and Robert Stam, *Film Theory: An Introduction* (Malden, MA: Blackwell, 2000). There is renewed interest in Münsterberg, and a new edition of his book has recently been published, edited by, and with an informative introduction by, Allan Langdale. The book also includes other writings on film by Münsterberg. See Hugo Münsterberg, *The Photoplay: A Psychological Study and Other Writings*, ed. Allan Langdale (New York and London: Routledge, 2002).

21 Mieke Bal, *Travelling Concepts in the Humanities: A Rough Guide*, Toronto: University of Toronto Press, 2002.

22 Noël Carroll, *Theorizing the Moving Image*, Cambridge: Cambridge University Press, 1996, xiii.

23 Carroll, *Theorizing*, xvi. Carroll and David Bordwell have been the major proponents of a "reconstruction" of film studies, and the reevaluation of basic premises and assumptions of film theory. See David Bordwell and Noël Carroll, eds., *Post-Theory: Reconstructing Film Studies* (Madison: University of Wisconsin Press, 1996). Reconstruction and reinvention are common themes within film studies and film theory now. See also Christine Gledhill and Linda Williams, eds., *Reinventing Film Studies* (London: Arnold, 2000).

24 Robert Stam, *Film Theory*, p. 7.

25 Casetti, *Theories of Cinema*, p. 2.

26 Hugo Münsterberg, *Hugo Münsterberg on Film: The Photoplay – A Psychological Study and Other Writings*. Ed. Allan Langdale, New York and London: Routledge, 2002, pp. 107 and 108.

27 Erwin Panofsky, "Style and Medium in the Moving Pictures," in Leo Braudy and Marshall Cohen, eds., *Film Theory and Criticism*, seventh edition (New York: Oxford University Press, 2009): 247.

28 Rudolf Arnheim, *Film Art* (Berkeley: University of California Press, 1967): 35.

29 This is from the translation by Hugh Gray, which is thought to be inadequate in many respects. Daniel Morgan, in the essay reprinted in this volume (Chapter 9), offers a new, more faithful translation of the passage: "The photographic image is the object itself, the object freed from temporal contingencies" (p. 108). See Morgan's essay for further corrections to Gray's original translations. A new English translation is also available. See André Bazin, *What is Cinema?*, trans. Timothy Barnard (Montreal: Caboose, 2009).

30 In the original French, Bazin writes: "D'autre part le cinéma est un langage." André Bazin, *Qu'est-ce que le cinéma?* (Paris: Édition Cerf, 2002 [1958]): 17. This is the same word, *langage*, that Christian Metz will use, rather than the alternative in French, which is

langue. The distinction was given a specifically technical sense in the structural linguistics of Ferdinand de Saussure, which Bazin is likely not trying to suggest, but which Metz will stress as fundamental in explaining cinematic expression.

31   Casetti, *Theories of Cinema*, p. 54. On the long and complex history of theories of "film language," see Casetti's Chapter 4.

32   "On peut évidement en conclure que le cinéma n'est pas un langage, ou qu'il l'est du moins dans un sens beaucoup trop figuré, et que par conséquent la semiologie n'a qu'à le laisser de coté." Christian Metz, *Essais sur la signification au cinéma*, Volume 1 (Paris: Klincksieck, 1971): 91.

33   Christian Metz, *The Imaginary Signifier*, trans. Celia Britton, Annwyl Williams, Ben Brewster, and Alfred Guzzetti (Bloomington: Indiana University Press, 1982): 18. Metz's debt to Lacan is explicit: "What I call psychoanalysis shall be the tradition of Freud and its still continuing developments, with original extensions such as those that revolve around the contributions of Melanie Klein in England and Jacques Lacan in France" (pp. 21–22).

34   Metz, *Imaginary Signifier*, p. 63.

35   Metz, *Imaginary Signifier*, p. 63.

36   An influential anthology, edited by Diane Carson, Linda Dittmar, and Janice R. Welsch, is, in fact, entitled *Multiple Voices in Feminist Film Criticism* (Minneapolis: University of Minnesota Press, 1995). An emphatic plurality is often emphasized in anthology titles, such as Laura Pietropaolo and Ada Testaferri, eds., *Feminisms in the Cinema* (Bloomington: Indiana University Press, 1995). The increasingly expansive view of feminist theory has also meant that the project has become increasingly interdisciplinary, extending beyond questions of cinema. For a recent view of the very broadly conceived project of feminist visual theory, see Amelia Jones, ed., *The Feminism and Visual Culture Reader* (New York and London: Routledge, 2003).

PART I

The future of film theory:
A debate

Chapter 1

D.N. Rodowick

AN ELEGY FOR THEORY

Éloge. n. m. (*1580: lat.* elogium, *pris au sens gr.* eulogia). *1. Discours pour célébrer qqn. ou qqch.* Éloge funèbre, académique. Éloge d'un saint.

(*Le Petit Robert*)

He sent thither his Theôry, or solemn legation for sacrifice, decked in the richest garments.

(George Grote, *A History of Greece*, 1862)

FROM THE LATE 1960S and throughout the 1970s, the institutionalization of cinema studies in universities in North America and Europe became identified with a certain idea of *theory*. This was less a "theory" in the abstract or natural scientific sense than an interdisciplinary commitment to concepts and methods derived from literary semiology, Lacanian psychoanalysis, and Althusserian Marxism, echoed in the broader influence of structuralism and post-structuralism on the humanities.

However, the evolution of cinema studies since the early 1980s has been marked both by a decentering of film with respect to media and visual studies and by a retreat from theory. No doubt this retreat had a number of salutary effects: a reinvigoration of historical research, more sociologically rigorous reconceptualizations of spectatorship and the film audience, and the placement of film in the broader context of visual culture and electronic media. But not all of these innovations were equally welcome. In 1996, the Post-Theory debate was launched by David Bordwell and Noël Carroll, who argued for the rejection of 1970s Grand Theory as incoherent. Equally suspicious of cultural and media studies, Bordwell and Carroll insisted on anchoring the discipline in film as an empirical object subject to investigations grounded in natural scientific methods. Almost simultaneously, other philosophical challenges to theory came from film scholars influenced by analytic philosophy and the later philosophy of Ludwig Wittgenstein. These debates emerged against the vexed backgrounds both of the culture wars of the 1990s and the rise of identity politics and cultural studies.

Confusing "theory" with Theory, often lost in these debates is the acknowledgment that judgments advanced—in history, criticism, or philosophy—in the absence of qualitative assessments of our epistemological commitments are ill-advised. To want to relinquish theory is more than a debate over epistemological standards; it is a retreat from reflection on the ethical stances behind our styles of knowing. In this respect, I want to argue not for a return to the 1970s concept of theory, but rather for a vigorous debate on what should constitute a philosophy of the humanities critically and reflexively attentive in equal measure to its epistemological and ethical commitments.

A brief look at the history of theory is no doubt useful for this project. Retrospectively, it is curious that early in the twentieth century film would become associated with theory, rather than with aesthetics or the philosophy of art. Already in 1924, Béla Balázs argues in *Der sichtbare Mensch* for a film theory as the compass of artistic development guided by the construction of concepts.[1] The evocation of theory here is already representative of a nineteenth-century tendency in German philosophies of art to portray aesthetics as a *Wissenschaft*, comparable in method and epistemology to the natural sciences. From this moment forward, one would rarely speak of film aesthetics or a philosophy of film, but rather, always, of film *theory*.

"Theory," however, has in the course of centuries been a highly variable concept. One finds the noble origins of theory in the Greek sense of *theoria* as viewing, speculation, or the contemplative life. For Plato it is the highest form of human activity; in Aristotle, the chief activity of the Prime Mover. For the Greeks, theory was not only an activity, but also an *ethos* that associated love of wisdom with a style of life or mode of existence.[2]

Bringing together *thea* [sight] and *theoros* [spectator], theory has often been linked to vision and spectacle. (Perhaps this is what Hegel meant in the *Aesthetics* when he names sight as the most theoretical of the senses.) In *Keywords*, Raymond Williams identifies four primary senses of the term emerging by the seventeenth century: spectacle, a contemplated sight, a scheme of ideas, and an explanatory scheme. With its etymological link to theater, no doubt it was inevitable that the young medium of film should call for theory. However, although the persistence of associating thought about film with theory might be attributed to the derivations of the term from spectating and spectacle, a contemporary commonsensical notion follows from the last two meanings. Theories seek to explain, usually by proposing concepts, but in this they are often distinguished from doing or practice. In this manner, Williams synthesizes "a scheme of ideas which explains practice."[3] This is certainly the way in which someone like Balázs or Sergei Eisenstein invoked the notion of theory.

In *The Virtual Life of Film*, I argue that one powerful consequence of the rapid emergence of electronic and digital media is that we can no longer take for granted what "film" is—its ontological anchors have come ungrounded—and thus we are compelled to revisit continually the question, What is cinema? This ungroundedness is echoed in the conceptual history of contemporary film studies by what I call the "metacritical attitude" recapitulated in cinema studies' current interest both in excavating its own history and in reflexively examining what film theory is or has been. The reflexive attitude toward Theory began, perhaps, with my own *Crisis of Political Modernism* and throughout the 1980s and '90s manifested itself in a variety of conflicting approaches: Carroll's *Philosophical Problems of Classical Film Theory* and *Mystifying Movies*, Bordwell's *Making Meaning*, Judith Mayne's *Cinema and Spectatorship*, Richard Allen's *Projecting Illusions*, Bordwell and Carroll's *Post-Theory: Reconstructing Film Studies*, Allen and Murray Smith's *Film Theory and Philosophy*, Francesco Casetti's *Theories of Cinema, 1945–95*, Allen and Malcolm Turvey's *Wittgenstein, Theory and the Arts*, and so on.[4]

In detaching "theory" as an object available for historical and theoretical examination, these books take three different approaches. Natural scientific models inspire one approach, both philosophical and analytic, which posit that the epistemological value of a well-constructed theory derives from a precise conceptual framework defined in a limited range of postulates. This approach assumes there is an ideal model from which all theories derive their epistemological value. Alternatively, Casetti's approach is both historical and socio-logical. Agnostic with respect to debates on epistemological value, it groups together state-ments made by self-described practitioners of theory, describing both the internal features of those statements and their external contexts. In *The Crisis of Political Modernism*, my own approach, inspired by Michel Foucault's *Archaeology of Knowledge*, assumes that the condition-ing of knowledge itself is historically variable. Discourse *produces* knowledge. Every theory is subtended by enunciative modalities that regulate the order and dispersion of statements by engendering or making visible groups of objects, inventing concepts, defining positions of address, and organizing rhetorical strategies. This approach analyzes how knowledge is produced in delimited and variable discursive contexts.

As a first move, it might indeed seem strange to associate theory with history. Intro-ducing a series of lectures at the Institute for Historical Research at the University of Vienna in 1998, I astonished a group of students by asserting that film theory *has* a history, indeed multiple histories. Here the analytic approach to theory, on one hand, and sociological and archaeological approaches on the other, part ways. The fact of having a history already distinguishes film theory, and indeed all aesthetic theory, from natural scientific inquiry, for natural and cultural phenomena do not have the same temporality. Aesthetic inquiry must be sensitive to the variability and volatility of human culture and innovation; their epistemol-ogies derive from (uneven) consensus and self-examination of what we already know and do in the execution of daily life. Examination of the natural world may presume a teleology where new data are accumulated and new hypotheses refined in modeling processes for which, unlike human culture, we have no prior knowledge.

* * *

I believe we need a more precise conceptual picture of how film became associated with theory in the early twentieth century, and how ideas of theory vary in different historical periods and national contexts. But let us return to the more recent, metacritical attitude toward theory.

By the mid-1990s, film theory and indeed the concept of "theory" itself were challenged from a number of perspectives. This contestation occurs in three overlapping phases. The first phase is marked by Bordwell's call throughout the 1980s for a "historical poetics" of film and culminates in the debates engendered by the publication of *Making Meaning: Inference and Rhetoric in the Interpretation of Cinema* and by the special issue of *iris* on "Cinema and Cognitive Psychology," both published in 1989. The capstone of the second phase is the 1996 publica-tion of *Post-Theory*. Subtitled *Reconstructing Film Studies*, the book represents an attempt to establish film studies as a discipline modeled on cognitivist science and historical poetics, and to recenter "theory" according to the epistemological ideals of natural scientific reasoning. If the second phase may be characterized by the attempt to return theory to a model of "scientific" investigation and explanation, the third phase subjects the association of theory with science to philosophical critique. As found in the recent work of Allen and Turvey, and deeply influenced by Wittgenstein's critique of theory in the *Philosophical Investigations*, this perspective calls for a new orientation in the examination of culture and the arts through a philosophy of the humanities. In this manner, throughout the 1980s and '90s there is a triple displacement of theory—by history, science, and, finally, philosophy.

It is important to appreciate Bordwell's contribution to what I have characterized as the metacritical or metatheoretical attitude in cinema studies. Among his generation, Bordwell was among the first to exhibit fascination with the history of film study itself, and to focus attention on problems of methodology with respect to questions of historical research and the critical analysis of film form and style. Throughout the 1980s, Bordwell produced a number of path-breaking methodological essays promoting a "historical poetics" of cinema.

From *Narration and the Fiction Film* (1985) to *Making Meaning*, the broad outlines of his approach are made apparent. Bordwell cannot be accused of a retreat from theory—no one's commitment to good theory building is greater or more admirable.[5] Instead, he wants to recast theory as history, or rather, to ground theory in the context of empirical historical research. In this way, Bordwell responds to what he perceives as the twin threats of cultural and media studies. On the one hand, there is a risk of methodological incoherence for a field whose interdisciplinary commitments had become too broad; on the other, the risk of diffusing, in the context of media studies, cinema studies' fundamental ground—film as a formal object delimiting specifiable effects. The aim of historical poetics, then, is to project a vision of methodological coherence onto a field of study perceived to be losing its center, and to restore an idea of film as a specifiable form to that center. In this respect, poetics concerns questions of form and style. It deals with concrete problems of aesthetic practice and describes the specificity of film's aesthetic function while recognizing the importance of social convention in what a culture may define as a work of art. In *Narration and the Fiction Film*, the *historical* side of poetics addresses the proliferation of distinct modes of narration (classical Hollywood, Soviet or dialectical materialist, postwar European art cinema, etc.) as delimitable in time and sensitive to national and/or cultural contexts. Here Bordwell makes his best case for basing the analysis of individual works upon sound historical investigation and explicit theoretical principles in a way that avoids arbitrary boundaries between history, analysis, and theory.

By 1989, however, Bordwell's attack on interpretation and his promotion of cognitivism as a model of "middle-level research" recast theory with respect to three particular propositions. First, his appeal to middle-level research calls for pulling back from broader concerns of ideology and culture to refocus attention on film's intrinsic structure and functions. Second, he promotes a comparable turn from psychoanalytic theories of the subject to the study of filmic comprehension as grounded in empirically delimitable mental and perceptual structures. Finally, his renewed emphasis on history also signals a withdrawal from high-level conceptual concerns to refocus research on the fundamental data of films themselves and the primary documentation generated from their production contexts. Thus, Bordwell accuses interpretation of reaching too high in grasping for abstract concepts to map semantically onto its object. Here the film-object itself disappears in its particularity, becoming little more than the example of a concept. Moreover, the interpreters are reflexively insensitive to the cognitive operations they execute. They produce no new knowledge, but rather only repetitively invoke the same heuristics to model different films.

The sometimes unruly responses to *Making Meaning* and *Cinema and Cognitive Psychology* demonstrate that Bordwell's criticisms touched a nerve, and there is little doubt that these works are a genuine and important response to the impasse in theory that cinema studies began to confront by the end of the 1980s. In the critique of so-called Grand Theory, what is most interesting here is the implicit alliance between historical poetics and analytical philosophy. In the two introductions to *Post-Theory*, Bordwell and Carroll promote strong views of what comprises good theory building in stark contrast to the then current state of contemporary film and cultural theory. Here I am less concerned with assessing their critique of contemporary film theory than in evaluating the epistemological ideals embodied in their common appeal to natural scientific models.[6] Looking at the reverse side of Bordwell and Carroll's criticisms, I think it is important to examine their ideal projection of "good theory" as the ethical appeal for a new mode of existence where, in their view, politics or ideology has not supplanted reason. Here "dialectics," as Carroll presents it, becomes the basis of an ideal research community of rational agents working on common problems and data sets with results that are falsifiable according to "ordinary standards" of truth and error.[7] But these ideals, I would argue, rest on no firmer philosophical grounds than the ideological theories they critique. For example, while Grand Theory is criticized for its obsession with an irrational and unconscious subject that cannot account for its actions, Bordwell promotes a "rational agent" theory of mental functioning, which is in fact the subject of good theory recognizing itself in the object it wants to examine.[8] The concept of the rational agent functions tautologically here as a projection where the ideal scientific subject seeks the contours of its own image in the model of mind it wishes to construct or to discover. In a perspective that strives to be free of ideological positioning and to assert an epistemology that is value-neutral, the introductions to *Post-Theory* nonetheless express the longing for a different world modeled on an idealized vision of scientific research: a community of researchers united by common epistemological standards who are striving for a universalizable and truthful picture of their object.

Richard Allen and Murray Smith's critique of contemporary film theory in *Film Theory and Philosophy* echoes Bordwell and Carroll's perspective. Accusing Theory of an "epistemological atheism" powered by an exaggerated ethical concern with the critique of a capitalist modernity, Allen and Smith's criticisms make clear a number of philosophical assumptions absent from the *Post-Theory* critique. From the analytic point of view, arguments for and against "theory" take place against the background of a philosophy of *science*. One engages in theory building or not according to an epistemological ideal based on natural scientific models. In employing the methods and forms of scientific explanation, however, philosophy becomes indistinguishable from science, at least with respect to theory construction. Philosophy disappears into science as "theory" becomes indistinguishable from scientific methodology.

In this manner, I want to argue that from the beginning of the twentieth century analytic philosophy has been responsible for projecting an epistemological ideal of theory derived from natural scientific methods. This ideal produced a disjunction between philosophy's ancient concern for balancing epistemological inquiry with ethical evaluation.[9] Here, theory, at least as it is generally conceived in the humanities, disappears in two ways. Not only is the activity of theory given over to science, but philosophy itself begins to lose its autonomy and self-identity—it would seem to have no epistemological function save in the light reflected from scientific ideals. Analytic philosophy attacks theory on more than one front. There is the implicit tendency to delegitimate extant *film* theory to the extent that it draws on concepts and methodologies influential in the humanities that fall outside of the reigning norm of what W.V. Quine would call a "naturalized philosophy." Consequently, because so little aesthetic thought on film conforms to scientific models, Carroll concludes that, for the most part, a *theory* of film does not yet exist, though it might at some future date. The conflict over theory in film studies thus reproduces in microcosm a more consequential debate, one that concerns both the role of epistemology and epistemological critique in the humanities and the place of philosophy with respect to science. Analytic philosophy wants to redeem "theory" for film by placing it in the context of a philosophy of science. At the same time, this implies that the epistemologies that were characteristic of the humanities for a number of decades are neither philosophically nor scientifically legitimate. And so the contestation of theory becomes a de facto epistemological dismissal of the humanities.

Throughout the 1990s, then, in cinema studies philosophy allies itself with science as a challenge to theory. In this phase of the debate, "theory" is the contested term. Very quickly, however, "science" becomes the contested term, as a philosophy of the humanities gives over theory to science and opposes itself to both. Important keys to this transition are the late works of Wittgenstein, especially his *Philosophical Investigations*, as well as G.H. von Wright's calls for a philosophy of the humanities in works like *The Tree of Knowledge, and Other Essays* (1993).

The interest of the later Wittgenstein for my project, and for the humanities in general, concerns his attack on the identification of philosophy with science. In asserting that "Philosophy is not one of the natural sciences" (*Tractatus Logico-Philosophicus* 4.111), he presents a formidable challenge to Bertrand Russell's conception of philosophy as allied with epistemological models drawn from the natural sciences. In contrast to Russell, Wittgenstein argues that science should not be the only model of explanation and knowledge, and so he insists on the specificity of philosophy as a practice. It is important to examine carefully Wittgenstein's attack on "theory" as an inappropriate form of explanation for the arts and humanities. However, my central concern here will be to explore arguments favoring a philosophy of the humanities as distinguishable from both science and theory.

If philosophy involves another mode of explaining and knowing, why does the alternative not amount to a theory? As Allen and Turvey summarize in their introduction to *Wittgenstein, Theory and the Arts*, philosophy differs from science in that its subject matter is not empirical in nature—only nature is subject to investigation by empirical methods. "Empirical" has a precise definition here as that of which we can have no prior knowledge. Alternatively, philosophy is concerned with problems of sense and meaning, and these problems are not empirical in the sense that language use and creative expression are already part of a commonly accessible stock of human knowledge.

This involves a second criterion: statements about empirical phenomenon are, and must be, necessarily falsifiable. Philosophical investigation, however, only concerns testing the limits of sense and meaning of given propositions. In this way, Wittgenstein's case for philosophy as the best alternative to theory for studying human behavior and creativity is based on what he calls the "autonomy of linguistic meaning." This concept is exemplified in the distinction between reasons and causes. In a causal explanation, each effect is presumed to have a cause identified by a hypothesis, which may and must be rejected or revised in light of further evidence. Causal explanations are legitimate in scientific contexts because actions have origins that derive from states of affairs of which we have no prior knowledge. Most human action and behavior, however, is ill served by causal explanation, for agents have the capacity to justify their behaviors with reasons. "Autonomy" now indicates that agents have the capacity for authoritative self-examination and self-justification. Therefore, a key difference between scientific and philosophical inquiry is that science tests its hypotheses against external phenomena, that is, the natural world. But philosophy admits only to internal or self-investigation. This is less a question of truth and error than judgments concerning the "rightness" of a proposition tested against prior experience and knowledge.

This is one way to begin to unravel the conceptual confusions surrounding the idea of theory in cinema studies; for example, why Bordwell and Carroll have been so wedded to a certain idea of science, but also why theory, even from a cultural or psychoanalytic perspective, remains so compelling for a great many fairly intelligent people. As Turvey puts the question, "Why is there a lack of basic empirical research in film theory if the nature and functions of cinema are like the laws governing natural phenomena? Why does such research, somehow, seem unnecessary to film theorists? And how is it that film theories ever convince anyone that they are plausible in the absence of such sustained research?"[10] Because these criteria are irrelevant for cultural investigation. Film theories, like all humanistic investigation, concern human activities and thus presume a high degree of prior, even self-, knowledge and examination. Like any cultural activity, cinema is a human creation and thus is embedded in practices and institutions that form the basis of our quotidian existence. We may not have conscious knowledge of these practices and institutions, nor any desire to construct theories about them in the form of propositions or concepts, yet we act on and through them in coherent and consistent ways. This is why cultural theories are able to solicit agreement in the absence of empirical research and experimentation. Their power and plausibility is based on the extent to which they seem to clarify for us what we already know and do on a daily basis. Here we need no external examination beyond the critical investigation of our own practices as they evolve historically. However, what film studies has called theory, in its multiple and variegate guises, might more appropriately be called aesthetics or philosophy. And indeed, perhaps we could achieve much methodological and conceptual clarification by setting aside "theory" provisionally in order to examine what a philosophy of the humanities, and, indeed, what a film philosophy might look like.

* * *

I would prefer to title this essay *Éloge de la théorie*, for in composing an elegy for theory I have kept in mind the subtle variations present in French. Combining the English sense of both eulogy and elegy, and something more besides, an *éloge* can be both praise song and funereal chant, panegyric and *chanson d'adieu*. (In addition, it conveys the second meaning of a legal judgment expressed in someone's favor.) Certainly I think the enterprise of theory is still a worthy one. Yet why, in contemporary critical discourse, are there so few left to praise and none to love it?

We must first examine the debate on theory from the point of view of competing epistemological stakes. Accused of "epistemological atheism," theory as a concept has been wrested from the Continent to be returned semantically to the shores of science and the terrain of British and American analytical philosophy. Initially, this debate was posed as a conflict between theory and philosophy. But the late Wittgenstein took this argument in another direction, one that also questioned theory but as a way of turning philosophy from science to restore it to the humanities. In so doing, Wittgenstein was less concerned with the epistemological perfectibility of philosophical language than with reclaiming philosophy's ancient task of *theoria*. If the politics and epistemology of theory have been subject to much soul searching and epistemological critique, it is important nonetheless to find and retain in theory the distant echo of its connection to philosophy, or to *theoria*, as restoring an ethical dimension to epistemological self-examination. As Wittgenstein tried to teach us, what we need after theory is not science, but a renewed dialogue between philosophy and the humanities wherein both refashion themselves in original ways.

Ultimately, I want to argue that Wittgenstein's attack on theory is both too broad and too restrictive, but here it is more important to foreground what the later Wittgenstein brings to a philosophy of the humanities. In liberating humanistic inquiry from the bonds of empirical and causal explanation, a philosophy of humanities may make propositional claims, but these claims need not be fallible—they only require suasion and clear, authoritative self-justification. This is because humanistic theories are culture-centered. Unlike the investigation of natural phenomena, philosophical investigations examine what human beings already know and do, and this knowledge is in principle public and accessible to all. In Bordwell's sense of the term, "naturalization," whether good or bad, has little relevance here as humanistic (self-) inquiry does not require finding new information, but rather only clarifying and evaluating what we already know and do, or know how to do, and understanding why it is of value to us. In its descriptive emphasis, Wittgenstein's philosophical investigations do support strongly one important aspect of historical poetics—the analysis of the internal norms of cultural objects and of our everyday sense-making activities in relation to those objects. Nonetheless, a "nonempirical" notion of history is wanted here, and for specific philosophical reasons. Natural laws are time-independent, at least in a human context, and thus are appropriately explored through falsifiable causal explanations. Alternatively, cultural knowledge is historical in a particular sense. It emerges and evolves in the context of multiple, diverse, and conflicting social interactions that require constant reevaluation on a human time scale. Human history and natural history may not be investigated by the same means, even if, with respect to certain problems, their domains may overlap. Unlike the scientist, the humanist must examine phenomena that may be shifting before her very eyes. She must account for change in the course of its becoming, while she herself might be in a process of self-transformation.

To what extent, then, is the enterprise of theory still possible? And how might we return to philosophy the specificity of its activity? The two questions are different yet related, and both are linked to the fate of humanities in the twenty-first century and the place of film in the future of the humanities. Possible answers begin in recognizing that epistemological atheism does not follow from an ethical critique of modernity. And indeed what links philosophy today to its most ancient origins are the intertwining projects of evaluating our styles of knowing with the examination of our modes of existence and their possibilities of transformation. I want to conclude by briefly exploring these questions in discussing two contemporary philosophers as exemplars of the twinned projects of ethical and epistemological evaluation: Gilles Deleuze and Stanley Cavell. Deleuze and Cavell are the two contemporary philosophers with the strongest commitment to cinema, yet with distinctly original conceptions of the specificity of philosophy and of philosophical expression in relation to film. Though an unlikely pairing, reading these two philosophers together can deepen and clarify their original contributions to our understanding of film and of contemporary philosophy. Here I want to make the case that a (film) philosophy may and should be distinguished from theory. At the same time, I want to distinguish for the humanities a fluid metacritical space of epistemological and ethical self-examination that we may continue to call "theory" should we wish to do so.

Deleuze's cinema books present two pairs of elements that show what a film philosophy might look like. These elements recur throughout Deleuze's philosophical work. On one hand, there is the relation of Concept to Image. Here the creation of Concepts defines the autonomy of philosophical activity, while the Image becomes the key to understanding subjectivity and our relation to the world. The second set involves Deleuze's original reconsideration of Nietzsche's presentation of ethical activity as philosophical interpretation and evaluation.

Deleuze ends *Cinema 2: The Time-Image* with a curious plaint for theory. Already in 1985, he argues, theory had lost its pride of place in thought about cinema, seeming abstract and unrelated to practical creation. But theory is not separate from the practice of cinema, for it is itself a practice or a constructivism of concepts:

> For theory too is something which is made, no less than its object. . . . A theory of cinema is not "about" cinema, but about the concepts that cinema gives rise to and which are themselves related to other concepts corresponding to other practices. . . . The theory of cinema does not bear on the cinema, but on the concepts of cinema, which are no less practical, effective or existent than cinema itself. . . . Cinema's concepts are not given in cinema. And yet they are cinema's concepts, not theories about cinema. So that there is always a time, midday–midnight, when we must no longer ask ourselves, "What is cinema?" but "What is philosophy?" Cinema itself is a new practice of images and signs, whose theory philosophy must produce as a conceptual practice.[11]

A slippage is obvious here with theory standing in for philosophy. But that being said, what does Deleuze wish to imply in complaining that the contemporary moment is weak with respect to creation and concepts? The most replete response comes from the most obvious successor to the problems raised in the cinema books—Deleuze and Félix Guattari's *What Is Philosophy?*

For Deleuze and Guattari, the three great domains of human creation are art, philosophy, and science. These are relatively autonomous domains, each of which involves acts of creation based on different modes of expression—perceptual, conceptual, or functional. The problem confronted in *What Is Philosophy?* is knowing how philosophical expression differs from artistic or scientific expression, yet remains in dialogue with them. Percepts, concepts, and functions are different expressive modalities, and each may influence the other, but not in a way that affects the autonomy of their productive activity. An artist or scientist no doubt profoundly engages in conceptual activity, and so is influenced by philosophy. Yet the outputs of that activity—percepts, functions—retain their autonomy and specificity.

From one perspective, the distinctiveness of these outputs is easy to explain. The aim of science is to create functions, of art to create sensuous aggregates, and of philosophy to create concepts, but the devil is in the details. In art, percepts refer to the creation of affective experience through constructions of sensuous materials. In painting, these expressive materials may be blocks of lines/colors; in cinema, blocks of movements/durations/sounds. Alternatively, the role of functions helps clarify the relation of philosophy to theory in the scientific sense. There is a function, Deleuze explains, as soon as two wholes are put into a fixed correspondence. Newton's inverse square law provides an apposite example. A function is a mathematical expression orienting thought (first whole) to a natural phenomenon (the propagation of energy). As expression, the function is not the specific phenomenon, of course, nor is it analogous to thinking. The function is a descriptor or algorithm. Its descriptiveness of behaviors in the natural world is important, but this is not the key to its specificity. It is abstract and general, and its generality derives from its time-independence. It produces descriptions, and these descriptions are valid for all times and all places—thus, the proposal of a second whole. In its predictiveness of future behaviors, then, the function is exemplary of what science calls "theory," and when this predictiveness becomes regular, functions become "laws."

Contrariwise, the concept is abstract yet singular—it relates to thought in its own temporality and human specificity. For these reasons, philosophy is much closer to art than it is to science. The expressiveness of art finds its instantiation in the sensuous products of art and its human affects, and the expressiveness of science finds its confirmation in the predicted behaviors of natural phenomena. But concepts express only thought and acts of thinking. Does this mean that thinking is purely an interior activity cut off from the sensuous and material world? Art provides important answers to this question in relating concepts to ideas, signs, and images.

In 1991, Deleuze gave an important lecture at FEMIS [*École nationale supérieure des métiers de l'image et du son*], the French national film and television school, an excerpt of which was published as "Having an Idea in Cinema." What does it mean to have an Idea in art and how do Ideas differ from Concepts? Ideas are specific to a domain, a milieu, or a material. And so Deleuze writes, "Ideas must be treated as potentials that are already engaged in this or that mode of expression and inseparable from it, so much so that I cannot say I have an idea in general. According to the techniques that I know, I can have an idea in a given domain, an idea in cinema or rather an idea in philosophy."[12] Now, ideas in philosophy are already oriented by a certain kind of image, what Deleuze calls the "image of thought," and so a connection or relation must link them. In *What Is Philosophy?* the image of thought is defined as the specific terrain or plane of immanence from which ideas emerge as preconceptual expression, or as "the image thought gives itself of what it means to think, to orient one's self in thought."[13] To have an idea, then, is to express thought through particular constructions, combinations, or linkages—what Deleuze calls signs. As Spinoza insisted, signs are not an expression of thought, but rather of our *powers* of thinking. Ideas are not separable from an autonomous sequence or sequencing of ideas in thought, what Spinoza calls *concatenatio*. This concatenation of signs unites form and material, constituting thought as a spiritual automation whose *potentia* expresses our powers of thinking, action, or creation.

The importance of Deleuze's cinema books is that they present his most complete account of a philosophical semiotic modeled on movement and time and show how images and signs in movement or time are conceptually innovative; that is, how they renew our powers of thinking. In this manner, art relates to philosophy in that images and signs involve preconceptual expression in the same way that the image of thought involves a protoconceptual expression—they prepare the terrain for new concepts to emerge. The cinema may be best able to picture thought and to call for thinking because like thought its ideas are comprised of movements, both spatial and temporal, characterized by connections and conjunctions of particular kinds. Every instance of art is expressive of an idea which implies a concept, and what philosophy does with respect to art is to produce new constructions or assemblages that express or give form to the concepts implied in art's ideas. It renders perspicuous and in conceptual form the automatisms that make a necessity of art's generative ideas.

There is also an ethical dimension to the various ways Deleuze characterizes image and concept in relation to the image of thought. For Deleuze, this implies a Nietzschean ethics encompassing two inseparable activities: interpretation and evaluation. "To interpret," Deleuze writes, "is to determine the force which gives sense to a thing. To evaluate is to determine the will to power which gives value to a thing."[14] What bridges Deleuze and Cavell here are not only their interest in Nietzsche, but also their original concept of ontology. Though Cavell uses the word and Deleuze does not, both are evaluating a particular way of Being. This is not the being or identity of film or what identifies film as art, but rather the ways of being that art provokes in us—or, more deeply, how film and other forms of art express for us or return to us our past, current, and future states of being. In both philosophers, the ethical relation is inseparable from our relation to thought. For how we think, and whether we sustain a relation to thought or not, is bound up with our modes of existence and our relations with others and to the world.

The key to grasping this relation in Deleuze is to understand the originality of his characterization of the image as both an ontological and ethical concept. Especially in the cinema books, the image is not the product of cinematic creation but rather its raw material, the worldly substance that it forms and to which it gives expression. Hence the key place of Henri Bergson's assertion from *Matter and Memory* that there is already photography in things. Like energy, images can neither be created nor destroyed—they are a state of the universe, an asubjective universal perception or luminosity that evolves and varies continuously. Human perception is therefore largely a process of subtraction. Because we must orient ourselves in this vast regime of universal change according to our limited perceptual context, we extract and form special images or perceptions according to our physiological limits and human needs. This image is the very form of our subjectivity and persists in the crossroads between our internal states and our external relations with the world.

The image is thus in relation with ourselves (interiority) and in relation with the world (exteriority) in an intimately interactive way. It is absurd to refer to subjectivity as pure interiority as it is ceaselessly engaged with matter and with the world. By the same token, thought is not interiority but our way of engaging with the world, orienting ourselves there and creating from the materials it offers us. Thus, another way of considering the autonomy of art, philosophy, and science is to evaluate the different though related images of thought they offer us. The percept is visually and acoustically sensuous, provoking affects or emotions in us. Concepts and functions are more abstract. What the function is to scientific expression, the sign is to aesthetic expression. Art's relation to thought, then, lies not in the substance of images, but in the logic of their combination and enchainment. No doubt every artistic image is an image of thought, a physical tracing and expression of thought given sensual form, no matter how incoherent or inelegant. However, while the aesthetic sign may imply a precise concept, it is nonetheless entirely affective and preconceptual. Yet there is a philosophical power in images. The artist's idea is not necessarily the philosopher's. But images not only trace thoughts and produce affects; they may also provoke thinking or create new powers of thinking. In so doing, we are thrown from sensuous to abstract thought, from an image of thought to a thought without image—this is the domain of philosophy. And in moving from one to the other, art may inspire philosophy to give form to a concept.

What does philosophy value in art? To ask this question is to demand what forces expressed in art, in images and signs, call for thinking? Philosophy parts ways with science to the extent that time is taken as an independent variable—in fact, the simplest way of describing Deleuze's (or Bergson's) philosophical project is as the will to reintroduce time and change to philosophy's image of thought. Philosophy finds inspiration in art because there the will to create is brought to its highest powers. Here, as in many other ways, Deleuze goes against the grain of contemporary philosophy. While happily science has never renounced its powers of creation, it has become less and less conceptual. And of course, it does not need concepts as philosophy does. Contrariwise, philosophy has moved closer and closer to art, and vice versa. This is the great untold story of twentieth-century philosophy that the twenty-first century must recount: that philosophy's greatest innovations were not made with respect to science, but in dialogue with art. And further, that the modern arts came closer and closer to philosophical expression while nonetheless amplifying their aesthetic powers.

That art may be considered philosophical expression is an important link between Deleuze and Cavell's interest in film. Like Deleuze, Cavell's cinema books are not studies of film but rather *philosophical* studies—they are works of philosophy first and foremost. Nonetheless, it may also be reasonable to read them as studies of film culture in their deep awareness of how cinema has penetrated the daily life of the mind and of being in the twentieth century. Though in very different ways, both Deleuze and Cavell comprehend cinema as expressing ways of being in the world and of relating to the world. In this respect, cinema is already philosophy, and a philosophy intimately connected to our everyday life. Deleuze exemplifies this idea in pairing Bergson's *Matter and Memory* with the early history of cinema. At the moment when philosophy returns to problems of movement and time in relation to thought and the image, the cinematic apparatus emerges neither as an effect of these problems nor in analogy with them. In its own way, it is the aesthetic expression of current and persistent philosophical problems. Nor should one say that Deleuze's thought is simply influenced by cinema. Rather, it is the direct philosophical expression, in the form of concepts and typologies of signs, of problems presented preconceptually in aesthetic form.

Cavell presents a similar perspective, though one more clearly framed by problems of ontology and ethics. In my view, Cavell's work is exemplary of a philosophy of and for the humanities, particularly in his original attempt to balance the concerns of epistemology and ethics. In this respect, two principal ideas unite Cavell's philosophical and film work. Moreover, these are less separate ideas than iterations of the same problem that succeed one another more or less chronologically, namely, the philosophical confrontation with skepticism and the concept of moral perfectionism. The question here is why film is so important as the companion or exemplification of this confrontation. One clue resides in the title of an important Cavell essay, "What Photography Calls Thinking."[15] What does it mean to say that art or images *think*, or that they respond to philosophical problems as a way of thinking or a style of thought? In the first phase of Cavell's film philosophy, represented by the period surrounding the publication of *The World Viewed*, the responses to this question are onto-logical and epistemological. But this ontology refers neither to the medium of art nor the identity of art works, but rather to how art expresses our modes of existence or ways of being in the world as the fall into and return from skepticism.

Here an ontology of film is less concerned with identifying the medium of film than with understanding how our current ways of being in the world and relating to it are "cinematic." In its very conditions of presentation and perception, cinema expresses a particular philosophical problem, that of skepticism and its overcoming. If, as Cavell argues, cinema presents "a moving image of skepticism," it neither exemplifies nor is analogous to the skeptical attitude.[16] Rather, cinema expresses both the problem and its possible overcom-ings. The quality of "movement" in this philosophical image is temporal or historical in a specific sense. In its very *dispositif* for viewing and encountering the world, cinema presents philosophy's historical dilemma (skepticism's perceptual disjunction from the world) as past, while orienting the modern subject toward a possible future. That skepticism should reproduce itself in a technology for seeing might mean that it is no longer the ontological air we breathe, but a passing phase of our philosophical culture. If, as Cavell argues, the reality that film holds before us is that of our own perceptual condition, then it opens the possibility of once again being present to self or acknowledging how we may again become present to ourselves. (Indeed Cavell's examination of cinema's relation to the fate of skepticism helps clarify a Deleuzian cinematic ethics as faith in this world and its possibilities for change.[17]) For these reasons, film may already be the emblem of skepticism in decline. Cinema takes up where philosophy leaves off, as the preconceptual expression of the passage to another way of being. This is why cinema is both a presentation of and withdrawal from skepticism—the almost perfect realization of the form of skeptical perception as a way, paradoxically, of reconnecting us to the world and asserting its existential force as past presence in time. The irony of this recognition now is that modernity may no longer characterize our modes of being or of looking, and we must then anticipate something else.

In the major books that follow, culminating in *Cities of Words*, the temporality of this epistemological condition is reconsidered as a question of art and ethical evaluation. The key concept of ethical evaluation is what Cavell calls moral perfectionism. Moral perfectionism is the nonteleological expression of a desire for change or becoming. Here our cinematic culture responds not to a dilemma of perception and thought, but rather a moral imperative. This trajectory from ontological to ethical questions is exemplary of how Cavell uses cinema to deepen his description of the subjective condition of modernity as itself suspended between a worldly or epistemological domain and a moral domain. In both cases, cinema confronts the problem of skepticism. In the first instance, this is an epistemological disap-pointment, in that we are disconnected from the world by our own subjectivity—all we can know of the world is from behind the screen of our consciousness. The second responds to a moral disappointment in the state of the world or with my current mode of existence. This division is not only formal; it is also, and perhaps primarily, temporal. As Kant posed the problem, the province of understanding, of knowledge of objects and their causal laws, defines the modern scientific attitude whose formidable power derives from making time an independent variable. What is unknown in the natural world could not become known through the powers of causal reasoning if the rules could change in the course of time. But the problem that so provoked Kant was that atemporal reason was in conflict with moral freedom. To be human is to experience change. So how might philosophy characterize humanity as at once subject of understanding and of reason, as subject to causal relations *and* expressive of moral freedom? Given that as material creatures we are in bondage to the empirical world and its causal laws, philosophy's task is to explain how we are also free to experience and to anticipate change in the projection of future existences.

Therefore, in Cavell's account moral perfectionism takes us from the form of skepticism to the possibilities of human change, and to the deeper moral problem of evaluating our contemporary mode of existence and transcending it in anticipation of a better, future existence. In the first stage, the problem is to overcome my moral despair of ever knowing the world; in the second, my despair of changing it and myself. Thus, Cavell's interest in Emerson (or in Wittgenstein, Nietzsche, or Freud) is to heal this rift in philosophy exemplified by Wittgenstein's disappointment with knowledge as failing to make us better than we are or to give us peace. Alternatively, moral perfectionism begins with this sense of ethical disappointment and ontological restlessness, catching up the modern subject in a desire for self-transformation whose temporality is that of a becoming without finality. "In Emerson and Thoreau's sense of human existence," Cavell writes, "there is no question of reaching a final state of the soul, but only and endlessly taking the next step to what Emerson calls 'an unattained but attainable self'—a self that is always and never ours—a step that turns us not from bad to good, or wrong to right, but from confusion and constriction toward self-knowledge and sociability."[18]

This idea forms the basis of Cavell's later books on comedies of remarriage and melodramas of the unknown woman. The interest of film here is to show it as the ordinary or quotidian expression of the deepest concerns of moral philosophy. And just as Wittgenstein sought to displace metaphysical expression into ordinary language and daily concerns, film brings moral philosophy into the context of quotidian dramatic expression:

> These films are rather to be thought of as differently configuring intellectual and emotional avenues that philosophy is already in exploration of, but which, perhaps, it has cause sometimes to turn from prematurely, particularly in its forms since its professionalization, or academization. . . . The implied claim is that film, the latest of the great arts, shows philosophy to be the often invisible accompaniment of the ordinary lives that film is so apt to capture.[19]

Where contemporary philosophy has reneged on its promise of moral perfectionism, film has responded, though in the preconceptual manner of all art and sensuous expression. Thus the great project of film philosophy today is not only to help reinvigorate this moral reflection, but to heal by example the rift in philosophy's relation to everyday life.

In the prologue to *Cities of Words*, Cavell reprises Thoreau's lament that "There are nowadays professors of philosophy, but not philosophers. Yet it is admirable to profess because it was once admirable to live." How well Thoreau foresaw the difficult life of philosophy in the twentieth and twenty-first centuries. If one must compose an elegy for theory, let us hope it awakens a new life for philosophy in the current millennium.

Notes

1   Béla Balázs, *Der sichtbare Mensch* (Frankfurt am Main: Suhrkamp, 2001). The original citation is: "Die Theorie ist, wenn auch nicht das Steuerruder, doch zumindest der Kompass einer Kunstentwicklung. Und erst wenn ihr euch einen Begriff von der guten Richtung gemacht habt, dürft ihr von Verirrungen reden. Diesen Begriff: die Theorie des Films, müsst ihr euch eben machen" (p. 12). Balázs does, however, associate this theory with a "film philosophy of art" (p. 1).

2   On the question of ethics as the will for a new mode of existence, see Pierre Hadot, *What Is Ancient Philosophy?*, trans. Michael Chase (Cambridge, Mass.: Harvard University Press, 2002). An influence on Michel Foucault's later works on the "care of the self," Hadot argues that the desire for a

philosophical life is driven first by an ethical commitment or a series of existential choices involving the selection of a style of life where philosophical discourse is inseparable from a vision of the world and the desire to belong to a community.

3   Raymond Williams, *Keywords: A Vocabulary of Culture and Society* (New York: Oxford University Press, 1976), p. 267.

4   See D.N. Rodowick, *Crisis of Political Modernism: Criticism and Ideology in Contemporary Film Theory* (1988; Berkeley and Los Angeles: University of California Press, 1994); Noël Carroll, *Philosophical Problems of Classical Film Theory* (Princeton, N.J.: Princeton University Press, 1988); Noël Carroll, *Mystifying Movies* (New York: Columbia University Press, 1998); David Bordwell, *Making Meaning* (Cambridge, Mass.: Harvard University Press, 1989); Judith Mayne, *Cinema and Spectatorship* (London: Routledge, 1993); Richard Allen, *Projecting Illusions* (Cambridge: Cambridge University Press, 1995); David Bordwell and Noël Carroll, eds., *Post-Theory: Reconstructing Film Studies* (Madison: University of Wisconsin Press, 1996); Richard Allen and Murray Smith, eds., *Film Theory and Philosophy* (Oxford: Clarendon Press, 1997); Francesco Casetti, *Theories of Cinema, 1945–95* (Austin: University of Texas Press, 1999); and Richard Allen and Malcolm Turvey, eds., *Wittgenstein, Theory and the Arts* (London: Routledge, 2001).

5   See especially Bordwell's introduction to *Cinema and Cognitive Psychology*, "A Case for Cognitivism," *iris* 5, no. 2 (1989), pp. 11–40. Here I am especially interested in Bordwell's characterization of theory as "good naturalization."

6   Ironically, one consequence of this appeal, strongly implicit in Carroll's contribution, is that film *theory* does not yet exist. Carroll, for example, criticizes both classical and contemporary film theory according to three basic arguments: they are essentialist or foundationalist, taking films as examples of a priori conditions; they are doctrine driven rather than data driven, meaning not susceptible to empirical examination and verification; and finally, they deviate too widely from *film*-based problems, that is, the concrete particularity of filmic problems disappears when they are taken up to illustrate broader concepts of ideology, subjectivity, or culture. Characterized by "ordinary standards of truth" as a regulative ideal, good theory seeks causal reasoning, deduces generalities by tracking regularities and the norm, is dialectical and requires maximally free and open debate, and, finally, is characterized by fallibilism. In this sense, good theory is "historical" in the sense of being open to revision through the successive elimination of error. In this respect, middle-level research presents the provisional ground for a theory or theories of film projected forward in a teleology of debate, falsification, and revision. The "post" in *Post-Theory* is a curious misnomer, then. For what has been characterized as Theory is epistemologically invalid, and, ironically, what comes after may only appear after a period of long debate and revisionism. A legitimate film theory remains to be constructed, the product of an indefinite future.

7   In a so-far-unpublished essay, "Film Theory and the Philosophy of Science," Meraj Dhir has presented an excellent defense of Carroll's position.

8   For related arguments, see Richard Allen's essay, "Cognitive Film Theory," in *Wittgenstein, Theory and the Arts*, pp. 174–209.

9   Bertrand Russell's 1914 essay "On Scientific Method in Philosophy" presents a succinct definition of this ideal: "A scientific philosophy such as I wish to recommend will be *piecemeal* and tentative like other sciences; above all, it will be able to *invent hypotheses* which, even if they are not wholly true, will yet remain fruitful after the necessary corrections have been made. This possibility of *successive approximations of the truth* is, more than anything else, the source of the triumphs of science, and to transfer this possibility to philosophy is to ensure a progress in method whose importance it would be almost impossible to exaggerate." In *Mysticism and Logic: and Other Essays* (New York: Longmans, Green and Co., 1918), p. 113 (my emphases). This is an admirably succinct summary of the epistemology to which Carroll subscribes. Theories are built piecemeal out of preliminary and falsifiable hypotheses, and one must establish the factual character of the parts before the whole can be understood. The theory then advances teleologically as successively closer approximations to the truth as hypotheses are further tested, refined, or rejected in light of new evidence.

10   Malcolm Turvey, "Can Science Help Film Theory?," *Journal of Moving Image Studies* 1, no. 1 (2001), http://www.uca.edu/org/ccsmi/journal/issue1_table_contents.htm. The passage reads differently in the latest published version of the essay. See Turvey, "Can Scientific Models of Theorizing Help Film Theory?," in *The Philosophy of Film: Introductory Texts and Readings*, ed. Angela Curren and Thomas E. Wartenberg (London: Blackwell, 2005), p. 25.

11   Gilles Deleuze, *Cinema 2: The Time-Image*, trans. Hugh Tomlinson and Robert Galeta (Minneapolis: University of Minnesota Press, 1989), p. 280.

12   Gilles Deleuze, "Having an Idea in Cinema," trans. Eleanor Kaufman, in *Deleuze and Guattari: New Mappings in Politics, Philosophy, and Culture*, ed. Eleanor Kaufman and Kevin Jon Heller (Minneapolis: University of Minnesota Press, 1998), p. 14.

13   Gilles Deleuze, *What Is Philosophy?*, trans. Hugh Tomlinson and Graham Burchell (New York: Columbia University Press, 1994), p. 37.

14   Gilles Deleuze, *Nietzsche and Philosophy*, trans. Hugh Tomlinson (New York: Columbia University Press, 1983), p. 54.

15   Stanley Cavell, "What Photography Calls Thinking," in *Cavell on Film*, ed. William Rothman (Albany: State University of New York Press, 2005), pp. 115–34.

16   Stanley Cavell, *The World Viewed: Reflections on the Ontology of Film*, enlarged edition (1971; Cambridge, Mass.: Harvard University Press, 1979), p. 188.

17   See my essay, "A World, Time," in *The Afterimage of Gilles Deleuze's Film Philosophy*, ed. D.N. Rodowick (Minneapolis: University of Minnesota Press, 2010).

18   Stanley Cavell, *Cities of Words: Pedagogical Letters on a Register of the Moral Life* (Cambridge, Mass.: Belknap Press of Harvard University Press, 2004), p. 13.

19   Ibid., p. 6.

Chapter 2

Malcolm Turvey

THEORY, PHILOSOPHY, AND FILM STUDIES: A RESPONSE TO D.N. RODOWICK'S "AN ELEGY FOR THEORY"

FROM *THE CRISIS OF POLITICAL MODERNISM* (1988) onward, David Rodowick has performed an invaluable service to scholars of film by identifying and clarifying crucial debates in film studies, often at moments when these debates have reached an impasse, and proposing novel, intriguing ways of moving beyond them. In his stimulating paper "An Elegy for Theory," he has done it again. For Rodowick is surely correct to claim that theory has become "a contested concept" in film studies since the 1980s, and his paper helpfully summarizes the debates about this concept over the last few decades. He also proposes a way of moving beyond these debates by turning to philosophy, specifically the philosophies of Gilles Deleuze and Stanley Cavell. Although I disagree with much of what he has to say about film theory and the role that philosophy should play in film studies, I want to thank Professor Rodowick for taking seriously the recent debates among film theorists and analytical philosophers about what film theory is, or should be, debates which have been largely ignored by film scholars in their turn toward history and cultural studies.

Rodowick, if I understand him correctly, makes the following arguments in his paper: (1) There has been a "retreat from theory" in film studies since the 1980s (p. 95 [p. 23 in this volume]).[1] (2) This retreat is due not only to the turn to history and cultural studies by film scholars, but the attack on theory, as it is practiced standardly in the humanities, by David Bordwell and Noël Carroll, as well as by Richard Allen and Murray Smith from the point of view of analytical philosophy in alliance with the natural sciences. For these scholars, the problem with film theory is that it has not been scientific enough. "Analytic philosophy wants to redeem 'theory' for film by placing it in the context of a philosophy of science. At the same time, this implies that the epistemologies that were characteristic of the humanities for a number of decades are neither philosophically nor scientifically legitimate. And so the contestation of theory becomes a de facto epistemological dismissal of the humanities" (p. 98 [p. 27 in this volume]). (3) This scientific conception of theory has in turn been attacked by Allen (in a later incarnation) and me from the Wittgensteinian point of view, which sees philosophy as discontinuous with science. Just as Wittgenstein rejected empirical, theoretical investigations into meaning, advocating instead the method of conceptual clarification, so Allen and I, according to Rodowick, argue that "we need no external examination beyond the critical investigation of our own practices as they evolve historically" (p. 100 [p. 29 in this volume]). (4) What is lost in this retreat from theory, according to Rodowick, is a reflection upon epistemological and ethical commitments: "often lost in these debates, is the acknowledgment that judgments advanced—in history, criticism, or philosophy—in the absence of qualitative assessments of our epistemological commitments are ill-advised. To want to relinquish theory is more than a debate over epistemological standards; it is a retreat from reflection on the ethical stances behind our styles of knowing" (p. 92 [p. 30 in this volume]). Hence, in his paper, Rodowick proposes a conception of theory that involves reflecting on epistemological and ethical commitments. "I want to distinguish for the humanities a fluid metacritical space of epistemological and ethical self-examination that we may continue to call 'theory' should we wish to do so" (p. 102 [p. 30 in this volume]). For Rodowick, this conception of theory is found in philosophy. "If the politics and epistemology of theory have been subject to much soul searching and epistemological critique, it is important nonetheless to find and retain in theory the distant echo of its connection to philosophy, or to *theoria*, as restoring an ethical dimension to epistemological self-examination" (p. 100 [p. 29 in this volume]). (5) Rodowick finds in the philosophies of Deleuze and Cavell a form of film theory that does restore "an ethical dimension to epistemological self-examination."

One of the problems with debates about theory is a lack of clarity about what, precisely, theory is. Rodowick notes correctly that various conceptions of theory have been employed in recent debates about the concept in film studies, although he mischaracterizes some of these. For example, he states that Bordwell and Carroll's conception of theory is "based on natural scientific models" of theory (p. 97 [p. 27 in this volume]) and is "grounded in natural scientific methods" (p. 92 [p. 23 in this volume]). In fact, this is not true. Neither employs natural scientific methods when theorizing, such as formal equations, predictive models, or laboratory experiments and other forms of rigorous empirical testing subject to falsification. Both define film theory simply as an explanatory generalization about film. Carroll states: "let anything count as film theorizing, so long as it involves the production of generalizations or general explanations or general taxonomies and concepts about film practice."[2] And Bordwell argues that "Most generally, 'film theory' refers to any reflection on the nature and functions of cinema."[3] Carroll turns to the natural sciences not as a model for film theory—he clearly says that he does not think that "film theory is a science, or that it can be or should be transformed into one"[4]—but as a model for film *theorizing*, for how film theory should be *practiced*, namely, dialectically. As in the natural sciences, film theories, he argues correctly in my view, should be formulated through dialectical criticism of rivals because it is only by proposing better theories of film that film theory can make progress, and it is this dialectical criticism that had been sorely lacking in film theory when it was dominated by psychoanalysis and semiotics. But he also points out that, while the natural sciences exemplify the practice of dialectical criticism, it "has been a basic route for theoretical inquiry at least since Plato."[5] In other words, theoretical inquiry in a variety of theoretical disciplines such as philosophy, the natural sciences, and the human sciences has advanced through dialectical criticism, so why shouldn't film theory? Rodowick, I take it, would agree with this modest proposal. For he offers his philosophical conception of theory through dialectically criticizing other conceptions, and views it as superior to these other conceptions because he thinks that it combines "projects of ethical and epistemological evaluation" (p. 101 [p. 30 in this volume]). This is dialectical theorizing in a nutshell. Whether it is persuasive is another matter.

Science plays a role in Bordwell and Carroll's work in a second way, namely, both turn to theories in the sciences, principally psychology, to explain various things about film and the viewer's response to it. But again, drawing on theories in the sciences does not mean that either thinks that film theory is, or should be, modeled on the natural sciences. A good example, as Rodowick points out, is Bordwell's use of "rational agent" theory. This is a theory that is employed widely in the human sciences, especially the social sciences and economics. Bordwell, however, does not employ it because he wants to model film theory on the natural sciences. Rather, he employs it, as do social scientists and economists, to explain human behavior. For him, filmmakers, like human beings in general according to rational agent theory, can be thought of as problem-solvers. They make certain choices rather than others in order to solve a wide variety of problems—aesthetic, economic, technical, etc.—arising in the contexts in which they are working.[6] Rodowick seems to find fault with this. "Bordwell promotes a 'rational agent' theory of mental functioning, which is in fact the subject of good theory recognizing itself in the object it wants to examine. The concept of the rational agent functions tautologically here as a projection where the ideal scientific subject seeks the contours of its own image in the model of mind it wishes to construct or to discover" (p. 97 [p. 27 in this volume]). But surely, in order to demonstrate that Bordwell's rational agent theory is an idealized "projection" onto film-makers, Rodowick would have to show that filmmakers are not, in fact, problem-solvers and that the examples that Bordwell cites of problem-solving in filmmaking can be better explained by a different conception of human agency. This he fails to do.

Rodowick also mischaracterizes the ramifications for the humanistic study of the arts of Wittgenstein's critique of theory, which Allen and I draw on in our work. Wittgenstein was opposed to the use of theory in philosophy in a very specific sense, namely, in a *reductive* sense.[7] A reductive theory is a form of explanation that reduces a range of apparently unconnected phenomena to an underlying explanatory principle that they all have in common and that is hidden from view. For Wittgenstein, natural scientific theorizing is the paradigm of reductive theorizing, but it is by no means found only in the natural sciences. For example, what he called the Augustinian picture of language exemplifies theory in this reductive sense, because it reduces the diverse uses of language to the underlying function of describing a state of affairs in the world, a function not necessarily visible to those who use language. Wittgenstein would have had no objection to Bordwell and Carroll's broader definition of theory as simply an explanatory generalization, for his work abounds in explanatory generalizations about concepts, such as the distinction between a reason and a cause that Rodowick himself cites. In the sense of offering explanatory generalizations about meaning. Wittgenstein was a theorist. Furthermore, the analytical tradition of conceptual analysis that he helped inaugurate is replete with examples of systematic theorizing in the sense of explanatory generalizations about concepts and our conceptual schemes, as any reader of Gilbert Ryle's *The Concept of Mind* (1949), Peter Strawson's *Individuals* (1959), or Anthony Kenny's *The Metaphysics of Mind* (1989) will know.[8]

In *Wittgenstein, Theory and the Arts*, Allen and I follow Wittgenstein in arguing that theory, in the reductive sense, is not a logically appropriate form of explanation for much of what humanistic scholars of the arts study. This is because, to put it crudely, if Wittgenstein is correct, then "meaning," including the meaning of human behavior, cannot be explained through reduction to hidden, unitary explanatory principles. This argument, however, in no way means that "we need no external examination beyond the critical investigation of our own practices as they evolve historically" (p. 100 [p. 29 in this volume]). For "our practices" are informed and constrained, to varying degrees, by nature.[9] Most obviously, the capacity to see motion in still images projected at a certain speed is the result of neurophysiological processes of which, pre-theoretically, we have little or no knowledge, and the same is true of a wide variety of perceptual features of interest to film scholars. In order to explain these features of perception, we need scientific theorizing. The claim that Allen and I make is simply that, when it comes to questions of meaning—the meanings of, say, our psycho-logical concepts, or the meanings of human actions, the reasons why human agents behave the way they do—theory in the reductive sense is the wrong method for answering such questions. Allen and I argue that the reductive model of theory is the major model of theorizing in the humanities, even among those who see themselves as opposed to science. Semioticians, psychoanalysts, and now cognitivists all attempt to explain film by appealing to hidden, unitary explanatory principles such as the structure underlying all human communication in structuralism, the unconscious drives and desires motivating all human behavior in psychoanalysis, and the inference from incomplete perceptual cues underlying all comprehension according to constructivist cognitivist psychologists. If we, or rather Wittgenstein, are correct, then they are at least in some respects profoundly mistaken in doing so. It is here that we part company with Bordwell, Carroll, psychoanalytical film theory, and much else.

Rather than repeat what Allen and I have argued at length elsewhere, I move now to the philosophical conception of theory that Rodowick recommends, one which involves epistemological and ethical reflection. As worthwhile as it might be to examine one's epistemological and ethical commitments from time to time, I do not think it is of much help in theorizing about film. This is because epistemological and ethical commitments typically *underdetermine* theories. In other words, the same epistemological and ethical commitments can give rise to many different, even conflicting theories. Reflecting on these commitments will not, therefore, usually help us to answer theoretical questions. Take epistemological realism, the anti-idealist position that what you know about the world exists independently of your thoughts and perceptions. Two different film theorists could be realists. Yet, one could quite happily subscribe to cognitivism and the other to psychoanalysis. There is nothing, in other words, about the epistemological commitment to realism that entails being either a cognitivist film theorist or a psychoanalytical one. Nor is there anything about it that entails being a Lacanian as opposed to a Kleinian psychoanalytical film theorist, or a cognitivist who believes in the "theory theory" as opposed to the "simulation theory" of empathy. The opposite is also true. Theories typically underdetermine epistemological commitments, and films theorists who subscribe to the same theory can have very different epistemological commitments. One might agree, for example, with Dziga Vertov's theory of the "camera eye" as being superior to the human eye without sharing his epistemological commitment to Marxism.

The same is true of ethical commitments (or epistemological commitments that seem to entail ethical ones). Let's assume that, like Deleuze, I share Bergson's radical antideterminism because I, like him, am epistemologically committed to the view that time is duration, and "duration means invention, the creation of forms, the continual elaboration of the absolutely new."[10] Hence, I believe that human beings are constantly evolving and changing in a process of self- and world-creation, that they are radically free and undetermined. This in no way entails that I have to accept Deleuze's theory of film, in which, as Rodowick puts it, the cinema is thought of as "best able to picture thought and to call for thinking because like thought its ideas are comprised of movements, both spatial and temporal, characterized by connections and conjunctions of particular kinds" (p. 104 [p. 32 in this volume]). For I might, as I in fact do, find the comparison between film and thinking totally unconvincing, even absurd. Indeed, I might instead follow Bergson himself, who would reject this comparison because a film is made up of separate, static images, and therefore exemplifies, according to him, the suppression of real duration that is typical of the Western tradition in general.[11] My point is that Bergson's metaphysics, and the epistemological and ethical commitments it appears to entail, underdetermine theories of film. Many theorists could agree with Bergson metaphysically, and arrive at very different theories of film. Ditto Cavell. Nothing about Cavell's epistemological and ethical commitment to "the truth of skepticism"—his argument that skepticism is always a "natural possibility" of language-use and that "our relation to the world as a whole, or to others in general, is not one of knowing, where knowing construes itself as being certain"[12]—entails accepting his film theory. For I might be a skeptic yet reject his claim, as indeed I do, that "the reality in a photograph is present to me, while I am not present to it; and a world I know, and see, but to which I am nevertheless not present (through no fault of my subjectivity), is a world past."[13] Nothing about a commitment to skepticism, in other words, entails viewing film as "a moving image of skepticism."[14] The converse is also true. Many theorists, Bazin being an obvious example, have subscribed to some kind of "presentation" theory of photography similar to Cavell's—in which photographs are thought of as making their referents present—without being committed to skepticism.

This, of course, does not rule out the possibility that a particular ethical or epistemological commitment might on occasion determine a particular film theory. If one is epistemologically committed to a dialectical conception of history, for instance, one will doubtless gravitate toward a dialectical theory of film history, such as André Bazin's theory of the history of film style as a dialectical struggle between those filmmakers who "put their faith in the image" and those who "put their faith in reality." But even in this case theorists might disagree about precisely what forces drive film history. Marxists, for example, have often dismissed Bazin's theory as "idealist" because it locates the forces of historical change in the superstructure of film style rather than the base of economic relations, even though they share his epistemological commitment to a dialectical conception of history. This commitment, in other words, does not provide an answer to the question about what forces drive (film) history.

If I am right, and turning to philosophy, or at least epistemology and ethics, is of little help to film theory because epistemological and ethical commitments typically underdetermine theories and vice-versa, then what role should philosophy play in film theory? I think it has two roles to play. First is the role it has been playing over the last twenty years, namely, as a *model* for film theorizing. Analytical philosophy as a theoretical discipline, introduced into film studies by the pioneering work of Noël Carroll in the 1980s, has taught a new generation of film theorists to theorize much better than their predecessors. The results have been impressive indeed. Although Rodowick's paper is an elegy for film theory, I would argue that film theory, due to the influence of analytical philosophy, has never been healthier even though, ironically, it has become a subfield largely ignored by the majority of film scholars. We now have powerful theories of film art, representation, narrative, suspense, stylistic techniques such as editing and point of view, sound, music, comprehension, interpretation, emotional response, character identification, perception, imagination, pleasure, ideology, and the list goes on and on.[15] This is because, while there is still much work to be done, film theory under the aegis of analytical philosophy has become much more dialectical, rigorous, and clear, ridding itself of much of the "fashionable nonsense" and dogma of psychoanalytical-semiotic film theory. This does not mean that film theorists have become analytical philosophers, for by and large we lack the training to do so. Rather, it means that we have learned from and borrowed at least some of the techniques of theory-building from analytical philosophy.

Second, Allen and I argue that philosophy also has a *propaedeutic* role to play in disciplines that study the arts such as film studies. By this, we mean that philosophy can help us clarify and therefore better understand the concepts, particularly the psychological concepts, we employ in theorizing about and studying film. For theorists routinely employ concepts, such as perceptual concepts, without a clear grasp of their meanings, with the result that our theories can stray beyond the bounds of sense. Here, Allen and I part company with the mainstream tradition in contemporary analytical philosophy, which has abandoned Wittgenstein's sharp distinction between the conceptual and the empirical, and which sees philosophy as allied with the sciences in improving upon our "folk" conceptual framework. This is not the place to essay this topic.[16] Instead, I will simply give a brief illustration of how philosophy, understood as conceptual clarification, can help us to root out conceptual confusion and nonsense in film theory by turning to one of Deleuze's film theoretical claims, namely, his claim about the cinema and perception.

Deleuze's theory of perception, like his philosophy in general, is derived from Bergson's. According to Bergson, reality is an indivisible, continuous whole in which everything is constantly interacting with everything else throughout time and space, a process he refers to as mobility.[17] Due to practical necessity, human perception is immobile ("to perceive is to immobilize"),[18] subtracting what is seen from its spatial and temporal connections to everything else.

> I should convert [objective reality] into representation if I could isolate it, especially if I could isolate its shell. . . . It [is] necessary, not to throw more light on the object, but, on the contrary, to obscure some of its aspects, to diminish it by the greater part of itself, so that the remainder, instead of being encased in its surroundings as a *thing*, should detach itself from them as a *picture*. . . . [Objects] becomes "perceptions" by their very isolation.[19]

Deleuze, like Jean Epstein before him, bases his film theory on this claim about the gap between reality and the way it appears to human sight.[20] However, again like Epstein, he departs from Bergson's philosophy by arguing that, rather than replicating the immobility of human vision, the cinema overcomes it, thereby revealing the mobility of reality to the film viewer. Although he never explains how, the cinema, Deleuze insists, does not artificially construct an imitation of movement, as human perception does according to Bergson. Rather, movement is an "immediate given" of the cinematic image, and he therefore calls it a "movement-image."[21] Furthermore, while framing does subtract what it frames from its spatial and temporal connections to the rest of reality, much like human sight, this is counteracted by camera movement and editing which, by revealing what is excluded by the frame, restore these spatial and temporal connections.

> If the cinema does *not* have natural subjective perception as its model, it is because the mobility of its centers and the variability of its framings always lead it to restore vast acentered and deframed zones. It then tends to return to the first regime of the movement-image: universal variation, total, objective, and diffuse perception.[22]

Hence, the cinema tends to oscillate between revealing and hiding the mobility of reality, between an "objective," "acentered" "perception," in which what is framed at any one moment is connected to the rest of reality by camera movement and editing, and a "subjective," "unicentered" "perception," in which what is framed is separated from its spatial and temporal connections to the rest of reality.[23]

This is a film theoretical claim in Bordwell and Carroll's sense. It is an explanatory generalization about the cinema's nature and functions. And like any film theoretical claim, it has to be evaluated in terms of whether it is a successful explanation of film. Reflecting on its underlying epistemological and ethical commitments will not help. Even if one shared Deleuze's epistemological and ethical commitment to Bergson's philosophy, one could still find fault—as Bergson himself would have done—with the claim that the cinema, rather than replicating the immobility of human vision, overcomes it. Bergson argued that, just as the cinema creates the impression of movement "artificially" through a succession of still photographs arranged uniformly on a strip of celluloid, so human "perception, intellection, language . . . take snapshots, as it were, of the passing reality," which we "string together on a becoming, abstract, uniform, and invisible." Far from overcoming the immobility of human perception, the cinema, much like human perception according to Bergson, merely "imitates" mobile reality through joining together a series of immobile representations of it.[24]

Allen and I argue that the role of philosophy in evaluating film theoretical claims should be a propaedeutic one, i.e. it should consist of clarifying the meaning of the concepts it employs. In this case, the central concept being employed is perception, and the correct philosophical question to ask is: is Deleuze using the concept of perception correctly, in a way that makes sense? I would say no. For Bergson, from whom Deleuze's conception of perception is borrowed, has an implausibly broad definition of perception. In *Matter and Memory*, he proposes an antirepresentationalist theory of perception, arguing that perception consists not of an internal representation of the external world but the "stimulation" of the brain and nervous system of a living creature by the external world. This stimulation is no different from the interactions taking place between all objects all of the time throughout the universe, he argues, and in this sense, all objects "perceive" all other objects, which is why Bergson calls them "images."[25] Deleuze accepts this theory unquestioningly, claiming at one point that atoms perceive, and indeed that they can perceive more than we humans can![26] But perceiving does not simply consist of the interaction between one thing and another. We do not say that a mirror perceives its environment simply because light rays from the objects around it are reflected on its surface. Rather, we say that something perceives on the basis of its *behavior* in appropriate contexts. As Wittgenstein pointed out, "Only of a living human being and what resembles (behaves like) a living human being can one say: it has sensations; it sees; is blind; hears; is deaf; is conscious or unconscious."[27] It is nonsensical to claim that atoms and mirrors perceive because they do not *behave* like sighted creatures such as ourselves in the appropriate contexts.

As a result of this broad definition of perception, Deleuze often talks about the cinema as if it can perceive, as we saw in the quotation above, or as if it is conscious, as in the following passage: "Given that it is a consciousness which carries out these divisions and reunions, we can say of the shot that it acts like a consciousness. But the sole cinematographic consciousness is not us, the spectator, nor the hero; it is the camera—sometimes human, sometimes inhuman or superhuman."[28] But even though a shot might be like human perception (as defined by Bergson) in that it separates what it frames from the rest of reality, this does not mean that it or the camera *is* a perception, or that it or the camera *perceives*, for a camera, let alone a shot, cannot behave like a sighted creature.[29] It cannot recognize or fail to recognize an object, identify or misidentify it, discover or overlook it, pay attention to or ignore it, watch it, observe it, scrutinize it, study it, or inspect it. Nor can it go blind or lose consciousness. It can certainly help human beings to do some of these things by recording and thereby enabling us to see what we would not be able to see otherwise. But this does not mean that *it* does them.[30] Hence, if Wittgenstein's explanatory generalization about the concept of perception is correct, it is pure nonsense to claim that the shot or the camera is a "perception" or a "consciousness."[31] This brief example is designed to show that, through clarifying the meaning of perception and other difficult concepts, philosophy can prevent film theorists from trafficking in the sort of conceptual confusion and nonsense—the incorrect use of concepts such as perception—that Deleuze does.

* * *

In this paper, I have tried to show that, while Professor Rodowick has done us a great service in identifying and clarifying the debates about film theory of the past few decades, he mischaracterizes some of the conceptions of theory employed in these debates, as well as some of their ramifications. Furthermore, the philosophical conception of theory that he recommends is of little use to film theory because the epistemological and ethical commitments he sees as central to film theorizing underdetermine theories and vice-versa. Instead, I have suggested that the role philosophy should play in film studies is as both a model for film theory, and, more controversially perhaps, as a propaedeutic that clarifies the meaning of important, difficult concepts such as perception, which we use in theorizing about film. This, however, does not mean that film theory should become a form of philosophy, because our expertise as film scholars is in film, and film is what we are trying to explain. As helpful as theories in philosophy, as well as various other disciplines such as sociology and economics, might be to us in film studies, most of us are not philosophers, sociologists, or economists but *film* scholars. What this means is that, at the end of the day, we have to use our expertise—gained from watching large numbers of films, observing them and the response of viewers to them carefully, and learning about the contexts in which they were made and exhibited—to evaluate the theories we take from other disciplines in terms of whether they successfully explain (or not) film.

As for film theory itself, contrary to Rodowick, I believe it is in a very healthy state, due largely to the influence of analytical philosophy, and not something we should compose an eulogy for, even though film scholars by and large ignore it. While Allen and I, following Wittgenstein, take issue with attempts to answer questions about meaning using the reductive model of theorizing, I see no problem with film theory conceived of, following Carroll and Bordwell, as an explanatory generalization about film formulated through dialectical criticism of rivals. Indeed, film theorizing in this sense seems to me to be an essential and valuable part of film studies, and one that is not going to come to an end any time soon.

Notes

1   Page numbers in the text refer to those in this issue of *October*. [—Ed.]
2   Noël Carroll, "Prospects for Film Theory: A Personal Assessment," in *Post-Theory: Reconstructing Film Studies*, ed. David Bordwell and Noël Carroll (Madison: University of Wisconsin Press, 1996), p. 39.
3   David Bordwell, *The Cinema of Eisenstein* (Cambridge, Mass.: Harvard University Press, 1993), p. 11.
4   Carroll, "Prospects for Film Theory," p. 59.
5   Ibid., p. 56.
6   See Bordwell, *Figures Traced in Light: On Cinematic Staging* (Berkeley and Los Angeles: University of California Press, 2005), chap. 6.
7   See our "Wittgenstein's Later Philosophy: A Prophylaxis against Theory," in our anthology *Wittgenstein, Theory and the Arts* (London: Routledge, 2001), pp. 1–35.
8   See P.M.S. Hacker, *Wittgenstein's Place in Twentieth-Century Analytic Philosophy* (London: Blackwell, 1996), chap. 6.
9   For a more detailed version of this argument, see my "Can Scientific Models of Theorizing Help Film Theory?," in *The Philosophy of Film: Introductory Texts and Readings*, ed. Angela Curran and Thomas E. Wartenberg (London: Blackwell, 2005), pp. 21–31.
10   Henri Bergson, *Creative Evolution* (1907; Mineola, N.Y.: Dover Publications, 1998), p. 11.
11   Ibid., p. 306.
12   Stanley Cavell, *The Claim of Reason: Wittgenstein, Skepticism, Morality, and Tragedy* (New York: Oxford University Press, 1979), pp. 47, 45.
13   Stanley Cavell, *The World Viewed: Reflections on the Ontology of Film*, enlarged edition (1971; Cambridge, Mass.: Harvard University Press, 1979), p. 23.
14   Ibid., p. 188. Cavell uses this particular phrase in the essay titled "More of The World Viewed," added to *The World Viewed* in the enlarged edition.

15   For a sampling, see the following anthologies: Richard Allen and Murray Smith, eds., *Film Theory and Philosophy* (Oxford: Clarendon Press, 1997); Curran and Wartenberg, eds. *The Philosophy of Film*; and Noël Carroll and Jinhee Choi, eds., *Philosophy of Film and Motion Pictures: An Anthology* (London: Blackwell, 2006).

16   For a recent overview of this debate, and a defense of Wittgenstein's position, see Oswald Hanfling, *Philosophy and Ordinary Language: The Bent and Genius of Our Tongue* (London: Routledge, 2000).

17   Henri Bergson, *Matter and Memory*, trans. N.M. Paul and W.S. Palmer (1896; New York: Zone Books, 1988), p. 208.

18   Ibid.

19   Ibid., p. 36.

20   I explore the influence of Bergson's philosophy on Epstein in chap. 1 of my *Doubting Vision: Film and the Revelationist Tradition* (New York: Oxford University Press, 2008).

21   Gilles Deleuze, *Cinema 1: The Movement Image*, trans. Hugh Tomlinson and Barbara Habberjam (1983; Minneapolis: University of Minnesota Press, 1986), p. 2.

22   Ibid., p. 64.

23   Ibid. See also p. 58.

24   Bergson, *Creative Evolution*, p. 306.

25   Bergson, *Matter and Memory*, pp. 30–31.

26   Deleuze, *Cinema 1*, pp. 63–64.

27   Ludwig Wittgenstein, *Philosophical Investigations*, ed. G.E.M. Anscombe and R. Rhees, trans. G.E.M. Anscombe, second edition (Oxford: Blackwell, 1958), §281. This claim has often led to the mistaken view that Wittgenstein was a behaviorist. For criticisms of this view, see P.M.S. Hacker, *Wittgenstein: Meaning and Mind*, vol. 3 of *An Analytical Commentary on the Philosophical Investigations, Part 1: Essays* (Oxford: Blackwell, 1993), chap. 6, "Behavior and Behaviorism."

28   Deleuze, *Cinema 1*, p. 20.

29   I explore this point in more depth in relation to Dziga Vertov's work in my "Can the Camera See? Mimesis in Man with a Movie Camera," *October* 89 (Summer 1999), pp. 25–50.

30   This may seem like nit-picking, but Deleuze's reckless attribution of psychological predicates to the cinema has major ramifications for his film theory, leading to his claim that, in Rodowick's words, the cinema is "best able to picture thought." Daniel Frampton takes this claim to its absurd extreme in *Filmosophy* (New York: Wallflower, 2006).

31   I point to other examples of Deleuze's misuse of perceptual concepts in chap. 4 of my *Doubting Vision*.

PART II

Arguments with early film theory

Hugo Münsterberg

THE PSYCHOLOGY OF THE PHOTOPLAY

Depth and movement

[Editor's note: This is an excerpt from Chapter 3 of *The Photoplay: A Psychological Study*.]

THE PROBLEM IS NOW quite clear before us. Do the photoplays furnish us only a photographic reproduction of a stage performance; is their aim thus simply to be an inexpensive substitute for the real theater, and is their esthetic standing accordingly far below that of the true dramatic art, related to it as the photograph of a painting to the original canvas of the master? Or do the moving pictures bring us an independent art, controlled by esthetic laws of its own, working with mental appeals which are fundamentally different from those of the theater, with a sphere of its own and with ideal aims of its own? If this so far neglected problem is ours, we evidently need not ask in our further discussions about all which books on moving pictures have so far put into the foreground, namely the physical technique of producing the pictures on the film or of projecting the pictures on the screen, or anything else which belongs to the technical or physical or economic aspect of the photoplay industry. Moreover it is then evidently not our concern to deal with those moving pictures which serve mere curiosity or the higher desires for information and instruction. Those educational pictures may give us delight, and certainly much esthetic enjoyment may be combined with the intellectual satisfaction, when the wonders of distant lands are unveiled to us. The landscape setting of such a travel film may be a thing of beauty, but the pictures are not taken for art's sake. The aim is to serve the spread of knowledge.

Our esthetic interest turns to the means by which the photoplay influences the mind of the spectator. If we try to understand and to explain the means by which music exerts its powerful effects, we do not reach our goal by describing the structure of the piano and of the violin, or by explaining the physical laws of sound. We must proceed to the psychology and ask for the mental processes of the hearing of tones and of chords, of harmonies and disharmonies, of tone qualities and tone intensities, of rhythms and phrases, and must trace how these elements are combined in the melodies and compositions. In this way we turn to the photoplay, at first with a purely psychological interest, and ask for the elementary excitements of the mind which enter into our experience of the moving pictures. We now disregard entirely the idea of the theater performance. We should block our way if we were to start from the theater and were to ask how much is left out in the mere photographic substitute. We approach the art of the film theater as if it stood entirely on its own ground, and extinguish all memory of the world of actors. We analyze the mental processes which this specific form of artistic endeavor produces in us.

To begin at the beginning, the photoplay consists of a series of flat pictures in contrast to the plastic objects of the real world which surrounds us. But we may stop at once: what does it mean to say that the surroundings appear to the mind plastic and the moving pictures flat? The psychology of this difference is easily misunderstood. Of course, when we are sitting in the picture palace we know that we see a flat screen and that the object which we see has only two dimensions, right–left, and up–down, but not the third dimension of depth, of distance toward us or away from us. It is flat like a picture and never plastic like a work of sculpture or architecture or like a stage. Yet this is knowledge and not immediate impression. We have no right whatever to say that the scenes which we see on the screen appear to us as flat pictures.

We may become more strongly conscious of this difference between an object of our knowledge and an object of our impression, if we remember a well-known instrument, the stereoscope. The stereoscope, which was quite familiar to the parlor of a former generation, consists of two prisms through which the two eyes look toward two photographic views of a landscape. But the two photographic views are not identical. The landscape is taken from two different points of view, once from the right and once from the left. As soon as these two views are put into the stereoscope the right eye sees through the prism only the view from the right, the left eye only the view from the left. We know very well that only two flat pictures are before us; yet we cannot help seeing the landscape in strongly plastic forms. The two different views are combined in one presentation of the landscape in which the distant objects appear much further away from us than the foreground. We feel immediately the depth of things. It is as if we were looking at a small plastic model of the landscape and in spite of our objective knowledge cannot recognize the flat pictures in the solid forms which we perceive. It cannot be otherwise, because whenever in practical life we see an object, a vase on our table, as a solid body, we get the impression of its plastic character first of all by seeing it with our two eyes from two different points of view. The perspective in which our right eye sees the things on our table is different from the perspective for the left eye. Our plastic seeing therefore depends upon this combination of two different perspective views, and whenever we offer to the two eyes two such one-sided views, they must be combined into the impression of the substantial thing. The stereoscope thus illustrates clearly that the knowledge of the flat character of pictures by no means excludes the actual perception of depth, and the question arises whether the moving pictures of the photoplay, in spite of our knowledge concerning the flatness of the screen, do not give us after all the impression of actual depth.

* * *

It may be said offhand that even the complete appearance of depth such as the stereoscope offers would be in no way contradictory to the idea of moving pictures. Then the photoplay would give the same plastic impression which the real stage offers. All that would be needed is this. When the actors play the scenes, not a single but a double camera would have to take the pictures. Such a double camera focuses the scene from two different points of view, corresponding to the position of the two eyes. Both films are then to be projected on the screen at the same time by a double projection apparatus which secures complete correspondence of the two pictures so that in every instance the left and the right view are overlapping on the screen. This would give, of course, a chaotic, blurring image. But if the apparatus which projects the left side view has a green glass in front of the lens and the one which projects the right side view a red glass, and every person in the audience has a pair of spectacles with the left glass green and the right glass red—a cardboard lorgnette with red and green gelatine paper would do the same service and costs only a few cents—the left eye would see only the left view, the right eye only the right view. We could not see the red lines through the green glass nor the green lines through the red glass. In the moment the left eye gets the left side view only and the right eye the right side view, the whole chaos of lines on the screen is organized and we see the pictured room on the screen with the same depth as if it were really a solid room set on the stage and as if the rear wall in the room were actually ten or twenty feet behind the furniture in the front. The effect is so striking that no one can overcome the feeling of depth under these conditions.

But while the regular motion pictures certainly do not offer us this complete plastic impression, it would simply be the usual confusion between knowledge about the picture and its real appearance if we were to deny that we get a certain impression of depth. If several persons move in a room, we gain distinctly the feeling that one moves behind another in the film picture. They move toward us and from us just as much as they move to the right and left. We actually perceive the chairs or the rear wall of the room as further away from us than the persons in the foreground. This is not surprising if we stop to think how we perceive the depth, for instance, of a real stage. Let us fancy that we sit in the orchestra of a real theater and see before us the stage set as a room with furniture and persons in it. We now see the different objects on the stage at different distances, some near, some far. One of the causes was just mentioned. We see everything with our right or our left eye from different points of view. But if now we close one eye and look at the stage with the right eye only, the plastic effect does not disappear. The psychological causes for this perception of depth with one eye are essentially the differences of apparent size, the perspective relations, the shadows, and the actions performed in the space. Now all these factors which help us to grasp the furniture on the stage as solid and substantial play their rôle no less in the room which is projected on the screen.

We are too readily inclined to imagine that our eye can directly grasp the different distances in our surroundings. Yet we need only imagine that a large glass plate is put in the place of the curtain covering the whole stage. Now we see the stage through the glass; and if we look at it with one eye only it is evident that every single spot on the stage must throw its light to our eye by light rays which cross the glass plate at a particular point. For our seeing it would make no difference whether the stage is actually behind that glass plate or whether all the light rays which pass through the plate come from the plate itself. If those rays with all their different shades of light and dark started from the surface of the glass plate, the effect on the one eye would necessarily be the same as if they originated at different distances behind the glass. This is exactly the case of the screen. If the pictures are well taken and the projection is sharp and we sit at the right distance from the picture, we must have the same impression as if we looked through a glass plate into a real space.

The photoplay is therefore poorly characterized if the flatness of the pictorial view is presented as an essential feature. That flatness is an objective part of the technical physical arrangements, but not a feature of that which we really see in the performance of the photoplay. We are there in the midst of a three-dimensional world, and the movements of the persons or of the animals or even of the lifeless things, like the streaming of the water in the brook or the movements of the leaves in the wind, strongly maintain our immediate impression of depth. Many secondary features characteristic of the motion picture may help. For instance, by a well-known optical illusion the feeling of depth is strengthened if the foreground is at rest and the background moving. Thus the ship passing in front of the motionless background of the harbor by no means suggests depth to the same degree as the picture taken on the gliding ship itself so that the ship appears to be at rest and the harbor itself passing by.

The depth effect is so undeniable that some minds are struck by it as the chief power in the impressions from the screen. Vachel Lindsay, the poet, feels the plastic character of the persons in the foreground so fully that he interprets those plays with much individual action as a kind of sculpture in motion. He says: "The little far off people on the old-fashioned speaking stage do not appeal to the plastic sense in this way. They are by comparison mere bits of pasteboard with sweet voices, while on the other hand the photoplay foreground is full of dumb giants. The bodies of these giants are in high sculptural relief." Others have emphasized that this strong feeling of depth touches them most when persons in the foreground stand with a far distant landscape as background—much more than when they are seen in a room. Psychologically this is not surprising either. If the scene were a real room, every detail in it would appear differently to the two eyes. In the room on the screen both eyes receive the same impression, and the result is that the consciousness of depth is inhibited. But when a far distant landscape is the only background, the impression from the picture and life is indeed the same. The trees or mountains which are several hundred feet distant from the eye give to both eyes exactly the same impression, inasmuch as the small difference of position between the two eyeballs has no influence compared with the distance of the objects from our face. We would see the mountains with both eyes alike in reality, and therefore we feel unhampered in our subjective interpretation of far distant vision when the screen offers exactly the same picture of the mountains to our two eyes. Hence in such cases we believe that we see the persons really in the foreground and the landscape far away.

Nevertheless we are never deceived; we are fully conscious of the depth, and yet we do not take it for real depth. Too much stands in the way. Some unfavorable conditions are still deficiencies of the technique; for instance, the camera picture in some respects exaggerates the distances. If we see through the open door of the rear wall into one or two other rooms, they appear like a distant corridor. Moreover we have ideal conditions for vision in the right perspective only when we sit in front of the screen at a definite distance. We ought to sit where we see the objects in the picture at the same angle at which the camera photographed the originals. If we are too near or too far or too much to one side, we perceive the plastic scene from a viewpoint which would demand an entirely different perspective than that which the camera fixated. In motionless pictures this is less disturbing; in moving pictures every new movement to or from the background must remind us of the apparent distortion. Moreover, the size and the frame and the whole setting strongly remind us of the unreality of the perceived space. But the chief point remains that we see the whole picture with both eyes and not with only one, and that we are constantly reminded of the flatness of the picture because the two eyes receive identical impressions. And we may add an argument nearly related to it, namely, that the screen as such is an object of our perception and demands an adaptation of the eye and an independent localization. We are drawn into this conflict of perception even when we look into a mirror. If we stand three feet from a large mirror on the wall, we see our reflection three feet from our eyes in the plate glass and we see it at the same time six feet from our eye behind the glass. Both localizations take hold of our mind and produce a peculiar interference. We all have learned to ignore it, but characteristic illusions remain which indicate the reality of this doubleness.

In the case of the picture on the screen this conflict is much stronger. *We certainly see the depth, and yet we cannot accept it.* There is too much which inhibits belief and interferes with the interpretation of the people and landscape before us as truly plastic. They are surely not simply pictures. The persons can move toward us and away from us, and the river flows into a distant valley. And yet the distance in which the people move is not the distance of our real space, such as the theater shows, and the persons themselves are not flesh and blood. It is a unique inner experience, which is characteristic of the perception of the photoplays. *We have reality with all its true dimensions; and yet it keeps the fleeting, passing surface suggestion without true depth and fullness, as different from a mere picture as from a mere stage performance.* It brings our mind into a peculiar complex state; and we shall see that this plays a not unimportant part in the mental make-up of the whole photoplay.

While the problem of depth in the film picture is easily ignored, the problem of movement forces itself on every spectator. It seems as if here the really essential trait of the film performance is to be found, and that the explanation of the motion in the pictures is the chief task which the psychologist must meet. We know that any single picture which the film of the photographer has fixed is immovable. We know, furthermore, that we do not see the passing by of the long strip of film. We know that it is rolled from one roll and rolled up on another, but that this movement from picture to picture is not visible. It goes on while the field is darkened. What objectively reaches our eye is one motionless picture after another, but the replacing of one by another through a forward movement of the film cannot reach our eye at all. Why do we, nevertheless, see a continuous movement? The problem did not arise with the kinetoscope only but had interested the preceding generations who amused themselves with the phenakistoscope and the stroboscopic disks or the magic cylinder of the zoötrope and bioscope. The child who made his zoötrope revolve and looked through the slits of the black cover in the drum saw through every slit the drawing of a dog in one particular position. Yet as the twenty-four slits passed the eye, the twenty-four different positions blended into one continuous jumping movement of the poodle.

But this so-called stroboscopic phenomenon, however interesting it was, seemed to offer hardly any difficulty. The friends of the zoötrope surely knew another little play-thing, the thaumatrope. Dr. Paris had invented it in 1827. It shows two pictures, one on the front, one on the rear side of a card. As soon as the card is quickly revolved about a central axis, the two pictures fuse into one. If a horse is on one side and a rider on the other, if a cage is on one and a bird on the other, we see the rider on the horse and the bird in the cage. It cannot be otherwise. It is simply the result of the positive afterimages. If at dark we twirl a glowing joss stick in a circle, we do not see one point moving from place to place, but we see a continuous circular line. It is nowhere broken because, if the movement is quick, the positive afterimage of the light in its first position is still effective in our eye when the glowing point has passed through the whole circle and has reached the first position again.

We speak of this effect as a positive afterimage, because it is a real continuation of the first impression and stands in contrast to the so-called negative afterimage in which the aftereffect is opposite to the original stimulus. In the case of a negative afterimage the light impression leaves a dark spot, the dark impression gives a light afterimage. Black becomes white and white becomes black; in the world of colors red leaves a green and green a red afterimage, yellow a blue and blue a yellow afterimage. If we look at the crimson sinking sun and then at a white wall, we do not see red light spots but green dark spots. Compared with these negative pictures, the positive afterimages are short and they last through any notice-able time only with rather intense illumination. Yet they are evidently sufficient to bridge the interval between the two slits in the stroboscopic disk or in the zoötrope, the interval in which the black paper passes the eye and in which accordingly no new stimulus reaches the nerves. The routine explanation of the appearance of movement was accordingly: that every picture of a particular position left in the eye an afterimage until the next picture with the slightly changed position of the jumping animal or of the marching men was in sight, and the afterimage of this again lasted until the third came. The afterimages were responsible for the fact that no interruptions were noticeable, while the movement itself resulted simply from the passing of one position into another. What else is the perception of movement but the seeing of a long series of different positions? If instead of looking through the zoötrope we watch a real trotting horse on a real street, we see its whole body in ever new progressing positions and its legs in all phases of motion; and this continuous series is our perception of the movement itself.

This seems very simple. Yet it was slowly discovered that the explanation is far too simple and that it does not in the least do justice to the true experiences. With the advance of modern laboratory psychology the experimental investigations frequently turned to the analysis of our perception of movement. In the last thirty years many researches, notably those of Stricker, Exner, Hall, James, Fischer, Stern, Marbe, Lincke, Wertheimer, and Korte, have thrown new light on the problem by carefully devised experiments. One result of them came quickly into the foreground of the newer view: the perception of movement is an independent experience which cannot be reduced to a simple seeing of a series of different positions. A characteristic content of consciousness must be added to such a series of visual impressions. The mere idea of succeeding phases of movement is not at all the original movement idea. This is suggested first by the various illusions of movement. We may believe that we perceive a movement where no actual changes of visual impressions occur. This, to be sure, may result from a mere misinterpretation of the impression: for instance when in the railway train at the station we look out of the window and believe suddenly that our train is moving, while in reality the train on the neighboring track has started. It is the same when we see the moon floating quickly through the motionless clouds. We are inclined to consider as being at rest that which we fixate and to interpret the relative changes in the field of vision as movements of those parts which we do not fixate.

But it is different when we come, for instance, to those illusions in which movement is forced on our perception by contrast and aftereffect. We look from a bridge into the flowing water and if we turn our eyes toward the land the motionless shore seems to swim in the opposite direction. It is not sufficient in such cases to refer to contrasting eye movements. It can easily be shown by experiments that these movements and counter-movements in the field of vision can proceed in opposite directions at the same time and no eye, of course, is able to move upward and downward, or right and left, in the same moment. A very characteristic experiment can be performed with a black spiral line on a white disk. If we revolve such a disk slowly around its center, the spiral line produces the impression of a continuous enlargement of concentric curves. The lines start at the center and expand until they disappear in the periphery. If we look for a minute or two into this play of the expanding curves and then turn our eyes to the face of a neighbor, we see at once how the features of the face begin to shrink. It looks as if the whole face were elastically drawn toward its center. If we revolve the disk in the opposite direction, the curves seem to move from the edge of the disk toward the center, becoming smaller and smaller, and if then we look toward a face, the person seems to swell up and every point in the face seems to move from the nose toward the chin or forehead or ears. Our eye which watches such an aftereffect cannot really move at the same time from the center of the face toward both ears and the hair and the chin. The impression of movement must therefore have other conditions than the actual performance of the movements, and above all it is clear from such tests that the seeing of the movements is a unique experience which can be entirely independent from the actual seeing of successive positions. The eye itself gets the impression of a face at rest, and yet we see the face in the one case shrinking, in the other case swelling; in the one case every point apparently moving toward the center, in the other case apparently moving away from the center. The experience of movement is here evidently produced by the spectator's mind and not excited from without.

We may approach the same result also from experiments of very different kind. If a flash of light at one point is followed by a flash at another point after a very short time, about a twentieth of a second, the two lights appear to us simultaneous. The first light is still fully visible when the second flashes, and it cannot be noticed that the second comes later than the first. If now in the same short time interval the first light moves toward the second point, we should expect that we would see the whole process as a lighted line at rest, inasmuch as the beginning and the end point appear simultaneous, if the end is reached less than a twentieth of a second after the starting point. But the experiment shows the opposite result. Instead of the expected lighted line, we see in this case an actual movement from one point to the other. Again we must conclude that the movement is more than the mere seeing of successive positions, as in this case we see the movement, while the isolated positions do not appear as successive but as simultaneous.

Another group of interesting phenomena of movement may be formed from those cases in which the moving object is more easily noticed than the impressions of the whole field through which the movement is carried out. We may overlook an area in our visual field, especially when it lies far to one side from our fixation point, but as soon as anything moves in that area our attention is drawn. We notice the movement more quickly than the whole background in which the movement is executed. The fluttering of kerchiefs at a far distance or the waving of flags for signaling is characteristic. All indicate that the movement is to us something different from merely seeing an object first at one and afterward at another place. We can easily find the analogy in other senses. If we touch our forehead or the back of our hand with two blunt compass points so that the two points are about a third of an inch distant from each other, we do not discriminate the two points as two, but we perceive the impression as that of one point. We cannot discriminate the one pressure point from the other. But if we move the point of a pencil to and fro from one point to the other we perceive distinctly the movement in spite of the fact that it is a movement between two end points which could not be discriminated. It is wholly characteristic that the experimenter in every field of sensations, visual or acoustical or tactual, often finds himself before the experience of having noticed a movement while he is unable to say in which direction the movement occurred.

We are familiar with the illusions in which we believe that we see something which only our imagination supplies. If an unfamiliar printed word is exposed to our eye for the twentieth part of a second, we readily substitute a familiar word with similar letters. Everybody knows how difficult it is to read proofs. We overlook the misprints, that is, we replace the wrong letters which are actually in our field of vision by imaginary right letters which correspond to our expectations. Are we not also familiar with the experience of supplying by our fancy the associative image of a movement when only the starting point and the end point are given, if a skillful suggestion influences our mind. The prestidigitator stands on one side of the stage when he apparently throws the costly watch against the mirror on the other side of the stage; the audience sees his suggestive hand movement and the disappearance of the watch and sees twenty feet away the shattering of the mirror. The suggestible spectator cannot help seeing the flight of the watch across the stage.

The recent experiments by Wertheimer and Korte have gone into still subtler details. Both experimenters worked with a delicate instrument in which two light lines on a dark ground could be exposed in very quick succession and in which it was possible to vary the position of the lines, the distance of the lines, the intensity of their light, the time exposure of each, and the time between the appearance of the first and of the second. They studied all these factors, and moreover the influence of differently directed attention and suggestive attitude. If a vertical line is immediately followed by a horizontal, the two together may give the impression of one right angle. If the time between the vertical and the horizontal line is long, first one and then the other is seen. But at a certain length of the time interval, a new effect is reached. We see the vertical line falling over and lying flat like the horizontal line. If the eyes are fixed on the point in the midst of the angle, we might expect that this movement phenomenon would stop, but the opposite is the case. The apparent movement from the vertical to the horizontal has to pass our fixation point and it seems that we ought now to recognize clearly that there is nothing between those two positions, that the intermediate phases of the movement are lacking; and yet the experiment shows that under these circumstances we frequently get the strongest impression of motion. If we use two horizontal lines, the one above the other, we see, if the right time interval is chosen, that the upper one moves downward toward the lower. But we can introduce there a very interesting variation. If we make the lower line, which appears objectively after the upper one, more intense, the total impression is one which begins with the lower. We see first the lower line moving toward the upper one which also approaches the lower; and then follows the second phase in which both appear to fall down to the position of the lower one. It is not necessary to go further into details in order to demonstrate that the apparent movement is in no way the mere result of an afterimage and that the impression of motion is surely more than the mere perception of successive phases of movement. The movement is in these cases not really seen from without, but is superadded, by the action of the mind, to motionless pictures.

The statement that our impression of movement does not result simply from the seeing of successive stages but includes a higher mental act into which the successive visual impressions enter merely as factors is in itself not really an explanation. We have not settled by it the nature of that higher central process. But it is enough for us to see that the impression of the continuity of the motion results from a complex mental process by which the various pictures are held together in the unity of a higher act. Nothing can characterize the situation more clearly than the fact which has been demonstrated by many experiments, namely, that this feeling of movement is in no way interfered with by the distinct consciousness that important phases of the movement are lacking. On the contrary, under certain circumstances we become still more fully aware of this apparent motion created by our inner activity when we are conscious of the interruptions between the various phases of movement.

We come to the consequences. What is then the difference between seeing motion in the photoplay and seeing it on the real stage? There on the stage where the actors move the eye really receives a continuous series. Each position goes over into the next without any interruption. The spectator receives everything from without and the whole movement which he sees is actually going on in the world of space without and accordingly in his eye. But if he faces the film world, *the motion which he sees appears to be a true motion, and yet is created by his own mind*. The afterimages of the successive pictures are not sufficient to produce a substitute for the continuous outer stimulation; the essential condition is rather the inner mental activity which unites the separate phases in the idea of connected action. Thus we have reached the exact counterpart of our results when we analyzed the perception of depth. We see actual depth in the pictures, and yet we are every instant aware that it is not real depth and that the persons are not really plastic. It is only a suggestion of depth, a depth created by our own activity, but not actually seen, because essential conditions for the true perception of depth are lacking. Now we find that the movement too is perceived but that the eye does not receive the impressions of true movement. It is only suggestion of movement, and the idea of motion is to a high degree the product of our own reaction. *Depth and movement alike come to us in the moving picture world, not as hard facts but as a mixture of fact and symbol. They are present and yet they are not in the things. We invest the impressions with them.* The theater has both depth and motion, without any subjective help; the screen has them and yet lacks them. We see things distant and moving, but we furnish to them more than we receive; we create the depth and the continuity through our mental mechanism.

Chapter 4

Noël Carroll

FILM/MIND ANALOGIES: THE CASE OF HUGO MÜNSTERBERG

THOUGH THERE IS A strong tendency in the writing of our culture to assimilate cinema to notions of reality and realism, there is another tradition, at least equally
persistent, that attempts to conceptualize cinema as an analog to the human mind—i.e. to
characterize cinematic processes as if they were modeled upon mental processes.

Neither of these traditions seems to me an adequate perspective from which to develop
satisfying film theories. However, neither tendency can be ignored, because both are so
entrenched in our thinking about film, that, if not explicitly confronted, they will continue
to haunt our thinking about cinema. The purpose of this article is to begin to challenge the
view that film can be profitably studied theoretically by analogizing it to mental processes.[1]

The attempt to develop a theoretically viable approach to cinema by means of film/
mind analogies was already in place in the second decade of this century, and it continues to
inform much of the most dominant strand of contemporary film theory—that of psychoanalytic semiotics. Readers more familiar with the analytic tradition in aesthetics will recall
a variant of the film/mind analogy in Suzanne Langer's conception of film as dream. Perhaps
the most elaborate working through of the film/mind analogy, with reference to the
cognitive-rational aspect of the mind, was developed by Hugo Münsterberg. In this essay,
I will be concerned with both the detailed way in which Münsterberg's project goes awry
and the way that the failure of his attempt may also shed light on the generic shortcomings of
any film/mind approach to film theory, including those of our contemporaries.

If Münsterberg is useful in terms of exemplifying a problematic of contemporary film
theory, he also illuminates the problematic of early film theory—the film theory of the silent
era. Thus, in discussing Münsterberg, it is not only my intent to scrutinize his attempt to
forge film/mind analogies, but also to consider his theory critically as illustrative of silent
film theory, particularly in virtue of the question of whether and by what means film could
be conceived of as an artform.

In early 1915, Hugo Münsterberg, a member of the Harvard Philosophy Department, a
leader in the field of applied psychology, and an adviser to the likes of Teddy Roosevelt,
Wilson, and Carnegie, saw Annette Kellerman in *Neptune's Daughter* and became enthralled
with the aesthetic possibilities of the nascent artform, the movies. He spent much of the
following summer in nickelodeons and visited the Vitagraph Studios in Brooklyn. Flattered

by the attentions of this distinguished academic, a student of Wilhelm Wundt and a protégé of William James, Adolph Zukor made him a contributing editor to the magazine *Paramount Pictograph*. Münsterberg took his role seriously and began to write a great deal about film—this activity culminating in 1916 in his *The Photoplay: A Psychological Study*.

Though by no means the first example of film theory, Münsterberg's text, now called *The Film: A Psychological Study*, was surely the most sustained of the early philosophical explanations and defenses of the film medium as an artform.[2] For many years, however, the book remained forgotten, perhaps because the German-born Münsterberg raised the ire of the popular press due to his strenuous efforts to stop America's entry into the First World War on behalf of the Allies. But when the treatise was reissued in 1970, it seemed almost prophetic, for Münsterberg's attempt to explain the workings of film processes through analogies with mental processes coincided, at least in a very general way, with the efforts of avant-garde filmmakers—like Alain Resnais, Stan Brakhage, and Michael Snow—to create works that were said to be modeled on or to objectify consciousness.

Today, Münsterberg's treatise remains interesting for several reasons. On the one hand, it is of exemplary historical value for, despite its early appearance, it manages to set out the underlying aesthetic problematic of silent film with a clarity that was rarely rivaled during the period. But it is also of contemporary interest. For in his use of mental analogies to explain both the particular power and the conventions of film, Münsterberg presages recent psychoanalytic explorations in film theory such as those of Christian Metz and Jean-Louis Baudry. Admittedly, Münsterberg's analogies were to, what might be thought of as, rational mental processes, whereas contemporary film theorists prefer analogs with irrational processes. However, Münsterberg can be seen as the pioneer of the mind/film analogy-approach to film theory, and his writings, therefore, can be discussed within the context of the contemporary debate about whether the mind/film paradigm is a useful one.

The most pressing problem for film theorists of the silent period was to show that film could be an artform, insofar as *art* was the only available cultural category through which the medium could claim serious attention. But, since film was photographic, detractors regarded it as a mere mechanical recording device. Either, it slavishly reproduced slices of reality (the early documentaries of the Lumières might be thought of as examples here), or, at best, it automatically recorded famous, and not so famous, plays. The point was that film was simply a copying machine, and nothing more. It blandly imitated whatever stood before the camera rather than creatively reconstituting it. In other words, it was presumed that imitation *simpliciter* was not a hallmark of art. And furthermore, since it was assumed that film—as a photographic medium—could do no more than imitate, then film could not be art.

Münsterberg, like other film theorists to come, agreed with the opponents of film that if a medium is to be an artform, it must do more than imitate. And this, in turn, entails that in order to show that film is an art, he must refute the assumption that all the film medium must do (given its photographic nature) is slavishly copy. This, however, involves showing two things: both that film need not necessarily copy reality *and* that films need not be mere mechanical reproductions of theatrical dramas.

Münsterberg pursues these demonstrations through an ingenious discussion of a series of cinematic devices—such as the close-up, parallel editing, flashbacks, and flashforwards—that were being refined and popularized during the period from 1908 to 1915. His review of these techniques—which at the time were considered innovations—put him in a position to claim not only that the filmmaker transformed what he photographed but also that he transformed it in a way that was uniquely cinematic (rather than theatrical). Moreover, Münsterberg's explanations of the way in which these devices functioned also enabled him to connect film—specifically, film's peculiar way of transforming the world—with that which Münsterberg, on independent grounds, took to be the purpose of art.

In a nutshell, then, there are three major items on the agenda in *The Photoplay*: first, to show that the film medium, despite its photographic provenance, could imaginatively reconstitute whatever it recorded; second, that the cinematic mode of transforming reality was different from the theatrical mode; and, third, that this mode of transformation implemented the general purposes of art—which purposes could be identified without reference to cinema.

After an "Introduction," in which he sketches the technological development of cinema, and its early stylistic breakthroughs, Münsterberg begins what he calls "The Psychology of the Photoplay." Essentially, this section is an analysis of cinematic devices (or processes of articulation) such as the close-up, parallel editing, and so on. This way of beginning—by focussing on characteristic cinematic processes of articulation—reminds one of the procedure of many future film theorists, such as Arnheim, and, in fact, the logical function this section performs also resembles that of opening portions of Arnheim's *Film as Art*. For what is to be shown here is that cinema is not the mere reproduction of anything, neither reality nor theater. (Incidentally, Münsterberg, again like Arnheim, opposes the sound film.)

First, Münsterberg examines the impressions of depth and motion in film, noting that in contradistinction with theater, film depth and film motion are, so to speak, *superadditions* that the mind supplies to a series of flat surfaces of still photos. Whereas "theater has both depth and motion, without subjective help," in film "we create the depth and continuity through our mental mechanism."[3]

The contrast with theater and the concern with the relation of cinematic processes to the mind continue throughout Münsterberg's discussion of cinematic devices. For example, in theater attention is directed by means of word and gesture. When an actor points an accusing finger at another character across the stage, my eye follows the line of movement and lands at the appropriate point of interest. But in film, attention can be directed by camera positioning. If you want the audience to attend to the key in *Notorious*, you can show a close-up of it. The close-up selects crucial dramatic elements—objects, faces, hands, etc.—and enlarges them, while eliminating surrounding details. What we do on our own in theater, it might be said, is done for us automatically in film. The film close-up is somehow equivalent to the psychological process of attention; it is an objectification or externalization of the process.

> Wherever our attention becomes focused on a special feature, the surrounding adjusts itself, eliminates everything in which we are not interested, and by the close-up heightens the vividness of that on which our mind is concentrated. It is as if that outer world were woven into our mind and were shaped not through its own laws but by the acts of our attention.[4]

Moreover, this account of the close-up not only purportedly explains its operation but also does so in a way which differentiates such devices from the means available in theater.

This notion of cinematic devices as the objectification of mental processes is central to the claims Münsterberg will make for film as an art. But it should be noted that there is a striking change in the manner of Münsterberg's analysis of cinematic depth and motion, on the one hand, and the analysis of the close-up, on the other. For in the matter of film depth and motion, the psychologist tells us we add something to the visual array, whereas with the close-up, the selecting is something that is done for us. That is, the mental process—attention—that Münsterberg discusses with respect to the close-up is, roughly speaking, in the film, not in us. A similar shift in direction occurs in the rest of Münsterberg's account of cinematic articulations.

In theater, later moments in a play may call to mind earlier ones; the scenes of Lear's desperation, for example, remind us of his earlier majesty. However, in film this sort of contrast can be literally visualized by means of a flashback. Where theater relies on the spectator's memory, the flashback in film is an analog or functional equivalent to memory. Likewise, when we see that proverbial gun in the first act of a play, we might be thought to imagine its going off in the last; but, in film, such predictions can be made by a flashforward, as in the case of the funeral barge in *Don't Look Now*. Where the flashback is the analog or objectification of memory, the flashforward correlates with the imagination.

Of course, these comparisons with the mental acts of the theater spectator do not fully characterize the functions of the cinematic devices in question because in film we can have flashbacks to scenes the audience never saw, close-ups of details not hitherto shown, and flashforwards to events never imagined. So we are not to think of these devices as substitutes for mental acts the audience would have performed had the action unfolded theatrically. Rather, it seems they must be taken as the operations of an externalized mind in which something is attended, something remembered, and something imagined. Moreover, these devices are modeled on generic acts of human attention, memory, and imagination so that the manner in which they work is thought to be explained by analogizing them to mental processes. Perhaps one way of thinking of this modeling is to recall the notion of objectification Suzanne K. Langer has in mind in *Feeling and Form*.

Parallel editing in film—cutting between two events that occur at the same time but in different places and which are generally related dramatically—also differs from standard theatrical procedures where such scenes would be narrated sequentially. For Münsterberg, this is, so to say, a reification of the capacity of the mind to split its attention or to distribute its interest over a number of events at roughly the same time.

Münsterberg also speculates on ways in which cinema might externalize emotional moods—for example, by the use of soft focus, rhythmical editing, and camera movement—though he regards his remarks here as tentative because these developments had not yet been fully cultivated by the cinema he knew.

One can read *The Film* primarily as an imaginative explanation of how *then* novel film devices function by means of mentalistic metaphors of the sort that V.I. Pudovkin would later employ to teach narrative film editing in terms of the shifting attention of an ideal spectator. However, Münsterberg himself has a larger project; he wants to use these analyses of film devices to show that the film medium can be an artform. To those who denied film could be art because it merely reproduces what it photographs, Münsterberg points out that a close look at these filmic structures, which constitute basic elements of the medium, shows they transform their photographic materials—specifically, they transform them in such a way that they appear *already* synthesized or molded by the human mind. So if it is a necessary condition for a medium to be art that it transform rather than imitate its referent, then film can be an art. Furthermore, since the mode of cinematic transformation is distinct from that of theater, then, if film is an art, it is an art distinct from theater. That is, for those worried that each art must differentiate itself from every other, film is not a theater clone. But the question remains why transforming reality in such a way that the resulting representation mimes the mind should count as artistic transformation. And to answer that Münsterberg needs to invoke his theory of art.

Münsterberg had worked out his view of art in *The Principles of Art Education* (1905). The fruits of this theorizing are applied to cinema in the second part of *The Film* under the heading of "The Esthetics of the Photoplay." Though many film scholars may find this section of the text disposably archaic, it is absolutely essential to Münsterberg's defense of film as an art. Indeed, since nowadays we take it as given that film is an art, the energies, not to mention the almost florid philosophizing, Münsterberg expends on this issue appear beside the point. And yet we must remember that the question of whether film could be art was *the* question of silent film theory.

Münsterberg's position on the nature of art can best be described as a de-Platonized variant on Schopenhauer. As one would expect, given Münsterberg's German heritage, it is deeply indebted to both rationalist and idealist aesthetics, though under his dispensation these receive a primarily psychological rather than a metaphysical twist. Münsterberg proceeds by drawing a contrast between two modes of thinking: the scientific and scholarly, on the one hand, and the artistic on the other. Sloganized, the difference, in Münsterberg's own words, is "connection is science, but the work of art is isolation."[5] That is, science discusses particular cases in order to connect them within larger systems by means of general laws; science subsumes. Art, on the other hand, places emphasis on the particular. Science yields general knowledge through studying cases. But for art, the particular itself is that which is valuable. Münsterberg, the epitome of the reasonable man, does not place one of these ways of knowing over the other; rather, for him, they are complementary.

The contrast Münsterberg has in mind is not unlike that of his contemporary Henri Bergson. Science is general; art particular. That Münsterberg should defend film by such a formula is particularly interesting in light of the history of film theory. For his fellow émigré, Siegfried Kracauer, will also develop a theory of film based on a contrast between a scientific way of approaching the world, which is generalizing, versus the particularizing mode of film which, for Kracauer, amounts to redeeming physical reality.

The origins of this view are deeply embedded in rationalist aesthetics. Perhaps it is first introduced by Baumgarten, who advises that representations be of particulars, albeit ones touched by perfection, as a means of coming to terms with the Leibnizian–Wolffian notion that the objects of sensitive knowledge (Baumgarten's term) are clear but indistinct. The notion that the object of art be particulars is also at least suggested by Kant's view that that which gives rise to the aesthetic perception of beauty is not subsumable under a concept.

Though the concept of disinterestedness is not so explicit in Münsterberg, he clearly has this Kantian commitment in mind when he writes:

> The lover of beauty seeks it in the contemplation of the single object; he isolates it from the world and by that act of isolation it does not come in question any more as means to an effect, as tool for an end, as product of a cause, as a steppingstone to something else, but merely in its own existence, and, therefore, because it does not suggest anything outside of itself, it brings a rest to the mind of the subject.[6]

If the notion, in this quotation, that the beautiful object lies outside the network of uses recalls the Kantian requirement of a divorce from practicality, the invocation of isolation, particularly of isolation as a means of inducing respite, reminds one of the radical form of Idealist aesthetics propounded by Schopenhauer. For Schopenhauer, aesthetic pleasure, in the main, derives from the deliverance of knowledge from the service of the will. The realm of the will comprises striving and, thus, is intimately bound up with causality. Beautiful objects present the viewer with objects lifted out of the network of relations of space, time, and causality, and afford a kind of objective knowledge not tied to the will and its needful concern with the interrelations of things. For Schopenhauer, this isolation from networks of space, time, and causality enables the particular to be viewed in a way that discloses the Platonic Form of the thing.

Echoing Schopenhauer, Münsterberg writes: "The work of art shows us the things and events perfectly complete in themselves, freed from all connections which lead beyond their own limits, that is, in perfect isolation."[7] Unlike Schopenhauer, Münsterberg does not correlate this isolation with the revelation of Platonic Ideas. Rather one finds solace in the particularity of the object abstracted from its relation to everything else. And the nature of this solace is specifically the kind of freedom from striving Schopenhauer emphasizes—the object "brings the desires to rest."[8] Such objects are not only isolated from relations with everything else but are marked by internal perfection, that is to say, they are harmonious wholes; they are unified by traditional organizing features such as plots.

Stated formulaically, Münsterberg holds that: "A work of art, by definition, is 1) a harmonious whole which is 2) divorced from practical interests by means of 3) being isolated from the networks of space, time and causality." Condition 2) states the troublesome but at least well-known requirement of aesthetic disinterest, inherited from such writers as Hutscheson and Kant, while condition 3) specifies that requirement more in the manner of Schopenhauer in terms of isolation from interconnection with everything else. Indeed, Münsterberg's language is even stronger than I have indicated, for he has in mind not only that the artwork is isolated from the rest of the world but that it *overcomes* what he calls the forms of the outer world, namely space, time, and causality. And this, in turn, is thought to result in a satisfying freedom from striving on the part of the viewer.

By this point, it may seem that we've drifted quite far from considering film. What can be the relation of film, specifically film as characterized by Münsterberg, and the view that art is the overcoming of forms of the outer world? Speaking of musical tones, Münsterberg says: "They have overcome the outer world and the social world entirely, they unfold our inner life, our mental play, with its feelings and emotions, its memories and fancies, in material tones which are fluttering and fleeting like our own mental states."[9] Here, it is clear that our inner life, our mental states are being contrasted with the outer world, and that something that imitates or in some sense reduplicates those states *overcomes* the outer world. With this in mind, the relation of Münsterberg's earlier analysis of filmic structures as analogs of mental processes and his theory of film fall in line. He writes: "the photoplay tells us a human story by overcoming the forms of the outer world, namely space, time and causality, by adjusting the events to the forms of the inner world, namely, attention, memory, imagination, and emotion." Film, that is, in virtue of constructing its structures as mental analogs, is an instance of art as theorized by Münsterberg.

The requirement that artworks be harmonious wholes can be satisfied by films by means of such features of plotting as unity of action and character, and by such pictorial attributes as balance. In sum, Münsterberg says:

> The photoplay shows us a significant conflict of human actions in moving pictures which, freed from the physical forms of space, time and causality, are adjusted to the free play of our mental experiences and which complete isolation from the practical world through the perfect unity of plot and pictorial appearance.[10]

The mention of the free play of the mind and separation from the practical again sound the Kantian chord, while Schopenhauer looms in the phrase "freed from the physical forms of space, time and causality."[11] Film is connected with a realm of freedom that has both psychological and metaphysical dimensions. Clearly, what Münsterberg is about here is linking film with existing conceptions of art in order to defend it against its detractors; and the conceptions of art he invokes do not tie the object in any essential way with the imitation of the outer world. Film does not copy the outer world, but rather reconstitutes it in the way that the mind does. This is a defense of the medium of film in general, rather than a defense of any particular film. Münsterberg has shown that film can be an art—under his modified, Idealist conception of art—without being committed to maintaining that the medium had, as yet, produced any masterpieces.

The logical structure of Münsterberg's theory is quite instructive for it is perhaps one of the first appearances of a model that will recur throughout the history of classical film theory.[12] At the general level, it attributes a purpose or role to cinema, here, the production of art. This, in turn, requires a specification of what art is which, for Münsterberg, most notably involves an overcoming of the physical forms of space, time, and causality. With this specification of the purpose of film, we are able to zero in on the determinant characteristic of the medium, that is, the characteristic that enables the medium to realize its purpose. For Münsterberg this is identified as the capacity for the medium to objectify the processes of the human mind (which, themselves, must be thought of as overcoming the forms of the outer world). A conception of the determinant feature of the medium, in turn, provides a framework for analyzing the medium's characteristic processes of articulation; specifically, these processes—such as the close-up, parallel editing, the flashback, etc.—are treated as instances of the determinant feature of film. The close-up exemplifies the capacity for the medium to objectify mental processes by being an analog for attention. And so on.

Though the logical structure of Münsterberg's theory is at least clear, neither its premises nor its presuppositions appear particularly reliable. Perhaps, the premise that film can serve the purposes of art is, by now, incontestable. But the rest of the philosophical superstructure of the theory is shaky. The dependence upon aesthetic disinterestedness is open to all the objections this hotly contested concept invites, and, thus, Münsterberg's theory incurs all the problems associated with what are called aesthetic definitions of art. But these difficulties appear almost minimal when compared to the sorts of pressure that can be brought to bear on the Schopenhauer-derived elements in the theory.

Works of art are said to overcome the outer forms of space, time, and causality. What could this possibly mean? One charitable gloss, one which has the virtue of making Münsterberg's view sound true, is that artworks characteristically come with things like frames, proscenium arches, curtains, and so on, which are thought of as conventional signs that inform audiences that whatever is enclosed by these devices is, in general, discontinuous with surrounding events and environments. The usher is not part of the play, nor does the red in the painting bear any significant relation to the red of the fire extinguisher that hangs next to it. The artwork, so to speak, has been lifted out of our everyday world. There is a technical sense, which undoubtedly would be tricky to articulate in full, in which for purposes of appreciation, the artwork is to be construed, at least in certain important respects, as outside our space–time continuum. Some may put this extravagantly by saying that the artwork is divorced from the real world and constitutes a world unto itself, where the verbiage here is to be taken as a mix of technical language, metaphor, and terms of art.

This interpretation would give us a very concrete way to think of art as a matter of isolation. And clearly Münsterberg has at least this view in mind. But he also means to claim much more, for art is said to *overcome* outer forms of space, time, and causality. But to be isolated, in certain very restricted senses, from the existing space–time continuum is not to be divorced from the forms of space, time, and causality. The forms of space, time, and causality may still have a relevance, in many different ways, to the internal structure of an artwork even if, for example, we regard the world of a fiction as discontinuous from the space, time, cause manifold of the everyday world which we inhabit.

A case in point is plotting, which Münsterberg himself adduces as a unity-making feature in films. Plotting does not overcome the forms of space, time, and causality but rather presupposes them. Münsterberg introduces his notion of "overcoming" with reference to music, which, for obvious reasons, was the highest form of art for Schopenhauer. And, with a great deal of music, the forms of space and causality, though not of time, may be irrelevant to the internal, artistic structure of the work. But for so many other arts the manipulation of the forms of space, time, and causality is integral to their structure. It seems incoherent to speak of artworks as overcoming the forms of space, time, and causality since so much art is involved with exploiting these very forms. Moreover, if the value of art is situated in a release from striving, which itself is seen to be engaged by the form of causality, then it is difficult to understand the way in which artforms that involve plots—novels, dramas, and, to Münsterberg's potential embarrassment, film—can liberate us in the appropriate way, since they will be parasitic upon the forms of causality.

It may be thought that this argument against Münsterberg is inadequate for it over-looks the fact that Münsterberg speaks of the overcoming of the *outer* forms of space, time, and causality. That is, mental processes and their analogous cinematic structures overcome something called the outer forms of space, time, and causality. But this sounds funny. One would have thought that our psychological processes were exactly what con-nected us to the outer forms of space, time, and causality. Indeed, some Kantians would identify these forms with mental forms. But, be that as it may, clearly mental processes do not stand in opposition to the forms of space, time, and causality, but are intimately connected to them. And these mental processes, in virtue of their deep connection with space, time, and causality, are what make practical activity possible; they do not stand against practical activity, they underlie practical activity. It appears incoherent to suggest that psychological processes overcome space, time, and causality since they connect us with these forms. Furthermore, it is incomprehensible that films in virtue of imitating the very psycho-logical processes that link us to space, time, and causality could be thought to liberate us from those self-same forms.

At this point, it might seem that what Münsterberg needs to do to is to drop the Schopenhauer-derived elements in his theory and explicate his notion of isolation solely in terms of the Kantian concept of aesthetic disinterestedness. But, of course, if that is done, then the tight logical connection between his analyses of cinematic devices and his concept of art will be severed.

A disjunction between outer forms of space, time, and causality and mental processes, then, is essential to Münsterberg's theory. But it is hard to see how it is to be drawn. Münsterberg might have something like the following in mind: we can imagine beings with different psychological make-ups than our own. Say that they have no memories, they cannot imagine or predict the future, they have no sense of causal regularities. They are sheer bodily existents and they live in a pure present. They are rather like amoebae; things just happen to them, they forget it, and then something else happens to them. Their psychology restricts them to an experience of the continuum of space, time, and causality on, so to speak, a moment to moment basis; if we had films depicting their experience, they would be long takes of whatever happened in front of the camera followed relentlessly by whatever happened next.

Our psychological processes, however, free us from the kind of pure-present experi-ence of the continuum of space, time, and causality of such sheer bodily entities through our powers of memory, prediction, and our ability to focus our attention. And, by extension, our movies, modeled on our psychological processes, might be said to liberate viewers from the mindless realism of sheer bodily filmmakers. So human psychology can be thought of as overcoming the kind of experience of outer forms of space, time, and causality that sheer bodily existents would have, and artforms, like film, that mime our psychological processes overcome the realism of baldly sequential, present states.

However, even if sense can be made of this interpretation of the way in which human psychological processes (and, by extrapolation, cinematic devices) can be said to overcome the forms of space, time, and causality, it remains questionable whether this can save Münsterberg's theory. Why? Well the theory has it that art, and film art, somehow release us from our ordinary experience of things with respect to space, time, and causality. But we do not ordinarily experience things as sheer bodily existents. So even if there were a contrast between the way we experience things and the way sheer bodily existents experience things, that contrast would appear to have little bearing on the issue. If films replicate our mental processes, then when we view them we will not encounter a contrasting way of seeing the world. That there might be a contrasting way of seeing, such as that of our sheer bodily existents, makes no difference for us when we encounter works of art organized in the ways we already negotiate the outer forms of space, time, and causality.

Another potential problem for Münsterberg resides in the contrast he develops between film and theater. For if film becomes an art in virtue of the way it transforms the spatio-temporal continuum of theater, then a question arises about whether theater remains an art. That is, Münsterberg must go on to explain the way in which theater overcomes space, time, and causality if he intends to count theater as an art. As it is, he appears to elevate film to the status of an art at the expense of theater. Undoubtedly, he mistakenly overlooks this problem because he has conflated two independent theoretical issues—the arguments that film is merely a reproduction of reality *and* that film is merely the reproduction of theater. Münsterberg treats these arguments as if they were one, effectively placing theater and reality in the same boat in a way that leaves us wondering how theater can be shown to be an art.

Of course, even if there are problems with the more philosophical aspects of Münsterberg's theory, it might be thought that there still may be something useful in his specific analyses of cinematic devices. That is, though his philosophy of art might leave too much to be desired, nevertheless his explanation of cinematic devices as analogs of mental processes could still be informative. And perhaps one could even go beyond Münsterberg and claim that audiences are able to readily assimilate cinematic conventions exactly because those conventions are modeled on prototypical psychological processes with which we are all already familiar.

However, even Münsterberg's mind/film analogies have come under recent attack.[13] If, for example, we take Münsterberg to be saying that any close-shot is analogous to the way in which one shifts attention, then it becomes crucial to determine what we mean by "way" here. That is, across what specific dimension of correspondence is the analogy being drawn? Mark Wicclair takes the relevant sense of "way" to be phenomenological; he presumes that for Münsterberg's analogs to succeed the appearance of cinematic devices, such as the close-up, must match the ways in which imagery appears to consciousness via the pertinent psychic process.[14] The close-up should have the same characteristics that objects of attention have in consciousness. And on these grounds, Wicclair finds Münsterberg's analogs wanting.

For example, a close-up involves moving in on an object in such a way that the screen size of the object is literally enlarged. This is quite different than attending to an object at a distance since it involves a scale change. Perhaps a more accurate way of miming attention would be to use a diaphanous mask or an iris shot. Likewise, the account of the flashback is subject to obvious disanalogies. If we remember something by means of an image, we entertain two percepts simultaneously, the memory image and the view of whatever is before our eyes. But flashbacks present images sequentially; they are phenomenologically disanalogous with imagistic memory. Perhaps, superimposition is more akin to such memory, though probably this is not quite right either. Similar problems can be generated with each of Münsterberg's analogies.

The upshot of this is that if we construe Münsterberg's analogies phenomenologically, then his account of cinematic structures is flawed. And given some of Münsterberg's descriptions, especially of the correlation of the close-up and attention, it does sound as though Münsterberg has phenomenological analogies in mind. However, the text is ambiguous in a way that might enable us to deflect Wicclair's objections.

Münsterberg, for instance, often speaks of functions. So rather than taking his analogies to be phenomenological, we might take them to be functional. That is, the close-up and attention are functionally analogous in regards to performing the same function—call it selective focussing—in different systems, the cinematic on the one hand, and the psychological on the other. In a similar vein, we might discriminate between two types of flashbacks—those that repeat earlier scenes, and those that present novel scenes of earlier events in the world of the film. The repetitive flashbacks could be said to perform the same function—i.e. retrieval—in the cinematic system that memory performs in the psychological system, while the novel flashbacks that fill in our fictions might be thought to perform the same function—here, postulating—that imagination does in our mental life. And, further functional analogs might be developed between mind and film.

However, despite the fact that we may save Münsterberg's explanations by emphasizing the importance of functional over phenomenological analogies, the real question is whether they are worth saving. For even if the analogies are meant to be functional analogies, it is far from clear that they explain anything about the operation of cinematic devices. For do we really learn anything by being told that the close-up is an analog to the psychological process of attention when we know so little about the way in which the psychological process of attention operates? And analogies to memory and to the imagination are on no firmer standing. Analogies to such processes have no explanatory force where we have so little grasp of the nature and structure of the mind.

The point here is crucial and it applies across the board to any mind/film analogy-approach to the cinema. In order to be instructive theoretically, an analogy must be such that one knows more about the term in the analogy that is supposed to be elucidating than the term that is supposed to be elucidated. That is, we need to know more, for example, about memory than we do about flashbacks if saying flashbacks are analogs to memory is to be informative. This requirement is fundamental to the logic of analogy. However, I am not convinced that this requirement is met by any of Münsterberg's analogies nor, for that matter, by any of the film/mind analogies propounded by film theorists so far.

Indeed, I suspect that the difficulty here is likely to persist into the foreseeable future, that is, for as long as the mind remains mysterious to us. Nor should film theorists be disheartened by this. For, in truth, we probably already know more about the operations of film than we do about the processes of the mind. This may appear to be an outlandish claim to film theorists. But it may be an occupational conceit on their part to envision film to be more unfathomable than it really is. In fact, we understand quite a lot about the way in which films work, about their conventions and their techniques. Far less is understood about the workings of attention, imagination, memory, and the emotions. Münsterberg manages to tell us virtually nothing by his analogies between film and the mind. The way a close-up works is really easily explained; to say it operates like attention actually complicates matters unless we understand how attention works; which, of course, we do not.[15]

These objections to Münsterberg's overall approach have a direct bearing on leading tendencies in contemporary film theory. For psychoanalytically inclined film theorists, like Baudry and Metz, have developed elaborate accounts of the working of film by means of mentalistic analogs: in Baudry's case, between the cinematic apparatus and night dream, and in Metz's, between film and daydreams.[16] These theories differ significantly from

Münsterberg's insofar as they press analogies between film and irrational mental processes while, for the most part, he relied on analogies with what might be thought of as rational or, at least, not irrational mental processes. Nevertheless, to the extent that these newer theories depend on mind/film analogies, they are susceptible to the same line of criticism just rehearsed with respect to Münsterberg.

One would not, of course, wish to deny that individual films might attempt to mime mental life. Brakhage's *Scenes from Under Childhood* and Resnais's *Last Year at Marienbad* are probably best explained critically in terms of the conceptions of the mind that they are meant to illustrate. A critic, that is, may be justified in exploring mind/film analogies where that supplies the most plausible interpretation of why a specific film is structured the way it is. However as a theoretical—as opposed to a critical—project, it is my contention that the mind/film analogy-approach is abjectly uninformative given our present state of knowledge—or, more aptly, lack of knowledge—about the mind, both in its rational and irrational aspects. We learn next to nothing from the claim that films are like daydreams or night dreams when we know so little about dreaming. No one really even knows why we sleep. Dreaming is much more inscrutable than the cinema.

One reason that films are not so obscure to us is that we make them. We make them to work in a certain way and, for the most part, they function in the way they are designed to work. In a very general sense, we tend to understand our own tools and inventions more readily than that which we have not created. I don't mean to say that we understand our creations perfectly, nor that we have no understanding of the physical universe (though that knowledge is derived from experiments which, of course, are the product of our invention). My point is rather the less controversial one that we know a great deal about what we create in virtue of making them to perform the tasks that they successfully perform.

Presently, the computer, a product of human invention, is being exploited by cognitive scientists as a model or analog for the mind. This is an eminently defensible strategy because having designed computers, we know a lot about them, and we can attempt to extrapolate that wealth of information to mental operations. In the past theater, recall Hume's metaphor of the stage, and even film, for example Husserl, provided at least suggestive analogs for the mind, though not ones as powerful as those currently advanced by experts in artificial intelligence. Here my point is not that when all is said and done, the best theories of the mind will be based on analogies with theater, film, or even artificial intelligence. But rather these theories have the correct logical structure whereas theories of film based on mentalistic analogs do not. For theater, film, and now computers are things that we know much of, for we invented them, whereas the mind is still obscure to us.

Münsterberg developed a very clear version of the mind/film analogy-approach to cinema early on in the evolution of film theory. One should not disparage his attempt. But perhaps what is best learned from his effort now is that this line of inquiry should be jettisoned.[17]

Notes

1   For a discussion of the problems of assimilating film to the notion of reality, see the second chapter of my *Philosophical Problems of Classical Film Theory* (Princeton University Press, 1988).

2   Hugo Münsterberg, *The Film: A Psychological Study* (New York: Dover Publications, 1970).

3   Ibid., p. 30.

4   Ibid., p. 39.

5   See Hugo Münsterberg, "Connection in Science and Isolation in Art," in *A Modern Book of Esthetics*,

3rd ed., ed. Melvin Rader (New York: Holt Rinehart and Winston, 1966), pp. 434–42. This is an excerpt from Münsterberg's *The Principles of Art Education.*

6   Ibid.

7   Münsterberg, *The Film*, p. 64.

8   Ibid., p. 66.

9   Ibid., p. 73.

10   Ibid., p. 81.

11   For an exploration of the Kantian aspect of Münsterberg's theory, see Donald Fredericksen, *The Aesthetic of Isolation in Film Theory: Hugo Münsterberg* (New York: Arno Press, 1977).

12   For a more detailed discussion of the structure of this type of film theory, see the introduction to my *Philosophical Problems of Classical Film Theory.*

13   See Mark Wicclair, "Film Theory and Hugo Münsterberg's *The Film: A Psychological Study*," in *The Journal of Aesthetic Education* 12 (July 1978): 33–50.

14   Ibid.

15   Upon hearing this assessment of Münsterberg's *The Film*, Mary Devereaux felt that I had overlooked what was really important about Münsterberg's contribution. She noted that one might take the notion of film as mind not as the basis of a theoretical research program, but as a rhetorical device, a metaphor, one meant to illuminate the new medium for a skeptical audience. Moreover, it was just the right kind of metaphor that the situation called for—one which got people thinking about film in contrast to reality or the slavish recording thereof. I would not want to deny that, as such a metaphor, the film as mind notion was rhetorically effective. My point is only that it could not be given a literal cash value—neither in Münsterberg's day nor in our own. And this is what renders the approach theoretically dubious, despite whatever might be its heuristic value.

16   For detailed, specific criticism of the theories of Metz and Baudry, see my *Mystifying Movies: Fads and Fallacies of Contemporary Film Theory* (Columbia University Press, 1988).

17   This essay was originally written as part of a series of retrospective reviews that the *Journal of Aesthetics and Art Criticism* planned of books written in this century before its inception. It has been somewhat reworked to be presented as an article independent of that series. This may account for some of its peculiarities; other peculiarities are traceable to me. Versions of this article were read at Vassar and at York University and I have benefitted from the criticisms of the faculties of both those schools, and, as well, particularly from the comments of Donald Fredericksen, Annette Michelson, Jesse Kalin, Mary Devereaux, Evan Cameron, David Bordwell, Peter Kivy, Ian Jarvie, and the referees of the *Journal of Aesthetics and Art Criticism*. Paul Guyer supplied especially useful information concerning the intricacies of rationalist-idealist aesthetics.

Chapter 5

Béla Balázs

VISIBLE MAN, OR THE CULTURE OF FILM

[Editor's note: This is from a new translation of Balázs' 1924 book, published originally in German as *Der sichtbare Mensch oder die Kultur des Films*. The full translation is forthcoming. See *Béla Balázs, Early Film Theory:* Visible Man and The Spirit of Film, trans. Rodney Livingstone (New York: Bergham Books, 2010).]

THE DISCOVERY OF PRINTING has gradually rendered the human face illegible. People have been able to glean so much from reading that they could afford to neglect other forms of communication.

Victor Hugo once wrote that the printed book has taken over the role of mediaeval cathedrals and has become the repository of the spirit of the people. But the thousands of books fragmented the single spirit of the cathedrals into a myriad different opinions. The printed word smashed the stone to smithereens and broke up the church into a thousand books.

In this way, the *visible spirit* was transformed into a legible spirit, and a *visual culture* was changed into a conceptual one. . . . Since the advent of printing the word has become the principal bridge joining human beings to one another. The soul has migrated into the word and become crystallized there. The body, however, has been stripped of soul and emptied.

The expressive surface of our bodies has been reduced to just our face. This is not simply because we cover the other parts of our bodies with clothes. Our face has now come to resemble a clumsy little semaphore of the soul, sticking up in the air and signalling as best it may. Sometimes, our hands help out a little, evoking the melancholy of mutilated limbs. The back of a headless Greek torso always reveals whether the lost face was laughing or weeping – we can still see this clearly. Venus's hips smile as expressively as her face, and casting a veil over her head would not be enough to stop us from guessing her thoughts and feelings. For in those days man was visible in his entire body. In a culture dominated by words, however, now that the soul has become audible, it has grown almost invisible. This is what the printing press has done.

Well, the situation now is that once again our culture is being given a radically new direction – this time by film. Every evening many millions of people sit and experience human destinies, characters, feelings and moods of every kind with their eyes, and without the need for words. For the intertitles that films still have are insignificant; they are partly the ephemeral rudiments of as yet undeveloped forms, and partly they bear a special meaning that does not set out to assist the visual expression. The whole of mankind is now busy relearning the long-forgotten language of gestures and facial expressions. This language is not the substitute for words characteristic of sign language for the deaf-and-dumb, but the visual corollary of human souls immediately made flesh. *Man will become visible once again.*

Modern philologists and historians of language have established that the origins of language are to be found in *expressive movements*. By this we mean that when man began to speak he began like a child, by moving his tongue and lips in the same way as his hands and his facial muscles; in other words, uttering sounds was not his original intention. Initially, the movements of his tongue and lips were no more than spontaneous gestures, on a par with other bodily gestures. The fact that he uttered sounds at the same time was a secondary phenomenon, one subsequently exploited for practical purposes. The immediately visible spirit was then transformed into a mediated audible spirit and much was lost in the process, as in all translation. But the language of gestures is the true mother tongue of mankind.

We are beginning to recall this language and are poised to learn it anew. As yet, it is still clumsy and primitive, and far from able to rival the subtleties of modern verbal art. But because its roots in human nature are older and deeper than the spoken language, and because it is nevertheless fundamentally new, its stammerings and stutterings often articulate ideas that the artists of the word strive in vain to express.

. . . The culture of words is dematerialized, abstract and over-intellectualized; it degrades the human body to the status of a biological organism. But the new language of gestures that is emerging at present arises from our painful yearning to be human beings with our entire bodies, from top to toe and not merely in our speech. We long to stop dragging our body around like an alien thing that is useful only as a practical set of tools. This new language arises from our yearning for the embodied human being who has fallen silent, who has been forgotten and has become invisible. . . .

[T]oday this visual man is in an in-between state: no longer there and not yet present. It is a law of nature that any organ that falls into disuse degenerates and atrophies. In the culture of words our bodies were not fully used and have lost their expressiveness in consequence. . . . Culture does not just refer to the beautiful poses of statues in the art galleries, but to the gait and the everyday gestures of people in the street or at their work. Culture means the penetration of the ordinary material of life by the human spirit, and a visual culture would have to find new and different forms with which to express people's behaviour in their daily intercourse with one another. The art of dance cannot do this; it is a task that will be accomplished by film. . . .

In general, culture appears to be taking the road from the abstract mind to the visible body. . . . Conscious knowledge turns into instinctive sensibility: *it is materialized as culture in the body*. The body's expressiveness is always the latest product of a cultural process. This means that however primitive and barbarous the film may be in comparison to *modern* literature, it nevertheless represents the cultural mainstream because it incorporates the direct transformation of spirit into body.

This path leads in two apparently opposite directions. At first glance, it appears as if the language of physiognomy could only increase and intensify the process of estrangement and alienation that started with the confusion of tongues in the Tower of Babel. This cultural path seemed to point towards the isolation of the individual, to loneliness. For after all, following the confusion of tongues in Babel, communities still survived who acquired the words and concepts of their common mother tongue, and a shared dictionary and grammar rescued human beings from the ultimate solitariness of mutual incomprehension. However, the language of gestures is far more individual and personal than the language of words. Admittedly, facial expressions have their own vocabulary of 'conventional' standard forms, so much so that we could and indeed should compile a comparative dictionary of these expressions on the model of comparative linguistics. However, although this language of gestures has its traditions, it is unlike grammar in that it lacks strict rules, whose neglect would be severely punished in school. This language is still so young that it can be smoothly moulded to fit the particular nature of each individual. It is still at the stage where it can be created by the mind, rather than mind being created by it.

On the other hand, the art of film seems to hold out the promise of redemption from the curse of Babel. The screens of the entire world are now starting to project the first *international language* . . . the language of gestures which has become standardized in film.

. . .

Sketches for a theory of film

. . .

Linguistic gesture and the language of gestures

Can we interpret expressive movement and the visual in general as the special province of film? After all, the stage actor also speaks with his whole body and stage decor likewise exists to be looked at.

But the facial expressions and other gestures of a speaking actor are different. They express only what is left over. *Whatever has to be said*, but will not go into words, is added with the aid of the actor's facial muscles and hands.

In film, however, the play of facial expressions is not an optional extra, and this distinction means not only that gestures in film are more explicit and detailed, but that they operate on an entirely different plane. For the speaker brings to light a different stratum of the soul from the one evoked by, say, the musician or dancer. Dependent as he is on language, the gestures that accompany his words spring from the same source as them. Optically, they may seem similar to a dancer's, but they are informed by a different spirit. A speaker's gestures have the same emotional content as his words, for the dimensions of the soul cannot be mixed. It is merely that they refer to words as yet unborn.

A dancer's gestures, however, have their origins elsewhere and they have a different meaning. They are the characteristic expression of a characteristic human being and hence the characteristic material of a characteristic form of art. They are as unrelated to the gestures of a speaker as they are to his words.

I would like to clarify this with an illustration. Every language has a musical component and every word its own melody. But the music of language, although similar acoustically to actual music, possesses no inner musicality. It has the atmosphere of concepts and helps to enhance the process of rational discrimination. However, music is not just an acoustic matter; it is a separate sphere of the soul. And indeed, facial expressions and gestures are themselves no mere optical matter.

I was speaking of dancers. But the film actor does not dance. Nevertheless, he is not dependent on words and plays no part in the rational world of concepts. There appears to be a third realm between the speaker's world of gestures and the decorative expressive movements of the dancer, and this realm has its own form of interiority. The *gestural language* of film is as far removed from the *linguistic gestures* of theatre as it is from dance.

. . .

The play of facial expressions

There was once a French film in which Suzanne Desprès played the lead even though she made no contribution to the 'plot'. The film went like this. In a short overture we see a beggar woman sitting with her dying child, beseeching fate to take pity. Death appears and tells the mother: 'I shall show you the predestined life of your child. Watch it and if you still want her to live, then so be it.' Then the actual film unfolds, the fate of the child a mundane, insignificant story. But the mother, Suzanne Desprès, watches. In the left-hand corner of the film we see her face as she is watching the film, like us, accompanying the adventures of her child with the play of her facial expressions. We watch for an hour and a half as hope, fear, joy, emotion, sadness, courage, the white heat of conviction and the blackness of despair pass across her face. The film's real drama, its essential content, is played out on her face. The 'story' was only the pretext.

. . . Gaumont knew what it was doing to pay Suzanne Desprès such a high fee for her role. For the public and the film business had already discovered something that our aesthetes and literati have not yet noticed. This is that *what matters in film is not the storyline but the lyrical*.

The narrative of feelings

The play of expressions expresses feelings; in other words it is lyrical. It is a form of lyricism that is incomparably richer and fuller of nuance than literary works of whatever kind. Facial expressions are vastly more numerous than words! And looks can express every shade of emotion far more precisely than a description! And how much more personal is the expression of a face than words that others too may use! And how much more concrete and unambiguous is physiognomy than concepts, which are always abstract and general!

It is here that we see the poetry of film at its most authentic and profound. A person who judges a film by its storyline seems to me to resemble someone who says of a love poem: 'What's so special about this poem? She is beautiful and he loves her!' Films, however wonderful, frequently have little more to say. But they say it in a way that poetry cannot match.

There are two particular reasons for this. One is that the meaning of words is in part more time-bound than facial expressions; the other is that since words are uttered in sequence, no simultaneous harmony, no meaningful chords, can arise. I shall explain this further.

There is a film in which Asta Nielsen is looking out of the window and sees someone coming. A mortal fear, a petrified horror, appears on her face. But she gradually realizes that she is mistaken and that the man who is approaching, far from spelling disaster, is the answer to her prayers. The expression of horror on her face is gradually modulated through the entire scale of feelings from hesitant doubt, anxious hope and cautious joy, right through to exultant happiness. We watch her face in closeup for some twenty metres of film. We see every hint of expression around her eyes and mouth and watch them relax one by one and slowly change. For minutes on end we witness the organic *development of her feelings*, and nothing beyond.

Such an emotional development cannot be depicted in words, however poetic. Every word signifies a separate stage, a process that gives rise to a staccato of isolated snapshots of the feelings. The fact is that one word has to have come to an end before another one can begin. *But a facial expression need not have been completed before another one starts to infiltrate it* and gradually displace it entirely. In the *legato* of visual continuity, past and future expressions merge into one another and display not just the individual states of the soul but also the mysterious process of development itself. This narrative of the feelings enables film to give us something unique.

The chords of the emotions

In general, facial expressions are more 'polyphonic' than language. The succession of words resembles the successive notes of a melody. But a face can display the most varied emotions *simultaneously*, like a chord, and the relationships between these different emotions is what creates the rich amalgam of harmonies and modulations. These are the chords of feeling whose essence is in fact their simultaneity. Such simultaneity cannot be expressed in words.

Pola Negri once acted Carmen.[1] She flirted with the truculent José and her face expressed joy and submissiveness at the same time, since she finds some pleasure in having to humble herself a little. But at the moment when José falls at her feet and she sees his weakness and helplessness, the look on her face becomes *superior* and *sad* at the same time. Moreover, she really has just one look in which these different elements cannot be separated out; each expression rubs off on the other. It points to the painful disappointment she feels at realizing that she is the stronger. The woman has lost the battle because she has emerged as victor. But by formulating what happens in words, we just cause a *single* expression to crumble. And as soon as we begin to speak, we somehow say something different.

. . .

The tempo of emotions

In *Way Down East*,[2] Lilian Gish plays a trusting girl who has been seduced. When the man tells her that he has deceived her and made a fool of her, she cannot believe her ears. She knows what he says is true, but wants to believe that he is just joking. And for five whole minutes she laughs and cries by turns, at least a dozen times.

We would need many printed pages to describe the storms that pass over this tiny, pale face. Reading them would also take up much time. But the nature of these feelings lies precisely in the crazy rapidity with which they succeed one another. The effect of this play of facial expressions lies in *its ability to replicate the original tempo of her emotions*.

That is something that words are incapable of. The description of a feeling always lasts longer than the time taken by the feeling itself. The rhythm of our inner turbulence will inevitably be lost in every literary narrative.

The visible possibilities and the morality of physiognomy

In *Fortune's Fool*,[3] Emil Jannings plays the part of the worst kind of profiteer. Every gesture, every facial expression shows him to be a bloodsucker, a remorseless shark. And yet! Somehow or other he remains a sympathetic character. There is something about his face that we cannot help liking. It is his naivety, something childlike, that persists as a covert decency *at the same time* as his dirty looks. It makes us believe that he is capable of kindness. At the end of the film, this better self becomes visible. But the fact that we can see these signs of goodness from the very outset even in his nastiest expressions is a miracle of polyphonic physiognomy.

A good film actor never presents us with surprises. Since film permits of no psychological explanations, the possibility of a change in personality must be plainly written in an actor's face from the outset. What is exciting is to discover a hidden quality, in the corner of the mouth, for example, and to see how from this germ the entire new human being grows and spreads over his entire face. Hebbel's remark, 'Whatever a man is capable of becoming, he already is', can and indeed must become physiognomical reality in the cinema.

The fact that a deeper face is both visible and hidden also provides a clue to the moral significance of physiognomy. For even in film a simple distinction between good people and bad is not enough. In literature the hidden moral qualities of a man can only be shown by loosening his mask or removing it altogether. What we find moving and also exciting in physiognomy, however, is its simultaneity, the fact that it is possible to discover goodness in the very expression of evil. Many a face surprises us with a deeper look, as if gazing out at us through the eyes of a mask.

There are many opportunities for producing tension in all this. A man may be depicted as a rogue and a scoundrel in all his actions. But his face tells us that it cannot be him. This contradiction creates a dilemma for the audience and we impatiently await its resolution. It endows a character with the vitality that only such an enigma can create.

The drama of facial expressions

The play of facial expressions in film is not just lyrical in its function. There are also ways of depicting the external action in purely physiognomic terms. Admittedly, this is a pinnacle that is only rarely attained in the cinema today. I shall give an example. A film by Joe May, *Die Tragödie der Liebe*,[4] contains a regular physiognomical duel. The examining magistrate sits across the bench from the accused. We do not learn what they say to each other. But both dissemble and disguise their true face behind expressions they have assumed. Each tries to discover what lies behind the other's mask. And by using their facial expressions to attack each other and to defend themselves, each strives to provoke his interlocutor into giving himself away by assuming a treacherous expression (just as one might try to induce someone to say more than he intends).

Such a duel of facial expressions is much more exciting than a verbal duel. A statement can be retracted or reinterpreted, but no statement is as utterly revealing as a facial expression.

In a truly artistic film the dramatic climax between two people will always be shown as a dialogue of facial expressions in closeup.

Closeup

I am speaking here of physiognomy and the play of facial expression as if they were a speciality and even a monopoly of film, and yet they also play a pivotal role in the theatre. But it is not to be compared with their importance in film. First, because in the theatre we listen to the words and so (both we and the actors) fail to concentrate on the characters' faces and notice only the crudest, most schematic, expressions. Second, the actor has to speak clearly for our ears and this impairs the spontaneous movements of the mouth and hence of the face as a whole. Third, because on the stage – for obvious technical reasons – we can never observe a face for so long, in such detail and as intensively as in a film closeup.

The closeup is the technical precondition for the art of facial expression and hence of the higher art of film in general. A face has to be brought really close to us and it must be isolated from any context that might distract our attention (likewise something that is not possible on the stage); we must be able to dwell on the sight so as to be able to read it properly. The film calls for a subtlety and assurance in depicting facial expressions of which actors who just appear on the stage can only dream. In closeups every wrinkle becomes a crucial element of character and every twitch of a muscle testifies to a pathos that signals great inner events. The closeup of a face is frequently used as the climax of an important scene; it must be the lyrical essence of the entire drama. If the sudden appearance of such an image is not to appear meaningless, we have to be able to recognize its links with the drama as a whole. The latter will be reflected in its features, just as a small lake reflects all the mountains that surround it. In the theatre, even the most important face is never more than one element in the play. In the film, however, when a face spreads over the entire screen in a closeup, this face becomes 'the whole thing' that contains the entire drama for minutes on end.

. . .

Closeups are film's true terrain. With the closeup the new territory of this new art opens up. It bears the name: 'The little things of life'. But even the biggest things of life consist of these 'little things', individual details and single moments, while the larger contours are mainly the result of the insensitivity and sloppiness with which we ignore the little things and blur their outlines. The abstract picture of the big things of life arises mainly from our myopia.

But the magnifying glass of the cinematograph brings us closer to the individual cells of life, it allows us to feel the texture and substance of life in its concrete detail. It shows you what your hand is doing, though normally you take no notice when it strokes someone or hits out at them. You live in it and pay no attention to it. The magnifying glass of the film camera will show you your shadow on the wall, something you live with without noticing, and it will show you the adventures and the ultimate fate of the cigar in your unsuspecting hand, and the secret – because unheeded – life of all the things that accompany you on your way and that taken together make up the events of your life. You have observed life much as a bad musician observes an orchestral piece. He hears only the leading melody and the rest of it merges into a general sound. Through its closeups a good film will teach you to read the score of the polyphony of life, the individual voices of all things which go to make up the great symphony.

In a good film, the decisive moment of the actual storyline is never shown in long shot. For in a long shot you can never see what is really happening. When I see a finger pulling the trigger and after that see the wound breaking open, then I have seen the start and finish of an action, its birth and transformation. Everything that comes between those two events is invisible, like a bullet in flight.

The director guides your gaze

What is specific to film about these closeups? After all, the theatre director could also carefully prepare such individual effects on the stage. The answer lies in the possibility of lifting the single image out of the whole. This not only enables us to see the minute atoms of life more clearly than anything on stage, but in addition the director uses them to guide our gaze. On the stage we always see the total picture in which these small moments dwindle into insignificance. But if they are emphasized, they lose the mood created by their very obscurity. By contrast, in film the director guides our gaze with the aid of closeups and also follows up the long shot with shots showing the hidden corners in which the mute life of things retains its secret mood.

The closeup in film is the art of emphasis. It is a mute pointing to important and significant detail, while at the same time providing an interpretation of the life depicted. Two films with the same plot, the same acting and the same long shots but with different closeups will express two different views of life.

The naturalism of love

Closeups are a kind of naturalism. They amount to the sharp observation of detail. However, such observation contains an element of tenderness, and I should like to call it the naturalism of love. For what you truly love, you also know well, and you gaze upon its minutest details with fond attentiveness. (Needless to say, there is also a sharp observation driven by hatred that we may likewise call naturalism.) In films with many good closeups you often gain the impression that these shots are not so much the product of a good eye as of a good heart. They radiate warmth, a diffuse lyricism whose particular artistic significance is that it moves us without lapsing into sentimentality. It remains impersonal and objective. A tender feeling towards things is aroused without being made explicit (or described in the usual clichés).

'Inserting' extreme closeups

Over and above the closeup, the tools with which to achieve emphasis include the concentration of lighting, 'effects lighting', and background shots. All of these present a director with the problem of visual linkage. . . . Linkage, in other words the sequence of images and their tempo, corresponds to style in literature. The fact that the same story can be told in very different ways and with different effects depends on the conciseness and the rhythm of the individual sentences. In the same way, linkage will give the film its rhythmic character. It will ensure that the images will flow smoothly and in a broad stream, like the hexameter in a classical epic, or else like a ballad, flaring up breathlessly and then dying down again, like a drama, rising inexorably towards a climax, or tingling capriciously. Linkage is the living breath of film and everything depends on it.

The first problem in linkage arises from the fact that the images cannot be conjugated. We can write, 'The hero *went* home, and when he entered . . .'. But an image exists only in the present and so the film can only show him *going*. Or else nothing at all. And the question is, 'What can and what should we leave out?'

Directors who come to film from the theatre often bring with them the prejudice about 'concentrating on essentials' and the need to 'focus' on large, detailed and crucial set-piece scenes. This means that there is always something of a chilling vacuum in the intervening scenes. The living, warm flow of life congeals into great blocks of ice.

However, the 'essentials' in a film are located elsewhere than on the stage, in a different dimension. The novelist knows full well why he does not present his story in three great concentrated acts, why he narrates a thousand little 'incidental' happenings. It is because he is interested in knitting together the texture of the atmosphere that is always ruptured and destroyed when the meaning of the action is revealed in a spectacular scene. This meaning may be the kernel of the entire work. But a kernel does not produce a fruit's juice and aroma.

Yet the words a novelist has to use are always clear-cut concepts whose sharp claws scratch an unambiguous meaning from everything, while the purely visual nature of film enables us to see that *indeterminate something* that can only ever appear between the lines even in the best of novelists. A good director will work with a 'thin flow' of images linking a number of subsidiary scenes in ways that will always seem surprising and new to us, like snapshots of movements that show us quite unfamiliar positions of the body. But the movement of life itself also consists of such unfamiliar positions (positions of the soul) that are easily obliterated by a focus on 'essentials', but that are revealed to us by film for the first time.

Interpolated images

The exclusively present nature of images means that our *experience of time* in a film is an especially problematic aspect of visual linkage. Because the original running time of an action is presented in a visually continuous sequence of images, the only way to 'let time pass' is to interrupt the scene by interpolating extra images. But the mere length of such interpolated images is not enough to enable the audience to gauge *how much* time has elapsed.

Length of time is a mood, not an objective fact to be measured by the clock. Whether we feel that one minute has passed or many hours depends on the rhythm of a scene, the space in which it is set and even the way it is lit. There are curious connections between our sense of time and space and they deserve closer psychological investigation. For example, the fact that *the further the location of an interpolated scene is from that of the principal scene, the greater is the illusion that a longer time has elapsed*. If we interrupt a scene in a room with another in the hall, however long the second scene lasts it does not suggest much more time has passed than the time taken by the scene itself. But if the interpolated scene leads us into a different town or even a foreign country, it will arouse the illusion of such a great shift of 'time–space' that we shall not find it easy to transport ourselves back into the original scene.

The twin necessities of interpolated scenes on the one hand and visual continuity on the other often appear to present an almost insoluble contradiction and turn visual linkage into the director's most delicate task. He has to know how to ensure that the mood of one scene continues to illuminate the mood of the following one. Just as the colour in a painting takes on a different hue depending on the colours adjacent to it, so too the mood of one scene will be influenced by the scene that precedes it. An interpolated scene, therefore, may diverge from the main action but must be related to it in mood.

This continuity of mood also helps to maintain the memory of what has gone before and also the general context, thus replacing the need to rely on the expedient of titles. Small motifs, objects, gestures and sometimes just the lighting can all evoke the associations of an earlier scene and, like visual leitmotifs that barely cross the threshold of consciousness, they enable us to grasp the main thrust of the plot.

Passageways

It is necessary here to say something about scenes of passage. These are transitional scenes that show us only how a character moves from one location to another. Many directors, especially those who come to cinema from the theatre, used to be strongly prejudiced against these scenes, regarding them as dead spaces in the film, clumsy expedients.

But passageways contain a film's lyrical element. The hero's solitary comings and goings before and after his great scene are his soliloquies, and in film these are not even 'unnatural'. Thanks to its *ritardando* effect, the hero's progress to the decisive scene can produce a preparatory tension, an atmospheric springboard, and the image of passage following the dramatic climax can present its impact, the emotional result. It can achieve this far more effectively than the climactic scene itself, where the events of the external action often obscure their internal ramifications.

In these performed monologues of walking, an actor can often display his art more fully than in the most turbulent dramatic scenes. The reason is that these latter scenes are full of gestures that have not merely an *inner motive* but also an *external purpose*. Such purposive gestures are not simply expressive in function; they are partly determined by the external action and hence do not provide an actor with the same opportunity to express emotions as an image of passage. When two men walk quietly side by side, their gait will reveal the differences in their characters. If they are fighting, however, even the wildest movements will cease to express the subtle differences of character and mood between them.

I can very well imagine an impressionist cinematic style – I might also term it a Maeterlinckian style – in which the principal scenes are not shown at all, but only the presentiments and lyrical after-effects of the events concerned – moments of passage.

In *The Phantom*,[5] Alfred Abel spends a lot of time wandering alone through the streets. But nowhere else in the film do we see so clearly that here is a lost soul, a deluded man who has gone astray, a man intoxicated by dreams who is doomed to fall into the abyss. In the scenes with other people we can still entertain the belief that the danger comes from them and that he might well be spared. But when he is alone, the way he walks tells us that the danger is in himself. He is inwardly wounded and he staggers around like a man who has been shot. (And in general, the way a protagonist walks expresses the gesture governing his destiny.)

And to see Conrad Veidt's walk! It is hard to imagine a film whose main dramatic scenes could equal the intensity of Veidt's images of passage. The way he walks as the sleepwalking medium in *Caligari* is like the slow, very slow, flight of an arrow bringing an ineluctable death. And in general, Veidt's gait resembles a spear cleaving the space in front of it and pointing to the direction fate intends to take.

In one film Lilian Gish plays a poor girl looking in vain for work and we see her walking along the street, exhausted and desperate. Every step she takes is like someone shutting her eyes, letting her head droop and falling under the wheels of a car.

Needless to say, passageways must not be treated as being of secondary importance. There are directors who prepare the decisive scenes with great care and ensure that they are played by the very best actors. But once the hero has left the room, the same directors may well ignore the servant who helps him into his coat or the chauffeur who opens the car door for him. Such interpolated scenes are treated as nothing more than dead linking material, as mere glue, and are not 'acted' at all. But such lifeless gaps act like a blast of cold air on the rest of the film; the audience does not notice where the cold comes from, but may feel the chill nonetheless. However, if directors keep a tight rein on even the tiniest scenes they will give the film a *continuity of illusion* that creates an atmospheric warmth that cannot be pinned down and that permeates the film as a whole.

Simultaneism and refrain

Visual linkage in film contains the most varied stylistic possibilities. I should like to refer to just two that I believe will play a special role in modern developments. The first style, one that can already be seen here and there, I should like to call 'simultaneism', after the most modern school of lyric poetry, with Walt Whitman as its most significant representative. For it is based on the same intention, namely the wish to present not merely a single image of the world at large, but a number of *simultaneous* events, even if there is no causal relationship between these events and the principal one, or among these simultaneous events themselves. By means of this cross-section of life as a *whole*, the aim is to create a cosmic impression, an impression of the entire world, since this alone can depict the world in its reality.

Abel Gance made attempts of this sort; he strove to depict not just an action but at the same time its entire context. For example, when we follow the fate of his hero in Paris, the narrative is constantly interrupted by momentary flashes in which we see villages, people working in the fields, or a girl at a window. None of these things is relevant to the plot, but they represent a simultaneous reality. In that reality life is going on as usual and that should not be forgotten.

I believe that the theoretical hopes placed in this style cannot be fulfilled in practice. They give the film *a false dimension*; a dimension of breadth instead of depth. To convey depth film should focus not on the neglected images of remote distances, but on the neglected images of things close to us, the invisible aspects of our own experienced moments. Furthermore, by inserting the action together with a number of motifs into a spatial perspective that evinces no sign of a before and after, such a simultaneous representation of the surrounding circumstances nullifies all sense of time.

   . . .

Tempo

In general, tempo is one of the most fascinating and important secrets of film. . . . A long take means something different from a short one. The length or brevity of a scene is not just a matter of rhythm, but rather it *determines its meaning*. (A doubtless vain reminder to distributors and cinema proprietors and all those who cut the director's work without his consent.) Every second counts. Just cut a metre of film and the scene – if it was a good one – will not only be shorter but have changed its meaning. It has been given a new mood-content.

Moreover, it often will have become shorter only in terms of physical length; in its mood it will have lengthened. The internal tempo of the images is entirely independent of the time required to show them in reality. There are scenes in which, by showing a large number of minor objects in closeup, the passing of the seconds produces the effect of dramatic tempo. When these details are cut, what remains is a general image that is no more than a lifeless frame. This may well take less time to see but it is not possible to fill such a frame with tension.

We can illustrate this situation with the aid of a simile that is perhaps not quite exact: if I look at the picture of an anthill in closeup, with the detailed images of its teeming activity, such images will have tempo. But if I shorten it by cutting out the closeups so that I am left with the generalized picture of an ant heap, a mere geometrical shape, the act of cutting will result only in filling the film with internal *longueurs*.

In the cinema every storyline resembles such an ant heap. The closer and more detailed our view, the more life and tempo it has. But when the events are just noted fleetingly, they are drained of all vitality. When an event just flits past, we merely *note its presence* without actually seeing it. It does not come to life before our eyes and has only the meaning of a kind of literature in hieroglyphs. Moreover, on its own even a concept, a word, can have no tempo, and the brief synopsis of a novel will always be more boring than the novel itself.

There are films that produce one interesting scene after another and yet are quite lacking in tension because scarcely have we reached one situation than the film's faulty tempo hustles us on to the next. A protracted duel makes for a more exciting scene than the lightning thrust of a dagger. It seems in general as if *the only thing that produces tempo in a scene is the mobility of the atoms of which it is composed*. This is because the spoken word can always call to mind the plot in its entirety, but it is only the momentary that enables us to *see*.

Notes

1   *Carmen / Gypsy Blood* (Ernst Lubitsch, 1918) was a film version not of Bizet's opera but of the story by Prosper Mérimée that had inspired it. This and all following notes are the translator's.
2   *Way Down East* (D.W. Griffith, 1920).
3   Also known as *Alles für Geld / All for Money* (Reinhold Schünzel, 1923).
4   *Die Tragödie der Liebe / The Tragedy of Love* (Joe May, 1923) featured Emil Jannings and, in a lesser role, Marlene Dietrich.
5   *The Phantom / Phantom* (F.W. Murnau, 1922), with Alfred Abel in the lead role, was based on a novel by Gerhart Hauptmann.

Chapter 6

Malcolm Turvey

BALÁZS: REALIST OR MODERNIST?

I

IN *THE WORLD VIEWED*, Stanley Cavell argues that "film is a moving image of skepticism."[1] Due to what he calls its "automatism," its removal of "the human agent from the
task of reproduction,"[2] film, he claims, satisfies the wish, born of skepticism and "intensify-
ing in the West since the Reformation, to escape subjectivity and metaphysical isolation—a
wish for the power to reach this world, having for so long tried, at last hopelessly, to
manifest fidelity to another."[3] By skepticism, it should be noted, Cavell does not mean a
rigorously theorized philosophical doctrine, but rather the somewhat vaguer idea, hugely
influential in modernity and still very much with us, that the ability of us human beings to
know the world around us is limited, that we are unable, or fail, to know reality as it really is.

The deep hold of this skeptical idea over film theorists and filmmakers has not, I think,
been given its due. The same is true of that which skepticism gives rise to: the wish to escape
the limits of human knowledge and access reality as it really is. Much film theory and
filmmaking informed by film theory, especially prior to the 1960s, is a euphoric expression
of the belief that in the cinema we finally have at our disposal an artistic medium that satisfies
the skeptical wish identified by Cavell, that overcomes the gulf created by skepticism
between subject and object, self and other, consciousness and nature—our "metaphysical
isolation," to use Cavell's felicitous phrase.

For most, however, it is not only what Cavell calls film's automatism that enables it to
"escape subjectivity" and "reach this world." In the context of film, skepticism has typically
taken the form of claims about the limits of human vision, about our inability to see reality as
it really is, which is unsurprising given that the cinema is widely considered to be a visual art.
And it is the cinema's capacity to reveal truths about reality invisible to human sight that is
viewed by many as the source of its power to escape the limits of human knowledge and access
reality. The major film theorists who conceive of the cinema in this way are Jean Epstein
(1897–1953), Dziga Vertov (1896–1954), Siegfried Kracauer (1889–1966), and Béla Balázs
(1884–1949) in the material from *Der sichtbare Mensch* (*The Visible Man*, 1924), his first book of
film theory, which he includes in *Theory of the Film* (1948), his third, and which he elaborates
on in other chapters of *Theory of the Film*, such as chapter eight, titled "The Face of Man."

Like Epstein, Vertov, and Kracauer (in *Theory of Film*, 1960), Balázs answers the question What is Cinema? in this material by arguing that one of the cinema's most significant properties is its capacity to reveal features of reality invisible to the naked human eye: "In the silent film facial expression, isolated from its surroundings [by the close-up], seemed to penetrate to a strange new dimension of the soul. It revealed to us a new world—a world of micro-physiognomy which could not otherwise be seen with the naked eye or in everyday life."[4] And again like these theorists, Balázs often compares the cinema to other visual technologies, in particular the microscope:

> The technique of the close-up . . . was able to make us feel nerve-rackingly the sultry tension underneath the superficial calm; the fierce storms raging under the surface were made tangible by mere microscopic movements, by the displacement of a hair. Such films were unsurpassed in showing the Strindbergian moods in the savagely antagonistic silences of human beings confined together in narrow spaces. The micro-tragedies in the peace and quiet of ordinary families were shown as deadly battles, just as the microscope shows the fierce struggles of micro-organisms in a drop of water.
>
> (TTF, pp. 84–85)

Like these theorists, Balázs also attaches considerable significance and value to the cinema's revelatory capacity. Indeed, he claims that this capacity has brought about the evolution of new perceptual and cognitive abilities in human beings: "The birth of film art led not only to the creation of new works of art but to the emergence of new human faculties with which to perceive and understand this new art" (TTF, p. 33). And he declares that it is the task of his film theory to "investigate and outline that sphere of the development of human sensibility which developed in mutual interaction with the evolution of the art of the film" (TTF, p. 33). Because it has led to the evolution of new perceptual and cognitive abilities, Balázs pronounces the invention of the cinema to be an epochal transformation for the better in human existence:

> The evolution of the human capacity for understanding, which was brought about by the art of the film, opened a new chapter in the history of human culture. . . . We were witnesses not only to the development of a new art but to the development of a new sensibility, a new understanding, a new culture in its public. . . . We have learned to see.
>
> (TTF, pp. 34–35)

But unlike Epstein and Vertov, Balázs argues (as does Kracauer in *Theory of Film*) that it is, in part, a *historical* limitation that normal human vision suffers from, a limitation from which it can potentially recover. For Epstein and Vertov, the eye is flawed and unreliable because of innate, physiological handicaps, which cannot be overcome (except perhaps by evolution). For Epstein, the eye shrouds reality in deceptive, anthropomorphic appearances:

> These [cinematic] experiments contradict and throw into confusion the sense of order which we have established at great cost in our conception of the universe. Yet it is hardly news that any classification has something of the arbitrary about it and that we abandon frameworks that seem overly artificial. The generalized sense of our own psychological time, which still varies very little, turns out to be an illusion that we have created in order to think more easily. The gaze

which cinematography lets us cast over nature, where such time is neither unique nor constant, is perhaps more fecund than the one we cast out of egocentric habit. . . . Not without some anxiety, man finds himself before that chaos which he has covered up, denied, forgotten, or thought was tamed. Cinema apprises him of a monster.[5]

In 1921, for example, Epstein evokes the scientific doctrine of "secondary qualities" to make this point:

The senses, of course, present us only with symbols of reality: uniform, proportionate, elective metaphors. And symbols not of matter, which therefore does not exist, but of energy; that is, of something which in itself seems not to be, except in its effects as they affect us. We say "red," "soprano," "sweet," "cypress," when there are only velocities, movements, vibrations.[6]

By contrast, the cinema is able to reveal what is hidden by such secondary qualities, namely, reality as it really is: the "waves invisible to us, and the screen's creative passion [which] contains what no other has ever had before; its proper share of ultraviolet."[7] For Vertov, meanwhile, the eye is very bad at processing visual data into organized, intelligible patterns. Hence, human beings are normally confused by what they see. Vertov gives as an example stage performances. "The viewer at a ballet follows, in confusion, now the combined legs of dancers, now random individual figures, now someone's legs—a series of scattered perceptions, different for each viewer."[8] The cinema, according to Vertov, is able to overcome this limitation, "bring[ing] clarity into the worker's awareness of the phenomena concerning him and surrounding him,"[9] because of the precision with which editing can be used to organize visual phenomena recorded on film into harmonious patterns—based upon geometrical principles—that can be understood by the viewer:

Within the *chaos* of movements, running past, away, running into and colliding—the eye, all by itself, enters life.

A day of visual impressions has passed. How is one to construct the impressions of the day into an effective whole, a visual study? If one films everything the eye has seen, the result, of course, will be a *jumble*. If one skillfully edits what's been photographed, the result will be clearer. If one scraps bothersome waste, it will be better still. One obtains an organized memo of the ordinary eye's impressions.[10]

But for Balázs, at least in part, human beings cannot see properly because they have forgotten how to, due to historically specific forces at work in modernity.

According to Balázs, the invention of the printing press made language and the printed word the dominant media through which human beings express their inner, mental lives in modernity, giving rise to what Balázs calls a "word culture": "The printing press has grown to be the main bridge over which the more remote interhuman spiritual exchanges take place and the soul has been concentrated and crystallized chiefly in the word" (TTF, p. 41). The result, for Balázs, is that within modernity, human beings have almost totally lost the capacity to express the inner with their faces and bodies: "The animals that do not chew lose their teeth. In the epoch of word culture we made little use of the expressive powers of our body and have therefore partly lost that power" (TTF, p. 42). The loss of this ability means that the dimension of the inner that used to be expressed by the face and body can no longer be expressed:

We had, however, when we neglected the body as a means of expression, lost more than mere corporal power of expression. That which was to have been expressed was also narrowed down by this neglect. For it is not the same spirit, not the same soul that is expressed once in words and once in gestures.

(TTF, p. 42)

While language is capable of expressing the inner, it cannot express the same dimension of the inner as facial expression and bodily behavior. Language and the body each express different realms of the inner.

> Those who do not speak may be brimming over with emotions which can be expressed only in forms and pictures, in gesture and play of feature. The man of visual culture uses these not as substitutes for words, as a deaf-mute uses his fingers. He does not think in words, the syllables of which he sketches in the air like the dots and dashes of the Morse code. The gestures of visual man are not intended to convey concepts which can be expressed in words, but such inner experiences, such non-rational emotions which would still remain unexpressed when everything that can be told has been told. Such emotions lie in the deepest levels of the soul and cannot be approached by words that are mere reflections of concepts; just as our musical experiences cannot be expressed in rationalized concepts. What appears on the face and in facial expression is a spiritual experience which is rendered immediately visible without the intermediary of words.
>
> (TTF, p. 40)

With the loss of the face and body's ability to express the inner comes a concomitant spiritual impoverishment in modernity. That realm of the inner that can only be expressed by the face and body—the realm of "non-rational emotions"—remains unexpressed, leaving just the "rational, conceptual culture" of the word (TTF, p. 43).

The loss of the capacity to use the face and body to express the inner in turn has an impact on normal human vision, and it is in describing this impact that the influence on Balázs of skepticism emerges. Human beings have forgotten how to see the face and body as expressive of the inner in the "word culture" of modernity, according to Balázs. They have lost this visual capacity or skill, because the face and body are no longer used to express the inner. Meanwhile, because the cinema lacks synchronized sound in the silent era, actors are forced to relearn how to express the inner through facial expression and bodily behavior. This is why Balázs in his early film theory believes that the cinema is bringing about the evolution of new perceptual and cognitive abilities in human beings.

> Now the film is about to inaugurate a new direction in our culture. Many million people sit in the picture houses every evening and purely through vision, experience happenings, characters, emotions, moods, even thoughts, without the need for many words. Humanity is already learning the rich and colorful language of gesture, movement, and facial expression. This is not a language of signs as a substitute for words, like the sign language of the deaf and dumb—it is the visual means of communication, without intermediary of souls clothed in flesh. Man has again become visible.
>
> (TTF, p. 41)

Due to the cinema's lack of synchronized sound, actors are forced to express the inner through the face and body. From them, human beings are once again relearning how to "read" the "language" of the face and body:

> Now we are beginning to remember and relearn this tongue. It is still clumsy and primitive and very far removed as yet from the refinements of word art. But already it is beginning to be able sometimes to express things that escape the artists of the word. How much of human thought would remain unexpressed if we had no music! The now developing art of facial expression and gesture will bring just as many submerged contents to the surface. Although these human experiences are not rational, conceptual contents, they are nevertheless neither vague nor blurred, but as clear and unequivocal as is music. Thus the inner man, too, will become visible.
>
> (TTF, p. 42)

According to Balázs, therefore, normal human vision suffers from a historical limitation specific to the "word culture" of modernity. Because this limitation is only historical, as opposed to physiological, the eye can potentially recover from it, and this is precisely what Balázs believed was starting to happen in the silent era. The cinema, he thought, was re-educating human beings in how to use and understand the language of facial expression and bodily behavior. What Balázs calls the "submerged," "unexpressed" realm of the inner was becoming visible again for the first time since the invention of the printing press. With the arrival of synchronized sound, however, all of this changed. Actors reverted to spoken language to express the inner, and the new education being offered by cinema in the silent era was cut short.

Balázs's skepticism about normal human vision is an idiosyncratic version of what can be called the "modern consciousness" theory, which has its roots in Romanticism. This argues that various forces in modernity—principally science, technology, and the putative penetration of "instrumental reason" into all spheres of human existence—have had a profound effect on human beings. These forces have actually altered the way that the average person's mind works, giving rise to a distinctively modern form of consciousness that is overly "rationalistic" and intrinsically divorced from the senses, the body, and nature in general. Rudolf Arnheim nicely summarizes key elements of this view at the beginning of *Art and Visual Perception* (1954):

> We have neglected the gift of comprehending things through our senses. Concept is divorced from precept, and thought moves among abstractions. Our eyes have been reduced to instruments with which to identify and to measure; hence we suffer a paucity of ideas that can be expressed in images and an incapacity to discover meaning in what we see. Naturally we feel lost in the presence of objects that make sense only to undiluted vision, and we seek refuge in the more familiar medium of words.[11]

We can unweave several strands in this familiar generalization about modern consciousness. First is the argument that it is divided into two realms, the mental and the physical, and that they are divorced from each other ("concept is divorced from precept"). Second is the suggestion that the overly rationalistic mental realm dominates the physical senses, particularly the eyes ("our eyes have been reduced to instruments with which to identify and measure"). As a result, human beings no longer attend to what the senses have to teach them independently of the mental realm ("we have neglected the gift of comprehending things through our senses"). Finally, there is the claim that people now typically "seek refuge" in the more familiar mental realm of "abstractions," "concept[s]," and the "medium of words," rather than the physical realm of the senses, because rationalistic consciousness no longer knows how to learn from "undiluted vision," namely, vision functioning independently of the mental.

Clearly, this theory evinces a deep skepticism about the normal exercise of the visual faculty, seeing it as part of a modern consciousness enslaved to rational, instrumental imperatives. Human beings have lost the capacity of gaining purely visual knowledge of reality in modernity ("the gift of comprehending things through our senses"; "undiluted vision"). Balázs modifies this theory by placing an intermediary stage—the use of language in place of the face and body to express the inner—in between the tendency to "seek refuge in the more familiar medium of words" and the failure to attend to what the senses have to teach independently of language. It is the use of language in place of the face and body, due to the dominance of language in the "word culture" of modernity, which results in human beings forgetting how to see the face and body of another as expressive of mind, according to Balázs.

As we shall see in a moment, this did not mean, however, that for Balázs the realm of the inner expressed by the face and body once again became "submerged" and "unexpressed" when synchronized sound arrived, as it had been prior to the invention of cinema. According to Balázs, normal human vision also suffers from a second limitation, namely, its failure to see details:

> By means of the close-up the camera in the days of the silent film revealed also the hidden mainsprings of a life that we had thought we already knew so well. Blurred outlines are mostly the result of our insensitive short-sightedness and superficiality. We skim over the teeming substance of life. The camera has uncovered that cell life of the vital issues in which all great events are ultimately conceived; for the greatest landslide is only the aggregate of the movements of single particles. A multitude of close-ups can show us the very instant in which the general is transformed into the particular. The close-up has not only widened our vision of life, it has also deepened it. In the days of the silent film it not only revealed new things, but showed us the meaning of the old.
>
> (TTF, p. 55)

Human beings, Balázs argues again and again, are very bad at noticing details. They tend to "skim over the teeming substance of life." They look at reality

> as a concert-goer ignorant of music listens to an orchestra playing a symphony. All he hears is the leading melody, all the rest is blurred into a general murmur. Only those who can really understand and enjoy the music can hear the contra-puntal architecture of each part in the score. This is how we see life: only its leading melody meets the eye.
>
> (TTF, p. 55)

It is not clear from these passages whether Balázs believes that the inability to notice details is an innate physiological limitation of normal human vision or a visual habit that can be corrected. But either way, it is a limitation that the cinema overcomes, primarily through the close-up: "But a good film with its close-ups reveals the most hidden parts in our polyphonous life, and teaches us to see the intricate visual details of life as one reads an orchestra score" (TTF, p. 55). Because it isolates and magnifies, the close-up reveals details that are invisible to sight: "An ant-heap is life-less if seen from a distance, but at close quarters it is teeming with busy life. The gray, dull texture of everyday life shows in its microdramatics many profoundly moving happenings, if we look at it carefully enough in close-up" (TTF, p. 86).

Because the naked eye cannot see details, it is unable to see the inner expressed in the details of the faces and bodies of others. But the close-up isolates, magnifies, and therefore renders visible the inner manifested in the details of a face or body; "But in the isolated close-up of the film we can see to the bottom of a soul by means of such tiny movements of facial muscles which even the most observant partner would never perceive" (TTF, p. 63). Thus, the realm of the inner expressed by the face and body did not once again become "submerged" and "unexpressed" when synchronized sound arrived. Although this happened to some extent, the use of the close-up in sound film ensured that this realm of the inner remained partially visible, even though actors were no longer forced to use their faces and bodies to express themselves because of synchronized dialogue. This is because the close-up, by isolating and magnifying the details of the faces and bodies it films, can reveal the inner expressed in those details—details that the naked eye cannot see unaided.

To summarize, though human beings cannot see details or the face and body as expressive of the inner due to the "word culture" of modernity, the cinema escapes these limits because, in the silent era, actors are forced to learn how to express themselves through their faces and bodies, thereby educating the film viewer to see the face and body as expressive of mind; and because the close-up isolates and magnifies details invisible to normal vision. It is for this reason that Balázs believes that the cinema can initiate an epochal transformation for the better in human existence. Its revelatory capacity rescues human beings from the particular type of blindness that, due to skepticism, he believes the naked eye to be suffering from: an inability to see other minds.

II

I have argued that Balázs, like Epstein, Vertov, and the later Kracauer, answers the question What is Cinema? by arguing that one of the cinema's most significant properties is its capacity to reveal truths about reality invisible to the naked human eye. This answer is different from the two answers to this question that have dominated film theorizing since it began. The first of these is that the cinema's most significant property, at least for the purpose of creating art, is "its capacity to manipulate reality, that is, to rearrange and thereby reconstitute the profilmic event (the event that transpires in front of the camera)."[12] This answer is identified as modernist because it is predicated on conceptions of art prevalent in modernism—anti-imitation, medium-specificity—and it was the most popular answer among film theorists until the 1930s, the period when the influence of modernism was at its height. Furthermore, like modernism, it reemerged with renewed vigor in the 1950s.

A famous example of this modernist answer is provided by Arnheim in his *Film as Art*, first published in 1932. According to Arnheim, if a filmmaker wishes to create a work of art, he cannot simply reproduce what is in front of the camera. Rather, he must express something about what is in front of the camera using uniquely cinematic techniques. This is because Arnheim has an anti-imitation and a medium-specificity conception of art, both prevalent in modernism:

> The film producer himself is influenced by the strong resemblance of his photo-graphic material to reality. As distinguished from the tools of the sculptor and the painter, which by themselves produce nothing resembling nature, the camera starts to turn and a likeness of the real world results mechanically. There

is serious danger that the filmmaker will rest content with such shapeless reproduction. In order that the film artist may create a work of art it is important that he consciously stress the peculiarities of his medium. This, however, should be done in such a manner that the character of the objects represented should not thereby be destroyed but rather strengthened, concentrated, and interpreted.[13]

Although they would not necessarily agree with Arnheim's expression conception of art— his claim that "the character of . . . objects represented should not . . . be destroyed but rather strengthened, concentrated, and interpreted"—many other modernist film theorists argue that the cinema's most significant property is its capacity to manipulate reality. They include German psychologist Hugo Münsterberg; Soviet montage filmmakers of the 1920s, such as Lev Kuleshov and Sergei Eisenstein; and most of the French Impressionist filmmakers of the 1920s, such as Germaine Dulac.

The second of the historically dominant answers to the question What is Cinema? is that the cinema's most significant property is its capacity to reproduce, rather than manipulate, reality. The most famous representative of this answer is probably André Bazin, who grew to maturity during the 1930s when realism renewed its influence on western artists and intellectuals. Bazin offers a number of arguments in his writings for why this is so. One focuses on the fact that photographs mechanically record reality. When exposed, the chemicals on the surface of a film automatically register the light emanating from whatever the camera is pointing toward. According to Bazin, a photograph therefore "shares, by virtue of the very process of its becoming, the being of the model of which it is the reproduction; it *is* the model."[14] This means that, for the first time in history, photographs allow human beings to "re-present" reality. Cinema goes one step further than still photography in re-presenting reality because, "for the first time, the image of things is likewise the image of their duration, change mummified as it were."[15] Because Bazin believes that human beings have "a basic psychological need . . . to have the last word in the argument with death by means of the form that endures,"[16] and because photography and cinema offer an unprecedented way of satisfying this need by re-presenting reality, he concludes that the cinema's most significant property, especially with the advent of synchronized sound, is its capacity to reproduce reality, not manipulate it.

While I do not dispute that these two answers—the modernist and the realist—to the question What is Cinema? are historically dominant in film theory even to this day, there are others, including the one advanced by Epstein, Vertov, Balázs, and Kracauer—namely, that the cinema's most significant feature is its capacity to reveal truths about reality invisible to the naked human eye. This answer constitutes a distinct alternative to the historically dominant ones of modernism and realism. For on the one hand, like the realist answer, it views the cinema's ability to reproduce reality as a valuable one, rather than denigrating it, as do modernists such as Arnheim. Epstein, Vertov, Balázs, and Kracauer constantly laud the cinema's capacity to reproduce reality as it really is.

However, as we have seen in the case of Balázs, these film theorists are influenced by a skepticism that takes the form of doubts about normal human vision. It is this that sets them apart from realists such as Bazin, who believe in the capacity of the human eye to see reality as it really is, who have faith in normal human vision. Linda Nochlin cites the writings of the painter Edgar Degas as an example of this faith in everyday sight in nineteenth-century realism:

In his notebooks, Degas reiterated in both words and sketches his passion for concrete, direct observation and notation of ordinary, everyday experience:

"Do every kind of worn object . . . corsets which have just been taken off . . . series on instruments and instrumentalists . . . for example, puffing out and hollowing of the cheeks of bassoons, oboes, etc. . . . . On the bakery, the bread: series on journeyman bakers, seen in the cellar itself or through the air vents from the street. . . . No one has ever done monuments or houses from below, from beneath, up close, as one sees them going by in the streets."[17]

In Bazin's writings, we often encounter a similar faith in normal human vision, and the view that certain films are realist art works because they imitate features of everyday sight. In an article on William Wyler, for example, Bazin argues that " 'Realism' consists not only of showing us a corpse, but also of showing it to us under conditions that re-create certain physiological or mental givens of natural perception."[18] And he celebrates directors such as Jean Renoir and Wyler because they use stylistic techniques such as the long take that, supposedly, better imitate the "givens of natural perception" than editing.

For Epstein, Vertov, Balázs, and Kracauer, the human eye is not to be trusted. It is not a reliable source of information about reality. Hence, contrary to Bazin, these theorists view those stylistic techniques that depart from everyday sight as most likely to reveal reality as it really is, techniques that modernists such as Arnheim typically celebrate due to their anti-imitation, medium-specific conceptions of art: slow motion, fast motion, reverse motion, extreme close-ups or long shots, editing, and so on. As Vertov puts it,

Until now many a cameraman has been criticized for having filmed a running horse moving with unnatural slowness on the screen (rapid cranking of the camera)—or for the opposite, a tractor plowing a field too swiftly (slow cranking of the camera), and the like.

These are chance occurrences, of course, but we are preparing a system, a deliberate system of such occurrences, a system of seeming irregularities to investigate and organize phenomena.

Until now, we have violated the movie camera and forced it to copy the work of the eye. And the better the copy, the better the shooting was thought to be. Starting today we are liberating the camera and making it work in the opposite direction—away from copying.[19]

However, unlike modernists such as Arnheim, Epstein, Vertov, Balázs, and Kracauer do not view these techniques as incompatible with recording and reproducing reality. Rather, they celebrate these techniques, including the cinema's capacity to record reality, because they better enable filmmakers to reproduce reality as it really is, not because they enable filmmakers to avoid "merely" reproducing reality, as they do for Arnheim and other modernists.

Because this answer—call it the revelationist answer—to the question What is Cinema? shares features with both the modernist and realist answers, there has been some debate about how to categorize the work of these film theorists. Dudley Andrew's *The Major Film Theories* (1976), for example, has been criticized by Sabine Hake for placing Balázs along with Arnheim in the "formative" or modernist tradition, and Kracauer in the realist.[20] However, if I am correct, Balázs and our other theorists belong neither in the one nor the other. Rather, they propose an answer to the question What is Cinema? that is distinct from the realist and modernist answers, even while it has features in common with them.[21]

Notes

1   Stanley Cavell, *The World Viewed: Reflections on the Ontology of Film*, Enlarged Edition (Cambridge, Mass.: Harvard University Press, 1979), p. 188. Cavell actually only uses this particular phrase in the essay added to the enlarged edition of *The World Viewed*, titled "More of The World Viewed."

2   Ibid., pp. 20, 23.

3   Ibid., p. 21.

4   Béla Balázs, *Theory of Film (Character and Growth of a New Art)*, trans. Edith Bone (New York: Arno Press, 1972), p. 65. Hereafter cited in the text as TTF.

5   Jean Epstein, "Photogénie and the Imponderable" (1935), in *French Film Theory and Criticism, A History/Anthology, Volume II, 1929–39*, ed. Richard Abel (Princeton, N.J.: Princeton University Press, 1988), p. 190.

6   Jean Epstein, "The Senses I (b)" (1921), in *French Film Theory and Criticism, A History/Anthology, Volume I, 1907–29*, ed. Richard Abel (Princeton, N.J.: Princeton University Press, 1988), p. 244.

7   Ibid.

8   Dziga Vertov, "Kinoks: A Revolution" (1923), in *Kino-Eye: The Writings of Dziga Vertov*, ed. Annette Michelson, trans. Kevin O'Brien (Berkeley: University of California Press, 1984), p. 16.

9   Vertov, "Kino-Eye" (1926), in ibid., p. 73.

10   Vertov, "Kinoks: A Revolution" (1923), pp. 18–19. My emphasis.

11   Rudolf Arnheim, *Art and Visual Perception: A Psychology of the Creative Eye* (Berkeley: University of California Press, 1974), new version, expanded and rev. ed., p. 1.

12   Noël Carroll, *Philosophical Problems of Classical Film Theory* (Princeton, N.J.: Princeton University Press, 1988), p. 7.

13   Rudolf Arnheim, *Film as Art* (1932; Berkeley: University of California Press, 1957), p. 35.

14   André Bazin, "The Ontology of the Photographic Image," in *What Is Cinema?*, vol. 1, trans. Hugh Gray (Berkeley: University of California Press, 1967), p. 14.

15   Ibid., p. 15.

16   Ibid., pp. 9–10.

17   Linda Nochlin, *Realism* (New York: Penguin Books, 1971), p. 19.

18   André Bazin, "William Wyler, or the Jansenist of Directing," in *Bazin at Work*, ed. Bert Cardullo, trans. Alain Piette and Bert Cardullo (New York: Routledge, 1997), p. 7.

19   Vertov, "Kinoks: A Revolution," pp. 15–16.

20   Sabine Hake, *Cinema's Third Machine: Writing on Film in Germany, 1907–33* (Lincoln: University of Nebraska Press, 1993), pp. 213–14.

21   I explore further this revelationist answer, as well as the influence of skepticism on film, in my forthcoming book *Film, Skepticism, and Revelation*.

Chapter 7

André Bazin

THE ONTOLOGY OF THE PHOTOGRAPHIC IMAGE

IF THE PLASTIC ARTS were put under psychoanalysis, the practice of embalming the dead might turn out to be a fundamental factor in their creation. The process might reveal that at the origin of painting and sculpture there lies a mummy complex. The religion of ancient Egypt, aimed against death, saw survival as depending on the continued existence of the corporeal body. Thus, by providing a defense against the passage of time it satisfied a basic psychological need in man, for death is but the victory of time. To preserve, artificially, his bodily appearance is to snatch it from the flow of time, to stow it away neatly, so to speak, in the hold of life. It was natural, therefore, to keep up appearances in the face of the reality of death by preserving flesh and bone. The first Egyptian statue, then, was a mummy, tanned and petrified in sodium. But pyramids and labyrinthine corridors offered no certain guarantee against ultimate pillage.

Other forms of insurance were therefore sought. So, near the sarcophagus, alongside the corn that was to feed the dead, the Egyptians placed terra cotta statuettes, as substitute mummies which might replace the bodies if these were destroyed. It is this religious use, then, that lays bare the primordial function of statuary, namely, the preservation of life by a representation of life. Another manifestation of the same kind of thing is the arrow-pierced clay bear to be found in prehistoric caves, a magic identity-substitute for the living animal, that will ensure a successful hunt. The evolution, side by side, of art and civilization has relieved the plastic arts of their magic role. Louis XIV did not have himself embalmed. He was content to survive in his portrait by Le Brun. Civilization cannot, however, entirely cast out the bogy of time. It can only sublimate our concern with it to the level of rational thinking. No one believes any longer in the ontological identity of model and image, but all are agreed that the image helps us to remember the subject and to preserve him from a second spiritual death. Today the making of images no longer shares an anthropocentric, utilitarian purpose. It is no longer a question of survival after death, but of a larger concept, the creation of an ideal world in the likeness of the real, with its own temporal destiny. "How vain a thing is painting" if underneath our fond admiration for its works we do not discern man's primitive need to have the last word in the argument with death by means of the form that endures. If the history of the plastic arts is less a matter of their aesthetic than of their psychology then it will be seen to be essentially the story of resemblance, or, if you will, of realism.

Seen in this sociological perspective photography and cinema would provide a natural explanation for the great spiritual and technical crisis that overtook modern painting around the middle of the last century. André Malraux has described the cinema as the furthermost evolution to date of plastic realism, the beginnings of which were first manifest at the Renaissance and which found its completest expression in baroque painting.

It is true that painting, the world over, has struck a varied balance between the symbolic and realism. However, in the fifteenth century Western painting began to turn from its age-old concern with spiritual realities expressed in the form proper to it, towards an effort to combine this spiritual expression with as complete an imitation as possible of the outside world.

The decisive moment undoubtedly came with the discovery of the first scientific and already, in a sense, mechanical system of reproduction, namely, perspective: the camera obscura of Da Vinci foreshadowed the camera of Niépce. The artist was now in a position to create the illusion of three-dimensional space within which things appeared to exist as our eyes in reality see them.

Thenceforth painting was torn between two ambitions: one, primarily aesthetic, namely the expression of spiritual reality wherein the symbol transcended its model; the other, purely psychological, namely the duplication of the world outside. The satisfaction of this appetite for illusion merely served to increase it till, bit by bit, it consumed the plastic arts. However, since perspective had only solved the problem of form and not of movement, realism was forced to continue the search for some way of giving dramatic expression to the moment, a kind of psychic fourth dimension that could suggest life in the tortured immobility of baroque art.[1]

The great artists, of course, have always been able to combine the two tendencies. They have allotted to each its proper place in the hierarchy of things, holding reality at their command and molding it at will into the fabric of their art. Nevertheless, the fact remains that we are faced with two essentially different phenomena and these any objective critic must view separately if he is to understand the evolution of the pictorial. The need for illusion has not ceased to trouble the heart of painting since the sixteenth century. It is a purely mental need, of itself nonaesthetic, the origins of which must be sought in the proclivity of the mind towards magic. However, it is a need the pull of which has been strong enough to have seriously upset the equilibrium of the plastic arts.

The quarrel over realism in art stems from a misunderstanding, from a confusion between the aesthetic and the psychological; between true realism, the need that is to give significant expression to the world both concretely and its essence, and the pseudorealism of a deception aimed at fooling the eye (or for that matter the mind); a pseudorealism content in other words with illusory appearances.[2] That is why medieval art never passed through this crisis; simultaneously vividly realistic and highly spiritual, it knew nothing of the drama that came to light as a consequence of technical developments. Perspective was the original sin of Western painting.

It was redeemed from sin by Niépce and Lumière. In achieving the aims of baroque art, photography has freed the plastic arts from their obsession with likeness. Painting was forced, as it turned out, to offer us illusion and this illusion was reckoned sufficient unto art. Photography and the cinema on the other hand are discoveries that satisfy, once and for all and in its very essence, our obsession with realism.

No matter how skillful the painter, his work was always in fee to an inescapable subjectivity. The fact that a human hand intervened cast a shadow of doubt over the image. Again, the essential factor in the transition from the baroque to photography is not the perfecting of a physical process (photography will long remain the inferior of painting in the reproduction of color); rather does it lie in a psychological fact, to wit, in completely satisfying our appetite for illusion by a mechanical reproduction in the making of which man plays no part. The solution is not to be found in the result achieved but in the way of achieving it.[3]

This is why the conflict between style and likeness is a relatively modern phenomenon of which there is no trace before the invention of the sensitized plate. Clearly the fascinating objectivity of Chardin is in no sense that of the photographer. The nineteenth century saw the real beginnings of the crisis of realism of which Picasso is now the mythical central figure and which put to the test at one and the same time the conditions determining the formal existence of the plastic arts and their sociological roots. Freed from the "resemblance complex," the modern painter abandons it to the masses who, henceforth, identify resemblance on the one hand with photography and on the other with the kind of painting which is related to photography.

Originality in photography as distinct from originality in painting lies in the essentially objective character of photography. [Bazin here makes a point of the fact that the lens, the basis of photography, is in French called the "objectif," a nuance that is lost in English.—Tr.] For the first time, between the originating object and its reproduction there intervenes only the instrumentality of a nonliving agent. For the first time an image of the world is formed automatically, without the creative intervention of man. The personality of the photographer enters into the proceedings only in his selection of the object to be photographed and by way of the purpose he has in mind. Although the final result may reflect something of his personality, this does not play the same role as is played by that of the painter. All the arts are based on the presence of man, only photography derives an advantage from his absence. Photography affects us like a phenomenon in nature, like a flower or a snowflake whose vegetable or earthly origins are an inseparable part of their beauty.

This production by automatic means has radically affected our psychology of the image. The objective nature of photography confers on it a quality of credibility absent from all other picture-making. In spite of any objections our critical spirit may offer, we are forced to accept as real the existence of the object reproduced, actually *re*-presented, set before us, that is to say, in time and space. Photography enjoys a certain advantage in virtue of this transference of reality from the thing to its reproduction.[4]

A very faithful drawing may actually tell us more about the model but despite the promptings of our critical intelligence it will never have the irrational power of the photograph to bear away our faith.

Besides, painting is, after all, an inferior way of making likenesses, an *ersatz* of the processes of reproduction. Only a photographic lens can give us the kind of image of the object that is capable of satisfying the deep need man has to substitute for it something more than a mere approximation, a kind of decal or transfer. The photographic image is the object itself, the object freed from the conditions of time and space that govern it. No matter how fuzzy, distorted, or discolored, no matter how lacking in documentary value the image may be, it shares, by virtue of the very process of its becoming, the being of the model of which it is the reproduction; it *is* the model.

Hence the charm of family albums. Those grey or sepia shadows, phantomlike and almost undecipherable, are no longer traditional family portraits but rather the disturbing presence of lives halted at a set moment in their duration, freed from their destiny; not, however, by the prestige of art but by the power of an impassive mechanical process: for photography does not create eternity, as art does, it embalms time, rescuing it simply from its proper corruption.

Viewed in this perspective, the cinema is objectivity in time. The film is no longer content to preserve the object, enshrouded as it were in an instant, as the bodies of insects are preserved intact, out of the distant past, in amber. The film delivers baroque art from its convulsive catalepsy. Now, for the first time, the image of things is likewise the image of their duration, change mummified as it were. Those categories of *resemblance* which determine the species *photographic* image likewise, then, determine the character of its aesthetic as distinct from that of painting.[5]

The aesthetic qualities of photography are to be sought in its power to lay bare the realities. It is not for me to separate off, in the complex fabric of the objective world, here a reflection on a damp sidewalk, there the gesture of a child. Only the impassive lens, stripping its object of all those ways of seeing it, those piled-up preconceptions, that spiritual dust and grime with which my eyes have covered it, is able to present it in all its virginal purity to my attention and consequently to my love. By the power of photography, the natural image of a world that we neither know nor can know, nature at last does more than imitate art: she imitates the artist.

Photography can even surpass art in creative power. The aesthetic world of the painter is of a different kind from that of the world about him. Its boundaries enclose a substantially and essentially different microcosm. The photograph as such and the object in itself share a common being, after the fashion of a fingerprint. Wherefore, photography actually contributes something to the order of natural creation instead of providing a substitute for it. The surrealists had an inkling of this when they looked to the photographic plate to provide them with their monstrosities and for this reason: the surrealist does not consider his aesthetic purpose and the mechanical effect of the image on our imaginations as things apart. For him, the logical distinction between what is imaginary and what is real tends to disappear. Every image is to be seen as an object and every object as an image. Hence photography ranks high in the order of surrealist creativity because it produces an image that is a reality of nature, namely, an hallucination that is also a fact. The fact that surrealist painting combines tricks of visual deception with meticulous attention to detail substantiates this.

So, photography is clearly the most important event in the history of plastic arts. Simultaneously a liberation and a fulfillment, it has freed Western painting, once and for all, from its obsession with realism and allowed it to recover its aesthetic autonomy. Impressionist realism, offering science as an alibi, is at the opposite extreme from eye-deceiving trickery. Only when form ceases to have any imitative value can it be swallowed up in color. So, when form, in the person of Cézanne, once more regains possession of the canvas there is no longer any question of the illusions of the geometry of perspective. The painting, being confronted in the mechanically produced image with a competitor able to reach out beyond baroque resemblance to the very identity of the model, was compelled into the category of object. Henceforth Pascal's condemnation of painting is itself rendered vain since the photograph allows us on the one hand to admire in reproduction something that our eyes alone could not have taught us to love, and on the other, to admire the painting as a thing in itself whose relation to something in nature has ceased to be the justification for its existence.

On the other hand, of course, cinema is also a language.

Notes

1   It would be interesting from this point of view to study, in the illustrated magazines of 1890–1910, the rivalry between photographic reporting and the use of drawings. The latter, in particular, satisfied the baroque need for the dramatic. A feeling for the photographic document developed only gradually.

2   Perhaps the Communists, before they attach too much importance to expressionist realism, should stop talking about it in a way more suitable to the eighteenth century, before there were such things as photography or cinema. Maybe it does not really matter if Russian painting is second-rate provided Russia gives us first-rate cinema. Eisenstein is her Tintoretto.

3   There is room, nevertheless, for a study of the psychology of the lesser plastic arts, the molding of
        death masks for example, which likewise involves a certain automatic process. One might consider
        photography in this sense as a molding, the taking of an impression, by the manipulation of light.

4   Here one should really examine the psychology of relics and souvenirs which likewise enjoy the
        advantages of a transfer of reality stemming from the "mummy-complex." Let us merely note in
        passing that the Holy Shroud of Turin combines the features alike of relic and photograph.

5   I use the term *category* here in the sense attached to it by M. Gouhier in his book on the theater
        in which he distinguishes between the dramatic and the aesthetic categories. Just as dramatic ten-
        sion has no artistic value, the perfection of a reproduction is not to be identified with beauty.
        It constitutes rather the prime matter, so to speak, on which the artistic fact is recorded.

Chapter 8

André Bazin

THE EVOLUTION OF THE LANGUAGE OF CINEMA

BY 1928 THE SILENT film had reached its artistic peak. The despair of its elite as they witnessed the dismantling of this ideal city, while it may not have been justified, is at least understandable. As they followed their chosen aesthetic path it seemed to them that the cinema had developed into an art most perfectly accommodated to the "exquisite embarrassment" of silence and that the realism that sound would bring could only mean a surrender to chaos.

In point of fact, now that sound has given proof that it came not to destroy but to fulfill the Old Testament of the cinema, we may most properly ask if the technical revolution created by the soundtrack was in any sense an aesthetic revolution. In other words, did the years from 1928 to 1930 actually witness the birth of a new cinema? Certainly, as regards editing, history does not actually show as wide a breach as might be expected between the silent and the sound film. On the contrary there is discernible evidence of a close relationship between certain directors of 1925 and 1935 and especially of the 1940s through the 1950s. Compare for example Erich von Stroheim and Jean Renoir or Orson Welles, or again Carl Theodore Dreyer and Robert Bresson. These more or less clear-cut affinities demonstrate first of all that the gap separating the 1920s and the 1930s can be bridged, and secondly that certain cinematic values actually carry over from the silent to the sound film and, above all, that it is less a matter of setting silence over against sound than of contrasting certain families of styles, certain basically different concepts of cinematographic expression.

Aware as I am that the limitations imposed on this study restrict me to a simplified and to that extent enfeebled presentation of my argument, and holding it to be less an objective statement than a working hypothesis, I will distinguish, in the cinema between 1920 and 1940, between two broad and opposing trends: those directors who put their faith in the image and those who put their faith in reality. By "image" I here mean, very broadly speaking, everything that the representation on the screen adds to the object there represented. This is a complex inheritance but it can be reduced essentially to two categories: those that relate to the plastics of the image and those that relate to the resources of montage, which, after all, is simply the ordering of images in time.

Under the heading "plastics" must be included the style of the sets, of the make-up, and, up to a point, even of the performance, to which we naturally add the lighting and, finally, the framing of the shot which gives us its composition. As regards montage, derived initially as we all know from the masterpieces of Griffith, we have the statement of Malraux in his *Psychologie du cinéma* that it was montage that gave birth to film as an art, setting it apart from mere animated photography, in short, creating a language.

The use of montage can be "invisible" and this was generally the case in the prewar classics of the American screen. Scenes were broken down just for one purpose, namely, to analyze an episode according to the material or dramatic logic of the scene. It is this logic which conceals the fact of the analysis, the mind of the spectator quite naturally accepting the viewpoints of the director which are justified by the geography of the action or the shifting emphasis of dramatic interest.

But the neutral quality of this "invisible" editing fails to make use of the full potential of montage. On the other hand these potentialities are clearly evident from the three processes generally known as parallel montage, accelerated montage, montage by attraction. In creating parallel montage, Griffith succeeded in conveying a sense of the simultaneity of two actions taking place at a geographical distance by means of alternating shots from each. In *La Roue* Abel Gance created the illusion of the steadily increasing speed of a locomotive without actually using any images of speed (indeed the wheel could have been turning on one spot) simply by a multiplicity of shots of ever-decreasing length.

Finally there is "montage by attraction," the creation of S.M. Eisenstein, and not so easily described as the others, but which may be roughly defined as the reenforcing of the meaning of one image by association with another image not necessarily part of the same episode—for example the fireworks display in *The General Line* following the image of the bull. In this extreme form, montage by attraction was rarely used even by its creator but one may consider as very near to it in principle the more commonly used ellipsis, comparison, or metaphor, examples of which are the throwing of stockings onto a chair at the foot of a bed, or the milk overflowing in H.G. Clouzot's *Quai des orfèvres*. There are of course a variety of possible combinations of these three processes.

Whatever these may be, one can say that they share that trait in common which constitutes the very definition of montage, namely, the creation of a sense or meaning not proper to the images themselves but derived exclusively from their juxtaposition. The well-known experiment of Kuleshov with the shot of Mozhukhin in which a smile was seen to change its significance according to the image that preceded it, sums up perfectly the properties of montage.

Montage as used by Kuleshov, Eisenstein, or Gance did not give us the event; it alluded to it. Undoubtedly they derived at least the greater part of the constituent elements from the reality they were describing but the final significance of the film was found to reside in the ordering of these elements much more than in their objective content.

The matter under recital, whatever the realism of the individual image, is born essentially from these relationships—Mozhukhin plus dead child equal pity—that is to say an abstract result, none of the concrete elements of which are to be found in the premises; maidens plus apple trees in bloom equal hope. The combinations are infinite. But the only thing they have in common is the fact that they suggest an idea by means of a metaphor or by an association of ideas. Thus between the scenario properly so-called, the ultimate object of the recital, and the image pure and simple, there is a relay station, a sort of aesthetic "transformer." The meaning is not in the image, it is in the shadow of the image projected by montage onto the field of consciousness of the spectator.

Let us sum up. Through the contents of the image and the resources of montage, the cinema has at its disposal a whole arsenal of means whereby to impose its interpretation of an event on the spectator. By the end of the silent film we can consider this arsenal to have been full. On the one side the Soviet cinema carried to its ultimate consequences the theory and practice of montage, while the German school did every kind of violence to the plastics of the image by way of sets and lighting. Other cinemas count too besides the Russian and German, but whether in France or Sweden or the United States, it does not appear that the language of cinema was at a loss for ways of saying what it wanted to say.

If the art of cinema consists in everything that plastics and montage can add to a given reality, the silent film was an art on its own. Sound could only play at best a subordinate and supplementary role: a counterpoint to the visual image. But this possible enhancement—at best only a minor one—is likely not to weigh much in comparison with the additional bargain-rate reality introduced at the same time by sound.

Thus far we have put forward the view that expressionism of montage and image constitute the essence of cinema. And it is precisely on this generally accepted notion that directors from silent days, such as Erich von Stroheim, F. W. Murnau, and Robert Flaherty, have by implication cast a doubt. In their films, montage plays no part, unless it be the negative one of inevitable elimination where reality superabounds. The camera cannot see everything at once but it makes sure not to lose any part of what it chooses to see. What matters to Flaherty, confronted with Nanook hunting the seal, is the relation between Nanook and the animal; the actual length of the waiting period. Montage could suggest the time involved. Flaherty, however, confines himself to showing the actual waiting period; the length of the hunt is the very substance of the image, its true object. Thus in the film this episode requires one set-up. Will anyone deny that it is thereby much more moving than a montage by attraction?

Murnau is interested not so much in time as in the reality of dramatic space. Montage plays no more of a decisive part in *Nosferatu* than in *Sunrise*. One might be inclined to think that the plastics of his image are impressionistic. But this would be a superficial view. The composition of his image is in no sense pictorial. It adds nothing to the reality, it does not deform it, it forces it to reveal its structural depth, to bring out the preexisting relations which become constitutive of the drama. For example, in *Tabu*, the arrival of a ship from left screen gives an immediate sense of destiny at work so that Murnau has no need to cheat in any way on the uncompromising realism of a film whose settings are completely natural.

But it is most of all Stroheim who rejects photographic expressionism and the tricks of montage. In his films reality lays itself bare like a suspect confessing under the relentless examination of the commissioner of police. He has one simple rule for direction. Take a close look at the world, keep on doing so, and in the end it will lay bare for you all its cruelty and its ugliness. One could easily imagine as a matter of fact a film by Stroheim composed of a single shot as long-lasting and as close-up as you like. These three directors do not exhaust the possibilities. We would undoubtedly find scattered among the works of others elements of nonexpressionistic cinema in which montage plays no part—even including Griffith. But these examples suffice to reveal, at the very heart of the silent film, a cinematographic art the very opposite of that which has been identified as "*cinéma par excellence*," a language the semantic and syntactical unit of which is in no sense the Shot; in which the image is evaluated not according to what it adds to reality but what it reveals of it. In the latter art the silence of the screen was a drawback, that is to say, it deprived reality of one of its elements. *Greed*, like Dreyer's *Jeanne d'Arc*, is already virtually a talking film. The moment that you cease to maintain that montage and the plastic composition of the image are the very essence of the language of cinema, sound is no longer the aesthetic crevasse dividing two radically different aspects of the seventh art. The cinema that is believed to have died of the soundtrack is in no sense "*the* cinema." The real dividing line is elsewhere. It was operative in the past and continues to be through thirty-five years of the history of the language of the film.

*   *   *

Having challenged the aesthetic unity of the silent film and divided it off into two opposing tendencies, now let us take a look at the history of the last twenty years.

From 1930 to 1940 there seems to have grown up in the world, originating largely in the United States, a common form of cinematic language. It was the triumph in Hollywood, during that time, of five or six major kinds of film that gave it its overwhelming superiority: (1) American comedy (*Mr. Smith Goes to Washington*, 1936); (2) the burlesque film (the Marx Brothers); (3) the dance and vaudeville film (Fred Astaire and Ginger Rogers and the Ziegfeld Follies); (4) the crime and gangster film (*Scarface*, *I Am a Fugitive from a Chain Gang*, *The Informer*); (5) psychological and social dramas (*Back Street*, *Jezebel*); (6) horror or fantasy films (*Dr. Jekyll and Mr. Hyde*, *The Invisible Man*, *Frankenstein*); (7) the western (*Stagecoach*, 1939). During that time the French cinema undoubtedly ranked next. Its superiority was gradually manifested by way of a trend towards what might be roughly called stark somber realism, or poetic realism, in which four names stand out: Jacques Feyder, Jean Renoir, Marcel Carné, and Julien Duvivier. My intention not being to draw up a list of prize-winners, there is little use in dwelling on the Soviet, British, German, or Italian films for which these years were less significant than the ten that were to follow. In any case, American and French production sufficiently clearly indicate that the sound film, prior to World War II, had reached a well-balanced stage of maturity.

First as to content: major varieties with clearly defined rules capable of pleasing a worldwide public, as well as a cultured elite, provided it was not inherently hostile to the cinema.

Secondly as to form: well-defined styles of photography and editing perfectly adapted to their subject matter; a complete harmony of image and sound. In seeing again today such films as *Jezebel* by William Wyler, *Stagecoach* by John Ford, or *Le Jour se lève* by Marcel Carné, one has the feeling that in them an art has found its perfect balance, its ideal form of expression, and reciprocally one admires them for dramatic and moral themes to which the cinema, while it may not have created them, has given a grandeur, an artistic effectiveness, that they would not otherwise have had. In short, here are all the characteristics of the ripeness of a classical art.

I am quite aware that one can justifiably argue that the originality of the postwar cinema as compared with that of 1938 derives from the growth of certain national schools, in particular the dazzling display of the Italian cinema and of a native English cinema freed from the influence of Hollywood. From this one might conclude that the really important phenomenon of the years 1940–50 is the introduction of new blood, of hitherto unexplored themes. That is to say, the real revolution took place more on the level of subject matter than of style. Is not neorealism primarily a kind of humanism and only secondarily a style of film-making? Then as to the style itself, is it not essentially a form of self-effacement before reality?

Our intention is certainly not to preach the glory of form over content. Art for art's sake is just as heretical in cinema as elsewhere, probably more so. On the other hand, a new subject matter demands new form, and as good a way as any towards understanding what a film is trying to say to us is to know how it is saying it.

Thus by 1938 or 1939 the talking film, particularly in France and in the United States, had reached a level of classical perfection as a result, on the one hand, of the maturing of different kinds of drama developed in part over the past ten years and in part inherited from the silent film, and, on the other, of the stabilization of technical progress. The 1930s were the years, at once, of sound and of panchromatic film. Undoubtedly studio equipment had continued to improve but only in matters of detail, none of them opening up new, radical possibilities for direction. The only changes in this situation since 1940 have been in photography, thanks to the increased sensitivity of the film stock. Panchromatic stock turned visual values upside down, ultrasensitive emulsions have made a modification in their structure possible. Free to shoot in the studio with a much smaller aperture, the operator could, when necessary, eliminate the soft-focus background once considered essential. Still there are a number of examples of the prior use of deep focus, for example in the work of Jean Renoir. This had always been possible on exteriors, and given a measure of skill, even in the studios. Anyone could do it who really wanted to. So that it is less a question basically of a technical problem, the solution of which has admittedly been made easier, than of a search after a style—a point to which we will come back. In short, with panchromatic stock in common use, with an understanding of the potentials of the microphone, and with the crane as standard studio equipment, one can really say that since 1930 all the technical requirements for the art of cinema have been available.

Since the determining technical factors were practically eliminated, we must look elsewhere for the signs and principles of the evolution of film language, that is to say by challenging the subject matter and as a consequence the styles necessary for its expression.

By 1939 the cinema had arrived at what geographers call the equilibrium-profile of a river. By this is meant that ideal mathematical curve which results from the requisite amount of erosion. Having reached this equilibrium-profile, the river flows effortlessly from its source to its mouth without further deepening of its bed. But if any geological movement occurs which raises the erosion level and modifies the height of the source, the water sets to work again, seeps into the surrounding land, goes deeper, burrowing and digging. Sometimes when it is a chalk bed, a new pattern is dug across the plain, almost invisible but found to be complex and winding, if one follows the flow of the water.

The evolution of editing since the advent of sound

In 1938 there was an almost universal standard pattern of editing. If, somewhat convention-ally, we call the kind of silent films based on the plastics of the image and the artifices of montage "expressionist" or "symbolistic," we can describe the new form of storytelling as "analytic" and "dramatic." Let us suppose, by way of reviewing one of the elements of the experiment of Kuleshov, that we have a table covered with food and a hungry tramp. One can imagine that in 1936 it would have been edited as follows:

1.   Full shot of the actor and the table.
2.   Camera moves forward into a close-up of a face expressing a mixture of amazement and longing.
3.   Series of close-ups of food.
4.   Back to full shot of person, who starts slowly towards the camera.
5.   Camera pulls slowly back to a three-quarter shot of the actor seizing a chicken wing.

Whatever variants one could think of for this scene, they would all have certain points in common:

1.   The verisimilitude of space in which the position of the actor is always determined, even when a close-up eliminates the decor.
2.   The purpose and the effects of the cutting are exclusively dramatic or psychological.

In other words, if the scene were played on a stage and seen from a seat in the orchestra, it would have the same meaning, the episode would continue to exist objectively. The changes of point of view provided by the camera would add nothing. They would present the reality a little more forcefully, first by allowing a better view and then by putting the emphasis where it belongs.

It is true that the stage director like the film director has at his disposal a margin within which he is free to vary the interpretation of the action but it is only a margin and allows for no modification of the inner logic of the event. Now, by way of contrast, let us take the montage of the stone lions in *The End of St. Petersburg*. By skillful juxtaposition a group of sculptured lions are made to look like a single lion getting to its feet, a symbol of the aroused masses. This clever device would be unthinkable in any film after 1932. As late as 1935 Fritz Lang, in *Fury*, followed a series of shots of women dancing the can-can with shots of clucking chickens in a farmyard. This relic of associative montage came as a shock even at the time, and today seems entirely out of keeping with the rest of the film. However decisive the art of Marcel Carné, for example, in our estimate of the respective values of *Quai des Brumes* or of *Le Jour se lève* his editing remains on the level of the reality he is analyzing. There is only one proper way of looking at it. That is why we are witnessing the almost complete disappearance of optical effects such as superimpositions, and even, especially in the United States, of the close-up, the too violent impact of which would make the audience conscious of the cutting. In the typical American comedy the director returns as often as he can to a shot of the characters from the knees up, which is said to be best suited to catch the spontaneous attention of the viewer—the natural point of balance of his mental adjustment.

Actually this use of montage originated with the silent movies. This is more or less the part it plays in Griffith's films, for example in *Broken Blossoms*, because with *Intolerance* he had already introduced that synthetic concept of montage which the Soviet cinema was to carry to its ultimate conclusion and which is to be found again, although less exclusively, at the end of the silent era. It is understandable, as a matter of fact, that the sound image, far less flexible than the visual image, would carry montage in the direction of realism, increasingly eliminating both plastic impressionism and the symbolic relation between images.

Thus around 1938 films were edited, almost without exception, according to the same principle. The story was unfolded in a series of set-ups numbering as a rule about 600. The characteristic procedure was by shot–reverse–shot, that is to say, in a dialogue scene, the camera followed the order of the text, alternating the character shown with each speech.

It was this fashion of editing, so admirably suitable for the best films made between 1930 and 1939, that was challenged by the shot in depth introduced by Orson Welles and William Wyler. *Citizen Kane* can never be too highly praised. Thanks to the depth of field, whole scenes are covered in one take, the camera remaining motionless. Dramatic effects for which we had formerly relied on montage were created out of the movements of the actors within a fixed framework. Of course Welles did not invent the in-depth shot any more than Griffith invented the close-up. All the pioneers used it and for a very good reason. Soft focus only appeared with montage. It was not only a technical must consequent upon the use of images in juxtaposition, it was a logical consequence of montage, its plastic equivalent. If at a given moment in the action the director, as in the scene imagined above, goes to a close-up of a bowl of fruit, it follows naturally that he also isolates it in space through the focusing of the lens. The soft focus of the background confirms therefore the effect of montage, that is to say, while it is of the essence of the storytelling, it is only an accessory of the style of the photography. Jean Renoir had already clearly understood this, as we see from a statement of his made in 1938 just after he had made *La Bête humaine* and *La Grande illusion* and just prior to *La Règle du jeu*: "The more I learn about my trade the more I incline to direction in depth relative to the screen. The better it works, the less I use the kind of set-up that shows two actors facing the camera, like two well-behaved subjects posing for a still portrait." The truth of the matter is, that if you are looking for the precursor of Orson Welles, it is not Louis Lumière or Zecca, but rather Jean Renoir. In his films, the search after composition in depth is, in effect, a partial replacement of montage by frequent panning shots and entrances. It is based on a respect for the continuity of dramatic space and, of course, of its duration.

To anybody with eyes in his head, it is quite evident that the sequence of shots used by Welles in *The Magnificent Ambersons* is in no sense the purely passive recording of an action shot within the same framing. On the contrary, his refusal to break up the action, to analyze the dramatic field in time, is a positive action the results of which are far superior to anything that could be achieved by the classical "cut."

All you need to do is compare two frames shot in depth, one from 1910, the other from a film by Wyler or Welles, to understand just by looking at the image, even apart from the context of the film, how different their functions are. The framing in the 1910 film is intended, to all intents and purposes, as a substitute for the missing fourth wall of the theatrical stage, or at least in exterior shots, for the best vantage point to view the action, whereas in the second case the setting, the lighting, and the camera angles give an entirely different reading. Between them, director and cameraman have converted the screen into a dramatic checkerboard, planned down to the last detail. The clearest if not the most original examples of this are to be found in *The Little Foxes*, where the *mise-en-scène* takes on the severity of a working drawing. Welles' pictures are more difficult to analyze because of his over-fondness for the baroque. Objects and characters are related in such a fashion that it is impossible for the spectator to miss the significance of the scene. To get the same results by way of montage would have necessitated a detailed succession of shots.

What we are saying then is that the sequence of shots "in depth" of the contemporary director does not exclude the use of montage—how could he, without reverting to a primitive babbling?—he makes it an integral part of his "plastic." The storytelling of Welles or Wyler is no less explicit than John Ford's but theirs has the advantage over his that it does not sacrifice the specific effects that can be derived from unity of image in space and time. Whether an episode is analyzed bit by bit or presented in its physical entirety cannot surely remain a matter of indifference, at least in a work with some pretensions to style. It would obviously be absurd to deny that montage has added considerably to the progress of film language, but this has happened at the cost of other values, no less definitely cinematic.

This is why depth of field is not just a stock in trade of the cameraman like the use of a series of filters or of such-and-such a style of lighting, it is a capital gain in the field of direction—a dialectical step forward in the history of film language.

Nor is it just a formal step forward. Well used, shooting in depth is not just a more economical, a simpler, and at the same time a more subtle way of getting the most out of a scene. In addition to affecting the structure of film language, it also affects the relationships of the minds of the spectators to the image, and in consequence it influences the interpretation of the spectacle.

It would lie outside the scope of this article to analyze the psychological modalities of these relations, as also their aesthetic consequences, but it might be enough here to note, in general terms:

1. That depth of focus brings the spectator into a relation with the image closer to that which he enjoys with reality. Therefore it is correct to say that, independently of the contents of the image, its structure is more realistic.
2. That it implies, consequently, both a more active mental attitude on the part of the spectator and a more positive contribution on his part to the action in progress. While analytical montage only calls for him to follow his guide, to let his attention follow along smoothly with that of the director, who will choose what he should see, here he is called upon to exercise at least a minimum of personal choice. It is from his attention and his will that the meaning of the image in part derives.

3.   From the two preceding propositions, which belong to the realm of psychology, there follows a third which may be described as metaphysical. In analyzing reality, montage presupposes of its very nature the unity of meaning of the dramatic event. Some other form of analysis is undoubtedly possible but then it would be another film. In short, montage by its very nature rules out ambiguity of expression. Kuleshov's experiment proves this *per absurdum* in giving on each occasion a precise meaning to the expression on a face, the ambiguity of which alone makes the three successively exclusive expressions possible.

On the other hand, depth of focus reintroduced ambiguity into the structure of the image, if not of necessity—Wyler's films are never ambiguous—at least as a possibility. Hence it is no exaggeration to say that *Citizen Kane* is unthinkable shot in any other way but in depth. The uncertainty in which we find ourselves as to the spiritual key or the interpretation we should put on the film is built into the very design of the image.

It is not that Welles denies himself any recourse whatsoever to the expressionistic procedures of montage, but just that their use from time to time in between sequences of shots in depth gives them a new meaning. Formerly montage was the very stuff of cinema, the texture of the scenario. In *Citizen Kane* a series of superimpositions is contrasted with a scene presented in a single take, constituting another and deliberately abstract mode of storytelling. Accelerated montage played tricks with time and space, while that of Welles, on the other hand, is not trying to deceive us; it offers us a contrast, condensing time, and hence is the equivalent, for example, of the French imperfect or the English frequentative tense. Like accelerated montage and montage of attractions these superimpositions, which the talking film had not used for ten years, rediscovered a possible use related to temporal realism in a film without montage.

If we have dwelt at some length on Orson Welles it is because the date of his appearance in the filmic firmament (1941) marks more or less the beginning of a new period and also because his case is the most spectacular and, by virtue of his very excesses, the most significant.

Yet *Citizen Kane* is part of a general movement, of a vast stirring of the geological bed of cinema, confirming that everywhere up to a point there had been a revolution in the language of the screen.

I could show the same to be true, although by different methods, of the Italian cinema. In Roberto Rossellini's *Paisà* and *Allemania Anno Zero* and Vittorio de Sica's *Ladri di Biciclette*, Italian neorealism contrasts with previous forms of film realism in its stripping away of all expressionism and in particular in the total absence of the effects of montage. As in the films of Welles and in spite of conflicts of style, neorealism tends to give back to the cinema a sense of the ambiguity of reality. The preoccupation of Rossellini when dealing with the face of the child in *Allemania Anno Zero* is the exact opposite of that of Kuleshov with the close-up of Mozhukhin. Rossellini is concerned to preserve its mystery. We should not be misled by the fact that the evolution of neorealism is not manifest, as in the United States, in any form of revolution in editing. They are both aiming at the same results by different methods. The means used by Rossellini and de Sica are less spectacular but they are no less determined to do away with montage and to transfer to the screen the *continuum* of reality. The dream of Zavattini is just to make a ninety-minute film of the life of a man to whom nothing ever happens. The most "aesthetic" of the neorealists, Luchino Visconti, gives just as clear a picture as Welles of the basic aim of his directorial art in *La Terra Trema*, a film almost entirely composed of one-shot sequences, thus clearly showing his concern to cover the entire action in interminable deep-focus panning shots.

However, we cannot pass in review all the films that have shared in this revolution in film language since 1940. Now is the moment to attempt a synthesis of our reflections on the subject.

It seems to us that the decade from 1940 to 1950 marks a decisive step forward in the development of the language of the film. If we have appeared since 1930 to have lost sight of the trend of the silent film as illustrated particularly by Stroheim, F.W. Murnau, Robert Flaherty, and Dreyer, it is for a purpose. It is not that this trend seems to us to have been halted by the talking film. On the contrary, we believe that it represented the richest vein of the so-called silent film, and precisely because it was not aesthetically tied to montage, but was indeed the only tendency that looked to the realism of sound as a natural development. On the other hand it is a fact that the talking film between 1930 and 1940 owes it virtually nothing save for the glorious and retrospectively prophetic exception of Jean Renoir. He alone in his searchings as a director prior to *La Règle du jeu* forced himself to look back beyond the resources provided by montage and so uncovered the secret of a film form that would permit everything to be said without chopping the world up into little fragments, that would reveal the hidden meanings in people and things without disturbing the unity natural to them.

It is not a question of thereby belittling the films of 1930 to 1940, a criticism that would not stand up in the face of the number of masterpieces, it is simply an attempt to establish the notion of a dialectic progress, the highest expression of which was found in the films of the 1940s. Undoubtedly, the talkie sounded the knell of a certain aesthetic of the language of film, but only wherever it had turned its back on its vocation in the service of realism. The sound film nevertheless did preserve the essentials of montage, namely discontinuous description and the dramatic analysis of action. What it turned its back on was metaphor and symbol in exchange for the illusion of objective presentation. The expressionism of montage has virtually disappeared but the relative realism of the kind of cutting that flourished around 1937 implied a congenital limitation which escaped us so long as it was perfectly suited to its subject matter. Thus American comedy reached its peak within the framework of a form of editing in which the realism of the time played no part. Dependent on logic for its effects, like vaudeville and plays on words, entirely conventional in its moral and sociological content, American comedy had everything to gain, in strict line-by-line progression, from the rhythmic resources of classical editing.

Undoubtedly it is primarily with the Stroheim–Murnau trend—almost totally eclipsed from 1930 to 1940—that the cinema has more or less consciously linked up once more over the last ten years. But it has no intention of limiting itself simply to keeping this trend alive. It draws from it the secret of the regeneration of realism in storytelling and thus of becoming capable once more of bringing together real time, in which things exist, along with the duration of the action, for which classical editing had insidiously substituted mental and abstract time. On the other hand, so far from wiping out once and for all the conquests of montage, this reborn realism gives them a body of reference and a meaning. It is only an increased realism of the image that can support the abstraction of montage. The stylistic repertory of a director such as Hitchcock, for example, ranged from the power inherent in the basic document as such, to superimpositions, to large close-ups. But the close-ups of Hitchcock are not the same as those of C.B. de Mille in *The Cheat* [1915]. They are just one type of figure, among others, of his style. In other words, in the silent days, montage evoked what the director wanted to say; in the editing of 1938, it described it. Today we can say that at last the director writes in film. The image—its plastic composition and the way it is set in time, because it is founded on a much higher degree of realism—has at its disposal more means of manipulating reality and of modifying it from within. The film-maker is no longer the competitor of the painter and the playwright, he is, at last, the equal of the novelist.

Chapter 9

Daniel Morgan

RETHINKING BAZIN: ONTOLOGY AND REALIST AESTHETICS

The word "realism" as it is commonly used does not have an absolute and clear meaning, so much as it indicates a certain tendency toward the faithful rendering of reality on film. Given the fact that this movement toward the real can take a thousand different routes, the apologia for "realism" *per se*, strictly speaking, means nothing at all. The movement is valuable only insofar as it brings increased meaning (itself an abstraction) to what is created.

(André Bazin, *Jean Renoir*, 1973)[1]

THE ADVANCE IN DIGITAL technologies of image production and manipulation has seriously challenged traditional views about photography and film. In the main, classical theories of these media defined them by their ability to automatically, even necessarily, provide a truthful image of what was in front of the camera at the moment the shutter clicked. Cinema, Jean-Luc Godard once remarked, is truth twenty-four times a second. Digital technologies, which allow for the almost total transformation and creation of images by means of binary coding, are thought to undermine the claim for the truthfulness of photographic media.[2] The classical theories now seem inadequate and irrelevant.

If we need to develop new theories to keep up with a rapidly changing media landscape, it is also important not to forget the ambitions of classical theories. Unlike much of contemporary media theory, classical theories are interested in the kind of physical objects images are. They start with the idea that the nature of the physical medium is a necessary part of our thinking about the images it supports. By contrast, it is often said that digital images as such have no physical existence, that they are merely contingently attached to various physical bases.[3] They are not things in the way photographs are.[4] This view, I think, involves a mistake. The materiality of the image cannot be avoided; it is crucial to how we think about the aesthetic possibilities, circulation, affective register, and so on of images of any sort.

In this essay, I am not going to offer a theory for new media so much as argue for the continuing value of classical theories of photography and film. They provide a needed corrective to recent theories by emphasizing the productive tension between the form in which an artist expresses subject matter and the kind of thing an image is, between style and ontology. To make this case, I will take a careful look at the important work of André Bazin, whose intelligence and insight in grappling with the difficult problems of style and ontology has been misunderstood and therefore mostly rejected. A more subtle interpretation of Bazin allows for elements in classical theory to emerge that are important for thinking about images however they are produced.[5]

Since the publication of the two-volume English translation of *Qu'est-ce que le cinéma?* (*What Is Cinema?*) in 1967 and 1971, Bazin has acquired a canonical, even foundational, position in cinema and media studies. Such is his importance that there is by now a generally accepted standard reading of his essays: a film is realist insofar as it comes closest to or bears fidelity to our perceptual experience of reality. Dudley Andrew speaks of Bazin's aesthetic as oriented around a "deep feeling for the integral unity of a universe in flux"[6] and elsewhere of realistic styles as "approximations of visible [or perceptual] reality."[7] Christopher Williams argues that, for Bazin, film has "the primary function of showing the spectator the real world," which he, like Andrew, glosses as "the aesthetic equivalent of human perception."[8] Peter Wollen goes so far as to assert that this realism constitutes an anti-aesthetic, the very negation of cinematic style and artifice: "the film could obtain radical purity only through its own annihilation."[9] The standard reading spells out Bazin's conception of realism in film as a list of attributes—for example, deep space, the long take—and directors or movements—for example, Jean Renoir, Orson Welles, and Italian neorealism—that fulfill this function in an exemplary way.[10]

Two propositions lie at the heart of this reading. First, Bazin argues for a necessary and determinate relation between the ontology of the photographic image and the realism of film. Second, Bazin gives an account of the ontology of the photographic image that is best understood in terms of a commitment, via the mechanical nature of the recording process of the camera, to the reproduction of an antecedent reality.

I'm going to argue that both propositions should be rejected. The first has led critics to be satisfied with a thin and impoverished picture of his conception of realism.[11] A closer examination of more of Bazin's critical writings on individual films will expand and transform the parameters of our understanding of how his realism works. The second proposition misconstrues the ontological argument at the heart of Bazin's account of film and photography. Proponents of this reading have assumed that his arguments can be described in semiotic terms. Dispensing with this assumption allows a different argument about the nature of the photographic image to emerge, which will have consequences for how realism is understood.

I want first to explain why we should reject the standard reading of Bazin's ontological argument and focus instead on his claim that objects in a photograph are ontologically identical to objects in the world. Part two of this essay discusses the standard reading of realism and its relation to this ontology, while parts three and four set out my own reading of Bazin on these topics. I will argue that, in contrast to Noël Carroll's caricature of a natural "entailment from representation to realism" (PP, p. 139; see also p. 136), Bazin sees a more complicated relation between style and reality. Though a film, to be realist, must take into account (or, as I will describe it, must acknowledge) the ontology of the photographic image, realism is not a particular style, lack of style, or set of stylistic attributes, but a process, a mechanism—an achievement. It turns out to cover a surprisingly large range of styles, even those that bear little affinity to the perceptual experience of reality. Part five considers two objections to this argument.

I hope to do more than simply provide a more accurate picture of Bazin's work. As long ago as 1973, Williams declared Bazin to be of interest only for historical and ideological readings.[12] This judgment was based on and supported by an inadequate understanding of both ontology and realism in Bazin's work. I will try to show that, by attending to the complexities of the relation between ontology and style in realist films, Bazin's position, properly understood, gives us a powerful and compelling account of the work realism can do as an analytic tool for film criticism.

1 The ontology of the photographic image

Bazin's early essay "The Ontology of the Photographic Image" is generally regarded as providing the theoretical foundation for his account of film. The essay divides into three rough sections. First, Bazin sketches a psychology of art based on the historical origins of the impulse to make representations. He locates it in what he calls the "mummy complex," where Egyptians sought to provide "a defense against the passing of time" by allowing the "corporeal body" to survive after death. Art emerges when this ambition moves away from preserving the actual body in favor of creating a representation of the dead person.[13] Second, there is an argument about aesthetics, which investigates the realistic or mimetic telos inherent in the psychology of art. Bazin introduces photography here as the technological development that "freed the plastic arts from their obsession with likeness" ("O," 1:12). Third, in the section that lies at the heart of discussions of the ontology of the photographic image, Bazin moves beyond the function of photography in the history of art to the question of what a photograph is.

The standard reading interprets the argument of the third section as providing an account of photography best understood in semiotic terms. Drawing heavily on the terminology of Charles S. Peirce, it generates the following picture. As a sign, a photograph mediates between the object (the referent) and the interpretant (the viewer); more simply: the image stands for the object in some relation to the viewer.[14] Peirce presents three possible ways a sign can stand in this relation: symbolically, iconically, and indexically. Symbolic relations are determined by convention; language is the best example of this (the word *car* only arbitrarily refers to or means a car). Iconic signs concern resemblance, the capacity a sign may have to represent its object by virtue of likeness: a portrait, for example. Indexical signs have to do with a direct, causal, and existential bond between sign and object: a footprint, a weather vane, a bullet hole, pulse rates. On the standard reading, photographs are primarily regarded as indexical signs; light reflects off an object and causes the photographic plate to react. A photograph's iconic properties are a function of its indexical status. I will call this view of the ontology of the photographic image the *index argument*.[15]

If the relation between object and photograph is indexical, three things follow. First, a photograph refers to an antecedent reality that is, as it were, "behind" the image.[16] Suppose I am shown a photograph of a car. Though I am tempted to say, "This is a car," or perhaps, "This is my car; see the dent in the fender?" I also know that it's not *really* my car, or even a car; it is an image or a sign of it. I cannot get into the car in the photograph and drive off; I cannot wash it. There is an ontological distinction between the object and the image: although the car is in some sense the cause of the photograph, they are not the same kind of thing. Our speech doesn't always make this distinction, but we know it to be there.

Second, the event or object to which a photograph refers is in the past. This is a general feature of indexical signs: a bullet hole refers to a past bullet, a sailor's gait to years spent at sea. On this model, a photograph is a record of how something (an object, a scene) looked at the time the image was taken; it is a direct record of a past state of affairs.

Third, for us to read a photograph correctly, we have to be aware of how it was produced, aware of its status as an indexical sign. We believe that a photograph is an accurate indication of the presence of objects in front of the camera at a past time not because of criteria of resemblance but because we know how the image was generated.[17]

Our knowledge enables what Bazin describes as "the irrational power of the photograph to bear away our faith" ("O," 1:14). If we understand the process of production—the fact that there is a direct relation between image and object—we will be able to say with certainty that what we see is faithful to what was there.[18]

There is evidence in the "Ontology" essay to support the index argument. Discussing the psychology of art, Bazin states that "no one believes any longer in the ontological identity of model and portrait" [*l'identité ontologique du modèle et du portrait*] ("O," 1:10), a remark which suggests that he is thinking of visual images as signs. He then tries to categorize different kinds of images according to the means by which they are produced, the relation between the image and the object it purports to represent. In painting, "no matter how skillful the painter, his work was always in fee to an inescapable subjectivity. The fact that a human hand intervened cast a shadow of doubt over the image" ("O," 1:12). For this reason, paintings do not have a direct relation to reality. What matters is not that there is mediation—a photograph has that as well—but that this mediation is human and intentional; the sign in the painting is not indexical.

Photography is different. Bazin claims that "for the first time, between the originating object and its reproduction there intervenes only the instrumentality of a nonliving agent. For the first time an image of the world is formed automatically, without the creative intervention of man" ("O," 1:13). The photographer has control over the selection of the object to be photographed (and other factors as well), but not over the formation of the image. This makes the photograph an indexical sign, pointing back in time towards its source in the objects behind the image. Bazin claims that "we are forced to accept as real the existence of the object reproduced, actually re-presented" ("O," 1:13–14).[19]

Despite such evidence, the index argument, and so the standard reading as well, does not capture the main argument of the "Ontology" essay; what Bazin argues is something far stronger, more powerful, and, in some deep ways, stranger. Immediately after the comments suggesting a semiotic model, Bazin begins to develop a new set of metaphors: "Photography affects us like a phenomenon in nature, like a flower or a snowflake" ("O," 1:13); "something more than a mere approximation, a decal or approximate tracing" [*un décalque approximatif*] ("O," 1:14). We are getting a different picture here. A snowflake and a flower do not *stand for* an absent object (though either can be interpreted in various ways, for example, to tell what season it is), nor do they refer to a past reality. Similarly, Bazin argues, objects in photographs are in the here and now, with a positive value: "Photography actually contributes something to the order of natural creation instead of providing a substitute for it" ("O," 1:15).

Bazin introduces the notion of "transfer" to elaborate this idea. He writes that, with photography, there is a "transfer of reality from the thing to its reproduction" [*un transfert de réalité de la chose sur sa reproduction*] ("O," 1:14).[20] It is a strong claim—how does *reality* move from one thing to another?—but it follows a logic in our ordinary uses of transfer: power is transferred from one location to another; we transfer between forms of public transportation; we transfer money between bank accounts; we are transferred from one division of a company to another; in a grim euphemism, populations are transferred wholesale to new locations.[21] In these uses of transfer, there is a movement from one position to another, the emphasis on the final destination rather than the starting point. Though a causal relation exists, recognizing the new position does not require a grasp of this relation.

The rhetoric of transfer suggests a fundamental incompatibility of Bazin's position with the index argument. A photograph, Bazin asserts, has a closer tie to its objects than simply being a sign of them, even an indexical one.[22] Thus, at the conclusion of the "Ontology" essay, he writes approvingly of surrealism's imperative that "every image is to be seen as an object and every object as an image" ("O," 1:15–16). The image is no longer wholly dependent on an antecedent object for its meaning.

As Bazin works through his argument, the rhetoric of a "transfer of reality" disappears. One might think Bazin sees a problem in the way transfer implies that reality goes from one thing to another. Does this mean that we should understand photographs as having a reality wrested from the objects themselves? It is clearly false that photographs somehow diminish the reality of the world.[23] Bazin, in fact, more frequently uses the formulation of ontological "identity" or "equivalence" to describe the relation between object and image.[24]

Bazin now sets out what I take to be the central position of the "Ontology" essay:

> The photographic image is the object itself, the object freed from temporal contingencies [*libéré des contingences temporelles*]. No matter how fuzzy, distorted, or discolored, no matter how lacking in documentary value the image may be, it proceeds, by virtue of its genesis, from the ontology of the model; it *is* the model [*elle procède par sa genèse de l'ontologie du modèle; elle* est *le modèle*].
>
> ["O," 1:14]

The basic postulate of the index argument is here: the image is formed by a causal process that depends for its effect not on criteria of resemblance but on the process of generation. But when Bazin says, "it *is* the model,"[25] how are we to understand *that*? No one argues that a footprint *is* a foot or that the barometer *is* the air pressure, despite the fact that there is a direct, nonsubjective causal relation between them. However we want to describe what it is that Bazin is arguing, and whatever we think of it as an argument, it is clear that we cannot account for his description of the photograph along the model of an indexical sign.[26]

It's not so much that the idea of ontological identity has been considered and rejected as that it has been ignored.[27] This is a bit of a puzzle, given what Bazin says. I suspect it has to do with the sometimes confusing translation by Hugh Gray[28] and, perhaps, with the fact that the idea seems on its face an uncomfortably strange one. But I want to take Bazin's claim seriously.

Bazin's denial of an ontological distinction between image and object raises an obvious question: what does it mean for an object in a photograph to be identical (ontologically, not just visually) to the object photographed? Bazin seems to say that our desire to speak of the content of a photograph as if we were present to it—"She's in front of the building," "He's wearing a red shirt," "See?"—registers not a temptation but an ontological fact. There are several ways to describe such a claim. It could mean that a car in a photograph is the same car as the car the photograph is of. Or that they are instances of the same kind of thing, namely, cars. Or is it that the car in the photograph is real in the same way that the car in the world is real?

It's not clear that any of these formulations, or similar ones we could construct to make sense of Bazin's claim, are coherent. One might try to avoid such problems by describing the identity relation differently. Rather than speaking about *ontological* identity, we could follow Carroll and try as a criterion the way "patterns of light from the image are identical with the pertinent patterns of light from the model, which also served as causal factors in the production of the image" (PP, p. 126). But this move has a number of problems, such as requiring Bazin to believe that photographs of the same object taken with different lenses are about different things because they emit different light patterns—and Bazin maintains that whatever relation there is holds regardless of the way the image looks.[29]

There are two reasons not to dismiss Bazin's formulation out of hand. First, there are no easy solutions to these ontological problems that he somehow misses. It's likely that the notion of ontological identity is a paraphrase of a claim about photography in Sartre's *L'Imaginaire*: "I say: 'This is the portrait of Pierre,' or, more briefly: 'This is Pierre.' "[30] Bazin, as I understand him, is dissatisfied with Sartre's ambiguous analysis, as Sartre resorts to notions like "quasi-person" and "irrational synthesis." Second, Bazin is not unaware of the inadequacy of his own formulations in the "Ontology" essay. We can find evidence of this in the sheer number of metaphors used across his essays to describe the relation between an object in a photograph and the object the photograph is of. Beyond transfer and identity, a partial list includes mummy, mold, death mask, mirror, equivalent, substitute, and asymptote. This proliferation signals an unwillingness or inability to give a clear, positive account of the ontology of the photographic image.

The fact that Bazin continually shifts metaphors, that he never gives a sustained definition of a photograph, suggests that he never finds an account that satisfies him. Each metaphor captures something important about what a photograph is, but each fails in some way. (The task of exegesis would be to figure out what goes right and what goes wrong with each metaphor and why, in light of the particular films he is discussing, Bazin is drawn to it.) But every one suggests an ontology that is stronger than the index argument allows.

Bazin's hesitancy and experimentation at this crucial point in his argument, then, should not be read as an evasion of the problems inherent in the model of ontological identity. His metaphors represent a series of attempts at understanding the peculiar ability of photographs to give us more than a representation, however direct and unmediated. Indeed, we might treat Bazin's situation as a practical example of what Stanley Cavell calls photography's ability to generate a condition of ontological restlessness.[31]

Bazin makes an important distinction within the terms of ontological identity. Although he says that the image is identical to the model, he does not claim that the two are identical in all respects. He says that the image is the object itself, but freed from temporal contingencies. It is easy to slide between the two positions—if the image is the object itself, it seems logical that they be identical on all counts—but the distinction is important. We can see this in Bazin's claims that "the photograph allows us . . . to admire in reproduction the original that our eyes alone could not have taught us to love" ("O," 1:16). The idea of being "freed from temporal contingencies" implies the possibility of forming relations to objects in photographs that are not possible with respect to objects in the world. Bazin doesn't think, as Philip Rosen claims, that the photograph "always provides the spectator with absolute brute knowledge that the objects visible in the frame *were at one time* in the spatial 'presence' of the camera, that they appear from an irrefutable past existence."[32] Bazin seems to be saying that photography removes the object from *any* specific position in time. The objects a photograph presents may not exist in the present, but they are not exactly in the past, nor are they in any other time. They are real but outside (historical) time altogether.

If we go back to the phrase "the photograph is the object itself," we get a fuller sense of the distinction being drawn. I take it that Bazin intends us to hear Kantian overtones in these words. According to Kant, we can perceive only what we can represent to our minds in space and time; these are a priori categories of the sensible intuition that we impose on every act of perception, not features of objects or the world as they exist outside us. Thus, Kant argues, we can never perceive an object as it really is, as a "thing in itself."[33] We can only know the external world insofar as it satisfies the general conditions of human knowledge, appearing to us in conformity with the constitution of our sensible intuition.

Bazin is *not* arguing that objects in a photograph exist in the realm of what Kant calls the noumenal—the realm of things in themselves—or that photography somehow grants us access to a metaphysical dimension. My purpose in making the analogy, and for suggesting the importance of hearing an affinity with Kantian turns of phrase, is to emphasize the extent to which photographed objects are, for Bazin, outside their embeddedness in ordinary perception.[34]

For Bazin, the separation is twofold. First, there are the general categories of space and time in which we experience an object. Bazin says that photography frees an object from "temporal contingencies," but he does not say the same with regard to space.[35] We generally see an object in a photograph located in a spatial context; even in an extreme close-up, where all we see is one object, that object still inhabits a space. A photograph does change something about space, but this has to do with contiguity to what is beyond the frame. Bazin's use of the image of an usher's flashlight as a metaphor for the contingency and instability of the frame suggests that, though it makes sense to ask what is beyond that boundary, there is no sure answer.[36] The connection to a world outside the frame is, if not exactly severed, at least loosened.

Second, there are individual habits, memories, and associations that we bring to perception, whether these are familiarities with the kind of object shown, economic desires, or other forms of attachment we might have. Bazin writes, "Only the impassive lens, stripping its object of all those ways of seeing it, those piled-up preconceptions, that spiritual dust and grime with which my eyes have covered it, is able to present it in all its virginal purity to my attention and consequently to my love" ("O," 1:15). Photography gives us the freedom to form new associations, to have different kinds of relations with the objects in a photograph than we do with the same objects in the world.

I take Bazin to have something like this in mind when he invokes surrealism towards the end of the "Ontology" essay. When he claims that, in surrealism, the distinction between image and object (or the imaginary and the real) disappears, the effects run both ways. It's not just that images are accorded objective reality, so that "photography . . . produces an image that is a reality of nature, namely, an hallucination that is also a fact" ("O," 1:16). Bazin is also interested in the "effect of the image on our imaginations" ("O," 1:15), so that the kinds of things we do with or to images are applicable to our engagement with objects. It is the latter movement that Bazin embraces as the surrealist project: the new relations formed with respect to images are transferred to reality.

2 Realism and the standard reading

For Bazin, the ontology of the photographic image is intimately related to his view of realism in film. Most tellingly, in a position he reiterates across his career, he claims that "the realism of the cinema follows directly from its photographic nature" ("TC," 1:108).[37] Such a claim, though, does not specify how the notion of realism should be understood or the specific way in which it follows from its photographic base. Proponents of the standard reading, following on from the index argument, have tended to understand Bazin's position literally: as hinging on the resemblance or correspondence of a film to the world outside it. Carroll, for example, argues that "Bazin seems to presuppose a view that realism is a two-term relation of correspondence between film and reality" (PP, p. 142).[38] The film/reality relation, in turn, has been described in two ways.

The first develops the relation in terms of visual resemblance, leaning on such remarks by Bazin as "the creation of an ideal world in the likeness of the real" ("O," 1:10). We can call this the model of *direct realism*; it emphasizes specific styles—or at least certain understandings of these styles—that appear to refuse stylization (artifice) in favor of preserving the authentic look of the world. Henderson describes it as a process of "coming closest to reality" (C, p. 39), Andrew as "closer and closer approximations of visible reality" (MFT, p. 139), while Wollen calls it the "annihilation" of cinema.[39]

Behind the logic of direct realism is the presupposition that the world of a realist film ought to look like what was before the camera when and where the film was made. But this view, partly because of its reliance on the index argument, quickly generates problems. One of these is how fictional worlds can be supported on film. If we hold it to be the case that the image necessarily refers to what was in front of the camera, then, as Carroll argues, we would seem forced to believe that "*M* is about Peter Lorre rather than about a psycho-pathic child killer; *The Creature from the Black Lagoon* is not about a rivulet off the Amazon but about Wakulla Springs, Florida. Films you thought were representations of castles, grave-yards, and forests are really about studio sets" (PP, p. 149). The world of a film needs to be separated from (the look of) the reality that caused it. Carroll notes, "if it always makes sense to ask what is adjacent to cinema images, we may arrive at some very screwy answers. 'What's next to the land of Oz?' 'The MGM commissary' " (PP, p. 147). The coherence of a film's world is broken by the implicit presence of the world outside its fictional domain.

Of course, it makes little sense if we respond that the MGM lot is next to Oz. The appropriate answer is the countryside, the yellow brick road, or whatever the film tells us is there. The question of what is beyond the frame, of what is adjacent to Oz, makes sense solely within the context of its fictional diegesis. Its world, for all intents and purposes, is reality. A theory that cannot account for this aspect of filmic experience is in trouble.

Bazin himself is careful to avoid the model of direct realism. Consider his discussion of a famous shot from Orson Welles's *Citizen Kane* (1941). When Susan Alexander tries to commit suicide in her room, Welles shows the entire scene in one shot:

> The screen opens on Susan's bedroom seen from behind the night table. In close-up, wedged against the camera, is an enormous glass, taking up almost a quarter of the image, along with a little spoon and an open medicine bottle. The glass almost entirely conceals Susan's bed, enclosed in a shadowy zone from which only a faint sound of labored breathing escapes, like that of a drugged sleeper. The bedroom is empty; far away in the background of this private desert is the door, rendered even more distant by the lens' false perspectives, and, *behind* the door, a knocking. . . . The scene's dramatic struc-ture is basically founded on the distinction between the two sound planes. . . . A tension is established between these two poles, which are kept at a distance from each other by the deep focus.[40]

Bazin's analysis of the scene draws attention to a use of sound that, combined with an image in deep focus, elucidates a specific relation between poles of dramatic interest. Welles's respect for the unity of space is the foundation for the shot's emotional resonance; Bazin suggests that the scene would lose its effect if broken down, via montage, into five or six shots.

There is a tempting criticism of this analysis. Because Welles uses a matte, there are in fact three different shots superimposed in one frame (the glass, Susan, and the door). What Bazin treats as the preservation of the integrity of space is actually the effect of internal montage. His argument seems invalid. This criticism, however, presumes the terms of direct realism. Bazin does not claim that Welles is being faithful to an antecedent reality but that he is producing an effect that allows "an *impression* to remain of continuous and homogeneous reality" (OW, p. 77; my emphasis). Bazin's interest in the shot—and its emotional power—has nothing to do with the faithful reproduction of a scene in front of the camera. His interest is in the effect the shot creates, which is based on an impression, but only an impression, of coherent space.

Such analyses lead to the most compelling version of the standard reading, what we can call the *perceptual* or *psychological* model of realism. Because it holds that the relation of a film's world to our world has less to do with visual resemblance than with experience, it is able to account for the problems of direct realism. Perceptual realism involves a reading of Bazin heavily indebted to a tradition of phenomenology. In a lecture that Bazin may have attended, Maurice Merleau-Ponty argued that "a movie has meaning in the same way that a thing does: neither of them speaks to an isolated understanding; rather, both appeal to our power to tacitly decipher the world or men and to coexist with them. . . . In the last analysis perception permits us to understand the meaning of the cinema."[41] A film's world, if it is to be sustained in the spectator's mind, must replicate the manner in which we experience our world.

Bazin's love of certain styles and filmmakers is often cited as the justification for perceptual realism, such as his advocacy of depth of field on the grounds that it "implies . . . a more active mental attitude on the part of the spectator." The spectator is not explicitly guided to what is important in the frame but allowed, as it were, to make a choice. Depth of field "brings the spectator into a relation with the image closer to that which he enjoys with reality" ("E," 1:35).[42] The use of deep space and the long take in Renoir's films, for example, are seen as techniques that are inherently realistic; neorealism, another favorite of Bazin's, involves the use of real locations, non-actors, natural light, and an emphasis on contingent and ordinary events. According to this account, these films not only provide an experience of the world of a film that replicates our habitual way of being in the world; they employ styles that emphasize it (see C, p. 37, and MFT, p. 157).

Proponents of perceptual realism do accept the index argument. But, rather than a strict insistence on a correspondence between a film and what was in front of the camera, they give a looser and more thematic interpretation. They suggest that, because there is a direct connection between image and world (on the model of the index), a realist film must aim at the "normal" experience of the world. It's almost a normative claim, reading Bazin's insistence that realism ought to follow from ontology as a quasi-moral position.

Bazin's discussion of the relation of the world on film to our world seems to support this view. He writes, for example, "We are prepared to admit that the screen opens upon an artificial world provided there exists a *common denominator* between the cinematographic image and the world we live in. Our experience of space is the structural basis for our concept of the universe" ("TC," 1:108; my emphasis). One might read "common denominator" as involving, in the manner of the index argument, the material bond connecting film to world. But Bazin means something other than direct realism here. It's not space so much as the "experience of space" that allows the world of the film to be held in place. This distinction emerges more clearly as Bazin emphasizes the autonomy of a film's world. A film is able to construct a world with its own "autonomous temporal destiny" [*un destin temporal autonome*] ("O," 1:10). And: "The world of the screen and our world cannot be juxtaposed. The screen of necessity substitutes for it since the very concept of universe is spatially exclusive. For a time, a film is the Universe, the world, or if you like, Nature" ("TC," 1:108–09).[43] I take Bazin to be suggesting that the world on the screen literally functions as reality—our reality—for as long as the film is being projected. For it to become our world, it has to allow us "normal" modes of perception and experience.

There are two basic objections to perceptual realism. First, Bazin does not describe the films of Renoir or neorealism as realist on grounds that they resemble the experience of reality. He not only rejects verisimilitude as an essential component of *realism*, at various points coming close to directly opposing it to realism.[44] He is also explicit that perceptual or psychological realism is an inadequate criterion for realism (see JR, p. 29). Second, Bazin describes as realist a large number of films that have little to do with resemblance predicated on the contingency, flux, and ambiguity of reality. Thus, the absolute white image at the end of Robert Bresson's *Diary of a Country Priest* (1956) is called "the triumph of cinematographic realism;" socialist realism is analyzed as a form of "historico-materialist realism;" and Eisenstein is, at some points, acknowledged as belonging and contributing to a general realist aesthetic.[45]

Ultimately, the problem with perceptual realism is not that it fails to describe what Bazin takes the world of a film to be: how it is constituted by the film and held in place by the viewer. Nor is it that Bazin never talks about realism in such terms. The problem lies in its equation of the creation of a coherent world on film with realism. What becomes apparent when we look at more examples of Bazin's criticism is that the correspondence of the world of a film to our world—the cornerstone of both versions of the standard reading—is simply *not* the criterion for realism. Bazin will be interested in realism in films where worlds do not form or at least do not self-evidently form. And where a world does form, realism will generally be used to describe something else. Getting an account of Bazin's view of realism requires taking a different route.

3 Bazin's realism

The difficulty of this task is that, while Bazin's realism is oriented by the ontology of the photographic image, it is not determined by that ontology and remains open to a range of styles and genres. As Bazin notes, "There is not one realism, but several realisms. Each period [or film] looks for its own, the technique and the aesthetics that will capture, retain, and render best what one wants from reality."[46]

It will be helpful to have available a better sense of the way Bazin uses realism in his critical practice. Let's start with his discussion of Renoir. Renoir was one of the most important directors for Bazin, giving him occasions for insights into both individual films and more general theoretical problems. Here, too, a standard reading exists. Andrew argues that Bazin advocates Renoir's use "of the long take, of reframing [rather than cutting], and of shooting in depth [because they] sanction not only a unity of place and of action, but also a potentially rich ambiguity of meaning" (MFT, p. 159).[47] Renoir's realism preserves the integrity of dramatic space, respecting the manner in which we ordinarily encounter the world in its openness.

It's not clear, however, that Bazin describes Renoir's style in such terms. Bazin does not treat the hallmarks of the standard reading, such as the long take, as having to do with the integrity of the depicted world.[48] One of Renoir's celebrated uses of a long take, which is combined with deep space and reframing, occurs towards the end of Le Crime de Monsieur Lange (1936). As Lange descends the staircase to confront Batala, the camera departs from his face and executes a counter clockwise pan of almost 360 degrees, moving in the opposite direction from Lange's walk. The camera takes in the entire courtyard, only to return to Lange as he comes up to Batala and shoots him [see Figure 1 in the original]. Bazin comments that, while the shot "has perhaps psychological or dramatic justification (it gives an impression of dizziness, of madness, of suspense) . . . its real *raison d'être* is more germane to the conception of the film: it is the pure spatial expression of the *mise en scène*" (JR, p. 46). Bazin earlier defined the *mise en scène* of the film as having to do with the creation of a sense of the cooperative, expressed in the establishment of a circular space (the courtyard) that serves as a thematic emblem for the communitarian politics of the Popular Front.[49] The work of the 360-degree pan is to literalize and make explicit—give "spatial expression" to—the thematic concerns of the film that are registered in the physical arrangement of its world.

Renoir's film repeatedly positions Lange within the community, a theme emphasized by showing the entire courtyard at the moment when the dramatic focus is on his seemingly individual decision. The shot attunes us to the larger effects Lange's action might have. One very real possibility is that the community will be shattered, its unity lost, and its primary source of income (Lange's comics) banished from its midst. But we can also read the murder as an evocation of communal will; Lange is not acting on his own desires (of jealousy or selfishness, for example) but on the desires of the entire courtyard. The point is not to decide in favor of one or the other (both are there and, I think, not incompatible) but to draw attention to the degree to which Renoir's style gives a dramatic, and spatial, situation its meaning. It does not simply provide a blank background (the ambiguity of reality) on which action takes place but makes us aware of the connection between the individual and the group, and the scale of the consequences an individual action may have.

We are starting to get a better sense of the kind of work realism does for Bazin. We can say that Renoir takes his film to say something about the social relations between both persons and classes (their differences, similarities, and interactions in a public sphere). The mere existence of the film gives these relations a physical reality. The work of style is to generate a social fact by taking up an attitude towards physical reality, showing it in a particular way. As Bazin notes, realism is a way of "giving reality meaning" (JR, p. 84).

It is crucial for my reading of Bazin that he describes Renoir's style as pertaining *only* to a specific form of realism that gives a particular interpretation of reality.[50] Bazin argues:

> The word "realism" as it is commonly used does not have an absolute and clear meaning, so much as it indicates a certain tendency toward the faithful rendering of reality on film. Given the fact that this movement toward the real can take a thousand different routes, the apologia for "realism" per se, strictly speaking, means nothing at all. The movement is valuable only insofar as it brings increased meaning (itself an abstraction) to what is created.
>
> [JR, p. 85]

He identifies Renoir's "genius" as the ability to bring a specific increase of meaning to an image of reality—to add something new to the reality, to give it an interpretation. The way Renoir does this defines his realism, but his alone; we cannot make it a more general model.

Along with Renoir's films of the 1930s, Italian neorealism is frequently cited as the style that most clearly fits Bazin's conception of realism (on the standard reading). Bazin is seen as holding the position Cesare Zavattini advocated, with neorealism as a cinema of authenticity, almost an anti-cinema, designed to correspond as closely as possible to the world the films are about.[51] Even when the fictional location isn't the real place of filming, there is an effort to provide an impression of authenticity and maintain a kind of "fidelity" to reality.[52] A typical list of neorealist features includes location shooting, the use of nonprofessional actors, contemporary political and social themes, technical roughness, and an episodic narrative form.

There are places where Bazin talks about neorealism in exactly these terms, as in his discussions of Vittorio de Sica's *The Bicycle Thieves* (1948). That film, Bazin argues, lives up to "the most exacting specifications of Italian neorealism. Not one scene shot in a studio. Everything was filmed in the streets. As for the actors, none had the slightest experience in theater or film." And: "No more actors, no more story, no more sets, which is to say that in the perfect aesthetic illusion of reality there is no more cinema."[53] This interpretation is generally taken to stand in for Bazin's view of neorealism more broadly. But, if we look at his other writings on neorealism, it turns out to pertain only to de Sica (and Zavattini). Bazin says different things about other neorealist filmmakers, such as Federico Fellini, Roberto Rossellini, and Luciano Visconti. With Rossellini, for example, Bazin explicitly refuses criteria of authenticity. He claims that Rossellini's films do not progressively fall away from neorealism just because they exhibit "less concern for social realism, for chronicling the events of daily life" ("BT," 2:96). Bazin also rejects the elimination of professional actors as a necessary feature of neorealism, even in light of the controversy over Ingrid Bergman's presence in *Stromboli* (1949).[54] Generally, when neorealist filmmakers used actors, they were not familiar faces—and most were cast, as with Anna Magnani and Aldo Fabrizi in *Rome: Open City* (1946), in roles they did not ordinarily play. Bergman, however, was already an international star and could under no circumstances be mistaken for a nonprofessional. Her presence was generally seen as introducing an unacceptable element of artifice into Rossellini's films. But the issue simply does not register for Bazin, even though he takes the role of nonprofessionals to be of real importance with de Sica.[55]

We find the logic behind Bazin's treatment of neorealism in an essay on Rossellini, where he argues that "the term neorealism should never be used as a noun, except to designate the neorealist directors as a body. *Neorealism as such does not exist*. There are only neorealist directors" ("DR," 2:99; my emphasis). De Sica's aesthetic differs from Rossellini's, and both differ from that of Fellini and Visconti. Because they each have their own style, Bazin suggests that they should be analyzed on their own terms.

In refusing to treat neorealism as a noun, Bazin is also saying that neorealism is not a list of things or a set of criteria that must be satisfied. Neither the content of the films nor an authentic relation between the fictional and the real world defines it. Instead, neorealism is a verb, an activity, a particular aesthetic relation that follows general contours but is specific to each filmmaker (and film). It denotes an attitude the filmmaker takes toward reality itself: "its realism is not so much concerned with the choice of subject as with a particular way of regarding things" ("DR," 2:97).[56]

It is at this point in his argument that Bazin introduces a new term: the fact. In neorealist films, Bazin argues, reality is turned into facts. A fact is not simply a term that refers to particular objects but to social phenomena as well: the relations a person has to the physical world, to other people, and, presumably, to institutions. A fact, Bazin writes, is "a fragment of concrete reality in itself multiple and full of ambiguity, whose meaning emerges only after the fact, thanks to other imposed facts between which the mind establishes certain relationships" ("AR," 2:37). We might say that a neorealist film starts with a particular fact that it treats as subject matter for the film, a sequence, or even a shot. It then constructs a style that functions as a response to that fact, a way of bringing out its meaning within the particular context in which it is placed.

Although the rhetoric of facts suggests an exclusive concern with social reality, Bazin is explicit that facts are based on physical reality. In his defense of Rossellini against his Italian critics, Bazin returns to the terms of the "Ontology" essay: a "photograph is not an image of reality. . . . There is ontological identity between the object and its photographic image" ("DR," 2:98). Neorealism, then, constitutes a particular mode of responding to and articulating facts while respecting the reality of objects in the image. Elsewhere, Bazin describes this achievement as the refusal to impose a viewpoint on reality: "The originality of Italian neorealism as compared with the chief schools of realism that preceded it and with the Soviet cinema, lies in never making reality the servant of some *a priori* point of view."[57] Facts do not enter a film with a preexistent meaning that is simply reproduced; they emerge in the way style confers (new) signification on physical reality.

Bazin describes Rossellini as an "*a posteriori*" filmmaker, one who presents reality and then takes a stance towards it. He writes, "The art of Rossellini consists in knowing what has to be done to confer on the facts what is at once their most substantial and their most elegant shape—not the most graceful, but the sharpest in outline, the most direct, or the most trenchant" ("DR," 2:101). It is not about reflecting the world, but taking its reality and using sound and image to give it meaning. Bazin often describes this as a dialectic between the concrete and the abstract, the physical level of reality and the style that gives it meaning (see "DR," 2:101; JR, p. 84; and "E," 1:39). Even at the basic level of the shot, reality is presented and an attitude, an interpretation, is taken.

To get a better sense of how this mechanism works, we will have to look in detail at an example. Bazin rarely engages in close analysis, but filling in what an analysis might be on his terms will show how his conception of realism aids a descriptive account of the work done by a film.

I want to turn, then, to the fact of Ingrid Bergman or, rather, to what Rossellini understands that fact to be. He seems to believe that Bergman almost automatically poses the problem of existence in a world that is not only physical but outside one's control. If Anna Magnani is at home amongst the physicality of objects, Bergman remains at a level of remove.[58] Rossellini's insight is that an entire drama can be built out of her confrontation with the material stuff of the world.

The change in Rossellini's use of Bergman from *Stromboli* to *Viaggio in Italia* (1954) reveals something about his understanding of this fact. In the first film, she is pitted against the bleak harshness of the island and the sheer sublimity of its volcano. Rossellini stages her encounter with the physical world in almost hyperbolic terms; it is only after being nearly annihilated by the volcano that she is able to accept a world that infringes on her sense of self and her desire to be separate from the corporeality of her environment. By *Viaggio in Italia*, though, Rossellini has become interested more in her relation to the physical world as such, a relation he brings out by placing her against ordinary, even innocuous, objects.

It is this more mundane treatment of Bergman's encounters with the world that structures the scene in *Viaggio in Italia* where Katherine (Bergman) encounters a series of statues at the Museo Archeologico Nazionale. Two aspects of its style are worth special attention: first, the camera is called to life by Katherine's gaze at the statues; second, it does not so much replicate her look as articulate a specific relation between her and the stone figures.

The first shot of the scene is from within the museum, as Katherine and her guide enter through a gate in the background. The camera pans with them as they move across the frame to the right, the guide providing the history of the museum while Katherine looks around, and then exit into the main hall. There is a dissolve to a close-up of an unidentified statue, the camera already in the process of pulling back from it. As it comes to a rest, the pair enter behind the statue and walk past from right to left. Katherine looks at it and, as she does so, the camera starts to track to the left, as if following her; there is a flurry of slightly mysterious and fantastic music.

This shot is worth attending to. The initial track backward from the statue is unique in the sequence, the only camera movement that occurs before Katherine has looked at a statue. It seems to be doing two things. First, it announces the autonomy of the camera from the looks of Katherine and her guide. In the shots that showed her driving to the museum, our views of the city and its inhabitants were restricted to her perspective; the same constraints do not apply here.[59] Second, it raises the question of what it is about these objects, and about art objects in general, that evokes such a response.[60] Why is the camera called into motion here, rather than when it looks at objects in the city or at other tourist locations? The terms of Rossellini's answer center around the capacity of the statues to provoke Katherine's imagination, to allow her to depart from and in a sense go beyond their physicality and the banality of the guide's remarks.[61] The drama of the sequence is the way these flights of fantasy are motivated but not entirely determined by the sculptures—the potential for a failed encounter exists and, as we will see, the conditions for it are built into the sequence.

Katherine's first encounter concludes as she and the guide walk to the left, towards a statue of a group of dancers. As she steps forward to get a better look, there is a cut to a closer shot of the dancers, the camera a tracking to the right across the faces of four statues and then tilting down to reveal Katherine looking up at them. The camera not only displays the statues but brings her, and her act of looking, into the frame as well. In a pattern that runs throughout the sequence, the camera's movement appears to be triggered by Katherine's gaze at a statue: we are shown a statue; she enters the frame and looks at it; the camera then begins to move around the object, as if articulating the tone of her look.

The next two shots, of the satyr and the drunken boy, continue this pattern. The first starts with a close-up of the statue. The guide passes behind it, moving to the right and talking, and Katherine follows; as she enters, looking at the satyr, the camera starts to track and pan to the left around the statue, keeping her and the figure within the same frame. Rossellini shows us the structure and duration of their encounter. The second shot also begins with the guide moving behind a statue. Katherine enters, looks over at the statue, and the camera tracks in towards her, going over the boy's head and swiveling to frame her briefly in a close-up from above (with the guide in the background). It then continues around her head to reframe the statue from behind her position.

Rossellini now begins to vary the pattern. There is a shot of Katherine walking directly at the camera, looking intently in front of her. A 180-degree cut leads to a quick track towards a statue of a discus thrower, staring above the camera into the distance; the camera stops slightly beneath the statue, looking up at it [see Figure 2 in the original]. The shot/ reverse-shot pairing generates a degree of intensity, almost suggesting that the statue looks back at her—or that it has, for Katherine at least, the capacity to do so. The power of these two shots then fades away as the next shot shows a longer view of her beside the statue as she starts to move away to the right; its magic (its aura?) is lost as her encounter with it comes to an end. Rossellini's camera registers the changing facts of the situation, not just by showing it but by articulating a series of views that brings out these facts.[62]

The three subsequent shots show busts of different emperors. A wipe establishes the first shot: the camera tracks into the statue and pivots around it. The same movement, though not always with the forward glide, is found in each of the next two shots. The camera embraces the different shapes, or looks, of the heads. Although we never see Katherine actually looking at these busts, we understand the shots according to the logic of her previous encounters. In the moment the camera starts to move, we infer the presence of her gaze; she is now looking. It's not that, as Sandro Bernardi suggests, these are "false point-of-view shots."[63] No person actually sees in this way. But they have a direct connection to her gaze; they are views inspired by the fact of her looking at, and in response to, the statues.

The shots of the emperors also tell us something about how to read the sequence in general. The movement of the camera tells us how she reacts to the statues; it responds to and evokes her mood. Our understanding of Katherine is based on a set of inferences from present effects to absent causes, from the movement of the camera to her psychological state. On the basis of what we see, and how we see it, we grasp something internal to her.

This logic is made explicit in the one encounter that fails. After the shots of the emperors, there is a cut to a stationary shot of a Venus, a reaction shot showing Katherine unmoved. Her irritation at the guide's semiflirtatious remarks—they remind her of the sexuality in the naked figure—results in the failure of this encounter to provoke her imagination. She remains at the level of the physicality of the world, the corporeality associated in *Stromboli* with sexuality, and we are stuck there with her. The stationary camera indicates the absence of the imaginative force that has been present so far. This is only an object, a thing with certain meanings associated with it. And yet, although the camera does not move, it is still responding to Katherine's look. She refuses to invest the Venus with new meaning, and Rossellini brings this out with the stationary camera.

The last two shots bring the sequence to a climax. The first shows the giant statue of the Farnese Hercules. Starting on the figure's right and slightly to its front, a framing that captures its bust, the camera swivels around in a crane shot to a position behind and above the statue, thereby also framing the guide and Katherine looking at it. The camera then slowly pulls back and settles into a stationary position; as it does, Katherine turns away to walk over to another statue in the background. In no other shot in the sequence is the encounter between her and a statue given such a dramatic handling. The movement of the camera traces the massive dimensions of the figure, investing it with a physical sensuousness that mirrors her exclamation, "Oh, it's wonderful!" If Katherine is overwhelmed by the physical imposition of the statue, she returns to herself in an imaginative act of encompassment; she is able to proclaim a judgment on the statue, albeit a trite one.

The final shot of the sequence shows several figures struggling with a bull. The camera tracks into the bull's head, moves left to frame a figure at the far right of the group, and then tilts down and pivots to reveal others underneath. Continuing onwards, it travels to the right across the front to show a dog looking up at the scene. Here, embedded in the final statue, is a kind of allegory for the sequence as a whole. Rossellini's mode of expression is based around a series of visual encounters, a figure outside the event looking in and responding to it.

The structure of the museum sequence in *Viaggio in Italia* emerges from Rossellini's weighing up, judging, and interpreting the fact of Bergman's physical and imaginative encounter with each statue. The structuring principle concerns the kinds of shots, or modes of expression, that best present the physical reality and social situation. On Bazin's terms, this counts as a neorealist sequence because the fact emerges not as a structure imposed on the world, or assumed to be already present, but as a form that responds to and, in so doing, defines its objects. Rossellini produces a "luminous mold" of the facts, a gesture adapted to their shape that serves to bring them out in greater relief.[64]

4 Realism as acknowledgment

So far, the difference between standard and revised models of Bazin's realism has had to do with his description and analysis of canonical realist films. If this were all, it might be possible to suitably modify the standard reading. But there are deeper issues here. On the one hand, we have Bazin's commitment to the realism of film as following from the ontology of the photographic image. On the other, we have a variety of styles that require an account that shows how and in what way Bazin thinks of them as realist. These are styles like Bresson's spiritualism and the Vasiliev brothers' Marxism that seem not to be predicated on a relation to visual or even physical reality. The task is to devise an account of how Bazin uses realism that accounts for both aspects of the term.

The standard reading can resolve this tension in one of two ways. The simplest is to ignore the moments when Bazin discusses "realist" styles that do not fit the conditions of direct or perceptual realism. But this leaves too much of Bazin's critical work unaccounted for.

The other option is to deny that considerations of ontology are central to Bazin's realism. This has at least the virtue of intellectual honesty. A sophisticated version of this position will note that Bazin himself insists on the connection between ontology and style but will argue that it is a theoretical mistake to do so and that his arguments about various films and stylistic movements are best understood apart from the ontological considerations (see C, p. 45).[65] Henderson has made the most extensive argument in this regard, dividing Bazin's work between systems of ontology and criticism (and then, within the latter field, between ontological and historical criticism). Henderson tries to show that, when examined, the two systems turn out to be irreconcilable and that the range of Bazin's criticism does not follow from or respond to the ontological arguments. He writes, "The history system involves far more complex, multifaceted judgments; as a structure of thought it is also far more difficult and complex than the ontology system. . . . It is not derivable from the ontology system" (C, p. 38).

The advantage of Henderson's account is that it is able to cover the range of styles that Bazin calls realist. He writes, "it is not the term 'realism' itself, but how Bazin qualifies that term that is the center of the critical act. Realism becomes the name of the problem to be solved, a kind of x. . . . Realism is Bazin's touchstone or basic critical concept; but it remains in itself a blank or open term" (C, p. 45).[66] Certainly, the openness of realism is the feature of Bazin's argument that is usually ignored by the standard reading.

Henderson's argument, though, fails on two counts. First, Bazin does not think that just any film can be realist; to his eyes, German expressionism is certainly not, and neither is Soviet cinema (sometimes). Second, the absence of the role of ontology comes at a cost. The trouble is not simply exegetical. The ontology of the photographic image is central to the productive tension between style and reality that lies at the heart of Bazin's understanding of realism. Bazin writes, "To define a film style, it is always necessary to come back to the dialectic between reality and abstraction, between the concrete and the ideal" (JR, p. 84). It is only by paying attention to the relation between style and ontology that we can discern why Bazin thinks certain films to be realist in the first place.

The initial definition of realism given above involved a film constructing a style that gives a meaning or significance to the physical reality it presents, turning it into facts. I've described this process in a set of loose phrases: the film "responds to," "takes into account," or "takes an attitude towards" the reality of objects in the images. I want to collect these under the general heading of *acknowledgment*, a concept that allows us to link the two aspects of realism together: its ontological foundation and its aesthetic variety.

The idea of acknowledgment is developed in Stanley Cavell's early work. In contrast to simply knowing something, for example, that someone is in pain, acknowledging involves actually doing something with that knowledge, responding to it in some way. Cavell writes, "Acknowledgment goes beyond knowledge. (Goes beyond not, so to speak, in the order of knowledge, but in its requirement that I *do* something or reveal something on the basis of that knowledge.)"[67] Cavell leaves the terms of this acknowledgment open, a troubling feature for a concept that is supposed to be foundational for ethical practice (sadism, for example, could be seen as relying on a perverse acknowledgment of another's pain). But what makes it problematic for ethics is exactly what is of value for aesthetics. The open-endedness of acknowledgment means that it avoids being defined as a particular set of terms, emphasizing instead the process by which a relation between style and reality is generated. It doesn't specify the content of the relation so much as the specific mechanism that produces it.

Michael Fried has provided the most extensive application of acknowledgment to aesthetics, using it to describe how certain modernist artists construct works in response to what they take to be the features "that cannot be escaped" of their medium. Fried notes that, for artists such as Kenneth Noland and Jules Olitski, "the continuing problem of *how* to acknowledge the literal character of the support—of *what counts* as that acknowledgment—has been at least as crucial to the development of modernist painting as the fact of its literalness."[68] The nature of the medium becomes the basis for the artwork; the work of the artist is to figure out the appropriate way, given the particular situation of the artwork (in a tradition, in a society), of acknowledging it.

Acknowledgment gives us a conceptual framework for conceiving how film can be oriented by its medium and at the same time produce a style that is not, strictly speaking, faithful to it. Recall Bazin's claim that an object in a photograph is ontologically identical to the object in the world (however murky this idea may be). This is the basic feature of photographic media, their "deep convention."[69] A film, if it is to be realist, must construct a style that counts as an acknowledgment of the reality conveyed through its photographic base; it must do something, in some way or other, with this knowledge of its medium. But what it does is left open for individual films to achieve. In the acknowledgment, a film produces a particular reading (an articulation or interpretation) of the reality in the photograph, thereby generating what Bazin, in his discussion of neorealism, calls a fact (a social fact, a political or moral fact, a spiritual fact, an existential fact, and so on).

This argument requires a distinction in the way Bazin talks about reality that is implicit, though not overt, in his writings. On the one hand, there is the brute or physical reality of objects in a photograph. On the other, there is what the film takes as its reality, which is already the result of the acknowledgment of physical reality. It is the latter use of reality that I have used the term *fact* to denote. The facts created in the acknowledgment can pertain to an understanding of social reality (Renoir), or they can demonstrate a certain feature about the world and one's existence in it (Rossellini). The kinds of facts developed, the second level of reality, *are* the forms the acknowledgment (of physical reality) takes—this is the mechanism underlying Bazin's theory of realism.[70]

The framework of acknowledgment allows us to see that Bazin's refusal to define "the real" is not, as Henderson argues, a crucial failing for realism but its greatest strength (C, p. 18). It leaves the stylistic resources of realism open, despite the grounding in the ontology of the photographic image. We cannot determine from contemplation of the medium itself what a realist style can be. Nor is it the case that there is only one fact that can be acknowledged by a given artwork, or only one way of doing the acknowledging. As Fried notes, "what, in a given instance, will count as acknowledgment remains to be discovered, to be made out."[71] The task is to discover, from looking at a film, what it is that its style is acknowledging—what it takes the fact of the film to be—and whether that involves doing something with the knowledge of its ontological foundation. Satisfying the latter condition brings the film under the general heading of realism; the form an acknowledgment takes specifies its kind of realism.

One of the strengths of the revised model of realism is its ability to cope with films that go beyond the film/reality correspondence of the standard reading. Take Bazin's description of the final image of Bresson's *Diary of a Country Priest*, a white background with the black outline of a cross and a text being read over it [see Figure 3 in the original]. He writes, "the screen, free of images and handed back to literature, is the triumph of cinematographic realism" ("SRB," 1:141). There seems to be a paradox here. Given the ontology of the photographic image, how are we to make sense of his claim that the lack of images, the very absence of physical reality, is the "triumph" of realism?

Bazin's argument, as I understand it, is twofold. First, the realism of the shot (and the film) involves the problem of showing spiritual grace or transcendence on film. Bazin is explicit, throughout his career, that genuinely religious cinema will not show this in visual terms, since grace does not have a physical manifestation. No external criteria can determine who is a saint and who isn't. Thus, since film is indelibly connected to the physical, Bazin will argue that the spiritual existence Bresson is interested in cannot be shown; as an inner state, it cannot take exterior form.[72] What Bresson does, as Bazin sees it, is give us this spiritual state, and at the same time acknowledge the ontology of the medium, by *negating* the visual dimension of the image. Because negation is not simple denial but a moment in a dialectic that implies the existence of the term being negated, there is still a relation to the physical reality (despite the absence of filmed images). Negation is not incompatible with acknowledgement.[73] Bazin writes, "The black cross on the white screen, as awkwardly drawn as on the average memorial card, the only trace left by the 'assumption' on the image, is a witness to something the reality of which is itself but a sign" ("SRB," 1:141). In the moment of the priest's transcendence (becoming a saint, as it were), Bresson turns *physical reality* itself into a mere sign, suggesting that what is happening is something that cannot be shown; it is spiritual, not of this world.

Second, Bazin argues that the film is not just about the inner salvation of a priest but about the relation of film to literature—the screen is "handed back to literature"—specifically the Bernanos novel on which it is based. He writes, "In this case the reality is not the descriptive content, moral or intellectual, of the text—it is the very text itself, or more properly, the style" ("SRB," 1:136). In saying that the film takes the text itself to be reality, Bazin depends on the distinction I've argued for: an adapted text does not have physical reality in the film—in this case, it seems like a metaphysical entity—but is a part of second-order reality (a fact). To make this explicit, Bazin qualifies himself and says that the reality that has to do with the text is not brute reality but the reality of the style, that is, the already interpreted reality.[74] Bresson enacts a "dialectic between fidelity and creation. . . . It is a question of building a secondary work with the novel as foundation. . . . It is a new aesthetic creation, the novel so to speak multiplied by cinema" ("SRB," 1:141–42). By negating the image and retaining the voice, Bresson articulates the prominence of word over image and thus novel over film.

In order to make sense of this and similar discussions in Bazin's work,[75] realism cannot be a limited and closed set of styles. What is at work is a relation between style and reality, but this can take many forms. Even films, like *Diary of a Country Priest*, that depend on a nonvisual style still acknowledge, by way of negation, the physical reality that objects in a photographic image have. With Hitchcock (a filmmaker he isn't fond of), Bazin argues that the narrative itself is taken to be part of the basic material of the world: "It is not merely a way of telling a story, but a kind of a priori vision of the universe, a predestination of the world for certain dramatic connections."[76] Hitchcock's work concerns how best to establish a relation to this stuff, to make it explicit (to acknowledge) that the film is about the way in which the story is told, the dramatic movement itself. Hence the importance of suspense. Hitchcock is described as a purveyor of a "light realism," with a delicacy of touch that serves as a counterpoint for the metaphysical status of narrative.[77]

Bazin's conception of realism opens up the wide range of ways in which physical reality is caught up in and mixed with rational, discursive, and spiritual facts (and the styles that generate them). If we apply his definition of neorealism to his own theory, we might say that realism, for Bazin, is not a noun, not any one thing, but an open set of styles that fall under a general heading because of a shared mode of approach: a way of interpreting, in acknowledgment, reality.

5 Objections: inadequacy and negative judgments

I can see two basic objections to this reading of Bazin. One is that it is inadequate because there are significant moments in Bazin's work where he proposes a different model of realism. Secondly, and more seriously, if it turns out to be the case that most films can be read to fall under the heading of realism, how do we account for Bazin's desire to say that certain styles, such as Soviet montage and German expressionism, are not realist? Does Bazin have valid grounds for negative judgments?

The most important source for the inadequacy objection is Bazin's essay "The Evolution of the Language of Cinema" (though examples can be found elsewhere), where he draws a distinction between "two broad and opposing trends" in film history. On the one side are realists who "put their faith in reality"; on the other, antirealists who "put their faith in the image" ("E," 1:24). Bazin's distinction centers on the location and fixity of a film's meaning. Bazin argues that, with F. W. Murnau, "The composition of his image is in no sense pictorial. It adds nothing to the reality, it does not deform it, it forces it to reveal its structural depth, to bring out the preexisting relations which become constitutive of the drama." Or, with Erich von Stroheim, "reality lays itself bare like a suspect confessing under the relentless examination of the commissioner of police" ("E," 1:27). The contrast is with montage-based style: "Montage as used by Kuleshov, Eisenstein, or Gance did not show the event; it alluded to it. . . . The final significance of the film was found to reside in the ordering of these elements [from reality] much more than in their objective content" ("E," 1:25). If realism allows the full ambiguity of reality to come through, expressionism and montage aesthetics artificially fix its meaning through stylistic impositions.

Consider, however, the ambitions of the essay. It is first of all a historical argument, analyzing "broad trends" rather than individual films. Bazin posits the historical development of cinema as culminating in what he sees as a contemporary turn to a form of realism that involves styles based on resemblance to reality: social realism of the 1930s (American as well as French) and postwar neorealism. These styles tend "to give back to the cinema a sense of the ambiguity of reality" ("E," 1:37). But this is not a contradiction of my reading of his realism. Bazin's defense of the "ambiguity" of reality can easily be read to fall under the more flexible model; for certain interests in reality, as with 1930s and 1940s social realism, the standard reading's version of realism counts as acknowledgment.[78]

The "Evolution" essay has a more specific ambition, however, and that is to defend sound cinema as a valid aesthetic form. Bazin is trying to rescue sound cinema, and realist cinema more generally, from theorists who treated silent film as the pinnacle of film art because of its distance or separation from reality. Rudolf Arnheim is an effective representative of such theories: "Film will be able to reach the heights of the other arts only when it frees itself from the bonds of photographic reproduction and becomes a pure work of man, namely, as animated cartoon or painting."[79] Arnheim believes that it is a historical fact of cinema that expressionism, and to some extent montage films as well, dies out with synchronized sound; by pinning the image down to a referent, sound prevents the kind of abstraction such films employed. The growing prominence of sound in cinema means that film loses aesthetic resources and moves farther away from becoming an authentic art.[80]

Bazin agrees that sound ties film more closely to a referent and also that this precludes a range of aesthetic forms, but, unlike Arnheim, he does not see this as a decline. Realism is understood to be the telos of cinema, with sound helping to bring out what was there all along: "Undoubtedly, the talkie sounded the knell of a certain aesthetic of the language of film, but only wherever it had turned its back on its vocation in the service of realism" ("E," 1:38). It is as if, in order to respond to writers like Arnheim, Bazin has to identify cinema's aim with a realism predicated on resemblance to reality.[81]

My sense is that Bazin winds up overstating his case—even on his own terms. We can see this in the way he talks about Eisenstein. In the "Evolution" essay, Eisenstein is opposed to the realist school of filmmaking. If filmmakers like Dreyer, Stroheim, Murnau, and Flaherty constitute the realistic tendency of the silent period, prefiguring the dominant aesthetic of sound cinema, Eisenstein is in the other camp: "the creation of a sense or meaning [is] not objectively contained in the images themselves but derived exclusively from their juxtaposition" ("E," 1:25). But Bazin equates Eisenstein with Dreyer at other points and elsewhere links the "search for realism that characterized the Russian films of Eisenstein, Pudovkin, and Dovjenko as revolutionary both in art and politics" to the ambitions of neorealism ("AR," 2:16).[82]

Bazin's strongest praise of Eisenstein comes in an early review of *Ivan the Terrible*.

He argues that it ranks "far above the best films from around the world that have been shown on French screens since the Liberation," but has trouble saying why, since "this film returns to the most conventional aesthetics of silent film . . . thus renouncing fifteen years of realistic cinema."[83] Bazin can't bring himself to like the film's style, but he is sure that Eisenstein has made a great film: "One is certainly entitled to consider the path Eisenstein takes in *Ivan the Terrible* as an offensive return to a dangerous aestheticism. . . . But such a hypothesis doesn't in itself give us leave to disregard the extraordinary mystery of this titan of the cinema, the genius of his camera in this, his latest film" ("B," p. 202).[84] What is striking is that Bazin tries to analyze *Ivan* with the tools of realism. At the end of the review, he puts forward a hypothesis that the film has such extravagant and baroque gestures because it is attempting to exhibit, to put on display, the fact that it is meant to serve a political enterprise: "Eisenstein may have consciously chosen a style for his film that rejected psychological realism from the start and that required for its own aesthetic realization the systematic magnification of a thesis, that is, the elaboration of a thesis without benefit of nuance" ("B," p. 203). This argument follows the model of realism as acknowledgment: Eisenstein takes a certain fact as the point of his film—namely, its status as propaganda—and makes that the basis of his aesthetic. The style is then an articulation of this fact through the acknowledgment of the reality of the image. By negation, Eisenstein makes us aware of the kind of reality the images ought to contain; he demonstrates the lack of fit between the world of *Ivan* (and, by analogy, the Stalinist world) and the reality it is supposed to engage.

There is, however, one group of films Bazin consistently designates as antirealist: German expressionist cinema. Here there is no need to modify the claims in the "Evolution" essay. But if we take a careful look at Bazin's position it's not clear that he has the right, given the critical tools at his disposal, to condemn what he calls "the expressionist heresy" ("AR," 2:26). This is the second objection, the problem of negative judgments.

Bazin's complaint is that German expressionism "did every kind of violence to the plastics of the image by way of sets and lighting," advocating a primacy of the image at the expense of physical reality ("E," 1:26; compare "SRB," 1:139). Even before an image is made, these films replace the world with something artificial, something that bears no relation to reality: the sets of *The Cabinet of Dr. Caligari* (1919), for example. Bazin's claim is that they have nothing to do with the ontology of the photographic image; they fail to acknowledge it.

The problem with this argument is that it is not a good reading of German expression-ism. Acknowledgment can take place by negation, which we have Bazin depend upon for his account of the final image of Bresson's *Diary of a Country Priest*. A similar argument might be made for an expressionist film. Cavell writes:

> Suppose that the only point of reality in these films is the ultimate point in any film, namely the actors—not a real animal or tree or sky or meadow or body of water to be found. Then what happens is that the locales of such films are given a specialized psychological or spiritual interpretation; we interpret them as projections of the characters', or some character's, state of soul, as their dreams, their fantasies, their madness. We interpret them in one direction or another, that is, as *competing* with our sense of reality. This means that the acting must be as stylized as the location; dictated by it, so to speak.[85]

If the fact of German expressionism is the actors, or characters, and their states of mind, a removal of physicality from the world would follow from it. The style of *Caligari*, then, could be seen as acknowledging the non-physical nature of this fact by negating the physical reality of the world it shows. Such a description is of a realist work.

To combat this, Bazin would have to argue that German expressionism constitutes a denial, rather than a negation, of physical reality and thereby fails to present a mode of acknowledgment. If negation recognizes the physical reality carried by the image, denial simply ignores it. The claim would be that, while both *Diary of a Country Priest* and *The Cabinet of Dr. Caligari* do not present physical reality as such, the former *does something* with its knowledge of the ontology of the photographic image. The latter does not; it is dead, mute, lifeless.[86]

This line of argument might lead us to treat Bazin's understanding of realism as implying a flexible but finite field, a continuum with a limit on either end. One pole would be German expressionism, with its denial of reality; the other would be a certain picture of documentary film, where reality is hypostatized and isolated, simply accepted as being there rather than acknowledged.[87]

I don't think this picture is satisfactory. It may be the case that some expressionist films constitute a denial of physical reality, but there is no reason why Bazin should think that all expressionist films do so. The same holds for documentary films, as Bazin himself makes clear. Discussing *Kon Tiki* (dir. Thor Heyerdahl; 1950), he argues that although the film takes as its reality the fact that "the actors in the drama" were there, the images don't have documentary authenticity on their own. Instead, the structure of the film works to acknowledge this fact: "whenever something of significance occurred, the onset of a storm for example, the crew were too busy to bother running a camera."[88] Rather than a hypostatization of reality, we are given a subtle engagement with it that generates an interpretation—a fact. Similar arguments could be made about other documentary films.

It's not clear that Bazin has the resources with which to make negative judgments. One possibility would be to base such judgments on criteria of coherence and consistency, as Bazin does with Hitchcock's *Shadow of a Doubt* (1943): "the writer and director obviously did not have the courage to follow their intent to the end."[89] We could also think of negative judgments in terms of quality: whether a film expressed its acknowledgment with subtlety, elegance, or dexterousness. But these options are neither robust nor critically exciting. And if we want to say that a film is bad, poorly made, barbarous, or uninteresting, that does not necessarily mean it fails to be realist on Bazin's terms.

We might also concede that Bazin was simply unable, for whatever reasons, to treat German expressionism with the kind of attention and complexity it deserves. The real difficulty, however, is more general. If the criterion for Bazin's dismissal of a film is that it does not in some sense acknowledge the fact that what is shown is in some sense real, there may be no films that, on a sympathetic reading, fail to do this. Bazin depends on the notion of realism to mark a specific feature of the way certain films work. If realism, for Bazin, is to be more than a rough synonym for films he likes, if it is meant to specify the kind of work only some films do, then it cannot be the case that, adequately described, any film can be read to fall under the heading of realism. Once negation is included within the critical vocabulary of realism—and a number of Bazin's arguments cannot do without it—it is difficult to think of how a film could fail to acknowledge the ontology of the photographic image.

If Bazin's conception of realism, as so many critics assert, does not live up to its own ambitions, it falls short on very different terms and for very different reasons than is commonly assumed. The problem is not that it is too restrictive, that it is founded on and so only recognizes a limited set of similar styles. Instead, realism now seems applicable to any and every film—Bazin at one point even hints at bringing animation under its aegis.[90] But this does not render realism tautological or irrelevant. There are other things it does than just provide criteria for classifying films as realist or non-realist. The work internal to a film that it helps us to see is vital to providing compelling accounts of what matters to a film and how this is shown.

6 Conclusion

I have been struggling against an established picture of Bazin, one which takes him to advocate a realism based on fidelity to an antecedent reality; it is a view on which realism is marked by the absence of stylization. According to this view, Bazin has an a priori set of criteria—long takes, deep space, respect for the integrity of a scene, ambivalent meaning—against which he measures an individual film. A film's status as a realist work depends on the extent to which it satisfies these criteria.

I have tried to set out an alternative understanding of Bazin's realism. Rather than marking out a set of features, realism describes the specific attitude a film takes to, on the one hand, the ontological basis of its medium, and, on the other, what the film holds as its central facts. I argued that we could best conceive this model in terms of acknowledgment and that doing so allowed us to see that what is being acknowledged by the film is only discovered by an investigation of its style. In *Viaggio in Italia*, for example, the movements of the camera tell us that the physical confrontation of Ingrid Bergman (and her imagination) with the statues is at stake and not, say, mere tourism. Realism becomes, in Bazin's work, an analytical tool, one that can get at the way a film works.

A final point. I have avoided an external reading, whether historical or ideological, of Bazin's writing. To engage these concerns directly would take us too far off topic. Still, what this essay should show is that, insofar as we treat Bazin's aesthetic as based on a moral or political foundation, we shouldn't take him to hold some set of implicit and abstract commitments.[91] Instead, we can think of Bazin as committed to a specific movement from image to reality. What we learn by watching and responding to films—films that are realist in the appropriate way—can be transferred to the way we engage reality. Bazin's moral imperative for films and film criticism goes something like this: It is only with things outside ourselves, things that stand freely of our capacity to impose an order on them, that we can establish meaningful kinds of relations—even if that involves their transcendence, as with Bresson. If film teaches us "to have a regard for reality" ("DR," 2:101), it does so by showing us something new about it, something worthy of our attentiveness and, as Bazin often says, our love.

Notes

1   André Bazin, *Jean Renoir*, trans. W.W. Halsey II and William H. Simon, ed. François Truffaut (New York, 1973), p. 85; hereafter abbreviated *JR*.

2   A representative example of this position is Fred Ritchin, "Photojournalism in the Age of Computers," in *The Critical Image: Essays on Contemporary Photography*, ed. Carol Squiers (Seattle, 1990), pp. 28–37.

3   The work of Timothy Binkley provides a clear exposition of this view. See Timothy Binkley, "Camera Fantasia: Computed Visions of Virtual Realities," *Millennium Film Journal* 20–21 (Fall–Winter 1988–89): 7–43; "The Quickening of Galatea: Virtual Creation without Tools or Media," *Art Journal* 49 (Fall 1990): 233–40; "Transparent Technology: The Swan Song of Electronics," *Leonardo* 28, no. 5 (1995): 427–32; and "The Vitality of Digital Creation," *Journal of Aesthetics and Art Criticism* 55 (Spring 1997): 107–16.

4   Whether a *film* is a thing like a photograph raises a different set of issues.

5   Miriam Hansen has made a similar attempt to reinterpret another classical film theorist, Siegfried Kracauer. See Miriam Bratu Hansen, introduction to Siegfried Kracauer, *Theory of Film: The Redemption of Physical Reality* (Princeton, N.J., 1997), pp. vii–xlv.

6   Dudley Andrew, *André Bazin* (New York, 1978), p. 21; hereafter abbreviated *AB*.

7   Andrew, *The Major Film Theories: An Introduction* (New York, 1976), p. 139; see also p. 157; hereafter abbreviated *MFT*.

8   *Realism and the Cinema: A Reader*, ed. Christopher Williams (London, 1980), pp. 35, 36.

9   Peter Wollen, *Signs and Meaning in the Cinema* (London, 1998), p. 89.

10   See Noël Carroll, *Philosophical Problems of Classical Film Theory* (Princeton, N.J., 1988), pp. 108–09, 111 n. 25, hereafter abbreviated *PP*; and Brian Henderson, *A Critique of Film Theory* (New York, 1980), p. 37, hereafter abbreviated *C*.

11   I mean to evoke here the sense in which Wittgenstein speaks of being in the grip of a picture: "A picture held us captive. And we could not get outside it, for it lay in our language and language seemed to repeat it to us inexorably" (Ludwig Wittgenstein, *Philosophical Investigations*, trans. G.E.M. Anscombe [1953; Oxford, 1997], §115).

12   See Williams, "Bazin on Neo-Realism," *Screen* 14 (Winter 1973–74): 61–68.

13   Bazin, "The Ontology of the Photographic Image," *What Is Cinema?*, trans. and ed. Hugh Gray, 2 vols. (Berkeley, 1967, 1971), 1:9; hereafter abbreviated "*O*." Gray's translations often obscure important aspects of Bazin's arguments; where necessary, I have modified them.

14   See Douglas Greenlee, *Peirce's Concept of Sign* (The Hague, 1973), p. 33.

15   This interpretation of Bazin began with Wollen, *Signs and Meaning in the Cinema*, pp. 79–106, and is still influential. For a recent example, see Mary Ann Doane, *The Emergence of Cinematic Time: Modernity, Contingency, the Archive* (Cambridge, Mass., 2002). For general challenges to indexicality as a descriptive category, see Joel Snyder and Neil Walsh Allen, "Photography, Vision, and Representation," *Critical Inquiry* 2 (Autumn 1975): 143–69, and Tom Gunning, "What's the Point of an Index? or, Faking Photographs," *Nordicom Review* 25, 1–2 (2004): 39–49.

16   This kind of phrasing often leads to the thought that photographs are somehow "transparent."

17   See Philip Rosen, "History of Image, Image of History: Subject and Ontology in Bazin," *Wide Angle* 9, no. 4 (1987): 13, and *MFT*, p. 138.

18   I am not suggesting that what I am calling the index argument is Peirce's own position but that he has been read in this way by a variety of film theorists. It may be the case that the thin reading of Peirce in film studies is due to an association of his thought with a particular picture of Bazin's arguments.

19   Doane summarizes this argument: "The fidelity of the image to its referent was no longer dependent upon the skill or honesty of a particular artist. The imprint of the real was automatically guaranteed by the known capability of the machine. For the first time, an aesthetic representation—previously chained to the idea of human control—could be made by accident" (Doane, *The Emergence of Cinematic Time*, p. 22).

20   The phrase "transfer of reality" also appears in Bazin's essay, "The Evolution of the Language of Cinema," *What Is Cinema?* 1:37; hereafter abbreviated "*E*."

21   Art practices also employ the idea of transfer. Lithography uses it to refer to the manner in which a design is moved onto a stone in order to make it available for more general reproduction. Photography, too, has the idea of transfer at various moments; an early example is the discussion in "The Talbotype.—Sun-Pictures," *The Art-Union* (June 1846): 143–44.

22   Insofar as the "Ontology" essay suggests an indexical reading, it is only as a moment in the logic of the general argument—a position that tempts us but that we need to go beyond.

23   Though it's not impossible to think so; people have thought that they could lose their souls if a photograph was taken. Poe's story "The Oval Portrait" dramatizes the transfer argument in the realm of painting, as does Jean Epstein's film *The Fall of the House of Usher* (1928).

24   See Bazin, "In Defense of Rossellini," *What Is Cinema?* 2:98, hereafter abbreviated "*DR*"; "On Realism," *French Cinema of the Occupation and Resistance: The Birth of a Critical Esthetic*, trans. Stanley Hochman, ed. Truffaut (New York, 1981), pp. 70–71; and "To Catch a Thief," *The Cinema of Cruelty: From Buñuel to Hitchcock*, trans. Sabine d'Estrée, ed. Truffaut (New York, 1982), p. 156.

25   David Bordwell makes a similar point regarding Bazin's account of the "mummy complex": "The mummy . . . is the prototype of all visual representation. The mummy is not a copy of the dead one; it is the dead one" (David Bordwell, *On the History of Film Style* [Cambridge, Mass., 1997], p. 71).

26   Bazin writes, for example, "In the [non-fiction] film about Manolete . . . we are present at the actual death of the famous matador and while our emotion may not be as deep as if we were actually present in the arena at that historic moment, its nature is the same" (Bazin, "Theater and Cinema—Part Two," *What Is Cinema?* 1:98; hereafter abbreviated "*TC*"). Bazin here draws a contrast between emotional presence—which can occur with a representation—and real, physical presence: the film gives us the thing/event itself.

27   Andrew and Carroll are the exceptions; see *MFT*, p. 140, and PP, p. 125.

28   Gray translates "*libéré des contingences temporelles*" as "freed from the conditions of space and time that

govern it" and "*elle procède par sa genèse de l'ontologie du modèle*" as "it shares, by virtue of the very process of its becoming, the being of the model of which it is the reproduction."

29   Which Carroll acknowledges; see PP, pp. 133–34.

30   Jean-Paul Sartre, *The Imaginary*, trans. Jonathan Webber (London, 2004), p. 22. Andrew has drawn attention to the importance of Sartre's book for Bazin; see Andrew, "Forward to the 2004 Edition," in Bazin, *What Is Cinema?* (Berkeley, 2005), pp. ix–xxiv. One might hear in these words older discussions of formal and objective reality. See René Descartes, "Meditations on First Philosophy," *Selected Philosophical Writings*, trans. John Cottingham, Robert Stoothoff, and Dugold Murdoch (Cambridge, 1988), p. 91.

31

> A photograph does not present us with "likenesses" of things; it presents us, we want to say, with the things themselves. But wanting to say that may well make us ontologically restless. "Photographs present us with things themselves" sounds, and ought to sound, paradoxical. . . . It is no less paradoxical or false to hold up a photograph of Garbo and say, "That is not Garbo," if all you mean is that the object you are holding up is not a human creature. Such troubles in notating so obvious a fact suggest that we do not know what a photograph is; we do not know how to place it ontologically. We might say that we don't know how to think of the connection between a photograph and what it is a photograph of [Stanley Cavell, *The World Viewed: Reflections on the Ontology of Film*
>
> (Cambridge, Mass., 1979), pp. 16–17].

32   Philip Rosen, *Change Mummified: Cinema, Historicity, Theory* (Minneapolis, 2001), p. 29; compare p. 168. See also PP, p. 145.

33   Kant writes, "But these *a priori* sources of knowledge [space and time], being merely conditions of our sensibility, just by this very fact determine their own limits, namely, that they apply to objects only in so far as objects are viewed as appearances, and do not present things as they are in themselves" (Immanuel Kant, *Critique of Pure Reason*, trans. Norman Kemp Smith [Boston, 1929], A39/B56, p. 80).

34   Though a photograph could re-create these conditions, the point is that it doesn't happen by necessity. See Janet Staiger, "*Theorist*, Yes, but What *Of*? Bazin and History," *iris* 2, no. 2 (1984): 105, and Cavell, *The World Viewed*, p. 24.

35   Gray's translation, given in note 28, obscures this point.

36   "We might say of the cinema that it is the little flashlight of the usher, moving like an uncertain comet across the night of our waking dream, the diffuse space without shape or frontiers that surrounds the screen" ("*TC*," 1:107). Bazin also compares the cinema to "the long prism of rigid light—the agile comet or the ray of moonlight from the projectionist's booth" (Bazin, "To Create a Public," *French Cinema of the Occupation and Resistance*, p. 69).

37   Andrew argues that Bazin was especially concerned with "the films that [the] ontology supported" (*AB*, p. 103). Compare C, p. 27.

38   See also Annette Michelson, review of *What Is Cinema?* by Bazin, *Artforum* 6 (Summer 1968): 70.

39   Wollen, *Signs and Meaning in the Cinema*, p. 89.

40   Bazin, *Orson Welles: A Critical View*, trans. Jonathan Rosenbaum (Los Angeles, 1991), pp. 77–78; hereafter abbreviated *OW*.

41   Maurice Merleau-Ponty, "The Film and the New Psychology," *Sense and Non-Sense*, trans. Hubert L. Dreyfus and Patricia Allen Dreyfus (Evanston, Ill., 1964), p. 58. For the claim about Bazin's attendance at this lecture, see Michelson, review of *What Is Cinema?* p. 70.

42   Elsewhere, Bazin writes, "Obliged to exercise his liberty and his intelligence, the spectator perceives the ontological ambivalence of reality directly, in the very structure of its appearances" (OW, p. 80). See *MFT*, p. 163.

43   Bazin will argue that a fantastic world, different from our own, is easily achieved by film: "Not only does some marvel or some fantastic thing on the screen not undermine the reality of the image, on the contrary it is its most valid justification. . . . It is based on the inalienable realism of that which is shown" ("*TC*," 1:108). I read Bazin's view of the autonomy of the film's world, like his use of the metaphor of transfer, as a conscious overstatement in order to emphasize the importance of treating the world on film as independent of the world outside the film. Perhaps his exaggeration issues from a feeling that the distinction between the two is harder to keep in mind, their separation rather than their connection.

44   Compare Bazin, "William Wyler, or the Jansenist of Directing," *Bazin at Work: Major Essays and Reviews from the Forties and Fifties*, trans. Alain Piette and Bert Cardullo, ed. Cardullo (London, 1997), p. 6 and "Farrebique, or the Paradox of Realism," *Bazin at Work*, pp. 103–08.

45   Bazin, "Le Journal d'un curé de campagne and the Stylistics of Robert Bresson," *What Is Cinema?* 1:141, hereafter abbreviated "*SRB*"; and "The Myth of Stalin in the Soviet Cinema," *Bazin at Work*, p. 23. See Bazin, "An Aesthetic of Reality: Neorealism," *What Is Cinema?* 2:25–26; hereafter abbreviated "*AR*."

46   Bazin, "William Wyler, or the Jansenist of Directing," p. 6.

47   Andrew notes that Bazin "loathed overplanned environments. . . . He sought the fortuitous, that provisory organization of the environment retaining the possibility of other organizations and harboring surprises and discoveries yet to be made" (*AB*, p. 12; see also p. 113). Jean Narboni notes Bazin's "preference for things that were alive, changing, becoming" (Jean Narboni, "André Bazin's Style," *Wide Angle* 9, no. 4 [1987]: 56).

48   He argues against both versions of the standard reading in his essays on Renoir: direct realism as well as a kind of psychological realism based on the believability of the characters and events. Thus, "what counts for [Renoir] is not verisimilitude but accuracy of detail" (*JR*, p. 81). And Renoir has a propensity to "dispense with psychological realism" (*JR*, pp. 38–39).

49   For a discussion of the recurrent motif of circular pans in Lange, see Alexander Sesonske, *Jean Renoir: The French Films, 1924–39* (Cambridge, Mass., 1980), pp. 191–92, 215–16. For a discussion of Lange in relation to Popular Front politics, see Christopher Faulkner, *The Social Cinema of Jean Renoir* (Princeton, N.J., 1986), pp. 58–71.

50

> But the function of depth of field is not only to allow more liberty to the director and the actors. It confirms the unity of the actor and décor, the total interdependence of everything real, from the human to the mineral. In the representation of space, it is a necessary modality of *this* realism which postulates a constant sensitivity to the world but which opens to a universe of analogies, of metaphors, or, to use Baudelaire's word in another, no less poetic sense, of correspondences [*JR*, p. 90; my emphasis].

51   See Cesare Zavattini, "Some Ideas on the Cinema," in *Film: A Montage of Theories*, ed. Richard Dyer MacCann (New York, 1966), pp. 216–28.

52   Peter Bondanella, for example, notes that "Rossellini's choice of locations combines authentic places that reveal the local color of precise geographical spots with artfully contrived locations that are so similar to the real thing that they have succeeded in fooling the critics for years" (Peter Bondanella, *The Films of Roberto Rossellini* [Cambridge, 1993], p. 66).

53   Bazin, "Bicycle Thief," *What Is Cinema?* 2:50, 60; hereafter abbreviated "*BT*."

54   See Stephen Gundle, "Saint Ingrid at the Stake: Stardom and Scandal in the Bergman–Rossellini Collaboration," in *Roberto Rossellini: Magician of the Real*, ed. David Forgacs, Sarah Lutton, and Geoffrey Nowell-Smith (London, 2000), pp. 64–79.

55   Discussing the possibility of Cary Grant playing the lead in *The Bicycle Thieves*, Bazin writes of its "absurdity": "Actually, Cary Grant plays this kind of part extremely well, but it is obvious that the question here is not one of playing a part but of getting away from the very notion of doing any such thing" (Bazin, "*BT*," 2:56).

56   And: "Neo-realism . . . is not characterized by a refusal to take a stand *vis-à-vis* the world, still less by a refusal to judge it; as a matter of fact, it always presupposes an attitude of mind: it is always reality as it is visible through an artist, as refracted by his consciousness" ("DR," 2:98). Gilles Deleuze, drawing explicitly on Bazin, gestures towards such a reading of neorealism with his idea of the "encounter"; see Gilles Deleuze, *Cinema 2: The Time-Image*, trans. Hugh Tomlinson and Robert Galeta (Minneapolis, 1989), pp. 1–10.

57   Bazin, "De Sica: Metteur en Scène," *What Is Cinema?* 2:64.

58   "From the beginning [of her career], Bergman was perceived as 'radiant,' 'spiritual,' 'natural' and 'pure' " (Gundle, "Saint Ingrid at the Stake," p. 69).

59   Laura Mulvey writes, "The director was clearly fascinated by these [statues], and the autonomous self-sufficient world of the fiction seems to collapse under their weight. That is to say, the combination of camera with music and editing that gives the sequence its aesthetic unity overwhelms Katherine and her fictional subjectivity. The camera is liberated from its subordination to her movements" (Laura Mulvey, "Vesuvian Topographies: The Eruption of the Past in Journey to Italy," in *Roberto Rossellini*, p. 104).

60   Another shot that has this kind of power and asks these kinds of questions occurs in the "Surrealist
      Overture" to George Franju's *The Blood of the Beasts* (1949). After a series of objects, we are shown a
      framed print of Renoir's *Jeunes Filles au piano*. At this moment, the nondiegetic music changes, and
      we hear the sound of a piano as if from within the painting itself. The print, initially just one thing
      among others in the outskirts of Paris, now seems more than that; Franju raises the question of why
      it is that we treat artworks differently than we do other objects.

61   Rossellini has located the role of the imagination at the heart of his films; see Roberto Rossellini,
      "A Discussion of Neorealism: An Interview with Mario Verdone," *My Method: Writings and Interviews*,
      trans. Annapaola Cancogni et al., ed. Adriano Apra (New York, 1995), p. 37.

62   Mulvey evokes "the discus thrower with his eyes looking straight into and challenging the camera. . . .
      It is as though the gaze of Medusa, or some other malign magician, had turned living movement into
      stone" (Mulvey, "Vesuvian Topographies," p. 105). The discus thrower actually stares slightly *above*
      the camera, presumably at Katherine. Is it significant that Rossellini, in *The Machine to Kill Bad People*
      (1948), shows photography as turning (bad) people into statues?

63   Sandro Bernardi, "Rossellini's Landscapes: Nature, Myth, History," in *Roberto Rossellini*, p. 59.

64   The model of fact and interpretation runs throughout Rossellini's career. In *Rome: Open City*
      and *Paisan* (1948), music functions as a kind of seduction, drawing us to the type of political actions
      we easily find glamorous and romantic. It tempts us to over invest in more romantic actions or
      ways of seeing and acting in the world. But the excessive emotions attached to these moments,
      the context in which they occur, and features of the way they are presented all work to prevent
      us from wholly identifying with them. Rossellini is able indirectly to call attention to what
      he conceives of as real political action: ordinary and routine events taken seriously and blended
      into the fabric of a larger political context. By giving so much emotion to the drama present
      in "false" political acts, the music winds up distancing us from them. It is a use so consistent as
      to almost be a code. We can see this in the Florentine episode in *Paisan*, where aspects of personal
      adventure are accompanied by music while the more mundane political activities are performed
      with only diegetic sound. In *Rome: Open City*, the actions of the children are given a romantic tenor—
      in both music and visual style—that contrasts with the sober, and ultimately more valuable, political
      work of Francesco. The work of the kids in their mock-revolutionary cells leads to their destruction
      of a German truck, but in doing so causes the death of members of the Resistance and the
      destruction of a real cell.

65   See also Michelson, review of *What Is Cinema?* p. 68.

66   See also Staiger, "*Theorist*, Yes, but What *of*?" p. 107.

67   Cavell, "Knowing and Acknowledging," *Must We Mean What We Say?* (Cambridge, 1969), p. 257.
      Other places where Cavell develops the idea of acknowledgment include Cavell, "The Avoidance of
      Love: A Reading of *King Lear*," *Must We Mean What We Say?* pp. 267–353, and *The Claim of Reason:
      Wittgenstein, Skepticism, Morality, and Tragedy* (Oxford, 1979), pp. 329–496.

68   Michael Fried, "Shape as Form: Frank Stella's Irregular Polygons," *Art and Objecthood* (Chicago,
      1998), pp. 78, 88. It is a running subtext of this section that the terms of modernist criticism,
      including those that came out of the writings of Clement Greenberg, can be of help in explaining the
      work of an ostensible realist like Bazin. Another direction this essay could take would be to show
      how Bazin offers us a more nuanced and compelling picture of such central modernist ideas as
      medium specificity and reflexivity.

69   Fried glosses "deep convention" as that aspect of a painting without which "the enterprise of painting
      would have to change so drastically that nothing more than the name would remain" (Michael Fried,
      "Art and Objecthood," *Art and Objecthood*, p. 169 n. 6).

70   The failure to see this distinction leads to criticisms like the following assertion: "Reality, if
      one reads Bazin carefully, sheds very quickly its material shell and is 'elevated' to a purely meta-
      physical (one could justifiably call it a theological) sphere" (James MacBean, *Film and Revolution*
      [Bloomington, Ind., 1975], p. 102).

71   Fried, "Jules Olitski," *Art and Objecthood*, p. 146 n. 12.

72   Describing another film's "phenomenology of sainthood," he writes of its "refusal not only to treat
      sainthood as anything but a fact, an event occurring in the world, but also to consider it from any
      point of view other than the external one. [The filmmaker] looks at sainthood from the outside, as
      the ambiguous manifestation of a spiritual reality that is absolutely impossible to prove" (Bazin, "A
      Saint Becomes a Saint Only after the Fact," *Bazin at Work*, p. 208). See also Bazin, "Cinema and
      Theology" and "La Strada," *Bazin at Work*, pp. 61–72, 113–20. Bazin describes Bresson's film as a
      "phenomenology of salvation and grace" ("*SRB*," 1:136).

73   See Cavell, "Knowing and Acknowledging," pp. 263–64. A similar understanding of the use of negation occurs in Adorno's remarks on Michelangelo Antonioni's *La notte* (1961). See Theodor W. Adorno, "Transparencies on Film," in *The Culture Industry*, ed. J.M. Bernstein (New York, 1991), p. 180.

74   I take Bazin's qualification as a way to avoid a regress to an antecedent reality. One might think that, since the novel resembles reality, for the film to be faithful to the text it must reproduce the look of the world. By placing emphasis on "style," Bazin makes it clear that the film takes the text *qua* text as its reality.

75   Another example would be Soviet cinema. Although Bazin sometimes criticizes it for a lack of realism, he tends to describe it as being realist *prior* to whatever film he is discussing at the moment. In "The Myth of Stalin in the Soviet Cinema," for example, he argues that realism does not fail until films are made in which Stalin's screen presence violates the basic canons of a Marxist analysis. Bazin opposes an authentic Marxist cinema, for which he coins the term "historico-materialist realism," to the films in which Stalin is presented as having "traits of omniscience and infallibility" (Bazin, "The Myth of Stalin in the Soviet Cinema," p. 29). Films in a Soviet realist tradition (Bazin gives *Chapayev* [1934] as an example) concern themselves with the relation between individuals and history. See Bazin, "The Myth of Stalin in the Soviet Cinema," pp. 23–40. For a similar argument about the role of the individual in a socialist realist film, see Sergei Eisenstein, *Beyond the Stars: The Memoirs of Sergei Eisenstein*, trans. William Powell, ed. Richard Taylor, vol. 4 of Eisenstein, *Selected Works* (London, 1995), pp. 751–71.

76   Bazin, "The Man Who Knew Too Much—1956," *The Cinema of Cruelty*, p. 166.

77   Ibid.

78   Bazin argues this more explicitly in "The Virtues and Limitations of Montage," *What Is Cinema?* 1:53–75. Moreover, in "The Evolution of the Language of Cinema," Bazin is talking about generalities, about large-scale film movements and trends, and it's not obvious how it relates to individual films. It is too simple to say that a film is realist only if it is in accord with dominant realist tendencies. His review of *The Bicycle Thieves*, for example, argues for its realism precisely because it differs from the established norm.

79   Rudolf Arnheim, "A New Laocoön: Artistic Composites and the Talking Film," *Film as Art* (Berkeley, 1957), p. 213.

80   For Arnheim's discussion of sound, see Arnheim, "Selections Adapted from Film," pp. 106–11.

81   The target of Bazin's polemic is evident when, after giving examples of films that "put their faith in reality," he writes, "these examples suffice to reveal, at the very heart of the silent film, a cinematographic art the very opposite of that which has been identified [by Arnheim and others] as '*cinéma par excellence*.' . . . The moment that you cease to maintain that montage and the plastic composition of the image are the very essence of the language of cinema, sound is no longer the aesthetic crevasse dividing two radically different aspects of the seventh art" ("E," 1:28).

82   See also Bazin, "The Passion of Joan of Arc," *The Cinema of Cruelty*, p. 21, "Day of Wrath," *The Cinema of Cruelty*, p. 25, and "*AR*," 2:25.

83   Bazin, "*Battle of the Rails* and *Ivan the Terrible*," *Bazin at Work*, pp. 197, 201; hereafter abbreviated "B."

84   And: "We must make a distinction between the value of the style as such and the quality of its individual execution" ("*B*," p. 202).

85   Cavell, *The World Viewed*, p. 196.

86   "Every sign by itself seems dead. What gives it life?—In use it is alive. Is life breathed into it there?—Or is the use its life?" (Wittgenstein, *Philosophical Investigations*, §432).

87   For a discussion of acknowledgment and hypostatization, see Fried, "Shape as Form," p. 92.

88   Bazin, "Cinema and Exploration," *What Is Cinema?* 1:161.

89   Bazin, "Shadow of a Doubt," *The Cinema of Cruelty*, p. 105.

90   This comes in a discussion of films of painting. See Bazin, "A Bergsonian Film: The Picasso Mystery," *Bazin at Work*, pp. 211–19.

91   As in MacBean, *Film and Revolution*, pp. 122, 322–25. For a recent example of this tendency, see Alan Stone, "Realism's Redemption," *Boston Review* 28 (Oct.–Nov. 2003): 65–66.

PART III

Classic debates

Chapter 10

Christian Metz

THE CINEMA: LANGUAGE OR LANGUAGE SYSTEM?

The era of "montage or bust"[i]

IN APRIL 1959, IN one of the famous interviews in the *Cahiers du cinema*[1] Roberto Rossellini—discussing, among other subjects, the problem of montage—expressed an opinion which was not new but to which, toward the end of the text, he gave a more personal twist. First, he made a commonplace observation: In the modern cinema, montage does not occupy the same place it did in the great period of 1925–30. Of course it remains an indispensable phase of film creation: One must select what one films, and what one has filmed must be combined. And, since one must edit and adjust, should one not do it in the best possible way and make the cut in the right place? However, continued the creator of *Paisà*, montage is no longer conceived of today as *all-powerful manipulation*. These are not the actual words of the Italian film-maker, but the formula does summarize Rossellini's most suggestive remarks.

Montage as supreme ordering—is that not the montage which, during its great period, lay claim to a persuasive power considered in some way absolute and which was "scientifically" guaranteed by Kuleshov's famous experiments? And is it not that montage whose effectiveness—overestimated perhaps, but nonetheless very real—made such a vivid impression on the young Eisenstein? Startled at first by the almost dishonest grossness of the efficacy[ii] it gave him, Eisenstein soon let his own mind be conquered by the desire to conquer other minds, and he became the leading theoretician of the "montage or bust" approach.[2] What followed was like a fireworks display. With Pudovkin, Alexandrov, Dziga Vertov, Kuleshov, Béla Balázs, Renato May, Rudolf Arnheim, Raymond J. Spottiswoode, André Levinson, Abel Gance, Jean Epstein—and how many others?—montage, through the enthusiastic and ingenious exploitation of all its combinations, through the pages and pages of panegyric in books and reviews, became practically synonymous with the cinema itself.

More direct than his fellows, Pudovkin was unwittingly close to the truth when he declared with aplomb[3] that the notion of montage, above and beyond all the specific meanings it is sometimes given (end-to-end joining, accelerated montage, purely rhythmic principle, etc.), is in reality the sum of filmic creation: The isolated shot is not even a small fragment of cinema; it is only raw material, a photograph of the real world. Only by montage can one pass from photography to cinema, from slavish copy to art. Broadly defined, montage is quite simply inseparable from the composition of the work itself.[4]

For the modern reader, a fanaticism, as it must indeed be called, of montage emerges from Eisenstein's great theoretical works, *Film Form* and *The Film Sense*. Micha rightly observes that, obsessed by that single idea, the Soviet film-maker saw montage everywhere and extended its boundaries disproportionately.[5] The histories of literature and painting, pressed en masse into the service of Eisenstein's theory, are used to furnish precursive examples of montage. It was enough that Dickens, Leonardo da Vinci, or any number of others combined two themes, two ideas, or two colors for Eisenstein to discover montage; the most obvious pictorial juxtaposition, the most properly literary effect of composition, were, to hear him, prophetically precinematographic. All is montage. There is something relentless, almost embarrassing at times, in Eisenstein's refusal to admit even the smallest place for continuous flows of creation; all he can see anywhere are prefragmented pieces, which ingenious manipulation will then join together. Furthermore, the manner in which he describes the creative work of all those he enlists as his forerunners does not fail, in certain truly improbable passages, to contradict even the slightest likelihood of any psychogenesis of creation.[6]

In the same way Eisenstein categorically refused to admit any kind of descriptive realism into the cinema. He would not accept that one could film a scene continuously, and he was full of scorn for what he called, depending on the passage, "naturalism," "purely objective representation," or narrative that is simply "informative" (as distinguished from "pathetic" or "organic," that is, in the final analysis, edited into montage sequence). He would not even consider that the continuous recording of a short scene that was itself composed and acted out could be a choice among others. No, one must fragment, isolate the close-ups, and then reassemble everything. Could not the filmed spectacle have its own beauty? One dare not say so. As if forever to reassure himself, that great artist whose genius and glory could have encouraged him a thousand times, manages to have beauty, which has been pitilessly rejected from every "profilmic"[iii] occasion, emerge without possible confusion from the filming, and only from the filming. Even more: from the montage, and only from the montage. For, on the level of each shot, there is filming, therefore composition. But Eisenstein never loses an opportunity to devalue, in favor of his concern for sequential arrangement, any element of art that might have intruded into the forming of the ordered segments.[iv]

The spirit of manipulation

A comparison suggests itself—and deserves more attention than the brief remarks that follow—between that obsession with breakdown analysis and montage and certain tendencies of the "modern" spirit and civilization. In its moments of excess, when inspiration would desert it, montage cinema (other than in Eisenstein's films) came at times very close to being a kind of mechanical toy—in a world, it is true, where erector sets are not the only syntagmatic toys to captivate our children, who acquire a taste for manipulation in their playing, which, if they later become engineers, specialists in cybernetics, even ethnographers and linguists, may be extended into a whole operational attitude, whose excellence of principle will be more evident here than in film. And, surely, we know anyway that an age is not defined by the state of mind of a few, just as "montage or bust" does not define all of the cinema. One man may be a cybernetics specialist, but another a farmer or a janitor; one film may be all montage, but another may unfold in large sections. A period, however, is shaped by all of its activities. If one chooses to emphasize one aspect of it, one is too often criticized for having at the same time neglected the others; the lack of ubiquity becomes a sin against intelligence. Nevertheless we must renounce discussing, along with our subject, all that is not our subject.

At the time of *Citizen Kane*, Orson Welles, whom the RKO producers had given an unusual freedom of means, would go into raptures, according to his biographer,[7] at all the apparatus he had been made master of: "That was the finest electric toy ever given to a boy." Erector set, electric train: both montage toys. Department stores sell electric trains in separate pieces: A new package of tracks acquired later on allows a small boy to reassemble his old switching in a new way; everything fits together. Catalogues list the different pieces one can buy (classifying them according to their functions in the over-all scheme): "right switch," "left switch," "ninety-degree angle crossing," "a twenty-two-degree angle crossing." You would think they were the parts of discourse according to Kuryglowicz, or a "text" spewed out by some American fanatic about distributional analysis. Still, toys are only an amusing example. There is also "photomontage," collage, paper cut-outs in the animated films of Borowizyk and Lenica, or certain "experimental" shows by the research teams of ORTF (French national television). Above all there are cybernetics and the theory of information, which has outdone even the most structuralist of linguistics: Human language is already fairly organized, much more in any case than many other code systems, such as the rules of politeness, art, custom; verbal language is enriched by a sufficiently rigorous paradigmatic category permitting the most varied syntagmatic arrangements. But, in the eyes of certain modern tendencies, it still bears too much "substance" and is not entirely organizable. Its double substantiality, phonemic and semantic (that is to say, twice human, through the body and the mind), resists exhaustive pigeon-holing. Thus the language we speak has become—very paradoxically if one thinks about it—what certain American logicians call "natural" or "ordinary" language, whereas no adjective is needed to describe the languages of their machines, which are more perfectly binary than the best analyses of Roman Jakobson. The machine has ground up human language and dispenses it in clean slices, to which no flesh clings. Those "binary digits," perfect segments, have only to be assembled (programmed) in the requisite order. The code triumphs and attains its perfection in the transmission of the *message*. It is a great feast for the syntagmatic mentality.

There are other examples. An artificial limb is to the leg as the cybernetic message is to the human sentence. And why not mention—for amusement and a change from erector sets—powdered milk and instant coffee? And robots of all kinds? The linguistic machine, at the forefront of so many modern preoccupations, remains nevertheless the privileged example.

The attitude that conceives and produces all these *products* is broadly the same: The natural object (whether human language or cow's milk) is considered as a simple point of departure. It is analyzed, literally and figuratively, and its constituent parts are isolated; this is the moment of *breakdown analysis*, as in the cinema. Then the parts are distributed into isofunctional categories:[8] straight tracks to one side, curved to the other. This is the paradigmatic aspect—and it is only preparatory, as was the filming of individual scenes for Eisenstein. The grand moment, which one has been waiting for and thinking about since the beginning, is the syntagmatic moment. One reassembles a duplicate of the original object, a duplicate which is perfectly grasped by the mind, since it is a pure product of the mind. It is the intelligibility of the object that is itself made into an object.

And one never takes into account that the natural object has been used as a *model*. Quite the contrary, the assembled object is taken as the model object—and let the natural object keep still! Thus the linguist[v] will try to apply the conditions of the theory of information to human language, while the ethnographer will call "model" not the reality he has studied but the formalization he has derived from that reality. Claude Lévi-Strauss is especially clear on this point.[9] The difference between the natural object and its reconstructed model is insisted upon, but somehow it is neutralized; the optional or individual variations of articulation in phonemics, for example, are "nonrelevant." The goal of the reconstruction, as Roland Barthes emphasizes, is not to reproduce reality; the reconstruction is not a reproduction, it does not attempt to imitate the concrete aspect of the original object; it is neither *poiesis* nor *pseudo-physis*, but a simulation, a product of *techne*.[10] That is to say: the result of a manipulation. As the structural skeleton of the object made into a second object, it remains a kind of prosthesis.

What Eisenstein wanted to do, what he dreamed of perpetually, was to make the lesson of events visually apparent, and through breakdown analysis and montage to make it itself an appreciable event. From this comes his horror of "naturalism." To Rossellini, who said, "Things are. Why manipulate them?" the Soviet film-maker might have replied, "Things are. They must be manipulated." Eisenstein never shows us the course of real events, but always, as he says, the course of real events refracted through an ideological point of view, entirely thought out, *signifying* from beginning to end. Meaning is not sufficient; there must also be signification.

Let there be no misunderstanding; this is not a matter of politics. It is not a question of opposing Eisenstein's political options to some kind of objectivity; nor is it a question of opposing to his purely narrative (nonpolitical) "prejudices" the possibility of some other reading, direct and mysteriously faithful to the deeper meaning of things, as André Bazin, more subtle than those who find fault with Eisenstein for being a Communist, has done.[11] It is a question only of semiotics: What we call the "meaning" of the event narrated by the film-maker would in any case have a meaning *for someone* (since no others exist). But from the point of view of the means of expression, one can distinguish between the "natural" meaning of things and beings (which is continuous, total, and without distinct signifiers: the expression of joy on the face of a child) and determined signification. The latter would be inconceivable if we did not live in a world of meaning; it is conceivable only as a distinct organizational act by which meaning is reorganized: Signification tends to make precise slices of discontinuous *significates* corresponding to so many discrete signifiers. By definition it consists in informing an amorphous semanticism. In *Potemkin*, three different lion statues filmed separately become, when placed in sequence, a magnificent syntagma; the stone animal seems to be rising and is supposed to yield an *unequivocal* symbol of the workers' revolt. It was not enough for Eisenstein to have composed a splendid sequence; he meant it to be, in addition, a fact of language (*fait de langue*).

How far can the taste for manipulation, one of the three forms of what Roland Barthes calls "sign imagination" ("*l'imagination du signe*") go?[12] Does not Moles anticipate a "permutational art" in which poetry, discarding the chaste mystery of inspiration, will openly reveal the portion of manipulation it has always contained, and will finally address itself to computers? The "poet" would program the machine, giving it a certain number of elements and setting limitations; the machine would then explore all the possible combinations, and the author would, at the end of the process, make his selection.[13] A utopia? Or prophecy? Moles does not say it will come tomorrow, and there is no reason why one cannot extrapolate from the premises of today. Prophecies are rarely fulfilled in their predicted forms, but they are nevertheless indicative. This essay springs from the conviction that the "montage or bust" approach is not a fruitful path for film (nor, for that matter, poetry). But it should be seen that that orientation is entirely consistent with a certain spirit of modernism, which, when called cybernetics or structural science, yields results that are much less questionable.

Thus, up to a certain point, "montage or bust" partakes of a state of mind peculiar to "structural man."[14] But no sooner is it established than this similarity must be qualified by two reservations, which might actually be only one. First is the point that the height of montage came well before the flood tide of the syntagmatic mind. The latter began really only after World War II, just at the time when "montage or bust" (1925–30) was being more and more criticized and rejected by film-makers and theoreticians.[15] Second, is it not paradoxical that the cinema should have been one of the areas in which the spirit of manipulation began its career? Is not the notion of a reconstructed reality, which seeks no literal resemblance, contrary to film's essential vocation? And is not the camera's role to restore to the viewer the object in its perceptual quasi-literalness, even if what it is made to film is only a preselected fragment of a total situation? Is not the close-up itself—the absolute weapon of the theoreticians of montage in their war against visual naturalism—on a smaller scale, as respectful of the object's aspect as is the establishing shot?[vi] Is not film the triumph of the "*pseudo-physis*" that the spirit of manipulation precisely rejects? Is it not entirely based on that famous "impression of reality," which no one challenges, which many have studied, and to which it owes its more "realistic" moments as well as its ability to realize the fantastic?[16]

In fact these two reservations are merely one: In the period when a certain form of intellect agent becomes more aware and sure of itself, it is natural that it should tend to abandon areas, such as the cinema, that restricted it, and should gather its forces elsewhere. Conversely, in order for it to exert a strong influence on the cinema, this mentality had to be as yet in its beginnings and not yet established.[vii]

From "*ciné-langue*" to cinema language

The preceding, somewhat cavalier[viii] view was not meant to explain everything. It was put forward as a hypothesis. The observation concluding it is negative and doubly so: Film did not lend itself well to manipulation, and the spirit of manipulation itself was not understood well. There remains a positive fact to account for: The cinema—which is not the only field in which manipulation may be, however imperfectly, conceived—the cinema, in preference to other fields, was chosen (and with what fanaticism!) by certain theoreticians of manipulation.

During the same period, to be sure, montage was being affirmed elsewhere than on the screen: in mechanical arts, in engineering techniques, and in the constructivist theater. Eisenstein was educated at the School for Public Works of St. Petersburg before 1917. He himself declared that his theory of the "montage of attractions" had been suggested to him by the assembling of tubular parts in engineering, as well as by the techniques of juxtaposition used in circuses and music halls.[17] He was actively engaged in the constructivist movement of the young Soviet theater. He was an admirer of the Kabuki theater, which he considered to be a pure product of montage. He wrote for *Lef*, Mayakovsky's review, staged Tretyakov, worked for the Prolecult (popular theater), for the Free Experimental Theater, for Meyerhold's theater, etc. But none of these influences and contagions[18] can exempt a truly cinematographic study from examining the factors that, in the nature of film itself, could produce—even if by some quasi-misunderstanding—the specifically filmic designs of the manipulative mind.

For the error was tempting: Seen from a certain angle, the cinema has all the appearances of what it is not.[ix] It is apparently a *kind of language* (une sorte de langage), but it was seen as something less, a specific *language system* (une langue).[x] It allows, it even necessitates, a certain amount of cutting and montage; its organization, which is so manifestly syntagmatic, could only be derived, one believed, from some embedded paradigmatic category, even if this paradigmatic category was hardly known. Film is too obviously a message for one not to assume that it is coded.

For that matter, any message, provided it is repeated often enough and with a sufficient number of variations—as is the case with film—becomes in time like a great river whose channels are forever shifting, depositing here and there along its course a string of islands: the disjointed elements of at least a partial code. Perhaps these islands, barely distinguishable from the surrounding flood, are too fragile and scattered to resist the sweep of the current that gave them birth and to which they will always be vulnerable. Nevertheless there are certain "syntactical procedures" that, after frequent use as *speech*, come to appear in later films as a language system: They have become conventional to a degree. Many people, misled by a kind of reverse anticipation, have antedated the language system; they believed they could understand the film because of its syntax, whereas one understands the syntax because one has understood, and only because one has understood, the film. The inherent intelligibility of a dissolve or a double exposure cannot clarify the plot of a film unless the spectator has already seen other films in which dissolves and double exposures were used intelligibly. On the other hand, the narrative force of a plot, which will always be understood only too well—since it communicates with us in images of the world and of ourselves—will automatically lead us to understand the double exposure and the dissolve, if not in the first film we see them, at least by the third or fourth. As Gilbert Cohen-Séat has said, the language of film will always have the advantage of being "already entirely written out in actions and in passions important to us."[19] All experiments on filmic intellection tend to prove this. The works of B. and R. Zazzo, Ombredane, Maddison, Van Bever, Mialaret, Méliès, Lajeunesse and Rossi, Rébeillard, etc. all share the idea that it is only those syntactical procedures that have become too conventionalized that cause difficulties of understanding among children or primitive subjects, unless the film's plot and its world of diegesis, which remain understandable in the absence of such procedures, are able to make the procedures themselves understandable.

After these digressions let us now return to Rossellini's interview. "Things are," he had said. "Why manipulate them?" Obviously he was not referring to the techniques of organization in their broadest sense, but only and explicitly to the actual cinematographic theory of "montage or bust." Thus he was echoing (to the utmost joy of *Cahiers du cinéma*, which was not interviewing him innocently) a whole tendency that the *Cahiers* had incubated and of which it was practically the incarnation. While the Italian director spoke, one thought of the French film-makers and writers. Was it not in connection with Rossellini's films[xi] that André Bazin had developed his famous theories on the sequence shot, depth of field, and continuity shooting?[20] As for all those comrades and friends, were they not all working towards the same goal, the death of a certain concept of the cinema: the erector-set film? If the cinema wants to be a true language, they thought, it must cease to be a caricature. Film has to say something? Well then, let it say it! But let it say it without feeling obliged to manipulate images "like words," arranging them according to the rules of a pseudo-syntax whose necessity seemed less and less evident to the mature minds of what is called—beyond the narrow sense of the "new wave"—the "modern" cinema? The days of Dziga Vertov's "*ciné phrase*" ("film sentence") and "*ciné-langue*" ("film language-system") were gone![21]

Thus André Bazin was not alone. There was Roger Leenhardt,[22] there was Jean Renoir with his many statements in favor of the sequence shot,[23] there was—to limit ourselves to film-makers who were also theoreticians—Alexandre Astruc, whose famous "*camera stylo*"[24] was, despite appearances, the exact opposite of the old notion of *ciné-langue*. A pen (*stylo*) only writes what it is made to write. What Astruc wanted was a cinema as free, personal, and sharp as some novels are, but he was careful to explain[25] that his "vocabulary" would be made up of the very aspect of things, "the impasto of the world." The "montage or bust" approach, on the contrary, consisted in dismantling the immanent perception of things in order to reel it off in slices, which would become simple signs to be used wherever one pleased. Around the same time, in a work whose title itself made cinema a language,[26] Marcel Martin observed in passing[27] that the reader would not find a strict system of signs. Then, following Merleau-Ponty's lecture on "Le Cinéma et la nouvelle psychologie,"[28] film began to be defined here and there, or at least approached, from what one called the "phenomenological" angle: A sequence of film, like a spectacle from life, carries its meaning within itself. The signifier is not easily distinguished from the significate. "It is the felicity of art to show how a thing begins to signify, not by reference to ideas that are already formed or acquired, but by the temporal and spatial arrangement of elements."[29] This is an entirely new concept of ordering. The cinema is the "phenomenological" art *par excellence*, the signifier is coextensive with the whole of the significate, the spectacle its own significa-tion, thus short-circuiting the sign itself: This is what was said, in substance, by Souriau, Soriano, Blanchard, Marcel, Cohen-Séat, Bazin, Martin, Ayfre, Astre, Cauliez, Dort, Vailland, Marion, Robbe-Grillet, B. and R. Zazzo, and many others in the course of one article or another. It is possible, even probable, that they went too far in this direction: For the cinema is after all not life; it is a created spectacle.[xii] But let us put these reservations aside for the moment, and simply record what was in fact a convergence in the historical evolution of ideas about film.

Rossellini's remarks, though they may not be very philosophical, nevertheless point in the same direction. Let us listen to him some more: The cinema, he says, is a language, if one means by that a "poetic language." But the theoreticians of silent film saw in it a real, specific *vehicle* (Rossellini's word) about which we are much more skeptical today. For the creator of *Open City*, who is not normally concerned with semiotics, this was a kind of conclusion. It was uttered somewhat haphazardly (in his choice of terms at any rate), spontaneously, but in fact with great felicity: It is unusual for a man of the profession, other than in his films, to suggest so many things in so few words.

A non-system language: film narrativity

When approaching the cinema from the linguistic point of view, it is difficult to avoid shuttling back and forth between two positions: the cinema as a language; the cinema as infinitely different from verbal language. Perhaps it is impossible to extricate oneself from this dilemma with impunity.

After analyzing the "logomorphic" nature[30] of film, Gilbert Cohen-Séat came to the provisional conclusion that one must at least overcome the temptation to consider the cinema as a language.[31] Film tells us continuous stories; it "says" things that could be conveyed also in the language of words; yet it says them differently: There is a reason for the possibility as well as for the necessity of adaptations.

To be sure, it has often been justly remarked[32] that, since film has taken the narrative road—or what F. Ricci calls the "novel's way" (*voie romanesque*)[33]—since the feature-length fiction film, which was only one of many conceivable genres, has taken over the greater part of total cinematic production, it could only be the result of a positive development in the history of film, and particularly in the evolution from Lumière to Méliès, from "cinema-tography" to cinema.[34] There was nothing unavoidable, or particularly natural, in this. Yet even those who emphasize the historical aspect of this growth never conclude that it was meaningless or haphazard. It had to happen, but it had to happen for a reason; it had to be that the very nature of the cinema rendered such an evolution if not certain at least probable.

There was the *demand*, what the spectator wanted. This is the main idea in Edgar Morin's analyses (which it would be superfluous to repeat with less talent). Although the spectatorial demand cannot mold the particular content of each film, Morin recently explained, it is perfectly capable of determining what one might call the spectacle's formula.[35] The ninety-minute show with its digressions (documentary, etc.) of lesser narrativity is one formula. It will perhaps not endure, but for the moment it is sufficiently pleasing; it is accepted. There have been other formulas, for example two "great movies" in a single showing. But these are all variations. The basic formula, which has never changed, is the one that consists in making a large continuous unit that tells a story and calling it a "movie." "Going to the movies" is going to see this type of story.

Indeed the cinema is eminently apt to assume this role; even the greatest demand could not have diverted it in any lasting way along a path that its inner semiological mechanism would have made improbable. Things could never have occurred so fast nor remained in the state we still find them, had the film not been a supreme story-teller and had its narrativity not been endowed with the nine lives of a cat. The total invasion of the cinema by novel-esque fiction is a peculiar, striking phenomenon, when one thinks that film could have found so many other possible uses which have hardly been explored by a society that is nevertheless forever in pursuit of technographic novelty.

The rule of the "story" is so powerful that the image, which is said to be the major constituent of film, vanishes behind the plot it has woven—if we are to believe some analy-ses[36]—so that the cinema is only in theory the art of images. Film, which by nature one would think adapted to a transversal reading, through the leisurely investigation of the visual content of each shot, becomes almost immediately the subject of a longitudinal reading, which is precipitous, "anxious," and concerned only with "what's next." The sequence does not string the individual shots; it suppresses them. Experiments on the memory retention of film—whether by Bruce, Fraisse and de Monmollin, Rébeillard, or Romano and Botson—all come to the same conclusion, though by different means: All one retains of a film is its plot and a *few images*. Daily experience confirms this, except of course for those who, seeing very few films, retain them entirely (the child's first movie; the farmer's one film of the year; and even then). On an entirely different level, Dreyfus[37] observes that the attempts to create a certain "language" in a type of modern film (Antonioni, Godard, etc.) occasionally produce a disturbing, however talented, overabundance, since the film track itself is already and always saying something.

Narrativity and logomorphism. It is as if a kind of induction current[38] were linking images among themselves, *whatever one did*, as if the human mind (the spectator's as well as the film-maker's) were incapable of not making a connection between two successive images.

Still photography—a close relative to film, or else some very old and very distant second cousin—was never intended to tell stories. Whenever it does, it is imitating the cinema, by spatially deploying the successivity that film unfolds in time. The eye proceeds down the page of the "picture romance" magazine in the prescribed order of the photo-graphs—which is the order they would have unreeled in on the screen. "Picture romances" are frequently used to retell the story of an existing film. This is the consequence of a deep similarity, which is in turn the result of a fundamental dissimilarity: Photography is so ill-suited to story-telling that when it wants to do so it becomes cinema. "Picture romances" are derived not from photography but from film. An isolated photograph can of course tell nothing! Yet why must it be that, by some strange correlation, two juxtaposed photographs must tell something? Going from one image to two images, is to go from image to language.

Kuleshov's experiments, as I said earlier, were considered for many years the "scientific" basis for the supremacy of montage. No one, however, has paid sufficient attention to the fact that, in the midst of the age of "montage or bust," there existed another interpretation of those famous experiments. An interpretation that seemed to provide yet more ammunition for the partisans of manipulation, but in fact implied a covertly discordant position (more modestly than it should have), which only the future was to bring to light. It was contained in Béla Balázs's book *Der Geist des Films* (1930).[39] With a kind of shrewdness peculiar to him, the Hungarian theoretician remarked that, if montage was indeed sovereign, it was so by necessity, for, when two images were juxtaposed purely by chance, the viewer would discover a "connection." That, and nothing else, is what Kuleshov's experiments demon-strated. Film-makers obviously understood this and decided that this "connection" would be their tool, to manipulate according to their will. Yet right from the beginning their hand was forced by the viewer, or rather, by a certain structure of the human mind, that obdurate diachronist. Listen to Balázs: "One presupposes an intention. . . . The viewer understands what he thinks montage wants him to understand. Images . . . are . . . linked together . . . internally through the inevitable induction of a current of signification. . . . The power [of montage] exists and is exerted, whether one wants it or not. It must be conscientiously used." In his *Esthétique et psychologie du cinéma* Jean Mitry elaborates in much greater detail an interpretation of the "Kuleshov effect" (pp. 283–85). He concludes that the famous experiments in no way authorize the theory of "montage or bust" (according to which the diegesis is marginal to the development of montage effects, which tend to produce an abstract logic, or piece of eloquence, independent of the film itself). They simply demonstrate the existence of a "logic of implication," thanks to which the image becomes language, and which is inseparable from the film's narrativity.

Thus, film montage—whether its role is the triumphant one of yesterday or the more modest one of today—and film narrativity—as triumphant now as it was in the past—are only the consequences of that current of induction that refuses not to flow whenever two poles are brought sufficiently close together, and occasionally even when they are quite far apart. The cinema is language, *above and beyond any particular effect of montage*. It is not because the cinema is language that it can tell such fine stories, but rather it has become language because it has told such fine stories.

Among the theoreticians and film-makers who have moved the cinema away from the spectacle to bring it closer to a novelistic "writing" capable of expressing everything—its author as well as the world—of repeating and sometimes replacing the novel in the multiple task it had assumed since the nineteenth century,[40] we find precisely, and by no accident, many of those who are the least concerned with "cinematographic syntax" and who have said so, not without talent at times, in their articles (Bazin, Leenhardt, Astruc, Truffaut) or have shown so in their films (Antonioni, Visconti, Godard, Truffaut). There are individual cases, of course: With Alain Resnais, with Jean-Luc Godard, there is a body of montage which reappears, but with a new meaning; the genius Orson Welles makes films beyond any restriction—a master of visual surprise, he can use, when necessary, continuous camera shots as involved and involving as a sentence of Marcel Proust's. But, whereas individual style is one thing, the evolution of cinematographic language is another, differing from it, not in substance (for it is the film-makers who make up the cinema), but in scale and in one's approach to it. One would need forty chapters to do justice to the first, whereas, for the latter, two suffice, at least for the present: *ciné-langue* (cinema language system) and cinema language. I have mentioned Antonioni, Visconti, Godard, and Truffaut because, of the directors having a style, they seem to me to belong among those, furthermore, in whom one can most clearly see the change from the will to system to the desire for language.[xiii] They frequently use the sequence shot where the partisans of montage would have cut and reassembled; they fall back on what is called, for better or worse, the "tracking shot" (and which implies nothing other than a noncodified mobility of the camera, a movement that is truly *free*)[xiv] where traditional film syntaxes distinguish between rear and forward "dolly," "pan," and "tilt," etc.[41]

Thus language is enriched by whatever is lost to system. The two phenomena are one. It is as if the code's signifying abundance were linked to that of the message in the cinema—or rather separated from it—by an obscurely rigorous relationship of inverse proportions: Code, when it is present, is crude—the great film-makers who believed in it were great despite it; the message, as it becomes refined, circumvents the code. At any given moment, the code could change or disappear entirely, whereas the message will simply find the means to express itself differently.[xv]

"Ciné langue" and verbal languages: the paradox of the talking movies

In the period when the cinema considered itself a veritable language system, its attitude toward verbal languages was one of utmost disdain. It feared their competition, which had come about only by its intrusion into their midst. One might think that before 1930 the very silence of film would have given it automatic protection against the detested verbal element. Like the deaf who sleep peacefully undisturbed by any noise, the silent cinema, deriving strength from its weakness, would lead, one might think, a still and tranquil life. But not at all! No period was ever more noisy than that of the silent movies. Manifestoes, vociferations, invectives, proclamations, and vaticinations succeeded each other in denouncing always the same, ghostlike enemy: speech—speech, which was radically absent—necessarily so—from film itself and which existed finally (as victim and executioner) only in the speeches delivered against it. The young Jean Epstein; the young René Clair; Louis Delluc (who died young); the cohorts of the "pure cinema" with their impetuous Egeria, Germaine Dulac; Béla Balázs; Charlie Chaplin; and naturally the legion in close formation of Soviet pioneers: They were all full of contempt for the word. And I have mentioned only the loudest.

Of course it is easy to smile at them. Yet there was more truth in their paradoxical anathemas than at first appears. The old verbal structures, although officially absent from film, were nevertheless a haunting presence. The attack was not without an object: Obviously there were the explanatory titles; above all there was the gesticulation in acting, whose true reason for being—we will have to return to this—was not, as has been wrongly said, in the infirmity of the silent image, or in acting habits mechanically inherited from the theater (how to explain that in some silent pictures there is no gesticulation?), but in a subconscious attempt to speak without words, and to say without verbal language not only what one would have said with it (which is never entirely impossible), but in *the same way* it would have been said. Thus there came into being a kind of silent gibberish, simultaneously overexcited and petrified, an exuberant gabbling whose every gesture, every bit of mimicry, stood with scrupulous and clumsy literalness for a linguistic unit, almost always a sentence whose absence, which would not otherwise have been catastrophic, became abundantly obvious when the gesticulated imitation so clearly emphasized it. Yet it was sufficient for a Stroheim[xvi]—reduced like his peers to silent pictures, and as anxious as they to express a great deal despite this limitation—to circumvent speech (instead of attacking it head on, while at the same time shamefully copying it) for film to be enriched and to become quieter, for the previously clumsily localized significations to become more continuous and to reveal a full, complex meaning.

Those for whom the silent film still spoke too much were thus not entirely wrong. They anticipated many truths; however, it was in the steps of a much broader development of thought—and one that was more obscure, and more deeply motivated. They were almost *afraid* of verbal language, for even as they were defining the cinema as a nonverbal language, they were still obscurely thinking of some pseudo-verbal system within their films. Obscurely, yet clearly enough for them to see the language of words as a powerful rival forever on the point of overstepping its bounds. An analysis of the theoretical writings of the period would easily show a surprising convergence of concepts: The image is like a word, the sequence like a sentence, for a sequence is made up of images like a sentence of words, etc. By assuming this position, the cinema, for all its proclamations of superiority, was condemning itself to perpetual inferiority. In contrast to a *refined* language (verbal language), it defined itself unwittingly as a coarser duplication. It only remained for it to sport its plebeian condition (many of Marcel L'Herbier's articles seem to have no other aim), in secret fear of a more distinguished older brother.

One can see how the paradox of the talking cinema was already rooted at the heart of the silent movies. But the greatest paradox was yet to come: The advent of the talking movies, which should have changed not only the films but the theories about them, in fact modified the latter in no way, at least during the first several years. Films talked, and yet one spoke about them as if they were silent. But there was an exception: A profoundly new tendency, unjustly scorned until Bazin began to rehabilitate it,[42] was being developed in the writings of Marcel Pagnol. This tendency came from outside the cinema, and its roots were not buried in the problems of the silent film (which is what aroused the fury of its enemies). Very significantly, it began to appear only after the arrival of the talking movies.[43] It was able to avoid what I have called the paradox of the talking cinema.

The introduction of speech into the cinema did not substantially modify the attendant theoretical positions. It is known that not a few lovers of cinematographic purity hesitated before accepting this newcomer to the filmic world. They gave their word here and there that they would not use it, or that they would use it as little as possible, and in any case never realistically; furthermore, the fashion would soon pass. There was also an attempt—both a diversion and a regression—which consisted in opposing "sound" to "talking." Noise and music were accepted but not speech, which, of all the sounds in the world, in whose midst it nevertheless exists, was kept—in theory—under a mysterious and specific taboo. This produced the "wordless talking film, the shy film, the film garnished with the creakings of doors and the tinkling of spoons; the moaning, shouting, laughing, sighing, crying, but never the talking film," as the Provençal dramatist expressed with such verve.[44] But all this was only episodic. The great debate on the statutory admission of speech into film was largely platonic, and one was hardly aware of it other than as something that occupied a large place in the theory of film. The films themselves were already talking: They began to do so very rapidly, almost all of them did so, and continued to do so.

Not the least part of the paradox is, in fact, the ease with which speech did in fact find its way into the films of all those whose pronouncements had indissolubly linked the survival of the art of film to the permanence of its silence.[45] Accepted in practice, speech was not accepted in theory. One persisted in explaining that nothing essential had changed—hardly a reasonable position!—and that the laws of cinematographic language remained what they had been in the past. Arnoux summarizes an opinion that was very common at the time when he affirms[46] that the good talking films were good for the same reason that the good silent films were, and that the "talkie" was after all only one of many technical improvements, less important all in all than the close-up shot, which had been "invented" long before.

From our greater distance in time, we can only be amazed at this obstinate refusal to see the arrival of speech as an occurrence of capital importance—at any rate an occurrence deserving to be given its place in theory, and consequently to displace older, accepted elements from their respective positions. This is the condition for any true change, as we know—linguists have shown this to be the case in diachronics, and Proust has demonstrated it with human feelings. But speech was simply added (if even that) to the theory of cinema, as if it were in excess and there were no more room for it—and this at the very time when the silent cinema (not to mention the "sound" cinema, that voluntary invalid, that stillborn child) was entirely disappearing from the screens.

This unwillingness to see, or rather to hear, is even to be found, though in a less sterile and caricatural form, among those who had the richest and most fruitful reaction to the birth of the talking film (Pagnol excepted). In the "Manifesto for Orchestral Counterpoint,"[47] Eisenstein, Alexandrov, and Pudovkin generously welcome the sound-track, in the absence of speech itself. Their attitude is positive. For them it is a matter of giving visual counterpoint an auditory dimension, of multiplying the old cinema by the new. However—and precisely because a healthy and intelligent reaction makes us regret its omission, since it provides them with such a rich frame—one notices that nowhere do the three Soviet directors take speech into consideration. For them the sound cinema is a cinema that is squared—multiplied by itself, and only by itself. The authors of the "Manifesto" were thinking of noise and music; for them a film remained an *uttered discourse*. They would not consider, they rejected, the idea that an uttering element, speech, could be inserted into film.

We should not blame them: It was more difficult to approach these subjects in 1928 than in 1964. But we can take advantage of our greater distance to note that the appearance of speech in film inevitably brought the cinema closer to the theater—contrary to an opinion too often held, and in spite of the numerous analyses (often correct in their own terms) that since 1930 have underlined the differences between cinematographic and theatrical speech. For the most part these analyses point to the same conclusion: In their different ways they all suggest that in the theater the *word* is sovereign, a constituent of the representation, whereas, in film, *speech* is governed and constituted by the diegesis. This is an important difference one can hardly challenge. In a deeper sense, nevertheless, any utterance, whether governing or governed, by nature tells us something *first*, whereas an image, or noise or music, even when it is "telling" us a great deal, must first be *produced*.

There is no way in which the division into active and passive aspects can occur in the same way for verbal language, which has always been bound to the human agent and to determined signification, and for the nonverbal "languages" of the image, of noise or even of music, which are for their part linked to the impassivity of the world and to the malleability of things; whatever one may say about it, a film dialogue is never entirely diegetic. Even if we set aside "film commentaries" (it is enough to note their existence), which would support us too easily, we observe that the verbal element is never entirely integrated into the film. It sticks out, necessarily. Speech is always something of a spokesman. It is never altogether *in* the film, but always a little *ahead* of it. The most brilliantly emphatic musical or pictorial compositions, on the contrary, never intervene between the film and the spectator; they are experienced as an integral part of the film: However rich they may be, they remain media.

Despite all that was questionable in his ideas about filmed theater, Marcel Pagnol was undoubtedly the least mistaken person during the years from 1927 to 1933, when it was indeed difficult not to be wrong. There were those who refused to admit sound. Others accepted it grudgingly. Still others had taken to it enthusiastically. Some—like the hostess who, wanting to have a great musician to dinner, invites his chattering wife as well, in the improbable hope that her dreaded manners might not after all be so dreadful—some, in a grand gesture of courageous acceptance, even considered letting a few words be added to the background noise they so highly prized. Pagnol was almost the only one to accept the *talking* cinema—that is to say, a cinema that talked.

After these few words of history, let us now try to define formally the paradox of the talking cinema, which Pagnol alone was able to avoid. When the cinema was silent, it was accused of "talking" too much. When it began to talk, one declared that it was still essentially silent and should remain so. Is there anything surprising, then, in the affirmation that, with the advent of the "talkie," nothing had changed? *And, in fact, for a certain kind of cinema, nothing had changed.* Before 1930, films chattered silently (pseudo-verbal gesticulation). After 1930, they were loquaciously silent: A torrent of words was superimposed over a structure of images which remained faithful to its old laws. *Ciné-langue* never was, and could not become, the talking cinema. Not in 1930 did films begin talking, but in 1940, or thereabouts, when little by little they changed in order to *admit* speech, which had remained waiting at the door, so to speak.[xvii]

But, one will say, it is well known that the first talking films talked too much. Certainly. But if this is so noticeable, it is because they did not really talk. Today, on the contrary, we are not shocked by speech in a film. Perhaps it is used more sparingly? Not always. But, say it is. In any event, the crux of the matter lies elsewhere: Today films talk better, and speech no longer surprises us, at least as a general rule. Let us make it clear that, as *films*, they talk better. The *text* has not necessarily improved, but it harmonizes better with the film.

For a cinema that claimed to be language but conceived of itself as a language system (a universal and "nonconventional" one, to be sure, but a language system, nevertheless, since it wanted to create a system that was fairly strict and that logically would precede any message), the verbal languages could only offer it an unwanted increase and an unseasonable rivalry: No one could think seriously of inserting, even less of fusing, them into the texture of images—one could hardly conceive of making them agree with the images. The cinema began to speak only after it had begun to conceive of itself as a language that was flexible, never predetermined, sufficiently sure of itself to do away with a permanent, ill-tempered guard in front of its own doors, and bountiful enough to be enriched by the wealth of others. The "sequence shot" did more for talking films than the advent of the talking cinema itself. As Étienne Souriau remarks in another context,[48] a technical invention can never resolve a problem in art; it can only state it, so that it can be resolved by a second, properly aesthetic, invention. This is the well-known dialectic of long-term progress and short-term regression.

In order to get a better understanding of the talking cinema, one should study a certain type of "modern" film,[49] particularly the work of the inseparable trio Alain Resnais, Chris Marker, and Agnes Varda. In their films, the verbal, even openly "literary," element is given great weight in the overall composition, which is nevertheless more authentically "filmic" than ever. In *Last Year at Marienbad*, the image and the text play a sort of game of hide-and-seek in which they give each other passing caresses. The sides are equal: Text becomes image, and image turns into text. This interplay of contexts gives the film its peculiar contexture.

One is reminded of the famous problem of "cinematographic specificity" about which André Bazin, in almost every one of his articles, makes at least one or two very enlightening statements. The overt self-affirmation of a strong personality is not always the trait of those who possess the strongest personalities: And thus it was for a certain type of cinema in the past.

A state of mind and a stage: criticism of *ciné-langue*

We forgive the cinema of the past for its excesses, because it has given us Eisenstein and a few others. But one always excuses genius. The concept of *ciné-langue* constituted a whole theoretical corpus and must be evaluated as such. The point is important, for the perspective of the critic or the historian does not coincide here with that of the theoretician. The theory is full of splendid deadends, concepts that have not survived, but while they were alive, gave us some of the greatest masterpieces of the screen.

Moreover, although a kind of "erector-set cinema" did exist, there never was an "erector-set film." The common trend in many films of the period was enshrined mainly in writings and manifestoes. It was never entirely invested in a particular film, unless perhaps in certain avant-garde productions on the borderline between normal cinema and pure experimentation. (Seeing these films today one begins to feel that the others were indeed normal. Let the critic evaluate the contribution of these experimental films.)

As for the historian, he will rightly observe that only through its excesses—theoretical as well as practical—could the cinema begin to gain a consciousness of itself. The cinema as a language system is also the birth of the cinema *as an art*, some time after the entirely technical invention of the cinematograph (as André Bazin said of the avant-garde in its strict sense).[50] This can be extended to include a good part of all the cinema of that period. Let the historian study everything positive—and that is a lot—in this crisis of adolescent originality.

In the broad sense used here, the language-system cinema produced a sizable portion of the best cinema of its period; through it there occurred something that affected both art and language. This is why I have spoken only about it. But one must not lose sight of the proportions: For each film of the language-system tendency, there were, as there are always, ten undistinguished films that managed to avoid the problems of the silent cinema and the paradox of the talking cinema. Before 1930, the grade-B movie director would go out and photograph African elephants; after 1930, he would record music-hall numbers, music and words included. Neither the presence or absence of speech could cramp his style.

There was another cinema, too, which was neither the *ciné-langue* nor the ordinary dud. At the height of the "montage or bust" era, Stroheim and Murnau were heralding the modern cinema. It was a matter of talent and personality, because their cinema had no theory and did not at first get a following. Ideologically, manipulation was supreme. And this is normal: Stages are made to be skipped by a talented minority.[xviii]

A seminal concept: cinematographic specificity

As Rossellini said, the cinema is a language of art rather than a specific vehicle. Born of the fusion of several pre-existing forms of expression, which retain some of their own laws (image, speech, music, and noise), the cinema was immediately obliged to *compose*, in every sense of the word. From the very beginning, threatened with extinction, it became an art. Its strength, or its weakness, is that it encompasses earlier modes of expression: Some, truly languages (the verbal element), and some, languages only in more or less figurative sense (music, images, noise).

Nevertheless, these "languages" are not all found on the same plane with respect to the cinema: Speech, noise, and music were annexed at a later time, but film was born with *image discourse*. A true definition of "cinematographic specificity" can therefore only be made on two levels: that of filmic discourse and that of image discourse.

As a totality, filmic discourse is specific through its composition. Resembling true languages as it does, film, with its superior instancy, is of necessity projected "upward" into the sphere of art—where it reverts to a specific language. The film total can only be a language if it is already an art.

But within this totality there is an even more specific core, which, contrary to the other constituent elements of the filmic universe, is not found in a separate state in other arts: It is the image discourse. The proportions in its case are reversed, because a sequence of images is a language first. Perhaps, being too far removed from the language we speak, it is only a figurative language? So be it. It is nevertheless a language, in such a way that Rossellini's characterization (which was obviously directed at film as a whole) cannot be applied to it. Image discourse *is* a specific vehicle. It did not exist before the cinema; until 1930 it alone was sufficient to define film. In technical or medical films it functions exclusively as a vehicle and is not linked to any attempt at artistic realization. On the other hand, in films of fiction the language of the image tends to become an art (within a vaster sphere of art)—just as verbal language, which has a thousand utilitarian applications, is able to become incantation, poetry, theater, or novel.

The specific nature of film is defined by the presence of a *langue* tending toward art, within an art that tends toward language.

We have two things, therefore. Not three. There is indeed language system, but neither the image discourse nor filmic discourse are language systems. Whether language or art, the image discourse is an open system, and it is not easily codified, with its nondiscrete basic units (the images), its intelligibility (which is too natural), its lack of distance between the significate and the signifier. Whether art or language, the composed film is an even more open system, with its whole sections of meaning directly conveyed to the audience.[xix]

Film as we know it is not an unstable compound, because its elements are not incompatible. And they are not incompatible because none of them are language systems. It is hardly possible to use two language systems simultaneously: If I am spoken to in English I am not spoken to in German. Languages on the other hand, are more tolerant of superimpositions, at least within certain limits: Whoever speaks to me by means of verbal language (English or German) can at the same time make use of gestures. As for the arts, they can be superimposed within even broader limits: Witness opera, ballet, and chanted poetry. Cinema gives us the impression—occasionally erroneous, by the way—of rendering everything compatible with everything else, because its field of action lies for the most part between language and art, and not within *langue*. The cinema as we know it—it may assume other shapes, some of which are already beginning to emerge in certain Cinerama spectacles—is a "formula" with many advantages: It joins consenting arts and languages in a durable union in which their individual faculties tend to become interchangeable. It is a commonwealth, as well as a marriage of love.

Film and linguistics

Does this mean, then, that the study of film—at a time when linguistics itself, faithful on the whole to the Saussurian teachings, is mainly concerned with language systems—cannot have a linguistic dimension?

I am persuaded on the contrary that the "filmolinguistic" venture is entirely justified, and that it must be fully "linguistic"—that is to say, solidly based on linguistics itself. But how is one to interpret this statement, since the cinema is not a language system? That is what I would now like to clarify.

The study of film is concerned with linguistics at two points, two separate moments of its procedure, and in the second, not quite with the same linguistics as in the first.

It was de Saussure, we know, who made the study of language the subject of linguistics.[51] But de Saussure also laid the foundation for a much broader science—semiotics—of which linguistics was to be only one branch, although an especially important one.[52] Conversely, there were those here and there who began to study the inner mechanism of nonverbal systems (traffic signals, cartographic conventions, numbers, the gestures of politeness), or of transverbal systems (the verbal formulas of politeness, poetry, folktales, myths), or even of certain systems bridging the verbal and the nonverbal (kinship as seen by Claude Lévi-Strauss, with its dual organization into "appellations" and "attitudes"),[53] and almost all of them were fervent readers, admirers, or direct disciples of the Swiss scholar. We will return to the point. But already we can notice a rather striking point: In theory, linguistics is only a branch of semiotics, but in fact semiotics was created from linguistics. In a way it is very normal: For the most part semiotics remains to be done, whereas linguistics is already well advanced. Nevertheless there is a slight reversal. The post-Saussurians are more Saussurian than de Saussure himself: They have taken the semiotics he foresaw and are squarely making it into a translinguistic discipline. And this is very good, for the older brother must help the younger, and not the other way around. Moreover, de Saussure himself hints at the possibility of such a cross-influence: Linguistics could be of great help to semiotics, he writes, if it became more semiological.[54]

By focusing its attention on human language, linguistics proper has been able to obtain a knowledge of its subject with an often enviable rigor. It has cast a bright light, which has (not paradoxically) illuminated neighboring topics. Thus broad aspects of the image discourse that a film weaves become comprehensible, or at least more comprehensible, when, in a first stage, they are as entities examined distinct from *langue*. To understand what film is not is to gain time, rather than to lose it, in the attempt to grasp what film is. The latter aim defines the second stage of film study. In practice, the two stages are not separable, for one always opens onto the other. I call one of them the "first stage" because it benefits from the capital of linguistics, which encourages one to begin with it. The "second stage" is properly semiological and translinguistic; it is less able to depend on previously acquired knowledge, so that, far from being helped, it must, on the contrary, participate—if it is able to—in work that is new. Thus it is condemned to suffer the present discomfort of semiotics.

Image discourse in relation to *langue*: the problem of cinematographic "syntax"

The second articulation [55]

There is nothing in the cinema that corresponds, even metaphorically, to the second articulation.[xx] This articulation is operative on the level of the signifier, but not on that of the significate: Phonemes and *a fortiori* "features" are distinctive units without proper signification. Their existence alone implies a great *distance* between "content" and "expression." In the cinema the distance is too short. The signifier is an image, the significate is what the image represents. Furthermore, the fidelity of the photographic process, which gives the image particular verisimilitude, and the psychological mechanisms of participation, which ensure the famous "impression of reality," shorten the distance even more—so that it is impossible to break up the signifier without getting isomorphic segments of the significate. Thus the impossibility of a second articulation: Film constitutes an entirely too "intrinsic seme," to use Eric Buyssens's terminology. If, in an image representing three dogs, I isolate the third dog, I am necessarily isolating both the signifying and the signified "third dog." The English logician and linguist Ryle makes fun of a certain naïve concept of language (which de Saussure already condemned), which he calls ironically the "FIDO—Fido theory": The name FIDO corresponds exactly to the dog, Fido; words stand in direct ratio to an equal number of pre-existing things. This point of view, very backward in linguistics, is less so in the cinema, where there are as many "things" in the filmic image as there were in the filmed spectacle.

The theoreticians of the silent film liked to speak of the cinema as a kind of Esperanto. Nothing is further from the truth. Certainly Esperanto does differ from ordinary languages, but that is because it accomplishes to perfection what they strive for but never attain: a system that is totally conventional, specific, and organized. Film also differs from true languages but in the opposite way. It would be more correct to say that the true languages are caught between two Esperantos: the true Esperanto (or the ido, or novial, or whatever), which is reached through an excess of linguisticity, and the other, the cinema, which has a dearth of linguisticity.

In short, the universality of the cinema is a two-fold phenomenon. Positive aspect: The cinema is universal because visual perception varies less throughout the world than languages do. Negative aspect: The cinema is universal because it lacks the second articulation. There is a solitary relationship between the two observations that must be emphasized: A visual spectacle entails a joining of the signifier to the significates, which in turn renders impossible their disjunction at any given moment and, therefore, the existence of a second articulation.

Strictly speaking, Esperanto is manufactured; it is a product of language. For the most part "visual Esperanto" is a raw material that precedes language. In this concept of filmic Esperanto there is, all the same, some truth: It is in the second articulation that languages differ most radically, one from another, and that men fail to understand each other.[56] As Roman Jakobson observes, the sentence is always more or less translatable.[57] That is because it corresponds to a real mental impulse, and not to a code unit. The word can still yield interlinguistic equivalences, imperfect to be sure, but sufficient to make dictionaries possible. The phoneme is completely untranslatable, since it is entirely defined by its position in the phonemic grid of each language. The absence of a meaning cannot be translated. Thus we return to the idea that image discourse needs no translation, and that is because, having no second articulation, it is already translated into all languages: The height of the translatable is the universal.

André Martinet believes that, strictly speaking, one cannot talk of language, except where there is double articulation.[58] In point of fact, the cinema is not a language but a language of art. The word language has numerous meanings, more or less strict, and each is in its own way justified. This polysemic multiplication tends—in my judgment—to branch out in two directions: Certain systems (even the least human ones) are called "languages" if their formal structure resembles that of our spoken languages: This is the case with the language of chess (which de Saussure found so interesting) or with the binary languages of computers. At the other pole, everything that expresses man to himself (even in the least organized and least linguistic way) is felt to be a "language": the language of flowers, the language of painting, even the language of silence. The semantic field of the word language seems to be organized along these two axes. Now it is in "language" in its most proper meaning (human phonic language) that these two vectors of metaphorical expansion are rooted: For verbal language is used by men to communicate among themselves, and it is highly organized. The two nodes of figurative meaning are already there. Keeping these conditions of usage in mind, which does not always allow us to abide by meanings one would like to be strict about, it seems appropriate to look at the cinema as a language without a system.

First articulation

The cinema has no phonemes; nor does it, whatever one may say, have words. Except on occasion, and more or less by chance, it is not subject to the first articulation. It should be shown that the almost insurmountable difficulties that film "syntaxes" launch themselves into are derived for the most part from an initial confusion: The image is defined as a word, the sequence as a sentence. The case is, however, that the image (at least in the cinema) corresponds to one or more sentences, and the sequence is a complex segment of *discourse*.

The word sentence of course, here and on the following pages, designates the oral and not the written sentence of grammarians (a complex statement with multiple assertions, contained between two marked punctuations). I am speaking of the linguists' sentence.[xxi] In his famous example, designed precisely to distinguish between the two types of sentence, Joseph Vendryes[59] maintains that there are five sentences (in the sense that interests us) in the following statement: "You see that man/ over there/ he's sitting on the sand/ well, I met him yesterday/ he was at the station." I do not want to suggest that a film sequence with the same contents would have exactly these five sentences (shots). I mean simply that the image in the cinema is a kind of "equivalent" to the spoken sentence, not to the written sentence. It is not impossible that certain shots or groups of shots might, in addition, correspond to the "written" type of sentence—but that is another problem. In many respects,[60] film recalls written expression a great deal more than spoken language. But at a certain point in the division into units, the shot, a "completed assertive statement," as Benveniste would call it,[61] is equivalent to an oral sentence.

Roman Jakobson writes[62] that Shimkin, in his work on proverbs, was brought to propose that, in the proverb, "the highest coded linguistic unit functions simultaneously with the smallest poetic unit." The image discourse of the cinema represents a nonverbal area (while the proverb is transverbal). Nevertheless the shot, a "sentence" and not a word (like the proverb), is indeed the smallest "poetic" entity.

How is one to understand this correspondence between the filmic image and the sentence? First of all, the shot, through its semantic content, through what Eric Buyssens would call its "substance,"[63] is closer, all things considered, to a sentence than to a word. An image shows a man walking down a street: It is equivalent to the sentence "A man is walking down the street." The equivalence is rough, to be sure, and there would be much to say about it; however, the same filmic image corresponds even less to the word "man," or the word "walk," or the word "street," and less still to the article "the" or to the zero-degree morpheme of the verb "walks."

The image is "sentence" less by its quantity of meaning (a concept too difficult to handle, especially in film) than by its assertive status. The image is *always actualized*. Moreover, even the image—fairly rare, incidentally—that might, because of its content, correspond to a "word" is still a sentence: This is a particular case, and a particularly revealing one. A close-up of a revolver does not mean "revolver" (a purely virtual lexical unit), but at the very least, and without speaking of the connotations, it signifies "Here is a revolver!" It carries with it a kind of *here* (a word which André Martinet rightly considers to be a pure index of actualization).[64] Even when the shot is a "word," it remains a kind of "sentence-word," such as one finds in certain languages.

Cinema and syntax

The image is therefore always speech, never a unit of language. It is not surprising that the authors of "cinematographic grammars" have found themselves at an impasse. They claimed to have written a syntax of film, but, in fact, with their image-word, they had been thinking of something half way between a lexicon and a morphology, something that does not exist in any language. The cinema is something else.

There is a syntax of the cinema, but it remains to be made and could be done only on a syntactical, and not a morphological, basis.[65] De Saussure observed[66] that syntax is only an aspect of the syntagmatic: A thought that should be meditated on by anyone concerned with film. The shot is the smallest unit of the filmic chain (one might perhaps call it a "taxeme," as Hjelmslev uses the term[67]); the sequence is a great syntagmatic whole. One should examine the richness, exuberance even, of the syntagmatic arrangements possible in film (which will bring one to see the problem of montage under a new light), and contrast it to the surprising poverty of the paradigmatic resources of the cinema.[xxii]

The paradigmatic category of film

In the writings of theoreticians, the word montage in its broad sense includes cutting, but the opposite never occurs. The moment of ordering (montage) in film is somehow more important—"linguistically" at least—than the choosing of the images (cutting), no doubt because the latter, being too open, is not a choice, but rather an act of decision, a kind of creation. That is why, on the *artistic level*, the content of each shot is of great importance (although the organization is itself an art). On the level of the visual subject, there is art, if anything. Art continues on the level of the sequence or of the composed shot, and "cinematographic language" begins. Hence the condemnation of "beautiful photography" in the cinema.

The image paradigm is fragile in film; often still-born, it is approximate, easily modified, and it can always be circumvented. Only to a slight degree does the filmic image assume meaning in relation to the other images that could have occurred at the same point along the chain. Nor can the latter be inventoried; their number is, if not limitless, at least more "open" than the "most open" linguistic inventory. There is no equivalent here to the "peribolic" unraveling whose importance in verbal language has been underlined by Guillaume.[68] Charles Bally[69] observed that certain units that are opposed to an unlimited and undefinable number of terms (dependent only on context, the speakers, and the association of ideas) are often in the long run unopposed, really, to any term: This is somewhat the case with the filmic image.

Everything is present in film: hence the obviousness of film, and hence also its opacity. The clarification of present by absent units occurs much less than in verbal language. The relationships *in præsentia* are so rich that they render the strict organization of *in-absentia* relationships superfluous and difficult. A film is difficult to explain because it is easy to understand. The image impresses itself on us, blocking everything that is not itself.

A rich message with a poor code, or a rich text with a poor system, the cinematographic image is primarily speech. It is all assertion. The word, which is the unit of language, is missing; the sentence, which is the unit of speech, is supreme. The cinema can speak only in neologisms. Every image is a *hapax*.[xxiii] It would be fruitless to search among images for true associative series or strict semantic fields. Even the cautious, flexible structuralism of a Stephen Ullmann,[70] for example, is out of place here, for it is lexicological, and a "filmo-linguistic" structuralism can only be syntactic.

There is a paradigmatic category of film. But the commutable units are large signifying units. Thus, in the scholarly work of J.L. Rieupeyrout on the history of the Western, we are told that there was a period when the "good" cowboy was indicated by his white clothes and the "bad" by his black costumes. The audience, apparently, always knew which was which. This allows us to establish a rudimentary commutation as much on the level of the signifier (white/black) as on that of the significates (good/bad). The two colors are already *predicated* (since attributed to present clothes), and so are the two qualities (since it is the cowboy in the image who is either good or bad), prior to the commutation, and this is the essential difference from a lexical and *a fortiori* phonological commutation. But that is not all: The paradigm, perhaps precisely because it is engaged too much in "speech," is unstable and fragile; the convention of the cowboy in white, or in black, did not last long. It was inevitable that one fine day a film-maker, bored with the routine, should get the idea of dressing his rider in gray, or in a white shirt and black pants, and so much for the paradigm! The poverty of the paradigm is the counterpart of a wealth distributed elsewhere: The film-maker can express himself by showing us directly the diversity of the world, and in this he differs from the reciter of tales. Thus the paradigm is very rapidly overwhelmed: This is another aspect of the kind of struggle, which occurs at certain points in the cinema, between code and message. The great directors (and is it not puerile to repeat always that the cinema is not them, for who else could it be?) have avoided the paradigm.

Or at least have avoided *certain* paradigms. For the "type" *cowboy in black/cowboy in white* defines only one kind of filmic paradigm. "Syntactic" by the syntagmatic extent of its commutable segments and by their assertive status, such an opposition, however, bears, by its contents, on affective impressions ("the cowboy is good") that retain something of a "levical" quality. Other filmic oppositions, also more or less commutable, are more rooted in syntax and bear more on kinds of "morphemes."[xxiv] A large number of *camera movements* (rear and forward dolly) or *techniques of punctuation* (dissolve or cut) can be considered in this light.[xxv] It is a case of one relationship opposed to another relationship. In addition to the commutable elements, there is always a kind of support[71] that is ideally invariable. Rear and forward dolly shots correspond to two intentions of a "seeing"—but that "seeing" always has an object; that which the camera moves away from or approaches. It is, therefore, to the theory of syn-categorematic terms that one should look here: Just as the word "but" never expresses the idea of the adversative as such, but always an adversative relationship between two realized units, a forward dolly expresses a concentration of attention, not on itself, but always on an object.

The duality of support and relationship, in a language that permits the simultaneity of several visual perceptions, explains why such procedures have something *supersegmental* to them: The support and the relationship are often perceived at the same time. Furthermore, in the cinema the "relationship" is often one and the same as the camera's (and the spectator's) "seeing" of the support object. A forward dolly on a face is a way of seeing that face. That is why so many materially unreal filmic procedures are psychologically convincing, as has been occasionally noted.[72] Consider, for example, the rapid forward dolly, which makes the object grow larger to our eyes, or oblique framing, or certain extreme close-ups—they are all instances in which the appearance of the object is hardly plausible. But the supersegmental aspect of the support-relationship pair displaces filmic "plausibility" toward the level of the living, constructive dynamism of perception, and away from that of the objective circumstances of the perceived situation, for in the same segment the film contains a perceived and a perceiving instance. There are many camera movements that work by bringing an implausible object to a "seeing" that makes it plausible.

Filming intellection[73]

A film is always more or less understandable. If by chance it is not at all understood, that is as a result of peculiar circumstances, and not of the semiological process proper to the cinema. Naturally the cryptic film, like the cryptic utterance, the extraordinary film, like the extraordinary book, the film that is too rich or too new, like an explanation that is too rich or too new, can very well become unintelligible. But as "language" a film is always grasped—except by abnormal persons who would not understand any other form of discourse any better, and often not as well; except by the blind, suffering from a selective impairment blocking reception of the signifier (like the deaf with speech); except, finally, in those cases where the actual substance of the signifier is materially damaged (the old film, scratched, yellowed, and undecipherable; the speaker whose voice is so hoarse he cannot be understood).

Aside from these cases, a film is always understood, but always *more or less so*, and this "more or less" is not easily quantifiable, for there are no discernible degrees, no units of signification that can be immediately counted. With two persons speaking different languages, one should—in principle, at least—be able to enumerate the quantitative degrees of their mutual understanding: *A* knows three words of the language spoken by *B*, and *B* six words of the language spoken by *A*. Within a given sentence, it is a particular word, and not its neighbor, that has not been understood; or it can be established that one certain word, by a kind of ricochet, has rendered the whole sentence unintelligible to the hearer. A linguistic unit is either *recognized* or not by the hearer, since it already exists in the language. Marcel Cohen's suggestion (to study the degrees of understanding between languages) can be successfully undertaken, despite great difficulties. But in the cinema the units—or rather, the elements—of signification that are present together in the image are too numerous and too continuous: Even the most intelligent viewer cannot discern them all. On the other hand it is sufficient to have generally understand the main elements to grasp the approximate, overall, and yet relevant meaning of the whole: Even the dimmest spectator will have roughly understood. There have been some rather interesting experiments,[74] thanks to which one has been able to isolate the *character* of what is easy or difficult to understand in film. But it cannot be inferred from this that the *degree* of understanding of a normal commercial film can easily be established for a particular viewer or category of viewers.

One must also set aside clearly all those cases—very numerous in the cinema, as well as in verbal language, literature, and even everyday life—in which the message is unintelligible because of the very nature of what is being said, without the semiological process being affected. Many films are incomprehensible (either entirely or in part and depending on the audience) because their *diegesis* contains realities or concepts that are too subtle, too exotic, or mistakenly thought to be familiar. The fact has not been sufficiently emphasized that, in these cases, it is not the film itself, but on the contrary what the film does not make clear, that is incomprehensible. And the reason this has not been emphasized is because the current fashion is to insist that *everything* is language, to such an extent that what is *said* is over-powered and reduced to nothing by how one *says* it. This is a very common illusion. The angry lover shouts to his faithless mistress, "You don't understand me!" But she understands him only too well; the case is simply that she no longer loves him. Whether filmic or verbal, language cannot suppress reality; on the contrary, it is rooted in reality. If men do not "understand" each other, it is not only because of words, but also because of what the words contain. How many "misunderstandings" are actually the result of too great an understanding! People always see a lack of understanding where there is real disagreement. A whole army of Korzybskis and "general semanticists"(!) cannot put a stop to antagonism, stupidity, and indifference. The audience of local shopkeepers[xxvi] who booed Antonioni's *L'Avventura* at the Cannes Film Festival had understood the film, but either they had not grasped, or were indifferent to, its message. Filmic intellection had nothing to do with their attitude; what bothered them was simply "life" itself. It is normal that the problems of the couple as stated by Antonioni should leave a large section of the audience indifferent, puzzled, or derisive.[xxvii]

Cinema and literature: the problem of filmic expressiveness

The cinema is not a language system, because it contradicts three important characteristics of the linguistic fact: a language is a *system* of *signs* used for *intercommunication*. Three elements to the definition.[75] Now, like all the arts, and because it is itself an art, the cinema is one-way communication. As we have already seen, it is only partly a system. Finally, it uses only very few true signs. Some film images, which, through long previous use in speech, have been solidified so that they acquire stable and conventional meanings, become kinds of signs. But really vital films avoid them and are still understood. Therefore the nerve center of the semiological process lies elsewhere.

The image is first and always an image. In its perceptual literalness it reproduces the signified spectacle whose signifier it is; and thus it becomes what it shows, to the extent that it does not have to *signify* it (if we take the word in the sense of *signum facere*, the special making of a sign). There are many characteristics to the filmic image that distinguish it from the preferred form of signs—which is arbitrary, conventional, and codified. These are the consequences of the fact that from the very first an image is not the indication of something other than itself, but the pseudopresence of the thing it contains.

The spectacle recorded by the film-maker may be natural ("realistic" films, scenes shot in the street, *cinéma verité*, etc.) or arranged (the film-operas of Eisenstein's last period, Orson Welles's films, and, in general, the cinema of the unreal, or of the fantastic, expressionist cinema, etc.). But it is basically all one thing. The *subject* of the film is either "realistic" or not; but, whatever the case, the film itself only shows whatever it shows. So we have a film-maker, realistic or not realistic, who films something. What happens? Whether natural or arranged, the filmed spectacle already had its own expressiveness, since it was after all a piece of the world, which always has a meaning. The words a novelist uses also have pre-existing meanings, since they are segments of language, which is always significant. Music and architecture have the advantage of being able to develop *immediately* their properly aesthetic expressiveness—their style—in materials (sound or stone) that are purely impressionable and do not *designate*.[76] But literature and the cinema are by their nature condemned to connotation,[77] since denotation always precedes their artistic enterprise.[xxviii]

Film, like verbal language, can be used merely as a vehicle, without any artistic intention, with designation (denotation) governing alone. Consequently, the art of the cinema, like verbal art, is, so to speak, driven one notch upward:[78] In the final analysis it is by the wealth of its connotations that Proust's great novel can be distinguished—in semiological terms—from a cookbook, or a film of Visconti's from a medical documentary.

Mikel Dufrenne believes that in any work of art the *world that is represented* (denoted) never constitutes the major part of what the author has to say. It is merely a threshold. In the nonrepresentational arts it is even missing: The art of stone and the art of sound do not designate anything. When it is present its function is only to introduce the *expressed world*:[79] the artist's style, the relationship of themes and values, a recognizable "accent"—in short, the connotative universe.

In this respect, however, there is an important difference between literature and the cinema. In the cinema, aesthetic expressiveness is grafted onto natural expressiveness—that of the landscape or face the film shows us. In the verbal arts, it is grafted, not onto any genuine prior expressiveness, but onto a conventional *signification*—that of language—which is generally inexpressive. Consequently the introduction of the aesthetic dimension—expressiveness added to expressiveness—into the cinema is made with ease: An easy art, the cinema is in constant danger of falling victim to this easiness. It is so easy to create an effect when one has available the natural expression of things, of beings, of the world! Too easy. The cinema is also a difficult art: For, Sisyphus-like, it is trapped under the burden of its facility. There are very few films which do not have a little art in them; fewer still contain a great deal of art. Literature—especially poetry—is a so much more improbable art! How can that insane craft ever succeed?—To bestow an aesthetic expressiveness (that is, *in a natural way*) upon those "words of the tribe" Mallarmé railed against—where linguists agree in recognizing only a small portion of expressiveness and a very large portion of arbitrary signification, even when one considers the modifications brought to the famous theory of the "arbitrary" since de Saussure (the presence in language of partial motivation—whether phonic, morphological, or semantic—brought to light principally by Ullmann; the motivations by the signifier and other "implicit associations" analyzed by Charles Bally; and, in general, the various studies on the "motivated" areas of language). But when the poet has succeeded in his initial alchemy and has made words expressive, the greater part of his task is done: In this respect, literature, which is a difficult art, enjoys at least that advantage. Its endeavor is so arduous that the weight it bears is hardly a danger. There are a great number of books entirely lacking in art; there are a few books possessing enormous art.

The concept of *expression* is used here as defined by Mikel Dufrenne. There is expression when a "meaning" is somehow immanent to a thing, is directly released from it, and merges with its very form.[xxix] Some of Eric Buyssens's "intrinsic semes" perhaps fall under this definition. *Signification*, on the contrary, links from the outside an isolable signifier to a significate that is itself—this has been known since de Saussure[80]—a concept and not a thing. These are the "extrinsic semes" Buyssens writes about.[81] A concept is signified; a thing is expressed. Being extrinsic, signification can only derive from a convention; it is of necessity obligatory, since one would deprive it of its only support—consensus—by rendering it optional. This, one recognizes, is the famous "thesis" of the Greek philosophers. There is *more than one difference* between expression and signification: One is natural, the other conventional; one is global and continuous, the other divided into discrete units; one is derived from beings and things, the other from ideas.[xxx]

The expressiveness of the world (of the landscape or face) and the expressiveness of art (the melancholy sound of the Wagnerian oboe) are ruled essentially by the same semiological mechanism: "Meaning" is naturally derived from the signifier as a whole, without resorting to a code. It is at the level of the signifier, and only there, that the difference occurs: In the first case the author is nature (expressiveness of the world) and in the second it is man (expressiveness of art).

That is why literature is an art of heterogeneous connotation (expressive connotation added to nonexpressive denotation), while the cinema is an art of homogeneous connotation (expressive connotation added to expressive denotation). The problem of cinematographic expressiveness should be studied from the point of view I have just outlined, for it would bring one to consider style, and therefore the author. In Eisenstein's *Que Viva Mexico*, there is a famous shot of the tortured, yet peaceful faces of three peons buried to their shoulders being trampled by the horses of their oppressors. It is a beautiful triangular composition, a well-known trademark of the great director. The denotative relationship yields a signifier (three faces) and a significate (they have suffered, they are dead). This is the "subject," the "story." There is natural expressiveness: Suffering is read on the peons' faces, death in their motionlessness. Over this is superimposed the connotative relationship, which is the beginning of art: The nobility of the landscape as it is structured by the triangle of the faces (*form* of the image) expresses what the author, by means of his style, wanted it to "say": The greatness of the Mexican people, his certainty of their eventual victory, a kind of passion in that man from the North for all that sunny splendor. Therefore, aesthetic expressiveness. And yet still "natural": The strong and savage grandeur rises very directly out of the plastic composition that turns suffering into beauty. Nevertheless, two languages exist side by side in this image, since one can identify two signifiers: (1) three faces in a barren stretch of land; (2) the landscape given a triangular shape by the faces—and two significates—(1) suffering and death; (2) grandeur and triumph. One notices that, as usual, the connoted expression is much "vaster" than the denoted expression, and is also disconnected from it.[82] One finds the denotative material (signifier and significate) functioning as the signifier of the connotation: The solemn, sorrowful victory that the image connotes is expressed by the three faces themselves (signifiers of denotation) as well as by the martyrdom they exhibit (significate of denotation). The signifier of the aesthetic language is the sum of the signifier–significate of a prior language (the anecdote, the subject) with which it is interlocked. This is precisely Hjelmslev's definition of connotation; the linguist, we know, does not use the terms "signifier" and "significate," but *expression* and *content* ("cénématique" and "plérématique"). However, for the student of the cinema the word *expression* (as distinct from *signification*) is too useful to be given the meaning of "signifier," for the result would be a very annoying polysemic collision. From our point of view, therefore, "expression" does not designate the signifier, but rather the relationship between a signifier and a significate, when that relationship is "intrinsic."[xxxi] It would even be possible, in the case of expressive semes, to use *expresser* and *expressed*, reserving "signifier" and "significate" for nonexpressive relationships (signification proper). But one hesitates dropping such established terms, which, since de Saussure, have been linked to so many important analyses, as the words *signifier* and *significate*.

Comparisons are frequently made between the cinema and "language," where the identity of the latter is uncertain and variable. At times it is literature (the art of language), and at other times it is ordinary language that one contrasts to film. In such a muddle it is impossible to see clearly. The art of words and the art of images, as we have seen, are located along the same semiological horizon; on the connotative level they are neighbors. If the art of the cinema is compared to ordinary language, however, everything is changed; the two members are no longer on the same plane. The cinema begins where ordinary language ends: at the level of the "sentence"—the film-maker's minimum unit and the highest properly linguistic unit of language. We then no longer have two arts; what we have is one art and one language (in this particular case, language itself). The strictly linguistic laws cease when nothing is any longer obligatory, when ordering becomes "free."[xxxii] But that is the point where film begins; it is immediately and automatically situated on the plane of rhetoric and poetics.

How then is one to explain such a curious lack of symmetry, a lack that insidiously confuses scholars and renders books obscure? On the verbal side two levels—verbal language and literature—are readily distinguished. On the filmic side there is only and always the "cinema." To be sure, one can make a distinction between films that are purely utilitarian (educational films, for example) and films that are artistic. Nevertheless one senses that this is not altogether satisfactory and that the distinction is not as clear cut as that between the poetic or dramatic word and a conversation in the street. There are, of course, borderline cases that obscure the division: The films of Flaherty, Murnau, or Painlevé, which are both documentaries (biological and ethnographic) and works of art. In the verbal order, however, one may find many equivalent examples. The crux of the matter must, therefore, lie elsewhere. In truth there is no totally aesthetic use of the cinema, for even the most connotative image cannot avoid being also a photographic representation. Even in the period when film-makers like Germaine Dulac dreamed of a "pure cinema," the most nonrealistic avant-garde films, the films that were the most resolutely devoted to the exclusive concerns of rhythmic composition, still represented something—whether it was the variations of changing cloud patterns, the play of light on water, or the ballet of pistons and connecting rods. Nor is there a totally "utilitarian" cinema, for even the most denotative image has some connotations. The most literal educational documentary cannot prevent itself from framing its images and organizing their sequence with at least something like an artistic concern; when a "language" does not already exist, one must be something of an artist to speak it, however poorly. For to speak it is partly to invent it, whereas to speak the language of everyday is simply to use it.

All this is derived from the fact that in the cinema connotation is homogeneous with denotation, and like it, is expressive. One is forever shifting from art to non-art, and vice-versa. The beauty of the film is governed to some extent by the same laws as the beauty of the filmed spectacle; in some cases it is impossible to tell which of the two is beautiful and which of the two is ugly. A film by Fellini differs from an American Navy film[xxxiii]—made to teach the art of tying knots to new recruits—through its talent and through its intention and not through its most intimate semiological workings. Purely vehicular films[xxxiv] are made in the same way others are, whereas a poem by Victor Hugo is not shaped in the same way as a conversation between two office workers: First of all, one is written while the other is oral; a film, however, is always filmed. But that is not the main point. It is because of its heterogeneous connotation (that is, the fact that it imparts a value to words that are in themselves nonexpressive) that the gap between the functional use of the verb and its aesthetic use came into being.[xxxv]

Thus the impression of having on the one hand two realities (ordinary language and literature) and on the other only one (the "cinema").[xxxvi] And thus—finally—the truth of that impression. Verbal language is used at every hour, at every moment. In order to exist, literature assumes that a book must first be written by a man—a special, costly act that cannot be diluted in ordinary activity. Whether "utilitarian" or "artistic," a film is always like a book and not like a conversation. It must always be created. Like a book still, and unlike the spoken sentence, a film does not automatically entail a direct answer from an interlocutor present to give an immediate reply in the same language; and in this sense film is expression rather than signification. There is a somewhat obscure but perhaps essential solidary relationship between *communication* (bilateral relation) and "arbitrary" signification; conversely, unilateral messages often depend on (nonarbitrary) expression—a relationship that is easier to grasp. A thing or a being yields its *singularity* through expression in a message that implies no answer. Even the most harmonious love is not a dialogue so much as it is a kind of duet. Jacques tells Nicole of his love for her; Nicole tells Jacques of her love for him. They are therefore not speaking about the same thing, and one says rightly that their love is "shared" (divided). They do not answer each other—indeed how can one really answer a person expressing himself?

Shared, their love is divided into two loves, which yield two expressions. For Jacques and Nicole, expressing as they did two different sentiments, to evolve, rather than the give-and-take of a dialogue, the agreement of a true encounter tending toward a fusion that abolishes all dialogue, there had to be a kind of coincidence—hence the rareness of the occurrence—rather than that interplay of influences and after-the-fact adjustments by which a dialogue is characterized. Like Jacques (without Nicole) or like Nicole (without Jacques), films and books express themselves and are not really answered. But if, using ordinary language, I ask, "What time is it?" and someone answers, "Eight o'clock," I have not been expressing myself; I have signified, I have communicated, and I have been answered.

It is therefore true that we identify only one cinema, unlike the double term literature–language, and furthermore that that one cinema resembles literature rather than language.

Cinema and translinguistics: the large signifying units

By initially casting light on what the cinema is not, and thanks to its analysis of language systems, linguistics—and especially that part of it which leads to translinguistics (semiotics)—gradually allows us to glimpse what the cinema is. The smallest filmic unit is the "sentence," the assertion, the actualized unit. This suggests certain comparisons.

A whole tendency of modern research, mostly in the straight line of the Saussurian enterprise, has come to be concerned precisely with the sentence. Joseph Vendryes[83] notes that a gesture of the hand is equivalent to a sentence rather than to a word. Eric Buyssens makes a similar observation[84] about traffic signs and, more generally, about all semes that cannot be broken down into signs. Claude Lévi-Strauss defines the smallest unit of the myth—the "*mythème*"—as the assigning of a predicate to a subject—that is to say, as an assertion; he even adds[85] that each *mythème* can perhaps, when it is first transcribed onto cards, be relevantly summarized by a sentence; and, at a later stage in formalization, the "*grand mythème*" is still, he says, a package of predicative relationships—in short, a set of sentences having a recurrent theme. In his study of proverbs, already mentioned, Shimkin sees the smallest poetic unit in the largest coded linguistic unit. Vladimir Propp's analysis of Russian folktales is undertaken in a similar spirit.[86] Roland Barthes has defined the modern myth as a unit of speech,[87] and has emphasized—precisely in relation to the cinema—the "large signifying units."[88] Georges Mounin[89] believes that certain "nonlinguistic systems of communication" have become so important in modern society that the time has arrived to undertake seriously the semiotic de Saussure had dreamt of (and this is what Eric Buyssens had been saying already in the very first lines of his book), instead of dispatching it in a few sentences clapped on to the end of textbooks of linguistics. Roman Jakobson believes that poetry could be studied in a more linguistic spirit, on the condition that linguistics in turn be concerned with units larger than those of the sentence.[90] These are all converging perspectives.[xxxvii]

The "nonlinguistic systems" Georges Mounin refers to[91] are those of numbers (telephone, social security, etc.), traffic signals, cartography, the symbology of tourist guidebooks, and advertising images. He does not speak of the cinema. Nevertheless he does observe that, in the modern world, the image tends gradually to lose its original decorative role and to acquire an informative function. Above all he underscores the fact that many of these nonlinguistic systems are ruled by a single articulation. "Semanteme by semanteme," he says,[92] "never phoneme by phoneme." However, it seems that many nonlinguistic systems are broken down into "sentences," rather than into semantemes. Many, but not all. Those Mounin mentions, which can be analyzed into words (like the symbols of international tourism signifying "restaurant," "hotel," or "garage"), do indeed exhibit a single articulation. It is these systems, as the author says, that justify André Martinet's question: Can a perfect "ideographic system" exist, "a language that would no longer be spoken but that one would continue to write," a "system in which the units of content would merge with those of expression"—whereas the second articulation divides discourse into expressive units without corresponding content? In the cinema, as in other nonlinguistic systems, the units of content are also "merged" with those of expression, but in a different sense—on the level of the "sentence."[xxxviii] Any traffic sign is a sentence in the imperative mode, rather than a semanteme. The jussive may actualize as clearly as the indicative. "Do Not Pass!" Two elements are identified: the lexeme (concept of "passing") and the imperative morpheme, which simultaneously actualizes and constitutes the sentence. This double function of "verbs" and more generally of predicates (which provide a lexemic content, and also constitute the statement as such) has been studied by linguists like Jean Fourquet, Louis Hjelmslev, Émile Benveniste, and André Martinet,[93] especially in relation to the famous problem of nominal sentences, which can be compared to the problem of close-ups in the cinema, or to the problem of sign boards and signals: A telephone sign does not just mean "telephone" (a purely lexical unit), but "telephone *here*." It is a self-sufficient statement, which implies the existence of something in reality; it is therefore not a word.

One can be misled, however, by the fact that in systems that are by nature *poor*, the breakdown of the "sememe" into sentences (and consequently the absence, really, of the first articulation itself) is not necessarily accompanied by a numerical multiplication of the units, which remain small in number and more or less stable. This makes it appear that there is an articulation—and in a certain sense there is one indeed, since it is true that the units are fairly stable and they can be at least approximately enumerated. But the discretion of discrete units does not prevent them from being "sentences." It is the natural poverty of the things signified that, in this case, guarantees a kind of automatic economy rendering the first articulation superfluous, and performing the same function as the articulation, yields the impression that the poverty has been derived from the articulation—for one lends only to the rich; furthermore, as André Martinet insists, the first articulation provides verbal language with a function of economy.[94] As for the sememes of sign boards, they benefit from a prior retrenchment, since the number of institutions designated is restricted: In this case it is the small number of the referents that functions as the first articulation. Since verbal language is a sememe containing many more "things that have to be said," it therefore requires the first articulation in order to reduce the infinite multiplication of sentences to the controlled amplitude of a lexicon. The cinema, like language, has much to say, but, like sign boards, it actually escapes the first articulation. It proceeds by "sentence," like sign boards, but, like verbal language, its sentences are unlimited in number. The difference is that the sentences of verbal language eventually break down into words, whereas, in the cinema, they do not: A film may be segmented into large units ("shots"), but these shots are not *reducible* (in Jakobson's sense) into small, basic, and specific units.

One can of course conclude that the cinema is not a language, or that it is so only in a sense that is altogether too figurative, and, consequently, it should not be dealt with through semiotics. But this is a very negative point of view, particularly in the case of a social fact as important as the cinema. The result of this attitude would be that one would study traffic signals because they have a very obvious paradigmatic structure, while paying no attention to a means of expression that after all carries a little more human weight than roadside signs! The alternative approach is to look at the semiological endeavor as open research, permitting the study of new forms; "language" (in the broad sense) is no simple thing—whole flexible systems may be studied as flexible systems, and with the appropriate methods.

Under these circumstances—and despite the fact that the names mentioned on these pages indicate a strong Saussurian legacy—problems of strict compliance can of course arise. But it suffices to point them out. Naturally, anything that even approximately resembles a *linguistics of speech* is a departure, it would seem, from the thought of the Genevan scholar. The objection had to be pointed out. It is, however, not insurmountable,[xxxix] and it would be to respect the great linguist very narrowly indeed if one were to block all innovative research under the pretext that one could not risk even grazing a study of speech. And I say: *grazing*. For it often happens in the study of nonverbal means of communication that the actual nature of the material under consideration causes one to resort to a "linguistics" that is neither that of language nor that of speech, but rather is one of *discourse* in Émile Benveniste's sense[95] (or even in the way Eric Buyssens used the word in a text in which he was attempting precisely to broaden the famous Saussurian bipartition in order to be able to analyze more diverse "language systems"). Between words—pure "sign events" as they are called in American semiotics, events that never occur twice and cannot give rise to a scientific study—and language (human language, or the more systematic and formalized language of machines), which is an organized, coherent instance, there is room for the study of "sign designs," sentence patterns,[96] transphrastic organizations, "writings" in the Barthesian sense, etc.—in short, *types of speech*.

Conclusion

There have been, up to now, four ways of approaching the cinema. I will leave aside the first two (film criticism and the history of the cinema), which are foreign to my purpose even if some of their basic notions, which fall under the category of "general cinematographic culture," are clearly indispensable to anyone who wants to speak about the cinema. One must go and see films, and one must of course have at least an approximate idea of their dates. The third approach is what has been called the "theory of cinema." Eisenstein, Béla Balázs, and André Bazin are its great names. The "theoreticians" were either film-makers, enthusiastic amateurs, or critics (and it has often been pointed out that criticism itself is a part of the cinematographic institution[97]): This is a fundamental point (about the cinema, or about film, according to the case), whose originality, whose interest, whose range, and whose very definition are after all derived from the fact that the theory was made within the cinematographic universe. The fourth approach is that of filmology—of the scientific study conducted from outside by psychologists, psychiatrists, aestheticians, sociologists, educators, and biologists. Their status, and their procedures, place them outside the institution: It is the cinematographic fact rather than the cinema, the filmic fact[98] rather than the film, which they consider. Theirs is a fruitful point of view. Filmology and the theory of film complement each other. There are even some borderline cases between the two, some of which are quite important: Who is to say whether Rudolf Arnheim, Jean Epstein, or Albert Laffay were "filmologists" or "theoreticians?" Filmology proper also has its great names: Gilbert Cohen-Séat and Edgar Morin. Both filmology and the theory of the cinema are indispensable to the approach I am proposing. Their division is justifiable only when it allows for a reciprocity of perspectives. If it becomes a true separation, if it is made into an antagonism, it can only be damaging. The major book Jean Mitry has just published, *Esthétique et psychologie du cinéma*, a true sum of all the thought that the cinema has provoked up to the present, is an example of the deep reconciliation of these two complementary approaches, which one can only applaud.

Very much to one side of both filmology and the theory of the cinema—unfortunately—is linguistics[xl] and its semiological extensions. The discipline is an old one—it was known by Bopp and Rask—and old age seems to suit it, since it is very much alive and well. It is sure of itself—therefore it inspires confidence. That is why one has sought its aid unhesitatingly—it can hardly be overburdened by a few extra demands placed on it, and in any case, the study of the cinema is far from being its only concern. It is a well-known fact that the busiest people are always those who find the time to concern themselves with others—as Proust remarked about Monsieur de Norpois.

These few pages were written in the belief that the time has come to start making certain conjunctions. An approach that would be derived as much from the writings of the great theoreticians of the cinema as from the studies of filmology and the methods of linguistics might, gradually—it will take a long time—begin to accomplish, in the domain of the cinema, and especially on the level of the large signifying units, the great Saussurian dream of studying the mechanisms by which human significations are transmitted in human society.

De Saussure did not live long enough to remark on the importance the cinema has assumed in our world. No one disputes this importance. The time has come for a semiotics of the cinema.

Notes

Roman numbering

i   The French is: *montage-roi*.—Editor.

ii   The word is used as defined by G. Cohen-Séat (*efficience*): not as the effectiveness of a particular approach or specific act, but as the power peculiar to a means of expression.

iii   As defined by Étienne Souriau. Whatever is placed in front of the camera, or whatever one shoots with the camera is "profilmic."

iv   We know that in his "last period" (*Alexander Nevsky* and *Ivan the Terrible*), Eisenstein was governed by a very different aesthetic, an aesthetic of the image much more than of montage. But this development has left only a faint trace in his theoretical writings, which concern us here. However, the unpublished manuscripts, which will be gradually published, will have to be seen.

v   Who is, incidentally, reticent at times and of two minds about these problems (consider André Martinet's attitude). Others, like P. Guiraud or Roman Jakobson, are more positive.

vi   In fact, though, not entirely; isolated and magnified, the fragment is occasionally unrecognizable. This has been pointed out already, with reason. But this nuance, which will have to be studied separately, may be temporarily neglected in a global study.

vii   It goes without saying that I am speaking here about cinematographic *creation*. For the author of this book is obviously in no position to maintain that syntagmatic methods are not suited to the *analysis* of film. This is somewhat like the problem of the "creator" and the "theoretician"—despite their closeness in the modern period, which, though it has often been pointed out, is still insufficient—who *necessarily* approach the same object by means that are so different that they are not always able to resist the pessimistic and oversimplifying illusion that it is not the same object.

viii   And which strikes me as being even more cavalier today than when this article was written.

ix   Despite the clumsy formulations of a man who was partly self-taught, which are scattered throughout his books (though not in his films), Eisenstein remains, to my mind, one of the greatest film theoreticians. His writings are crammed full of ideas. His thoughts on language systems (in spite of an exuberant and somewhat unfocused vocabulary), however, will have to be restated in terms of language.

x A language system (*langue*) is a highly organized code. Language itself covers a much broader area: de Saussure said that language is the sum of *langue* plus speech (*parole*). The concept of a "fact of language" (*fait de language*) in Charles Bally or Émile Benveniste points in the same direction. If we were to define things and not words, we might say that language, in its broadest reality, is manifest every time something is said with the intention of saying it (see Charles Bally, "Qu'est-ce-qu'un signe?" in *Journal de psychologie normale et pathologique*, Paris, vol. 36, 1939, nos. 3 and 4, pp. 161–74, and especially p. 165). Of course, the distinction between verbal language (language proper) and other "sign systems" (semes) (sometimes called "languages in the figurative sense") comes to mind, but it must not confuse the issue. It is natural that semiotics be concerned with all "languages," without pre-establishing the extent and the limits of the semic domain. Semiotics can and must depend heavily on linguistics, but it must not be confused with linguistics.

xi And also in relation to Italian neorealism in general, and to certain aspects of Orson Welles, William Wyler, Jean Renoir, Erich von Stroheim, Friederich Murnau, etc.

xii In *Esthétique et psychologie du cinéma* (Paris: Éditions Universitaries, vol. 1, 1963), Jean Mitry states matters more vigorously: After having been everything, montage now tends to be nothing, at least in some theories. But the cinema is inconceivable without a minimum of montage, which is itself contained within a larger field of language phenomena (pp. 10–11). The analogy and the quasi-fusion of the signifier and the significate do not define all of film, but only one of its constituents—the photographic material—which is no more than a point of departure. A film is made up of many images, which derive their meaning in relation to each other in a whole interplay of reciprocal implications, symbols, ellipses, etc. Thus the signifier and the significate are given a greater distance, and so there is indeed a "cinematographic language" (see especially pp. 119–23 [in the original]). I mention this in order to insist on the difference between such a "language" and a "film language-system." The partisans of what is called "non-montage" (the Bazin tendency), even if they have occasionally made statements on the aesthetics of film that are too exclusive, at least can be credited—on the level of a sort of intuitive and spontaneous semiotics—with rejecting any concept of the cinema as *langue* and affirming the existence of a cinematographic *language*.

xiii This text was written in the beginning of 1964; today there would be many names to add to it.

xiv A very successful example: the sequence of the travel agency in *Breathless* by Jean-Luc Godard.

xv Today I would no longer state the relationship between the code and the message in such strictly antagonistic terms. It now appears to me that the realities codes possess are more complex, more various, subtler—and therefore more compatible, so to speak, with the richness of messages. On these points, see the whole of Chapter 5 [in the original], "Problems of Denotation in the Fiction Film," as well as passages from "The Modern Cinema and Narrativity." See also "*Problèmes actuels de théorie du cinéma*," (not reprinted here), *Revue d'esthétique* (special issue: "Le Cinéma") vol. xx, no. 2–3 (especially p. 221 [in the original]).

xvi Think of the magnificent seduction scene in *Wedding March* (1927), which was entirely constructed from the imperceptible facial play of the actor-*auteur*. Not a gesture, but what expressiveness!

xvii Today I would qualify this statement. There were good talking films right from the beginning of the talkies; the period 1930–33 was fairly rich. A little later there were also certain American comedies. Etc. . . . .

xviii I have said nothing about the period prior to 1920, which is nevertheless of capital importance for the genesis of cinematographic language (especially D.W. Griffith). But the problems this period poses are foreign to the intent of these pages, which do not pretend to give a historical account. It is quite apparent that a director like Feuillade, to take one example out of many, is exempt from the kind of excesses for which I am blaming the *ciné-langue attitude*. The question that interests me (language or language system?) was conceivable only after the first *theories* of film made their appearance, roughly in 1920. Before then, the cinema was too busy being created. Lumière invented the cinematograph; he did not invent "film" as we know it today (a complex narrative body of considerable magnitude). The great pioneers before 1920 invented the cinema (see Mitry, *Esthétique et psychologie du cinéma, op. cit.*, pp. 267–85 of vol. I). Before the problems of semiotics raised here could even have meaning, let alone an object, the cinema had first to exist, and it had to begin thinking of itself in terms of theory.

xix Today I would not use the words "natural" and "directly." Or at least I would use them more circumspectly. See second footnote p. 78 [in the original; note xxx here].

xx   Rather than to the cinema, this affirmation should in fact be applied to "cinematographic language," i.e. to the *specific level* of codification that is constituted by the signifying organizations proper to film and common to all films. Therefore it would be more correct to say that the cinema *as such* has no second articulation (and, as we will see further, no first articulation either). But the "cinema" as a totality—the sum of all that is said in films, as well as of all the signifying organizations (perceptual, intellectual, iconological, ideological, "symbolic," etc.) that affect the understanding of a whole film—the cinema as a totality represents a much vaster phenomenon, within which cinematographic language constitutes only one among many signifying levels. To that extent, it is not impossible that certain cinematographic significations are ruled by systems that, in one way or another, contain several articulations. The concept of *cinematographic language* is a methodological abstraction: This language is never present alone in films but is always in combination with various other systems of signification: cultural, social, stylistic, perceptual, etc.

Secondly, it is appropriate to note that, in the linguistic sense of the term, the articulations—i.e. what is called the "double articulation"—are not the only conceivable types of articulation.

For either one of these two reasons, one must make a careful distinction between two affirmations: The first, which is advanced in this text, consists in saying that cinematographic language in itself exhibits nothing resembling the double linguistic articulation. The second, for which I assume no responsibility, would consist in saying that the cinema has no articulations.

Indeed, there would be nothing absurd in supposing—and this is only an example—that the total cinematographic message brings five main levels of codification into play, each one of which would be a kind of articulation: (1) perception itself (systems for structuring space, "figures," and "backgrounds," etc.), to the degree that it already constitutes a system of acquired intelligibility, which varies according to different "cultures"; (2) recognition and identification of visual or auditive objects appearing on the screen—that is to say, the ability (which is also culturally acquired) to manipulate correctly the denoted material of the film; (3) all the "symbolisms" and connotations of various kinds attach themselves to objects (or to relationships between objects) outside of films—that is to say, in culture; (4) all the great narrative structures (in Claude Brémond's sense) which obtain outside of films (but in them as well) within each culture; and, finally, (5) the set of properly cinematographic systems that, in a specific type of discourse, organize the diverse elements furnished to the spectator by the four preceding instances.

We know that Umberto Eco has recently formulated an interesting hypothesis according to which the cinematographic message taken as a whole would involve only three main levels of articulation (*Appunti per une semiologica delle comunicazioni visivi*, University of Florence, Bompiani, 1967, pp. 139–52). In the preface of his work, *Le Cru et le cuit* (Plon, 1964, p. 31, notably; *The Raw and the Cooked* [New York: Harper & Row, 1969]), one recalls, as well, Claude Lévi-Strauss distinguished two main levels of organization in pictorial art—and it is easy to apply this to cinematographic art: On one hand the objects that are represented on the canvas, and on the other hand the properly pictorial composition into which they enter. For his part, Pier Paolo Pasolini sees two principal levels of articulation in the pictorial message, somewhat like those discerned by Lévi-Strauss (*La lingua scritta dell'azione*, paper contributed to the Second Festival of New Cinema, *Pesaro II*, Italy, June 1966, reprinted in *Nuovi Argomenti*, new series, no. 2, April–June 1966, pp. 67–103).

Without going into the details of these several analyses, I will remark simply that, in principle, they do not contradict the ideas here expressed. For it is obvious that the authors I have mentioned (1) bring into their account aside from cinematographic language itself one or another system of signification that is mainly cultural and extends beyond the cinema, although it does come into play in the deciphering of the film as totality; (2) they have in mind levels of articulation of which they ask only that they be authentic—and I agree with them that they are—but of which they demand no equivalence to linguistic articulations (whereas, I want to insist precisely on the absence of these equivalences, without, however, maintaining that cinema has no articulation at all).

Similarly, it can be remarked that my "large syntagmatic category of the image-track," which will be outlined further on (Chapter 5 [in the original]) by its very existence constitutes a specific articulation: It resembles neither the first, nor the second articulation of verbal language—since it does not divide the film into units comparable to phonemes or monemes—but it undoubtedly has the effect of *articulating* (in another way—that is to say, on the level of the discourse) the cinematographic message.

xxi   This distinction between two kinds of sentence seems less important to me today than it did when I wrote this article. First of all, from a purely linguistic point of view, Vendryes's analysis, which I used to support my argument, is subject to a number of reservations, particularly since Noam Chomsky's work has progressively shed new light on the problem of the sentence. Secondly, from a properly cinematographic point of view, it is in any case impossible to say whether the "shot" corresponds to *one* or to several sentences: The question of knowing whether these sentences would be of the "written" or "oral" type, "simple" or "complex," is therefore quite secondary. One can say simply that a film "shot" is very different from a word, that it always constitutes an actualized unit of discourse, and that consequently it is to be situated *on the level* of the sentence. And that is indeed the observation I made in this text; but it should have exempted me from looking for more precise equivalences between the shot and one or another type of *internal phrastic structure* observable in languages. Since the shot is *not made of words*, it can "correspond" only *externally* to the sentence, i.e. in relation to discourse (see Chapter 5, part 3 [in the original]). As long as one seeks internal equivalences, one will be led into an impasse: Let us indeed suppose that in certain circumstances a shot can appear to be equivalent to several sentences (a thing that will not fail to occur): How are we to know if these sentences, in a written text, have always been separate sentences or if, for example, they had at one time been different "clauses" of a single complex sentence?

xxii   I am no longer of the opinion, as I reread this, that the two aspects of the problem can be strictly speaking "*contrasted.*" For, as I have said—but not sufficiently clearly—in the text reprinted here, they are not situated on the same level: One can speak of "paradigmatic poverty" in relation to the *image* (see pp. 65–67 [in the original]) and of "syntagmatic richness" in relation to the *structuring of images* (see p. 67 [in the original]). At the same time, however, it should be remarked that the existence of several types of image-ordering has the effect of creating (on the level of discourse) a specific paradigmatic category, which is constituted precisely by the total system of the different syntagmas. One cannot indeed conceive of a syntagmatic category with no corresponding paradigmatic category on the *same level* (that is, a paradigmatic category related to units of the same magnitude), nor of a paradigmatic category with no corresponding syntagmatic category on the same level: by definition the syntagmatic categories and paradigmatic categories are strict correlatives. I will return to these problems in Chapter 5 [in the original].

    Second observation: One must not exclude the possibility that *between the images themselves* there are different kinds of paradigmatic associations, since in all human groups one finds various cultural "symbolisms" that relate to iconography. These paradigms, however, are not peculiar to cinematographic language.

    Third and final observation: One must keep in mind when distinguishing between the "image" and the "structuring of images" that the first term can designate either the shot (as opposed to the sequence) or the filmed subject (as opposed to the shot, which is already the product of an initial composing or arrangement). In either case, what we call "image" is really the *photographic fact* (or phonographic fact, if we are referring to the sound-track), and what it is contrasted to is the *filmic fact*. The latter indeed unfolds on two levels: within the shot, from "subject" to "subject"; within the sequence, from shot to shot. For more on this point, see Chapter 5 [in the original], particularly part 6.

xxiii   It is becoming less and less certain, in fact—especially since one has begun to understand Chomsky's work—that the sentence is a unit of speech. In one way the sentence is even the unit of language *par excellence*, since a language is a system that allows one to make sentences.

    As for the filmic image, which is only a "sentence" because of its function in discourse, and not because of its internal structure, it does indeed remain a "hapax," but it also is contained by larger units that are not hapaxes. I was therefore only partially correct in saying that the cinema can only talk by neologism. I should have said that, *in order to speak*, the cinema is able to use only neologism as its basic material, but that, *in speaking* it integrates these neologisms (without, however, altering them in their details) into a second order not governed by the single law of proliferation. On these problems, see Chapter 5, parts 3 and 4 [in the original].

xxiv   The word is taken here in the sense in which it is opposed to the term "semanteme," or the more current "lexeme," and not in the sense: minimum unit having its own signification. It seems to me that I did not sufficiently insist, in the passage above, on the fact that paradigms of this second variety—precisely because they come closer to those of true grammar—are much less easily judged than the others in terms of "originality" or "banality" when one encounters them in films. It is these paradigms that constitute "cinematographic language" itself, whereas the systems like that of the cowboy in black or white only affect a few film subjects, and only for a restricted period. I return to this problem later, in Chapter 6 [in the original] (see especially pp. 221–23, including note on p. 223 [in the original]).

xxv   And, even more so, many *codified montage orderings* (see "Problems of Denotation in the Fiction Film," especially pp. 119–33). That is why I am indeed less skeptical today about the paradigmatic category of film than I was when I wrote this article; what I had not seen is that a major part of the paradigmatic category of film must be sought for in the syntagmatic category itself— that is to say in the interplay between various different image orderings. On this point see also "Problems of Denotation. . . ."

xxvi   They are given free tickets by the municipality of Cannes and constitute what one refers to as the Festival audience.

xxvii   In this passage reprinted here, the material has been considered too exclusively from the *point of view of the cinema*, and I have not paid sufficient attention to the possibilities of a general semiotics of culture. To be sure, it was not the cinematographic language in *L'Avventura* (which was utilized in a particularly clear fashion) that put off the Cannes "shopkeepers"; in this sense one can say that it was the subject of the film, and therefore "life," that had annoyed them. If all that is wanted is to show that the particular problem of filmic intellection is not relevant in such cases, the argument suffices. But if one wants to go further, one must then indeed observe that the "subject" of the film (as well as "life" itself) is, in turn, liable to be more or less understood— again depending on the audience, and on the form in which it is presented—*according to a set of cultural systems* that, though they are foreign to the cinema, nevertheless do constitute organized systems of signifiers.

In other words, the distinction referred to between what is said and how it is said should be made relative: One can identify what pertains to the "saying" and what belongs to the "said" only in relation to the instance of "saying" with which one is occupied in each particular analysis. When analyzing another set of signifiers, one might well find that what was part of the "saying" now comes under the "said." In every human phenomenon of some magnitude—the cinema included—various cultural systems intervene together and overlap in complex ways. A "content" determined by one of these systems can be annexed by another (which encloses it although it did not determine it) within the same overall "message." What we call "the cinema" is not only cinematographic language itself; it is also a thousand social and human significations that have been wrought elsewhere in culture but that occur also in films. Furthermore, the "cinema" is also each individual film as a unique composition, with signifying and signified elements distinct from those of cinematographic language in general. In the case of *L'Avventura*, one can isolate at least three autonomous factors of signification (sets of signifiers) that are present at the level of the concrete message: (1) cinematographic language (a much larger category but one that does not exclude the film); (2) *L'Avventura* as a work of art (which, on both the levels of expression and content, *adds* to cinematographic language many particular structures that do not belong to the general "writing" of the cinema); and (3) a peculiar ideology (that of the "modern couple," of the "exhaustion of feeling," etc.) derived from a historical and sociocultural situation foreign to the cinema, but liable to be reflected in films. The insufficiently educated audience in my example did not understand the film, not because it could not grasp system 1, but surely because it was unable to decipher correctly systems 2 and 3. The cinematographic "saying" was not responsible. But nor was the "said" entirely so either—or, if it was, it was so only in relation to the previous "saying"—since it comprised on the one hand a particular "Antonionian" content and on the other a certain "socio-ideological" content. So that, in a way, it is still true that the cause lay with the "saying" and not with what was "said"; yet in another way the responsibility was in the "said" and not in the "saying." In the study of a determined signifying system many things that appear to be pure substance actually correspond to significations derived from elsewhere, where they existed as forms and not as substances. Unless one entirely abandons the endeavor to speak about Man, one cannot avoid the enclosing of meaning. The reason that the cinema as a totality gives a first impression of being a collective body lacking in any kind of strict organization is in large part because it is one of the locations where a very large number of signifying systems, each having its relative autonomy, come together from the four corners of culture: cinematographic language itself is only one of those systems. Whatever cinematographic language does not account for is not necessarily condemned to formlessness; simply, it has been formed elsewhere.

xxviii   "Prior" to literature, denotation is secured through *idiom*. "Prior" to the art film, it is secured:

(1) through perceptual analogy; (2) through the cinema language that contains a partial denotative code (derived incidentally from the earlier search for connotations). On this point see Chapter 5, pp. 117–19 [in the original].

xxix   Gestalt, and not graphic contour.

xxx   Today, I would say rather that expressiveness is a meaning established without recourse to a *special* and explicit code. But not without recourse to vast and complex sociocultural *organizations*, which are represented by other forms of codification. On this point, see Chapter 5, pp. 110–14 and 140–42 [in the original]. In general, if the sum of the effects of meaning we call *expressive*, or *motivated*, or *symbolic*, etc. appears to be "natural"—and is indeed so in a certain way, for example to a phenomenology or a psychology of meaning—it is mainly because the effects are very deeply rooted in cultures, and because they are rooted at a level that, in these cultures, lies far beyond the various explicit, specialized, and properly informative codes. One can of course argue whether these deep significatory organizations existing at these distant levels can rightly be considered as proper codes. But, whatever the case, they are more or less organized systems, which can convey meaning and vary from one human group to another. If as a general rule the system-user experiences them not as codes but as effects of natural meaning, that is because he has sufficiently "assimilated" them to the extent that he does not possess them *in a separate state*. Thus, as a paradoxical consequence, the deepest cultural codifications are experienced as the most natural. Other codifications—which are cultural too, but are more superficial or more specialized—are, on the contrary, much more easily identified by the user as conventional and separate systems.

In the text above, I gave, among other examples of *expressiveness*, what we quite rightly call "facial expression." Certainly it is not through the effect of "cinematographic language" (nor of any other explicitly informative code) that the film spectator is able to decipher the expressions he reads on the hero's face. However, it is not through the effect of nature itself either, for the expressions of the face have meanings that vary considerably from one civilization to another (think of the difficulty one experiences in trying to understand the facial expressions in a Japanese film). Nevertheless it remains true that in films of our own culture we understand them quite naturally—that is to say, through the effect of a knowledge that is very old and very deep in us, that functions by itself, and that—for us—is henceforth merged with perception itself.

xxxi   This terminological problem does not seem as serious to me today; it suffices to indicate clearly in each case what one is talking about. Moreover the relationship between expression and signification no longer seems to me to be as adversative; the distinction retains all of its value for a phenomenology of meaning, but for a semiological analysis it may be a matter of codified organizations in both cases, although each has a different character and is situated at a different level. See Chapter 5, pp. 110–14 [in the original].

xxxii   The quotation marks were placed around the word "free" to indicate that the freedom I am talking about is never total—since in the next sentence I mention "rhetoric and poetics" (to which one might add, incidentally, the various Barthesian "writings"). In many ways "cinematographic language" is one of these "writings"—on this point, see note, Chapter 6, p. 223 [in the original]. Simply, it is true, as Roman Jakobson noted, that as one considers syntagmatic units of increasing magnitude the portion of freedom available to the speaker becomes increasingly important. In this respect, the *level of the sentence* is a kind of threshold, below which the speaker is ruled (for the most part anyway) by the law of idiom, beyond which he falls under various laws of "composition," "rhetoric," etc., which are less restrictive—or perhaps have other restrictions?—than those of idiom. One can, if not ignore them, at least circumvent them, play with them, bend them, etc. That is indeed why the most authentic creativity (or "originality") is by no means inseparable from a total *freedom*: The French classical writers of the seventeenth century understood this perfectly, and it was bourgeois romanticism that made us forget it.

xxxiii   Let us not forget that there are thousands of films of this type.

xxxiv   Like those of the American Navy I have just mentioned, or even like the technical films of the French Institut de Filmologie, or technological films in general. The documentaries one sees in movie theaters are something else; they are, in purpose at least, already art films.

xxxv   In fact, even in the verbal order, pure denotation is very rare. Everyday language carries strong connotations. In *Le Language et la vie* (Geneva, 1926), Charles Bally analyzes the spontaneous expressiveness of everyday or "popular" language at length and shows that in essence it is no different from literary or poetic expressiveness. But this is another problem. The "gap" I am referring to still exists—in the verbal order, not in the cinema—between expressive connotation (whether it is "literary" or "ordinary") and pure denotation (i.e. the inexpressive code of *language*).

xxxvi   In *Esthétique et psychologie du cinéma*, vol. I, Jean Mitry notes quite rightly (p. 48) that the word "cinema" designates three different things: a means of mechanical recording, which lies this side of art (animated photography); cinematographic art, which is also language (filmic fact); and, finally, a means of broadcasting (cinematographic fact).

xxxvii   Since this article was written (February 1964) this trend has become even more pronounced. One would now have to add to the list—to mention only those contributions of a general, theoretical nature, and more especially those applicable to significatory bodies other than verbal languages—the work of Algirdas Julien Greimas and Luis J. Prieto, whose precise significance has become more clearly apparent now that each writer has outlined his thought in a coherent, overall exposé: *Sémantique structurale* (1966) for Greimas, and *Messages et signaux* (also 1966) for Prieto. Similarly, the gathering of several of Émile Benveniste's articles into a single volume, *Problèmes de linguistique generale* (again 1966) has contributed to clarifying the notion of *discourse*. Also, since 1964 a number of semiological investigations have been undertaken, which, on questions such as narration and discourse, partly overlap on the semiotics of film: literary studies, mythological studies, studies of narrativity, etc., in France (see, for example, *Communications*, no. 8, special issue on the structural analysis of the narrative, 1966), as well as elsewhere (Italy, the United States, Poland, the Soviet Union, Czechoslovakia, etc. . . . with various resulting conferences). As for the cinema itself, the successive roundtable discussions (1965, 1966, 1967) conducted within the framework of the *New Cinema Festival* (Pesaro, Italy) have allowed various contributions to come to light, like those of Pier Paolo Pasolini or of Umberto Eco, which are mentioned elsewhere in this book. There was also the second volume of Jean Mitry's *Esthétique et psychologie du cinéma* (1965). Etc.

xxxviii   I am not suggesting that each *shot* equals a *single* sentence. That is why I have placed the word *sentence* between quotation marks throughout this passage. The "correspondence" between shot and sentence is on a global scale and is derived from the fact that a shot is an actualized unit, a unit of discourse, and is inherently dissimilar to the word. The filmic shot is of the *magnitude of the sentence*, so to speak.

This is not the case—it is a notable difference within a deeper resemblance—with traffic signs, which are discussed a little further on in the text: They are also of the magnitude of the sentence, but, in addition, it is possible to find more precise equivalences between a highway sign and a sentence (like my example, "Do Not Pass"). Among other things, this obviously derives from the fact that a traffic sign constitutes a signifying unit that is poorer and easier to analyze than cinematographic language. That is why I hesitate to use the word *seme* in connection with the cinema (and particularly with the shot). This term—in one of its acceptations at least, for authors like Bernard Pottier and Greimas use it differently—is the one that Eric Buyssens and Luis Prieto use to designate precisely the *units of signification of the magnitude of the statement*, such as one finds in various signifying systems; the statement proper thus becomes the specifically linguistic form of the seme. (On this problem, see my article "Sème" in *Supplément scientifique à la Grande Encyclopédie Larousse*, 1968, and "Remarque sur le mot et le chiffre. À Propos des conceptions de Luis J. Prieto," in *La Linguistique*, 1967, vol. 2—texts that are not reprinted in this book.) In many nonlinguistic signifying bodies one finds units clearly different from the "word," and clearly on the magnitude of the sentence—up to this point, exactly as in the cinema—but which are, moreover, finite in number, relatively easy to enumerate, and each one of which is equivalent, through its semantic substance, to a sentence that can be more or less reconstructed (as is the case with sign boards). The concept of the "seme," particularly since it has been remarkably developed by Luis Prieto, seems to me to be henceforth "ready" for the analyses of all instances of this kind (and there are many). On the other hand the concept of the seme in its present form could not be applied to signifying bodies like cinematographic language where one encounters units which, although they are of the magnitude of the statement, are infinite in number, impossible to enumerate, and none of which permits an exact equivalence with *a* sentence, but only very vague "equivalences" with a large segment of linguistic discourse comprising an indeterminate number of successive sentences. I have, incidentally, nothing better to suggest for "replacing" the concept of the seme in such cases; one can only note that the general history of semiotics has nothing to offer on this point so far (at least to my knowledge); that is why I use paraphrases like "units of the magnitude of the sentence, but which . . . etc." For that matter it may be that this lacuna is permanent (that it is not really a lacuna), and that the difficulty derives simply from the fact that "cinematographic language" has no specific units *on the level of the image*, but only on the level of the ordering of images.

xxxix   In the present state of research in linguistics and semiotics, it is becoming less and less insurmountable. The fact that Chomsky's work—and, among other contributions, his reformulation of the "language system/speech" duality in terms of "competence/performance," with all that this implies—is now better known in France is only one of the reasons. There is also the concept of *discourse* (neither pure language system nor pure speech) in Émile Benveniste; Zellig Harris's *discourse analysis*; Greimas's *transphrastic* analysis; Luis Prieto's concept of the seme (extralinguistic unit of the same order as the statement), etc. A certain, too brutal, or too literally Saussurian, concept of the "language system/speech" dichotomy is becoming less and less tenable.

xl   In his *Essais sur les principes . . . (op. cit.)*, G. Cohen-Séat had very clearly indicated what importance the linguistic approach would have for the filmic fact. But there has been no development since then. One still speaks innocently about "language" in the cinema as if no one had ever studied language. Was Meillet then a service-station attendant, and Trubetskoy a butcher?

Arabic numbering

1   *Cahiers du cinéma*, no. 94, April 1959. The interview was conducted by F. Hoveyda and J. Rivette.

2   J. Carta has analyzed Eisenstein's early conversion to montage. See "L'Humanisme commence au langage," in *Esprit*, June 1960, pp. 1113–32, and especially pp. 1114–16.

3   Pudovkin, in *Cinéa-Ciné pour tous*, Jan. 1, 1924. Reprinted in Pierre Lherminier's selection, *L'Art du cinéma* (Paris, 1960), pp. 189–200.

4   *Ibid.*, p. 190 in Lherminier's book.

5   R. Micha, "Le Cinéma, art du montage?" in *Critique*, Aug.–Sept. 1951, no. 51–52, pp. 710–24. For the idea I am discussing, see pp. 723–24.

6   See particularly the comparison between Griffith and Dickens in "Dickens, Griffith and the Film Today," Eisenstein's contribution to *Amerikanskaya Kinematografyia: D.U. Griffit* (Moscow, 1944). Reprinted in Jay Leyda's edition of *Film Form* combined with *The Film Sense* (New York: Harcourt, Brace, and Meridian, 1957), pp. 195–255.

7   R.A. Fowler, "Les Débuts d'O. Welles à Hollywood," in *Revue du cinéma*, second series, no. 3, Dec. 1946, p. 13.

8   The concept is used here in a broadened sense derived from J. Kurylowicz, "Linguistique et théorie du signe," in *Journal de psychologie normale et pathologique*, vol. 42, 1949, p. 175. Besides, the idea of subordinating morphology to syntax, which is dear to this author, points in the same direction.

9   See Claude Lévi-Strauss, "La Notion de structure en ethnologie," paper delivered at the symposium on Social Structure, New York, 1952. Reprinted in *Structural Anthropology*.

10   Roland Barthes, "L'Activité structuraliste," in *Lettres nouvelles*, Feb. 1963, pp. 71–81.

11   Vol. III of *Qu'est-ce que le cinéma?* (*Cinéma et sociologie*, 1961), pp. 172–73 (in a passage of the article "La Cybernetique d'André Cayette," which was originally published in *Cahiers du cinéma*, no. 36, 1954). [This article was not included in Hugh Gray's selection.—Translator.]

12   Barthes, in *Arguments*, no. 27–28, 3d and 4th quarters, 1962, pp. 118–20.

13   A. Moles, "Poésie expérimentale, poétique et art permutationnel," in *Arguments*, no. 27–28, pp. 93–97.

14   Roland Barthes's expression.

15   See the next section, "From *ciné-langue* to cinema language," for the overall historical development.

16   The impression of reality is a factor common to both the realistic and fantastic film content. Many film theoreticians had felt this, suggested it, half said it before Edgar Morin established it solidly in *Le Cinéma ou L'Homme imaginaire*. See Chapter 1 of this book [the original].

17   In his manifesto on the montage of attractions (*Lef*, May 1923, Moscow). This idea was further developed by Eisenstein in *Notes of a Film Director*, R. Yurenev, translated by X. Danko (Foreign Language Publications, Moscow, 1958).

18   Which Eisenstein's personal remarks (*passim.*) reflect, as do the works of Jay Leyda, B. Amengual, Jean Mitry, and others on Eisenstein.

19   G. Cohen-Séat, *Essai sur les principes d'une philosophie du cinéma*, rev. ed. (Paris: Presses Universitaires de France, 1958), p. 13.

20   Bazin speaks of them everywhere. His basic writing on the subject is "L'Evolution du langage cinématographique" (a synthesis of three earlier articles) in *Qu'est-ce que le cinéma?*, vol. I (*Ontologie*

et langage, 1958). This essay is included in *What Is Cinema? op. cit.* ("The Evolution of the Language of Cinema"), pp. 23–40.

21   These terms of Dziga Vertov's summarize perfectly the concept of "montage or bust." The first (*ciné phrase, film sentence*) is found in "Kinoki-Pereverot," the manifesto of the "Soviet Tronkh" (Vertov's "Group of the Three"), which was published in *Lef* (Mayakovsky's review), May–June 1923 (the same issue that published Eisenstein's manifesto), reprinted in French in *Cahiers du cinéma*, no. 144 (June 1963) and 146 (Aug. 1963). The passage quoted is from p. 33 of *Cahiers* no. 144. The second term ("*ciné-langue*") is found in *Cinéoeil* (Moscow, 1924) and is reprinted in M. Lapierre's *Anthologie du cinéma, op. cit.*, pp. 207–09.

22   Leenhardt, "Ambiguïté du cinéma," lecture delivered on Sept. 2, 1957, and reprinted in *Cahiers du cinéma*, no. 100, Oct. 1959, pp. 27–38.

23   Jean Renoir, in *Radio-cinéma-télévision* (Nov. 22, 1959), *Cahiers du cinéma*, no. 100, Oct. 1959, and in many "remarks" elsewhere. What is more remarkable, he said the same thing as early as 1938, in *Point* (Dec. issue).

24   Astruc, manifesto published in *L'Écran français*, March 30, 1948.

25   Astruc, in *Ciné-Digest*, no. 1, 1949.

26   Marcel Martin, *Le Langage cinématographique*, Paris, 1955.

27   Ibid., pp. 236–37.

28   Merleau-Ponty, lecture at the IDHEC (Institut des Hautes Études Cinématographiques), March 13, 1945. Published in *Sens et nonsens*.

29   Ibid.

30   Cohen-Séat, *Essai sur les principes . . .*, p. 128.

31   Ibid., p. 119.

32   Especially Edgar Morin, *Le Cinéma ou L'Homme imaginaire, op. cit.*, pp. 55–90 (i.e. all of ch. 3).

33   F. Ricci, "Le Cinéma entre l'imagination et la réalité," in *Revue internationale de filmologie*, no. 2, Sept.–Oct. 1947, pp. 161–63.

34   The concept and the terminology are from Edgar Morin, *op. cit.*

35   Morin, in "Le Rôle du cinéma," *Esprit*, vol. 38, June 1960, pp. 1069–79. For the point considered here, see p. 1071.

36   See especially L. Sceve, "Cinéma et méthode" in *Revue internationale de filmologie*, no. 1 (July–Aug. 1947), no. 2 (Sept.–Oct. 1947) and no. 3–4 (Oct. 1948). For the point considered: no. 2, pp. 172–74.

37   D. Dreyfus, "Cinéma et langage," in *Diogene*, no. 35, July–Sept. 1961.

38   Béla Balázs's expression (cf. further).

39   The passage was published (in a French translation) in P. Lherminier's anthology *L' Art du cinéma, op. cit.* See p. 208, for the idea I am discussing. Lherminier's text is based on the German edition of 1949, *Der Film* (Vienna, Globus Verlag), in which the author gathered together and condensed *Der Geist des Films* and *Der sichtbare Mensch oder die Kultur des Films*. [A selection of Balázs's main theoretical writings has been published in English: *Theory of the Film*, translated by Edith Bone (London, 1953)–Translator.]

40   See F.R. Bastide, "Le Roman à l'echafaud," *Esprit*, vol. 28, June 1960, pp. 1133–41. For the point considered here: p. 1139.

41   This phenomenon has been well analyzed by F. Chevassu, in *Le Langage cinématographique* (Ligue Française de l'Enseignement, Paris, 1962), pp. 36–37.

42   Bazin, "Le Ces Pagnol," in *Qu'est-ce que le cinéma? op. cit.*, vol. II, pp. 119–25. (This text is not included in Gray's selection.)

43   M. Pagnol's first manifesto: 1930. Second manifesto: 1933.

44   From Pagnol's second manifesto, "Cinématurgie de Paris," *Les Cahiers du film*, Dec. 15, 1933.

45   This was noted by R. Leenhardt in "Ambiguïté du cinéma" (*op. cit.*). See *Cahiers du cinéma*, no. 100, p. 28.

46   Arnoux, in an article later included in *Du Muet au parlant* (new edition, 1946). My reference is to P. Lherminier's selection (*op. cit.*), in which it appears with no references.

47   In *Zhizn Iskusstva* (Leningrad), no. 32, Aug. 5, 1928.

48   Souriau was speaking about "new film techniques" (Cinemascope, etc.) for the symposium on film effects in relation to new techniques (*Symposium sur les effèts de film en fonction de techniques nouvelles*, of the Second International Congress on Film, Paris, Feb. 1955). Reprinted in *Revue internationale de filmologie*, no. 20–24 (1955), pp. 92–95. The above passage refers to p. 94.

49   Here and there the work has been begun: by B. Pingaud and J. Ricardou on Alain Resnais (*Premier*

plan, no. 18, Oct. 1961); J. Carta on Resnais, Agnès Varda, and Chris Marker (*Esprit*, June 1960); and R. Bellour on the same film-makers (*Artsept*, no. 1, quarter, 1963).

50 Bazin, in "L'Avant-garde nouvelle" (*Festival du film maudit*, limited edition published in 1949 on the occasion of this same festival), reprinted in *Cahiers du cinéma*, no. 10, March, 1952, pp. 16–17.

51 De Saussure, *Course in General Linguistics*, translated by Wade Baskin (New York, 1959), p. 9.

52 Ibid., p. 16.

53 C. Lévi-Strauss, "Structural Analysis in Linguistics and Anthropology," *Word*, Aug. 1945. Reprinted in *Structural Anthology* (New York, 1963).

54 De Saussure, *Course . . .*, *op. cit.*, p. 17.

55 In a text not included in this book, I have dwelt on the problem of the "articulations" in relation to non-linguistic semiotics: "Les Sémiotiques, ou sémies. À propos de travaux de Louis Hjelmslev et d'André Martinet," *Communications*, no. 7, 1966.

56 See "On the Impression of Reality in the Cinema" (Chapter 1 of this book [the original]).

57 R. Jakobson, "On Linguistic Aspects of Translation," in *On Translation*, R.A. Brower, ed. (Harvard Studies in Comparative Literature, 1959).

58 "Arbitraire linguistique et double articulation," in *Cahiers F. de Saussure*, 15, 1957, pp. 105–16. Reprinted in *La Linguistique synchronique* (Paris, 1965), pp. 21–35. Passage mentioned: pp. 26–27.

59 J. Vendryes, ed., in *Le Langage, introduction linguistique à l'histoire*, Renaissance du livre, 1921.

60 See further on, "Cinema and Literature" (pp. 75–84).

61 E. Benveniste, "La Phrase nominale," *Bulletin de la Société de Linguistique de Paris*, vol. XLVI, 1950. Reprinted in *Problèmes de linguistique générale* (Gallimard, Paris, 1966), pp. 151–67.

62 Jakobson, "Results of the Conference of Anthropologists and Linguists," in *Supplement to International Journal of American Linguistics*, vol. 19, no. 2, April 1953.

63 E. Buyssens, *Les Langages et le discours*, Office de publicité, Brussels, 1943, ch. II, Paragraph A, pp. 8–12.

64 A. Martinet, *Elements of General Linguistics*, translated by Elisabeth Palmer (London: Faber and Faber, 1960), p. 118.

65 From this point of view, Jean Mitry's book (*Esthétique et psychologie du cinéma*, vol. 1) represents considerable progress on many earlier works on the theory of the cinema.

66 De Saussure, p. 137.

67 L. Hjelmslev, "Stratification in Language," *Word*, 10, 1954. Reprinted in French in *Essais linguistiques* (Copenhagen, 1959). For the taxeme, see pp. 40 and 58 of the *Essais. . . .*

68 G. Guillaume, "Observation et explication dans les sciences du langage," in *Études philosophiques*, 1958, pp. 446–62. Passage under consideration: pp. 446–47.

69 C. Bally, "Sur la Motivation des signes linguistiques," in *Bulletin de la Société de Linguistique de Paris*, 1940, vol. XLI, pp. 75 ff., and specifically p. 87.

70 S. Ullman, pp. 341–43 of *Journal de psychologie normale et pathologique*, 1958 ("Orientations nouvelles en semantique"). See also *Précis de semantique française*, Bern, 1952, *passim*.

71 Already noted by Roland Barthes in "Les Unités traumatiques au cinéma," *Revue internationale de filmologie*, no. 34, July–Sept. 1960.

72 Notably by M. Martin, *Langage cinématographique*, pp. 152–54.

73 I have already spoken about filmic intellection elsewhere. In addition, pp. 194–200 of Edgar Morin's book (*Le Cinéma ou L'Homme imaginaire*) are very enlightening on this question.

74 See pp. 40–42 of this book.

75 Gilbert Cohen-Séat, *Essai sur les principes . . .*, pp. 145–46.

76 Cf. Étienne Souriau's famous distinction between the representational and the nonrepresentational arts, also with a remark in the same vein in connection with the cinema and its poetry in D. Dreyfus, "Cinéma et langage" and in connection with the cinema, as early as 1927, L. Landry, "Formation de la sensibilité," *L'Art cinématographique*, no. 2, p. 60.

77 The terms are used in Hjelmslev's sense. See all of the last part of *Prolegomena to a Theory of Language*, Indiana University Publications in Anthropology and Linguistics, 1953 (the English translation of a work originally published in Danish in 1943).

78 See Jean Mitry, *Esthétique et psychologie du cinéma*, "Le Mot et l'image," pp. 65–104 of vol. 1.

79 Mikel Dufrenne, *Phénoménologie de l'expérience esthétique*, Paris: Presses Universitaires de France, 1953, vol. 1 (*L'Objêt esthétique*), pp. 240 ff.

80 De Saussure, *Course . . .*, p. 66.

81 E. Buyssens, *Les Langages et le discours*, ch. 5, pp. 44–48.

82 See Roland Barthes's diagram at the end of *Mythologies* (Paris, 1957), p. 222.

83   J. Vendryes, "Langage oral et langage par gestes," *Journal de psychologie normale et pathologique*, vol. XLII, 1950, pp. 7–33; passage referred to on p. 22.

84   E. Buyssens, *Les Langages et le discours*, ch. IV, paragraph A, pp. 34–42.

85   C. Lévi-Strauss, "The Structural Study of Myths," *Myth, a Symposium*. Reprinted in *Structural Anthropology* (New York, 1963).

86   V. Propp, *Morphology of the Folktale* (Mouton and Co., 1958). Each one of the "functions" the folktale is divided into is characterized by an abstract substantive (prohibition, transgression, pursuit, etc. . . .); each of the abstract substantives corresponds to the substantiation of a sentence predicate as Walter Porzig, for example, has shown ("Die Leistung der Abstrakta in der Sprache," *Blätter für deutsche Philosophie* IV, 1930, pp. 66–67).

87   Barthes, *Mythologie, op. cit.*, pp. 215–17 ("Le Mythe est une parole").

88   "Entretien avec Roland Barthes," an interview with Barthes conducted by M. Delahaye and J. Rivette for *Cahiers du cinéma*, no. 147, Sept. 1963, pp. 22–31. Passage referred to: pp. 23–24 ("Macrosemantique").

89   G. Mounin, "Les Systèmes de communication non-linguistiques et leur place dans la vie du ving-tième siecle," *Bulletin de la Société de Linguistique de Paris*, vol. LIV, 1959 (the entire article).

90   R. Jakobson, "Closing Statements: Linguistics and Poetics," *Style and Language*, Th. A. Seboek, ed. (MIT Press, 1960), pp. 352–53.

91   Mounin, "Les Systèmes de communications non-linguistiques . . .," *op. cit.*

92   Ibid., p. 187.

93   Jean Fourquet, "La Notion du verbe," *Journal de psychologie normale et pathologique*, 1950, pp. 74–98. Louis Hjelmslev, "Le Verbe et la phrase nominale," *Mélanges de philologie, de littérature et d'histoire offerts à J. Marouzeau*, 1948, pp. 253–81, reprinted in *Essais linguistiques* (*op. cit.*), pp. 165–91. (The verb as "clause connecting," p. 190). Émile Benveniste, "La Phrase nominale," *Bulletin de la Société de Linguistique de Paris*, vol. XLVI, 1950; reprinted in *Problèmes de linguistique generale* (*op. cit.*), pp. 151–67. (The double "verbal function:" cohesive and assertive; the verb as "predicate of reality.") André Martinet, "La Construction ergative," *Journal de psychologie normale et pathologique*, July–Sept. 1958; reprinted in *La Linguistique synchronique* (Paris, 1965), pp. 206–22. (The concept of the "predicate of existence," in connection with Basque syntax.)

94   A. Martinet, *Elements of General Linguistics*, p. 23.

95   É. Benveniste, *Les Langages* . . ., ch. III, paragraph C, pp. 30–33 ("Parole, discours, langue").

96   Eric Buyssens's term.

97   "Principes de bibliographie et de documentation," a study by Claude Brémond summarized by Gilbert Cohen-Séat in *Problèmes actuels du cinéma et de l'information visuelle* (Paris, 1959), vol. 2, pp. 79–88. Passage referred to: p. 79.

98   This is Gilbert Cohen-Séat's famous distinction; see *Essais sur les principes* . . ., p. 54.

Chapter 11

Peter Wollen

THE SEMIOLOGY OF THE CINEMA

IN RECENT YEARS A considerable degree of interest has developed in the semiology of the cinema, in the question whether it is possible to dissolve cinema criticism and cinema aesthetics into a special province of the general science of signs. It has become increasingly clear that traditional theories of film language and film grammar, which grew up spontaneously over the years, need to be re-examined and related to the established discipline of linguistics. If the concept of 'language' is to be used it must be used scientifically and not simply as a loose, though suggestive, metaphor. The debate which has arisen in France and Italy, round the work of Roland Barthes, Christian Metz, Pier Paolo Pasolini and Umberto Eco, points in this direction.

The main impulse behind the work of these critics and semiologists springs from Ferdinand de Saussure's *Course in General Linguistics*. After Saussure's death in 1913 his former pupils at the University of Geneva collected and collated his lecture outlines and their own notes and synthesised these into a systematic presentation, which was published in Geneva in 1915. In the *Course* Saussure predicted a new science, the science of semiology:

> A science that studies the life of signs within society is conceivable; it would be part of social psychology and consequently of general psychology; I shall call it *semiology* (from Greek *semeion*, 'sign'). Semiology would show what constitutes signs, what laws govern them. Since the science does not yet exist, no one can say what it would be; but it has a right to existence, a place staked out in advance. Linguistics is only a part of the general science of semiology; the laws discovered by semiology will be applicable to linguistics, and the latter will circumscribe a well-defined area within the mass of anthropological facts.[1]

Saussure, who was impressed by the work of Emile Durkheim (1858–1917) in sociology, emphasised that signs must be studied from a social viewpoint, that language was a social institution which eluded the individual will. The linguistic system – what might nowadays be called the 'code' – pre-existed the individual act of speech, the 'message'. Study of the system therefore had logical priority.

Saussure stressed, as his first principle, the arbitrary nature of the sign. The signifier (the sound-image *o-k-s* or *b-ö-f*, for example) has no natural connection with the signified (the concept 'ox'). To use Saussure's term, the sign is 'unmotivated'. Saussure was not certain what the full implications of the arbitrary nature of the linguistic sign were for semiology:

> When semiology becomes organised as a science, the question will arise whether or not it properly includes modes of expression based on completely natural signs, such as pantomime. Supposing the new science welcomes them, its main concern will still be the whole group of systems grounded on the arbitrariness of the sign. In fact, every means of expression used in society is based, in principle, on collective behaviour or – what amounts to the same thing – on convention. Polite formulas, for instance, though often imbued with a certain natural expressiveness (as in the case of a Chinese who greets his emperor by bowing down to the ground nine times), are none the less fixed by rule; it is this rule and not the intrinsic value of the gestures that obliges one to use them. Signs that are wholly arbitrary realise better than the others the ideal of the semiological process; that is why language, the most complex and universal of all systems of expression, is also the most characteristic; in this sense linguistics can become the master-pattern for all branches of semiology although language is only one particular semiological system.[2]

Linguistics was to be both a special province of semiology and, at the same time, the master-pattern ('le patron général') for the various other provinces. All the provinces, however – or, at least, the central ones – were to have as their object systems 'grounded on the arbitrariness of the sign'. These systems, in the event, proved hard to find. Would-be semiologists found themselves limited to such micro-languages as the language of traffic-signs, the language of fans, ships' signalling systems, the language of gesture among Trappist monks, various kinds of semaphore and so on. These micro-languages proved extremely restricted cases, capable of articulating a very sparse semantic range. Many of them were parasitic on verbal language proper. Roland Barthes, as a result of his researches into the language of costume, concluded that it was impossible to escape the pervasive presence of verbal language. Words enter into discourse of another order either to fix an ambiguous meaning, like a label or a title, or to contribute to the meaning that cannot otherwise be communicated, like the words in the bubbles in a strip-cartoon. Words either anchor meaning or convey it.

It is only in very rare cases that non-verbal systems can exist without auxiliary support from the verbal code. Even highly developed and intellectualised systems like painting and music constantly have recourse to words, particularly at a popular level: songs, cartoons, posters. Indeed, it would be possible to write the history of painting as a function of the shifting relation between words and images. One of the main achievements of the Renaissance was to banish words from the picture-space. Yet words repeatedly forced themselves back; they reappear in the paintings of El Greco, for instance, in Dürer, in Hogarth: one could give countless examples. In the twentieth century words have returned with a vengeance. In music, words were not banished until the beginning of the seventeenth century; they have asserted themselves in opera, in oratorio, in *Lieder*. The cinema is another obvious case in point. Few silent films were made without intertitles. Erwin Panofsky has recollected his cinema-going days in Berlin around 1910:

> The producers employed means of clarification similar to those we find in medieval art. One of these were printed titles or letters, striking equivalents of

the medieval *tituli* and scrolls (at a still earlier date there even used to be explainers who would say, *viva voce*, 'Now he thinks his wife is dead but she isn't' or 'I don't wish to offend the ladies in the audience but I doubt that any of them would have done that much for her child').[3]

In Japan, 'explainers' of this kind formed themselves into a guild, which proved strong enough to delay the advent of the talkie.

In the end Barthes reached the conclusion that semiology might be better seen as a branch of linguistics, rather than the other way round. This seems a desperate conclusion. The province turns out to be so much 'the most complex and universal' that it engulfs the whole. Yet our experience of cinema suggests that great complexity of meaning can be expressed through images. Thus, to take an obvious example, the most trivial and banal book can be made into an extremely interesting and, to all appearances, significant film; reading a screenplay is usually a barren and arid experience, intellectually as well as emotionally. The implication of this is that it is not only systems exclusively 'grounded on the arbitrariness of the sign' which are expressive and meaningful. 'Natural signs' cannot be so readily dismissed as Saussure imagined. It is this demand for the reintegration of the natural sign into semiology which led Christian Metz, a disciple of Barthes, to declare that cinema is indeed a language, but a language without a code (without a *langue*, to use Saussure's term). It is a language because it has texts; there is a meaningful discourse. But, unlike verbal language, it cannot be referred back to a preexistent code. Metz's position involves him in a considerable number of problems which he never satisfactorily surmounts; he is forced back to the concept of 'a "logic of implication" by which the image becomes language'[4]; he quotes with approval Béla Balázs's contention that it is through a 'current of induction' that we make sense of a film. It is not made clear whether we have to learn this logic or whether it is natural. And it is difficult to see how concepts like 'logic of implication' and 'current of induction' can be integrated into the theory of semiology.

What is needed is a more precise discussion of what we mean by a 'natural sign' and by the series of words such as 'analogous', 'continuous', 'motivated', which are used to describe such signs, by Barthes, Metz and others. Fortunately the groundwork necessary for further precision has already been accomplished, by Charles Sanders Peirce, the American logician. Peirce was a contemporary of Saussure; like Saussure his papers were collected and published posthumously, between 1931 and 1935, twenty years after his death in 1914. Peirce was the most original American thinker there has been, so original, as Roman Jakobson has pointed out, that for a great part of his working life he was unable to obtain a university post. His reputation now rests principally on his more accessible work, principally his teachings on pragmatism. His work on semiology (or 'semiotic' as he himself called it) has been sadly neglected. Unfortunately, his most influential disciple, Charles Morris, travestied his position by coupling it with a virulent form of Behaviourism. Severe criticisms of Behaviourism in relation to linguistics and aesthetics, from writers such as E.H. Gombrich and Noam Chomsky, have naturally tended to damage Peirce by association with Morris. However, in recent years, Roman Jakobson has done a great deal to reawaken interest in Peirce's semiology, a revival of enthusiasm long overdue.

The main texts which concern us here are his *Speculative Grammar*, the letters to Lady Welby and *Existential Graphs* (sub-titled 'my *chef d'œuvre*' by Peirce). These books contain Peirce's taxonomy of different classes of sign, which he regarded as the essential semiological foundation for a subsequent logic and rhetoric. The classification which is important to the present argument is that which Peirce called 'the second trichotomy of signs', their division into icons, indices and symbols. 'A sign is either an *icon*, an *index* or a *symbol*.'[5]

An icon, according to Peirce, is a sign which represents its object mainly by its similarity to it; the relationship between signifier and signified is not arbitrary but is one of resemblance or likeness. Thus, for instance, the portrait of a man resembles him. Icons can, however, be divided into two sub-classes: images and diagrams. In the case of images 'simple qualities' are alike; in the case of diagrams the 'relations between the parts'. Many diagrams, of course, contain symboloid features; Peirce readily admitted this, for it was the dominant aspect or dimension of the sign which concerned him.

An index is a sign by virtue of an existential bond between itself and its object. Peirce gave several examples:

> I see a man with a rolling gait. This is a probable indication that he is a sailor.
> I see a bowlegged man in corduroys, gaiters and a jacket. These are probable
> indications that he is a jockey or something of the sort. A sundial or clock
> indicates the time of day.[6]

Other examples cited by Peirce are the weathercock, a sign of the direction of the wind which physically moves it, the barometer, the spirit-level. Roman Jakobson cites Man Friday's footprint in the sand and medical symptoms, such as pulse-rates, rashes and so on. Symptomatology is a branch of the study of the indexical sign.

The third category of sign, the symbol, corresponds to Saussure's arbitrary sign. Like Saussure, Peirce speaks of a 'contract' by virtue of which the symbol is a sign. The symbolic sign eludes the individual will. 'You can write down the word "star", but that does not make you the creator of the word, nor if you erase it have you destroyed the word. The word lives in the minds of those who use it.'[7] A symbolic sign demands neither resemblance to its object nor any existential bond with it. It is conventional and has the force of a law. Peirce was concerned about the appropriateness of calling this kind of sign a 'symbol', a possibility which Saussure also considered but rejected because of the danger of confusion. However, it seems certain that Saussure over-restricted the notion of sign by limiting it to Peirce's 'symbolic'; moreover, Peirce's trichotomy is elegant and exhaustive. The principal remaining problem, the categorisation of such so-called 'symbols' as the scales of justice or the Christian cross is one that is soluble within Peirce's system, as I shall show later.

Peirce's categories are the foundation for any advance in semiology. It is important to note, however, that Peirce did not consider them mutually exclusive. On the contrary, all three aspects frequently – or, he sometimes suggests, invariably – overlap and are co-present. It is this awareness of overlapping which enabled Peirce to make some particularly relevant remarks about photography:

> Photographs, especially instantaneous photographs, are very instructive, because
> we know that in certain respects they are exactly like the objects they represent.
> But this resemblance is due to the photographs having been produced under
> such circumstances that they were physically forced to correspond point by
> point to nature. In that aspect then, they belong to the second class of signs,
> those by physical connection.[8]

That is, to the indexical class. Elsewhere he describes a photographic print as a 'quasi-predicate', of which the light-rays are the 'quasi-subject'.

Among European writers on semiology Roland Barthes reaches somewhat similar conclusions, though he does not use the category 'indexical', but sees the photographic print simply as 'iconic'. However, he describes how the photographic icon presents 'a kind of natural *being-there* of the object'. There is no human intervention, no transformation, no code, between the object and the sign; hence the paradox that a photograph is a message without a code. Christian Metz makes the transition from photography to cinema. Indeed Metz verges upon using Peirce's concepts, mediated to him through the work of André Martinet:

> A close-up of a revolver does not signify 'revolver' (a purely potential lexical unit) — but signifies *as a minimum*, leaving aside its connotations, 'Here is a revolver.' It carries with it its own actualisation, a kind of 'Here is' ('*Voici*': the very word which André Martinet considers to be a pure index of actualisation).[9]

It is curious that Metz, in his voluminous writings, does not lay much greater stress on the analysis of this aspect of the cinema, since he is extremely hostile to any attempt to see the cinema as a symbolic process which refers back to a code. In fact, obscured beneath his semiological analysis is a very definite and frequently overt aesthetic *parti pris*. For, like Barthes and like Saussure, he perceives only two modes of existence for the sign: natural and cultural. Moreover, he is inclined to see these as mutually exclusive, so that a language must be either natural or cultural, uncoded or coded. It cannot be both. Hence Metz's view of the cinema turns out like a curious inverted mirror-image of Noam Chomsky's view of verbal language; whereas Chomsky banishes the ungrammatical into outer darkness, Metz banishes the grammatical. The work of Roman Jakobson, influenced by Peirce, is, as we shall see, a corrective to both these views. The cinema contains all three modes of the sign: indexical, iconic and symbolic. What has always happened is that theorists of the cinema have seized on one or other of these dimensions and used it as the ground for an aesthetic firman. Metz is no exception.

In his aesthetic preferences, Metz is quite clearly indebted to André Bazin, the most forceful and intelligent protagonist of 'realism' in the cinema. Bazin was one of the founders of *Cahiers du cinéma* and wrote frequently in *Esprit*, the review founded by Emmanuel Mounier, the Catholic philosopher, originator of Personalism and the most important intellectual influence on Bazin. Many people have commented on the way in which Bazin modelled his style, somewhat abstruse, unafraid of plunging into the problems and terminology of philosophy, on that of Mounier. Bazin became interested in the cinema during his military service at Bordeaux in 1939. After his return to Paris he organised, in collaboration with friends from *Esprit*, clandestine film-shows; during the German Occupation he showed films such as Fritz Lang's *Metropolis* and the banned works of Chaplin. Then, after the Liberation, he became one of the dominant figures in orientating the fantastic efflorescence of cinema culture which grew up in the clubs, in Henri Langlois's magnificent *Cinémathèque*, in the commercial cinema, where American films once again reappeared. During this time, perhaps most important of all, Bazin developed his aesthetics of the cinema, an aesthetics antithetical to the 'pure cinema' of Delluc and the 'montage' theory of Malraux's celebrated article in *Verve*. A new direction was taken.

Bazin's starting-point is an ontology of the photographic image. His conclusions are remarkably close to those of Peirce. Time and again Bazin speaks of photography in terms of a mould, a death-mask, a Veronica, the Holy Shroud of Turin, a relic, an imprint. Thus Bazin speaks of 'the lesser plastic arts, the moulding of death-masks for example, which likewise involves a certain automatic process. One might consider photography in this sense as a moulding, the taking of an impression, by the manipulation of light'.[10] Thus Bazin repeatedly stresses the existential bond between sign and object which, for Peirce, was the determining characteristic of the indexical sign. But whereas Peirce made his observation in order to found a logic, Bazin wished to found an aesthetic. 'Photography affects us like a phenomenon in nature, like a flower or a snowflake whose vegetable or earthly origins are an inseparable part of their beauty.'[11] Bazin's aesthetic asserted the primacy of the object over the image, the primacy of the natural world over the world of signs. 'Nature is always photogenic': this was Bazin's watchword.

Bazin developed a bi-polar view of the cinema. On the one hand was Realism ('The good, the true, the just', as Godard was later to say of the work of Rossellini); on the other hand was Expressionism, the deforming intervention of human agency. Fidelity to nature was the necessary touchstone of judgement. Those who transgressed, Bazin denounced: Fritz Lang's *Nibelungen*, *The Cabinet of Dr Caligari*. He recognised the Wagnerian ambitions of Eisenstein's *Ivan the Terrible* and wrote: 'One can detest opera, believe it to be a doomed musical genre, while still recognising the value of Wagner's music.' Similarly, we may admire Eisenstein, while still condemning his project as 'an aggressive return of a dangerous aestheticism'.[12] Bazin found the constant falsification in *The Third Man* exasperating. In a brilliant article he compared Hollywood to the Court at Versailles and asked where was its *Phèdre*? He found the answer, justly, in Charles Vidor's *Gilda*. Yet even this masterpiece was stripped of all 'natural accident'; an aesthetic cannot be founded on an 'existential void'.

In counterposition to these recurrent regressions into Expressionism, Bazin postulated a triumphal tradition of Realism. This tradition began with Feuillade, spontaneously, naïvely, and then developed in the 1920s in the films of Flaherty, Von Stroheim and Murnau, whom Bazin contrasted with Eisenstein, Kuleshov and Gance. In the 1930s the tradition was kept alive principally by Jean Renoir. Bazin saw Renoir stemming from the tradition of his father, that of French Impressionism. Just as the French Impressionists – Manet, Degas, Bonnard – had reformulated the place of the picture-frame in pictorial composition, under the influence of the snapshot, so Renoir *fils* had reformulated the place of the frame in cinematic composition. In contrast to Eisenstein's principle of montage, based on the sacrosanct close-up, the significant image centred in the frame, he had developed what Bazin called *re-cadrage* ('re-framing'): lateral camera movements deserted and recaptured a continuous reality. The blackness surrounding the screen masked off the world rather than framed the image. In the 1930s Jean Renoir alone

> forced himself to look back beyond the resources provided by montage and so uncover the secret of a film form that would permit everything to be said without chopping the world up into little fragments, that would reveal the hidden meanings in people and things without disturbing the unity natural to them.[13]

In the 1940s the Realist tradition reasserted itself, though divided between two different currents. The first of these was inaugurated by *Citizen Kane* and continued in the later films of Welles and of Wyler. Its characteristic feature was the use of deep focus. By this means, the spatial unity of scenes could be maintained, episodes could be presented in their physical entirety. The second current was that of Italian Neo-realism, whose cause Bazin espoused with especial fervour. Above all, he admired Rossellini. In Neo-realism Bazin recognised fidelity to nature, to things as they were. Fiction was reduced to a minimum. Acting, location, incident: all were as natural as possible. Of *Bicycle Thieves* Bazin wrote that it was the first example of pure cinema. No more actors, no more plot, no more *mise en scène*: the perfect aesthetic illusion of reality. In fact, no more cinema. Thus the film could obtain radical purity only through its own annihilation. The mystical tone of this kind of argument reflects, of course, the curious admixture of Catholicism and Existentialism which had formed Bazin. Yet it also develops logically from an aesthetic which stresses the passivity of the natural world rather than the agency of the human mind.

Bazin hoped that the two currents of the Realist tradition – Welles and Rossellini – would one day reconverge. He felt that their separation was due only to technical limitations: deep focus required more powerful lighting than could be used on natural locations. But when Visconti's *La Terra Trema* appeared, a film whose style was for the first time the same 'both *intra* and *extra muros*', the most Wellesian of Neo-realist films, nevertheless Bazin was disappointed. The synthesis, though achieved, lacked fire and 'affective eloquence'.[14] Probably Visconti was too close to the opera, to Expressionism, to be able to satisfy Bazin. But in the late 1940s and 1950s his concept of Realism did develop a step further, towards what, in a review of *La Strada*, he was to call 'realism of the person' ('de la personne').[15] The echo of Mounier was not by chance. Bazin was deeply influenced by Mounier's insistence that the interior and the exterior, the spiritual and the physical, the ideal and the material were indissolubly linked. He re-orientated the philosophical and socio-political ideas of Mounier and applied them to the cinema. Bazin broke with many of the Italian protagonists of Neo-realism when he asserted that 'Visconti is Neorealist in *La Terra Trema* when he calls for social revolt and Rossellini is Neo-realist in the *Fioretti*, which illustrates a purely spiritual reality'.[16] In Bresson's films Bazin saw 'the outward revelation of an interior destiny', in those of Rossellini 'the presence of the spiritual' is expressed with 'breath-taking obviousness'.[17] The exterior, through the transparence of images stripped of all inessentials, reveals the interior. Bazin emphasised the importance of physiognomy, upon which – as in the films of Dreyer – the interior spiritual life was etched and printed.

Bazin believed that films should be made, not according to some *a priori* method or plan, but, like those of Rossellini, from 'fragments of raw reality, multiple and equivocal in themselves, whose meaning can only emerge *a posteriori* thanks to other facts, between which the mind is able to see relations'. Realism was the vocation of the cinema, not to signify but to reveal. Realism, for Bazin, had little to do with mimesis. He felt that cinema was closer to the art of the Egyptians, which existed, in Panofsky's words, 'in a sphere of magical reality', than to that of the Greeks, 'in a sphere of aesthetic ideality'.[18] It was the existential bond between fact and image, world and film, which counted for most in Bazin's aesthetic, rather than any quality of similitude or resemblance. Hence the possibility – even the necessity – of an art which could reveal spiritual states. There was for Bazin a double movement of impression, of moulding and imprinting: first, the interior spiritual suffering was stamped upon the exterior physiognomy; then the exterior physiognomy was stamped and printed upon the sensitive film.

It would be difficult to overestimate the impact of Bazin's aesthetic. His influence can be seen in the critical writing of Andrew Sarris in the United States, in the theories of Pier Paolo Pasolini in Italy, in Charles Barr's lucid article on CinemaScope (published in *Film Quarterly*, Summer 1963, but written in England), in Christian Metz's articles in *Communications* and *Cahiers du cinéma*. That is to say, all the most important writing on cinema in the last ten or twenty years has, by and large, charted out the course first set by Bazin. For all these writers Rossellini occupies a central place in film history. 'Things are there. Why manipulate them?' For Metz, Rossellini's question serves as a kind of motto; Rossellini, through his experience as a film-maker, had struck upon the same truth that the semiologist achieved by dint of scholarship. Both Metz and Barr contrast Rossellini with Eisenstein, the villain of the piece. They even fall into the same metaphors. Thus Barr, writing of Pudovkin, who is used interchangeably with Eisenstein, describes how he

> reminds one of the bakers who first extract the nourishing parts of the flour, process it, and then put back some as 'extra goodness': the result may be eatable, but it is hardly the only way to make bread, and one can criticise it for being unnecessary and 'synthetic'. Indeed one could extend the culinary

analogy and say that the experience put over by the traditional aesthetic is essentially a *predigested* one.[19]

And Metz: 'Prosthesis is to the leg as the cybernetic message is to the human phrase. And why not also mention – to introduce a lighter note and a change from Meccano – powdered milk and Nescafé? And all the various kinds of robot?'[20] Thus Rossellini becomes a natural wholemeal director while Eisenstein is an *ersatz*, artificial, predigested. Behind these judgements stands the whole force of Romantic aesthetics: natural versus artificial, organic versus mechanical, imagination versus fancy.

But the Rossellini versus Eisenstein antinomy is not so clear-cut as might appear. First, we should remember that for Bazin it was Expressionism that was the mortal foe: *The Cabinet of Dr Caligari* rather than *Battleship Potemkin* or *October*. And, then, what of a director like Von Sternberg, clearly in the Expressionist tradition? 'It is remarkable that Sternberg managed to stylise performances as late into the talkies as he did.' Andrew Sarris's observation immediately suggests that Von Sternberg must be arrayed against Rossellini. Yet, in the same paragraph, Sarris comments upon Von Sternberg's eschewal of 'pointless cutting within scenes', his achievements as a 'non-montage director'.[21] This is the same kind of problem that Bazin met with Dreyer, whose work he much admired, including its studio sequences. 'The case of Dreyer's *Jeanne d' Arc* is a little more subtle since at first sight nature plays a non-existent role.' Bazin found a way out of the dilemma through the absence of make-up. 'It is a documentary of faces. . . . The whole of nature palpitates beneath every pore.'[22] But his dyadic model had been dangerously shaken.

The truth is that a triadic model is necessary, following Peirce's trichotomy of the sign. Bazin, as we have seen, developed an aesthetic which was founded upon the indexical character of the photographic image. Metz contrasts this with an aesthetic which assumes that cinema, to be meaningful, must refer back to a code, to a grammar of some kind, that the language of cinema must be primarily symbolic. But there is a third alternative. Von Sternberg was virulently opposed to any kind of Realism. He sought, as far as possible, to disown and destroy the existential bond between the natural world and the film image. But this did not mean that he turned to the symbolic. Instead he stressed the pictorial character of the cinema; he saw cinema in the light, not of the natural world or of verbal language, but of painting. 'The white canvas on to which the images are thrown is a two-dimensional flat surface. It is not startlingly new, the painter has used it for centuries.' The film director must create his own images, not by slavishly following nature, by bowing to 'the fetish of authenticity', but by imposing his own style, his own interpretation. 'The painter's power over his subject is unlimited, his control over the human form and face despotic.' But 'the director is at the mercy of his camera'; the dilemma of the film director is there, in the mechanical contraption he is compelled to use. Unless he controls it, he abdicates. For 'verisimilitude, whatever its virtue, is in opposition to every approach to art'. Von Sternberg created a completely artificial realm, from which nature was rigorously excluded (the main thing wrong with *The Saga of Anatahan*, he once said, is that it contained shots of the real sea, whereas everything else was false) but which depended, not on any common code, but on the individual imagination of the artist. It was the iconic aspect of the sign which Von Sternberg stressed, detached from the indexical in order to conjure up a world, comprehensible by virtue of resemblances to the natural world, yet other than it, a kind of dream world, a heterocosm.[23]

The contrast to Rossellini is striking. Rossellini preferred to shoot on location; Von Sternberg always used a set. Rossellini avers that he never uses a shooting-script and never knows how a film will end when he begins it; Von Sternberg cut every sequence in his head before shooting it and never hesitated while editing. Rossellini's films have a rough-and-ready, sketch-like look; Von Sternberg evidently paid meticulous attention to every detail. Rossellini uses amateur actors, without make-up; Von Sternberg took the star system to its ultimate limit with Marlene Dietrich and revelled in hieratic masks and costumes. Rossellini speaks of the director being patient, waiting humbly and following the actors until they reveal themselves: Von Sternberg, rather than wishing humbly to reveal the essence, seeks to exert autocratic control: he festoons the set with nets, veils, fronds, creepers, lattices, streamers, gauze, in order, as he himself puts it, 'to conceal the actors', to mask their very existence.

Yet even Von Sternberg is not the extreme: this lies in animated film, usually left to one side by theorists of the cinema. But the separation is not clear-cut. Von Sternberg has recounted how the aircraft in *The Saga of Anatahan* was drawn with pen and ink. He also sprayed trees and sets with aluminium paint, a kind of extension of make-up to cover the whole of nature, rather than the human face alone. In the same way, Max Ophuls painted trees gold and the road red in his masterpiece, *Lola Montès*. Alain Jessua, who worked with Ophuls, has described how he took the logical next step forward and, in *Comic Strip Hero*, tinted the film. John Huston has made similar experiments. And Jessua has also introduced the comic-strip into the cinema. There is no reason at all why the photographic image should not be combined with the artificial image, tinted or drawn. This is common practice outside the cinema, in advertising and in the work of artists such as El Lissitsky, George Grosz and Robert Rauschenberg.

Semiologists have been surprisingly silent on the subject of iconic signs. They suffer from two prejudices: firstly, in favour of the arbitrary and the symbolic, secondly in favour of the spoken and the acoustic. Both these prejudices are to be found in the work of Saussure, for whom language was a symbolic system which operated in one privileged sensory band. Even writing has persistently been assigned an inferior place by linguists who have seen in the alphabet and in the written letter only 'the sign of a sign', a secondary, artificial, exterior sub-system. These prejudices must be broken down. What is needed is a revival of the seventeenth-century science of characters, comprising the study of the whole range of communication within the visual sensory band, from writing, numbers and algebra through to the images of photography and the cinema. Within this band it will be found that signs range from those in which the symbolic aspect is clearly dominant, such as letters and numbers, arbitrary and discrete, through to signs in which the indexical aspect is dominant, such as the documentary photograph. Between these extremes, in the centre of the range, there is a considerable degree of overlap, of the co-existence of different aspects without any evident predominance of any one of them.

In the cinema, it is quite clear, indexical and iconic aspects are by far the most powerful. The symbolic is limited and secondary. But from the early days of the film there has been a persistent, though understandable, tendency to exaggerate the importance of analogies with verbal language. The main reason for this, there seems little doubt, has been the desire to validate cinema as an art.

Clearly, a great deal of the influence which Bazin has exerted has been due to his ability to see the indexical aspect of the cinema as its essence – in the same way as its detractors – yet, at the same time, celebrate its artistic status. In fact, Bazin never argued the distinction between art and non-art within the cinema; his inclination was to be able to accept anything as art: thus, for example, his praise of documentary films such as *Kon-Tiki* and *Annapurna* which struck him forcefully. Christian Metz has attempted to fill this gap in Bazin's argument, but by no means with striking success. 'In the final analysis, it is on account of its wealth of connotations that a novel of Proust can be distinguished from a cookbook or a film of Visconti from a medical documentary.'[24] Connotations, however, are uncoded, imprecise and nebulous: he does not believe that it would be possible to dissolve them into a rhetoric. In the last resort, the problem of art is the problem of style, of the author, of an idiolect. For Metz aesthetic value is purely a matter of 'expressiveness'; it has nothing to do with conceptual thought. Here again Metz reveals the basic Romanticism of his outlook.

In fact, the aesthetic richness of the cinema springs from the fact that it comprises all three dimensions of the sign: indexical, iconic and symbolic. The great weakness of almost all those who have written about the cinema is that they have taken one of these dimensions, made it the ground of their aesthetic, the 'essential' dimension of the cinematic sign, and discarded the rest. This is to impoverish the cinema. Moreover, none of these dimensions can be discounted: they are co-present. The great merit of Peirce's analysis of signs is that he did not see the different aspects as mutually exclusive. Unlike Saussure he did not show any particular prejudice in favour of one or the other. Indeed, he wanted a logic and a rhetoric which would be based on all three aspects. It is only by considering the interaction of the three different dimensions of the cinema that we can understand its aesthetic effect.

Exactly the same is true of verbal language, which is, of course, predominantly a symbolic system. This is the dimension which Saussure illuminated so brilliantly, but to the exclusion of every other. He gave short shrift, for instance, to onomatopoeia. 'Onomatopoeia might be used to prove that the choice of signifier is not always arbitrary. But onomatopoeic formations are never organic elements of a linguistic system. Besides, their number is much smaller than is generally supposed.'[25] In recent years, the balance has been somewhat redressed by Roman Jakobson, who has made persistent efforts to focus attention once again on the work of Peirce. Jakobson has pointed out that whereas Saussure held that 'signs that are wholly arbitrary realise better than the others the ideal of the semiological process',[26] Peirce believed that in the most perfect of signs the iconic, the indexical and the symbolic would be amalgamated as nearly as possible in equal proportions.

Jakobson has himself written on several occasions about the iconic and indexical aspects of verbal language. The iconic, for instance, is manifest not only in onomatopoeia, but also in the syntactic structure of language. Thus a sentence like 'Veni, vidi, vici' reflects in its own temporal sequence that of the events which it describes. There is a resemblance, a similitude, between the syntactic order of the sentence and the historic order of the world. Again, Jakobson points out that there is no known language in which the plural is represented by the subtraction of a morpheme, whereas, of course, in very many a morpheme is added. He also investigates the role of synesthesia in language. In a brilliant article, on 'Shifters, verbal categories, and the Russian verb', Jakobson discusses the indexical dimensions of language. He focuses particular attention on pronouns, whose meaning – at one level – varies from message to message. This is because it is determined by the particular existential context. Thus when I say 'I', there is an existential bond between this utterance and myself, of which the hearer must be aware to grasp the significance of what is being said. Pronouns also have a symbolic aspect – they denote the 'source' of an utterance, in general terms – which makes them comprehensible on one level, at least, even when the actual identity of the source is unknown. The indexical aspect also comes to the fore in words such as 'here,' 'there', 'this', 'that' and so on. Tenses are also indexical; they depend for full intelligibility on knowledge of the point in time at which a message was uttered.[27]

Jakobson has also pointed out how these submerged dimensions of language become particularly important in literature and in poetry. He quotes with approval Pope's 'alliterative precept' to poets that 'the sound must seem an Echo of the sense' and stresses that poetry 'is a province where the internal nexus between sound and meaning changes from latent into patent and manifests itself most intensely and palpably'.[28] The same is surely true, *mutatis mutandis*, of the cinema. Unlike verbal language, primarily symbolic, the cinema is, as we have seen, primarily indexical and iconic. It is the symbolic which is the submerged dimension. We should therefore expect that in the 'poetry' of the cinema, this aspect will be manifested more palpably.

In this respect, the iconography of the cinema (which, in Peirce's terms, is not the same as the iconic) is particularly interesting. Metz has minimised the importance of iconography. He discusses the epoch in which good cowboys wore white shirts and bad cowboys black shirts, only in order to dismiss this incursion of the symbolic as unstable and fragile. Panofsky has also doubted the importance of iconography in the cinema:

> There arose, identifiable by standardised appearance, behaviour and attributes, the well-remembered types of the Vamp and the Straight Girl (perhaps the most convincing modern equivalents of the medieval personifications of the Vices and Virtues), the Family Man and the Villain, the latter marked by a black moustache and walking-stick. Nocturnal scenes were printed on blue or green film. A checkered table-cloth meant, once for all, a 'poor but honest' milieu; a happy marriage, soon to be endangered by the shadows from the past, was symbolised by the young wife's pouring the breakfast coffee for her husband; the first kiss was invariably announced by the lady's gently playing with her partner's necktie and was invariably accompanied by her kicking out her left foot.[29]

But as audiences grew more sophisticated, and particularly after the invention of the talking film, these devices 'became gradually less necessary'. Nevertheless, 'primitive symbolism' does survive, to Panofsky's pleasure, 'in such amusing details as the last sequence of *Casablanca* where the delightfully crooked and right-minded *préfet de police* casts an empty bottle of Vichy water into the waste-paper-basket'.[30]

In fact, I think, both Metz and Panofsky vastly underestimate the extent to which 'primitive symbolism' does survive, if indeed that is the right word at all, with its hardly muffled condemnation to death. Counter to the old post-Eisenstein over-valuation of the symbolic there has developed an equally strong prejudice *against* symbols. Barthes, for example, has commented on the 'peripheral zone' in which a kernel of rhetoric persists. He cites, as an instance, calendar pages torn away to show the passage of time. But recourse to rhetoric, he feels, means to welcome mediocrity. It is possible to convey 'Pigalle-ness' or 'Paris-ness' with shots of neon, cigarette-girls and so on, or with boulevard cafés and the Eiffel Tower, but for us rhetoric of this kind is discredited. It may still hold good in the Chinese theatre where a complicated code is used to express, say, weeping, but in Europe 'to show one is weeping, one must weep'. And, of course, 'the rejection of convention entails a no less draconian respect for nature'. We are back in familiar territory: cinema is *pseudo-physis*, not *techne*.[31]

Thus Roland Barthes sweeps away the American musical, *It's Always Fair Weather* and *On The Town*, condemned to mediocrity by their recourse to rhetoric to convey 'New York-ness'. And what about Hitchcock: *The Birds* or *Vertigo*? The symbolic structure of the ascent and fall in *Lola Montès*? or *La Ronde*? Welles? The sharks, the wheelchair, the hall of mirrors in *Lady from Shanghai*? Buñuel? *The Man Who Shot Liberty Valance*? The extraordinary symbolic scenes in the films of Douglas Sirk, *Imitation of Life* or *Written on the Wind*? Eisenstein's peacock is by no means the length and breadth of symbolism in the cinema. It is impossible to neglect this whole rich domain of meaning. Finally, Rossellini: what are we to say of the Vesuvian lovers in *Voyage to Italy*, the record of Hitler's voice playing among the ruins in *Germany Year Zero*, the man-eating tiger in *India*?

At this point, however, we must go forward with caution. Words such as *symbol* carry with them the risk of confusion. We have seen how Saussure's usage is not compatible with Peirce's. For Peirce the linguistic sign is a symbol, in a narrow and scientific sense. For Saussure, the linguistic sign is arbitrary, whereas one characteristic of the symbol is that it is never wholly arbitrary; it is not empty, for there is the rudiment of a natural bond between the signifier and the signified. The symbol of justice, a pair of scales, could not be replaced by just any other symbol, such as a chariot.[32]

The confusion has been increased still further by Hjelmslev and the Copenhagen school:

> From the linguistic side there have been some misgivings about applying the term *symbol* to entities that stand in a purely arbitrary relationship to their interpretation. From this point of view, *symbol* should be used only of entities that are isomorphic with their interpretation, entities that are depictions or emblems, like Thorwaldsen's *Christ* as a symbol for compassion, the hammer and sickle as a symbol for Communism, scales as a symbol for justice, or the onomatopoetica in the sphere of language.[33]

Hjelmslev, however, chose to use the term in a far broader application; as he put it, games such as chess, and perhaps music and mathematics, are symbolic systems, as opposed to semiotics. He suggested that there was an affinity between isomorphic symbols, such as the hammer and sickle, and the pieces in a game, pawns or bishops. Barthes complicated the issue still more by stressing that symbols had no adequate or exact meaning: 'Christianity "outruns" the cross.'

What should we say about the hammer and sickle, the Christian cross, the scales of justice? First, unlike Hjelmslev, we must distinguish clearly between a depiction or image, as Peirce would say, and an emblem. An image is predominantly iconic. An emblem, however, is a mixed sign, partially iconic, partially symbolic. Moreover, this dual character of the emblematic or allegorical sign can be overtly exploited: Panofsky cites the examples of Dürer's portrait of Lucas Paumgartner as St George, Titian's Andrea Doria as Neptune, Reynolds's Lady Stanhope as Contemplation. Emblems are unstable, labile: they may develop into predominantly symbolic signs or fall back into the iconic. Lessing, in the *Laocoön*, saw the problem with great clarity. The symbolic or allegorical, he held, are necessary to painters but redundant to poets, for verbal language, which has priority, is symbolic in itself:

> Urania is for the poets the Muse of Astronomy; from her name, from her functions, we recognise her office. The artist in order to make it distinguishable must exhibit her with a pointer and celestial globe, this attitude of hers provides his alphabet from which he helps us to put together the name Urania. But when the poet would say that Urania has long ago foretold his death by the stars – 'Ipsa diu positis letum praedixerat astris Urania' – why should he, thinking of the painter, add thereto, Urania, the pointer in her hand, the celestial globe before her? Would it not be as if a man who can and may speak aloud should at the same time still make use of the signs which the mutes in the Turk's seraglio have invented for lack of utterance?[34]

Lessing described a scale of representations between the purely iconic and the purely symbolic. The bridle in the hand of Temperance and the pillar on which Steadfastness leans are clearly allegorical:

> The scales in the hand of Justice are certainly less purely allegorical, because the right use of the scales is really a part of justice. But the lyre or flute in the hand

of a Muse, the spear in the hand of Mars, the hammer and tongs in the hand of Vulcan, are not symbols at all, but mere instruments.[35]

Painters should minimise the symbolic – the extreme case, 'the inscribed labels which issue from the mouths of the persons in ancient Gothic pictures', Lessing disapproved of entirely. He looked forward to an art which would be more purely iconic, much more than he ever anticipated: Courbet, the *plein air* painters, the Impressionists. In fact, what happened is that, as the symbolic was ousted, the indexical began to make itself felt. Painters began to be interested in optics and the psychology of perception.

Indeed, Courbet sounds strangely like Bazin:

> I maintain, in addition, that painting is an essentially *concrete* art and can only consist of the representation of *real and existing* things. It is a completely physical language, the words of which consist of all visible objects; an object which is *abstract*, not visible, non-existent, is not within the realm of painting. . . . The beautiful exists in nature and may be encountered in the midst of reality under the most diverse aspects. As soon as it is found there, it belongs to art, or rather, to the artist who knows how to see it there. As soon as beauty is real and visible, it has its artistic expression from these very qualities. Artifice has no right to amplify this expression; by meddling with it, one only runs the risk of perverting and consequently of weakening it. The beauty provided by nature is superior to all the conventions of the artist.[36]

One current in the history of art has been the abandonment of the lexicon of emblems and the turn to nature itself, to the existential contiguity of painter and object which Courbet demanded. At the end of this road lay photography; under its impact painting began to oscillate violently.

The iconic sign is the most labile; it observes neither the norms of convention nor the physical laws which govern the index, neither *thesis* nor *nomos*. Depiction is pulled towards the antinomic poles of photography and emblematics. Both these undercurrents are co-present in the iconic sign; neither can be conclusively suppressed. Nor is it true, as Barthes avers, that the symbolic dimension of the iconic sign is not adequate, not conceptually fixed. To say that 'Christianity "outruns" the cross' is no different in order from saying that Christianity outruns the word Christianity or divinity outruns the mere name of *God*. To see transcendent meanings is the task of the mystic, not the scientist. Barthes is dangerously close to Barth, with his 'impenetrable incognito' of Jesus Christ. There is no doubt that the cross can serve as a phatic signal and as a degenerate index, triggering off an effusive and devout meditation, but this should be radically distinguished from the conceptual content articulated by the symbolic sign.

It is particularly important to admit the presence of the symbolic – hence conceptual – dimension of the cinema because this is a necessary guarantee of objective criticism. The iconic is shifting and elusive; it defies capture by the critic. We can see the problem very clearly if we consider a concrete example: Christian Metz's interpretation of a famous shot from Eisenstein's *Que Viva Mexico!* Metz describes the heads of three peasants who have been buried in the sand, their tormented yet peaceful faces, after they have been trampled upon by the hooves of their oppressors' horses. At the denotative level the image means that they have suffered, they are dead. But there is also a connotative level: the nobility of the landscape, the beautiful, typically Eisensteinian, triangular composition of the shot. At this second level the image expresses 'the grandeur of the Mexican people, the certainty of final victory, a kind of passionate love which the northerner feels for the sun-drenched splendour of the scene'.[37] The Italian writer on aesthetics Galvano della Volpe has argued that this kind of interpretation has no objective validity, that it could never be established and argued like the paraphrasable meaning of a verbal text. There is no objective code; therefore there can only be subjective impressions. Cinema criticism, Della Volpe concludes, may exist *de facto*, but it cannot exist *de jure*.

There is no way of telling what an image *connotes* in the sense in which Metz uses the word, even less accurate than its sense in what Peirce called 'J. S. Mill's objectionable terminology'. Della Volpe is right about this. But, like Metz, he too underestimates the possibility of a symbolic dimension in the cinematic message, the possibility, if not of arriving at a *de jure* criticism, at least of approaching it, maximising lucidity, minimising ambiguity. For the cinematic sign, the language or semiotic of cinema, like the verbal language, comprises not only the indexical and the iconic, but also the symbolic. Indeed, if we consider the origins of the cinema, strikingly mixed and impure, it would be astonishing if it were otherwise. Cinema did not only develop technically out of the magic lantern, the Daguerreotype, the phenakistoscope and similar devices – its history of Realism – but also out of strip-cartoons, Wild West shows, automata, pulp novels, barn-storming melodramas, magic – its history of the narrative and the marvellous. Lumière and Méliès are not like Cain and Abel; there is no need for one to eliminate the other. It is quite misleading to validate one dimension of the cinema unilaterally at the expense of all the others. There is no pure cinema, grounded on a single essence, hermetically sealed from contamination.

This explains the value of a director like Jean-Luc Godard, who is unafraid to mix Hollywood with Kant and Hegel, Eisensteinian montage with Rossellinian Realism, words with images, professional actors with historical people, Lumière with Méliès, the documentary with the iconographic. More than anybody else Godard has realised the fantastic possibilities of the cinema as a medium of communication and expression. In his hands, as in Peirce's perfect sign, the cinema has become an almost equal amalgam of the symbolic, the iconic and the indexical. His films have conceptual meaning, pictorial beauty and documentary truth. It is no surprise that his influence should proliferate among directors throughout the world. The film-maker is fortunate to be working in the most semiologically complex of all media, the most aesthetically rich. We can repeat today Abel Gance's words four decades ago: 'The time of the image has come.'[38]

Editor's notes

1   Ferdinand de Saussure, *Course in General Linguistics*, trans. Wade Baskin (New York: McGraw-Hill, 1966): 16.
2   Ibid., 68.
3   Erwin Panofsky, "Style and Medium in the Motion Pictures," in *Three Essays on Style*, ed. Irving Lavin (Cambridge, MA: MIT Press, 1995): 112.
4   Christian Metz, "Cinema: Language or Language System," p. 47 in this volume.
5   Charles Sanders Peirce, *Collected Papers*, vols. II, eds. C. Hartshorne, P. Weiss, and A. Burks (Cambridge, MA: Harvard University Press, 1931): 2.247–49. (Standard referencing format for the *Collected Papers* is to note volume and paragraph number.)
6   Ibid., 2.285.
7   Ibid., 2.301.
8   Ibid., 2.281.
9   Christian Metz, "Cinema: Language or Language System," p. 67 (in a slightly different English translation) in this volume.
10   André Bazin, "Ontology of the Photographic Image," p. 12 in this volume.
11   André Bazin, "Ontology of the Photographic Image," p. 13 in this volume.
12   André Bazin, "*Battle of the Rails* and *Ivan the Terrible*," in *Bazin at Work: Major Essays and Reviews from the*

Forties and Fifties, ed. Bert Cardullo, trans. Alain Piette and Bert Cerdullo (New York and London: Routledge, 1997): 202.

13   André Bazin, "Evolution of the Language of Cinema," p. 38 in this volume.

14   See André Bazin, "*La Terra Trema*," in *What Is Cinema?*, vol. II, trans. Hugh Gray (Berkeley: University of California Press, 1971): 41–46.

15   André Bazin, "*La Strada*," in *Bazin at Work: Major Essays and Reviews from the Forties and Fifties*, ed. Bert Cardullo, trans. Alain Piette and Bert Cerdullo (New York and London: Routledge, 1997): 117.

16   André Bazin, "In Defense of Rossellini," *What Is Cinema?*, vol. II, trans. Hugh Gray (Berkeley: University of California Press, 1971): 99–100.

17   Ibid. See also André Bazin, "*Le Journal d'un curé de campagne* and the Stylistics of Robert Bresson," *What Is Cinema?*, vol. I, trans. Hugh Gray (Berkeley: University of California Press, 1967): 125–43.

18   Erwin Panofsky, "The History of the Theory of Human Proportions as a Reflection of the History of Styles," in *Meaning in the Visual Arts* (Garden City, NY: Doubleday Anchor Books, 1955): 61–62.

19   Charles Barr, "CinemaScope: Before and After," *Film Quarterly* 16.4 (Summer 1963): 16–17.

20   Christian Metz, "Cinema: Language or Language System," p. 35 (in a slightly different English translation) in this volume.

21   See Andrew Sarris, *The Films of Josef von Sternberg* (New York: Museum of Modern Art, 1966).

22   André Bazin, "Theatre and Cinema—Part 2," *What Is Cinema?*, vol. I, trans. Hugh Gray (Berkeley: University of California Press, 1967): 109–10.

23   Josef von Sternberg, *Fun in a Chinese Laundry* (London: Secker and Warburg, 1967), n.p.

24   Christian Metz, "Cinema: Language or Language System," pp. 76–7 (in a slightly different English translation) in this volume.

25   Ferdinand de Saussure, *Course in General Linguistics*, trans. Wade Baskin (New York: McGraw-Hill, 1966): 69.

26   Ibid., 68.

27   Roman Jakobson, "Shifters, Verbal Categories and the Russian Verb," in *Selected Writings, Vol. II: Word and Language* (The Hague and Paris: Mouton, 1971): 130–47.

28   Roman Jakobson, "Linguistics and Poetics," in *Style in Language*, ed. Thomas Sebeok (Cambridge, MA: MIT Press, 1960): 373.

29   Erwin Panofsky, "Style and Medium in the Motion Pictures," *Three Essays on Style*, ed. Irving Lavin (Cambridge, MA: MIT Press, 1995): 112.

30   Erwin Panofsky, "Style and Medium in the Motion Pictures," in *Three Essays on Style*, ed. Irving Lavin (Cambridge, MA: MIT Press, 1995): 113.

31   See Roland Barthes, *Mythologies*, trans. Annette Lavers (New York: Hill and Wang, 1972).

32   Ferdinand de Saussure, *Course in General Linguistics*, trans. Wade Baskin (New York: McGraw-Hill, 1966): 68.

33   Cited in Umberto Eco, *Theory of Semiotics* (Bloomington: Indiana University Press, 1976): 189.

34   Gotthold Ephraim Lessing, *Laocoon: An Essay upon the Limits of Painting and Poetry*, trans. Ellen Frothingham (New York: Noonday Press, 1957): 67.

35   Ibid., 70.

36   Gustave Courbet, *Letters of Gustav Courbet*, ed. and trans. Petra ten-Doesschatte Chu (Chicago: University of Chicago Press, 1992): 204.

37   Christian Metz, "Cinema: Language or Language System," p. 80 (in a slightly different English translation) in this volume.

38   Abel Gance, "Le Temps de l'image est venu," *L'Art cinématographique*, vol. 2, 1927. Translated as, "The Era of the Image Has Arrived," in *Rediscovering French Film*, ed. and trans. Mary Lea Bandy (New York: Museum of Modern Art, 1983): 53–4.

Chapter 12

Gilles Deleuze

RECAPITULATION OF IMAGES AND SIGNS

1

IT IS NECESSARY TO carry out a recapitulation of the images and signs in the cinema at this point. This is not merely a pause between the movement-image and another kind of image, but an opportunity to deal with the most pressing problem, that of the relations between cinema and language. In fact, the possibility of a semiology of the cinema seems to be dependent on these relations. Christian Metz has taken a number of precautions on this point. Instead of asking, 'In what way is the cinema a language (the famous universal language of humanity)?', he poses the question 'Under what conditions should cinema be considered as a language?' And his reply is a double one, since it points first to a fact, and then to an approximation. The historical fact is that cinema was constituted as such by becoming narrative, by presenting a story and by rejecting its other possible directions. The approximation which follows is that, from that point, the sequences of images and even each image, a single shot, are assimilated to propositions or rather oral utterances: the shot will be considered as the smallest narrative utterance. Metz himself underlines the hypothetical character of this assimilation. But it could be said that he takes more precautions only to allow himself a decisive recklessness. He posed a very rigorous question of right (*quid juris?*), and he replies with a fact and an evaluation. Substituting an utterance for the image, he can and must apply to it certain determinations which do not belong exclusively to the language system [*langue*], but condition the utterances of a language [*langage*], even if this language is not verbal and operates independently of a language system. The principle according to which linguistics is only a part of semiology is thus realized in the definition of languages without a language system (semes), which includes the cinema as well as the languages of gestures, clothing or music. There is therefore no reason to look for features in cinema that only belong to a language system, like double articulation. On the other hand, language features which necessarily apply to utterances will be found in the cinema, as rules of use, in the language system and outside it: the syntagm (conjunction of present relative units) and the paradigm (disjunction of present units with comparable absent units). The semiology of cinema will be the discipline that applies linguistic models, especially syntagmatic ones, to images as constituting one of their principal 'codes'. We are moving in a strange circle here, because syntagmatics assumes that the image can in fact be assimilated to an utterance, but it is also what makes the image by right assimilable to the utterance. It is a typically Kantian vicious circle: syntagmatics applies because the image is an utterance, but the image is an utterance because it is subject to syntagmatics. The double of utterances and 'grand syntagmatics' has been substituted for that of images and signs, to the point where the very notion of sign tends to disappear from this semiology. It obviously disappears, clearly, to the benefit of the signifier. The film appears as a text, with a distinction comparable to that made by Julia Kristeva, between a 'phenotext' of utterances which actually appear and a 'genotext' of structuring, constitutive or productive syntagms and paradigms.[1]

The first difficulty concerns narration: this is not an evident [apparent] given in cinematographic images in general, even ones which are historically established. There can certainly be no quarrel with the passages in which Metz analyses the historical fact of the American model which was constituted as cinema of narration.[2] And he recognizes that this narration itself indirectly presupposes montage: the fact is that there are many linguistic codes that interfere with the narrative code or the syntagmatics (not only montages, but punctuations, audio-visual connections, camera movements . . .). Similarly, Christian Metz has no insurmountable difficulty in accounting for the deliberate disturbances of narration in modern cinema: it is enough to point to changes of structure in the syntagmatics.[3] The difficulty is therefore elsewhere: it is that, for Metz, narration refers to one or several codes as underlying linguistic determinants from which it flows into the image in the shape of an evident given. On the contrary, it seems to us that narration is only a consequence of the visible [apparent] images themselves and their direct combinations – it is never a given. So-called classical narration derives directly from the organic composition of movement-images [montage], or from their specification as perception-images, affection-images and action-images, according to the laws of a sensory-motor schema. We shall see that the modern forms of narration derive from the compositions and types of the time-image: even 'readability'. Narration is never an evident [apparent] given of images, or the effect of a structure which underlies them; it is a consequence of the visible [apparent] images themselves, of the perceptible images in themselves, as they are initially defined for themselves.

The root of the difficulty is the assimilation of the cinematographic image to an utterance. From that point on, this narrative utterance necessarily operates through resemblance or analogy, and, in as much as it proceeds through signs, these are 'analogical signs'. Semiology thus needs to have a double transformation: on the one hand, the reduction of the image to an analogical sign belonging to an utterance; on the other hand, the codification of these signs in order to discover the (non-analogical) linguistic structure underlying these utterances. Everything will take place between the utterance by analogy, and the 'digital' or digitalized structure of the utterance.[4]

But at the very point that the image is replaced by an utterance, the image is given a false appearance, and its most authentically visible characteristic, movement, is taken away from it.[5] For the movement-image is not analogical in the sense of resemblance: it does not resemble an object that it would represent. This is what Bergson showed from the first chapter of *Matter and Memory*: if movement is taken from the moving body, there is no longer any distinction between image and object, because the distinction is valid only through immobilization of the object. The movement-image is the object; the thing itself caught in movement as continuous function. The movement-image is the modulation of the object itself. We encounter 'analogical' again here, but in a sense which now has nothing to do with resemblance, and which indicates modulation, as in so-called analogical machines. It may be objected that modulation in turn refers on the one hand to resemblance, even if only to evaluate degrees in a continuum, and on the other hand to a code which is able to 'digitalize' analogy. But, here again, this is true only if movement is immobilized. The similar and the digital, resemblance and code, at least have in common the fact that they are *moulds*, one by perceptible form, the other by intelligible structure: that is why they can so easily have links with each other.[6] But *modulation* is completely different; it is a putting into variation of the mould, a transformation of the mould at each moment of the operation. If it refers to one or several codes, it is by grafts, code-grafts that multiply its power (as in the electronic image). By themselves, resemblances and codifications are poor methods; not a great deal can be done with codes, even when they are multiplied, as semiology endeavours to do. It is modulation that nourishes the two moulds and makes them into subordinate means, even if this involves drawing a new power from them. For modulation is the operation of the Real, in so far as it constitutes and never stops reconstituting the identity of image and object.[7]

In this respect, Pasolini's highly complex thesis is in danger of being misunderstood. Umberto Eco reproached him for his 'semiological naïveté'. This incensed Pasolini. It is the fate of the trick to appear too naive to those who are naive but over-clever. Pasolini seems to want to go still further than the semiologists: he wants cinema to be a language system, to be provided with a double articulation (the shot, equivalent to the moneme, but also the objects appearing in the frame, 'cinemes' equivalent to phonemes). It is as if he wants to return to the theme of a universal language system. Except that he adds: it is the language system . . . of reality. 'Descriptive science of reality', this is the misunderstood nature of semiotics, beyond 'existing languages', verbal or otherwise. Does he not mean that the movement-image (the shot) consists of a first articulation in relation to a change or becoming which the movement expresses, but also a second articulation in relation to the objects between which it is established, which have become at the same time integral parts of the image (cinemes)? It would, therefore, be pointless to object to Pasolini that the object is only a referent, and the image a portion of the signified: the objects of reality have become units of the image, at the same time as the movement-image has become a reality which 'speaks' through its objects.[8] The cinema, in this sense, has constantly achieved a language of objects, in very varied ways; in Kazan the object is behavioural function; in Resnais it is mental function; in Ozu formal function or still life; in Dovzhenko first, then in Paradjanov, material function, ponderous matter roused by the spirit (*Sayat Nova* is definitely the masterpiece of a material language of object).

In fact, this language system of reality is not at all a language. It is the system of the movement-image, which, as we saw in Volume 1, was defined on vertical and horizontal axes which have nothing to do with paradigm and syntagm, but constitute two 'processes'. On the one hand, the movement-image expresses a whole which changes, and becomes established between objects: this is a process of *differentiation*. The movement-image (the shot) thus has two sides, depending on the whole that it expresses and depending on the objects between which it passes. The whole constantly divides depending on the objects, and constantly combines the objects into a whole [*tout*]: 'everything' [*tout*] changes from one to the other. On the other hand, the movement-image includes intervals: if it is referred to an interval, distinct kinds of image appear, with signs through which they are made up, each in itself and all of them together (thus the perception-image is at one end of the interval, the action-image at the other end and the affection-image in the interval itself). This is a process of *specification*. These components of the movement-image, from the dual point of view of specification and differentiation, constitute a *signaletic material* which includes all kinds of modulation features, sensory (visual and sound), kinetic, intensive, affective, rhythmic, tonal and even verbal (oral and written). Eisenstein compared them first to ideograms, then, more profoundly, to the internal monologue as proto-language or primitive language system. But, even with its verbal elements, this is neither a language system nor a language.

It is a plastic mass, an a-signifying and a-syntaxic material, a material not formed linguistic-ally even though it is not amorphous and is formed semiotically, aesthetically and pragmatic-ally.[9] It is a condition, anterior by right to what it conditions. It is not an enunciation, and these are not utterances. It is an *utterable*. We mean that, when language gets hold of this material (and it necessarily does so), then it gives rise to utterances which come to dominate or even replace the images and signs, and which refer in turn to pertinent features of the language system, syntagms and paradigms, completely different from those we started with. We therefore have to define, not semiology, but 'semiotics', as the system of images and signs independent of language in general. When we recall that linguistics is only a part of semiotics, we no longer mean, as for semiology, that there are languages without a language system, but that the language system only exists in its reaction to a *non-language-material* that it transforms. This is why utterances and narrations are not a given of visible images, but a consequence which flows from this reaction. Narration is grounded in the image itself, but it is not given. As for the question of knowing if there are specific and intrinsic cinemato-graphic utterances – written in silent cinema, oral in talking cinema – it is a completely different question, which has to do with the specificity of these utterances, and with the conditions on which they belong to the system of images and signs, in short, on the reverse reaction.

2

Peirce's strength, when he invented semiotics, was to conceive of signs on the basis of images and their combinations, not as a function of determinants which were already linguistic. This led him to the most extraordinary classification of images and signs, of which we offer only a brief summary. Peirce begins with the image, from the phenomenon or from what appears. The image seems to him to be of three kinds, no more: firstness (something that only refers to itself, quality or power, pure possibility; for instance, the red that we find identical to itself in the proposition 'You have not put on your red dress' or 'You are in red'); secondness (something that refers to itself only through something else, existence, action–reaction, effort–resistance); thirdness (something that refers to itself only by comparing one thing to another, relation, the law, the necessary). It will be noted that the three kinds of images are not simply ordinal – first, second, third – but cardinal: there are two in the second, to the point where there is a firstness in the secondness, and there are three in the third. If the third marks the culmination, it is because it cannot be made up with dyads, but also because combinations of triads on their own or with the other modes can produce any multiplicity. This said, the sign in Peirce apparently combines the three kinds of image, but not in any kind of way: the sign is an image which stands for another image (its object), through the relation of a third image which constitutes 'its interpretant', this in turn being a sign, and so on to infinity. Hence Peirce, by combining the three modes of the image and the three aspects of the sign, produces nine sign elements, and ten corresponding signs (because all the combinations of elements are not logically possible).[10] If we ask what the function of the sign is in relation to the image, it seems to be a cognitive one: not that the sign makes its object known; on the contrary, it presupposes knowledge of the object in another sign, but adds new elements of knowledge to it as a function of the interpretant. It is like two processes to infinity. Or rather, what amounts to the same thing, the sign's function must be said to 'make relations efficient': not that relations and laws lack actuality *qua* images, but they still lack that efficiency which makes them act 'when necessary', and that only know-ledge gives them.[11] But, on this basis, Peirce can sometimes find himself as much a linguist as the semiologists. For, if the sign elements still imply no privilege for language, this is no longer the case with the sign, and linguistic signs are perhaps the only ones to constitute a pure knowledge, that is, to absorb and reabsorb the whole content of the image as consciousness or appearance. They do not let any material that cannot be reduced to an utterance survive, and hence reintroduce a subordination of semiotics to a language system. Peirce would thus not have maintained his original position for very long; he would have given up trying to make semiotics a 'descriptive science of reality' (logic).

This is because, in his phenomenology, he claims the three types of image as a fact, instead of deducing them. We saw in Volume 1 that firstness, secondness and thirdness corresponded to the affection-image, the action-image and the relation-image. But all three are deduced from the movement-image as material, as soon as it is related to the interval of movement. Now this deduction is possible only if we first assume a perception-image. Of course, perception is strictly identical to every image, in so far as every image acts and reacts on all the others, on all their sides and in all their parts. But, when they are related to the interval of movement which separates, within *one* image, a received and an executed movement, they now vary only in relation to this one image, which will be called 'perceiving' the movement received, on one of its sides, and 'carrying out' the movement executed, on another side or in other parts. A special perception-image is therefore formed, an image which no longer simply expresses movement, but the relation between movement and the interval of movement. If the movement-image is already perception, the perception-image will be perception of perception, and perception will have two poles, depending on whether it is identified with movement or with its interval (variation of all the images in their relations with each other, *or* variation of all the images in relation to one of them). And perception will not constitute a first type of image in the movement-image without being extended into the other types, if there are any: perception of action, of affection, of relation, etc. The perception-image will therefore be like a degree zero in the deduction which is carried out as a function of the movement-image: there will be a 'zeroness' before Peirce's firstness. As for the question: are there types of image in the movement-image other than the perception-image?, it is resolved by the various aspects of the interval: the perception-image received movement on one side, but the affection-image is what occupies the interval (firstness), the action-image what executes the movement on the other side (secondness), and the relation-image what reconstitutes the whole of the movement with all the aspects of the interval (thirdness functioning as closure of the deduction). Thus the movement-image gives rise to a sensory-motor whole which grounds narration in the image.

Between the perception-image and the others, there is no intermediary, because perception extends by itself into the other images. But, in the other cases, there is necessarily an intermediary which indicates the extension as passage.[12] This is why, in the end, we find ourselves faced with six types of perceptible visible images that we see, not three: *perception-image, affection-image, impulse-image* (intermediates between affection and action), *action-image, reflection-image* (intermediate between action and relation), *relation-image.* And since, on the one hand, deduction constitutes a genesis of types, and, on the other, its degree zero, the perception-image, gives the others a bipolar composition appropriate to each case, we shall find ourselves with at least two signs of composition, and at least one sign of genesis for each type of image. We therefore take the term 'sign' in a completely different way from Peirce: it is a particular image that refers to a type of image, whether from the point of view of its bipolar composition, or from the point of view of its genesis. It is clear that all this involves the discussion in Volume 1: the reader may, then, skip it, as long as he keeps in mind the recapitulation of signs set out earlier, where we borrowed from Peirce a certain number of terms whilst changing their meaning. Thus the signs of composition for the perception-image are the *dicisign* and the *reume*. The dicisign refers to a perception of perception, and usually appears in cinema when the camera 'sees' a character who is seeing;

it implies a firm frame, and so constitutes a kind of solid state of perception. But the reume refers to a fluid or liquid perception which passes continuously through the frame. The *engramme*, finally, is the genetic sign or the gaseous state of perception, molecular perception, which the two others presuppose. The affection-image has the *icon* as sign of composition, which can be of quality or of power; it is a quality or a power which are only expressed (for example, a face) without being actualized. But it is the *qualisign* or the *potisign* which constitute the genetic element because they construct quality or power in an any-space-whatever, that is, in a space that does not yet appear as a real setting. The impulse-image, intermediate between affection and action, is composed of *fetishes*, fetishes of Good or Evil: these are fragments torn from a derived setting, but which refer genetically to the *symptom* of an originary world operating below the setting. The action-image implies a real actualized setting which has become sufficient, so that a global situation will provoke an action, or on the contrary an action will disclose a part of the situation: the two signs of composition, therefore, are the *synsign* and the *index*. The internal link between situation and action, in any case, constitutes the genetic element or the *imprint*. The reflection-image, which goes from action to relation, is composed when action and situation enter into indirect relations: the signs are then *figures*, of attraction or inversion. And the genetic sign is *discursive*, that is, a situation or an action of discourse, independent of the question: is the discourse itself realized in a language? Finally, the relation-image relates movement to the whole that it expresses, and makes the whole vary according to the distribution of movement: the two signs of composition will be the *mark*, or the circumstance, through which two images are united, according to a habit ('natural' relation), and the *demark*, the circumstance through which an image finds itself torn from its natural relation or series; the sign of genesis the *symbol*, the circumstance through which we are made to compare two images, even arbitrarily united ('abstract' relation).

The movement-image is matter [*matière*] itself, as Bergson showed. It is a matter that is not linguistically formed, although it is semiotically, and constitutes the first dimension of semiotics. In fact, the different kinds of image which are necessarily deduced from the movement-image, the six kinds, are the elements that make this matter into a signaletic material [*matière signalétique*]. And the signs themselves are the features of expression that compose and combine these images, and constantly re-create them, borne or carted along by matter in movement [*la matière en mouvement*].

A final problem then arises: why does Peirce think that everything ends with thirdness and the relation-image and that there is nothing beyond? This is undoubtedly true from the point of view of the movement-image: this is framed by the relations which relate it to the whole that it expresses, so much so that a logic of relations seems to close the transformations of the movement-image by determining the corresponding changes of the whole. We have seen, in this sense, that a cinema like that of Hitchcock, taking relation as its explicit object, completed the circuit of the movement-image and brought to its logical perfection what could be called classical cinema. But we have encountered signs which, eating away at the action-image, also brought their effect to bear above and below, on perception and relation, and called into question the movement-image as a whole: these are opsigns or sonsigns. The interval of movement was no longer that in relation to which the movement-image was specified as perception-image, at one end of the interval, as action-image at the other end, and as affection-image between the two, so as to constitute a sensory-motor whole. On the contrary the sensory-motor link was broken, and the interval of movement produced the appearance as such of *an image other than the movement-image*. Sign and image thus reversed their relation, because the sign no longer presupposed the movement-image as material that it represented in its specified forms, but set about presenting the other image whose material it was itself to specify, and forms it was to constitute, from sign to sign. This was the second dimension of pure, non-linguistic semiotics. There was to arise a whole series of new signs, constitutive of a transparent material, or of a time-image irreducible to the movement-image, but not without a determinable relationship with it. We could no longer consider Peirce's thirdness as a limit of the system of images and signs, because the opsign (or sonsign) set everything off again, from the inside.

3

The movement-image has two sides, one in relation to objects whose relative position it varies, the other in relation to a whole – of which it expresses an absolute change. The positions are in space, but the whole that changes is in time. If the movement-image is assimilated to the shot, we call framing the first facet of the shot turned towards objects, and montage the other facet turned towards the whole. Hence a first thesis: it is montage itself which constitutes the whole, and thus gives us the image *of* time. It is therefore the principal act of cinema. Time is necessarily an indirect representation, because it flows from the montage which links one movement-image to another. This is why the connection cannot be a simple juxtaposition: the whole is no more an addition than time is a succession of presents. As Eisenstein said over and over again, montage must proceed by alterations, conflicts, resolutions and resonances, in short an activity of selection and co-ordination, in order to give time its real dimension, and the whole its consistency. This position of principle implies that movement-image is itself in the present, and nothing else. That the present is the sole direct time of the cinematographic image seems to be almost a truism. Pasolini will again rely on it to maintain a very classical notion of montage: precisely because it selects and co-ordinates 'significant moments', montage has the property of 'making the present past', of transforming our unstable and uncertain present into 'a clear, stable and desirable past', in short of achieving time. It is useless for him to add that this is the operation of death, not a death that is over and done with, but a death in life or a being for death ('death achieves a dazzling montage of our life').[13] This black note reinforces the classic, grandiose concept of the montage king: time as indirect representation that flows from the synthesis of images.

But this thesis has another aspect, which seems to contradict the first: the synthesis of movement-images *must* rely on characteristics intrinsic to each of them. Each movement-image expresses the whole that changes, as a function of the objects between which movement is established. The shot must therefore already be a potential montage, and the movement-image, a matrix or cell of time. From this point of view, time depends on movement itself and belongs to it: it may be defined, in the style of ancient philosophers, as the number of movement. Montage will therefore be a relation of number, variable according to the intrinsic nature of the movements considered in each image, in each shot. A uniform movement in the shot appeals to a simple measure, but varied and differential movements to a rhythm; intensive movements proper (like light and heat) to a tonality, and the set of all the potentialities of a shot, to a harmony. Hence Eisenstein's distinctions between a metrical, rhythmic, tonal and harmonic montage. Eisenstein himself saw a certain opposition between the synthetic point of view, according to which time flowed from the montage, and the analytic point of view, according to which the time set up was dependent on a movement-image.[14] According to Pasolini, 'the present is transformed into past' by virtue of montage, but this past 'still appears as a present' by virtue of the nature of the image. Philosophy had already encountered a similar opposition, in the notion of 'number of movement', because number appeared sometimes like an independent instance, sometimes like a simple dependence on what it measured. Should we not, however, maintain both points of view, as the two poles of an indirect representation of time: time depends on movement, but through the intermediary of montage; it flows from montage, but as if subordinate to movement? Classical reflection turns on this kind of alternative, montage *or* shot.

It is still necessary for movement to be normal: movement can only subordinate time, and make it into a number that indirectly measures it, if it fulfils conditions of normality. What we mean by normality is the existence of centres: centres of the revolution of movement itself, of equilibrium of forces, of gravity of moving bodies, and of observation for a viewer able to recognize or perceive the moving body, and to assign movement. A movement that avoids centring, in whatever way, is as such abnormal, aberrant. Antiquity came up against these aberrations of movement, which even affected astronomy, and which became more and more pronounced when one entered the sub-lunar world of men (Aristotle). Now, aberrant movement calls into question the status of time as indirect representation or number of movement, because it evades the relationships of number. But, far from time itself being shaken, it rather finds this the moment to surface directly, to shake off its subordination in relation to movement and to reverse this subordination. Conversely, then, a direct presentation of time does not imply the halting of movement, but rather the promotion of aberrant movement. What makes this problem as much a cinematographic as a philosophical one is that the movement-image seems to be in itself a profoundly aberrant and abnormal movement. Epstein was perhaps the first to focus theoretically on this point, which viewers in the cinema experienced practically: not only speeded up, slowed down and reversed sequences, but the non-distancing of the moving body ('a deserter was going flat out, and yet remained face to face with us'), constant changes in scale and proportion ('with no possible common denominator') and false continuities of movement (what Eisenstein called 'impossible continuity shots').[15]

More recently, Jean-Louis Schefer, in a book in which the theory forms a kind of great poem, showed that the ordinary cinema-viewer, the man without qualities, found his correlate in the movement-image as extraordinary movement. The movement-image does not reproduce a world, but constitutes an autonomous world, made up of breaks and disproportion, deprived of all its centres, addressing itself as such to a viewer who is in himself no longer centre of his own perception. The *percipiens* and the *percipi* have lost their points of gravity. Schefer draws the most rigorous consequence from this: the aberration of movement specific to the cinematographic image sets time free from any linkage; it carries out a direct presentation of time by reversing the relationship of subordination that time maintains with normal movement; 'cinema is the sole experience where time is given to me as a perception'. Certainly Schefer points to a primordial crime with an essential link to this condition of cinema, just as Pasolini invoked a primordial death for the other situation. It is a homage to psychoanalysis, which has only ever given cinema one sole object, one single refrain, the so-called primitive scene. But there is no other crime than time itself. What aberrant movement reveals is time as everything, as 'infinite opening', as anteriority over all normal movement defined by motivity [*motricité*]: time has to be anterior to the controlled flow of every action, there must be 'a birth of the world that is not completely restricted to the experience of our motivity' and 'the most distant recollection of image must be separated from all movement of bodies'.[16] If normal movement subordinates the time of which it gives us an indirect representation, aberrant movement speaks up for an anteriority of time that it presents to us directly, on the basis of the disproportion of scales, the dissipation of centres and the false continuity of the images themselves.

What is in question is the obviousness on the basis of which the cinematographic image is in the present, necessarily in the present. If it is so, time can be represented only indirectly, on the basis of a present movement-image and through the intermediary of montage. But is this not the falsest obviousness, in at least two respects? First, there is no present which is not haunted by a past and a future, by a past which is not reducible to a former present, by a future which does not consist of a present to come. Simple succession affects the presents which pass, but each present coexists with a past and a future without which it would not itself pass on. It is characteristic of cinema to seize this past and this future that coexist with the present image. To film what is *before* and what is *after* . . . Perhaps it is necessary to make what is before and after the film pass inside it in order to get out of the chain of presents. For example, the characters: Godard says that it is necessary to know what they were before being placed in the picture, and will be after. 'That is what cinema is, the present never exists there, except in bad films.'[17] This is very difficult, because it is not enough to eliminate fiction, in favour of a crude reality which would lead us back all the more to presents which pass. On the contrary, it is necessary to move towards a limit, to make the limit of before the film and after it pass into the film and to grasp in the character the limit that he himself steps over in order to enter the film and leave it, to enter into the fiction as into a present which is inseparable from its before and after (Rouch, Perrault). We shall see that this is precisely the aim of *cinéma-vérité* or of direct cinema: not to achieve a real as it would exist independently of the image, but to achieve a before and an after as they coexist with the image, as they are inseparable from the image. This is what direct cinema must mean, to the point where it is a component of all cinema: to achieve the direct presentation of time.

Not only is the image inseparable from a before and an after which belong to it, which are not to be confused with the preceding and subsequent images; but in addition it itself tips over into a past and a future of which the present is now only an extreme limit, which is never given. Take, for example, the depth of field in Welles: when Kane is going to catch up with his friend the journalist for the break, it is in time that he moves, he occupies a place in time rather than changing place in space. And when the investigator at the beginning of *Mr Arkadin* emerges into the great courtyard, he literally emerges from time rather than coming from another place. Take Visconti's tracking shots: at the beginning of *Sandra*, when the heroine returns to the house where she was born, and stops to buy the black headscarf that she will cover her head with, and the cake that she will eat like magic food, she does not cover space, she sinks into time. And in a film a few minutes long, *Appunti su un Fatto di Cronaca*, a slow tracking shot follows the empty path of the raped and murdered school-girl, and comes back to the fully present image to load it with a petrified perfect tense, as well as with an inescapable future perfect.[18] In Resnais too it is time that we plunge into, not at the mercy of a psychological memory that would give us only an indirect representation, nor at the mercy of a recollection-image that would refer us back to a former present, but following a deeper memory, a memory of the world directly exploring time, reaching in the past that which conceals itself from memory. How feeble the flashback seems beside explorations of time as powerful as this, such as the silent walk on the thick hotel carpet which each time puts the image into the past in *Last Year in Marienbad*. The tracking shots of Resnais and Visconti, and Welles's depth of field, carry out a temporalization of the image or form a direct time-image, which realizes the principle: the cinematographic image is in the present only in bad films. 'Rather than a physical movement, it is a question above all of a displacement in time.'[19] And undoubtedly there are many possible ways of proceeding: it is, on the contrary, the crushing of depth and the planitude of the image, which, in Dreyer and other authors, will directly open the image on to time as fourth dimension. This is, as we shall see, because there are varieties of the time-image just as there were types of the movement-image. But the direct time-image always gives us access to that Proustian dimension where people and things occupy a place in time which is incommensurable with the one they have in space. Proust indeed speaks in terms of cinema, time mounting its magic lantern on bodies and making the shots coexist in depth.[20] It is this build-up, this emancipation of time, which ensures the rule of impossible continuity and aberrant movement. The postulate of 'the image in the present' is one of the most destructive for any understanding of cinema.

But were these characteristics not clear in the cinema at an early stage (Eisenstein, Epstein)? Is Schefer's theme not valid for the whole of the cinema? How are we to delineate a modern cinema which would be distinct from 'classical' cinema or from the indirect representation of time? We might once more rely on an analogy in thought: if it is true that aberrations of movement were recognized at an early stage, they were in some sense corrected, normalized, 'elevated', and brought into line with laws which saved movement, extensive movement of the world or intensive movement of the soul, and which maintained the subordination of time. In fact we will have to wait for Kant to carry out the great reversal: aberrant movement became the most everyday kind, everydayness itself, and it is no longer time that depends on movement, but the opposite . . . A similar story appears in cinema. For a long time aberrations of movement were recognized, but warded off. The intervals of movement first called its communication into question and introduced a gap or disproportion between a received movement and an executed one. Even so, related to such an interval, the movement-image finds in it the principle of its differentiation into the perception-image (received movement) and the action-image (executed movement). What was aberration in relation to the movement-image ceases to be so in relation to these two images: the interval itself now plays the role of centre, and the sensory-motor schema restores the lost proportion, re-establishes it in a new mode, between perception and action. The sensory-motor schema moves forward by selection and co-ordination. Perception is organized in obstacles and distances to be crossed, while action invents the means to cross and surmount them, in a space which sometimes constitutes an 'encompasser', sometimes a 'line of the universe': movement is saved by becoming relative. And this status, of course, does not exhaust the movement-image. As soon as it stops being related to an interval as sensory-motor centre, movement finds its absolute quality again, and every image reacts with every other one, on all their sides and in all their parts. This is the regime of universal variation, which goes beyond the human limits of the sensory-motor schema towards a non-human world where movement equals matter, or else in the direction of a super-human world which speaks for a new spirit. It is here that the movement-image attains the sublime, like the absolute condition of movement, whether in the material sublime of Vertov, in the mathematical sublime of Gance or in the dynamic sublime of Murnau or Lang. But in any event the movement-image remains primary, and gives rise only indirectly to a representation of time, through the intermediary of montage as organic composition of relative movement, or supra-organic recomposition of absolute movement. Even Vertov, when he carries perception over into matter, and action into universal interaction, peopling the universe with micro-intervals, points to a 'negative of time' as the ultimate product of the movement-image through montage.[21]

Now, from its first appearances, something different happens in what is called modern cinema: not something more beautiful, more profound or more true, but something different. What has happened is that the sensory-motor schema is no longer in operation, but at the same time it is not overtaken or overcome. It is shattered from the inside. That is, perceptions and actions ceased to be linked together, and spaces are now neither co-ordinated nor filled. Some characters, caught in certain pure optical and sound situations, find themselves condemned to wander about or go off on a trip. These are pure seers, who no longer exist except in the interval of movement, and do not even have the consolation of the sublime, which would connect them to matter or would gain control of the spirit for them. They are rather given over to something intolerable which is simply their everyday-ness itself. It is here that the reversal is produced: movement is no longer simply aberrant, aberration is now valid in itself and designates time as its direct cause. 'Time is out of joint': it is off the hinges assigned to it by behaviour in the world, but also by movements of world. It is no longer time that depends on movement; it is aberrant movement that depends on time. The relation, *sensory-motor situation* → *indirect image of time* is replaced by a non-localizable relation, *pure optical and sound situation* → *direct time-image*. Opsigns and sonsigns are direct presentations of time. False continuity shots are the non-localizable relation itself: characters no longer jump across them, they are swallowed up in them. Where has Gertrud gone? Into the false continuity shots . . .[22] Of course they have always been there, in the cinema like aberrant movements. But what makes them take on a specifically new value, to the point where *Gertrud* was not understood at the time and still offends perception? We can choose between emphasizing the continuity of cinema as a whole, or emphasizing the difference between the classical and the modern. It took the modern cinema to re-read the whole of cinema as already made up of aberrant movements and false continuity shots. The direct time-image is the phantom which has always haunted the cinema, but it took modern cinema to give a body to this phantom. This image is virtual, in opposition to the actuality of the movement-image. But, if virtual is opposed to actual, it is not opposed to real, far from it. Again, this time-image will be said to presuppose montage, just as much as indirect representation did. But montage has changed its meaning, it takes on a new function: instead of being concerned with movement-images from which it extracts an indirect image of time, it is concerned with the time-image, and extracts from it the relations of time on which aberrant movement must now depend. To adopt a word of Lapoujade's, montage has become 'montrage'.[23]

What seems to be broken is the circle in which we were led from shot to montage and from montage to shot, one constituting the movement-image, the other the indirect image of time. Despite all its efforts (and especially those of Eisenstein), the classical conception had difficulty in getting rid of the idea of a vertical construction going right to the edge in both directions, where montage worked on movement-images. It has often been pointed out, in modern cinema, that the montage was already in the image, or that the components of an image already implied montage. There is no longer an alternative between montage and shot (in Welles, Resnais or Godard). Sometimes montage occurs in the depth of the image, sometimes it becomes flat: it no longer asks how images are linked, but 'What does the image *show*?'[24] This identity of montage with the image itself can appear only in conditions of the direct time-image. In a text with important implications Tarkovsky says that what is essential is the way time flows in the shot, its tension or rarefaction, 'the pressure of time in the shot'. He appears to subscribe to the classical alternative, shot *or* montage, and to opt strongly for the shot ('the cinematographic figure only exists inside the shot'). But this is only a superficial appearance, because the force or pressure of time goes outside the limits of the shot, and montage itself works and lives in time. What Tarkovsky denies is that cinema is like a language working with units, even if these are relative and of different orders: montage is not a unit of a higher order which exercises power over unit-shots and which would thereby endow movement-images with time as a new quality.[25] The movement-image can be perfect, but it remains amorphous, indifferent and static if it is not already deeply affected by injections of time which put montage into it, and alter movement. 'The time in a shot must flow independently and, so to speak, as its own boss': it is only on this condition that the shot goes beyond the movement-image, and montage goes beyond indirect representation of time, to both share in a direct time-image, the one determining the form or rather force of time in the image, the other the relations of time or of forces in the succession of images (relations that are no more reducible to succession than the image is to movement). Tarkovsky calls his text 'On the cinematographic figure', because he calls figure that which expresses the 'typical', but expresses it in a pure singularity, something unique. This is the sign, it is the very function of the sign. But, as long as signs find their material in the movement-image, as long as they form the singular expressional features, from a material in movement, they are in danger of evoking another generality which would lead to their being confused with a language. The representation of time can be extracted from this only by association and generalization, or as concept (hence Eisenstein's bringing together of montage and concept). Such is the ambiguity of the sensory-motor schema, agent of abstraction. It is only when the sign opens directly on to time, when time provides the signaletic material itself, that the type, which has become temporal, coincides with the feature of singularity separated from its motor associations. It is here that Tarkovsky's wish comes true: that 'the cinematographer succeeds in fixing time in its indices [in its signs] perceptible by the senses'. And, in a sense, cinema had always done this; but, in another sense, it could only realize that it had in the course of its evolution, thanks to a crisis of the movement-image. To use a formula of Nietzsche's, it is never at the beginning that something new, a new art, is able to reveal its essence; what it was from the outset it can reveal only after a detour in its evolution.

Notes

1   On all these points, reference may be made to Christian Metz, *Essais sur la signification au cinéma*, Klincksieck (particularly Vol. I, 'Langue ou langage?' ["The Cinema: Language or Language System" (this volume)], and 'Problèmes de dénotation', which analyses the eight syntagmatic types). Raymond Bellour's book *L'Analyse du film*, Albatros, is also essential. In an unpublished work, André Parente makes a critical study of this semiology, underlining the hypothesis of narrativity: *Narrativité et non-narrativité filmiques*.

2   Metz, op. cit., I, pp. 96–99, and 51 [p. 139, this volume]: Metz takes up Edgar Morin's theme, which is that the 'cinematograph' became 'cinema' by committing itself to a narrative direction. cf. Morin, *Le Cinéma ou l'homme imaginaire*, Editions de Minuit, ch. 3.

3   Metz had begun by underlining the weakness of paradigmatics, and the predominance of syntagmatics in the narrative code of cinema (*Essais*, I, pp. 73, 102). But his followers propose to show that, if the paradigm assumes a specifically cinematographic importance (and likewise other structural factors), there result new modes of narration, 'dysnarrative' ones. Metz returns to the question in *Psychoanalysis and the Cinema: the imaginary signifier*, trans. Celia Britton *et al.*, London: Macmillan, 1983. For all this, nothing changed in the hypothesis of semiology, as we shall see.

4   On this view, it must first be shown that a judgement of resemblance or analogy is already subject to codes. However, these codes are not specifically cinematographic but socio-cultural in general. It must therefore be shown in addition that the analogical utterances themselves, in each area, refer to specific codes which no longer determine resemblance but internal structure: 'It is not only from the outside that the visual message is partly invested by a language system . . . but equally from the inside and in its very visuality, which is only intelligible because its structures are partly non-visual . . . Not everything is iconic in the icon . . .' Once one has opted for analogy by resemblance, one moves necessarily to a 'beyond analogy'; cf. Christian Metz, *Essais*, II, pp. 157–59; and Umberto Eco, 'Sémiologie des messages visuels', *Communications*, no. 15, 1970.

5   It is odd that, in order to distinguish the cinematographic image from a photo, Metz points, not to movement, but to narrativity (I, p. 53: 'To go from one image to two images is to go from the image to language'). Moreover, semiologists explicitly appeal to a suspension of movement, in contrast, as they put it, to the 'cinephilic gaze'.

6   On this 'analogical–digital' circularity, cf. Roland Barthes, *Elements of Semiology*, trans. Annette Lavers and Colin Smith, New York: Hill & Wang, 1978, pp. 51–54 (II.4.3).

7   We shall see that the notion of the 'model' (modelling) in Bresson, elaborated as a result of the problem of the actor, but going far beyond this problem, is close to modulation. Similarly the 'type' or 'typing' in Eisenstein. These notions cannot be understood without contrasting them with the workings of the mould.

8   See the whole second part of Pasolini's book *L'Expérience hérétique*, Payot. Pasolini shows *on what conditions* real objects should be considered as constituting the image, and the image as constitutive of

reality. He refuses to talk of an 'impression of reality' given by cinema: it is simply reality (p. 170), 'cinema represents reality through reality', 'I always stay within the framework of reality', without interrupting it because of a symbolic or linguistic system (p. 199). It is the study of the preliminary conditions that Pasolini's critics have not understood: it is conditions of principle [de droit] that constitute 'cinema', even though cinema does not actually exist outside particular films. So the object can indeed be just a referent in the image, and the image an analogical image which in turn refers to codes. But there is nothing to stop film in practice overtaking itself towards principle [droit], towards cinema as 'Ur-code' which, independently of any language system, makes the phoneme of the image from real objects and the moneme of reality from the image. Pasolini's whole thesis loses all sense as soon as this study of the conditions of principle [de droit] is ignored. If it is worth making a philosophical comparison, Pasolini might be called post-Kantian (the conditions of legitimacy are the conditions of reality itself), whilst Metz and his followers remain Kantians (bringing principle down to fact).

9   Eisenstein quickly abandons his theory of the ideogram for a notion of internal monologue, to which he thinks cinema gives an even greater extension than literature: 'Film form, new problems', *Film Form*, trans. Jay Leyda, London: Dennis Dobson, 1951, pp. 122–31. He first compares internal monologue to a primitive language system or a proto-language, as certain linguists of the Marr school had (cf. Eichenbaum's text on cinema, in 1927, *Cahiers du cinéma*, nos 220–21, juin 1970). But the internal monologue is rather closer to a visual and sound method loaded with various expressional features: the great sequence in *The General Line*, after the success of the cream-making machine, would be a classic case. Pasolini, also, moved from the idea of primitive language system to that of material constituting an internal monologue: it is not arbitrary 'to say that cinema is based on a system of signs different from a system of written–spoken language systems, that is, that cinema is another language system. But not another language system in the sense that Bantu is different from Italian' (pp. 161–62). The linguist Hjelmslev calls 'content' [*matière*] precisely this element which is not linguistically formed although it is perfectly formed from other points of view. He says 'not semiotically formed' because he identifies the semiotic function with the linguistic one. This is why Metz tends to exclude this material in his interpretation of Hjelmslev (cf. *Language and Cinema*, trans. Donna Jean Umiker-Sebeck, The Hague: Mouton, 1974, ch. 10). But its specificity as signaletic material is none the less presupposed by a language: in contrast to the majority of linguists and critics of cinema inspired by linguistics, Jakobson attaches a great deal of importance to the notion of internal monologue in Eisenstein ('Entretien sur le cinéma', in *Cinéma, théorie, lectures*, Klincksieck).

10   Peirce, *Ecrits sur le signe*, commentary by Gérard Deledalle, Seuil: we reprint Deledalle's table (p. 240):

	First	*Second*	*Third*
Representamen	Qualisign (1.1)	Synsign (1.2)	Legisign (1.3)
Object	Icon (2.1)	Index (2.2)	Symbol (2.3)
Interpretant	Rheme (3.1)	Dicisign (3.2)	Argument (3.3)

11   Peirce, *ibid.*, p. 30.

12   In Peirce, there are no intermediaries, but only 'degenerate' or 'accretive' types: cf. Deledalle, *Théorie et pratique du signe*, Payot, pp. 55–64.

13   Pasolini, op. cit., pp. 211–12. We already find in Epstein, from the same point of view, a fine discussion of cinema and death: 'death makes its promises to us by cinematograph' (*Ecrits sur le cinéma*, Seghers, 1, p. 199).

14   Eisenstein sometimes criticizes himself for having given too much importance to montage or co-ordination in relation to the parts co-ordinated and their 'analytic deepening': as in the text 'Montague 1938', *Film Form*. But we shall see how difficult it is, in Eisenstein's texts, to distinguish what is genuine and what is a show for Stalinist critics. In practice, from the outset, Eisenstein emphasized the need to consider the image or shot as an organic 'cell', and not as an indifferent element: in a text from 1929, 'Methods of montage', rhythmic, tonal and harmonic methods already consider the intrinsic content of each shot, according to deepening which takes increasing account of

all the 'potentialities' of the image. It none the less remains true that the two points of view – that of montage and that of image or shot – enter into an oppositional relation, even if this opposition has to be 'dialectically' resolved.

15   Epstein, *Ecrits*, Seghers, pp. 184, 199 (and on 'moving spaces', 'floating periods' and 'dangling causes', pp. 364–79). On 'impossible continuity shots', cf. Eisenstein, p. 59. Noël Burch gives an analysis of the false continuities in the priest's scene in *Ivan the Terrible*, in *Praxis du cinéma*, Gallimard, pp. 61–63.

16   Jean-Louis Schefer, *L'Homme ordinaire du cinéma*, Cahiers du cinéma/Gallimard.

17   Godard, in connection with *Passion*, *Le Monde*, 27 mai 1982.

18   Cf. Claude Beylie's analysis in *Visconti, Etudes cinématographiques*.

19   René Prédal, *Alain Resnais, Etudes cinématographiques*, p. 120.

20   Proust, *A la Recherche du temps perdu*, Pléiade, III, p. 924.

21   Vertov, *Articles, journaux, projets*, Paris: UGE, pp. 129–32. 'Negative' is obviously not to be understood in the sense of negation, but of indirect or derived: it is the derivative of the 'visual equation' of movement, which also allows the resolution of this primitive equation. The solution will be 'the communist deciphering of reality'.

22   Cf. Narboni, Sylvie Pierre and Rivette, 'Montage', *Cahiers du cinéma*, no. 210, mars 1969.

23   Robert Lapoujade, 'Du Montage au montrage', in 'Fellini', *L'Arc*.

24   Bonitzer, *Le Champ aveugle*, Cahiers du cinéma/Gallimard, p. 130: 'Montage becomes the order of the day again, but in an interrogative form that Eisenstein never gave it.'

25   Tarkovsky, 'De la Figure cinématographique', *Positif*, no. 249, décembre 1981: 'Time in cinema becomes the basis of bases, like sound in music, colour in painting . . . Montage is far from producing a new quality . . .' Cf. Michel Chion's comments on this text of Tarkovsky, *Cahiers du cinéma*, no. 358, avril 1984, p. 41: 'His profound intuition about the essence of cinema, when he refuses to assimilate it to a language which combines units such as shot, images, sounds, etc.'

Chapter 13

Laura Mulvey

VISUAL PLEASURE AND
NARRATIVE CINEMA

I Introduction

(a) A political use of psychoanalysis

THIS PAPER INTENDS TO use psychoanalysis to discover where and how the fascination of film is reinforced by pre-existing patterns of fascination already at work within the individual subject and the social formations that have moulded him. It takes as its starting-point the way film reflects, reveals and even plays on the straight, socially established interpretation of sexual difference which controls images, erotic ways of looking and spectacle. It is helpful to understand what the cinema has been, how its magic has worked in the past, while attempting a theory and a practice which will challenge this cinema of the past. Psychoanalytic theory is thus appropriated here as a political weapon, demonstrating the way the unconscious of patriarchal society has structured film form.

The paradox of phallocentrism in all its manifestations is that it depends on the image of the castrated women to give order and meaning to its world. An idea of woman stands as linchpin to the system: it is her lack that produces the phallus as a symbolic presence, it is her desire to make good the lack that the phallus signifies. Recent writing in *Screen* about psychoanalysis and the cinema has not sufficiently brought out the importance of the representation of the female form in a symbolic order in which, in the last resort, it speaks castration and nothing else. To summarise briefly: the function of woman in forming the patriarchal unconscious is twofold: she firstly symbolises the castration threat by her real lack of a penis and secondly thereby raises her child into the symbolic. Once this has been achieved, her meaning in the process is at an end. It does not last into the world of law and language except as a memory, which oscillates between memory of maternal plenitude and memory of lack. Both are posited on nature (or on anatomy in Freud's famous phrase). Woman's desire is subjugated to her image as bearer of the bleeding wound; she can exist only in relation to castration and cannot transcend it. She turns her child into the signifier of her own desire to possess a penis (the condition, she imagines, of entry into the symbolic). Either she must gracefully give way to the word, the name of the father and the law, or else struggle to keep her child down with her in the half-light of the imaginary. Woman then stands in patriarchal culture as a signifier for the male other, bound by a symbolic order in which man can live out his fantasies and obsessions through linguistic command by imposing them on the silent image of woman still tied to her place as bearer, not maker, of meaning.

There is an obvious interest in this analysis for feminists, a beauty in its exact rendering of the frustration experienced under the phallocentric order. It gets us nearer to the roots of our oppression, it brings closer an articulation of the problem, it faces us with the ultimate challenge: how to fight the unconscious structured like a language (formed critically at the moment of arrival of language) while still caught within the language of the patriarchy? There is no way in which we can produce an alternative out of the blue, but we can begin to make a break by examining patriarchy with the tools it provides, of which psychoanalysis is not the only but an important one. We are still separated by a great gap from important issues for the female unconscious which are scarcely relevant to phallocentric theory: the sexing of the female infant and her relationship to the symbolic, the sexually mature woman as non-mother, maternity outside the signification of the phallus, the vagina. But, at this point, psychoanalytic theory as it now stands can at least advance our understanding of the *status quo*, of the patriarchal order in which we are caught.

(b) Destruction of pleasure as a radical weapon

As an advanced representation system, the cinema poses questions about the ways the unconscious (formed by the dominant order) structures ways of seeing and pleasure in looking. Cinema has changed over the last few decades. It is no longer the monolithic system based on large capital investment exemplified at its best by Hollywood in the 1930s, 1940s and 1950s. Technological advances (16mm and so on) have changed the economic conditions of cinematic production, which can now be artisanal as well as capitalist. Thus it has been possible for an alternative cinema to develop. However self-conscious and ironic Hollywood managed to be, it always restricted itself to a formal *mise en scène* reflecting the dominant ideological concept of the cinema. The alternative cinema provides a space for the birth of a cinema which is radical in both a political and an aesthetic sense and challenges the basic assumptions of the mainstream film. This is not to reject the latter moralistically, but to highlight the ways in which its formal preoccupations reflect the psychical obsessions of the society which produced it and, further, to stress that the alternative cinema must start specifically by reacting against these obsessions and assumptions. A politically and aesthetically avant-garde cinema is now possible, but it can still only exist as a counterpoint.

The magic of the Hollywood style at its best (and of all the cinema which fell within its sphere of influence) arose, not exclusively, but in one important aspect, from its skilled and satisfying manipulation of visual pleasure. Unchallenged, mainstream film coded the erotic into the language of the dominant patriarchal order. In the highly developed Hollywood cinema it was only through these codes that the alienated subject, torn in his imaginary memory by a sense of loss, by the terror of potential lack in fantasy, came near to finding a glimpse of satisfaction: through its formal beauty and its play on his own formative obsessions. This article will discuss the interweaving of that erotic pleasure in film, its meaning and, in particular, the central place of the image of woman. It is said that analysing pleasure, or beauty, destroys it. That is the intention of this article. The satisfaction and reinforcement of the ego that represent the high point of film history hitherto must be attacked. Not in favour of a reconstructed new pleasure, which cannot exist in the abstract, nor of intellectualised unpleasure, but to make way for a total negation of the ease and plenitude of the narrative fiction film. The alternative is the thrill that comes from leaving the past behind without simply rejecting it, transcending outworn or oppressive forms, and daring to break with normal pleasurable expectations in order to conceive a new language of desire.

II Pleasure in looking/fascination with the human form

A The cinema offers a number of possible pleasures. One is scopophilia (pleasure in looking). There are circumstances in which looking itself is a source of pleasure, just as, in the reverse formation, there is pleasure in being looked at. Originally, in his *Three Essays on Sexuality*, Freud isolated scopophilia as one of the component instincts of sexuality which exist as drives quite independently of the erotogenic zones. At this point he associated scopophilia with taking other people as objects, subjecting them to a controlling and curious gaze. His particular examples centre on the voyeuristic activities of children, their desire to see and make sure of the private and forbidden (curiosity about other people's genital and bodily functions, about the presence or absence of the penis and, retrospectively, about the primal scene). In this analysis scopophilia is essentially active. (Later, in 'Instincts and Their Vicissitudes', Freud developed his theory of scopophilia further, attaching it initially to pregenital auto-eroticism, after which, by analogy, the pleasure of the look is transferred to others. There is a close working here of the relationship between the active instinct and its further development in a narcissistic form.) Although the instinct is modified by other factors, in particular the constitution of the ego, it continues to exist as the erotic basis for pleasure in looking at another person as object. At the extreme, it can become fixated into a perversion, producing obsessive voyeurs and Peeping Toms whose only sexual satisfaction can come from watching, in an active controlling sense, an objectified other.

At first glance, the cinema would seem to be remote from the undercover world of the surreptitious observation of an unknowing and unwilling victim. What is seen on the screen is so manifestly shown. But the mass of mainstream film, and the conventions within which it has consciously evolved, portray a hermetically sealed world which unwinds magically, indifferent to the presence of the audience, producing for them a sense of separation and playing on their voyeuristic fantasy. Moreover the extreme contrast between the darkness in the auditorium (which also isolates the spectators from one another) and the brilliance of the shifting patterns of light and shade on the screen helps to promote the illusion of voyeuristic separation. Although the film is really being shown, is there to be seen, conditions of screening and narrative conventions give the spectator an illusion of looking in on a private world. Among other things, the position of the spectators in the cinema is blatantly one of repression of their exhibitionism and projection of the repressed desire onto the performer.

B The cinema satisfies a primordial wish for pleasurable looking, but it also goes further, developing scopophilia in its narcissistic aspect. The conventions of mainstream film focus attention on the human form. Scale, space, stories are all anthropomorphic. Here, curiosity and the wish to look intermingle with a fascination with likeness and recognition: the human face, the human body, the relationship between the human form and its surroundings, the visible presence of the person in the world. Jacques Lacan has described how the moment when a child recognises its own image in the mirror is crucial for the constitution of the ego. Several aspects of this analysis are relevant here. The mirror phase occurs at a time when children's physical ambitions outstrip their motor capacity, with the result that their recognition of themselves is joyous in that they imagine their mirror image to be more complete, more perfect than they experience in their own body. Recognition is thus overlaid with misrecognition: the image recognised is conceived as the reflected body of the self, but its misrecognition as superior projects this body outside itself as an ideal ego, the alienated subject which, re-introjected as an ego ideal, prepares the way for identification with others in the future. This mirror moment predates language for the child.

Important for this article is the fact that it is an image that constitutes the matrix of the imaginary, of recognition/misrecognition and identification, and hence of the first articulation of the I, of subjectivity. This is a moment when an older fascination with looking (at the mother's face, for an obvious example) collides with the initial inklings of self-awareness. Hence it is the birth of the long love affair/despair between image and self-image which has found such intensity of expression in film and such joyous recognition in the cinema audience. Quite apart from the extraneous similarities between screen and mirror (the framing of the human form in its surroundings, for instance), the cinema has structures of fascination strong enough to allow temporary loss of ego while simultaneously reinforcing it. The sense of forgetting the world as the ego has come to perceive it (I forgot who I am and where I was) is nostalgically reminiscent of that pre-subjective moment of image recognition. While at the same time, the cinema has distinguished itself in the production of ego ideals, through the star system for instance. Stars provide a focus or centre both to screen space and screen story where they act out a complex process of likeness and difference (the glamorous impersonates the ordinary).

C Sections A and B have set out two contradictory aspects of the pleasurable structures of looking in the conventional cinematic situation. The first, scopophilic, arises from pleasure in using another person as an object of sexual stimulation through sight. The second, developed through narcissism and the constitution of the ego, comes from identification with the image seen. Thus, in film terms, one implies a separation of the erotic identity of the subject from the object on the screen (active scopophilia), the other demands identification of the ego with the object on the screen through the spectator's fascination with and recognition of his like. The first is a function of the sexual instincts, the second of ego libido. This dichotomy was crucial for Freud. Although he saw the two as interacting and overlaying each other, the tension between instinctual drives and self-preservation polarises in terms of pleasure. But both are formative structures, mechanisms without intrinsic meaning. In themselves they have no signification, unless attached to an idealisation. Both pursue aims in indifference to perceptual reality, and motivate eroticised phantasmagoria that affect the subject's perception of the world to make a mockery of empirical objectivity.

During its history, the cinema seems to have evolved a particular illusion of reality in which this contradiction between libido and ego has found a beautifully complementary fantasy world. In *reality* the fantasy world of the screen is subject to the law which produces it. Sexual instincts and identification processes have a meaning within the symbolic order which articulates desire. Desire, born with language, allows the possibility of transcending the instinctual and the imaginary, but its point of reference continually returns to the traumatic moment of its birth: the castration complex. Hence the look, pleasurable in form, can be threatening in content, and it is woman as representation/image that crystallises this paradox.

III Woman as image, man as bearer of the look

A In a world ordered by sexual imbalance, pleasure in looking has been split between active/male and passive/female. The determining male gaze projects its fantasy onto the female figure, which is styled accordingly. In their traditional exhibitionist role women are simultaneously looked at and displayed, with their appearance coded for strong visual and erotic impact so that they can be said to connote *to-be-looked-at-ness*. Woman displayed as sexual object is the *leitmotif* of erotic spectacle: from pin-ups to striptease, from Ziegfeld to Busby Berkeley, she holds the look, and plays to and signifies male desire. Mainstream film neatly combines spectacle and narrative. (Note, however, how in the musical song-and-dance numbers interrupt the flow of the diegesis.) The presence of woman is an indispensable element of spectacle in normal narrative film, yet her visual presence tends to work against the development of a story-line, to freeze the flow of action in moments of erotic contemplation. This alien presence then has to be integrated into cohesion with the narrative. As Budd Boetticher has put it:

> What counts is what the heroine provokes, or rather what she represents. She is the one, or rather the love or fear she inspires in the hero, or else the concern he feels for her, who makes him act the way he does. In herself the woman has not the slightest importance.

(A recent tendency in narrative film has been to dispense with this problem altogether; hence the development of what Molly Haskell has called the 'buddy movie', in which the active homosexual eroticism of the central male figures can carry the story without distraction.) Traditionally, the woman displayed has functioned on two levels: as erotic object for the characters within the screen story, and as erotic object for the spectator within the auditorium, with a shifting tension between the looks on either side of the screen. For instance, the device of the show-girl allows the two looks to be unified technically without any apparent break in the diegesis. A woman performs within the narrative; the gaze of the spectator and that of the male characters in the film are neatly combined without breaking narrative verisimilitude. For a moment the sexual impact of the performing woman takes the film into a no man's land outside its own time and space. Thus Marilyn Monroe's first appearance in *The River of No Return* and Lauren Bacall's songs in *To Have and Have Not*. Similarly, conventional close-ups of legs (Dietrich, for instance) or a face (Garbo) integrate into the narrative a different mode of eroticism. One part of a fragmented body destroys the Renaissance space, the illusion of depth demanded by the narrative; it gives flatness, the quality of a cut-out or icon, rather than verisimilitude, to the screen.

B An active/passive heterosexual division of labour has similarly controlled narrative structure. According to the principles of the ruling ideology and the psychical structures that back it up, the male figure cannot bear the burden of sexual objectification. Man is reluctant to gaze at his exhibitionist like. Hence the split between spectacle and narrative supports the man's role as the active one of advancing the story, making things happen. The man controls the film fantasy and also emerges as the representative of power in a further sense: as the bearer of the look of the spectator, transferring it behind the screen to neutralise the extradiegetic tendencies represented by woman as spectacle. This is made possible through the processes set in motion by structuring the film around a main controlling figure with whom the spectator can identify. As the spectator identifies with the main male protagonist, he projects his look onto that of his like, his screen surrogate, so that the power of the male protagonist as he controls events coincides with the active power of the erotic look, both giving a satisfying sense of omnipotence. A male movie star's glamorous characteristics are thus not those of the erotic object of the gaze, but those of the more perfect, more complete, more powerful ideal ego conceived in the original moment of recognition in front of the mirror. The character in the story can make things happen and control events better than the subject/spectator, just as the image in the mirror was more in control of motor co-ordination.

In contrast to woman as icon, the active male figure (the ego ideal of the identification process) demands a three-dimensional space corresponding to that of the mirror recognition, in which the alienated subject internalised his own representation of his imaginary existence. He is a figure in a landscape. Here the function of film is to reproduce as accurately as possible the so-called natural conditions of human perception. Camera technology (as exemplified by deep focus in particular) and camera movements (determined by the action of the protagonist), combined with invisible editing (demanded by realism), all tend to blur the limits of screen space. The male protagonist is free to command the stage, a stage of spatial illusion in which he articulates the look and creates the action. (There are films with a woman as main protagonist, of course. To analyse this phenomenon seriously here would take me too far afield. Pam Cook and Claire Johnston's study of *The Revolt of Mamie Stover* in Phil Hardy (ed.), *Raoul Walsh* (Edinburgh, 1974), shows in a striking case how the strength of this female protagonist is more apparent than real.)

C1 Sections III A and B have set out a tension between a mode of representation of woman in film and conventions surrounding the diegesis. Each is associated with a look: that of the spectator in direct scopophilic contact with the female form displayed for his enjoyment (connoting male fantasy) and that of the spectator fascinated with the image of his like set in an illusion of natural space, and through him gaining control and possession of the woman within the diegesis. (This tension and the shift from one pole to the other can structure a single text. Thus both in *Only Angels Have Wings* and in *To Have and Have Not*, the film opens with the woman as object of the combined gaze of spectator and all the male protagonists in the film. She is isolated, glamorous, on display, sexualised. But as the narrative progresses she falls in love with the main male protagonist and becomes his property, losing her outward glamorous characteristics, her generalised sexuality, her show-girl connotations; her eroticism is subjected to the male star alone. By means of identification with him, through participation in his power, the spectator can indirectly possess her too.)

But in psychoanalytic terms, the female figure poses a deeper problem. She also con-notes something that the look continually circles around but disavows: her lack of a penis, implying a threat of castration and hence unpleasure. Ultimately, the meaning of woman is sexual difference, the visually ascertainable absence of the penis, the material evidence on which is based the castration complex essential for the organisation of entrance to the symbolic order and the law of the father. Thus the woman as icon, displayed for the gaze and enjoyment of men, the active controllers of the look, always threatens to evoke the anxiety it originally signified. The male unconscious has two avenues of escape from this castration anxiety: preoccupation with the re-enactment of the original trauma (investigating the woman, demystifying her mystery), counterbalanced by the devaluation, punishment or saving of the guilty object (an avenue typified by the concerns of the *film noir*); or else complete disavowal of castration by the substitution of a fetish object or turning the repre-sented figure itself into a fetish so that it becomes reassuring rather than dangerous (hence overvaluation, the cult of the female star).

This second avenue, fetishistic scopophilia, builds up the physical beauty of the object, transforming it into something satisfying in itself. The first avenue, voyeurism, on the contrary, has associations with sadism: pleasure lies in ascertaining guilt (immediately associated with castration), asserting control and subjugating the guilty person through punishment or forgiveness. This sadistic side fits in well with narrative. Sadism demands a story, depends on making something happen, forcing a change in another person, a battle of will and strength, victory/defeat, all occurring in a linear time with a beginning and an end. Fetishistic scopophilia, on the other hand, can exist outside linear time as the erotic instinct is focused on the look alone. These contradictions and ambiguities can be illustrated more simply by using works by Hitchcock and Sternberg, both of whom take the look almost as the content or subject matter of many of their films. Hitchcock is the more complex, as he uses both mechanisms. Sternberg's work, on the other hand, provides many pure examples of fetishistic scopophilia.

C2 Sternberg once said he would welcome his films being projected upside-down so that

story and character involvement would not interfere with the spectator's undiluted appreciation of the screen image. This statement is revealing but ingenuous: ingenuous in that his
films do demand that the figure of the woman (Dietrich, in the cycle of films with her, as the
ultimate example) should be identifiable; but revealing in that it emphasises the fact that for
him the pictorial space enclosed by the frame is paramount, rather than narrative or identification processes. While Hitchcock goes into the investigative side of voyeurism, Sternberg
produces the ultimate fetish, taking it to the point where the powerful look of the male
protagonist (characteristic of traditional narrative film) is broken in favour of the image in
direct erotic rapport with the spectator. The beauty of the woman as object and the screen
space coalesce; she is no longer the bearer of guilt but a perfect product, whose body,
stylised and fragmented by close-ups, is the content of the film and the direct recipient of the
spectator's look.

Sternberg plays down the illusion of screen depth; his screen tends to be one-
dimensional, as light and shade, lace, steam, foliage, net, streamers and so on reduce the
visual field. There is little or no mediation of the look through the eyes of the main male
protagonist. On the contrary, shadowy presences like La Bessière in *Morocco* act as surrogates
for the director, detached as they are from audience identification. Despite Sternberg's
insistence that his stories are irrelevant, it is significant that they are concerned with situation,
not suspense, and cyclical rather than linear time, while plot complications revolve around
misunderstanding rather than conflict. The most important absence is that of the controlling
male gaze within the screen scene. The high point of emotional drama in the most typical
Dietrich films, her supreme moments of erotic meaning, take place in the absence of the
man she loves in the fiction. There are other witnesses, other spectators watching her on the
screen, their gaze is one with, not standing in for, that of the audience. At the end of *Morocco*,
Tom Brown has already disappeared into the desert when Amy Jolly kicks off her gold
sandals and walks after him. At the end of *Dishonoured*, Kranau is indifferent to the fate of
Magda. In both cases, the erotic impact, sanctified by death, is displayed as a spectacle for the
audience. The male hero misunderstands and, above all, does not see.

In Hitchcock, by contrast, the male hero does see precisely what the audience sees.
However, although fascination with an image through scopophilic eroticism can be the subject of the film, it is the role of the hero to portray the contradictions and tensions experienced by the spectator. In *Vertigo* in particular, but also in *Marnie* and *Rear Window*, the look is
central to the plot, oscillating between voyeurism and fetishistic fascination. Hitchcock has
never concealed his interest in voyeurism, cinematic and non-cinematic. His heroes are
exemplary of the symbolic order and the law – a policeman (*Vertigo*), a dominant male
possessing money and power (*Marnie*) – but their erotic drives lead them into compromised
situations. The power to subject another person to the will sadistically or to the gaze
voyeuristically is turned onto the woman as the object of both. Power is backed by a
certainty of legal right and the established guilt of the woman (evoking castration, psychoanalytically speaking). True perversion is barely concealed under a shallow mask of ideological correctness – the man is on the right side of the law, the woman on the wrong.
Hitchcock's skilful use of identification processes and liberal use of subjective camera from
the point of view of the male protagonist draw the spectators deeply into his position,
making them share his uneasy gaze. The spectator is absorbed into a voyeuristic situation
within the screen scene and diegesis, which parodies his own in the cinema.

In an analysis of *Rear Window*, Douchet takes the film as a metaphor for the cinema.
Jeffries is the audience, the events in the apartment block opposite correspond to the screen.
As he watches, an erotic dimension is added to his look, a central image to the drama. His
girlfriend Lisa had been of little sexual interest to him, more or less a drag, so long as she
remained on the spectator side. When she crosses the barrier between his room and the

block opposite, their relationship is reborn erotically. He does not merely watch her through his lens, as a distant meaningful image, he also sees her as a guilty intruder exposed by a dangerous man threatening her with punishment, and thus finally giving him the opportunity to save her. Lisa's exhibitionism has already been established by her obsessive interest in dress and style, in being a passive image of visual perfection; Jeffries's voyeurism and activity have also been established through his work as a photo-journalist, a maker of stories and captor of images. However, his enforced inactivity, binding him to his seat as a spectator, puts him squarely in the fantasy position of the cinema audience.

In *Vertigo*, subjective camera predominates. Apart from one flashback from Judy's point of view, the narrative is woven around what Scottie sees or fails to see. The audience follows the growth of his erotic obsession and subsequent despair precisely from his point of view. Scottie's voyeurism is blatant: he falls in love with a woman he follows and spies on without speaking to. Its sadistic side is equally blatant: he has chosen (and freely chosen, for he had been a successful lawyer) to be a policeman, with all the attendant possibilities of pursuit and investigation. As a result, he follows, watches and falls in love with a perfect image of female beauty and mystery. Once he actually confronts her, his erotic drive is to break her down and force her to *tell* by persistent cross-questioning.

In the second part of the film, he re-enacts his obsessive involvement with the image he loved to watch secretly. He reconstructs Judy as Madeleine, forces her to conform in every detail to the actual physical appearance of his fetish. Her exhibitionism, her masochism, make her an ideal passive counterpart to Scottie's active sadistic voyeurism. She knows her part is to perform, and only by playing it through and then replaying it can she keep Scottie's erotic interest. But in the repetition he does break her down and succeeds in exposing her guilt. His curiosity wins through; she is punished.

Thus, in *Vertigo*, erotic involvement with the look boomerangs: the spectator's own fascination is revealed as illicit voyeurism as the narrative content enacts the processes and pleasures that he is himself exercising and enjoying. The Hitchcock hero here is firmly placed within the symbolic order, in narrative terms. He has all the attributes of the patriarchal superego. Hence the spectator, lulled into a false sense of security by the apparent legality of his surrogate, sees through his look and finds himself exposed as complicit, caught in the moral ambiguity of looking. Far from being simply an aside on the perversion of the police, *Vertigo* focuses on the implications of the active/looking, passive/looked-at split in terms of sexual difference and the power of the male symbolic encapsulated in the hero. Marnie, too, performs for Mark Rutland's gaze and masquerades as the perfect to-be-looked-at image. He, too, is on the side of the law until, drawn in by obsession with her guilt, her secret, he longs to see her in the act of committing a crime, make her confess and thus save her. So he, too, becomes complicit as he acts out the implications of his power. He controls money and words; he can have his cake and eat it.

IV Summary

The psychoanalytic background that has been discussed in this article is relevant to the pleasure and unpleasure offered by traditional narrative film. The scopophilic instinct (pleasure in looking at another person as an erotic object) and, in contradistinction, ego libido (forming identification processes) act as formations, mechanisms, which mould this cinema's formal attributes. The actual image of woman as (passive) raw material for the (active) gaze of man takes the argument a step further into the content and structure of representation, adding a further layer of ideological significance demanded by the patriarchal order in its favourite cinematic form – illusionistic narrative film. The argument must return again to the psychoanalytic background: women in representation can signify castration, and activate voyeuristic or fetishistic mechanisms to circumvent this threat. Although none of these interacting layers is intrinsic to film, it is only in the film form that they can reach a perfect and beautiful contradiction, thanks to the possibility in the cinema of shifting the emphasis of the look. The place of the look defines cinema, the possibility of varying it and exposing it. This is what makes cinema quite different in its voyeuristic potential from, say, striptease, theatre, shows and so on. Going far beyond highlighting a woman's to-be-looked-at-ness, cinema builds the way she is to be looked at into the spectacle itself. Playing on the tension between film as controlling the dimension of time (editing, narrative) and film as controlling the dimension of space (changes in distance, editing), cinematic codes create a gaze, a world and an object, thereby producing an illusion cut to the measure of desire. It is these cinematic codes and their relationship to formative external structures that must be broken down before mainstream film and the pleasure it provides can be challenged.

To begin with (as an ending), the voyeuristic–scopophilic look that is a crucial part of traditional filmic pleasure can itself be broken down. There are three different looks associated with cinema: that of the camera as it records the pro-filmic event, that of the audience as it watches the final product, and that of the characters at each other within the screen illusion. The conventions of narrative film deny the first two and subordinate them to the third, the conscious aim being always to eliminate intrusive camera presence and prevent a distancing awareness in the audience. Without these two absences (the material existence of the recording process, the critical reading of the spectator), fictional drama cannot achieve reality, obviousness and truth. Nevertheless, as this article has argued, the structure of looking in narrative fiction film contains a contradiction in its own premises: the female image as a castration threat constantly endangers the unity of the diegesis and bursts through the world of illusion as an intrusive, static, one-dimensional fetish. Thus the two looks materially present in time and space are obsessively subordinated to the neurotic needs of the male ego. The camera becomes the mechanism for producing an illusion of Renaissance space, flowing movements compatible with the human eye, an ideology of representation that revolves around the perception of the subject; the camera's look is disavowed in order to create a convincing world in which the spectator's surrogate can perform with verisimilitude. Simultaneously, the look of the audience is denied an intrinsic force: as soon as fetishistic representation of the female image threatens to break the spell of illusion, and the erotic image on the screen appears directly (without mediation) to the spectator, the fact of fetishisation, concealing as it does castration fear, freezes the look, fixates the spectator and prevents him from achieving any distance from the image in front of him.

This complex interaction of looks is specific to film. The first blow against the monolithic accumulation of traditional film conventions (already undertaken by radical filmmakers) is to free the look of the camera into its materiality in time and space and the look of the audience into dialectics and passionate detachment. There is no doubt that this destroys the satisfaction, pleasure and privilege of the 'invisible guest', and highlights the way film has depended on voyeuristic active/passive mechanisms. Women, whose image has continually been stolen and used for this end, cannot view the decline of the traditional film form with anything much more than sentimental regret.

Chapter 14

E. Ann Kaplan

IS THE GAZE MALE?

SINCE THE BEGINNING OF the recent women's liberation movement, American feminists have been exploring the representation of female sexuality in the arts – literature, painting, film, and television.[1] The first wave of feminist critics adopted a broadly sociological approach, looking at sex roles women were seen to occupy in all kinds of imaginative works, from high art to mass entertainment. Roles were assessed as 'positive' or 'negative' according to some externally constructed criteria for the fully autonomous, independent woman.

Feminist film critics were the first to object to this prevailing critical approach, largely because of the general developments taking place in film theory at the beginning of the 1970s.[2] They noted the lack of awareness about the way images are constructed through the mechanism of whatever artistic practice is involved; representations, they pointed out, are mediations, embedded through the art form in the dominant ideology. Influenced by the work of Claude Lévi-Strauss, Roland Barthes, Jacques Lacan, Christian Metz, Julia Kristeva and others, women began to apply the tools of psychoanalysis, semiology and structuralism in analysing the representation of women in film.[3] I will not duplicate the history of these theoretical developments here; let it suffice to note, by way of introduction, that increasing attention has been given first, to cinema as a signifying practice, to *how meaning is produced* in film rather than to something that used to be called its 'content'; and second, to the links between the processes of psychoanalysis and those of cinema.[4] Feminists have been particularly concerned with how sexual difference is constructed psychoanalytically through the Oedipal process, especially as this is read by Lacan. For Lacan, woman cannot enter the world of the symbolic, of language, because at the very moment of the acquisition of language, she learns that she lacks the phallus, the symbol that sets language going through a recognition of difference; her relation to language is a negative one, a lack. In patriarchal structures, thus, woman is located as other (enigma, mystery), and is thereby viewed as outside (male) language.[5]

The implications of this for cinema are severe: dominant (Hollywood) cinema is seen as constructed according to the unconscious patriarchy, which means that film narratives are constituted through a phallocentric language and discourse that parallels the language of the unconscious. Women in film, thus, do not function as signifiers for a signified (a real woman) as sociological critics have assumed, but signifier and signified have been elided into a sign that represents something in the male unconscious.[6]

Two basic Freudian concepts – voyeurism and fetishism – have been used to explain what exactly woman represents and the mechanisms that come into play for the male spectator watching a female screen image. (Or, to put it rather differently, voyeurism and fetishism are mechanisms the dominant cinema uses to *construct* the male spectator in accordance with the needs of his unconscious.) The first, voyeurism, is linked to the scopophilic instinct (i.e. the male pleasure in his own sexual organ transferred to pleasure in watching other people having sex). Critics argue that the cinema relies on this instinct, making the spectator essentially a voyeur. The drive that causes little boys to peek through keyholes of parental bedrooms to learn about their sexual activities (or to get sexual gratification by thinking about these activities) comes into play when the male adult watches films, sitting in a dark room. The original eye of the camera, controlling and limiting what can be seen, is reproduced by the projector aperture that lights up one frame at a time; and both processes (camera and projector) duplicate the eye at the keyhole, whose gaze is confined by the keyhole 'frame'. The spectator is obviously in the voyeur position when there are sex scenes on the screen, but screen images of women are sexualized no matter what the women are doing literally, or what kind of plot may be involved.

According to Laura Mulvey (the British filmmaker and critic whose theories are central to new developments), this eroticization of women on the screen comes about through the way the cinema is structured around three explicitly male looks or gazes: there is the look of the camera in the situation where events are being filmed (called the profilmic event) – while technically neutral, this look, as we have seen, is inherently voyeuristic and usually 'male' in the sense of a man doing the filming; there is the look of the men within the narrative, which is structured so as to make women objects of their gaze; and finally there is the look of the male spectator that imitates (or is necessarily in the same position as) the first two looks.[7]

But if women were simply eroticized and objectified, things might not be too bad, since objectification may be an inherent component of both male and female eroticism. (As I will show later on, however, things in this area are not symmetrical.) But two further elements enter in: to begin with, men do not simply look; their gaze carries with it the power of action and of possession that is lacking in the female gaze. Women receive and return a gaze, but cannot act on it. Second, the sexualization and objectification of women is not simply for the purposes of eroticism; from a psychoanalytic point of view, it is designed to annihilate the threat that woman (as castrated, and possessing a sinister genital organ) poses. In her 1932 article 'The Dread of Woman', Karen Horney goes to literature to show that 'men have never tired of fashioning expressions for the violent force by which man feels himself drawn to the woman, and side by side with his longing, the dread that through her he might die and be undone'.[8] Later on, Horney conjectures that even man's glorification of women 'has its source not only in his cravings for love, but also in his desire to conceal his dread. A similar relief, however, is also sought and found in the disparagement of women that men often display ostentatiously in their attitudes.'[9] Horney goes on to explore the basis of the dread of women not only in castration (more related to the father), but in fear of the vagina.

But psychoanalysts agree that, for whatever reason – the fear of castration (Freud), or the attempt to deny the existence of the sinister female genital (Horney) – men endeavour to find the penis in women.[10] Feminist film critics have seen this phenomenon (clinically known as fetishism) operating in the cinema; the camera (unconsciously) fetishizes the female form, rendering it phallus-like so as to mitigate woman's threat. Men, that is, turn 'the represented figure itself into a fetish so that it becomes reassuring rather than dangerous' (hence overvaluation, the cult of the female star).[11]

The apparently contradictory attitudes of glorification and disparagement pointed out by Horney thus turn out to be a reflection of the same ultimate need to annihilate the dread that woman inspires. In the cinema, the twin mechanisms of fetishism and voyeurism represent two different ways of handling this dread. As Mulvey points out, fetishism 'builds up the physical beauty of the object, turning it into something satisfying in itself', while voyeurism, linked to disparagement, has a sadistic side, and is involved with pleasure through control or domination, and with punishing the woman (guilty for being castrated).[12] For Claire Johnston, both mechanisms result in woman's not being presented qua *woman* at all. Extending the *Cahiers du cinéma* analysis of *Morocco*, Johnston argues that Sternberg represses 'the idea of woman as a social and sexual being', thus replacing the opposition man/woman with male/nonmale.[13]

With this brief look at feminist film theories as background, we can turn to the question of the gaze: as it stands, current work using psychoanalysis and semiology has demonstrated that the dominant cinematic apparatus is constructed by men for a male spectator. Women as women are absent from the screen *and* from the audience. Several questions now arise: first, is the *gaze necessarily* male (i.e. for reasons inherent in the structure of language, the unconscious, all symbolic systems, and thereby all social structures)? Or would it be possible to structure things so that women own the gaze? Second, would women want to own the gaze, if it were possible? Third, in either case, what does it mean to be a female spectator? Women are in fact present in audiences: what is happening to them as they watch a cinematic apparatus that constructs a male viewer? Does a woman spectator of female images have any choice other than either identifying as female object of desire, or if subject of desire, then appropriating the male position? Can there be such a thing as the female subject of desire? Finally, if a female subject is watching images of lesbians, what can this mean to her? How do such images inform women's actual, physical relations with other women?[14]

It is extremely important for feminist film critics to begin to address these questions. First, behind these questions, posed largely in structural terms, lie the larger questions concerning female desire and female subjectivity: Is it possible for there to be a female voice, a female discourse? What can a feminine specificity mean? Second, those of us working within the psychoanalytic system need to find a way out of an apparently overwhelming theoretical problem that has dramatic consequences for the way we are constituted, and constitute ourselves, not just in representation but also in our daily lives. Is there any escape from the overdetermined, phallocentric sign? The whole focus on the materialization of the signifier has again brought daily experience and art close together. Now critics read daily life as structured according to signifying practices (like art, 'constructed', not naively experienced), rather than the earlier oversimplification of seeing art as a mere reflection/imitation of lived experience (mirroring it, or, better, presenting it as through a transparent pane of glass).

Finally, the growing interest in psychoanalytic and semiological approaches has begun to polarize the feminist film community,[15] and I want to begin by addressing some objections to current theoretical work, since they will lead us back to the larger questions of the female gaze and female desire. In a roundtable discussion in 1979, some women voiced their displeasure with theories that were themselves originally devised by men, and with women's preoccupation with how we have been seen/placed/positioned by the dominant male order. Julia LeSage, for instance, argues that the use of Lacanian criticism has been destructive in reifying women 'in a childlike position that patriarchy has wanted to see them in'; for LeSage, the Lacanian framework establishes 'a discourse which is totally male'.[16] And Ruby Rich objects to theories that rest with the apparent elimination of women from both screen and audience. She asks how we can move beyond our placing, rather than just analysing it.[17]

As if in response to Rich's request, some feminist film critics have begun to take up the challenge of moving beyond the preoccupation with how women have been constructed in patriarchal cinema. In a recent paper on *Gentlemen Prefer Blondes*, Lucie Arbuthnot and Gail Seneca attempt to appropriate for themselves some of the images hitherto defined as repressive. They begin by expressing their dissatisfaction not only with current feminist film theory as outlined above, but also with the new theoretical feminist films, which, they say, 'focus more on denying men their cathexis with women as erotic objects than in connecting women with each other'. In addition, these films, by 'destroying the narrative and the possibility for viewer identification with the characters, destroy both the male viewer's pleasure and our pleasure'.[18] Asserting their need for identification with strong female screen images, they argue that Hollywood films offer many examples of pleasurable identification; in a clever analysis, the relationship between Marilyn Monroe and Jane Russell in *Gentlemen Prefer Blondes* is offered as an example of strong women, who care for one another, providing a model we need.

However, looking at the construction of the film as a whole, rather than simply isolating certain shots, it is clear that Monroe and Russell are positioned, and position themselves, as objects for a specifically male gaze. The men's weakness does not mitigate their diegetic power, leaving to the women merely the limited control they can wield through their sexuality. The film constructs them as 'to-be-looked-at', and their manipulations end up merely comic, since 'capturing' the men involves their 'being captured'. The images of Monroe show her fetishized placement, aimed at reducing her sexual threat, while Russell's stance is a parody of the male position.[19] The result is that the two women repeat, in exaggerated form, dominant gender stereotypes.

Yet Arbuthnot and Seneca begin from important points: first, the need for films that construct *women* as the spectator and yet do not offer *repressive* identifications (as, for example, Hollywood women's films do);[20] and second, the need for feminist films that satisfy our craving for *pleasure*. In introducing the notion of pleasure. Arbuthnot and Seneca pinpoint a central and little-discussed issue. Mulvey was aware of the way feminist films as counter-cinema would deny pleasure, but she argued that this denial was a necessary prerequisite for freedom, and did not go into the problems involved.[21] Arbuthnot and Seneca locate the paradox in which feminist film critics have been caught without realizing it: namely, that we have been analysing Hollywood (rather than, say, avant-garde) films, largely because they bring us pleasure; but we have (rightly) been wary of admitting the degree to which the pleasure comes from identifying with our own objectification. Our positioning as 'to-be-looked-at', as object of the gaze, has, through our positioning, come to be sexually pleasurable.

However, it will not do to simply enjoy our oppression unproblematically; to appropriate Hollywood images to ourselves, taking them out of the context of the total structure in which they appear, will not get us very far. In order to fully understand *how it is* that women take pleasure in the objectification of women, one has to have recourse to psychoanalysis. Since criticisms like those voiced by LeSage, Rich, and Arbuthnot and Seneca are important, and reflect the deepening rift in the feminist film community, it is worth dwelling for a moment on why psychoanalysis is necessary as a feminist tool at this point in our history.

As Christian Metz, Stephen Heath and others have shown, the processes of cinema mimic in many ways those of the unconscious. The mechanisms Freud distinguishes in relation to dream and the unconscious have been likened to the mechanisms of film.[22] In this analysis, film narratives, like dreams, symbolize a latent, repressed content, only now the 'content' refers not to an individual unconscious but to that of patriarchy in general. If psychoanalysis is a tool that will unlock the meaning of dreams, it should also unlock that of films.

But of course the question still remains as to the ideology of psychoanalysis: is it true, as Talking Lips argues at the start of the film *Sigmund Freud's Dora*, that psychoanalysis is a discourse shot through with bourgeois ideology, functioning 'almost as an Ideological State Apparatus', with its focus on the individual, 'outside of real history and real strug-gle'?[23] Or is psychoanalysis, although developed at a time when bourgeois capitalism was the dominant form, a theory that applies *across* history rather than being *embedded* in history?

Of these two possibilities, the first seems to me to be true. Psychoanalysis and cinema are inextricably linked both to each other and to capitalism, because both are products of a particular stage of capitalist society. The psychic patterns created by capitalist social and interpersonal structures (especially the nuclear family) required at once a machine for their unconscious release and an analytic tool for understanding and adjusting disturbances caused by the structures confining people. To this extent, both mechanisms support the status quo; but they are not eternal and unchanging, being rather inserted in history and linked to the particular social formation that produced them.

For this very reason, we have to begin by using psychoanalysis if we want to understand how we have been constituted, and the kind of linguistic and cultural universe we live in. Psychoanalysis may indeed have been used to oppress women, in the sense of forcing us to accept a positioning that is inherently antithetical to subjectivity and autonomy; but if that is the case, we need to know exactly *how* this has functioned to repress what we could potentially become. Given our positioning as women raised in a historical period dominated by Oedipal structuring and discourse, we must start by examining the psychoanalytic pro-cesses as they have worked to position us as other (enigma, mystery), and as eternal and unchanging, however paradoxical this may appear. For it is only in this way that we can begin to find the gaps and fissures through which we can reinsert woman in history, and begin to change ourselves as a first step toward changing society.

Let us now return to the question of women's pleasure in being objectified and see what we can learn about it through psychoanalysis. We saw earlier that the entry of the father as the third term disrupts the mother/child dyad, causing the child to understand the mother's castration and possession by the father. In the symbolic world the girl now enters she learns not only subject/object positions but the sexed pronouns 'he' and 'she'. Assigned the place of object (since she lacks the phallus, the symbol of the signifier), she is the recipient of male desire, the passive recipient of his gaze. If she is to have sexual pleasure, it can only be constructed around her objectification; it cannot be a pleasure that comes from desire for the other (a subject position) – that is, her desire is to be desired.

Given the male structuring around sadism that I have already discussed, the girl may adopt a corresponding masochism.[24] In practice, this masochism is rarely reflected in more than a tendency for women to be passive in sexual relations; but in the realm of fantasy, masochism is often quite prominent. In an interesting paper, 'The "Woman's Film": Posses-sion and Address', Mary Ann Doane has shown that in the one film genre that constructs a female spectator, that spectator is made to participate in what is essentially a masochistic fantasy. Doane notes that in the major classical genres, the female body *is* sexuality, provid-ing the erotic object for the male spectator. In the woman's film, the gaze must be de-eroticized (since the spectator is now assumed to be female), but in doing this the films effectively disembody their spectator. The repeated masochistic scenarios are designed to immobilize the female viewer, refuse her the imaginary identification that, in uniting body and identity, gives back to the male spectator his idealized (mirror) self, together with a sense of mastery and control.[25]

Later on in her paper, Doane shows that Freud's 'A Child Is Being Beaten' is important in distinguishing the way a common masochistic fantasy works out for boys and for girls. In the male fantasy, 'sexuality remains on the surface' and the man 'retains his own role and his own gratification in the context of the scenario. The "I" of identity remains'. But the female fantasy is, first, desexualized, and, second, 'necessitates the woman's assumption of the position of spectator, outside of the event'. In this way, the girl manages, as Freud says, 'to escape from the demands of the erotic side of her life altogether'.[26]

Perhaps we can phrase this a little differently and say that in locating herself in fantasy in the erotic, the woman places herself as either passive recipient of male desire, or, at one remove, positions herself as *watching* a woman who is passive recipient of male desires and sexual actions. Although the evidence we have to go on is slim, it does seem that women's sexual fantasies would confirm the predominance of these positionings. Nancy Friday's volumes, for instance, provide discourses on the level of dream, and, however questionable as scientific evidence, show narratives in which the woman speaker largely arranges the scenario for her sexual pleasure so that things are done to her, or in which she is the object of men's lascivious gaze.[27] Often, there is pleasure in anonymity, or in a strange man approaching her when she is with her husband. Rarely does the dreamer initiate the sexual activity, and the man's large, erect penis usually is central in the fantasy. Nearly all the fantasies have the dominance–submission pattern, with the woman in the latter place.

It is significant that in the lesbian fantasies that Friday has collected women occupy *both* positions, the dreamer excited either by dominating another woman, forcing her to have sex, or enjoying being so dominated. These fantasies suggest either that the female positioning is not as monolithic as critics often imply, or that women occupy the 'male' position when they become dominant. Whichever the case may be, the prevalence of the dominance–submission pattern as a sexual turn-on is clear. At a discussion about pornography organized by Julia LeSage at the Northwestern Conference on Feminist Film Criticism, gay and straight women admitted their pleasure (in both fantasy and actuality) in being 'forced' or 'forcing' someone else. Some women claimed that this was a result of growing up in Victorian-style households where all sexuality was repressed, but others denied that it had anything to do with patriarchy. Women wanted, rightly, to accept themselves sexually, whatever the turn-on mechanism.[28] But to simply celebrate whatever gives us sexual pleasure seems to me both problematic and too easy: we need to analyse how it is that certain things turn us on, how sexuality has been constructed in patriarchy to produce pleasure in the dominance–submission forms, before we advocate these modes.

It was predictable that many of the male fantasies in Friday's book *Men in Love* would show the speaker constructing events so that he is in control: again, the 'I' of identity remains central, as it was not in the female narrations.[29] Many male fantasies focus on the man's excitement arranging for his woman to expose herself (or even give herself) to other men, while he watches. The difference between this male voyeurism and the previous female form is striking: the women do not own the desire, even when they watch; their watching is to place responsibility for sexuality at yet one more remove, to distance themselves from sex; the man, on the other hand, owns the desire and the woman, and gets pleasure from exchanging the woman, as in Lévi-Strauss' kinship system.

Yet some of the fantasies in Friday's book show men's wish to be taken over by an aggressive woman who would force them to become helpless, like the little boy in his mother's hands. The Women Against Pornography guided trip around Times Square corroborated this; after a slide show that focused totally on male sadism and violent sexual exploitation of women, we were taken on a tour that showed literature and film loops expressing as many fantasies of male as of female submission. The situations were the predictable ones, showing young boys (but sometimes men) seduced by women in a form of authority – governesses, nursemaids, nurses, schoolteachers, stepmothers. (Of course, it is significant that the corresponding dominance–submission female fantasies have men in authority positions that carry much more status – professors, doctors, policemen, executives: these men seduce the innocent girls, or young wives, who cross their paths.)

Two interesting things emerge from all this: one is that dominance–submission patterns are apparently a crucial part of both male and female sexuality as constructed in western capitalism. The other is that men have a far wider range of positions available: more readily both dominant and submissive, they vacillate between supreme control and supreme abandonment. Women, meanwhile, are more consistently submissive, but not excessively abandoned. In their own fantasies, women do not position themselves as exchanging men, although a man might find being exchanged an exciting fantasy.

But the important question remains: when women are in the dominant position, are they in the *masculine* position? Can we envisage a female dominant position that would differ qualitatively from the male form of dominance? Or is there merely the possibility for both sex genders to occupy the positions we now know as masculine and feminine?

The experience of recent films of the 1970s and 1980s would support the latter possibility, and explain why many feminists have not been excited by the so-called liberated woman on the screen, or by the fact that some male stars have recently been made to seem the object of the female gaze. Traditionally male stars did not necessarily (or even primarily) derive their glamour from their looks or their sexuality, but from the power they were able to wield within the filmic world in which they functioned (i.e. John Wayne); these men, as Laura Mulvey has shown, became ego ideals for the men in the audience, corresponding to the image in the mirror, who was more in control of motor coordination than the young child looking in. 'The male figure', Mulvey notes, 'is free to command the stage . . . of spatial illusion in which he articulates the look and creates the action'.[30]

Recent films have begun to change this pattern: a star like John Travolta (*Saturday Night Fever*, *Urban Cowboy*, *Moment by Moment*) has been rendered the object of woman's gaze and in some of the films (i.e. *Moment by Moment*) placed explicitly as a sexual object to a woman who controlled the film's action. Robert Redford likewise has begun to be used as the object of female desire (i.e. in *Electric Horseman*). But it is significant that in all these films, when the man steps out of his traditional role as the one who controls the whole action, and when he is set up as a sex object, the woman then takes on the masculine role as bearer of the gaze and initiator of the action. She nearly always loses her traditionally feminine characteristics in so doing – not those of attractiveness, but rather of kindness, humaneness, motherliness. She is now often cold, driving, ambitious, manipulating, just like the men whose position she has usurped.

Even in a supposedly feminist film like *My Brilliant Career* the same processes are at work. The film is interesting because it places in the foreground the independent minded heroine's dilemma in a clearly patriarchal culture: in love with a wealthy neighbour, the heroine makes him the object of her gaze, but the problem is that, as female, her desire has no power. Men's desire naturally carries power with it, so when the hero finally concedes his love for her, he comes to get her. However, being able to conceive of 'love' only as 'submission', an end to autonomy and to her life as a creative writer, the heroine now refuses. The film thus plays with established positions, but is unable to work through them to something else.

What we can conclude from the discussion so far is that our culture is deeply committed to clearly demarcated sex differences, called masculine and feminine, that revolve on, first, a complex gaze-apparatus; and, second, dominance–submission patterns. This positioning of the two sex genders clearly privileges the male through the mechanisms of voyeurism and fetishism, which are male operations, and because his desire carries power/action, where woman's usually does not. But as a result of the recent women's movement, women have been permitted in representation to assume (step into) the position defined as masculine, as long as the man then steps into *her* position, so as to keep the whole structure intact.

It is significant, of course, that while this substitution is made to happen relatively easily in the cinema, in real life any such 'swapping' is fraught with the immense psychological difficulties that only psychoanalysis can unravel. In any case, such 'exchanges' do not do much for either sex, since nothing has essentially changed: the roles remain locked into their static boundaries. Showing images of mere reversal may in fact provide a safety valve for the social tensions that the women's movement has created by demanding a more dominant role for women.

We have thus arrived at the point where we must question the necessity for the dominance–submission structure. The gaze is not necessarily male (literally), but to own and activate the gaze, given our language and the structure of the unconscious, is to be in the masculine position. It is for this reason that Julia Kristeva and others have said that it is impossible to know what the feminine might be; while we must reserve the category 'women' for social demands and publicity, Kristeva says that by 'woman' she means 'that which is not represented, that which is unspoken, that which is left out of meanings and ideologies'.[31] For similar reasons, Sandy Flitterman and Judith Barry have argued that feminist artists must avoid claiming a specific female power residing in the body of women that represents 'an inherent feminine artistic essence which could find expression if allowed to be explored freely'. The impulse toward this kind of art is understandable in a culture that denies satisfaction in being a woman, but it results in motherhood's being redefined as the seat of female creativity, while women 'are proposed as the bearers of culture, albeit an alternative one'.[32]

Barry and Flitterman argue that this form of feminist art, along with some others that they outline, is dangerous in not taking into account 'the social contradictions involved in "femininity" '. They suggest that 'a radical feminist art would include an understanding of how women are constituted through social practices in culture', and argue for 'an aesthetics designed to subvert the production of "woman" as commodity', much as Claire Johnston and Laura Mulvey had earlier stated that to be feminist, a cinema had to be a counter-cinema.[33]

The problem with all these arguments is that they leave women trapped in the position of negativity – subverting rather than positing. Although the feminists asserting this point of view are clearly right in placing in the foreground women's repression in representation and culture (and in seeing this work as a necessary first step), it is hard to see how women can move forward from these awarenesses. If certain feminist groups (i.e. Women Against Pornography) err on the side of eliding reality with fantasy (i.e. in treating an image's violating of women on the same level as a literal act of violation on the street), feminist critics err on the side of seeing a world constructed only of signifiers, of losing contact with the 'referred' world of the social formation.

The first error was in positing an unproblematic relationship between art and life in the sense that (1) art was seen as able simply to imitate life, as if through a transparent pane of glass; and (2) that representation was thought to affect social behaviour directly; but the second error is to see art and life as both equally 'constructed' by the signifying practices that define and limit each sphere. The signifier is here made material, in the sense that it is all there is to know. Discussing semiology in relation to Marxism, Terry Eagleton points out the dangers of this way of seeing for a Marxist view of history. History evaporates in the new scheme; since the signified can never be grasped, we cannot talk about our reality as human subjects. But, as he goes on to show, more than the signified (which in Saussure's scheme obediently followed the signifier, despite its being arbitrary) is at stake: 'It is also', he says, 'a question of the referent, which we all long ago bracketed out of being. In re-materializing the sign, we are in imminent danger of de-materializing its referent; a linguistic materialism gradually reverts itself into a linguistic idealism'.[34]

Eagleton no doubt overstates the case when he talks about 'sliding away from the referent', since neither Saussure nor Althusser denied that there *was* a referent. But it is true that while semiologists talk about the eruption of 'the real' (i.e. accidents, death, revolution), on a daily basis they tend to be preoccupied with life as dominated by the prevailing signifying practices of a culture. It may be true that all lived experience is mediated through signifying practices, but we should not therefore pay exclusive attention to this level of things. In attempting to get rid of an unwelcome dualism, inherent in western thought at least since Plato, and rearticulated by Kant on the brink of the modern period, some semiologists run the danger of collapsing levels of things that need to remain distinct if we are to work effectively in the political arena to bring about change.

Thus while it is essential for feminist film critics to examine signifying processes carefully in order to fully understand the way women have been constructed in language and the non-verbal arts, it is equally important not to lose sight of the need to find strategies for changing discourse, since these changes would, in turn, affect the structuring of the social formation.

Some feminist film critics have begun to face this challenge. The directors of *Sigmund Freud's Dora*, for example, suggest that raising questions is the first step toward establishing a female discourse, or, perhaps, that asking questions is the only discourse available to women as a resistance to patriarchal domination. Since questions lead to more questions, a kind of movement is in fact taking place, although it is in a nontraditional mode. Sally Potter structured her film *Thriller* around this very notion, and allowed her heroine's investigation of herself as heroine to lead to some (tentative) conclusions. And Laura Mulvey has suggested that even if one accepts the psychoanalytic positioning of women, all is not lost, since the Oedipus complex is not completed in women; she notes that 'there is some way in which women aren't colonized', having been 'so specifically excluded from culture and language'.[35]

From this position, psychoanalytic theory allows us to see that there is more possibility for women to change themselves (and perhaps to bring about social change) just because they have not been processed, as have little boys, through a clearly defined, and ultimately simple, set of psychic stages. The girl's relationship to her mother remains forever unresolved, incomplete; in heterosexuality, she is forced to turn away from her primary love object, destined never to return to it, while the boy, through marrying someone like his mother, can regain his original plenitude in another form. The girl must transfer her need for love to the father, who, as Nancy Chodorow has shown, never completely satisfies.[36]

Mulvey thus suggests that patriarchal culture is not monolithic, not cleanly sealed. There are gaps, fissures through which women can begin to ask questions and introduce change. The directors of *Sigmund Freud's Dora* end their film with a series of letters from a daughter (who is sometimes called Dora) read out by her mother, some of which deal with the place of the mother in psychoanalysis. The daughter's comments illuminate the fact that Freud dismisses Dora's mother (in his famous account of the case history), instead of talking about her 'as the site of the intersection of many representations' (of which the historical mother is just one). She suggests that Freud's omission was not merely an oversight, but, given his system, a necessity.

Mulvey and Wollen's earlier film, *Riddles of the Sphinx*, confronted the repression of mothering in patriarchal culture directly; the film argued that women 'live in a society ruled by the father, in which the place of the mother is repressed. Motherhood, and how to live it or not to live it, lies at the root of the dilemma'.[37] In an interview, Mulvey noted the influence of psychoanalysis on her conception of the mother–child exchange ('the identification between the two, and the implications that has for narcissism and recognition of the self in the "other" '), but she went on to say that this is an area rarely read from the mother's point of view.[38]

Motherhood thus becomes one place from which to begin to reformulate our position as women, just because men have not dealt with it theoretically or in the social realm (i.e. by providing free child care, free abortions, maternal leave, after-school child programs, etc.). Motherhood has been repressed on all levels except that of hypostatization, romanticization and idealization.[39] Yet women have been struggling with lives as mothers – silently, quietly, often in agony, often in bliss, but always on the periphery of a society that tries to make us all, men and women, forget our mothers.

But motherhood, and the fact that we were all mothered, will not be repressed; or, if the attempt is made, there will be effects signalling 'the return of the repressed'. The entire construction of woman in patriarchy as a lack could be viewed as emerging from the need to repress mothering and the painful memory traces it has left in the man. The phallus as signified can be set in motion only given the other with a lack, and this has resulted in the male focus on castration. But is it possible that this focus was designed to mask an even greater threat that mothering poses? And if we look from the position of women, need this lack in reality have the dire implications men would have us believe? The focus on women as (simply) sex object, or (more complexly) as fetishized (narcissistic male desire) that we have been tracing through Hollywood films, may be part of the apparatus that represses mothering. The insistence on rigidly defined sex roles, and the dominance–submission, voyeurism–fetishism mechanisms may be constructed to this end.

In placing the problem of mothering in the foreground in this way one is not necessarily falling into the trap of essentialism. First, I am not denying that motherhood has been constructed in patriarchy by its very place as repressed; nor, second, am I saying that women are inherently mothers; nor, third, that the only ideal relationship that can express female specificity is mothering. I am saying, rather, that motherhood is one of the areas that has been left vague, allowing us to reformulate the position as given, rather than discovering a specificity outside the system we are in.[40] It is a place to start rethinking sex-difference, not an end.

Let me review briefly some of the main ways in which motherhood can be thought of within psychoanalysis. First, and most conservatively, motherhood has been analysed as an essentially narcissistic relationship, and as involved with the problem of castration. In this way, it parallels male fetishism; just as men fetishize women in order to reduce their threat (finding themselves thus in the other), so women fetishize the child, looking in the child for the phallus to 'make up' for castration; second, motherhood can be seen as narcissistic, not in the sense of finding the phallus in the child, but of finding *the self* in the child (this parallels male fetishizing of women in another way); women here do not relate to the child as other, but as an extension of their own egos; third, and most radically (but this is also the position that can lead to essentialism), one could argue that since the law represses mothering, a gap is left through which it may be possible to subvert patriarchy.

The problem with this latter (and most hopeful) position, however, is that of how to express motherhood after the period of the imaginary. One could argue that women are faced with an impossible dilemma: to remain in blissful unity with the child in the imaginary (or to try to hold onto this realm as long as possible), or to enter the symbolic in which mothering is repressed, cannot be 'spoken', cannot represent a position of power. Here the only resistance is silence.[41]

But is this not one of those places where a rigid adherence to the theoretical formulation of imaginary and symbolic betrays the inadequacy of the theory? Is not mothering, in fact, now being 'spoken', even through patriarchal discourse? Both Dorothy Dinnerstein and Nancy Chodorow 'speak' a discourse about mothering that, while remaining within psychoanalysis, breaks new ground.[42] And the feminist films about mothering now appearing begin to investigate and move beyond patriarchal representations.[43]

On the social/historical level, in addition, we are living in a period in which mothers are increasingly living alone with their children, offering the possibility for new psychic patterns to emerge; fathers are increasingly becoming involved with childrearing, and also living alone with their children. Freud's own kind of science (which involved studying the people brought up in strict Victorian, bourgeois households) applied rigorously to people today results in very different conclusions. Single mothers are forced to make themselves subject in relation to their children; they are forced to invent new symbolic roles, which combine positions previously assigned to fathers with traditional female ones. The child cannot position the mother as object to the father's law, since in single-parent households *her* desire sets things in motion.

A methodology is often not *per se* either revolutionary or reactionary, but open to appropriation for a variety of usages. At this point, feminists may have to use psychoanalysis, but in a manner opposite to the traditional one. Other kinds of psychic processes obviously can exist and may stand as models for when we have worked our way through the morass that confronts us as people having grown up in western capitalist culture. Julia Kristeva, for example, suggests that desire functions in a very different manner in China, and urges us to explore Chinese culture, from a very careful psychoanalytic point of view, to see what is possible.[44]

Many of the mechanisms we have found in Hollywood films which echo deeply embedded myths in western capitalist culture are thus not inviolable, eternal, unchanging or inherently necessary. They rather reflect the unconscious of patriarchy, including a fear of the pre-Oedipal plenitude with the mother. The domination of women by the male gaze is part of men's strategy to contain the threat that the mother embodies, and to control the positive and negative impulses that memory traces of being mothered have left in the male unconscious. Women, in turn, have learned to associate their sexuality with domination by the male gaze, a position involving a degree of masochism in finding their objectification erotic. We have participated in and perpetuated our domination by following the pleasure principle, which leaves us no options, given our positioning.

Everything, thus, revolves around the issue of pleasure, and it is here that patriarchal repression has been most negative. For things have been structured to make us forget the mutual, pleasurable bonding that we all, male and female, enjoyed with our mothers. Some recent experimental (as against psychoanalytic) studies have shown that the gaze is first set in motion in the mother–child relationship.[45] But this is a *mutual* gazing, rather than the subject–object kind that reduces one of the parties to the place of submission. Patriarchy has worked hard to prevent the eruption of a (mythically) feared return of the matriarchy that might take place were the close mother–child bonding returned to dominance, or allowed to stand in place of the law of the father.

This is by no means to argue that a return to matriarchy would be either possible or desirable. What rather has to happen is that we move beyond long-held cultural and linguistic patterns of oppositions: male/female (as these terms currently signify); dominant/submissive; active/passive; nature/civilization; order/chaos; matriarchal/patriarchal. If rigidly defined sex differences have been constructed around fear of the other, we need to think about ways of transcending a polarity that has only brought us all pain.[46]

Notes

1   See works by Kate Millett, Linda Nochlin, Molly Haskell, articles in the few issues of *Women in Film* (1972–75), and articles in *Screen* and *Screen Education* throughout the 1970s. For a summary of early developments across the arts, see Lucy Arbuthnot's PhD diss., New York University, 1982.

2   See especially work by Christian Metz, Jean-Louis Comolli, Raymond Bellour, Roland Barthes and essays in *Cahiers du cinéma* in France; in England, the work by Stephen Heath, Colin McCabe, Paul Willemen and others in *Screen* and elsewhere.

3   See especially the work of Claire Johnston, Pam Cook and Laura Mulvey from England, and subsequent work by the *Camera Obscura* group.

4   Christine Gledhill, 'Recent Developments in Feminist Film Criticism', *Quarterly Review of Film Studies*, 3: 4 (1978), 458–93; E. Ann Kaplan, 'Aspects of British Feminist Film Criticism', *Jump Cut*, nos. 12–13 (Dec. 1976), 52–56; and Kaplan, 'Integrating Marxist and Psychoanalytic Concepts in Feminist Film Criticism', *Millennium Film Journal*, April 1980, 8–17.

5   Jacques Lacan, 'The Mirror Phase as Formative of the Function of the "I" ' (1949), in *New Left Review*, 51 (Sept.–Oct. 1968), 71–77. See also essays on Lacan in Anthony Wilden, *System and Structure: Essays in Communication and Exchange* (London: Tavistock Publications, 1972).

6   For a background to semiological concepts, see work by Roland Barthes, Julia Kristeva and Umberto Eco, among others. Terence Hawkes, *Structuralism and Semiology* (London: Methuen, 1977), and Rosalind Coward and John Ellis, *Language and Materialism* (London: Routledge and Kegan Paul, 1977), provide useful summaries of relevant material.

7   Laura Mulvey, 'Visual Pleasure and Narrative Cinema', *Screen*, 16: 3 (Autumn 1975), 16–18.

8   Karen Horney, 'The Dread of Woman' (1932), in *Feminine Psychology* (New York: W.W. Norton, 1967), 134.

9   Ibid., 136.

10   For a useful discussion of fetishism, see Otto Fenichel, *The Psychoanalytic Theory of Neurosis* (New York: W.W. Norton, 1945), 341–45.

11   Mulvey, 'Visual Pleasure', 14.

12   Ibid.

13   Claire Johnston, 'Woman's Cinema as Counter-Cinema', in *Notes on Women's Cinema*, ed. Claire Johnston (London: Screen Pamphlet, 1973), 26.

14   Some of these questions are raised in the letters read by a mother toward the end of the film *Sigmund Freud's Dora*, made by Anthony McCall, Andrew Tyndall, Claire Pajaczkowska and Jane Weinstock.

15   This has been evident in feminist film sessions at various conferences, but was particularly clear at the Lolita Rodgers Memorial Conference on Feminist Film Criticism, held at Northwestern University, 14–16 Nov. 1980. For a report of some differences, see Barbara Klinger, 'Conference Report', *Camera Obscura*, 7 (Spring 1981), 137–43.

16   'Women and Film: A Discussion of Feminist Aesthetics', *New German Critique*, 13 (Winter 1978), 93.

17   Ibid., 87.

18   Lucy Arbuthnot and Gail Seneca, 'Pre-Text and Text in *Gentlemen Prefer Blondes*', paper delivered at the Conference on Feminist Film Criticism, Northwestern University, Nov. 1980.

19   See Maureen Turim, 'Gentlemen Consume Blondes', in *Wideangle*, 1: 1 (1979), 52–59. Carol Rowe also (if somewhat mockingly) shows Monroe's phallicism in her film *Grand Delusion*.

20   See Mary-Anne Doane, 'The Woman's Film: Possession and Address', paper delivered at the Conference on Cinema History, Asilomar, Monterey, May 1981.

21   Mulvey, 'Visual Pleasure', 7–8, 18.

22   See the essays in *Edinburgh Magazine*, 1 (1977), by Coward, Metz, Heath and Johnston. Also the issue of *Screen*, 16: 2 (Summer 1975), on 'Psychoanalysis and Cinema', especially the piece by Metz.

23   See E. Ann Kaplan, 'Feminist Approaches to History, Psychoanalysis, and Cinema in *Sigmund Freud's Dora*', *Millennium Film Journal*, 7/8/9 (Fall/Winter 1979), 173–85.

24   Charles Brenner offers perhaps the most accessible account of Freud's notion of the Oedipus complex in his *An Elementary Textbook of Psychoanalysis* (New York: Anchor Books, 1957), 108–41.

25   Freud's work is central to any discussion of sadism and masochism. Since I wrote this paper, these issues have been discussed by Kaja Silverman in 'Masochism and Subjectivity', *Framework*, 12 (1981), 2–9, and by Joel Kovel, *The Age of Desire* (New York: Pantheon, 1981).

26   Doane, 'The Woman's Film', 3–8.

27   Nancy Friday, *My Secret Garden: Women's Sexual Fantasies* (New York: Pocket Books, 1981).

28   Unpublished transcript of a discussion, organized by Julia LeSage, at the Conference on Feminist Criticism, Northwestern University, Nov. 1980. See also, for discussion of dominance–submission patterns, Pat Califa, 'Feminism and Sadomasochism', *Heresies 12*, 32ff.

29   Nancy Friday, *Men in Love* (New York: Dell, 1980).

30   Mulvey, 'Visual Pleasure', 12–13.

31   Julia Kristeva, 'La Femme, ce n'est jamais ça', trans. Marilyn A. August, in *New French Feminisms*, ed. E. Marks and I. de Courtivron (Amherst: University of Massachusetts Press, 1980), 37.

32   Sandy Flitterman and Judith Barry, 'Textual Strategies: The Politics of Art-Making', *Screen*, 2: 3 (Summer 1980), 37.

33   Ibid., 36.

34   Terry Eagleton, 'Aesthetics and Politics', *New Left Review* (1978).

35   'Women and Representation: A Discussion with Laura Mulvey' (collective project by Jane Clarke, Sue Clayton, Joanna Clelland, Rosie Elliott and Mandy Merck), *Wedge* (London), 2 (Spring 1979), 49.

36   Nancy Chodorow, 'Psychodynamics of the Family', in *The Reproduction of Mothering* (Berkeley: University of California Press, 1978), 191–209.

37   '*Riddles of the Sphinx*: A Film by Laura Mulvey and Peter Wollen; Script', *Screen*, 18: 2 (Summer 1977), 62.

38   Jacquelyn Suter and Sandy Flitterman, 'Textual Riddles: Woman as Enigma or Site of Social Meanings? An Interview with Laura Mulvey', *Discourse*, 1 (Fall 1979), 107.

39   Ibid., 109–20.

40   Ibid., 116–19.

41   Mulvey, 'Women and Representation', 49.

42   Dinnerstein, *The Mermaid and the Minotaur* (New York: Harper and Row, 1976), and Chodorow, *The Reproduction of Mothering*.

43   See for example, films by Laura Mulvey and Peter Wollen, Michelle Citron, Marjorie Keller and Helke Sander.

44   Kristeva, 'Les Chinoises à "contre-courant" ', *New French Feminisms*, 240.

45   Eleanor Maccoby and John Martin, 'Parent–Child Interaction', in *Handbook of Child Psychology*, ed. E. M. Hetherington (New York: John Wiley & Sons: in press). One has obviously to be careful here about introducing discourses that work on an entirely different level than the theoretical, psychoanalytic discourse that I have mainly been considering. It may be, however, that the confronting of the psychoanalytic discourse with more empirically based kinds of discourse could lead to an opening up of the theory, to suggestions for a way out of the theoretical impasse in which psychoanalytic frameworks place women.

46   See the important essay by Jessica Benjamin, 'Master and Slave: The Fantasy of Erotic Domination', in Ann Snitow (ed.), *Powers of Desire* (New York: Monthly Review Press, 1983).

Chapter 15

Laura Mulvey

AFTERTHOUGHTS ON 'VISUAL PLEASURE AND NARRATIVE CINEMA'

SO MANY TIMES OVER the years since my 'Visual Pleasure and Narrative Cinema' article was published in *Screen*, I have been asked why I only used the *male* third person singular to stand in for the spectator. At the time, I was interested in the relationship between the image of woman on the screen and the 'masculinisation' of the spectator position, regardless of the actual sex (or possible deviance) of any real live moviegoer. In-built patterns of pleasure and identification impose masculinity as 'point of view'; a point of view which is also manifest in the general use of the masculine third person. However, the persistent question 'what about the women in the audience?' and my own love of Hollywood melodrama (equally shelved as an issue in 'Visual Pleasure') combined to convince me that, however ironically it had been intended originally, the male third person closed off avenues of inquiry that should be followed up. Finally, *Duel in the Sun* and its heroine's crisis of sexual identity brought both areas together.

I still stand by my 'Visual Pleasure' argument, but would now like to pursue the other two lines of thought. First (the 'women in the audience' issue), whether the female specta- tor is carried along, as it were by the scruff of the text, or whether her pleasure can be more deep-rooted and complex. Second (the 'melodrama' issue), how the text and its attendant identifications are affected by a *female* character occupying the centre of the narrative arena. So far as the first issue is concerned, it is always possible that the female spectator may find herself so out of key with the pleasure on offer, with its 'masculinisation', that the spell of fascination is broken. On the other hand, she may not. She may find herself secretly, unconsciously almost, enjoying the freedom of action and control over the diegetic world that identification with a hero provides. It is *this* female spectator that I want to consider here. So far as the second issue is concerned, I want to limit the area under consideration in a similar manner. Rather than discussing melodrama in general, I am concentrating on films in which a woman central protagonist is shown to be unable to achieve a stable sexual identity, torn between the deep blue sea of passive femininity and the devil of regressive masculinity.

There is an overlap between the two areas, between the unacknowledged dilemma faced in the auditorium and the dramatic double bind up there on the screen. Generally it is dangerous to elide these two separate worlds. In this case, the emotions of those women accepting 'masculinisation' while watching action movies with a male hero are illuminated by the emotions of a heroine of a melodrama whose resistance to a 'correct' feminine position is the critical issue at stake. Her oscillation, her inability to achieve a stable sexual identity, is echoed by the woman spectator's masculine 'point of view'. Both create a sense of the difficulty of sexual difference in cinema that is missing in the undifferentiated spectator of 'Visual Pleasure'. The unstable, oscillating difference is thrown into relief by Freud's theory of femininity.

Freud and femininity

For Freud, femininity is complicated by the fact that it emerges out of a crucial period of parallel development between the sexes; a period he sees as masculine, or phallic, for both boys and girls. The terms he uses to conceive of femininity are the same as those he has mapped out for the male, causing certain problems of language and boundaries to expression. These problems reflect, very accurately, the actual position of women in patriarchal society (suppressed, for instance, under the generalised male third person singular). One term gives rise to a second as its complementary opposite, the male to the female, in that order. Some quotations:

> In females, too, the striving to be masculine is ego-syntonic at a certain period – namely in the phallic phase, before the development of femininity sets in. But it then succumbs to the momentous process of repression, as so often has been shown, that determines the fortunes of a woman's femininity.[1]

> I will only emphasise here that the development of femininity remains exposed to disturbances by the residual phenomena of the early masculine period. Regressions to the pre-Oedipus phase very frequently occur; in the course of some women's lives there is a repeated alternation between periods in which femininity and masculinity gain the upper hand.[2]

> We have called the motive force of sexual life 'the libido'. Sexual life is dominated by the polarity of masculine–feminine; thus the notion suggests itself of considering the relation of the libido to this antithesis. It would not be surprising if it were to turn out that each sexuality had its own special libido appropriated to it, so that one sort of libido would pursue the aims of a masculine sexual life and another sort those of a feminine one. But nothing of the kind is true. There is only one libido, which serves both the masculine and the feminine functions. To it itself we cannot assign any sex; if, following the conventional equation of activity and masculinity, we are inclined to describe it as masculine, we must not forget that it also covers trends with a passive aim. Nevertheless, the juxtaposition 'feminine libido' is without any justification. Furthermore, it is our impression that more constraint has been applied to the libido when it is pressed into the service of the feminine function, and that – to speak teleologically – Nature takes less careful account of its [that function's] demands than in the case of masculinity. And the reason for this may lie – thinking once again teleologically – in the fact that the accomplishment of the aim of biology has been entrusted to the aggressiveness of men and has been made to some extent independent of women's consent.[3]

One particular point of interest in the third passage is Freud's shift from the use of active/

masculine as *metaphor* for the function of the libido to an invocation of Nature and biology that appears to leave the metaphoric usage behind. There are two problems here: Freud introduces the use of the word *masculine* as 'conventional', apparently simply following an established social-linguistic practice (but which, once again, confirms the masculine 'point of view'); however, secondly, and constituting a greater intellectual stumbling-block, the feminine cannot be conceptualised as different, but rather only as *opposition* (passivity) in an antinomic sense, or as *similarity* (the phallic phase). This is not to suggest that a hidden, as yet undiscovered femininity exists (as is perhaps implied by Freud's use of the word 'Nature') but that its structural relationship to masculinity under patriarchy cannot be defined or determined within the terms offered. This shifting process, this definition in terms of opposition or similarity, leaves women also shifting between the metaphoric opposition 'active' and 'passive'. The correct road, *femininity*, leads to increasing repression of 'the active' (the 'phallic phase' in Freud's terms). In this sense Hollywood genre films structured around masculine pleasure, offering an identification with the *active* point of view, allow a woman spectator to rediscover that lost aspect of her sexual identity, the never fully repressed bedrock of feminine neurosis.

Narrative grammar and trans-sex identification

The 'convention' cited by Freud (active/masculine) structures most popular narratives, whether film, folk-tale or myth (as I argued in 'Visual Pleasure'), where his metaphoric usage is acted out literally in the story. Andromeda stays tied to the rock, a victim, in danger, until Perseus slays the monster and saves her. It is not my aim, here, to debate the rights and wrongs of this narrative division of labour or to demand positive heroines, but rather to point out that the 'grammar' of the story places the reader, listener or spectator *with* the hero. The woman spectator in the cinema can make use of an age-old cultural tradition adapting her to this convention, which eases a transition out of her own sex into another. In 'Visual Pleasure' my argument took as its axis a desire to identify a pleasure that was specific to cinema, that is, the eroticism and cultural conventions surrounding the look. Now, on the contrary, I would rather emphasise the way that popular cinema inherited traditions of story-telling that are common to other forms of folk and mass culture, with attendant fascinations other than those of the look.

Freud points out that 'masculinity' is, at one stage, ego-syntonic for a woman. Leaving aside, for the moment, problems posed by his use of words, his general remarks on stories and day-dreams provide another angle of approach, this time giving a cultural rather than psychoanalytic insight into the dilemma. He emphasises the relationship between the ego and the narrative concept of the hero:

> It is the true heroic feeling, which one of our best writers has expressed in the inimitable phrase, 'Nothing can happen to me!' It seems, however, that through this revealing characteristic of invulnerability we can immediately recognise His Majesty the Ego, the hero of every day-dream and every story.[4]

Although a boy might know quite well that it is most *unlikely* that he will go out into the world, make his fortune through prowess or the assistance of helpers, and marry a princess, the stories describe the male fantasy of ambition, reflecting something of an experience and expectation of dominance (the active). For a girl, on the other hand, the cultural and social overlap is more confusing. Freud's argument that a young girl's day-dreams concentrate on the erotic ignores his own position on her early masculinity and the active day-dreams necessarily associated with this phase. In fact, all too often, the erotic function of the woman is represented by the passive, the waiting (Andromeda again), acting above all as a formal closure to the narrative structure. Three elements can thus be drawn together: Freud's concept of 'masculinity' in women, the identification triggered by the logic of a narrative grammar, and the ego's desire to fantasise itself in a certain, active, manner. All three suggest that, as desire is given cultural materiality in a text, for women (from childhood onwards) trans-sex identification is a *habit* that very easily becomes *second nature*. However, this Nature does not sit easily and shifts restlessly in its borrowed transvestite clothes.

The Western and Oedipal personifications

Using a concept of character function based on V. Propp's *Morphology of the Folk-tale*, I want to argue for a chain of links and shifts in narrative pattern, showing up the changing function of 'woman'. The Western (allowing, of course, for as many deviations as one cares to enumerate) bears a residual imprint of the primitive narrative structure analysed by Vladimir Propp in folk-tales. Also, in the hero's traditional invulnerability, the Western ties in closely with Freud's remarks on day-dreaming. (As I am interested primarily in character function and narrative pattern, not in genre definition, many issues about the Western as such are being summarily side-stepped.) For present purposes, the Western genre pro-vides a crucial node in a series of transformations that *comment* on the function of 'woman' (as opposed to 'man') as a narrative signifier and sexual difference as personification of 'active' or 'passive' elements in a story.

In the Proppian tale, an important aspect of narrative closure is 'marriage', a function characterised by 'princess' or equivalent. This is the only function that is sex-specific, and thus essentially relates to the sex of the hero and his marriageability. This function is very commonly reproduced in the Western, where, once again, 'marriage' makes a crucial contribution to narrative closure. However, in the Western the function's presence has also come to allow a complication in the form of its opposite, 'not marriage'. Thus, while the social integration represented by marriage is an essential aspect of the folk-tale, in the Western it can be accepted . . . or not. A hero can gain in stature by refusing the princess and remaining alone (Randolph Scott in the Ranown series of movies). As the resolution of the Proppian tale can be seen to represent the resolution of the Oedipus complex (integration into the symbolic), the rejection of marriage personifies a nostalgic celebration of phallic, narcissistic omnipotence. Just as Freud's comments on the 'phallic' phase in girls seemed to belong in limbo, without a place in the chronology of sexual development, so, too, does this male phenomenon seem to belong to a phase of play and fantasy difficult to integrate exactly into the Oedipal trajectory.

The tension between two points of attraction, the symbolic (social integration and marriage) and nostalgic narcissism, generates a common splitting of the Western hero into two, something unknown in the Proppian tale. Here two functions emerge, one celebrating integration into society through marriage, the other celebrating resistance to social demands and responsibilities, above all those of marriage and the family, the sphere represented by woman. A story such as *The Man Who Shot Liberty Valance* juxtaposes these two points of attraction, and spectator fantasy can have its cake and eat it too. This particular tension between the double hero also brings out the underlying significance of the drama, its relation to the symbolic, with unusual clarity. A folk-tale story revolves around conflict between hero and villain. The flashback narration in *Liberty Valance* seems to follow these lines at first. The narrative is generated by an act of villainy (Liberty rampages, dragon-like, around the countryside). However the development of the story acquires a complication. The issue at stake is no longer how the villain will be defeated, but how the villain's defeat will be inscribed into history, whether the *upholder* of law as a symbolic system (Ranse) will be seen to be victorious or the *personification* of law in a more primitive manifestation (Tom), closer to the good or the right. *Liberty Valance*, as it uses a flashback structure, also brings out the poignancy of this tension. The 'present-tense' story is precipitated by a funeral, so that the story is shot through with nostalgia and sense of loss. Ranse Stoddart mourns Tom Doniphon.

This narrative structure is based on an opposition between two irreconcilables. The two paths cannot cross. On one side there is an encapsulation of power, and phallic attributes, in an individual who has to bow himself out of the way of history; on the other, an individual impotence rewarded by political and financial power, which, *in the long run*, in fact becomes history. Here the function 'marriage' is as crucial as it is in the folk-tale. It plays the same part in creating narrative resolution, but is even more important in that 'marriage' is an integral attribute of the upholder of the law. In this sense Hallie's choice between the two men is predetermined. Hallie equals princess equals Oedipal resolution rewarded, equals repression of narcissistic sexuality in marriage.

Woman as signifier of sexuality

In a Western working within these conventions, the function 'marriage' sublimates the erotic into a final, closing, social ritual. This ritual is, of course, sex-specific, and the main rationale for any female presence in this strand of the genre. This neat *narrative* function restates the propensity for 'woman' to signify 'the erotic' already familiar from *visual* representation (as, for instance, argued in 'Visual Pleasure'). Now I want to discuss the way in which introducing a woman as central to a story shifts its meanings, producing another kind of narrative discourse. *Duel in the Sun* provides the opportunity for this.

While the film remains visibly a 'Western', the generic space seems to shift. The landscape of action, although present, is not the dramatic core of the film's story; rather it is the interior drama of a girl caught between two conflicting desires. The conflicting desires, first of all, correspond closely with Freud's argument about female sexuality quoted above, that is: an oscillation between 'passive' femininity and regressive 'masculinity'. Thus, the symbolic equation, woman = sexuality, still persists, but now rather than being an image or a narrative function, the equation opens out a narrative area previously suppressed or repressed. Woman is no longer the signifier of sexuality (function 'marriage') in the 'Western' type of story. Now the female presence as centre allows the story to be actually, *overtly*, about sexuality: it becomes a melodrama. It is as though the narrational lens had zoomed in and opened up the neat function 'marriage' ('and they lived happily . . .') to ask 'what next?' and to focus on the figure of the princess, waiting in the wings for her one moment of importance, to ask 'what does *she* want?' Here we find the generic terrain for melodrama, in its woman-orientated strand. The second question ('what does *she* want?') takes on greater significance when the hero function is split, as described above in the case of *Liberty Valance*, where the heroine's choice puts the seal of married grace on the upholder of the law. *Duel in the Sun* opens up this question.

In *Duel in the Sun* the iconographical attributes of the two male (oppositional) characters, Lewt and Jesse, conform very closely to those of Tom and Ranse in *Liberty Valance*. But now the opposition between Ranse and Tom (which represents an abstract and allegorical conflict over Law and history) is given a completely different twist of meaning. As Pearl is at the centre of the story, caught between the two men, their alternative attributes acquire meaning *from* her, and represent different sides of her desire and aspiration. They personify the split in *Pearl*, not a split in the concept of *hero*, as argued previously for *Liberty Valance*.

However, from a psychoanalytic point of view, a strikingly similar pattern emerges, Jesse (attributes: books, dark suit, legal skills, love of learning and culture, destined to be Governor of the State, money and so on) signposts the 'correct' path for Pearl, towards learning a passive sexuality, learning to 'be a lady', above all sublimation into a concept of the feminine that is socially viable. Lewt (attributes: guns, horses, skill with horses, Western get-up, contempt for culture, destined to die an outlaw, personal strength and personal power) offers sexual passion, not based on maturity but on a regressive, boy/girl mixture of rivalry and play. With Lewt, Pearl can be a tomboy (riding, swimming, shooting). Thus the Oedipal dimension persists, but now illuminates the sexual ambivalence it represents for femininity.

In the last resort, there is no more room for Pearl in Lewt's world of misogynist machismo than there is room for her desires as Jesse's potential fiancée. The film consists of a series of oscillations in her sexual identity, between alternative paths of development, between different desperations. Whereas the regressive phallic male hero (Tom in *Liberty Vallance*) had a place (albeit a doomed one) that was stable and meaningful, Pearl is unable to settle or find a 'femininity' in which she and the male world can meet. In this sense, although the male characters personify Pearl's dilemma, it is their terms that make and finally break her. Once again, however, the narrative drama dooms the phallic, regressive resistance to the symbolic. Lewt, Pearl's masculine side, drops out of the social order. Pearl's masculinity gives her the 'wherewithal' to achieve heroism and kill the villain. The lovers shoot each other and die in each other's arms. Perhaps, in *Duel*, the erotic relationship between Pearl and Lewt also exposes a dyadic interdependence between hero and villain in the primitive tale, now threatened by the splitting of the hero with the coming of the Law.

In *Duel in the Sun*, Pearl's inability to become a 'lady' is highlighted by the fact that the perfect lady appears, like a phantasmagoria of Pearl's failed aspiration, as Jesse's perfect future wife. Pearl recognises her and her rights over Jesse, and sees that she represents the 'correct' road. In an earlier film by King Vidor, *Stella Dallas* (1937), narrative and iconographic structures similar to those outlined above make the dramatic meaning of the film although it is not a Western. Stella, as central character, is flanked on each side by a male personification of her instability, her inability to accept correct, married 'femininity' on the one hand, or find a place in a macho world on the other. Her husband, Stephen, demonstrates all the attributes associated with Jesse, with no problems of generic shift. Ed Munn, representing Stella's regressive 'masculine' side, is considerably emasculated by the loss of the Western's accoutrements and its terrain of violence. (The fact that Stella is a mother, and that her relationship to her child constitutes the central drama, undermines a possible sexual relationship with Ed.) He does retain residual traces of Western iconography. His attributes are mapped through associations with horses and betting, the racing scene. However, more importantly, his relationship with Stella is regressive, based on 'having fun', most explicitly in the episode in which they spread itching powder among the respectable occupants of a train carriage. In *Stella Dallas*, too, a perfect wife appears for Stephen, representing the 'correct' femininity that Stella rejects (very similar to Helen, Jesse's fiancée in *Duel in the Sun*).

I have been trying to suggest a series of transformations in narrative pattern that illuminate, but also show shifts in, Oedipal nostalgia. The 'personifications' and their iconographical attributes do not relate to parental figures or reactivate an actual Oedipal moment. On the contrary, they represent an internal oscillation of desire, which lies dormant, waiting to be 'pleasured' in stories of this kind. Perhaps the fascination of the classic Western, in particular, lies in its rather raw touching on this nerve. However, for the female spectator the situation is more complicated and goes beyond simple mourning for a lost fantasy of omnipotence. The masculine identification, in its phallic aspect, reactivates for her a fantasy of 'action' that correct femininity demands should be repressed. The fantasy 'action' finds expression through a metaphor of masculinity. Both in the language used by Freud and in the male personifications of desire flanking the female protagonist in the melodrama, this metaphor acts as a strait-jacket, becoming itself an indicator, a litmus paper, of the problems inevitably activated by any attempt to represent the feminine in patriarchal society. The memory of the 'masculine' phase has its own romantic attraction, a last-ditch resistance, in which the power of masculinity can be used as postponement against the power of patriarchy. Thus Freud's comments illuminate both the position of the female spectator and the image of oscillation represented by Pearl and Stella:

> in the course of some women's lives there is a repeated alternation between periods in which femininity and masculinity gain the upper hand.
>   . . . (the phallic phase) . . . then succumbs to the momentous process of repression as has so often been shown, that determines the fortunes of women's femininity.

I have argued that Pearl's position in *Duel in the Sun* is similar to that of the female spectator as she temporarily accepts 'masculinisation' in memory of her 'active' phase. Rather than dramatising the success of masculine identification, Pearl brings out its sadness. Her 'tomboy' pleasures, her sexuality, are not fully accepted by Lewt, except in death. So, too, is the female spectator's fantasy of masculinisation at cross-purposes with itself, restless in its transvestite clothes.

Notes

1   S. Freud, 'Analysis Terminable and Interminable', *Standard Edition*, vol. XXIII (London: The Hogarth Press, 1964).
2   S. Freud, 'Femininity', *Standard Edition*, vol. XXII (London: The Hogarth Press, 1964).
3   Ibid.
4   S. Freud, 'Creative Writers and Day Dreaming', *Standard Edition*, vol. IX (London: The Hogarth Press, 1964).

bell hooks

THE OPPOSITIONAL GAZE: BLACK FEMALE SPECTATORS

WHEN THINKING ABOUT BLACK female spectators, I remember being punished as a child for staring, for those hard intense direct looks children would give grown-ups, looks that were seen as confrontational, as gestures of resistance, challenges to authority. The "gaze" has always been political in my life. Imagine the terror felt by the child who has come to understand through repeated punishments that one's gaze can be dangerous. The child who has learned so well to look the other way when necessary. Yet, when punished, the child is told by parents, "Look at me when I talk to you." Only, the child is afraid to look. Afraid to look, but fascinated by the gaze. There is power in looking.

Amazed the first time I read in history classes that white slave-owners (men, women, and children) punished enslaved black people for looking, I wondered how this traumatic relationship to the gaze had informed black parenting and black spectatorship. The politics of slavery, of racialized power relations, were such that the slaves were denied their right to gaze. Connecting this strategy of domination to that used by grown folks in southern black rural communities where I grew up, I was pained to think that there was no absolute difference between whites who had oppressed black people and ourselves. Years later, reading Michel Foucault, I thought again about these connections, about the ways power as domination reproduces itself in different locations employing similar apparatuses, strategies, and mechanisms of control. Since I knew as a child that the dominating power adults exercised over me and over my gaze was never so absolute that I did not dare to look, to sneak a peep, to stare dangerously, I knew that the slaves had looked. That all attempts to repress our/black peoples' right to gaze had produced in us an overwhelming longing to look, a rebellious desire, an oppositional gaze. By courageously looking, we defiantly declared: "Not only will I stare. I want my look to change reality." Even in the worse circumstances of domination, the ability to manipulate one's gaze in the face of structures of domination that would contain it, opens up the possibility of agency. In much of his work, Michel Foucault insists on describing domination in terms of "relations of power" as part of an effort to challenge the assumption that "power is a system of domination which controls everything and which leaves no room for freedom." Emphatically stating that in all relations of power "there is necessarily the possibility of resistance," he invites the critical thinker to search those margins, gaps, and locations on and through the body where agency can be found.[1]

Stuart Hall calls for recognition of our agency as black spectators in his essay "Cultural Identity and Cinematic Representation." Speaking against the construction of white representations of blackness as totalizing, Hall says of white presence: "The error is not to conceptualize this 'presence' in terms of power, but to locate that power as wholly external to us—as extrinsic force, whose influence can be thrown off like the serpent sheds its skin."[2] What Frantz Fanon reminds us, in *Black Skin, White Masks*, is how power is inside as well as outside:

> the movements, the attitudes, the glances of the Other fixed me there, in the sense in which a chemical solution is fixed by a dye. I was indignant; I demanded an explanation. Nothing happened. I burst apart. Now the fragments have been put together again by another self. This "look," from—so to speak—the place of the Other, fixes us, not only in its violence, hostility and aggression, but in the ambivalence of its desire.[3]

Spaces of agency exist for black people, wherein we can both interrogate the gaze of the Other but also look back, and at one another, naming what we see. The "gaze" has been and is a site of resistance for colonized black people globally. Subordinates in relations of power learn experientially that there is a critical gaze, one that "looks" to document, one that is oppositional. In resistance struggle, the power of the dominated to assert agency by claiming and cultivating "awareness" politicizes "looking" relations—one learns to look a certain way in order to resist.

When most black people in the United States first had the opportunity to look at film and television, they did so fully aware that mass media was a system of knowledge and power reproducing and maintaining white supremacy. To stare at the television, or mainstream movies, to engage its images, was to engage its negation of black representation. It was the oppositional black gaze that responded to these looking relations by developing independent black cinema. Black viewers of mainstream cinema and television could chart the progress of political movements for racial equality *via* the construction of images, and did so. Within my family's southern black working-class home, located in a racially segregated neighborhood, watching television was one way to develop critical spectatorship. Unless you went to work in the white world, across the tracks, you learned to look at white people by staring at them on the screen. Black looks, as they were constituted in the context of social movements for racial uplift, were interrogating gazes. We laughed at television shows like *Our Gang* and *Amos 'n' Andy*, at these white representations of blackness, but we also looked at them critically. Before racial integration, black viewers of movies and television experienced visual pleasure in a context where looking was also about contestation and confrontation.

Writing about black looking relations in "Black British Cinema: Spectatorship and Identity Formation in Territories," Manthia Diawara identifies the power of the spectator: "Every narration places the spectator in a position of agency; and race, class and sexual relations influence the way in which this subjecthood is filled by the spectator."[4] Of particular concern for him are moments of "rupture" when the spectator resists "complete identification with the film's discourse." These ruptures define the relation between black spectators and dominant cinema prior to racial integration. Then, one's enjoyment of a film wherein representations of blackness were stereotypically degrading and dehumanizing co-existed with a critical practice that restored presence where it was negated. Critical discussion of the film while it was in progress or at its conclusion maintained the distance between spectator and the image. Black films were also subject to critical interrogation. Since they came into being in part as a response to the failure of white-dominated cinema to represent blackness in a manner that did not reinforce white supremacy, they too were critiqued to see if images were seen as complicit with dominant cinematic practices.

Critical, interrogating black looks were mainly concerned with issues of race and racism, the way racial domination of blacks by whites overdetermined representation. They were rarely concerned with gender. As spectators, black men could repudiate the reproduction of racism in cinema and television, the negation of black presence, even as they could feel as though they were rebelling against white supremacy by daring to look, by engaging phallocentric politics of spectatorship. Given the real life public circumstances wherein black men were murdered/lynched for looking at white womanhood, where the black male gaze was always subject to control and/or punishment by the powerful white Other, the private realm of television screens or dark theaters could unleash the repressed gaze. There they could "look" at white womanhood without a structure of domination overseeing the gaze, interpreting, and punishing. That white supremacist structure that had murdered Emmet Till after interpreting his look as violation, as "rape" of white womanhood, could not control black male responses to screen images. In their role as spectators, black men could enter an imaginative space of phallocentric power that mediated racial negation. This gendered relation to looking made the experience of the black male spectator radically different from that of the black female spectator. Major early black male independent filmmakers represented black women in their films as objects of male gaze. Whether looking through the camera or as spectators watching films, whether mainstream cinema or "race" movies such as those made by Oscar Micheaux, the black male gaze had a different scope from that of the black female.

Black women have written little about black female spectatorship, about our movie-going practices. A growing body of film theory and criticism by black women has only begun to emerge. The prolonged silence of black women as spectators and critics was a response to absence, to cinematic negation. In "The Technology of Gender," Teresa de Lauretis, drawing on the work of Monique Wittig, calls attention to "the power of discourses to 'do violence' to people, a violence which is material and physical, although produced by abstract and scientific discourses as well as the discourses of the mass media."[5] With the possible exception of early race movies, black female spectators have had to develop looking relations within a cinematic context that constructs our presence as absence, that denies the "body" of the black female so as to perpetuate white supremacy and with it a phallocentric spectatorship where the woman to be looked at and desired is "white." (Recent movies do not conform to this paradigm but I am turning to the past with the intent to chart the development of black female spectatorship.)

Talking with black women of all ages and classes, in different areas of the United States, about their filmic looking relations, I hear again and again ambivalent responses to cinema. Only a few of the black women I talked with remembered the pleasure of race movies, and even those who did, felt that pleasure interrupted and usurped by Hollywood. Most of the black women I talked with were adamant that they never went to movies expecting to see compelling representations of black femaleness. They were all acutely aware of cinematic racism—its violent erasure of black womanhood. In Anne Friedberg's essay "A Denial of Difference: Theories of Cinematic Identification" she stresses that "identification can only be made through recognition, and all recognition is itself an implicit confirmation of the ideology of the status quo."[6] Even when representations of black women were present in film, our bodies and being were there to serve—to enhance and maintain white womanhood as object of the phallocentric gaze.

Commenting on Hollywood's characterization of black women in *Girls on Film*, Julie Burchill describes this absent presence:

> Black women have been mothers without children (Mammies—who can ever
> forget the sickening spectacle of Hattie MacDaniels waiting on the simpering

Vivien Leigh hand and foot and enquiring like a ninny, "What's ma lamb gonna wear?") . . . Lena Horne, the first black performer signed to a long term contract with a major (MGM), looked gutless but was actually quite spirited. She seethed when Tallulah Bankhead complimented her on the paleness of her skin and the non-Negroidness of her features.[7]

When black women actresses like Lena Horne appeared in mainstream cinema most white viewers were not aware that they were looking at black females unless the film was specifically coded as being about blacks. Burchill is one of the few white women film critics who has dared to examine the intersection of race and gender in relation to the construction of the category "woman" in film as object of the phallocentric gaze. With characteristic wit she asserts: "What does it say about racial purity that the best blondes have all been brunettes (Harlow, Monroe, Bardot)? I think it says that we are not as white as we think."[8] Burchill could easily have said "we are not as white as we want to be," for clearly the obsession to have white women film stars be ultra-white was a cinematic practice that sought to maintain a distance, a separation between that image and the black female Other; it was a way to perpetuate white supremacy. Politics of race and gender were inscribed into mainstream cinematic narrative from *Birth of a Nation* on. As a seminal work, this film identified what the place and function of white womanhood would be in cinema. There was clearly no place for black women.

Remembering my past in relation to screen images of black womanhood, I wrote a short essay, "Do you remember Sapphire?" which explored both the negation of black female representation in cinema and television and our rejection of these images. Identifying the character of "Sapphire" from *Amos 'n' Andy* as that screen representation of black femaleness I first saw in childhood, I wrote:

> She was even then backdrop, foil. She was bitch—nag. She was there to soften images of black men, to make them seem vulnerable, easygoing, funny, and unthreatening to a white audience. She was there as man in drag, as castrating bitch, as someone to be lied to, someone to be tricked, someone the white and black audience could hate. Scapegoated on all sides. *She was not us.* We laughed with the black men, with the white people. We laughed at this black woman who was not us. And we did not even long to be there on the screen. How could we long to be there when our image, visually constructed, was so ugly. We did not long to be there. We did not long for her. We did not want our construction to be this hated black female thing—foil, backdrop. Her black female image was not the body of desire. There was nothing to see. She was not us.[9]

Grown black women had a different response to Sapphire; they identified with her frustrations and her woes. They resented the way she was mocked. They resented the way these screen images could assault black womanhood, could name us bitches, nags. And in opposition they claimed Sapphire as their own, as the symbol of that angry part of themselves white folks and black men could not even begin to understand.

Conventional representations of black women have done violence to the image. Responding to this assault, many black women spectators shut out the image, looked the other way, accorded cinema no importance in their lives. Then there were those spectators whose gaze was that of desire and complicity. Assuming a posture of subordination, they submitted to cinema's capacity to seduce and betray. They were cinematically "gaslighted." Every black woman I spoke with who was/is an ardent moviegoer, a lover of the Hollywood film, testified that to experience fully the pleasure of that cinema they had to close down critique, analysis; they had to forget racism. And mostly they did not think about sexism. What was the nature then of this adoring black female gaze—this look that could bring pleasure in the midst of negation? In her first novel, *The Bluest Eye*, Toni Morrison constructs a portrait of the black female spectator; her gaze is the masochistic look of victimization. Describing her looking relations, Miss Pauline Breedlove, a poor working woman, maid in the house of a prosperous white family, asserts:

> The onliest time I be happy seem like was when I was in the picture show. Every time I got, I went, I'd go early, before the show started. They's cut off the lights, and everything be black. Then the screen would light up, and I's move right on in them picture. White men taking such good care of they women, and they all dressed up in big clean houses with the bath tubs right in the same room with the toilet. Them pictures gave me a lot of pleasure.[10]

To experience pleasure, Miss Pauline sitting in the dark must imagine herself transformed, turned into the white woman portrayed on the screen. After watching movies, feeling the pleasure, she says, "But it made coming home hard."

We come home to ourselves. Not all black women spectators submitted to that spectacle of regression through identification. Most of the women I talked with felt that they consciously resisted identification with films—that this tension made moviegoing less than pleasurable; at times it caused pain. As one black woman put it, "I could always get pleasure from movies as long as I did not look too deep." For black female spectators who have "looked too deep" the encounter with the screen hurt. That some of us chose to stop looking was a gesture of resistance, turning away was one way to protest, to reject negation. My pleasure in the screen ended abruptly when I and my sisters first watched *Imitation of Life*. Writing about this experience in the "Sapphire" piece, I addressed the movie directly, confessing:

> I had until now forgotten you, that screen image seen in adolescence, those images that made me stop looking. It was there in *Imitation of Life*, that comfortable mammy image. There was something familiar about this hardworking black woman who loved her daughter so much, loved her in a way that hurt. Indeed, as young southern black girls watching this film, Peola's mother reminded us of the hardworking, church-going, Big Mamas we knew and loved. Consequently, it was not this image that captured our gaze; we were fascinated by Peola.[11]

Addressing her, I wrote:

> You were different. There was something scary in this image of young sexual sensual black beauty betrayed—that daughter who did not want to be confined by blackness, that "tragic mulatto" who did not want to be negated. "Just let me escape this image forever," she could have said. I will always remember that image. I remembered how we cried for her, for our unrealized desiring selves. She was tragic because there was no place in the cinema for her, no loving pictures. She too was absent image. It was better then, that we were absent, for when we were there it was humiliating, strange, sad. We cried all night for you, for the cinema that had no place for you. And like you, we stopped thinking it would one day be different.[12]

When I returned to films as a young woman, after a long period of silence, I had developed an oppositional gaze. Not only would I not be hurt by the absence of black female presence, or the insertion of violating representation, I interrogated the work, cultivated a way to look past race and gender for aspects of content, form, language. Foreign films and U.S. independent cinema were the primary locations of my filmic looking relations, even though I also watched Hollywood films.

From "jump," black female spectators have gone to films with awareness of the way in which race and racism determined the visual construction of gender. Whether it was *Birth of a Nation* or Shirley Temple shows, we knew that white womanhood was the racialized sexual difference occupying the place of stardom in mainstream narrative film. We assumed white women knew it to. Reading Laura Mulvey's provocative essay, "Visual Pleasure and Narrative Cinema," from a standpoint that acknowledges race, one sees clearly why black women spectators not duped by mainstream cinema would develop an oppositional gaze. Placing ourselves outside that pleasure in looking, Mulvey argues, was determined by a "split between active/male and passive/female."[13] Black female spectators actively chose not to identify with the film's imaginary subject because such identification was disenabling.

Looking at films with an oppositional gaze, black women were able to critically assess the cinema's construction of white womanhood as object of phallocentric gaze and choose not to identify with either the victim or the perpetrator. Black female spectators, who refused to identify with white womanhood, who would not take on the phallocentric gaze of desire and possession, created a critical space where the binary opposition Mulvey posits of "woman as image, man as bearer of the look"[14] was continually deconstructed. As critical spectators, black women looked from a location that disrupted, one akin to that described by Annette Kuhn in *The Power of the Image*:

> the acts of analysis, of deconstruction and of reading "against the grain" offer an additional pleasure—the pleasure of resistance, of saying "no": not to "unsophisticated" enjoyment, by ourselves and others, of culturally dominant images, but to the structures of power which ask us to consume them uncritically and in highly circumscribed ways.[15]

Mainstream feminist film criticism in no way acknowledges black female spectatorship. It does not even consider the possibility that women can construct an oppositional gaze via an understanding and awareness of the politics of race and racism. Feminist film theory rooted in an ahistorical psychoanalytic framework that privileges sexual difference actively suppresses recognition of race, reenacting and mirroring the erasure of black womanhood that occurs in films, silencing any discussion of racial difference—of racialized sexual difference. Despite feminist critical interventions aimed at deconstructing the category "woman" which highlight the significance of race, many feminist film critics continue to structure their discourse as being about "women" when in actuality it speaks only about white women. It seems ironic that the cover of the recent anthology *Feminism and Film Theory* edited by Constance Penley has a graphic that is a reproduction of the photo of white actresses Rosalind Russell and Dorothy Arzner on the 1936 set of the film *Craig's Wife* yet there is no acknowledgment in any essay in this collection that the woman "subject" under discussion is always white. Even though there are photos of black women from films reproduced in the text, there is no acknowledgment of racial difference.

It would be too simplistic to interpret this failure of insight solely as a gesture of racism. Importantly, it also speaks to the problem of structuring feminist film theory around a totalizing narrative of woman as object whose image functions solely to reaffirm and reinscribe patriarchy. Mary Ann Doane addresses this issue in the essay "Remembering Women: Psychical and Historical Constructions in Film Theory":

> This attachment to the figure of a degeneralizible Woman as the product of the apparatus indicates why, for many, feminist film theory seems to have reached an impasse, a certain blockage in its theorization . . . In focusing upon the task of delineating in great detail the attributes of woman as effect of the apparatus, feminist film theory participates in the abstraction of women.[16]

The concept "Woman" effaces the difference between women in specific socio-historical contexts, between women defined precisely as historical subjects rather than as *a* psychic subject (or non-subject). Though Doane does not focus on race, her comments speak directly to the problem of its erasure. For it is only as one imagines "woman" in the abstract, when woman becomes fiction or fantasy, can race not be seen as significant. Are we really to imagine that feminist theorists writing only about images of white women, who subsume this specific historical subject under the totalizing category "woman," do not "see" the whiteness of the image? It may very well be that they engage in a process of denial that eliminates the necessity of revisioning conventional ways of thinking about psychoanalysis as a paradigm of analysis and the need to rethink a body of feminist film theory that is firmly rooted in a denial of the reality that sex/sexuality may not be the primary and/or exclusive signifier of difference. Doane's essay appears in a very recent anthology, *Psychoanalysis and Cinema*, edited by E. Ann Kaplan, where, once again, none of the theory presented acknowledges or discusses racial difference, with the exception of one essay, "Not Speaking with Language, Speaking with No Language," which problematizes notions of orientalism in its examination of Leslie Thornton's film *Adynata*. Yet in most of the essays, the theories espoused are rendered problematic if one includes race as a category of analysis.

Constructing feminist film theory along these lines enables the production of a discursive practice that need never theorize any aspect of black female representation or spectatorship. Yet the existence of black women within white supremacist culture problematizes, and makes complex, the overall issue of female identity, representation, and spectatorship. If, as Friedberg suggests, "identification is a process which commands the subject to be displaced by an other; it is a procedure which breaches the separation between self and other, and, in this way, replicates the very structure of patriarchy."[17] If identification "demands sameness, necessitates similarity, disallows difference"—must we then surmise that many feminist film critics who are "over-identified" with the mainstream cinematic apparatus produce theories that replicate its totalizing agenda? Why is it that feminist film criticism, which has most claimed the terrain of woman's identity, representation, and subjectivity as its field of analysis, remains aggressively silent on the subject of blackness and specifically representations of black womanhood? Just as mainstream cinema has historically forced aware black female spectators not to look, much feminist film criticism disallows the possibility of a theoretical dialogue that might include black women's voices. It is difficult to talk when you feel no one is listening, when you feel as though a special jargon or narrative has been created that only the chosen can understand. No wonder then that black women have for the most part confined our critical commentary on film to conversations. And it must be reiterated that this gesture is a strategy that protects us from the violence perpetuated and advocated by discourses of mass media. A new focus on issues of race and representation in the field of film theory could critically intervene on the historical repression reproduced in some arenas of contemporary critical practice, making a discursive space for discussion of black female spectatorship possible.

When I asked a black woman in her twenties, an obsessive moviegoer, why she thought we had not written about black female spectatorship, she commented: "we are afraid to talk about ourselves as spectators because we have been so abused by 'the gaze'." An aspect of that abuse was the imposition of the assumption that black female looking relations were not important enough to theorize. Film theory as a critical "turf" in the United States has been and continues to be influenced by and reflective of white racial domination. Since feminist film criticism was initially rooted in a women's liberation movement informed by racist practices, it did not open up the discursive terrain and make it more inclusive. Recently, even those white film theorists who include an analysis of race show no interest in black female spectatorship. In her introduction to the collection of essays *Visual and Other Pleasures*, Laura Mulvey describes her initial romantic absorption in Hollywood cinema, stating:

> Although this great, previously unquestioned and unanalyzed love was put in crisis by the impact of feminism on my thought in the early 1970s, it also had an enormous influence on the development of my critical work and ideas and the debate within film culture with which I became preoccupied over the next fifteen years or so. Watched through eyes that were affected by the changing climate of consciousness, the movies lost their magic.[18]

Watching movies from a feminist perspective, Mulvey arrived at that location of disaffection that is the starting point for many black women approaching cinema within the lived harsh reality of racism. Yet her account of being a part of a film culture whose roots rest on a founding relationship of adoration and love indicates how difficult it would have been to enter that world from "jump" as a critical spectator whose gaze had been formed in opposition.

Given the context of class exploitation, and racist and sexist domination, it has only been through resistance, struggle, reading, and looking "against the grain," that black women have been able to value our process of looking enough to publicly name it. Centrally, those black female spectators who attest to the oppositionality of their gaze deconstruct theories of female spectatorship that have relied heavily on the assumption that, as Doane suggests in her essay "Woman's Stake: Filming the Female Body," "woman can only mimic man's relation to language, that is assume a position defined by the penis-phallus as the supreme arbiter of lack." Identifying with neither the phallocentric gaze nor the construction of white womanhood as lack, critical black female spectators construct a theory of looking relations where cinematic visual delight is the pleasure of interrogation. Every black woman spectator I talked to, with rare exception, spoke of being "on guard" at the movies. Talking about the way being a critical spectator of Hollywood films influenced her, black woman filmmaker Julie Dash exclaims, "I make films because I was such a spectator!" Looking at Hollywood cinema from a distance, from that critical politicized standpoint that did not want to be seduced by narratives reproducing her negation, Dash watched mainstream movies over and over again for the pleasure of deconstructing them. And of course there is that added delight if one happens, in the process of interrogation, to come across a narrative that invites the black female spectator to engage the text with no threat of violation.

Significantly, I began to write film criticism in response to the first Spike Lee movie, *She's Gotta Have It*, contesting Lee's replication of mainstream patriarchal cinematic practices that explicitly represents woman (in this instance black woman) as the object of a phallo-centric gaze. Lee's investment in patriarchal filmic practices that mirror dominant patterns makes him the perfect black candidate for entrance to the Hollywood canon. His work mimics the cinematic construction of white womanhood as object, replacing her body as text on which to write male desire with the black female body. It is transference without transformation. Entering the discourse of film criticism from the politicized location of resistance, of not wanting, as a working-class black woman I interviewed stated, "to see black women in the position white women have occupied in film forever," I began to think critically about black female spectatorship.

For years I went to independent and/or foreign films where I was the only black female present in the theater. I often imagined that in every theater in the United States there was another black woman watching the same film wondering why she was the only visible black female spectator. I remember trying to share with one of my five sisters the cinema I liked so much. She was "enraged" that I brought her to a theater where she would have to read subtitles. To her it was a violation of Hollywood notions of spectatorship, of coming to the movies to be entertained. When I interviewed her to ask what had changed her mind over the years, led her to embrace this cinema, she connected it to coming to critical conscious-ness, saying, "I learned that there was more to looking than I had been exposed to in ordinary (Hollywood) movies." I shared that though most of the films I loved were all white, I could engage them because they did not have in their deep structure a subtext reproducing the narrative of white supremacy. Her response was to say that these films demystified "white," since the lives they depicted seemed less rooted in fantasies of escape. They were, she suggested, more like "what we knew life to be, the deeper side of life as well." Always more seduced and enchanted with Hollywood cinema than me, she stressed that unaware black female spectators must "break out," no longer be imprisoned by images that enact a drama of our negation. Though she still sees Hollywood films – because "they are a major influence in the culture"—she no longer feels duped or victimized.

Talking with black female spectators, looking at written discussions either in fiction or academic essays about black women, I noted the connection made between the realm of representation in mass media and the capacity of black women to construct ourselves as subjects in daily life. The extent to which black women feel devalued, objectified, dehuman-ized in this society determines the scope and texture of their looking relations. Those black women whose identifies were constructed in resistance, by practices that oppose the domin-ant order, were most inclined to develop an oppositional gaze. Now that there is a growing interest in films produced by black women and those films have become more accessible to viewers, it is possible to talk about black female spectatorship in relation to that work. So far, most discussions of black spectatorship that I have come across focus on men. In "Black Spectatorship: Problems of Identification and Resistance" Manthia Diawara suggests that "the components of 'difference' " among elements of sex, gender, and sexuality give rise to different readings of the same material, adding that these conditions produce a "resisting" spectator.[19] He focuses his critical discussion on black masculinity.

The recent publication of the anthology *The Female Gaze: Women as Viewers of Popular Culture*, edited by Lorraine Gamman and Margaret Marshment, excited me, especially as it included an essay, "Black Looks" by Jacqui Roach and Petal Felix, that attempts to address black female spectatorship. The essay posed provocative questions that were not answered: Is there a black female gaze? How do black women relate to the gender politics of representa-tion? Concluding, the authors assert that black females have "our own reality, our own history, our own gaze—one which sees the world rather differently from 'anyone else.' "[20] Yet, they do not name/describe this experience of seeing "rather differently." The absence of definition and explanation suggests they are assuming an essentialist stance wherein it is presumed that black women, as victims of race and gender oppression, have an inherently different field of vision. Many black women do not "see differently" precisely because their perceptions of reality are so profoundly colonized, shaped by dominant ways of knowing. As Trinh T. Minh-ha points out in "Outside In, Inside Out": "Subjectivity does not merely consist of talking about oneself . . . be this talking indulgent or critical."[21]

Critical black female spectatorship emerges as a site of resistance only when individual black women actively resist the imposition of dominant ways of knowing and looking. While every black woman I talked to was aware of racism, that awareness did not automatic-ally correspond with politicization, the development of an oppositional gaze. When it did, individual black women consciously named the process. Manthia Diawara's "resisting spectatorship" is a term that does not adequately describe the terrain of black female spectatorship. We do more than resist. We create alternative texts that are not solely reactions. As critical spectators, black women participate in a broad range of looking relations, contest, resist, revision, interrogate, and invent on multiple levels. Certainly when I watch the work of black women filmmakers Camille Billops, Kathleen Collins, Julie Dash, Ayoka Chenzira, Zeinabu Davis, I do not need to "resist" the images even as I still choose to watch their work with a critical eye.

Black female critical thinkers concerned with creating space for the construction of radical black female subjectivity, and the way cultural production informs this possibility, fully acknowledge the importance of mass media, film in particular, as a powerful site for critical intervention. Certainly Julie Dash's film *Illusions* identifies the terrain of Hollywood cinema as a space of knowledge production that has enormous power. Yet, she also creates a filmic narrative wherein the black female protagonist subversively claims that space. Inverting the "real-life" power structure, she offers the black female spectator representations that challenge stereotypical notions that place us outside the realm of filmic discursive practices. Within the film she uses the strategy of Hollywood suspense films to undermine those cinematic practices that deny black women a place in this structure. Problematizing the question of "racial" identity by depicting passing, suddenly it is the white male's capacity to gaze, define, and know that is called into question.

When Mary Ann Doane describes in "Woman's Stake: Filming the Female Body" the way in which feminist filmmaking practice can elaborate "a special syntax for a different articulation of the female body," she names a critical process that "undoes the structure of the classical narrative through an insistence upon its repressions."[22] An eloquent description, this precisely names Dash's strategy in *Illusions*, even though the film is not unproblematic and works within certain conventions that are not successfully challenged. For example, the film does not indicate whether the character Mignon will make Hollywood films that subvert and transform the genre or whether she will simply assimilate and perpetuate the norm. Still, subversively, *Illusions* problematizes the issue of race and spectatorship. White people in the film are unable to "see" that race informs their looking relations. Though she is passing to gain access to the machinery of cultural production represented by film, Mignon continually asserts her ties to black community. The bond between her and the young black woman singer Esther Jeeter is affirmed by caring gestures of affirmation, often expressed by eye-to-eye contact, the direct unmediated gaze of recognition. Ironically, it is the desiring objectifying sexualized white male gaze that threatens to penetrate her "secrets" and disrupt her process. Metaphorically, Dash suggests the power of black women to make films will be threatened and undermined by that white male gaze that seeks to reinscribe the black female body in a narrative of voyeuristic pleasure where the only relevant opposition is male/ female, and the only location for the female is as a victim. These tensions are not resolved by the narrative. It is not at all evident that Mignon will triumph over the white supremacist capitalist imperialist dominating "gaze."

Throughout *Illusions*, Mignon's power is affirmed by her contact with the younger black woman whom she nurtures and protects. It is this process of mirrored recognition that enables both black women to define their reality, apart from the reality imposed upon them by structures of domination. The shared gaze of the two women reinforces their solidarity. As the younger subject, Esther represents a potential audience for films that Mignon might produce, films wherein black females will be the narrative focus. Julie Dash's recent feature-length film *Daughters of the Dust* dares to place black females at the center of its narrative. This focus caused critics (especially white males) to critique the film negatively or to express many reservations. Clearly, the impact of racism and sexism so overdetermine spectatorship—not only what we look at but who we identify with—that viewers who are not black females find it hard to empathize with the central characters in the movie. They are adrift without a white presence in the film.

Another representation of black females nurturing one another *via* recognition of their common struggle for subjectivity is depicted in Sankofa's collective work *Passion of Remembrance*. In the film, two black women friends, Louise and Maggie, are from the onset of the narrative struggling with the issue of subjectivity, of their place in progressive black liberation movements that have been sexist. They challenge old norms and want to replace them with new understandings of the complexity of black identity, and the need for liberation struggles that address that complexity. Dressing to go to a party, Louise and Maggie claim the "gaze." Looking at one another, staring in mirrors, they appear completely focused on their encounter with black femaleness. How they see themselves is most important, not how they will be stared at by others. Dancing to the tune "Let's Get Loose," they display their bodies not for a voyeuristic colonizing gaze but for that look of recognition that affirms their subjectivity—that constitutes them as spectators. Mutually empowered they eagerly leave the privatized domain to confront the public. Disrupting conventional racist and sexist stereotypical representations of black female bodies, these scenes invite the audience to look differently. They act to critically intervene and transform conventional filmic practices, changing notions of spectatorship. *Illusions*, *Daughters of the Dust*, and *Passion of Remembrance* employ a deconstructive filmic practice to undermine existing grand cinematic narratives even as they retheorize subjectivity in the realm of the visual. Without providing "realistic" positive representations that emerge only as a response to the totalizing nature of existing narratives, they offer points of radical departure. Opening up a space for the assertion of a critical black female spectatorship, they do not simply offer diverse representations, they imagine new transgressive possibilities for the formulation of identity.

In this sense they make explicit a critical practice that provides us with different ways to think about black female subjectivity and black female spectatorship. Cinematically, they provide new points of recognition, embodying Stuart Hall's vision of a critical practice that acknowledges that identity is constituted "not outside but within representation," and invites us to see film "not as a second-order mirror held up to reflect what already exists, but as that form of representation which is able to constitute us as new kinds of subjects, and thereby enable us to discover who we are."[23] It is this critical practice that enables production of feminist film theory that theorizes black female spectatorship. Looking and looking back, black women involve ourselves in a process whereby we see our history as counter-memory, using it as a way to know the present and invent the future.

Editor's notes

1   Raúl Fornet-Betancourt, Helmut Becker, Alfredo Gomez-Müller and J.D. Gauthier, "The Ethic of Care for the Self as a Practice of Freedom: An Interview with Michel Foucault on January 20, 1984," *Philosophy & Social Criticism* 12.2–3 (1987): 124.

2   Stuart Hall, "Cultural Identity and Cinematic Representation," *Framework* 36 (1989): 78.

3   Frantz Fanon, *Black Skin, White Masks* (New York: Grove Press, 1967): 109.

4   Manthia Diawara, "Black British Cinema: Spectatorship and Identity Formation in *Territories*," *Public Culture* 3.1 (Fall 1990): 33.

5   Teresa de Lauretis, *Technologies of Gender: Essays on Theory, Film and Fiction* (Bloomington: Indiana University Press, 1987): 17.

6   Anne Friedberg, "A Denial of Difference: Theories of Cinematic Identification," in *Psychoanalysis and Cinema*, ed. E. Ann Kaplan (London: Routledge, 1990): 45.

7   Julie Burchill, *Girls on Film* (New York: Pantheon, 1986): np.

8   Ibid.
9   bell hooks, "Do You Remember Sapphire?" Originally published in *Sexism, Colonialism, Misrepresenta-tion*, a special issue of *Motion Picture Magazine*, ed. B. Reynaud (New York: Collective for Living Cinema, 1990): np.
10   Toni Morrison, *The Bluest Eye* (New York: Holt, Rinehart and Winston, 1970): 95.
11   bell hooks, "Do You Remember Sapphire?"
12   bell hooks, "Do You Remember Sapphire?"
13   Laura Mulvey, "Visual Pleasure and Narrative Cinema," *Visual and Other Pleasures* (Bloomington: Indiana University Press, 1989): 19; p. 203 in this volume.
14   Ibid.; p. 203 in this volume.
15   Annette Kuhn, *Power of the Image: Essays on Representation and Sexuality* (New York: Routledge, 1989).
16   Mary Ann Doane, "Remembering Women: Psychical and Historical Constructions in Film Theory," in *Psychoanalysis and Cinema*, ed. E. Ann Kaplan (London: Routledge, 1990): 47.
17   Friedberg, Anne Friedberg, "A Denial of Difference": 36.
18   Laura Mulvey, *Visual and Other Pleasures* (Bloomington: Indiana University Press, 1989): xiii.
19   Manthia Diawara, "Black Spectatorship: Problems of Identification and Resistance," *Screen* 29.4 (1988): 67.
20   Jacqui Roach and Petal Felix, "Black Looks," in *Female Gaze: Women as Viewers of Popular Culture*, ed. Lorraine Gamman and Margaret Marshment (Seattle: Real Comet Press, 1989): 142.
21   Trinh T. Minh-ha, Outside in, Inside Out," in *Questions of Third Cinema*, ed. Jim Pines and Paul Willeman (London: British Film Institute, 1989): 147.
22   Mary Ann Doane, "Woman's Stake: Filming the Female Body," in *Feminism and Film Theory*, ed. Constance Penley (New York: Routledge, 1988): 227.
23   Stuart Hall, "Cultural Identity and Cinematic Representation," *Framework* 36 (1989): 80.

References

Burchill, Julie. *Girls on Film*. New York: Pantheon, 1986.
de Lauretis, Teresa. *Technologies of Gender: Essays on Theory Film, and Fiction*. Bloomington, IN: Indiana University Press, 1987.
Diawara, Manthia. "Black Spectatorship: Problems of Identification and Resistance." *Screen*, Vol. 29, No. 4 (1988).
———. "Black British Cinema: Spectatorship and Identity Formation in Territories." *Public Culture*, Vol. 1, No. 3 (Summer 1989).
Doane, Mary Ann. "Woman's Stake: Filming the Female Body." In *Feminism and Film Theory*, edited by Constance Penley. New York: Routledge, 1988.
———. "Remembering Women: Psychical and Historical Constructions in Film Theory." In *Psycho-analysis & Cinema*, edited by E. Ann Kaplan. London: Routledge, 1990.
Fanon, Frantz. *Black Skin, White Masks*. New York: Monthly Review, 1967.
Foucault, Michel. *Language, Counter-memory, Practice: Selected Essays and Interviews*. Edited by Donald F. Bouchard, translated by Bouchard and Sherry Simon. Ithaca, NY: Cornell University Press, 1977.
———. *Power/Knowledge: Selected Interviews and Other Writings*. Edited by Colin Gordon, translated by Gordon et al. New York: Pantheon, 1980.
Friedberg, Anne. "A Denial of Difference: Theories of Cinematic Identification." In *Psychoanalysis & Cinema*, edited by E. Ann Kaplan. London: Routledge, 1990.
Gamman, Lorraine and Margaret Marshment. *Female Gaze: Women as Viewers of Popular Culture*. Seattle, WA: Real Comet Press, 1989.
Hall, Stuart. "Cultural Identity and Cinematic Representation." *Framework*, 36 (1989): 68–81.
hooks, bell. *Ain't I a Woman: Black Women and Feminism*. Boston: South End Press, 1981.
———. *Feminist Theory: From Margin to Center*. Boston: South End Press, 1984.
———. *Talking Back: Thinking Feminist, Thinking Black*. Boston: South End Press, 1989.
———. *Yearning: Race, Gender, and Cultural Politics*. Boston: South End Press, 1990.
Kaplan, E. Ann, ed. *Psychoanalysis & Cinema: AFI Film Readers*. New York: Routledge, 1989.
Kuhn, Annette. *Power of the Image. Essays on Representation and Sexuality*. New York: Routledge, 1985.

Minh-ha, Trinh. "Outside In, Inside Out." In *Questions of Third World Cinema*, edited by Jim Pines. London: British Film Institute, 1989.

Morrison, Toni. *The Bluest Eye*. New York: Holt, Rinehart and Winston, 1970.

Mulvey, Laura. *Visual and Other Pleasures*. Bloomington, IN: Indiana University Press, 1989.

Penley, Constance. *Feminism and Film Theory*. New York: Routledge, 1988.

PART IV

Recent arguments

Chapter 17

Lev Manovich

DIGITAL CINEMA AND THE HISTORY OF A MOVING IMAGE

Cinema, the art of the index

MOST DISCUSSIONS OF CINEMA in the computer age have focused on the possibilities of interactive narrative. It is not hard to understand why: Since the majority of viewers and critics equate cinema with storytelling, computer media are understood as something that will let cinema tell its stories in a new way. Yet as exciting as the idea of a viewer participating in a story, choosing different paths through the narrative space, and interacting with characters may be, it addresses only one aspect of cinema that is neither unique nor, as many will argue, essential to it—narrative.

The challenge that computer media pose to cinema extends far beyond the issue of narrative. Computer media redefine the very identity of cinema. In a symposium that took place in Hollywood in the spring of 1996, one of the participants provocatively referred to movies as "flatties" and to human actors as "organics" and "soft fuzzies."[1] As these terms accurately suggest, what used to be cinema's defining characteristics are now just default options, with many others available. Now that one can "enter" a virtual three-dimensional space, viewing flat images projected on a screen is no longer the only option. Given enough time and money, almost everything can be simulated on a computer; filming physical reality is but one possibility.

This "crisis" of cinema's identity also affects the terms and categories used to theorize cinema's past. French film theorist Christian Metz wrote in the 1970s that "most films shot today, good or bad, original or not, 'commercial' or not, have as a common characteristic that they tell a story; in this measure they all belong to one and the same genre, which is, rather, a sort of 'supergenre' [sur-genre]."[2] In identifying fictional film as a "super-genre" of twentieth-century cinema, Metz did not bother to mention another characteristic of this genre because at that time it was too obvious: Fictional films are *live-action* films; that is, they largely consist of unmodified photographic recordings of real events that took place in real, physical space. Today, in the age of photorealistic 3-D computer animation and digital compositing, invoking this characteristic becomes crucial in defining the specificity of twentieth-century cinema. From the perspective of a future historian of visual culture, the differences between classical Hollywood films, European art films, and avant-garde films (apart from abstract ones) may appear less significant than this common feature—their reliance on lens-based recordings of reality. This section is concerned with the effect of computerization on cinema as defined by its "super-genre," fictional live-action film.[3]

During cinema's history, a whole repertoire of techniques (lighting, art direction, the use of different film stocks and lenses, etc.) was developed to modify the basic record obtained by a film apparatus. Yet behind even the most stylized cinematic images, we can discern the bluntness, sterility, and banality of early nineteenth-century photographs. No matter how complex its stylistic innovations, the cinema has found its base in these deposits of reality, these samples obtained by a methodical and prosaic process. Cinema emerged out of the same impulse that engendered naturalism, court stenography, and wax museums. Cinema is the art of the index; it is an attempt to make art out of a footprint.

Even for director Andrey Tarkovsky, film-painter par excellence, cinema's identity lies in its ability to record reality. Once, during a public discussion in Moscow sometime in the 1970s, he was asked whether he was interested in making abstract films. He replied that there can be no such thing. Cinema's most basic gesture is to open the shutter and to start the film rolling, recording whatever happens to be in front of the lens. For Tarkovsky, an abstract cinema is thus impossible.

But what happens to cinema's indexical identity if it is now possible to generate photorealistic scenes entirely on a computer using 3-D computer animation; modify individual frames or whole scenes with the help a digital paint program; cut, bend, stretch, and stitch digitized film images into something with perfect photographic credibility, even though it was never actually filmed?

This section will address the meaning of these changes in the filmmaking process from the point of view of the larger cultural history of the moving image. Seen in this context, the manual construction of images in digital cinema represents a return to the pro-cinematic practices of the nineteenth century, when images were hand-painted and hand-animated. At the turn of the twentieth century, cinema was to delegate these manual techniques to animation and define itself as a recording medium. As cinema enters the digital age, these techniques are again becoming commonplace in the filmmaking process. Consequently, cinema can no longer be clearly distinguished from animation. It is no longer an indexical media technology but, rather, a subgenre of painting.

This argument will be developed in two stages. I will first follow a historical trajectory from nineteenth-century techniques for creating moving images to twentieth-century cinema and animation. Next I will arrive at a definition of digital cinema by abstracting the common features and interface metaphors of a variety of computer software and hardware that are currently replacing traditional film technology. Seen together, these features and metaphors suggest the distinct logic of a digital moving image. This logic subordinates the photographic and the cinematic to the painterly and the graphic, destroying cinema's identity as a media art. In the beginning of the next section, "New language of cinema" [not included in this volume], I will examine different production contexts that already use digital moving images—Hollywood films, music videos, CD-ROM-based games, and other stand-alone hypermedia—to see if and how this logic has begun to manifest itself.

A brief archeology of moving pictures

As testified by its original names (kinetoscope, cinematograph, moving pictures), cinema was understood from its birth as the art of motion, the art that finally succeeded in creating a convincing illusion of dynamic reality. If we approach cinema in this way (rather than as the art of audio-visual narrative, or the art of the projected image, or the art of collective spectatorship, etc.), we can see how it superseded earlier techniques for creating and displaying moving images.

These earlier techniques share a number of common characteristics. First, they all relied on hand-painted or hand-drawn images. Magic-lantern slides were painted at least until the 1850s, as were the images used in the Phenakistiscope, the Thaumatrope, the Zootrope, the Praxinoscope, the Choreutoscope, and numerous other nineteenth-century pro-cinematic devices. Even Muybridge's celebrated Zoopraxiscope lectures of the 1880s featured not actual photographs but colored drawings painted from photographs.[4]

Not only were the images created manually, they were also manually animated. In Robertson's *Phantasmagoria*, which premiered in 1799, magic-lantern operators moved behind the screen to make projected images appear to advance and withdraw.[5] More often an exhibitor used only his hands, rather than his whole body, to put the images in motion. One animation technique involved using mechanical slides consisting of a number of layers. An exhibitor would slide the layers to animate the image.[6] Another technique was to move a long slide containing separate images slowly in front of a magic-lantern lens. Nineteenth-century optical toys enjoyed in private homes also required manual action to create move-ment—twirling the strings of the Thaumatrope, rotating the Zootrope's cylinder, turning the Viviscope's handle.

It was not until the last decade of the nineteenth century that the automatic generation of images and automatic projection were finally combined. A mechanical eye was coupled with mechanical heart; photography met the motor. As a result, cinema—a very particular regime of the visible—was born. Irregularity, nonuniformity, the accident, and other traces of the human body that previously had inevitably accompanied moving-image exhibitions, were replaced by the uniformity of machine vision.[7] A machine, like a conveyer belt, now spat out images, all sharing the same appearance and the same size, all moving at the same speed, like a line of marching soldiers.

Cinema also eliminated the discrete character of both space and movement in moving images. Before cinema, the moving element was visually separated from the static back-ground, as with a mechanical slide show or Reynaud's Praxinoscope Theater (1892).[8] The movement itself was limited in range and affected only a clearly defined figure rather than the whole image. Thus, typical actions would include a bouncing ball, a raised hand or raised eyes, a butterfly moving back and forth over the heads of fascinated children—simple vectors charted across still fields.

Cinema's most immediate predecessors share something else. As the nineteenth-century obsession with movement intensified, devices that could animate more than just a few images became increasingly popular. All of them—the Zootrope, Phonoscope, Tachyscope, and Kinetoscope—were based on loops, sequences of images featuring complete actions that can be played repeatedly. Throughout the nineteenth century, the loops grew progressively longer. The Thaumatrope (1825), in which a disk with two different images painted on each face was rapidly rotated by twirling strings attached to it, was, in essence, a loop in its most minimal form—two elements replacing one another in succession. In the Zootrope (1867) and its numerous variations, approximately a dozen images were arranged around the perimeter of a circle.[9] The Mutoscope, popular in America throughout the 1890s, increased the duration of the loop by placing a larger number of images radially on an axle.[10] Even Edison's Kinetoscope (1892–96), the first modern cinematic machine to employ film, continued to arrange images in a loop.[11] Fifty feet of film translated to an approximately twenty-second-long presentation—a genre whose potential development was cut short when cinema adopted a much longer narrative form.

From animation to cinema

Once the cinema was stabilized as a technology, it cut all references to its origins in artifice. Everything that characterized moving pictures before the twentieth century—the manual construction of images, loop actions, the discrete nature of space and movement—was delegated to cinema's bastard relative, its supplement and shadow—animation. Twentieth-century animation became a depository for nineteenth-century moving-image techniques left behind by cinema.

The opposition between the styles of animation and cinema defined the culture of the moving image in the twentieth century. Animation foregrounds its artificial character, openly admitting that its images are mere representations. Its visual language is more aligned to the graphic than to the photographic. It is discrete and self-consciously discontinuous—crudely rendered characters moving against a stationary and detailed background, sparsely and irregularly sampled motion (in contrast to the uniform sampling of motion by a film camera—recall Jean-Luc Godard's definition of cinema as "truth 24 frames per second"), and finally space constructed from separate image layers.

In contrast, cinema works hard to erase any traces of its own production process, including any indication that the images that we see could have been constructed rather than simply recorded. It denies that the reality it shows often does not exist outside the film image, an image arrived at by photographing an already impossible space, itself put together with the use of models, mirrors, and matte paintings, and then combined with other images through optical printing. It pretends to be a simple recording of an already existing reality—both to the viewer and to itself.[12] Cinema's public image stressed the aura of reality "captured" on film, thus implying that cinema was about photographing what existed before the camera rather than creating the "never-was" of special effects.[13] Rear-projection and blue-screen photography, matte paintings and glass shots, mirrors and miniatures, push development, optical effects, and other techniques that allowed filmmakers to construct and alter moving images, and thus could reveal that cinema was not really different from animation, were pushed to cinema's periphery by its practitioners, historians, and critics.[14]

In the 1990s, with the shift to computer media, these marginalized techniques moved to the center.

Cinema redefined

A visible sign of this shift is the new role that computer-generated special effects have come to play in the Hollywood industry in the 1990s. Many blockbusters have been driven by special effects; feeding on their popularity, Hollywood has even created a new minigenre of "The Making of . . . ," videos and books that reveal how special effects are created.

I will use special effects from 1990s' Hollywood films as illustrations of some of the possibilities of digital filmmaking. Until recently, Hollywood studios were the only ones who had the money to pay for digital tools and for the labor involved in producing digital effects. However, the shift to digital media affects not just Hollywood, but filmmaking as a whole. As traditional film technology is universally being replaced by digital technology, the logic of the filmmaking process is being redefined. What I describe below are the new principles of digital filmmaking that are equally valid for individual or collective film productions, regardless of whether they are using the most expensive professional hardware and software or amateur equivalents.

Consider, the following principles of digital filmmaking:

1. Rather than filming physical reality, it is now possible to generate film-like scenes directly on a computer with the help of 3-D computer animation. As a result, live-action footage is displaced from its role as the only possible material from which a film can be constructed.

2. Once live-action footage is digitized (or directly recorded in a digital format), it loses its privileged indexical relationship to prefilmic reality. The computer does not distinguish between an image obtained through a photographic lens, an image created in a paint program, or an image synthesized in a 3-D graphics package, since they are all made from the same material—pixels. And pixels, regardless of their origin, can be easily altered, substituted one for another, and so on. Live-action footage is thus reduced to just another graphic, no different than images created manually.[15]

3. If live-action footage were left intact in traditional filmmaking, now it functions as raw material for further compositing, animating, and morphing. As a result, while retaining the visual realism unique to the photographic process, film obtains a plasticity that was previously only possible in painting or animation. To use the suggestive title of a popular morphing software, digital filmmakers work with "elastic reality." For example, the opening shot of *Forrest Gump* (Zemeckis, Paramount Pictures, 1994; special effects by Industrial Light and Magic) tracks an unusually long and extremely intricate flight of a feather. To create the shot, the real feather was filmed against a blue background in different positions; this material was then animated and composited against shots of a landscape.[16] The result: a new kind of realism, which can be described as "something which looks exactly as if it could have happened, although it really could not."

4. In traditional filmmaking, editing and special effects were strictly separate activities. An editor worked on ordering sequences of images; any intervention within an image was handled by special-effects specialists. The computer collapses this distinction. The manipulation of individual images via a paint program or algorithmic image processing becomes as easy as arranging sequences of images in time. Both simply involve "cut and paste." As this basic computer command exemplifies, modification of digital images (or other digitized data) is not sensitive to distinctions of time and space or to differences in scale. So, reordering sequences of images in time, compositing them together in space, modifying parts of an individual image, and changing individual pixels become the same operation, conceptually and practically.

Given the preceding principles, we can define digital film in this way:

digital film = live action material + painting + image processing + compositing +
2-D computer animation + 3-D computer animation

Live-action material can either be recorded on film or video or directly in a digital format.[17] Painting, image processing, and computer animation refer to the processes of modifying already existent images as well as creating new ones. In fact, the very distinction between creation and modification, so clear in film-based media (shooting versus darkroom processes in photography, production versus postproduction in cinema), no longer applies to digital cinema, given that each image, regardless of its origin, goes through a number of programs before making it into the final film.[18]

Let us summarize these principles. Live-action footage is now only raw material to be manipulated by hand—animated, combined with 3-D computer generated scenes, and painted over. The final images are constructed manually from different elements, and all the elements are either created entirely from scratch or modified by hand. Now we can finally answer the question "What is digital cinema?" *Digital cinema is a particular case of animation that uses live-action footage as one of its many elements.*

This can be reread in view of the history of the moving image sketched earlier. Manual construction and animation of images gave birth to cinema and slipped into the margins . . . only to reappear as the foundation of digital cinema. The history of the moving image thus makes a full circle. *Born from animation, cinema pushed animation to its periphery, only in the end to become one particular case of animation.*

The relationship between "normal" filmmaking and special effects is similarly reversed. Special effects, which involved human intervention into machine-recorded footage and which were therefore delegated to cinema's periphery throughout its history, become the norm of digital filmmaking.

The same logic applies to the relationship between production and postproduction. Cinema traditionally involved arranging physical reality to be filmed through the use of sets, models, art direction, cinematography, and so forth. Occasional manipulation of recorded film (for instance through optical printing) was negligible compared to the extensive manipulation of reality in front of the camera. In digital filmmaking, shot footage is no longer the final point, it is merely raw material to be manipulated on a computer, where the real construction of a scene will take place. In short, production becomes just the first stage of postproduction.

The following example illustrates this new relationship between different stages of the filmmaking process. Traditional on-set filming for *Stars Wars: Episode 1—The Phantom Menace* (Lucas, 1999) was done in just sixty-five days. The postproduction, however, stretched over two years, since 95 percent of the film (approximately 2,000 shots out of the total 2,200) was constructed on a computer.[19]

Here are two further examples illustrating the shift from rearranging reality to rearranging its images. From the analog era: for a scene in *Zabriskie Point* (1970), Michaelangelo Antonioni, trying to achieve a particularly saturated color, ordered a field of grass to be painted. From the digital era: To create the launch sequence in *Apollo 13* (Howard, 1995; special effects by Digital Domain), the crew shot footage at the original location of the launch at Cape Canaveral. The artists at Digital Domain scanned the film and altered it on computer workstations, removing recent building construction, adding grass to the launch pad and painting the skies to make them more dramatic. This altered film was then mapped onto 3-D planes to create a virtual set that was animated to match a 180-degree dolly movement of a camera following a rising rocket.[20]

The last example brings us to another conceptualization of digital cinema—as painting. In his study of digital photography, Mitchell focuses our attention on what he calls the inherent mutability of the digital image: "The essential characteristic of digital information is that it can be manipulated easily and very rapidly by computer. It is simply a matter of substituting new digits for old . . . Computational tools for transforming, combining, altering, and analyzing images are as essential to the digital artist as brushes and pigments to a painter."[21] As Mitchell points out, this inherent mutability erases the difference between a photograph and a painting. Since a film is a series of photographs, it is appropriate to extend Mitchell's argument to digital film. Given that an artist is easily able to manipulate digitized footage either as a whole or frame by frame, a film in a general sense becomes a series of paintings.[22]

Hand-painting digitized film frames, made possible by a computer, is probably the most dramatic example of the new status of cinema. No longer strictly locked in the photographic, cinema opens itself toward the painterly. Digital hand-painting is also the most obvious example of the return of cinema to its nineteenth-century origins—in this case, the hand-crafted images of magic-lantern slides, the Phenakistiscope, and Zootrope.

We usually think of computerization as automation, but here the result is the reverse: What was previously recorded by a camera automatically now has to be painted one frame at a time. And not just a dozen images, as in the nineteenth century, but thousands and thousands. We can draw another parallel with the practice of manually tinting film frames in different colors according to a scene's mood, a practice common in the early days of silent cinema.[23] Today, some of the most visually sophisticated digital effects are often achieved using the same simple method: painstakingly altering thousands of frames by hand. The frames are painted over either to create mattes ("hand-drawn matte extraction") or to change the images directly, as, for instance, in *Forrest Gump*, where President Kennedy is made to speak new sentences by altering the shape of his lips, one frame at a time.[24] In principle, given enough time and money, one can create what will be the ultimate digital film: 129,600 frames (ninety minutes) completely painted by hand from scratch, but indistinguishable in appearance from live photography.

The concept of digital cinema as painting can also be developed in a different way. I would like to compare the shift from analog to digital filmmaking to the shift from fresco and tempera to oil painting in the early Renaissance. A painter making a fresco has limited time before the paint dries, and once it has dried, no further changes to the image are possible. Similarly, a traditional filmmaker has limited means of modifying images once they are recorded on film. Medieval tempera painting can be compared to the practice of special effects during the analog period of cinema. A painter working with tempera could modify and rework the image, but the process was painstaking and slow. Medieval and early Renaissance masters would spend up to six months on a painting only a few inches tall. The switch to oils greatly liberated painters by allowing them to quickly create much larger compositions (think, for instance, of the works by Veronese and Titian) as well as to modify them as long as necessary. This change in painting technology led the Renaissance painters to create new kinds of compositions, new pictorial space, and new narratives. Similarly, by allowing a filmmaker to treat a film image as an oil painting, digital technology redefines what can be done with cinema.

If digital compositing and digital painting can be thought of as an extension of cell animation techniques (since composited images are stacked in depth parallel to each other, as cells on a animation stand), the newer method of computer-based postproduction makes filmmaking a subset of animation in a different way. In this method, the live-action photographic stills and/or graphic elements are positioned in a 3-D virtual space, thus giving the director the ability to move the virtual camera freely through this space, dollying and panning. Thus cinematography is subordinated to 3-D computer animation. We may think of this method as an extension of the multiplane animation camera. However, if the camera mounted over a multiplane stand could only move perpendicular to the images, now it can move in an arbitrary trajectory. An example of a commercial film that relies on this newer method, which one day may become the standard of filmmaking (because it gives the director the most flexibility), is Disney's *Aladdin*; an example of an independent work that fully explores the new aesthetic possibilities of this method without subordinating it to traditional cinematic realism is Waliczky's *The Forest*.

In the "Compositing" section [not included in this volume], I pointed out that digital compositing can be thought off as an intermediary step between 2-D images and 3-D computer representation. The newer postproduction method represents the next logical step toward completely computer-generated 3-D representations. Instead of the 2-D space of "traditional" composite, we now have layers of moving images positioned in a virtual 3-D space.

The reader who has followed my analysis of the new possibilities of digital cinema may wonder why I have stressed the parallels between digital cinema and the pro-cinematic techniques of the nineteenth century, but have not mentioned twentieth-century avant-garde filmmaking. Did not the avant-garde filmmakers already explore many of these new possibilities? To take the notion of cinema as painting, Len Lye, one of the pioneers of abstract animation, was painting directly on film as early as 1935; he was followed by Norman McLaren and Stan Brackage, the latter extensively covering shot footage with dots, scratches, splattered paint, smears, and lines in an attempt to turn his films into equivalents of Abstract Expressionist paintings. More generally, one of the major impulses in all avant-garde filmmaking from Leger to Godard was to combine the cinematic, the painterly, and the graphic—by using live-action footage and animation within one film or even a single frame, by altering this footage in a variety of ways, or by juxtaposing printed texts and filmed images.

When the avant-garde filmmakers collaged multiple images within a single frame, or painted and scratched film, or revolted against the indexical identity of cinema in other ways, they were working against "normal" filmmaking procedures and the intended uses of film technology. (Film stock was not designed to be painted on.) Thus they operated on the periphery of commercial cinema not only aesthetically but also technically.

One general effect of the digital revolution is that avant-garde aesthetic strategies came to be embedded in the commands and interface metaphors of computer software.[25] In short, *the avant-garde became materialized in a computer*. Digital-cinema technology is a case in point. The avant-garde strategy of collage reemerged as the "cut-and-paste" command, the most basic operation one can perform on digital data. The idea of painting on film became embedded in the paint functions of film-editing software. The avant-garde move to combine animation, printed texts, and live-action footage is repeated in the convergence of animation, title generation, paint, compositing, and editing systems into all-in-one packages. Finally, the move to combine a number of film images within one frame (for instance, in Leger's 1924 *Ballet Mechanique* or in *Man with a Movie Camera*) also becomes legitimized by technology, given that all editing software, including Photoshop, Premiere, After Effects, Flame, and Cineon, assume by default that a digital image consists of a number of separate image layers. All in all, what used to be exceptions for traditional cinema have become the normal, intended techniques of digital filmmaking, embedded in technology design itself.[26]

From kino-eye to kino-brush

In the twentieth century, cinema played two roles at once. As a media technology, its role was to capture and store visible reality. The difficulty of modifying images once recorded was precisely what lent it value as a document, assuring its authenticity. This same rigidity has defined the limits of cinema as a "super-genre" of *live-action* narrative. Although cinema includes within itself a variety of styles—the result of the efforts of numerous directors, designers, and cinematographers—these styles share a strong family resemblance. They are all children of a recording process that uses lenses, regular sampling of time, and photographic media. They are all children of a machine vision.

The mutability of digital data impairs the value of cinema recordings as documents of reality. In retrospect, we can see that twentieth-century cinema's regime of visual realism, the result of automatically recording visual reality, was only an exception, an isolated accident in the history of visual representation, which has always involved, and now again involves, the manual construction of images. Cinema becomes a particular branch of painting—painting in time. No longer a kino-eye, but a kino-brush.[27]

The privileged role played by the manual construction of images in digital cinema is one example of a larger trend—the return of pro-cinematic moving-image techniques. Although marginalized by the twentieth-century institution of live-action, narrative cinema, which relegated them to the realms of animation and special effects, these techniques are reemerging as the foundation of digital filmmaking. What was once supplemental to cinema becomes its norm; what was at the periphery comes into the center. Computer media return to us the repressed of the cinema.

As the examples in this section suggest, directions that were closed off at the turn of the century when cinema came to dominate the modern moving-image culture are now again beginning to be explored. The moving-image culture is being redefined once again; cinematic realism is being displaced from the dominant mode to merely one option among many.

Notes

1   Scott Billups, presentation during the "Casting from Forest Lawn (Future of Performers)" panel at "The Artists Rights Digital Technology Symposium '96," Los Angeles, Directors Guild of America, 16 February 1996. Billups was a major figure in bringing together Hollywood and Silicon Valley by way of the American Film Institute's Apple Laboratory and Advanced Technologies Programs in the late 1980s and early 1990s. See Paula Parisi, "The New Hollywood Silicon Stars," *Wired* 3.12 (December 1995), 142–45, 202–10.

2   Christian Metz, "The Fiction Film and Its Spectator: A Metapsychological Study," Trans. Alfred Guzzetti, *New Literary History* 8, 1 (Autumn 1976), 75–105.

3   Cinema as defined by its "super-genre" of fictional live-action film belongs to the media arts, which, in contrast to traditional arts, rely on recordings of reality as their basis. Another term not as popular as "media arts" but perhaps more precise is "recording arts." For the use of this term, see James Monaco, *How to Read a Film*, rev. ed. (New York: Oxford University Press, 1981), 7.

4   Charles Musser, *The Emergence of Cinema: The American Screen to 1907* (Berkeley: University of California Press, 1994), 49–50.

5   Musser, *The Emergence of Cinema*, 25.

6   C.W. Ceram, *Archeology of the Cinema* (New York: Harcourt, Brace and World, 1965), 44–45.

7   The birth of cinema in the 1890s is accompanied by an interesting transformation: While the body as the generator of moving pictures disappears, it simultaneously becomes their new subject. Indeed, one of the key themes of early films produced by Edison is a human body in motion—a man sneezing, the famous bodybuilder Sandow flexing his muscles, an athlete performing a somersault, a woman dancing. Films of boxing matches play a key role in the commercial development of Kinetoscope. See Musser, *The Emergence of Cinema*, 72–79, and David Robinson, *From Peep Show to Palace: The Birth of American Film* (New York: Columbia University Press, 1996), 44–48.

8   Robinson, *From Peep Show to Palace*, 12.

9   This arrangement was previously used in magic-lantern projections; it is described in the second edition of Althanasius Kircher's *Ars magna* (1671). See Musser, *The Emergence of Cinema*, 21–22.

10   Ceram, *Archeology of the Cinema*, 140.

11   Musser, *The Emergence of Cinema*, 78.

12   The extent of this lie is made clear by the films of Andy Warhol from the early 1960s—perhaps the only real attempt to create cinema without language.

13   I have borrowed this definition of special effects from David Samuelson, *Motion Picture Camera Techniques* (London: Focal Press, 1978).

14   The following examples illustrate this disavowal of special effects; other examples can be easily found. The first example is from popular discourse on cinema. A section entitled "Making the Movies" in Kenneth W. Leish's *Cinema* (New York: Newsweek Books, 1974) contains short stories from the history of the movie industry. The heroes of these stories are actors, directors, and producers; special-effects artists are mentioned only once. The second example is from an academic source: The authors of the authoritative *Aesthetics of Film* state, "The goal of our book is to summarize from a synthetic and didactic perspective the diverse theoretical attempts at examining these empirical notions [terms from the lexicon of film technicians], including ideas like frame vs. shot, terms from production crews' vocabularies, the notion of identification produced by critical vocabulary, etc." The fact that the text never mentions special-effects techniques reflects the general lack of any

historical or theoretical interest in the topic by film scholars. Bordwell and Thompson's *Film Art: An Introduction*, which is used as a standard textbook in undergraduate film classes, is a little better as it devotes three of its five hundred pages to special effects. Finally, a relevant statistic: A library of the University of California, San Diego, contains 4,273 titles catalogued under the subject "motion pictures" and only sixteen titles under "special effects cinematography." For the few important works addressing the larger cultural significance of special effects by film theoreticians, see Vivian Sobchack and Scott Bukatman. Norman Klein is currently working on a history of special-effects environments. Kenneth W. Leish, *Cinema* (New York: Newsweek Books, 1974); Jacques Aumont, Alain Bergala, Michel Marie, and Marc Vernet, *Aesthetics of Film*, trans. Richard Neupert (Austin: University of Texas Press, 1992), 7; David Bordwell and Kristin Thompson, *Film Art: An Introduction*, 5th edn. (New York: McGraw Hill, 1997); Vivian Sobchack, *Screening Space: The American Science Fiction Film*, 2nd ed. (New York: Ungar, 1987); Scott Bukatman, "The Artificial Infinite," in *Visual Display*, eds. Lynne Cooke and Peter Wollen (Seattle: Bay Press, 1995).

15   For a discussion of the subsumption of the photographic by the graphic, see Peter Lunenfeld, "Art Post-History: Digital Photography and Electronic Semiotics," *Photography after Photography*, eds. Hubertus von Amelunxen, Stefan Iglhaut, and Florian Rötzer, 58–66 (Munich: Verlag der Kunst, 1995).

16   For a complete list of people at ILM who worked on this film, see *SIGGRAPH '94 Visual Proceedings* (New York: ACM SIGGRAPH, 1994), 19.

17   In this respect, 1995 can be called the last year of digital media. At the 1995 National Association of Broadcasters convention, Avid showed a working model of a digital video camera that records not on a videocassette but directly onto a hard drive. Once digital cameras become widely used, we will no longer have any reason to talk about digital media since the process of digitization will have been eliminated.

18   Here is another, even more radical definition: Digital film $= f(x,y,t)$. This definition would be greeted with joy by the proponents of abstract animation. Since a computer breaks down every frame into pixels, a complete film can be defined as a function that, given the horizontal, vertical, and time location of each pixel, returns its color. This is actually how a computer represents a film, a representation that has a surprising affinity with a certain well-known avant-garde vision of cinema! For a computer, a film is an abstract arrangement of colors changing in time, rather than something structured by "shots," "narrative," "actors," and so on.

19   Paula Parisi, "Grand Illusion," *Wired 7.05* (May 1999), 137.

20   See Barbara Robertson, "Digital Magic: Apollo 13," *Computer Graphics World* (August 1995), 20.

21   William J. Mitchell, *The Reconfigured Eye: Visual Truth in the Post-Photographic Era* (Cambridge, MA: MIT Press, 1992), 7.

22   The full advantage of mapping time into 2-D space, already present in Edison's first cinema apparatus, is now realized: One can modify events in time by literally painting on a sequence of frames, treating them as a single image.

23   See Robinson, *From Peep Show to Palace*, 165.

24   See "Industrial Light and Magic Alters History with MATADOR," promotion material by Parallax Software, SIGGRAPH 95 Conference, Los Angeles, August 1995.

25   See my "Avant-Garde as Software" (http://visarts.ucsd.edu/~manovich).

26   For the experiments in painting on film by Lye, McLaren, and Brackage, see Robert Russett and Cecile Starr, *Experimental Animation* (New York: Van Nostrand Reinhold, 1976), 65–71, 117–28; P. Adams Smith, *Visionary Film*, 2nd ed. (Oxford: Oxford University Press), 230, 136–227.

27   Dziga Vertov coined the term "kino-eye" in the 1920s to describe the cinematic apparatus's ability "to record and organize the individual characteristics of life's phenomena into a whole, an essence, a conclusion." For Vertov, it was the presentation of film "facts," based as they were on materialist evidence, that defined the very nature of the cinema. See *Kino-Eye: The Writings of Dziga Vertov*, ed. Annette Michelson, trans. Kevin O'Brien (Berkeley: University of California Press, 1984). The quotation above is from "Artistic Drama and Kino-Eye," originally published in 1924, 47–49, 47.

Chapter 18

Tom Gunning

MOVING AWAY FROM THE INDEX: CINEMA AND THE IMPRESSION OF REALITY

Indexical realism and film theory

WHILE CINEMA HAS OFTEN been described as the most realistic of the arts, cinematic realism has been understood in a variety of ways: from an aspect of a sinister ideological process of psychological regression to infantile states of primal delusion, to providing a basis for evidentiary status for films as historical and even legal documents. Cinematic realism has been praised as a cornerstone of film aesthetics, denounced as a major ploy in ideological indoctrination, and envied as a standard for new media. I believe the time has come to return to this issue without some of the polemics that have previously marked it but with a careful and historically informed discussion of cinema's uses and definitions of the impression of reality. In film theory over the last decades, realist claims for cinema have often depended on cinema's status as an index, one of the triad of signs in the semiotics of Charles Sanders Peirce. Film's indexical nature has almost always (and usually exclusively) been derived from its photographic aspects. In this essay I want to explore alternative approaches that might ultimately provide new ways of thinking about the realistic aspects of cinema.

Peirce defined the index as a sign that functions through an actual existential connection to its referent "by being really and in its individual existence connected with the individual object" ("Prolegomena" 251). Thus, frequently cited examples of indices are the footprint, the bullet hole, the sundial, the weathervane, and photographs—all signs based on direct physical connection between the sign and its referent—the action of the foot, impact of the bullet, the movement of the sun, the direction of the wind, or the light bouncing from an object (*Philosophical* 106–11). A number of these examples (such as the weather vane and the sundial) perform their references simultaneously to the action of their referents. This fact reveals that the identification of the photographic index with the pastness of the trace (made by several theorists) is not a characteristic of all indices (and one could point out that it only holds true for a fixed photograph, but not of the image that appears within a camera obscura).

For Peirce the index functions as part of a complex system of interlocking concepts that comprise not only a philosophy of signs but a theory of the mind and its relation to the world. Peirce's triad of signs (icon, index, and symbol), rather than being absolutely opposed to each other, are conceived to interact in the process of signification, with all three operating in varying degrees in specific signs. However (with the exception of Gilles Deleuze, for whom Peirce's system, rather than the index, is primary), within theories of cinema, photography, and new media, the index has been largely abstracted from this system, given a rather simple definition as the existential trace or impression left by an object, and used to describe (and solve) a number of problems dealing with the way what we might call the light-based image media refer to the world. In fact, Peirce's discussion of the index includes a large range of signs and indications, including "anything which focuses attention" (*Philosophical* 108) and the general hailing and deixic functions of language and gesture. Peirce therefore by no means restricts the index to the impression or trace. I do not claim to have a command of the range of Peirce's complex semiotics, but it is perhaps important to point out that the use of the index in film theory has tended to rely on a small range of the possible meanings of the term.

I have no doubt that Peirce's concept has relevance for film and that (although more complex than generally described) the index also provides a useful way of thinking through some of these problems; indeed, even the restricted sense of the index as a trace has supplied insights into the nature of film and photography. However, I also think that what we might call a diminished concept of the index may have reached the limits of its usefulness in the theory of photography, film, and new media.[1] The nonsense that has been generated specifically about the indexicality of digital media (which, due to its digital nature, has been claimed to be nonindexical—as if the indexical and the analog were somehow identical) reveals something of the poverty of this approach. But I also feel the index may not be the best way, and certainly should not be the only way, to approach the issue of cinematic realism. Confronting questions of realism anew means that contemporary media theory must still wrestle with its fundamental nature and possibilities. I must confess that this essay attempts less to lay a logical foundation for these discussions than to launch a polemic calling for such a serious undertaking and to reconnoiter a few of its possibilities.

It is worth reviewing here the history of the theoretical discourse by which a relation was forged between cinematic realism and the index. Without undertaking a thorough historiographic review of the concept of the index in film and media theory, the first influential introduction of the concept of the index into film theory came in Peter Wollen's groundbreaking comparison of Peirce to the film theory of André Bazin (125–26 [p. 175, this volume]). But to understand this identification, a review of certain aspects of Bazin's theory of film is needed. Bazin introduced in his essays and critical practice an argument for the realism of cinema that was, as he termed it in his most quoted theoretical essay, "ontological." The complexity and indeed the dialectical nature of Bazin's critical description of a realist style have become increasingly recognized.[2] For Bazin, realism formed the aesthetic basis for the cinema, and most of his discussion of cinematic realism dealt with visual, aural, and narrative style. Although Bazin never argued the exact relation between his theories of ontology and of style systematically (and indeed, one could claim that Bazin's discussion of realism across his many essays contains both contradictions and also a possible pattern of evolution and change in his work taken as a whole—not to mention multiple interpretations), at least in the traditional reception of Bazin's theory, cinematic realism depended on the medium's photographic nature.

A number of frequently quoted statements containing the essence of Bazin's claim for the ontology of the photographic image and presumably for motion picture photography warrant consideration. Bazin's account of the realism of photography rests less on a correspondence theory (that the photograph resembles the world, a relation Peirce would describe as iconic), than on what he describes as "a transference of reality from the thing to its reproduction," referring to the photograph as "a decal or approximate tracing."[3] Bazin extends these comments, saying:

The photographic image is the object itself, the object freed from temporal contingencies. No matter how fuzzy, distorted, or discolored, no matter how lacking in documentary value the image may be, it proceeds, by virtue of its genesis, from the ontology of the model; it is the model.[4]

He adds shortly after this:

The photograph as such and the object in itself share a common being, after the fashion of a fingerprint. Wherefore, photography actually contributes something to the order of natural creation instead of providing a substitute for it.

("Ontology" 18 [p. 93, this volume])

To cite one more famous description from another essay, Bazin also describes the photograph as "the taking of a veritable luminous impression in light—to a mold. As such it carries with it more than a mere resemblance, namely a kind of identity" ("Theater" 91).

Bazin's descriptions are both evocative and elusive, and Wollen was, I think, the first to draw a relation between Bazin's ideas and Peirce's concept of the index. In his pioneering essay on "Semiology of the Cinema," Wollen said of Bazin:

His conclusions are remarkably close to those of Peirce. Time and again Bazin speaks of photography in terms of a mould, a death-mask, a Veronica, the Holy Shroud of Turin, a relic, an imprint. [. . .] Thus Bazin repeatedly stresses the existential bond between sign and object, which, for Peirce, was the determining characteristic of the indexical sign.

(125–26 [p. 175, this volume])

The traditional reception of Bazin's film theory takes his account of the ontology of the photographic image as the foundation of his arguments about the relation between film and the world. Wollen's identification of Bazin's photographic ontology with Peirce's index has been widely accepted (although critics have rarely noted Wollen's important caveat: "But whereas Peirce made his observation in order to found a logic, Bazin wished to found an aesthetic" [126 [p. 175, this volume]]).

I must state that I think one can make a coherent argument for reading Bazin's ontology in terms of the Peircean index, as Wollen did. However, I have also claimed elsewhere that this reading of Bazin in terms of Pierce does some disservice to the full complexity of Bazin's aesthetic theory of realism ("What's the Point"). Likewise, in a recent essay Daniel Morgan makes a convincing and fully argued case (different from mine) that Bazin's theory of cinematic realism should not be approached through the theory of the index at all ("Rethinking"). I would still maintain, however, that parallels between aspects of Bazin's theory of cinematic realism and the index do exist, even if they cannot explain the totality of his theory of cinematic realism (or, as Morgan would argue, its most important aspects).

I do not intend to rehearse here either my own or others' arguments about why the index might not supply a complete understanding of Bazin's theory of cinematic realism, but some summary remarks are in order. The chief limitation to the indexical approach to Bazin comes from the difference between a semiotics that approaches the photograph (and therefore film) as a sign and a theory like Bazin's that deals instead with the way a film creates an aesthetic world. When Bazin claims that "photography actually contributes something to the order of natural creation instead of providing a substitute for it," [p. 93, this volume] he denies the photograph the chief characteristic of a sign, that of supplying a substitute for a referent. While it would be foolish to claim that a photograph cannot be a sign of something (it frequently does perform this function), I would claim that signification does not form the basis of Bazin's understanding of the ontology of the photographic image and that his theory of cinematic realism depends on a more complex (and less logical) process of spectator involvement. Bazin describes the realism of the photograph as an "irrational power to bear away our faith" ("Ontology" 14 [p. 92, this volume]). This "magical" understanding of photographic ontology is clearly very different from a logic of signs. In Peirce's semiotics, the indexical relation falls entirely into the rational realm.

Beyond the index: cinematic realism and medium promiscuity

The indexical argument no longer supplies the only way to approach Bazin's theory. Rather than assuming that the invocation of Peirce's concept of the index solves the question of film's relation to reality, I think we must now raise again the question that Bazin asked so passionately and subtly (even if he never answered definitively): what is cinema? What are cinema's effects and what range of aspects relates to its oft-cited (and just as variously defined) realistic nature? Given the historically specific nature of Bazin's arguments for cinematic realism as an aesthetic value (responding as he did to technical innovations such as deep focus cinematography and to new visual and narrative styles such as Italian Neo-realism), it makes sense for a contemporary theory of cinematic realism to push beyond those aspects of cinematic realism highlighted by Bazin. Specifically, we need to ask in a contemporary technical and stylistic context: what are the bounds that cinema forges with the world it portrays? Are these limited to film's relation to photography? Is the photographic process the only aspect of cinema that can be thought of as indexical, especially if we think about the term more broadly than as just a trace or impression? If the claim that digital processing by its nature eliminates the indexical seems rather simplistic, one must nonetheless admit that computer-generated images (CGI) do not correspond directly to Bazin's description of the "luminous mold" that the still photograph supposedly depends on. But can these CGI images still be thought of as in some way indexical? In what way has the impression of reality been attenuated by new technology, and in what ways is it actually still functioning (or even intensified)? But setting aside the somewhat complex case of computer-generated special effects, is it not somewhat strange that photographic theories of the cinema have had such a hold on film theory that much of film theory must immediately add the caveat that they do not apply to animated film? Given that as a technical innovation cinema was first understood as "animated pictures" and that computer-generated animation techniques are now omni-present in most feature films, shouldn't this lacuna disturb us? Rather than being absorbed in the larger categories of cultural studies or cognitive theory, shouldn't the classical issues of film theory be reopened? I will not attempt to answer all these questions in this essay, but I think they are relevant to the issues I will raise.

Within the academy, the study of film theory has often been bifurcated between "classical film theory" and "contemporary film theory." Insofar as this division refers to something more than an arbitrary sense of the past and present, "classical" film theories have been usefully defined as theories that seek to isolate and define the "essence" of cinema, while "contemporary" theories rely on discourses of semiotics and psychoanalysis to describe the relation between film and spectator (Carroll 10–15). While the classical approach has been widely critiqued as essentialist, it seems to me that a pragmatic investigation of the characteristics of film as developed and commented on through time hardly needs to involve a proscriptive quest for the one pure cinema. Therefore, if I call for new descriptions of the nature(s) of the film medium, I am not at all calling for a return to classical film theory (and even less to a neo-classicism!). But I do think the time has come to take stock of the historical and transforming nature of cinema as a medium and of its dependence and differentiation from other media.

Considering historically the definitions of film as a medium helps us avoid the dilemma of either proscriptively (and timelessly) defining film's essence or the alternative of avoiding any investigation into the diverse nature of media for fear of being accused of promoting an idealist project. As a new technology at the end of the nineteenth century, cinema did not immediately appear with a defined essence as a medium, but rather, displayed an amazing promiscuity (if not polymorphic perversity) in both its models and uses. Cinema emerged within a welter of new inventions for the recording or conveying of aspects of human life previously felt to be ephemeral, inaudible, or invisible: the telephone, the phonograph, or the X-ray are only a few examples. Before these devices found widespread acceptance as practical instruments, they existed as theatrical attractions, demonstrated on stage before paying audiences. Indeed, the X-ray, which appeared almost simultaneously with the projection of films on the screen, seemed at one point to be displacing moving pictures as a popular attraction, and a number of showmen exchanged their motion picture projectors for the new apparatus that showed audiences the insides of their bodies (and unknowingly gave themselves and their collaborators dangerous doses of radiation). It is in this competitive context of novel devices that Antoine Lumière, the father of Louis and Auguste Lumière, who managed the theatrical exhibition of his sons' invention, warned a patron desirous of purchasing a Cinématographe that it was an "invention without a future" (quoted in Chardère 313).

Rather than myths of essential origins, historical research uncovers a genealogy of cinema, a process of emergence and competition yielding the complex formation of an identity. But cinema has always (and not only at its origin) taken place within a competitive media environment, in which the survival of the fittest was in contention and the outcome not always clear. As a historian I frequently feel that one of my roles must be to combat the pervasive amnesia that a culture based in novelty encourages, even within the academy. History always responds to the present, and changes in our present environment allow us to recognize aspects of our history that have been previously obscured or even repressed. At the present moment, cinema finds itself immersed in another voraciously competitive media environment. Is cinema about to disappear into the maw of undefined and undifferentiated image media, dissolved into a pervasive visual culture? To be useful in such an investigation where theory and history intertwine, the discussion of cinematic realism cannot be allowed to ossify into a dogmatic assertion about the photographic nature of cinema or an assumption about the indexical nature of all photography.

My history lesson resists either celebration or paranoia at the prospect of a new media environment, seeing in our current situation not only a return to aspects of cinema's origins but a dynamic process that has persisted in varying degrees throughout the extent of film's history—an interaction with other competing media, with mutual borrowings, absorptions, and transformation among them. Cinema has never been one thing. It has always been a point of intersection, a braiding together of diverse strands: aspects of the telephone and the phonograph circulated around the cinema for almost three decades before being absorbed by sound cinema around 1928, while simultaneously spawning a new sister medium, radio; a variety of approaches to color, ranging from tinting to stencil coloring, existed in cinema as either common or minority practices until color photography became pervasive in the 1970s; the film frame has changed its proportions since 1950 and is now available in small, medium, and supersized rectangles (television, cinemascope, imax, for example); cinema's symbiotic relation to television, video, and other digital practices has been ongoing for nearly half a century without any of these interactions and transformations—in spite of numerous predictions—yet spelling the end of the movies. Thus anyone who sees the demise of the cinema as inevitable must be aware they are speaking only of one form of cinema (or more likely several successive forms whose differences they choose to overlook).

Film history provides a challenge to rethinking film theory, arguing for the importance of using the recent visibility of film's multiple media environment as a moment for reflection and perhaps redefinition. In contemporary film theory, *a priori* proscriptions as well as *a posteriori* definitions that privilege only certain aspects of film have given way to approaches (like semiotics, psychoanalysis, or cognitivism) that seem to ignore or minimize differences between media in favor of broader cultural or biological conditions. My view of cinema as a braid made of various aspects rather than a unified essence with firm boundaries would seem to offer a further argument against the essentialist approach of classical film theory.

But we also increasingly need to offer thick descriptions of how media work, that is, phenomenological approaches that avoid defining media logically before examining the experience of their power. And while I maintain the various media work in concert and in contest rather than isolation, I also maintain that the formal properties of a specific medium convey vital aesthetic values and do not function as neutral channels for functional equivalents. An attempt to isolate a single essence of cinema remains not only an elusive task but possibly a reactionary project, yet most earlier attempts by theorists to define the essence of cinema can also be seen as attempts to elucidate the specific possibilities of cinema within a media environment that threatens to obscure or dismiss the particular powers that film holds. In other words, while the naming of a specific aspect of cinema as its essence must always risk being partial, it once had the polemical value of drawing attention to those aspects, allowing theorists to describe their power. This was true of the emphasis given to editing by the Soviet theorists in the twenties, who established that film could function not simply as a mode of mechanical reproduction but that it could create a poetics and a rhetoric that resembled a language. Partly as a corrective to this earlier claim that editing formed the essence of film as a creative form, the emphasis on film's relation to photography found after World War II in the work of Bazin, Siegfried Kracauer, and Stanley Cavell also performed this sort of vital function of attracting attention to a neglected aspect of cinema. In the current environment, probing the power of cinema, its affinities with and differentiations from other media, must again take a place on our agenda.

What really moves me . . .

Photography's relation to cinema comprises one of the central concepts in classical film theory's attempt to characterize the nature of cinema, and it remains a rich area for investigation. However, to offer alternative paradigms, I want to return to the generation of film theorists of the twenties, primarily the work of filmmaker theorists such as Sergei Eisenstein, Jean Epstein, and Germaine Dulac,[5] who wrote before the dominance of photography that marks the work of Bazin and Kracauer (and arguably Walter Benjamin). Although photography played a key role in film theories of the twenties as well (especially in the concept of *Photogénie*—the claim that film produced a unique image of the world more revelatory than other forms of imagery—championed by Epstein, Dulac, and Louis Delluc), I want to focus on the centrality of cinematic motion in the discussions of cinema's nature that marked this foundational period of classical film theory. Dulac declared in 1925, "*Le cinéma est l'art du mouvement et de la lumière*" [Cinema is the art of movement and light]. In her writings and her innovative abstract films, she envisioned a pure cinema uncontaminated by the other arts (although aspiring to the condition of music), which she described as "a visual symphony, a rhythm of arranged movements in which the shifting of a line or of a volume in a changing cadence creates emotion without any crystallization of ideas" (394).[6]

The concerns that preoccupied both the French Impressionist filmmakers and the Soviet montage theorists of the 1920s—cinematic rhythm as a product of editing, camera movement, and composition; the physical and emotional reactions of film spectators as shaped by visual rhythms; even the visual portrayal of mental states and emotions—were all linked to cinema's ability both to record and create motion.[7]

The role of motion in motion pictures initially appears to be something of a tautology. Rather than simply recycling this seemingly obvious assumption—that the movies *move*—theories of cinematic motion can help us reformulate a number of theoretical and aesthetic issues, including film spectatorship, film style, and the confluence of a variety of new media. Further, a renewed focus on cinematic motion directly addresses what I feel is one of the great scandals of film theory, which I previously mentioned as an aporia resulting from the dominance of a photographic understanding of cinema: the marginalization of animation.[8] Again and again, film theorists have made broad proclamations about the nature of cinema, and then quickly added, "excluding, of course, animation." Perhaps the boldest of new media theorists, Lev Manovich, has recently inverted this cinematic prejudice, claiming that the arrival of new digital media reveals cinema as simply an event within the history of animation. While I appreciate the polemic value of this proclamation, I would point out (as Manovich's archeology of the cinema also indicates) that, far from being a product of new media, animation has always been part of cinema and that only the over-emphasis given to the photographic basis of cinema in recent decades can explain in the neglect this historical and technological fact has encountered.

Stressing, as Manovich does, the nonreferential nature of animation implies that only photography can be referential—a major error that comes from a diminished view of the index. But if cinema should be approached as a form of animation, then cinematic motion rather than photographic imagery becomes primary. Spectatorship of cinematic motion raises new issues, such as the physical reactions that accompany the watching of motion. Considering this sensation of kinesthesia avoids the exclusive visual and ideological emphasis of most theories of spectatorship and acknowledges instead that film spectators are embodied beings rather than simply eyes and minds somehow suspended before the screen. The physiological basis of kinesthesia exceeds (or supplements) recent attempts to reintroduce emotional affect into spectator studies. We do not just *see* motion and we are not simply affected emotionally by its role within a plot; we *feel* it in our guts or throughout our bodies.

Theories of cinema's difference from the other arts that appeared in the twenties derived from the excitement that filmmakers of the teens and twenties experienced in their new-found ability to affect viewers physiologically as well as emotionally through such motion-based sequences as chase scenes involving galloping horses or racing locomotives, rapid camera movement, or accelerated rhythmic editing. While kinesthetic effects still play a vital role in contemporary action cinema, nowadays these devices of motion rarely generate theoretical speculation or close analysis. Nonetheless, critical attention to cinematic motion need not be limited to action films, however rich this mainstay of film practice may be. Motion, as Eisenstein's analysis of the methods of montage makes clear, can shape and trigger the process of both emotional involvement and intellectual engagement.[9] Analysis of motion in cinema should address a complete gamut of cinema, from the popular action film to the avant-garde work of filmmakers such as Stan Brakhage, Maya Deren, or Abigail Child.

In many ways these avant-garde filmmakers took up the legacy of Dulac's pure cinema and explored the possibilities of filmic motion outside of narrative development. Although Deren in particular stressed the importance of the photographic basis of film in her theoretical writings, she made the analysis and transformation of motion essential to all her films, especially her later films inspired by dance and ritualized bodily movement such as *Ritual in*

Transferred Time (1946), *Choreography for the Camera* (1945), *Meditation on Violence* (1948), and *The Very Eye of Night* (1958).[10] Brakhage's use of hand-held camera movement and complex editing patterns, as well as frenetic kinetic patterns created by painting directly on celluloid, produced patterns of motion that evoked a crisis of perception and lyrical absorption in the processes of vision.[11] Filmmaker Abigail Child's recent volume of writings on film and poetry is actually titled *This Is Called Moving*, testifying to her commitment to cinema as a means of deconstructing the dominant cultural forms of media through an intensification of cinematic perception that relies in part on new patterns of motion, often created through editing. As cinematic experience, motion can play an intense role both in sensations of intense diegetic absorption fostering involvement with dramatic, suspenseful plots à la Hitchcock and in kinetic abstraction, thrusting viewers into unfamiliar explorations of flexible coordinates of space and time.

Theoretical exploration of cinematic motion need not contradict, but can actually supplement, photographic theories of cinema such as those of Kracauer and Bazin. Kracauer in particular deals extensively with cinema's affinities with motion (discussing especially the cinematic possibilities of the chase, dancing, and the transformation from stillness to motion [41–45]) as a part of cinema's mission to capture and redeem physical reality. Even if movement never receives a detailed discussion as a theoretical issue within Bazin's work, he clearly sees camera movement as an essential tool within a realist style, as in his analysis of the extended track and pan in Jean Renoir's *The Crime of M. Lange* (*Jean* 43–46), or his description of the shot in Friedrich Murnau's *Tabu* in which "the entrance of a ship from left screen gives an immediate sense of destiny at work, so that Murnau has no need to cheat in any way on the uncompromising realism of a film whose settings are completely natural ("Evolution" 27 [p. 97, this volume]).[12]

Metz and cinematic movement

While Bazin and Kracauer saw motion as contributing to (or at least not contradicting) the inherent realism of the film medium, another film theorist went farther and made movement the cornerstone of cinema's impression of reality. I want to turn now to a neglected essay by a theorist usually associated with postclassical film theory, Christian Metz. "On the Impression of Reality in the Cinema," a short essay that directly superimposes the issues of motion and cinematic realism, opens the first volume of Metz's writings and is among Metz's presemiotic essays that the section heading characterizes as "phenomenological" (and that most theorists have zoomed past, treating as juvenilia).

Metz attempts in this essay to account for the "impression of reality" that the movies offer ("Films release a mechanism of affective and perceptual *participation* in the spectator [. . .] films have the *appeal* of a presence and of a proximity" [4–5]). While later apparatus theorists (including Metz himself in later writings) would see realism as a dangerous ideological illusion (while Bazin, on the contrary, would deepen cinematic realism into the possibility of grasping the mysteries of Being), in this early essay Metz simply attempts to give this psychological effect a phenomenological basis. Metz begins by contrasting media, claiming this degree of spectator participation and investment does not occur in still photography. Following Roland Barthes, Metz claims that still photography is condemned to a perceptual past tense ("This has been there"), while the movie spectator becomes absorbed by "a sense of 'There it is' " (6).

Metz locates the realistic effect of cinematic motion in its "participatory" effect. "Participation" seems to be a magic word in theories of realism that seek to overcome the dead ends encountered by correspondence theories of cinema. For Bazin, participation describes the relation between the photographic image and its object. Likewise, his description of the spectator's active role in the cinematic style that makes use of depth-of-field composition ("it is from [the spectator's] attention and his will that the meaning of the image in part derives" ["Evolution" 36 [p. 101, this volume]]) indicates an active participation by the viewer. For Metz, similarly, participation in the cinematic image is both "affective and perceptual," engendering "a very direct hold on perception," "an appeal of a presence and proximity" ("Impression" 4).

Metz points out that "participation, however, must be engendered" (5). What subtends this sense of immediacy and presence in the cinema? "An answer immediately suggests itself: It is *movement* [. . .] that produces the strong impression of reality" (7). While Metz admits other factors in film's effect on spectators, he ascribes a particular affect to the perception of motion, "a general law of psychology that movement is always perceived as real—unlike many other visual structures, such as volume, which is often very readily perceived as unreal" (8). In terms that seem to recall Bazin's claim that a photograph "is the object," Metz adds:

> The strict distinction between object and copy, however, dissolves on the threshold of motion. Because movement is never material but is always visual, to reproduce its appearance is to duplicate its reality. In truth, one cannot even "reproduce" a movement; one can only re-produce it in a second production belonging to the same order of reality, for the spectator as the first. [. . .] In the cinema the impression of reality is also the reality of the impression, the real presence of motion.
>
> (9)

Metz gives here a very compressed account of a complex issue, and his assumptions would take some time to isolate and explicate (such as exactly what the "reality of an impression" might be and the begging of the question through the assertion that cinema delivers "the real presence of motion"). But the relation he draws between motion and the impression of reality provides us with a radical course of thought. We experience motion on the screen in a different way than we look at still images, and this difference explains our participation in the film image, a sense of perceptual richness or immediate involvement in the image. Spectator participation in the moving image depends, Metz claims, on perceiving motion and the perceptual, cognitive, and physiological effects this triggers. The nature of cinematic motion, its continuous progress, its unfolding nature, would seem to demand the participation of a perceiver.

Although Metz does not refer directly to Henri Bergson's famous discussion of motion, I believe Bergson developed the most detailed description of the need to participate in motion in order to grasp it. Bergson claims, "In order to advance with the moving reality, you must replace yourself within it" (308).[13] For Bergson, discontinuous signs, such as language or ideas, cannot grasp the continuous flow of movement, but must conceive of it as a series of successive static instants, or positions. Only motion, one can assume, is able to convey motion. Therefore, to perceive motion, rather than represent it statically in a manner that destroys its essence, one must participate in the motion itself. Of course, analysis provides a means of conceptual understanding, and Bergson actually refers to our tendency to conceive of motion through a series of static images—a distortion he claims our habits of mind and language demand of us—as "cinematographic." Great confusion (which I feel Deleuze increases rather than dispels) comes if we do not realize that the analytical aspect of the cinematograph that Bergson took as his model for this tendency to conceive of motion in terms of static instants derives from the *film strip*, in which motion is analyzed into a succession of frames, not the *projected image* on the screen, in which synthetic motion is recreated.

Cinema, the projected moving image, demands that we participate in the movement we perceive. Analysis of perceiving motion can only offer some insights into the way the moving image exceeds our contemplation of a static image. Motion always has a projective aspect, a progressive movement in a direction, and therefore invokes possibility and a future. Of course, we can project these states into a static image, but with an actually moving image we are swept along with the motion itself. Rather than imagining previous or anterior states, we could say that through a moving image, the progress of motion is projected onto us. Undergirded by the kinesthetic effects of cinematic motion, I believe "participation" properly describes the increased sense of involvement with the cinematic image, a sense of presence that could be described as an impression of reality.

Metz claims that the motion we see in a film is real, not a representation, a claim I take to be close to Bergson's discussion of the way movement cannot be derived simply from a static presentation of successive points. According to Metz, what we see when we see a moving image on the screen should not be described as a "picture" of motion, but instead as an experience of seeing something truly moving. In terms of a visual experience of motion, therefore, no difference exists between watching a film of a ball rolling down a hill, say, and seeing an actual ball rolling down a hill. One might object to this identification of motion and its visual sensation by pointing out that our sensation of motion (kinesthesia) does not depend entirely on vision but on a range of bodily sensations. But I believe Metz could respond to this in two ways. First, the most extreme sort of kinesthesia primarily refers to the sensation of ourselves moving bodily, traversing space, not simply watching a moving object. Insofar as we do experience kinesthesia when we observe a moving object other than ourselves, the same sensations seem to occur when we watch a moving object in a film. Thus, perceiving motion in the cinema, while triggered by visual perception, need not be restricted to visual effects. Clearly, cinema cannot move us, as viewers, physically (we don't, for instance, leave our seats or get transported to another place, even if we have a sensation of ourselves moving as we watch films in which the camera moves through space). However, while acknowledging that Metz can only claim that cinema possesses visual motion, not literal movement through space—a change of place—the fact remains that even visual motion, such as camera movement, doesn't only affect us visually but does produce the physiological effect of kinesthesia.

Metz questions whether there could be a "portrayal of motion" that did not actually involve motion, a representation parallel, say, to the use of perspective drawing to render volumes. In a way, it is not hard to conceive of such a portrayal. A diagram conveying the trajectory of a moving object, such as a graph of the parabola described by a baseball hit by David Ortiz, could be said to portray motion. The speed lines used by comic book artists to indicate a running figure also portray the idea of motion visually but in static form. Indeed, the chronophotographs of Étienne-Jules Marey, with their composite and successive figures tracing the path of human movement, or the blurred image of simple actions like turning a head found in the photo-dynamist photographs of Futurist Anton Guilio Bragaglia, all portray motion without actually moving. But that is the point, precisely. These diagrammatic portrayals of motion strike us very differently from actual motion pictures. Such portrayals of motion recall Bergson's descriptions of attempts to generate a sense of motion from tracing a pattern of static points or positions, which miss the continuous sweep of motion. In contrast to these diagrams of the successive phases of motion or indications of its pathways, we could say, perhaps now with even more clarity, that cinema shows us motion, not its portrayal.

Ultimately, I think there is little question that phenomenologically we see movement on the screen, not a "portrayal" of movement. But what does it mean to say the movement is "real"? As I understand Metz's claim, it does not at all commit us to the nonsensical position that we take the cinema image for reality, that we are involved in a hallucination or "illusion" of reality that could cause us to contemplate walking into the screen, or interacting physically with the fictional events we see portrayed. In the cinema, we are dealing with realism, not "reality." As Metz makes clear, "on the one hand, there is the impression of reality; on the other, the perception of reality" (13). Theater, for instance, makes use of real materials, actual people and things, to create a fiction world. Cinema works with images that possess an impression of reality, not its materiality. This distinction is crucial.

The realistic motion of fantasy

Metz's description of cinematic motion supplies at least part of (and probably a central part of) an alternative theory of the realistic effect of the cinema (one I find much more compelling and flexible than the ideological explanation of psychological regression offered by Jean-Louis Baudry and, in a sense, the later Metz of *The Imaginary Signifier*). But we should keep in mind that this is a theory of the impression of reality (based, as he says, on the reality of the impression), rather than an argument for a realist aesthetic such as that offered by Bazin or Kracauer. Part of the flexibility of Metz's theory of the reality of cinematic motion lies in its adaptability to a range of cinematic styles. As Metz indicates, the "feeling of credibility" film offers "operates on us in films of the unusual and of the marvelous, as well as in those that are 'realistic' " ("Impression" 8). But his description also shows that movement can be an important factor in describing a realist style (one need only think of the role of camera movement in Welles and Rossellini, undertheorized by Bazin, or in Renoir, which Bazin describes beautifully). But the fantastic possibilities of motion, or rather its role in rendering the fantastic believable, and I would say visceral, shows the mercurial role motion can play in film spectatorship and film style.

It is this mercurial, protean, indeed *mobile* nature of cinematic motion that endows it with power as a concept for film theory and analysis. Not only does the concept of cinematic movement unite photographic-based films and traditional animated films (not to mention the hybrid synthesis of photographic and animation techniques that Computer Generated Images represents), movement displays a flexibility that avoids the proscriptive nature of much of classical film theory.[14] While the formal aspects of cinematic movement (and the range of ways it can be used, or even the number of aspects of cinematic motion possible) make it an important tool for aesthetic analysis (and even useful in a polemical argument like Dulac's or Bazin's for a particular style of film), nothing restricts movement to a single style.

The impression of reality that cinematic movement carries can underwrite a realist film style (think of the use of hand-held camera movement in the films of the Dogma 95 movement), a highly artificial fantasy dependent on special effects (the importance of kinesis in the *Star Wars* films), or an abstract visual symphony (animator Oskar Fischinger). Metz describes the role of the impression of reality enabled by cinematic motion as "to inject the reality of motion into the unreality of the image and thus to render the world of imagination more real than it had ever been" (15). Like Mercury, winged messenger of the gods, cinematic motion crosses the boundaries between heaven and earth, between the embodied senses and flights of fancy, not simply playing the whole gamut of film style but contaminating one with the other, endowing the fantastic with the realistic impression of visual motion.

The extraordinary writings Sergei Eisenstein produced in the 1930s on the animated films of Walt Disney accent this double valence of movement, tending not only toward realism but also, as the animated film and new digital processes demonstrate, toward fantasy.

Movement in the cinema not only generates the visual sense of realism that Metz describes, but bodily sensations of movement can engage spectator fantasy through perceptual and physical participation. Thus, movement created by animation, freed from photographic reference, can endow otherwise "impossible" motion and transformations with the immediacy of perception that Metz claims movement entails. In some ways this returns us to Dulac's concept of a pure cinema based entirely on the motion of forms (and the forms of motion). In his writings on Disney, Eisenstein focuses on the possibility of the animated line to invoke precisely this aspect of motion, which he calls "plasmaticness" and defines as "a rejection of once-and-forever allotted form, freedom from ossification, the ability to dynamically assume any form" (27). Rather than simply endowing familiar forms with the solidity and credibility that Metz describes, movement can extend beyond familiarity to fantasy and imagination, creating the impossible bodies that throng the works of animation, from the early cartoons of Emile Cohl to the digital manipulation of Gollum in *The Lord of the Rings*.[15] While flaunting the rules of physical resemblance, such animation need not remain totally divorced from any reference to our lived world. As I once heard philosopher Arthur Danto explain, the cartoon body can reveal primal phenomenological relations we have to our physical existence, our sense of grasping, stretching, exulting.[16] For Eisenstein, this plasmatic quality invokes

> [a] lost changeability, fluidity, suddenness of formations—that's the "subtext" brought to the viewer who lacks all this by these seemingly strange traits which permeate folktales, cartoons, the spineless circus performer and the seemingly groundless scattering of extremities in Disney's drawings.
>
> (21)

Motion therefore need not be realistic to have a "realistic" effect, that is, to invite the empathic participation, both imaginative and physiological, of viewers. Eisenstein's discussion of motion as a force that does not simply propel forms but actually creates them not only refers back to the theories of Bergson but makes clear the multiple nature of the participation that motion invokes, from the perceptual identity described by Metz to the realm of anticipation, speculation, and imagination of the possibly transforming aspects of line described by Eisenstein. Unlike the literalness of pointing to an actual individual that a narrow adherence to the diminished indexical theory of film and photography forces on us, as Metz emphasizes, the cinematic impression of reality affects the diegesis, the fictional world created by the film, and thus escapes the straitjacket of exclusive correspondence or reference to any preexisting reality. Metz's concept of cinematic movement's "novel power to convince [. . .] was all to the advantage of the imagination" ("Impression" 14).

The realist claim offered for cinema's indexical quality, based in still photography, actually operates in a diametrically different direction than the role Metz outlines for cinematic movement in the medium's impression of reality. An indexical argument, as it has been developed, based in the photographic trace, points the image back into the past, to a preexisting object or event whose traces could only testify to its having already been. Metz's concept of the impression of reality moves in the opposite direction, toward a sensation of the present and of presence. The indexical argument can be invoked most clearly (and usefully) for films used as historical evidence. It remains unclear, however, how the index functions within a fiction film, where we are dealing with a diegesis, a fictional world, rather than a reference to a reality. Laura Mulvey, in her extremely important discussion of indexicality in film, has pointed out how it relates to the phenomenon of the Star, clearly an existing person beyond the fictional character he or she plays and therefore a reference outside the film's diegesis.[17] The effect of an index in guaranteeing the actual existence of its reference depends on the one who makes this connection invoking a technical knowledge of photography, understanding the effect of light on the sensitive film. Metz's cinematic impression of reality depends on "forgetting" (that is, on distracting the viewer's attention away from—not literally repressing the knowledge of) the technical process of filming in favor of an experience of the fictional world as present. As he claims, "The movie spectator is absorbed, not by a 'has been there' but by a sense of 'There it is' " (6).

Even if the indexical claim for cinema is granted, I am not sure it really supplies the basis for a realist aesthetic. Although Bazin invokes something that sounds like an index in his description of the ontology of the photographic image, maintaining the exact congruence of his claims with a strictly indexical claim seems fraught with difficulty. Rather than an argument about signs, Bazin's ontology of the photographic and filmic image seems to assert a nearly magical sense of the presence delivered by the photographic image. In any case, at best, the index would only function as one aspect of Bazin's realist aesthetic.[18] Once again, I am not claiming no use exists for the index in theories of film and photography, but simply that it has been entrusted with tasks it cannot fulfill and that reading it back into classical realist theories of the cinema probably obscures as much as it explains.

But I would also have to admit that "motion," even when specified as "cinematic motion," probably includes multiple aspects, not just one perceptible factor. The extreme spectator involvement that movement can generate needs further study, both in terms of perceptual and cognitive processes (which I think call for both experimental and phenomenological analysis) and in relation to broader aesthetic styles. Metz's description is based on the classical fiction film: what role does motion play in nonclassical films? (I have, of course, argued for its vital role in avant-garde film.) I am offering only a prolegomena to a larger investigation; my comments here aspire to be provocative rather than definitive. Motion, I am arguing, needs to be taken more seriously in our exploration of the nature of film and our account of how film style functions. At the same time, giving new importance to movement (or restoring it) builds a strong bridge between cinema and the new media that some view as cinema's successors. Like the animated line Germaine Dulac described, whose movement directly creates an emotion, motion involves both transformation and continuity (film history involves both the transformation of its central medium and a recognition of an ever-shifting continuity, a trajectory, to this transformation). As an art of motion, cinema has affinities to other media: dance, action painting, instantaneous photography, kinetic sculpture. But it also possesses its own trajectory, one in which I suspect the new media of motion arts will also find a place, or at least an affinity.

Notes

1   In a series of carefully argued and provocative articles, historian and theorist of photography Joel Snyder has questioned the usefulness of the index argument in describing photography.

2   For a recent reevaluation of Bazin, once dismissed as a naive realist, one could cite Philip Rosen, esp. 1–42.

3   I use here the translation proposed by Daniel Morgan in his essay "Rethinking Bazin: Ontology and Realist Aesthetics," which revises the widely available translation by Hugh Gray. Gray translates this as "a decal or transfer" ("Ontology" 14 [p. 92, this volume]). The original French is "transfert de réalité de la chose sur la reproduction" and "un décalique approximatif" ("Ontologie" 16). Unless otherwise noted, translations are Gray's.

4   Again, this is Morgan's revised translation (450 [p. 108, this volume]). Gray has: "The photographic image is the object itself, the object freed from the conditions of time and space that govern it. No matter how fuzzy, distorted, or discolored, no matter how lacking in documentary value the image may be, it shares, by virtue of the very process of its becoming, the being of the model of which it is the reproduction; it is the model" (14 [p. 92, this volume]). Morgan discusses the misinterpretation

inherent in Gray's addition of the phrase "and space" (absent in Bazin) in "Rethinking Bazin." The original French reads "cet objet lui-même, mais libéré des contingences temporelles. L'image peut être floue, déformée, décolorée, sans valeur documentaire, elle procède par sa genèse de l'ontologie du modèle; elle est le modèle" ("Ontologie" 16).

5   Key essays by Dulac and Epstein can be found in Abel. An excellent selection of Eisenstein's essays is in Leyda.

6   The French original appears in Dulac, *Écrits* 98–105.

7   The recuperation of motion in contemporary film theory will immediately evoke Deleuze's two-volume philosophical work *Cinema: The Movement-Image* and *Cinema: The Time-Image*. There is much to learn from this work, although its background in and understanding of itself as an essay in philosophy, rather than film theory or history, should be taken seriously. I do not want to undertake a full-scale discussion of Deleuze's work here, since I feel that will pull us away from the issue of movement to a consideration of Deleuze's methods, terms, and assumptions. As Deleuze announces about his work in his preface, "This is not a history of the cinema. It is a taxonomy, an attempt at the classification of images and signs" (1: xiv). Although a number of Deleuze's taxonomic distinctions provide insights into cinematic motion, an in-depth discussion of them would lead us astray from this issue. I want instead to consider the discussion of cinematic motion that preceded Deleuze, emerging primarily from film practice and theory. Most of the issues I want to raise here, while having a relation to Deleuze, remain marginal to his discussions, while they are central to the earlier theorists I will refer to. The best treatment of Deleuze's book, fully informed of the history and theory of film, is by Rodowick.

8   Notably, Deleuze devotes no real discussion to animation.

9   A key essay in this regard by Eisenstein would be "Methods of Montage."

10   See also *Essential Deren*.

11   A fine collection of Brakhage's writing is *Essential Brakhage*, edited by Bruce R. McPherson. See also the discussion of Brakhage in Sitney, *Visionary Films*, and his work in progress "Eyes Upside Down."

12   Morgan's detailed discussion of the camera movement in Rossellini's *Voyage to Italy* in "Rethinking Bazin" shows one way camera movement can function within Bazin's realist aesthetic. See pages 465–68 [pp. 116–18, this volume].

13   The discussion of motion extends over pages 297–314.

14   Would a focus on movement entail a proscriptive definition that all films must include motion? Insofar as we are referring to the movement of the apparatus, the film traveling through the projector gate, this might be tautological. Duration as a measure of this motion of the film certainly provides the sine qua non for cinematic motion and all cinema, technically defined. However, I think we can certainly conceive of films that exclude motion, made entirely of still images. Interestingly, many films that use still images seem to do so to comment on movement. Clearly, the dialectical relation between stillness and movement provides one of the richest uses of motion in film. But I think it would be an essentialist mistake to assume a film could not avoid cinematic motion, even if the examples of such are very rare and possibly debatable.

15   See my discussion of Gollum and CGI-generated characters in "Gollum and Golem: Special Effects and the Technology of Artificial Bodies."

16   Danto discussed this more than a decade ago at the Columbia Film Seminar in New York City. He specifically referred, as I recall, to the way Mickey Mouse and other cartoon characters often have fewer than five fingers but cogently convey the role of the hand in grasping. If my memory is faulty, I apologize to Mr. Danto (with humble admiration).

17   See esp. 54–66.

18   Kracauer's argument for the realist mission of cinema, although also based in its photographic legacy, most certainly exceeds, if it implies at all, the index.

References

Abel, Richard. *French Film Theory and Criticism: 1907–39, A History/Anthology.* 2 vols. Princeton, NJ: Princeton UP, 1988.

Baudry, Jean-Louis. "The Apparatus: Metapsychological Approaches to the Impression of Reality in the Cinema." *Narrative, Apparatus, Ideology.* Ed. Philip Rosen. New York: Columbia up, 1986. 690–707.

Bazin, Andre. "Evolution." *What Is Cinema?* 1: 23–41.

——— . *Jean Renoir.* New York: Da Capo, 1992.

——— . "Ontologie de l'image photographique." *Qu'est-ce que le Cinéma? Vol. 1. Ontologie et langage.* Paris: Cerf, 1958. 11–19.

——— . "The Ontology of the Photographic Image." *What Is Cinema?* 1: 9–16.

——— . "Theater and Cinema." *What Is Cinema?* 1: 76–124.

——— . *What Is Cinema?* 2 vols. Ed. and trans. Hugh Gray. Berkeley: U of California P, 1967.

Bergson, Henri. *Creative Evolution.* Trans. Arthur Mitchell. Lanham: UP of America, 1983.

Brakhage, Stan. *Essential Brakhage: Selected Writings on Filmmaking.* Ed. Bruce R. McPherson. Kingston, New York: Documentext, 2001.

——— . "Eyes Upside Down." Unpublished ms.

Carroll, Noël. *Philosophical Problems of Classical Film Theory.* Princeton, NJ: Princeton UP, 1988.

Cavell, Stanley. *The World Viewed: Reflections on the Ontology of Film.* Cambridge, MA: Harvard UP, 1979.

Chardère, Bernard. *Le Roman des lumières.* Paris: Gallimard, 1995.

Child, Abigail. *This Is Called Moving: A Critical Poetics of Film.* Tuscaloosa: U of Alabama P, 2005.

Deleuze, Gilles. *Cinema 1: The Movement-Image.* Trans. Hugh Tomlinson and Barbara Habberjam. Minneapolis: U of Minnesota P, 1986.

——— . *Cinema 2: The Time-Image.* Trans. Hugh Tomlinson and Barbara Habberjam. Minneapolis: U of Minnesota P, 1989.

Deren, Maya. *Essential Deren: Collected Writings on Film.* Ed. Bruce R. McPherson. Kingston, New York: Documentext, 2005.

Dulac, Germaine. "Aesthetics, Obstacles, Integral Cinegraphie." Trans. Stuart Liebman. Abel 1: 394.

——— . *Écrits sur le cinema, 1919–37.* Ed. Prosper Hillairet. Paris: Paris Expérimental, 1994. 98–105.

Eisenstein, Sergei. *Eisenstein on Disney.* Ed. and Trans. Jay Leyda. London: Methuen, 1988.

——— . *Film Form: Essays in Film Theory.* Ed. and Trans. Jay Leyda. New York: Harcourt, 1949.

——— . "Methods of Montage." *Film Form* 72–83.

Gunning, Tom. "Gollum and Golem: Special Effects and the Technology of Artificial Bodies." Eds. Ernest Mathijs and Murray Pomerance. *From Hobbits to Hollywood: Essays on Peter Jackson's Lord of the Rings.* Amsterdam: Rodopi, 2006.

——— . "What's the Point of an Index? Or Faking Photographs." *Still Moving.* Ed. Karen Beckman and Jean Ma. Durham, NC: Duke UP, forthcoming.

Kracauer, Siegfried. *Theory of Film: The Redemption of Physical Reality.* Princeton, NJ: Princeton UP, 1960.

Manovich, Lev. *The Language of New Media.* Cambridge, MA: MIT P, 2001.

Metz, Christian. *The Imaginary Signifier: Psychoanalysis and Cinema.* Trans. Celia Britton, Annwyl Williams, Ben Brewster, and Alfred Guzzetti. Bloomington: U of Indiana P, 1982.

——— . "On the Impression of Reality in the Cinema." *Film Language: A Semiotics of the Cinema.* Trans. Michael Taylor. New York: Oxford UP, 1974. 315.

Morgan, Daniel. "Rethinking Bazin: Ontology and Realist Aesthetics." *Critical Inquiry* 32 (2006): 441–81.

Mulvey, Laura. *Death 24x a Second: Stillness and the Moving Image.* London: Reaktion, 2006.

Peirce, Charles Sanders. *Philosophical Writings of Peirce.* Ed. Justus Buchler. New York: Dover, 1955.

——— . "Prolegomena to an Apology for Pragmaticism." *Peirce on Signs.* Ed. James Hoopes. Chapel Hill: U of North Carolina P, 1991. 249–52.

Rodowick, D.N. *Gilles Deleuze's Time Machine.* Durham, NC: Duke UP, 1997.

Rosen, Philip. *Change Mummified: Cinema, Historicity, Theory.* Minneapolis: U of Minnesota P, 2001.

Sitney, P. Adams. *Visionary Films: The American Avant-Garde, 1943–2000.* New York: Oxford UP, 2001.

Snyder, Joel. "Res Ipsa Books Loquitur." *Things That Talk: Object Lessons from Art and Science.* Ed. Lorraine Daston. New York: Zone, 2004. 195–222.

——— . "Picturing Vision." *Critical Inquiry* 6 (1980): 499–526.

——— . "Pointless." *Photography Theory.* Ed. James Elkins. New York: Routledge, 2006. 369–400.

——— . "Visualization and Visibility." *Picturing Science, Producing Art.* Ed. Peter Galison and Caroline Jones. London: Reaktion, 1998. 379–400.

Snyder, Joel, and Neil Walsh Allen. "Photography, Vision, and Representation." *Critical Inquiry* 2 (1975): 143–69.

Wollen, Peter. "The Semiology of the Cinema." *Signs and Meaning in the Cinema.* Bloomington: U of Indiana P, 1969. 116–54.

Chapter 19

Anne Friedberg

THE END OF CINEMA: MULTIMEDIA AND TECHNOLOGICAL CHANGE

THE SCREEN FEATURED HERE [see the original] faces its audience: the regimented rows of a computer keyboard, each key in the fixed position of a cinema spectator. The image—of the transformative moment in *Metropolis* when the metallic robot Maria is infused with the life-force of electricity—suggests another moment of transformation. The cinema screen has been replaced by its digital other, the computer screen.

As this millennium draws to an end, the cinema—a popular form of entertainment for almost a century—has been dramatically transformed. It has become embedded in—or perhaps lost in—the new technologies that surround it. One thing is clear: we can note it in the symptomatic discourse, inflected with the atomic terms of "media fusion" or "convergence" or the pluralist inclusiveness of "multimedia"—the differences between the media of movies, television, and computers are rapidly diminishing. This is true both for technologies of production (that is, film is commonly edited on video; video is transferred to film; computer graphics and computer-generated animation are used routinely in both film and television production) and for technologies of reception and display (that is, we can watch movies in digitized formats on our computer screens or in video formats on our television screens). The movie screen, the home television screen, and the computer screen retain their separate locations, yet the types of images you see on each of them are losing their medium-based specificity.

When Marshall McLuhan proclaimed "the medium is the message" in 1964, this sound-bite aphorism drew attention not only to the *media*tion that the media incurred but also to the specificity of each separate medium. McLuhan inveighed against content-based studies: "The 'content' of any medium," McLuhan wrote, "blinds us to the characteristics of the medium." Instead, he prescribed an account of the effects—"the change of scale or pace or pattern"—that each particular medium might produce. McLuhan analyzed the interrelated-ness of media in an evolutionary scheme ("The content of any medium is always another medium"), and he insisted that each new medium would "institute new ratios, not only among our private senses, but among themselves, when they interact among themselves" (McLuhan, 1964: 8–9, 53). In the new media environment of the 1990s, the media of radio, telephone, television, movies, computer not only interact among themselves, but their cross-purposed interactions pose new questions about their technological specificities. German media theorist Friedrich Kittler anticipated this convergence of media when he wrote: "The general digitalization of information and channels erases the difference between individual media" (1986: 102). Yet Kittler predicted that the installation of fiber-optic cable was the technology that would turn film, music and phone-calls into a "single medium." Given the suggested reconfiguration of screens and their spectators in the image of *Metropolis* on the computer monitor figured here [see original], we must now ask: how have the material differences between cinematic, televisual, and computer media been altered as *digital* technologies transform them?

Nicholas Negroponte answers this question with a counter-polemical aphorism, turning McLuhan's "the medium is the message" on its head. "The medium is not the message in the digital world," declares Negroponte. "It is an embodiment of it. A message might have several embodiments automatically derivable from the same data" (1995: 71). Digital imaging, delivery, and display effectively erase the "messages" implicit in the source "medium." The digitized *Metropolis* illustrates how almost all of our assumptions about the cinema have changed: its image is digital, not photographically based, its screen format is small and not projection-based, its implied interactivity turns the spectator into a "user."

The following chapter addresses two related issues. The first part examines a number of technologies introduced in the 1970s and 1980s which began to erode the historical differences between television and film. The video cassette recorder, the television remote control, and the growth of cable television significantly altered the terms of both televisual and cinematic viewing. As I will argue, these technologies led to a convergence of film and television technology that began without fiber-optic cable, occurred before the digitalization of imagery, and preceded the advent of the home computer.

Secondly, as a result of these initial reconfigurations and as our visual field has been transformed by newer technologies, the field of "film studies" finds itself at a transitional moment. We must add computer screens (and digital technologies), television screens (and interactive video formats) to our conceptualization (both historical and theoretical) of the cinema and its screens. *Screens* are now "display and delivery" formats—variable in versions of projection screen, television screen, computer screen, or headset device. *Film* is a "storage" medium—variable in versions of video, computer disks, compact discs (CDs), high-density compact video-disc players (DVDs), databanks, on-line servers. *Spectators* are "users" with an "interface"—variable in versions of remotes, mice, keyboards, touch screens, joysticks, goggles, and gloves and body suits. Just as the chemically based "analog" images of photography have been displaced by computer-enhanced digital images, the apparatus we came to know as "the cinema" is being displaced by systems of circulation and transmission which abolish the projection screen and begin to link the video screens of the computer and television with the dialogic interactivity of the telephone. Multimedia home stations combining telephone, television, and computer (what will we call these: tele-puters? image-phones?) will further reduce the technical differentiation of film, television, and the computer.

It now seems that a singular history of "the film" without its dovetailing conspirators— the telephone, the radio, the television, the computer—provides a too-narrowly constructed geneology. Once thought to be the province of "information science" and not part of the study of "visual culture," histories of the telephone and the computer become significant tributaries in the converging multimedia stream.[1] In this way, perhaps, Charles Babbage's 1832 "analytical engine" could be measured as as significant in the contemporary remaking of visual imagery as Joseph Plateau's 1832 phenakistiscope. Babbage's "analytical engine"—a mechanical precursor to modern digital computing—could store a number, retrieve it, modify it, and then store it in another location. Plateau's phenakistiscope—an optical toy now considered a key pre-cinematic apparatus—demonstrated how movements analyzed into their static components could be perceived as moving images when perceived through the slits of a spinning disc. The "analytical engine" turned information into discrete, manipulable units; the phenakistiscope turned images into discrete and manipulable units. The historical coincidence between these two devices only emerges as significant in light of recent technologies of digital imaging and display.

The new media environment

But there were a number of pre-digital technologies that significantly changed our concept of film-going and television-viewing before the digital "revolution." The video cassette recorder (VCR), cable television, and the television remote control have prepared us for the advent of computer screens with wired (Internet) connections—for interactive "usage" instead of passive spectatorship—and continue to produce profound changes to our sense of temporality.[2] If television's innate "liveness"—its ability to collapse the time of an event with the time of its transmission—was one of its key apparatical distinctions from the movies, the VCR collapsed these separations. Television's mode of absolute presence, as Jane Feuer has eloquently argued, became a key determinant of televisual aesthetics (1983: 12–22). The VCR demolished the aura of live television and the broadcast event, freeing the television screen from its servitude to the metaphysics of presence. Whereas the cinematic apparatus had the potential for re-seeing a film built into its means of mechanical reproduction, television had to await the advent of videotape recording and playback features of the VCR. The VCR introduced the potential to "time-shift" (to view what you want, when you want), to "zip" (to fast-forward and/or reverse the video cassette, effectively skipping portions of the taped program (with televised programming, this usually meant commercials)), and also made it easier to re-see a film or program over (and over) again. With the VCR, both the cinematic and the televisual past became more easily accessible and interminably recyclable.

Cable television not only changed the quality of and criteria for television reception, but expanded its offerings with increased channel choice, effectively breaking the monopolies of network broadcasting. In turn, the television remote control allowed the viewer instantaneously to change televised channels (to "zap"), to fast-forward and/or reverse the video cassette (to "zip"), to switch between live and taped programming, and to eliminate the lure or distraction of television's sound (to "mute"). As a result of these technologies, the premises of cinema spectatorship and televisual viewing changed radically.[3]

The VCR

The time-shift machine

As the VCR became widely available in the mid-1980s, the number of VCR households grew in a parallel "penetration" of the American home to the growth of television in the 1950s. In 1952 fewer than 250,000 sets were owned by American households; by 1960, 80 percent of American homes had television; by 1993 there were 93.1 million television households, with a near total saturation, in the high 90 percent. The marketing of the VCR followed this curve. While there were a variety of video cassette systems marketed in the 1970s, it was not until the early 1980s that the VCR became a common household appliance. In 1985, only 20 percent of American households had VCRs; in 1989 the figure was 65.5 percent.

But by 1993 the total reached 80 percent, and by 1997, 88 percent of American homes had VCRs (Lipton, 1991; Nielsen, 1996).

A videotape machine with the capacity for recording and playback on video cassettes, the VCR not only solved broadcast television's reception difficulties, but also freed the television viewer from its programming limitations and rigid timetable. In 1970, there were six competing "cassette TV" systems in development, set for target marketing dates in mid-1971 or early 1972. [Five of these—Avco, Sony, Ampex, Magnavox, Norelco—relied on videotape. CBS' EVR—Electronic Video Recording—used a photographic film which was scanned and converted to a television signal (Kern, 1970: 46–55).] The Sony Betamax, introduced in 1975, used ½ inch videotape in a cassette format that could record for an hour; and a competing ½ inch format VHS (Video Home System) was introduced in 1976. The VHS format initially had the advantage of recording for up to two hours. Since cassette recorders were first used primarily for recording broadcast feature films, the two-hour cassette made a difference in the competitive market (Lardner, 1987).

VCRs were first used for recording off the air, but through the 1980s as more and more pre-recorded video cassettes became available, a rental market (an entirely new industry) developed for movies, exercise videos, educational, and self-help material. Hence, the VCR—originally intended by its marketers to be used as a recording and "time-shifting" device—became essentially a playback device. Both formats—Betamax and VHS—quickly adopted (1) pause buttons so that the viewer could eliminate commercials while recording; (2) timers that allowed the viewer to record while not at home; (3) devices that allowed the viewer to view one program while taping another; and (4) still frame and variable-speed playback features. The sales of VCRs soared beyond expectations.[4] As the major film studios sold video rights to their archives, slowly, through the 1980s, most films—even foreign— were transferred to video.

There was only a small cloud over the steamrolling success of the VCR in the market-place: the issue of copyright. In 1976, Universal and Disney sued the Sony Corporation claiming that any machine that could record, hence "copy," copyrighted material was in violation of basic copyright laws and should not be manufactured. In 1979, a federal judge sided with Sony, declaring that recording and viewing television program material in the home were "fair use." An appeals court reversed this decision, and it was not until a 1984 Supreme Court decision ruled that home taping does not violate copyright laws that the machine itself was in the clear.[5]

As the VCR became a fixture in American living rooms, its penetration of the global market also proceeded apace. A 1983 study showed that VCR penetration of the Third World exceeded television growth. VCRs were used for viewing videotapes, especially of banned material: Indian films in Pakistan and Bangladesh, Western films in Eastern Europe, pornography everywhere. VCRs became an easy "open door" for cultural contraband— material kept out of cinemas and off television but available for viewing on this playback box. Video cassettes and VCRs also penetrated countries bereft of television; offering uncensored mass entertainment by supplying the immediacy of television without its political impedi-ments. [Statistics from 1982 demonstrated some interesting things about cross-cultural usage: 92 percent of television homes in Kuwait had VCRs; 82 percent in Panama, 70 percent in Oman, 43 percent in Bahrain, whereas in 1984, in France the figure was 10 percent, Japan 26 percent, Singapore 62 percent, United Arab Emirates 75 percent, UK 30 percent (Ganley and Ganley, 1987).]

Despite the initial fear of theater owners and film producers that VCRs would detract from their box-office receipts, the statistical evidence from the 1980s did not support this fear: movie-goers attended in record numbers and still rented videos. While 40 percent of feature-film viewing is done on VCRs, movie attendance is still strong; as if the use of VCRs actually stimulates movie-orientated activity. Nielsen reports that movie rentals cut into only a small percentage of total television use (Nielsen, 1996). So, if the statisticians have it right, television use has not decreased, movie attendance has not decreased, while VCR usage has increased. This would lead us to conclude that in the past 15 years we have spent more time watching television and films and videotapes of both.

A new temporality: when will then be now? Soon!

Now that "time" is so easily electronically "deferred" or "shifted" one can ask: Has the VCR produced a new temporality, one that has dramatically affected our concept of history and our access to the past? The VCR treats films or videotapes as objects of knowledge to be explored, investigated, deconstructed as if they were events of the past to be studied.[6] The 1987 film *Spaceballs* (Mel Brooks, 1987) parodies some of the changes in movie reception produced by the VCR and the rental marketing of video cassettes. In the film, Dark Helmet (Rick Moranis) and his commander, Colonel Sanders, chase an intergalactic "winnebago" driven by a space-bum-for-hire Lone Star (Bill Pullman) and his canine sidekick, Barf (John Candy). Dark Helmet and Colonel Sanders stand by the spaceship's video scanner screen when Sanders introduces a "new breakthrough in video marketing—instant cassettes." The riff between Helmet and Sanders toys with the new temporality produced by the video cassette: "Prepare to fast-forward . . . go past this part . . . the part on ridiculous speed." When they suddenly stop the tape at a frame that matches the moment they are in, they do a double take between the screen and each other:

> "When does this happen? Then?"
> "Now."
> "When will then be now?"
> "Soon!"

The jumbled tenses of present and past here form a parody on the very paradoxes of televisual presence ("Now") and the VCR's deeper challenges to time and memory ("When will then be now?" "Soon!").

Paul Virilio has described the new temporality made possible by the VCR:

> The machine, the VCR, allows man [sic] to organize a time which is not his own, *a deferred time*, a time which is somewhere else—and to capture it . . . The VCR . . . creates two days: a reserve day which can replace the ordinary day, the lived day.
>
> (1988)

For Virilio, the VCR produces a time that is shifted, borrowed, made asynchronous. The VCR is like an electronic melatonin, resetting the viewer's internal clock to a chosen moment from the past.

While these new attributes of televisual time often lead to liberatory rhetoric about the VCR—freeing its viewers from the tyranny of standard time and broadcast choices with button-pushing empowerment—there remain limits to the choices available. Richard Dienst forecloses any emancipatory potential of this new temporality, reminding us that the privilege of individual prerogative ultimately profits "paranational . . . conglomerates":

> VCRS do nothing but extend the range of still and automatic time, offering an additional loop of flexibility in the circulation of images, bringing new speeds

and greater turnover . . . video allows people to operate another series of switches, a privilege bought with more time, money and subjective attachment . . . who profits from this new and immense expansion in the volume of overall televisual time? . . . paranational electronic manufacturers and entertainment conglomerates.

(1994: 165–66)

And now that the VCR has become a well-entrenched consumer durable, electronics companies are trying to supplant it with laser disc technology, hoping that the DVD player will become the next VCR, just as audio CD machines have supplanted record players in the past decade (Bauman and Harmon, 1994). DVD technology offers some advantages: as with the larger laser disc formats, one can access a different section of the disc in a near instant; there is no fast-forwarding or rewinding required. But owing to more sophisticated image compression algorithms, a DVD, unlike larger laser discs and CD-ROM technology, can hold an entire feature film on a single disc. [. . .] CD-ROM technology promised to bring "movies" to your computer, with new playback possibilities, but the DVD may be the format that succeeds in doing so.

Cable television

Cable television is almost as old as commercial broadcast television. Because broadcast television required a clear "line of sight" between the transmitter and the receiving set for adequate "reception," cable television developed in areas where broadcast television was not easily received, where antennae could not "see" each other, and where alternative methods were needed for transmitting broadcast signals. But cable television also offered some additional advantages: because it delivered television signals on coaxial cable it could carry more than one channel on the coaxial cable and import distant signals which were received by one master antenna (or, later, by one master satellite dish) and retransmit them.

In 1975—the year that began the Betamax/VHS format wars—a dramatic change in cable programming occurred: Home Box Office (HBO) began distributing special events (beginning with the Ali–Frazier "Thriller in Manila" fight) and movies via satellite. Shortly after HBO launched its service, Viacom launched a competing pay television service (Showtime) in 1976, and Warner Communication followed with The Movie Channel (which showed movies 24 hours a day) in 1979. These "pay" or "premium" cable channels relied heavily on the programming of feature films.

And not long after HBO began using satellite transmission, the owner of a low-rated UHF station in Atlanta put his station's signal on satellite to be seen nationwide. This station, WTBS, owned by Ted Turner, became known as a "superstation" because of its national availability. Turner's "superstation" was a "cable network" which made economic sense both to subscribers and to local cable companies. Cable subscribers were not charged for an extra station, the local cable company was only charged a dime a month per subscriber, and the extra service increased subscribers. And even though the revenues from the local cable companies did not cover the superstation's costs, the superstation could charge higher advertisement fees because it could boast a bigger audience. The core programming on WTBS consisted of Hollywood's movie past. [In 1986 Turner bought MGM and its film library; in 1987 Turner bought rights to an additional 800 RKO films (Gomery, 1992: 263–75).]

In the late 1970s and early 1980s cable television grew phenomenally. Most of what we know now as "basic cable"—CNN, MTV, Nickelodeon, C-Span, the superstations TBS, WOR, USA Network—were born within a timespan of a few years. In 1993, 64 percent of television owners subscribed to cable; by 1996, the figure was 68.5 percent (Nielsen, 1996). While studies on the movie-going habits of basic and pay cable subscribers have shown mixed results, indicating both a decrease and increase in movie-going (Austin, 1986: 93–94), one thing is certain: the increase in VCR users and cable subscribers meant that the cinematic spectator became a televisual viewer.

The television remote control

A third technology that transformed televisual viewing (and exacerbated its differences from film spectatorship) is the television remote control. The television remote control pene-trated the American household as rapidly as VCRs and cable: in 1976, 9.5 percent of televisions were sold with remote controls; by 1990, 90 percent of them were (Napoli, 1999); in 1985, only 29 percent of households had remote controls, in 1996, 90 percent of US household had at least one (Nielsen, 1996). Versions of the television "remote" control device were marketed in the 1950s—first tethered to a wire and later as a wireless light-sensor remote—but these offered fewer options to the couch-bound viewer of 1950s' broadcast television than the same device did for the later VCR or cable subscriber. With a television remote control, the viewer becomes a *montagiste*, editing at will with the punch of a fingertip, "zipping," "zapping," and "muting." Television programmers have noted that to capture the armchair channel-surfer requires more and more "visual" programming—relying less on plot and characterization and more on fast rhythmic editing. Some studies have shown that this form of viewing even changes the ability to follow linear arguments (Meyerowitz, 1985). And, as if to demonstrate its teleological relation to computer usage, the television remote control is now—retronymically—referred to as an "air mouse."

The film screen, the television screen, the computer screen

Certainly, much of the early competition between film and television centered around screen size and format; the television providing a 10–12 inch screen tailored to the domestic scale of the home, the movie screen differentiating its offerings with color, three-dimensional, and wider screen formats, compensating for what the black-and-white flat screens of television could not supply. Television "viewing" altered some of the protocols of cinema "spectatorship": unlike the cinema spectator, the television viewer watches a light-emanating cathode ray box in a partially darkened room. The optics of television do not rely on persistence of vision and projection but on scanning and transmission. [Our eyes have grown accustomed to NTSC 525 lines per image at 30 frames per second; or phase alteration line (PAL) at 624 lines at 25 frames per second; high definition television (HDTV) has 1125 lines per image.] And, as television scholars are quick to note, the placement of televisions in the home significantly alters the function of such spectatorship. Lynn Spigel, for example, likens the television's screen—a form of "home theater"—to the 1950s' architectural use of the picture window, a "window-wall" designed to bring the outside in (1992: 102).

Although both the content and the form of television competed with the film industry for viewers, television also became a delivery system for motion pictures—first in broadcast and syndicated format and later in basic and premium cable movie channels (Gomery, 1992: 247–75). As films were shown on television, changes in cinema screen aspect ratios meant that films were either panned and scanned or—more appropriately—"letterboxed" to fit in the 4:3 rectangular format of the television screen. The television "viewer" could now view films in a space that was, as Roland Barthes described it, "familiar, organized, tamed" (Barthes, 1975). In 1974, Raymond Williams predicted: "The major development of the late seventies may well be the large screen receiver: first the screen of four by six feet which is already in development; then the flat-wall receiver" (Williams, 1974: 136). As HDTV flat screen technology improves and screens replace real windows with a kind of "inhabited television," a "windows environment" may come to mean a virtual "window-wall."

The scale and domestic place of the television have prepared us for the screens of the "personal" computer. Computer "users" are not spectators, not viewers. Immobile with focused attention on a cathode ray screen, the computer "user" interacts directly with the framed image on a small flat screen, "using" a device—keyboard, mouse, or, in the case of touch screens, the finger—to manipulate what is contained within the parameter of the screen.[7] While computers have been designed to "interface" with humans in ways that emulate the associative patterns of human thought (Bush, 1945), to become dyadic partners in a metaphysical relationship (Turkle, 1995), complaints about the awkwardness of this relationship are surfacing. As one critic has proclaimed: "Using computers is like going to the movie theater and having to watch the projector instead of the film" (Kline, 1997).

Reinventing "film studies"

As the field of "film studies" has been redefining itself, both revising its internal historical accounts and opening up its field to the emerging multiplicities of "cultural studies" and "visual studies," much of this work has been coincident with the campaign for the academic legitimacy of film studies as a republic separate from its former disciplinary overlords. But as new technologies trouble the futures of cinematic production and reception, "film" as a discrete object becomes more and more of an endangered species, itself in need of asserting its own historicity. In the past decade or so, first with the VCR and more recently with on-line and digital technologies, the methods and source material for film and television scholarship have been radically transformed.[8]

Here it seems necessary to describe the following historiographical conundrum: David Bordwell and Kristin Thompson, arbiters of film history-as-text (and as text-book) have marked the history of film as a field of academic research "no more than thirty years old" (1994: xxvi). Yet in the past several decades, while film scholars have been reworking the histories of cinema's past—adjusting or refuting its teleologies, challenging its grand narratives—our concept of and access to not just the cinema's past but the past itself have also radically been transformed and this due in no small part to the cinema. Hence, there is a troubling paradox in the way in which the ascendency of film historical discourse in the past several decades may have worked to mask the very *loss* of history that the film itself inflicted. What I am invoking here are a familiar set of historiographic questions about the ways in which we can know the past, the truth claims of histories, and the nature of historical knowledge. As the field of "film history" has flourished in its vitality, the concomitant changes to our concept of the past produce a reflexive problematic. Cinema spectatorship, as one of its essential features, has always produced experiences that are not temporally fixed, has freed the spectator to engage in the fluid temporalities of cinematic construction—flashbacks, ellipses, achronologies—or to engage in other time frames (other than the spectator's moment in historical time, whether watching the diegetic fiction of a period drama or simply a film from an earlier period).

Without the discourse of film history, films would lose their historical identity, would slip into the fog of uncertain temporality. (As an exercise in my undergraduate film history classes, I ask them to turn on TNT in the middle of the night, without their television guides in hand, and to try to identify a rough production date for the films they are watching.) But even with the discourse of film history, films continue to reconstitute our sense of historical past. Recent films which have digitally "revised" film footage from the 1960s— *Nixon*, *JFK*, *Forrest Gump*—illustrate the compelling urge to reprogram popular memory. And as the past is dissolved as a real referent and reconstituted by cinematic images which displace it, Charles Baudelaire's 1859 cynical prophesy about photography's "loathing for history"[9] meets Fredric Jameson's (1983) dystopic syptomology of history's "disappearance."[10]

And just as soon as film scholars have undone the set of teleologies which read film history backward from the classical Hollywood model, a newly constructed teleology seems to be in the making. If a 1995 *New York Times* front-page story, "If the medium is the message, the message is the Web," is any indication, a new *telos* is beginning to appear. In a feature-spread headlined "How the earlier media achieved critical mass," separate articles on the printing press, the motion picture, radio, and television were juxtaposed, suggesting a synergy of the mythic moments that have transformed each medium from one with technological potential into one with "critical mass," that is, into a medium of mass reception. In this article, Molly Haskell's account of "the defining moment for motion pictures as a mass medium" formulaically replays *Birth of a Nation*'s New York premiere as the event "that catapulted the medium from its 19th century peep-show origins into its status as the great new popular art form of the 20th century" (1995: C5). While *The New York Times* did not directly assert the World Wide Web as *the* heir to the cultural centrality of the motion pictures and television ("there will be no certainty that this medium will achieve the critical mass that capitalism demands of its mass media"), the Web was positioned as a challenging successor which, unlike "each previous mass medium . . . does not require its audience to be merely passive recipients of information." Certainly, as the World Wide Web has become the *modem* (*modus*) *operandi* of everyday life, media savants have had to change their predictions about the electronic future of the 500-channel information highway and adjust for a much more computer-based key to the electronic future (Levy, 1995).

And now as the cynical futurologists prophesy the future of each new technology, it is worth recalling that in 1895, Louis Lumière boasted, "the cinema is an invention with no future." While we have some indications of where new technologies might take us, we still have no clear sense of what will be a "sustainable" technology in market terms. Even the current storage and display media—CD-ROMs and video cassettes—may be seen as transitional technologies as films and other visual material move on-line. And yet it is more than apparent that with the speed of such rapid and radical transformations, our technological environments cannot be conclusively theorized.

The history of "film studies" in its own way parallels the history of film itself, with a lag of perhaps 40 years. In what has been called the "classical" Hollywood period of film history there was a consensus not only as to what constituted narrative "content" but also as to the size, shape, color, and scope of the screen. Similarly, during the "classical" period of film studies there has been a general agreement as to what constitutes the size, shape, and scope of the discipline's objects. Now, a variety of screens—long and wide and square, large and small, composed of grains, composed of pixels—compete for our attention without any arguments about hegemony. Not only does our concept of "film history" need to be reconceptualized in light of these changes in technology, but our assumptions about "spectatorship" have lost their theoretical pinions as screens have changed, as have our relations to them.

Notes

1   In the United States, the 1995 Telecommunications Bill introduced pro-competitive deregulatory policies which encouraged the merging of technology industries, thus erasing many of the historical bases for their separation.

2   These three technologies fit as examples of Raymond Williams's tripartite typology of communication technologies as: *amplificatory* (distributing messages), *durative* (storing messages), and *alternative* (altering the form of messages) (Williams, 1980). In this way, the VCR is "durative," cable television is "amplificatory," and the television remote is "alternative."

3   Hence, the schoolyard epithet: "Your folks are so old, they get up to change the channels." More recently, as "picture in picture" television sets allow for the simultaneous viewing of multiple channels, the sequential tide of television "flow" no longer applies.

4   The VCR became a basic household appliance, but the puzzle of programming a VCR became a running national gag. President George Bush joked at a commencement speech at Caltech in 1991: "The seventh goal of education should be that by the turn of the century, Americans must be able to get their VCRs to stop flashing 12:00" (Ferguson, 1993: 72).

5   Soon after Sony won the copyright battle it lost the format battle. Betamax was a format that—although it offered better picture quality—lost its market share as the majority of new VCR buyers bought VHS.

6   The Mia Farrow character, Cecilia, in *Purple Rose of Cairo* (Woody Allen, 1985) was a pre-VCR viewer who had a viewing repetition compulsion made possible by the cinematic potential for re-seeing/re-experiencing the identical film over and over.

   There seems to be little statistical evidence on how often films were re-viewed by the same viewer, or how often the same viewer re-viewed a film over time—in its original release and then again in its re-release, or its release in repertory. Television viewing was always thought of as more transient. The pleasures of re-viewing television programs, once only available on the cycle of summer re-runs, have been more fully discovered since cable networks become repertories for revisiting the televisual past and since the VCR has made it technologically possible to capture and replay them on videotape. In this regard, it is worth considering how we commonly listen to an audio recording repeatedly, while visual media is thought to be more disposable and, in fact, is often constructed as such.

7   When Microsoft trademarked its second-generation software as Windows#tm they emphasized the metaphoric nature of much of our computer usage—"mice" which scurry under our fingers at the fluid command of wrist and palm; "desktops" which defy gravity and transform the horizontal desk into a vertical surface with an array of possible colors and digital textures. The computer "window" is only a portion of the computer screen, scalable in size. Windows can overlap, stack, or abut each other. The windows "environment" makes the screen smaller and allows for simultaneous applications. As an "interface," Windows#tm extends screen space by overlapping screens of various sizes; each "window" can run a different application; you can scroll through a text within a "window," arrange windows on your screen in stacked or overlapping formations, decorate your windows (with wallpapers, textured patterns). A paradox begins to emerge: the more the image becomes digital, the more the interface tries to compensate for its departure from reality-based representation by adopting the metaphors of familiar objects in space.

8   For example: as part of an on-line collection deemed "American Memory" the Library of Congress has made films in its "Early Motion Picture Collection" available for downloading off the World Wide Web along with hyperlinked texts detailing the historical context of "America at the turn of the century," complete with a selected bibliography. (Although conclusions drawn from these films have to take into account that in their digitized format, 5–10 percent of the original film frames are lost in the transfer.)

9   In 1859, Charles Baudelaire indicted photography as being a "cheap method of disseminating a loathing for history." Baudelaire was an early declaimer of the dangerous transformations of history and memory that the photographic image would produce. Despite photography's "loathing for history," Baudelaire also recognized it as a technique that could preserve "precious things whose form is dissolving and which demand a place in the archives of our memory" (1862: 153).

10   In a 1983 essay, Fredric Jameson, one of the key diagnosticians of postmodernity, catalogued some of its symptoms as:

the disappearance of history, the way in which our entire contemporary social system has little by little begun to *lose its capacity to retain its own past*, has begun to live in a perpetual present and in a perpetual change that obliterates traditions.

(1983: 125, emphasis added)

References

Bruce A. Austin 1986: The film industry, its audiences, and new communications technologies. In *Current research in film: audiences, economics and law*, Vol. 2. Ed. Bruce A. Austin. Norwood, NJ: Ablex, 80–116.

Roland Barthes 1975: En Sortant du Cinéma. *Communications* 23, translated by Bertrand Augst and Susan White, in *Apparatus*, edited by Theresa Hak Kyung Cha. New York: Tanam Press, 1980, 1–4.

Charles Baudelaire 1862: The salon of 1859. In *Art in Paris 1845–1862: salons and other exhibitions*, translated and edited by Jonathan Mayne. Oxford: Phaidon Press, 1965, 144–216.

Adam S. Bauman and Amy Harmon 1994: Rival systems of VCR "Replacement" could spark standards war. *Los Angeles Times*, 14 September 1, D1, D4.

Robert V. Bellamy, Jr and James R. Walker 1996: *Television and the remote control: grazing on a vast wasteland*. New York: Guilford Press.

David Bordwell and Kristin Thompson 1994: *Film history: an introduction*. New York: McGraw-Hill, xxvi.

Vannevar Bush 1945: As we may think. *Atlantic Monthly*, July.

Sean Cubitt 1991: *Time shift: on video culture*. New York: Routledge.

Richard Dienst 1994: *Still life in real time: theory after television*. Durham, NC: Duke University Press, 165–66.

Andrew Ferguson 1993: Charge of the couch brigade. *National Review* 45(19), 4 October.

Jane Feuer 1983: The concept of live television: ontology as ideology. In E. Ann Kaplan, ed., *Regarding television*. Los Angeles, CA: American Film Institute Monographs, 12–22.

Gladys D. Ganley and Oswald H. Ganley 1987: *Global political fallout: the VCR's first decade*. Cambridge, MA: Program on Information and Resources Policy, Harvard University.

Douglas Gomery 1992: *Shared pleasures: a history of movie presentation in the United States*. Madison, WI: University of Wisconsin Press.

Molly Haskell 1995: 'The Birth of a Nation', the birth of serious film. *The New York Times*, 20 November: C5.

Frederic Jameson 1983: Postmodernism and consumer society. In Hal Foster, ed., *The anti-aesthetic*. Port Townsend, WA: Bay Press, 111–25.

Edward Kern 1970: Cassette TV: the good revolution. *Life* 69(16) (16 October): 46–55.

Friedrich Kittler 1986: *Grammophon, film, typewriter*. Berlin: Brinkmann and Bose. Translated by Dorthea Von Mücke with the assistance of Philippe L. Similon, as 'Gramophone, film, typewriter', *October* 41: 101–18.

David Kline 1997: The embedded Internet. *Wired Magazine* 5:2, February.

James Lardner 1987: *Fast forward: Hollywood, the Japanese, and the VCR wars*. New York: New American Library.

Steven Levy 1995: *The New York Times*, 24 September.

Lauren Lipton 1991: VCR: very cool revolt. *Los Angeles Times*, TV Times cover story, 'How we tape', 4 August.

Marshall McLuhan 1964: *Understanding media*. Cambridge, MA: MIT Press, 1994.

Joshua Meyerowitz 1985: *No sense of place: the impact of electronic media on social behavior*. New York: Oxford University Press.

Lisa Napoli 1999: A gadget that taught a nation to surf: the TV remote control. *The New York Times*, 11 February: D10.

Nicolas Negroponte 1995: *Being digital*. New York: Alfred Knopf.

The New York Times, 1995: If the medium is the message, the message is the Web. 20 November, pp. A1, C5.

A.C. Nielsen 1996: *The home technology report*. A.C. Nielsen Company, July.

Lynn Spigel 1992: *Make room for TV: television and the family ideal in postwar America*. Chicago, IL: University of Chicago Press.

Sherry Turkle 1995: *Life on the screen: identity in the age of the Internet.* New York: Simon and Schuster.

Paul Virilio 1988: The third window: an interview with Paul Virilio. *Cahiers du Cinema,* translated by Yvonne Shafir, in *Global Television,* edited by Cynthia Schneider and Brian Wallis. Cambridge, MA: MIT Press: 185–97.

Raymond Williams 1974: *Television: technology as cultural form.* New York: Schocken.

—— 1980: Means of communication as means of production. In *Problems of materialism and culture.* London: New Left Books.

Chapter 20

John Belton

DIGITAL CINEMA: A FALSE REVOLUTION

ANDRÉ BAZIN WAS INTRIGUED by the "delay" in the invention of the cinema. Noting that the *idea* of the cinema—the duplication of external reality in sound, color, and relief—had existed for centuries, he was amazed at the slow pace at which technology was developed to make that idea a reality. What is interesting about Bazin's theory of technological development is not entirely his notion of "an integral realism" toward which the cinema teleologically evolves, but his acknowledgment of a counterforce, an "obstinate resistance" that is innate to the cinema and that steadfastly thwarts its development. Bazin's theory is both idealist and materialist, though his focus is ultimately idealist—on the drive toward what he called "total cinema."[1] I want to explore the implications of the materialist thrust of Bazin's argument, to look at the significance of certain delays in technological development. (I shall be using the terms "invention, innovation, and diffusion," introduced to film studies by Douglas Gomery. "Invention" refers to the phase in which the necessary technology is developed; "innovation" to the manufacturing and marketing of the technology; "diffusion" to its widespread adoption by the industry.)[2]

During the period of the cinema's actual invention—the two decades prior to 1900—motion pictures were made in sound, color, and widescreen (and even in 3-D). But, of course, sound wasn't successfully innovated and diffused until the late 1920s and it was not until the mid-1950s that widescreen cinema became the norm. Though color was more or less continuously being innovated and more or less successfully marketed in the mid-1930s in the form of Technicolor, it was not until 1965, when an ancillary market for color features opened up on network television, that Hollywood had an economic incentive to make most films in color.[3]

Clearly, the diffusion of new technology depends upon a variety of factors. No one technology takes quite the same path to full diffusion as another. Nor do they necessarily ever achieve full diffusion. In our attempts to understand this uneven development of new technologies, it has become clearer to me over the years that we cannot look to the path taken by one technology to explain or understand that of another. That is because the conditions within which technological change takes place are continually changing. This is why contemporary comparisons of the advent of digital cinema to the coming of sound in the late 1920s are not only misleading but wrong.

The latest so-called technological revolution is the digital revolution, which, it would seem, is taking place in quite distinct phases—not all at once, as was the case for earlier technologies. For audiences, it began in the realm of special effects—a field that is now dominated by computer-generated imagery. Then there was digital sound. Now we are seeing a very slow movement toward digital production using digital cameras and digital projection. Within the history of digital sound, there has not yet been full diffusion of the technology. The number of theaters worldwide that have digital sound readers is under 50 percent. Moreover, every print carrying a digital sound track continues to rely on a backup track of analog sound, usually Dolby SVA.

The digital revolution is more clearly being driven by home theater and home entertainment software and hardware technologies, and by corporate interests in marketing, than it is by any desire—as in the past—to revolutionize the *theatrical* moviegoing experience. In short, the digital revolution is part of a new corporate synergy within Hollywood, driven by the lucrative home entertainment market.

The first stage of this revolution within the cinema was the digitization of special effects. Digital technology has transformed the photographic image into a truly "plastic" object that can be molded and remolded into whatever shape is desired. As Lev Manovich has argued, digital technology has made the cinema a subset of animation.[4] It is a world inhabited by the liquid-metal man, as in *Terminator 2* (1991) or multiple Eddie Murphys interacting with one another in *The Klumps* (2000). Computer-generated graphics have enabled filmmakers to realize fantasy in a way that was only dreamed of a few years ago.

Digital special effects led the way, but digital sound was not far behind. With the commercial popularity of the compact disc, film sound went digital. Audiences expected it; analog was dead. As one motion picture exhibitor put it, "digital means progress and customers want it."[5] The digital revolution was and is all about economics—all about marketing new digital consumer products to a new generation of consumers—all about the home electronics industry using the cinema to establish a product line with identifiable brand names for home entertainment systems.

Among digital motion picture technologies, sound was most driven by consumer demand. In a marketplace in which the word "digital" sells consumer products, it is digital sound that marks, for consumers, the entry of motion pictures into the digital era.

Digital sound was introduced in 1990 with the release of *Dick Tracy*, then with *Edward Scissorhands* (1990), *The Doors* (1991), and *Terminator 2*. Because of the compact disc, the public increasingly associated digital sound with state-of-the-art sound. The marketability of digital sound drove its development, and the advent of Cinema Digital Sound (CDS) clearly prompted Dolby and others within the industry to accelerate work on their own digital systems. At the same time, the sudden shift in 1990 to digital from analog in the development of a High Definition Television standard undoubtedly encouraged Dolby and others to try to dominate this potential market as well. Indeed, with the shift from analog to digital HDTV, Dolby's status in the highly profitable home electronics industry was suddenly in jeopardy. By 1992, Dolby had perfected a digital track that could be placed alongside an analog Dolby Stereo track. It was introduced with the premiere of *Batman Returns*. Digital Theatre Systems (DTS) introduced a different digital system in 1993 with the release of *Jurassic Park*. DTS is owned, in part, by Steven Spielberg and Universal/MCA and has been used on all Universal and Amblin Entertainment pictures. DTS is a double-system format in which a standard, stereo optical print is distributed with a special time code on it that is synched up with a compact disc.

Dolby began working on a digital sound format in 1987. Perfected in 1992 and introduced with the release of *Batman Returns*, Dolby digital, known as Dolby SRD, combined a conventional Dolby SR track in the standard sound track area alongside the image with a digital track that was located between the sprocket holes at the edge of the film. This permitted a single print inventory for distributors and provided immediate backup, via the analog track, in case of system failure. Although *Jurassic Park* provided a big send-off for the DTS system, DTS made a number of crucial mistakes in promoting the system. DTS encouraged theaters to play back the sound louder than they had with Dolby SR, in large part because DTS (and other digital systems) claimed to have greater headroom. The additional volume strained the amplifiers and loudspeakers, resulting in amplifier clipping, general system shock, and tweeter failure. The result was a harsh, metallic playback of the dialogue. DTS moved fairly quickly to control this potential disaster. And by 1994, DTS had secured an exclusive contract with MGM/UA and had contracted to do a series of films for New Line Cinema. DTS was owned, in part, by MCA, at that time a property of the Japanese electronics giant Matsushita, which manufactured Panasonic equipment. Matsushita's chief rival was Sony. The emergence of digital sound in the theater served as a lightning rod to galvanize the electronics industry—especially the Japanese electronics industry—which was struggling to retain its dominance in the home entertainment market. In fact, as Paul Rayton has suggested, it is possible to view experiments with digital sound in the theater as the preliminary battle for the potentially much more lucrative market of digital sound in the home.[6] It was a battle that took place on the level of both hardware and software. If MCA (or Sony) could produce enough box-office hits in DTS (or SDDS), it could effectively market playback hardware and film software to home consumers.

By the end of 1994, most studios were releasing exclusively in one format or another. However, during the summer of 1995, more and more studios began releasing their films in multiple digital formats in an attempt to take advantage of the different systems in the majority of digitally equipped theaters. Each of the three systems uses different areas of the release print to encode information. Digital sound has evolved into a three-system standard. As long as most digital theaters can get most big films in digital, the multistandard is likely to continue. Dolby's strategy of overseas domination guarantees its survival in a market dominated by software giants such as Universal, Columbia, and Tri-Star. The bulk of a studio's profits come from overseas distribution; domestic rentals are considered strong if they earn back negative, print, and distribution cost. Dolby is thus uniquely positioned. In order to reap these overseas profits, studios will ultimately need to make overseas prints available in Dolby. About 25,000 theaters worldwide are equipped to play Dolby Stereo. Since Dolby's analog optical track continues to be placed on most digital prints, theaters will undoubtedly resist digital and continue to rely on four-channel Dolby systems. The fact that all digital systems retain a stereo analog track means that all theaters can run these films without converting to 5.1 digital.

What has emerged is thus a marketplace in which all three systems exist alongside one another. The coming of digital sound is consequently quite unlike other, previous "revolutions" in motion picture technology. The initial transition to sound (1926–29) led to a single standard—sound on film—that was met by a handful of proprietary technologies (Movietone, RCA Photophone, generic Western Electric). Digital sound is a technology of the new era of Macintosh and IBM; two standards can coexist in the digital marketplace. Consumers have adjusted/adapted to multiple standards; so long as they can run their computer programs or play back their home entertainment programs, they will tolerate multiple standards.

The history of digital sound suggests a need to rethink traditional models of technological determinism. In this particular instance, consumer demand for novelty drove the expansion of the technology. Technology did not determine the demand in the traditional linear, cause/effect pattern. Rather, there was an overlapping of technologies (computers, CDs) and an overlapping of demands (for commodifying/marketing information, for consumer entertainment). These overlapping technologies and demands mutually determined one another in a process of back-and-forth negotiation.

One of the legacies of digital sound has been the death of 70mm as an exhibition format. Digital sound was, of course, not necessarily any better than Dolby's six-track stereo magnetic sound. But it was cheaper. It cost over $12,000 to strike and stripe a 70mm print from a 35mm negative; 35mm six-track digital prints cost almost the same as standard 35mm prints—about $2,000. This particular phase of the digital technological revolution was more of a cost-saving effort on the part of the studios than anything else, although, undoubtedly, the upgrade in 35mm sound from four to six tracks and the quality of digital sound did constitute significant improvements over standard 35mm Dolby SVA in the audience's theatrical experience. Even so, all it offered was what we already had in 70mm, Dolby Stereo presentations. And the projected image was far inferior to that of a 70mm print.

At the end of 1999, with the celebration of the faux-millennium, came the advent of a new, "revolutionary" technology—digital projection. Spearheaded by George Lucas, whose *Star Wars: The Phantom Menace* was projected digitally in four theaters in the US in June 1999, digital projection was heralded as the newest technological revolution—a revolution that would change the face of the industry. Admittedly, the production and postproduction of many Hollywood blockbusters had grown more and more dependent on digital technology, and most films—even those without digital imaging—were currently being edited on computer. But this reliance on the digital domain was relatively invisible to the average moviegoer. The potential for a totally digital cinema—digital production, postproduction, distribution, and exhibition—caught the attention and imagination of the media. At the supposed turn of the millennium, the one-hundred-plus-year reign of celluloid was over; film was dead; digital was It. The *New York Times*, *Wall Street Journal*, *Los Angeles Times*, and several national news magazines heralded the dawning of the new digital age, proclaiming that it was no longer a matter of *whether* it would happen but *when*. One writer noted that the age of Edison was over—the phonograph had been replaced by the compact disc, and film by digital signals; all that remained was Edison's lightbulb.[7] Strategically, it was the perfect moment to introduce the new technology, since the popular media was looking for symbolic events to mark the advent of the new millennium.

George Lucas quickly emerged as digital cinema's poster boy. Lucas wrote that "In the twentieth century, cinema was celluloid; the cinema of the twenty-first century will be digital. . . . Film is going to be photographed and projected digitally. The recorded image will go automatically into a computer and most postproduction will take place in a computer. . . . We made it through the silent era to the sound era and from the black-and-white era to the color era, and I'm sure we'll make it through to the digital era. . . . The creator's palette has been continually widened."[8] Like others, Lucas compared the digital revolution to earlier revolutions in motion picture technology.

Sound designer Walter Murch, who did the sound for Lucas's *American Graffiti* (1973) and Coppola's *The Conversation* (1974) and *Apocalypse Now* (1979), had won an editing and sound-mixing Oscar for *The English Patient* (1996). He now joined in the millennial hype. For Murch, the digital revolution, which had already swept the fields of film editing and film sound, was perfectly positioned to overthrow "the two last holdouts of film's nineteenth-century, analog-mechanical legacy"—projection and original photography.[9]

Theaters showing *The Phantom Menace* digitally displayed banners linking it with other technological revolutions in the cinema—with the projection of the first motion picture, the introduction of sound, color film, CinemaScope widescreen, and digital audio. Interestingly, Cinerama was absent from this list, replaced by the development of CinemaScope, which was erroneously dated as 1955, the year that the Todd–AO Process was premiered. Rick McCallum, one of the producers of *Phantom Menace*, referred to the premiere as "a milestone in cinematic history" and said that "like the introduction of sound and color, these digital screenings represent the beginning of a new era in film presentation."[10] Russell Wintner of CineComm Digital Cinema likened the premiere to that of *The Jazz Singer* in 1927 and the excitement generated by the coming of sound.

If the digital revolution begun in Hollywood's special-effects laboratories was completed in the digitization of projection, then it was hardly a technological revolution on the order of those to which it has been compared. It is really not quite clear in what way it *is* a technological revolution. It does indeed threaten to overthrow the dominance of 35mm film, which has been the chief format of the motion picture industry for over one hundred years. But it is not revolutionary in the way that these other technological revolutions were. Digital projection as it exists today does not, in any way, transform the nature of the motion picture experience. Audiences viewing digital projection will not experience the cinema differently, as those who heard sound, saw color, or experienced widescreen and stereo sound for the first time did. Cinerama, for example, did transform the theatrical experience, producing a dramatic sense of audience participation. It was as if the audience, surrounded with image and sound, had entered the space of the picture. This sense of participation was exploited in Cinerama publicity photos that depicted spectators, sitting in their theater seats, going over Niagara Falls, water skiing, or sitting in Milan's La Scala opera house.

Digital projection is not a new experience for the audience. What is being offered to us is simply something that is potentially equivalent to the projection of traditional 35mm film. This, in fact, is what Steven Morley, vice-president of technology at Qualcomm, which has perfected techniques for delivering digitized motion pictures from studios to theaters via on-site servers or satellite, says was Qualcomm's mission. He writes that the goal of Digital Cinema is "to provide the image quality of a first run motion picture on 35mm film stock projected on opening night at a premier theater."[11] The advantages of "digital"—whatever they may be—are not being exploited in the theater. Current digital projection technology is not interactive. It does not enable audiences to relate to the cinema in ways similar to those provided by the computer or the Internet. It may be digital for George Lucas and Walter Murch at their end of the film chain, but it might just as well be analog for us, since it does not give the audience the empowerment of digital. For it to be truly digital, it must be digital for the audience as well. There would have to be a computer mouse or a virtual reality glove at every seat in the theater. All that the proponents of digital projection are claiming is that it is comparable to 35mm. That does not sound like a revolutionary technology. As far as I can see, the only transformation of the motion picture experience for audiences that has taken place in the last forty years or so has been the development of stadium seating!

If this is not a real revolution, what exactly is it? What is going on? *The Phantom Menace* had "nearly 2,200 digitally generated shots, making up 90 percent of the movie."[12] Lucas is currently filming the next episode of *Star Wars* entirely in digital, using a Sony, twenty-four-frame progressive-scan electronic camera.[13] For George Lucas, digital cinema is clearly the realization of *his* dreams, a revolution in *filmmaking*. His commitment to sci-fi demands that he find new ways of realizing fantasy. In the wake of *Star Wars* (1977), *Close Encounters of the Third Kind* (1977), *E. T. the Extra-Terrestrial* (1982), the *Terminator* films (1984–) and others, sci-fi has emerged as a major Hollywood genre. Sci-fi and special-effects blockbusters from *Star Wars* to *Titanic* (1997) have transformed the motion picture industry. Big budget block-busters have driven up negative cost so that it currently hovers at around $55 million. They have spawned saturation ad campaigns and saturation booking, so that these films now regularly open in as many as 3,500 theaters or more on the same day. This saturation marketing strategy has driven up advertising and prints costs to an average of over $27 million per film.[14] Sci-fi and special-effects action films have become the dogs that wag Hollywood's tail. But it is not the only dog in Hollywood; there are still other genres. Other filmmakers rely less upon special effects and fantasy; there are scores of directors like Woody Allen, Martin Scorsese, Robert Altman, Stephen Frears, John Sayles, Paul Schrader, and Mike Leigh, who make films about more or less realistically conceived characters in more or less realistic settings. There is no reason for the digital fantasies of sci-fi to drive an industry that, since the sci-fi blockbusters of the late 1970s and early '80s, has become increasingly diverse in terms of narrative content. Indeed, the danger is that an all-digital cinema might very well lead to an all-fantasy cinema—to essentially one genre. Of course, filmmakers do not have to use digital technology as Lucas does, but if they want to "be digital" and demonstrate what digital cinema can do, then they will surely be tempted to follow in Lucas's footsteps.

To be fair, digital cinema has not necessarily become the sole property of Lucas, James Cameron, and big-budget, commercial Hollywood. It has spawned a countercinema of sorts. The relative cheapness of the technology has brought new opportunities for making independent films to a variety of filmmakers. *Timecode* (2000), which cost only $4 million, not only takes advantage of digital video to present events in a continuous way that outdoes Alfred Hitchcock's *Rope* (1948) by a factor of three, but it foregrounds the new technology in its script. The character played by Kyle McLaughlin introduces his client, a filmmaker named Ana, in apocalyptic terms: "Armed with nothing more than a digital camera and an incredible vision . . . Ana is prepared to drag us kicking and screaming into the new millennium." His remarks are suitably punctuated by one of the film's several earthquakes.

Francis Ford Coppola's Zoetrope Studios have gone digital, and he encourages independent filmmakers to work in that format. Next Wave Films, a subsidiary of the Independent Film Channel that furnishes finishing funds to independent filmmakers, has seen a dramatic increase in digital submissions for funding; roughly 51 percent of the films submitted are shot digitally.[15] Sundance, Vancouver, and other independent film festivals have also seen a rise in the number of digital films—and have begun to project these films digitally as well. The question is what ultimate effect the "democratization" of the means of production will have—whether independent films will, as they did in the 1990s, evolve by becoming more and more like commercial Hollywood films, or whether they will be able to use the new technology for a different kind of film practice.

The pattern of acquisitions and mergers that has characterized Hollywood in the 1980s and 1990s may explain the fervor for digitization. As the major players in the industry divested themselves of companies that had little or no relation to the emerging media industry, they sought "synergy." Hardware producers of VCRs such as Sony and Matsushita bought software producers such as Columbia and Universal. Publishers, such as the *Time* organization, merged with studios (Warner) and cable companies (Turner) to create vertically integrated entertainment providers. The buzz word in the past few years has shifted slightly from "synergy" to "convergence." "Convergence" refers to "the union of audio, video and data communications into a single source, received on a single device, delivered by a single connection."[16] Convergence looks back to economic structures of yore, such as the vertical integration of the motion picture industry in the 1920s–1940s. Convergence consists of "three subsidiary convergences: content (audio, video and data); platforms (PC, TV, Internet appliance, and game machine); and distribution (how the content gets to your platform)."[17] The recent $100 billion merger of Time Warner with AOL is an example of both synergy and "convergence." The content provider *Time* and its publishing affiliates can distribute its material on film via Warner, on cable via Turner, and on-line via AOL. In this Age of Information, Hollywood has begun to redefine itself as an information provider and is currently building systems for the delivery of that information, expanding from television and cable to satellites and the Internet. Indeed, AOL Time Warner has stated its long-range intentions that studios use AOL's digital networks to distribute movies to theaters.

"Convergence" depends upon the development of broadband wired or wireless transmission. With the exception of satellite transmission or fiber optic cable, broadband transmission seems fairly far off.

As the motion picture industry digitizes, it explores new markets that have arisen around digital technology. Most new films are being digitized for release on DVD. More and more of the studio's profits derive from ancillary markets such as video, cable, and broadcast television release. Indeed, 70 percent of the revenues generated by a film now come from these non-theatrical, ancillary markets.[18] Profits from video retail in 2000 were $20 billion, while box-office receipts from theaters totaled only $7.7 billion.[19] Digital projection finds the studios and digital projection companies situating themselves for a new marketplace in which the theater may well become an expendable casualty.

Currently, theaters play a crucial role in providing an initial platform for films, generating public interest in them and providing "buzz" that creates a mass market for future sales. But the role of theatrical release could slowly disappear; the economics of synergy and convergence could lead studios to release films directly to the home, relying upon existing techniques of saturation ad campaigns to bypass the theaters.

In short, digital cinema is a revolutionary technological innovation for filmmakers like Lucas and for the interests of corporate synergy that currently drive Hollywood. As we shall see, it is also a potential boon—in the form of cost saving—for film distributors. But it is not yet clear that it can do anything for motion picture audiences aside from eliminating jitter, weave, dirt, and scratches from the projected image. Even if we concede that these improvements result in better projection, they are not significant enough for them to be declared "revolutionary" in terms of the audience's experience of motion pictures.

On June 18, 1999, *Star Wars: The Phantom Menace* was projected digitally in four theaters in the United States using two different projection systems. CineComm Digital Cinema and its Hughes/JVC projector ran the film at Pacific's Winnetka Theater in Chatsworth near Los Angeles and at Loews' Route 4 Theater in Paramus, New Jersey. A Texas Instruments projector was used at AMC's Burbank 14 Multiplex and at Loews' Meadows 6 in Secaucus, New Jersey. Critical response to the Hughes/JVC system was fairly damning. *Variety* critic Todd McCarthy noted that "the imprecision of the system was woefully apparent the moment the *Star Wars* scene-setting backstory scrolled up the screen—pixilation was readily visible in the letters, which weren't well defined. In the film proper, the darker areas of the frames were murky, colors were flat, there were noticeable blurs in some movements and a general softness was prevalent in the images. Overall effect was akin to a so-so color photocopy."[20] In a special edition of *Widegauge*, Scott Marshall reviewed both systems and noted that the Hughes system "looked like very good video projection" but was "not like film at all. Color registration seemed perfect all the way to the corners, but there was a 'ringing' in the video that added sharp artificial contours to vertical edges, contributing to the 'video look' . . . There was a faint flickering of horizontal lines in the closing credit scroll, a giveaway that the image was interlaced and not progressive scan."[21]

The Texas Instruments Digital Light Processing cinema projector emerged as the clear winner in the digital cinema projector wars. McCarthy noted that DLP projection was "exceedingly sharp" and "bright." The "process has a cool, clear, hard-edged look."[22] Scott Marshall, who subtitled his review of the DLP "A 70mm for the next generation?", attended the screening skeptical of claims that had been circulating that digital was as good as 35mm. When the previews of coming attractions began, he noted that he "was immediately astonished by the spectacularly bright image that also seemed very sharp and with excellent contrast and deeply saturated colors. . . . The picture was absolutely stunning, with deep reds, yellows, and oranges, convincing flesh tones, and sharp, steady superimposed titles. The picture had no dust, dirt, jitter, weave, scratches, or flicker. It was something like a beautifully exposed, new Kodachrome slide, only in motion. It gave me the same feeling in my gut that I get when I watch a perfect 70mm print of a 65mm film."[23] Marshall was a bit less blown away by *The Phantom Menace*—mostly because of flaws in the original photographic style of the film itself.

The Texas Instruments DLP projector is essentially a picture head that is mounted on an existing theater projection lamphouse. This head is twenty inches wide and weighs seventy-four pounds; the projection lens weighs another five to ten pounds. The current method of data delivery to the theater projector is through optical disks. The film is stored on a server, consisting of as many as twenty or more eighteen-gigabyte hard drives. The digital sound track is separate and was, for the *Phantom Menace*, played back on a Tascam MMR-8 eight-channel digital tape deck. Since the sound does not need to be digitally encoded on the film, it is not compressed and resembles, in quality, the track heard by the sound engineer in the film's final mix. Steve Morley notes that "it's possible to send sound tracks of six, eight, or more channels of full bandwidth audio, such as 24-bit, 48kHz sampled tracks directly compatible with the formats used by postproduction sound mixing facilities."[24]

Digital information from the Texas Instruments server is decompressed and decrypted and then sent to the projector. The heart of the projector is a digital light processing chip—actually three chips in the cinema projector—known as the Digital Micromirror Device or DMD. A formatter board translates the digital signal into a pure digital bit stream. The chip functions as a digital light switch. Each chip has over 1.3 million tiny aluminum mirrors sixteen by sixteen micrometers square. Each mirror is mounted on a pair of hinges that tilt the mirror plus or minus ten degrees in response to binary code. Each mirror can switch on or off more than 5,000 times per second, depending upon the signal its gets. Amazingly, there have been no mirror or hinge failures to date, and Texas Instruments analysts put the life of these chips at twenty years of more or less continuous use.

Light from the lamphouse hits the mirror; if the mirror is in one position, the light is reflected through the lens and onto the screen. If it is in another position, the light is deflected and absorbed by the interior of the DMD; no light reaches the screen; the result is the projection of a black pixel on the screen. Texas Instruments has recently developed a new, so-called "dark chip." This chip is better than earlier chips in absorbing light. As a result, it can generate blacker blacks on the screen and improve contrast ratio.[25] The function of the chip is to convert a digital electronic input into digital light, which is then projected on the screen. The spectator's eye performs the digital to analog conversion. In other words, what gets to the screen is digital light, not an electronic video image.

Over the past few years, a number of other companies have begun research and development on digital projection. Several of these display their wares regularly at ShoWest, the annual gathering of movie exhibitors. Several big-name movie companies have become involved in digital projection. IMAX, for example, has purchased Digital Projection International. Through this subsidiary, IMAX will build and market digital projectors using the TI [Texas Instrument] chips. Technicolor has also become involved in the development of digital projection technology using the DLP chips. Teaming up with Qualcomm, Technicolor is offering to distribute digital films for studios and to pay for the installation of digital projection in theaters for a small fee. Technicolor is also interested in offering alternative programming—such as rock concerts and sporting events—to theaters using digital trans-mission and projection.[26] Texas Instruments, which brings its DLP projector to ShoWest each year and which has taken a commanding lead in the field, has campaigned to get the industry to establish standards for digital compression, encryption, and projection, possibly hoping that its dominance in the field will result in the adoption of standards compatible with its system. An SMPTE [Society of Motion Picture and Television Engineers] task force is currently working on establishing industry-wide standards. However, no standards currently exist, and this lack of standards is one of the chief roadblocks to the innovation and diffusion of digital projection technology.

Digital cinema is still very much a question mark on the cinema horizon. Although its proponents claim that within five or ten or twenty years it will have replaced film, this seems unlikely. The compelling reasons for digital cinema lie in the financial benefits it can provide to motion picture distributors and in the creative flexibility it can offer to a handful of very important Hollywood filmmakers like Lucas, Cameron, and others. Of course, the film-makers who desire it already have the digital advantage in production and postproduction. It would appear to be the film distributors who would benefit the most from digital distribu-tion and exhibition. The cost of 35mm prints—$2,000 each—multiplied by the number of prints currently used on today's saturation market—3,000 to 5,000 (7,000 prints were struck for *Godzilla*)—add up to $6–$10 million per title. Qualcomm's Steve Morley calcu-lates that the cost to supply 100 or 10,000 theaters is roughly the same with digital cinema—approximately "$450 per screen per year, compared to the previously computed film cost exceeding $22,000 per screen per year."[27] The chief selling point of Qualcomm and others is cost-saving for distributors.

But it is not clear, however, that exhibitors are willing to go along with this. Theaters are not necessarily reluctant to go digital. To some extent the idea appeals to them. John Fithian notes that the core of moviegoers is in the twelve- to twenty-four-year-old range. They account for 39 percent of all tickets sold. He points out that the kids today are the children of the baby-boom generation and that their numbers will crest in 2010, producing more teenagers in the United States than at any other time in history. He believes that this population will have considerable influence over what happens in the theater. "Their life is digitized," he says. The fact that this new generation of "moviegoers" has grown accustomed to watching film on TV monitors and has probably never seen films at their optimum—projected on a big screen in 70mm with six-track Dolby stereo sound—means that they will have nothing to compare digital projection to but standard 35mm, third-generation release prints, which can be fairly poor, especially if they were printed on today's high-speed printers that run at the rate of 2,000 feet per minute.

The question is not one of exhibitors wanting digital. The fact is that they simply cannot afford it. The boom in theater construction that has seen the number of screens climb to around 37,000 has left many theater chains in massive debt. Nine of the largest theater chains in the country have filed for Chapter Eleven bankruptcy protection over the past few years.[28] According to John Fithian, the new president of NATO [National Association of Theater Owners], the only way digital projection will get into the theater is if "those who are making the savings pay for it." That means the studios and distributors will have to foot the bill. At a cost of $100,000 per screen that comes to $3.7 billion. Recent cost estimates for projectors run from $150,000 to $180,000 each, which would increase that estimate from $3.7 to $5.6 billion. And potential costs do not stop there. Hollywood just barely breaks even on domestic rentals. Profits—more than 50 percent of a film's total revenues—come from exhibition overseas, where there are an additional 22,000 screens in Europe and the UK alone.[29] Distributors will need to foot the bill for digital projection in these and other theaters around the world as well.

Over the past year, Boeing aircraft began negotiations with several theaters to fund the installation of digital projection equipment in the expectation that these theaters would use Boeing's satellite-based delivery system as a distributor. Boeing did participate in the suc-cessful satellite delivery of *Bounce* to the AMC 25 theater in Times Square in November 2000 and of Miramax's *Spy Kids* to a recent ShoWest convention in March 2001.

And since digital technology changes every year—how many computer upgrades have we had to make in the last ten years?—these costs are not one-time costs, but will involve continual renegotiation. Fithian also insists that before theaters even think of converting to digital, industry-wide compression, encryption, and delivery standards need to be established. In this matter, NATO and the MPAA [Motion Picture Association of America] are surely in agreement. At the same time, he argues that the delivery of digital cinema to the theater must be competitively structured. There can be no single gatekeeper; there must be multiple suppliers, if the film industry is to avoid the mistakes of the past associated with the Bell Telephone monopoly.[30] Fithian also fears that exhibitors might lose control of the "show" and that the operations of their theaters might be under remote control of the studios.[31]

Theaters have played a pivotal role in the innovation of revolutionary film technologies, but theaters have generally been dragged to the revolution against the exhibitors' will. Neither the major studios nor their theaters wanted the coming of sound, but when Warner Bros. and Fox forced the issue, the studios found that they had no choice. And, since most of the theaters were then owned by the studios, exhibitors made the transition as well. Color cost exhibitors nothing in terms of technological upgrade, though rental rates were more than for black-and-white films. But it was not until the 1950s that the resistance of exhibitors to costly new technology became a significant negative factor in the innovation of that technology. By this time, U.S. studios were no longer permitted to own theaters, and exhibitors were often cast in the role of adversaries to producers and distributors. The majority of exhibitors capitulated to the widescreen revolution, but they revolted en masse against the costly conversion to stereo magnetic sound that was packaged together with these new widescreen images. In the 1970s, the relatively inexpensive equipment required to provide Dolby Stereo made an upgrade in theater sound affordable for most theaters. The most recent wave of digital sound technology, which, like Dolby Stereo, is relatively inexpensive, has found a place in many American theaters. However, even six or seven years after this revolution, only about 25 percent of European theaters have converted to digital sound. If theaters have to pay for it, they will not convert to digital projection.

Digital equipment manufacturers try to sell theaters on digital by reviving the dream of theater television and the new revenue streams it was always predicted to provide. Digital theaters could provide big-screen presentations of sporting events, such as prizefights, World Cup matches, or rock concerts, and other Pay-Per-View cable fare. But theater television has never become a viable entertainment format in the past. This was due in part to technological obstacles that digital projection has solved. But it is also due to the difficulty in marketing these events to a public that increasingly expects to see them at home on television either for free or for a modest Pay-Per-View charge.

One of the major threats facing digital cinema is film piracy. Several years ago, Jack Valenti noted that "unless we find suitable technological armor to protect the digital movie, we will soon be standing in the ruins of a once-great enterprise."[32] The studios lose close to $2.5 billion a year in piracy. Qualcomm boasts that it can put "watermarks" into its digital projection that can be used to identify when and where the copy was made. This might help track down the pirates. Encryption of the digital original is designed to protect it on its path from the studio to the theater. According to Dan Sweeney, Qualcomm has an expertise in "military-level encryption" for satellite delivery. It relies on a 128-bit key length and has "a provision for changing keys during transmission several thousands of times." Each key, it is said, would take weeks to crack on a mainframe.[33] But does encryption work? In the fall of 1999, the encryption code for the Digital Video Disc system was broken by a Norwegian teenager, who was a member of a radical group known as MoRE (Masters of Reverse Engineering). He then distributed the algorithms of the code on the Internet. Having been assured that DVDs could not be copied, Hollywood was traumatized by the event, realizing that millions of perfect copies of popular films could now flood the market.

Given the industry's concern about piracy, it is extremely unlikely that it will embrace satellite delivery of digital cinema, even though it is the cheapest and most efficient way of delivering digital films to the theater. For the present, it would seem that the physical delivery of disks to the theater—and high security storage of them there—or sending them on secure fiber optic lines would be the only viable means of getting digital films to the theater. (Fiber optics were used to deliver *Titan A.E.* [2000] from Hollywood to a theater in Atlanta.)

At present, the digital projection revolution is stalled, lacking product and theaters to show it in. Only thirty-eight screens in the country (two at the AMC 25 in New York City) are equipped with digital projectors, and only thirty-two major motion pictures have been made available for digital projection, including—in addition to those already mentioned—*Tarzan, Toy Story 2, The Perfect Storm, Dinosaur, Fantasia 2000, 102 Dalmatians, Mission to Mars, Vertical Limit, Shrek, Jurassic Park III, Final Fantasy: The Spirits Within, Planet of the Apes*, and *Monsters, Inc.*

Film critic Roger Ebert, who saw a demonstration of digital projection at the May 1999 Cannes Film Festival, is one of the few people speaking out against digital cinema. Ebert's chief objection is that digital projection cannot duplicate the *experience* of 35mm film. In this respect, his argument is much subtler than my own in that all I am saying is that digital projection does not offer audiences a *new experience* in the theater.

Perhaps the most important concern about the digitization of the cinema is its implications for film preservation. At the moment, polyester safety film is the ideal medium for long-term storage of motion picture images and sound tracks. Its longevity is estimated at about one hundred years—longer if it is placed in cold storage facilities. Digital data has been stored, for the most part, on magnetic tape or disc—a format that has an effective media life of five to ten years and an estimated time until obsolescence of only five years. Studios would be crazy to use digital formats for archiving their holdings. Films made digitally could be stored in that format, but they would have to be converted to a new format every five years. It would make more sense for them to be transferred to celluloid and stored as films. Given the rapid obsolescence of various past digital formats, is it not clear that digital information can be retrieved in the future.

One obvious problem with digital cinema is that it has no novelty value, at least not for film audiences. This being the case, what will drive its future development? Meanwhile, predictions by Lucas, Murch, and others of an all-digital cinema tend to ignore the often conflicting material forces of the marketplace that regularly reshape and even reject new technology. Nor do they take into account the inevitable development of other, nonfilm technologies that might impact upon the evolution of film, altering its ultimate form. Their predictions are idealist, not materialist. They take no note of what Bazin did factor into his quasi-idealist notions of technological development—the obstinate resistance of matter.

Notes

1   "Total cinema" is a term that describes a cinema capable of creating "a total and complete representation of reality." André Bazin, *What Is Cinema?*, vol. 1, trans. Hugh Gray (Berkeley: University of California Press, 1967), pp. 17, 20.

2   Douglas Gomery, "The Coming of Sound: Technological Change in the American Film Industry," in Elisabeth Weis and John Belton, eds. *Film Sound: Theory and Practice* (New York: Columbia University Press, 1985), pp. 5–6.

3   Brad Chisholm, "Red, Blue, and Lots of Green: The Impact of Color Television on Feature Film Production," in Tino Balio, ed. *Hollywood in the Age of Television* (Boston: Unwin Hyman, 1990), p. 227.

4   Lev Manovich, "What Is Digital Cinema?", at http://www.apparitions.ucsd.edu/_manovich/text/digital-cinema.html. See *Perspectives of Media Art*, eds. Jeffrey Shaw and Hans Peter Schwartz (Ostfildern, Germany: Cantz Verlag, 1996). [This was republished in Manovich, *The Language of New Media*, as the chapter that is reprinted in this volume. See p. 251 –Ed.]

5   Gary Reber, "Sound Wars at a Theatre Near You: Round Five," *Widescreen Review* 3, no. 2 (April/May 1994), p. 72.

6   Conversation with the author, 1993.

7   Rob Sabin, "Taking Film out of Films," *New York Times*, September 5, 1999.

8   George Lucas, "Movies Are an Illusion," *Premiere*, February 1999, p. 60.

9   Walter Murch, "A Digital Cinema of the Mind?," *New York Times*, May 2, 1999, 2A, p. 1.

10   Texas Instruments 1999 Press Release.

11   Steven A. Morley, "Making Digital Cinema Actually Happen—What It Takes and Who's Going to Do It," QUALCOMM, 1998. Presented at SMPTE 140th Technical Conference, Pasadena, Calif., October 31, 1999.

12   Sabin, "Taking Film out of Films."

13   *Daily Variety*, February 18, 2000, p. A10.

14   Jack Valenti Press Release, March 9, 1999 at http://www.mpaa.org Web site. See also Jill Goldsmith, "Pix Tix Get Swift Kick," *Daily Variety*, March 8, 2000. MPAA stats for 1999 put the figure at $24.5 million, down from previous years.

15   "Moviemaking in Transition," *Scientific American* (November 2000), p. 62.

16   Peter Forman and Robert W. Saint John, "Creating Convergence," *Scientific American* (November 2000), p. 50.

17   Ibid.

18   Conversation with John Fithian, president of NATO, February 29, 2000.

19   Perry Sun, "The Future of Movies: Part 6," *Widescreen Review* 50 (July 2001), p. 80; "Vid Flips Lid with $20 bil in Revenue," Scott Hetrick, *Daily Variety* (January 5, 2001), p. 39.

20   "Digital Cinema Is the Future . . . or Is It?", *Daily Variety*, June 25, 1999.

21   Scott Marshall, "Texas Instruments 'DLP' Digital Projection," *Widegauge* 4, no. 1 (Summer 1999), pp. 10–11.

22   Todd McCarthy, "Digital Cinema."

23   Marshall, "Texas Instruments," p. 10.

24   Morley, "Making Digital Cinema Actually Happen," p. 9.

25   "Focus on New Tech," *Daily Variety*, March 6, 2000, p. A4.

26   Perry Sun, *Widescreen Review* 50, p. 82.

27   Morley, "Making Digital Cinema Actually Happen," p. 12.

28   This includes Regal, Loews Cineplex, UA, Carmike Theaters, General Cinemas, Edwards Cinemas, Silver Cinemas, and others. John Fithian, "Digital Cinema—Promising Technology, Serious Issues," National Institute of Standards & Technology Conference, January 11–12, 2001. See also the following *Daily Variety* issues for 2000: May 22, July 13, August 9, September 11, September 19, September 22, November 12.

29   DTS news release, November 20, 1998.

30   Conversation with the author, February 29, 1999.

31   Fithian, "Digital Cinema."

32   Valenti Press Release at http://www.mpaa.org.

33   Dan Sweeney, "Electronic Cinema: A Parricide's Progress," *The Perfect Vision*, July/August 1999, p. 27.

Index

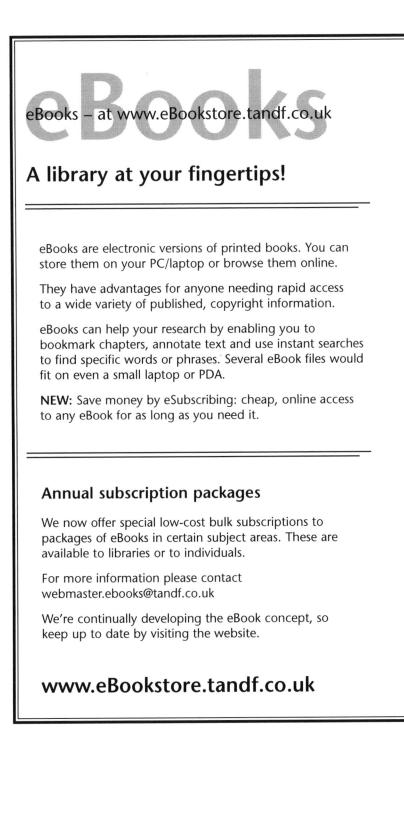

Related Film titles from Routledge

Analysing the Screenplay
Edited by Jill Nelmes

Most producers and directors acknowledge the crucial role of the screenplay, yet the film script has received little academic attention until recently, even though the screenplay has been in existence since the end of the 19th century.

Analysing the Screenplay highlights the screenplay as an important form in itself, as opposed to merely being the first stage of the production process. It explores a number of possible approaches to studying the screenplay, considering the depth and breadth of the subject area, including:

- the history and early development of the screenplay in the United States, France and Britain
- the process of screenplay writing and its peculiar relationship to film production
- the assumption that the screenplay is standardised in form and certain stories or styles are universal
- the range of writing outside the mainstream, from independent film to story ideas in Bhutanese film production to animation
- possible critical approaches to analysing the screenplay.

Analysing the Screenplay is a comprehensive anthology, offering a global selection of contributions from internationally renowned, specialist authors. Together they provide readers with an insight into this fascinating yet complex written form.

This anthology will be of interest to undergraduate and postgraduate students on a range of Film Studies courses, particularly those on scriptwriting.

ISBN13: 978–0–415–55634–7 (pbk)
ISBN13: 978–0–415–55633–0 (hbk)
ISBN13: 978–0–203–84338–3 (ebk)

Available at all good bookshops
For ordering and further information please visit:
www.routledge.com

Related Film titles from Routledge

Film and Ethics
Foreclosed Encounters
Lisa Downing and Libby Saxton

Film & Ethics considers a range of films and texts of film criticism alongside disparate philosophical discourses of ethics by Levinas, Derrida, Foucault, Lacanian psychoanalysts and postmodern theorists.

While an ethics of looking is implicitly posited in most strands of cinema theory, there is no established body of work that might be called ethical film criticism. This book, therefore, redresses the reluctance of many existing works to address cinema from an explicitly ethical perspective.

Readings range across popular Hollywood films such as *Thelma and Louise*, Alfred Hitchcock's canonical corpus, and films from European and World cinemas, including Dreyer's *The Passion of Joan of Arc* and the little-known African film *Bamako*. The book engages with debates concerning censorship and pornography; the ethical implications of 'positive representation'; the ethics of making and viewing images of atrocity and suffering; and the relationship between ethics and aesthetics.

Lisa Downing and Libby Saxton re-invigorate debates in film studies by foregrounding the ethical dimensions of the moving image, and create dialogues between ostensibly incompatible philosophical and political trends of thought, without seeking to reconcile their differences.

ISBN13: 978–0–415–40927–8 (pbk)
ISBN13: 978–0–415–40926–1 (hbk)
ISBN13: 978–0–203–87201–7 (ebk)

Available at all good bookshops
For ordering and further information please visit:
www.routledge.com

Related Film titles from Routledge

Encyclopedia of Early Cinema
Edited by Richard Abel

'A unique reference that will be welcomed by serious students of film history. It is a fascinating story and this reference will help students and other interested readers explore its full scope.' – *Against the Grain*

'This definitive new encyclopedia provides an essential reference tool ... This work represents a long-awaited accumulation of knowledge on the international emergence of cinema. Highly recommended for all reference collections.' – *Choice*

'It's a great pleasure to report that such an *Encyclopedia* has now been published, and that the job has been uncommonly well done ... both for the newcomer and for the specialist, the *Encyclopedia of Early Cinema* is highly recommended ... this is a book that deserves a place on virtually any film enthusiast's bookshelf.' – *Nineteenth Century Theatre & Film*

The *Encyclopedia of Early Cinema*, now in a new paperback edition, is a unique one-volume reference work which explores the first 25 years of cinema's development, from the early 1890s to the mid-1910s. These early years of the history of cinema have lately been the subject of resurgent interest and a growing body of scholarship, and have come to be recognized as an extraordinarily diverse period, when moving pictures were quite unlike the kind of cinema that later emerged as the dominant norm.

The *Encyclopedia of Early Cinema* is an invaluable and fascinating resource for students and researchers interested in the history of cinema.

ISBN13: 978–0–415–77856–5 (pbk)